THE MAYA 6
HANDBOOK

THE MAYA 6 HANDBOOK

ADAM WATKINS

CHRIS NEUHAHN

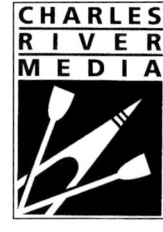

CHARLES RIVER MEDIA, INC.

Hingham, Massachusetts

Publisher: Jenifer Niles
Cover Design: The Printed Image
Cover Image: Chris Neuhahn

CHARLES RIVER MEDIA, INC.
10 Downer Avenue
Hingham, Massachusetts 02043
781-740-0400
781-740-8816 (FAX)
info@charlesriver.com
www.charlesriver.com

This book is printed on acid-free paper.

Adam Watkins and Chris Neuhahn. *The Maya 6 Handbook.*
ISBN: 1-58450-351-3

Library of Congress Cataloging-in-Publication Data
Watkins, Adam.
 The Maya 6 handbook / Adam Watkins and Chris Neuhahn.— 1st ed.
   p. cm.
  ISBN 1-58450-351-3 (pbk. : alk. paper)
 1. Maya (Computer file) 2. Computer animation. I. Neuhahn, Christopher. II. Title.
 TR897.7.W385 2005
 006.6'96—dc22

                          2004019398

Printed in the United States of America
04 7 6 5 4 3 2 First Edition

AUTHOR BIOS

Adam Watkins is the director of Computer Arts at the University of the Incarnate Word in San Antonio, Texas. He has a BFA in theater set and lighting design, and an MFA in graphic design. He is also the author of *The Maya 4.5 Handbook, The Cinema 4D R8 Handbook,* and the *Final Cut Pro 3 & DVD Studio Pro Handbook.* He currently teaches a number of 3D graphics courses, including several on Maya.

Chris Neuhahn is a professional animator of seven years. He has generated graphics and animation for courtroom presentations, medical illustration, cinematics for many popular video games (*Myst III: Exile, Pitfall Harry, Shrek 2, Medal of Honor,* and *Shark Tale*), and a children's television show. He is currently working on an animated series of short films called Vacant Planet (*www.vacantplanet.com*).

CONTENTS

CHAPTER 11   ANIMATION   **327**

APPENDIX A   WHICH HARDWARE TO USE   **345**

APPENDIX B   CUSTOMIZING THE MAYA USER INTERFACE   **355**

APPENDIX C   CREATING EFFECTIVE TEXTURE MAPS   **379**

APPENDIX D   ABOUT THE CD-ROM   **391**

INDEX   **393**

ACKNOWLEDGMENTS

I'd like to give special thanks to Jenifer for giving me the opportunity to do this book, and Dave for introducing me.

People think I'm a pitch man for Dell computers, but they make wonderful and stable machines, and that makes an animator very, very happy.

Thanks to Josh Book (*www.joshbook.com*) for his assistance. Also, thanks to Mo at Brain Zoo Studios, for keeping me well fed.

PREFACE

All the major players in 3D software have created very powerful tools. But from creating content for games all the way to commercials and movies—even for medical illustration—Maya is practically synonymous with 3D animation.

With feature lists that read like novels, Maya™ 6 is extremely powerful and complex. Despite its intuitive interface, it can be daunting to gaze at the screen and wonder where to start.

This book will teach you the core of the program and the theory behind the Maya work flow. It will not cover all the deepest dark recesses of Maya, because that would require a volume closer to the size of a Volvo. But by learning the vital aspects of Maya, you will have the confidence to create your own projects and even brave some of those deeper, more powerful areas of the program.

The tutorials in this book have been developed by Adam through class experimentation at the University of the Incarnate Word, and have been expanded from Chris's more than seven years of professional animation experience.

Though most of the improvements in Maya 6 are advanced features beyond the scope of this book, we have added some crucial new tutorials covering the creation, rigging, and animation of a cartoon bird.

Included with the explanations and tutorials, you will find screenshots and renders of the projects as we work. The grayscale images printed in this book are usually sufficient to guide you along. However, if you wish to enjoy them in glorious 24-bit color, all the images are also on the CD-ROM.

In addition, the results of the tutorials and several in-process versions of tutorial files are included on the CD-ROM. Sometimes, picking apart an already altered file can teach volumes.

ORGANIZATION

For the most part, this book assumes that you have a good understanding of 3D. Perhaps this knowledge comes from using another software package. Although we look at a few general ideas behind 3D and how they relate to Maya, we will not spend a lot of time on general vocabulary or concepts.

This book is organized so that you can jump ahead to any area. The contents of this book are largely geared toward newer users of Maya, though intermediate users will find some new things not previously covered. If you are just starting out with the program, start from the beginning of the book. We'll look at how Maya organizes its Workspace, how it "thinks" of digital space, and how to work within that space. Immediately after, we will dive into the many levels of modeling within Maya. After modeling, we will jump into Maya's shading methods, then onto animation, and finally character animation.

As Maya is a node-based program, this book is a node-based volume. Each node (modeling, shading, and animation) has its own eccentricities and can be used powerfully by itself. However, to create the most powerful effects, all the nodes have a synergistic effect when used together. A quick look through the book will show you that the projects are interdependent; one builds on the next. So, if you jump to a different place in the book, be mindful that sometimes core information has been presented earlier.

Keep in mind that although this is not a reference book, there are some sections included in the appendices that can be used as reference sections. Largely, the appendices are short articles that cover issues of what hardware is needed to run Maya effectively, how to change the Maya interface, and information about the machine used to create this book.

RATIONALE

The idea behind this volume is to give you the ability to expand upon the tutorials and even create new projects from scratch. You cannot use book tutorials in demo reels; after all, your portfolio would like just like everyone else's who followed the book. If you feel you've missed the concept of a section, reread it. The goal is to gain a fundamental understanding of the techniques, not an understanding of how to follow tutorial instructions.

Each chapter and tutorial includes a lot of detail. Because Maya runs on both Macs and PCs, there are occasional differences in instructions, so watch for platform-specific quirks that may pop up.

CONVENTIONS

Because of Maya's slightly unconventional method of hiding different parts of its toolset, it will be important to point out some conventions we will use in the process of this volume.

- Keystrokes, hotkeys, keyboard shortcuts (for things like Marking Menus) will be in bold. For example the keystroke for duplicating an object is **Ctrl-D**.
- Maya hides different collections of tools depending on which module you are in. Do not worry about what module means now, but if you look at the interface, in the top left corner is a pull-down menu that allows you to change the module you are in (Animation, Modeling, Dynamics, Rendering, and so on). To make sure you are always in the correct module, when pull-down menus are listed, if they are module-specific, the module will be listed as Modeling | Surfaces > Loft. This means, "Make sure you are in the Modeling module, go to the Surfaces pull-down, and select Loft."

Using the mouse is complex in Maya.

LMB: = Left mouse button
MMB: = Middle mouse button
RMB: = Right mouse button
LMMB: = Left and middle mouse button at the same time.
Click or double-click: Unless otherwise stated, this means to click the LMB.

CONCLUSION

Above all, make sure that this is all fun. If it ceases to be fun, never underestimate the power of a good break. Having a monitor's bright eye staring at you all day is trying even to us seasoned animators. So, take a break on occasion.

Something that seems obvious to one writer or reader may be a brain bender to another. Please be patient with things that move too slowly and other parts that move too quickly.

So, enough dry pontificating, let's learn Maya 6. There are miles of ground to cover and the thrill of new discovery to be had.

MAYA WORK FLOW AND INTERFACE

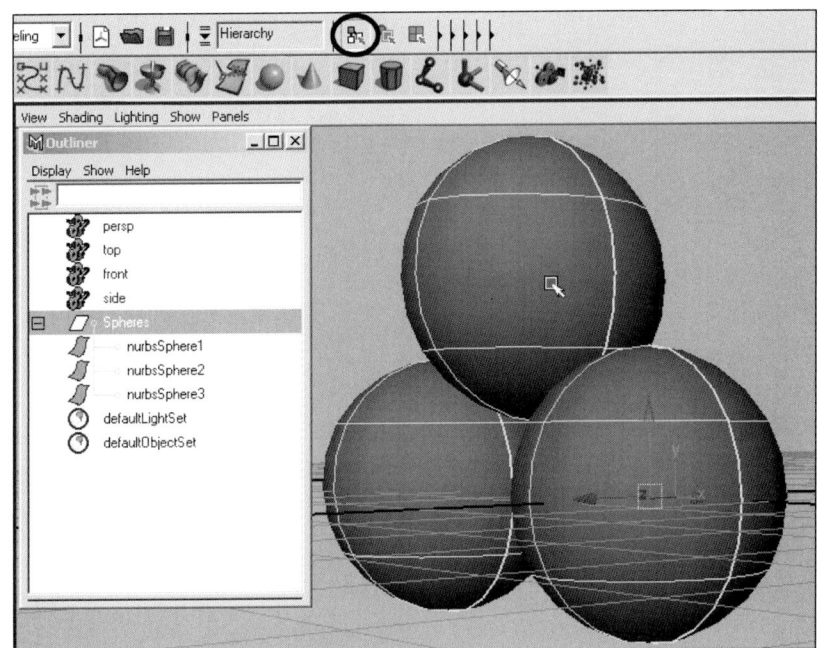

Later in this chapter, we will examine the organization of Maya's interface. This will help define why the interface has been often admired and imitated. But to better understand the reasoning behind the organization, it's important to first look briefly at a general 3D work flow and specifically, at Maya's work flow. Through the process, we will have an opportunity to discuss Maya's working paradigm: the rationale behind the software as well as the benefits and drawbacks of this way of thinking.

A GENERAL 3D WORK FLOW

Every 3D artist works a little differently than the next. The goal of this section is not to set a definitive step-by-step progression, because the steps may shift depending on your project or your team. In general, however, most 3D projects can be broken down into the following steps.

Step 1: Project Conceptualization

Okay, so this is actually a huge step and includes an incredible amount of sub-steps including research, sketches, storyboards, perhaps clay models, and a video asset collection. The importance of building, defining, and refining a solid concept is immense. The process is also highly individualized. What needs to happen before a project "goes digital" depends largely on an animator's strengths and weaknesses. Because of this, we will leave this discussion at that. But if you are just getting started in 3D, make sure you build the habit of playing with ideas on paper before pounding polygons. Usually, a couple of hours in traditional pencil and paper land can save you many, many hours in the digital realm.

For further information on general work flow in 3D creation, see the book, *3D Animation: From Models to Movies* (©2000, Charles River Media, Inc.).

Step 2: Modeling

Modeling is a specific term that covers many concepts and techniques. At its simplest, modeling is the process of constructing the virtual shapes that make up your scene. These objects can be anything from clouds to worms to furniture to caricatures to photo-realistic people.

How these objects are constructed largely depends on a myriad of variables including what the object is, how it's going to move, if it's going to move, how it needs to be textured, how detailed it is, and what the final output is—games, TV, movies, etc. Basically, the idea here is that before anything else can be done on the project—including lighting, shading, or animation—there must first be models with which to work.

Over the course of this volume, we will be talking about several modeling methods. Of course, these are by no means exhaustive, and many artists use techniques and methods that are specific to their style or the pipeline of their workplace. So, take these techniques as a very general look at basic building blocks. Put them together in ways that make sense to you and create new methods.

Step 3: Shading (Texturing)

Texturing is the process of giving the gray models created in earlier steps surface characteristics including color, specular highlights, luminance, diffuse, and others. Tactile characteristics like bumps are also controlled through the texturing process. Most of these texturing processes are a type of veneer—a flat kind of painting across the surface of the model; however, there are some texturing techniques such as displacement that actually alter the geometry of the model.

Basically, texturing makes a volleyball look different than a bowling ball, which looks different than a tennis ball, which is still different than an eyeball. Maya's texturing capabilities are incredibly powerful and deep. Again, we will take time to explore many interesting techniques for using Maya's texturing tools. Once again, this will not be an exhaustive exploration—just enough to introduce you to many of the levers of this texturing tool; you will even get to pull a few. Mastering the texture techniques will be up to you.

Step 4: Lighting

Virtual lighting is one of the most fun but most challenging parts of 3D. Not many people take enough time with it and, unfortunately, that means not very many people do it well. A well-lit scene can hide problems or highlight strengths. Lighting is largely a subconscious aesthetic, so folks do not often understand that they are being affected by it.

Lighting in 3D has some interesting challenges, because virtual lights don't behave quite like "real" lights. Because of the different rules of light in a virtual world, a bit of different thinking must go into your virtual lighting design. Throughout this volume, we'll look closely at how Maya's lighting tools work and how we can manipulate them to produce the desired image.

Step 5: Animation

Perhaps the most fun, dynamic, and difficult part of the whole process is animation. Everyone thinks they can do it, but few people are really very good at it. Animation is the process of making the objects modeled earlier move, or even making objects such as lights or virtual cameras move. The key to it all is movement.

The problem is that movement is very hard to cover in a book. It's very hard to teach in general and requires quite a bit of physical face-to-face time. So, we won't be going into the physics of movement much. Neither will we go much beyond a cursory look at movement aesthetics and issues of timing. What we'll cover are the tools that Maya provides to allow you to make your textured, lit models come to life.

Maya's animation tools—especially the character animation tools—are truly at the top of their class. We'll look at the core of this robust animation tool set over the course of this book. The animations we'll create will be basic but sound. You can use the techniques and skill set from these tutorial animations to create great masterpieces that will amaze your family and impress your friends.

Step 6: Rendering

You're the god of the 3D world you're creating. You define the objects therein, what characteristics they have, and how they move. When you've finished creating and animating your world, you then tell Maya (the camera) how to take a picture or draw the world you've created. You can define all sorts of minute details of how Maya will understand the light, how large it'll draw or render the image, how many images in a second it's going to draw to create movement, and how much detail to put into the final rendering. The core idea is that Maya, under your direction, is drawing or rendering the world you've created. You define the rules, but Maya does little without you telling it to.

The truth is, Maya's rendering isn't as intuitive as many of the 3D applications that you might be coming from. The power is great within the renderer but with this power comes endless options, each of which can tweak your project closer to the illustrative perfection you see in your mind's eye.

Work Flow Wrap-up

Now of course the steps outlined so far are a gross underrepresentation of the cyclical nature of the creation process. Hardly any of the steps outlined are completed and then totally left behind for the remainder of the creation process. Usually, you model, texture, rework the model, rework the texture, then light a bit, then rework a texture or two, touch up the model a bit, then readjust the lighting, and so on. But in general, it's nice to think of your project in this linear process.

As we work through the book, we'll follow this general process. We'll start out by looking at the general layout of the tools. Then we'll move right into creating some objects through various modeling techniques. After we have our mini-worlds created, we'll color them through the texturing process. Then we'll illuminate the world through lighting, animate some of the characters in this world, and finally have Maya render the whole thing out for us. It's a complex and fun process but it will take a while. So, let's move right into how Maya organizes the tools it gives us to create our virtual worlds.

AN INTERFACE OVERVIEW

3D interfaces have come a long way over the years. The trend has shifted and evolved as the interface aesthetic has changed. An interesting development is the tendency to mimic Maya's interface. This is especially true of mid-range 3D applications. It's no wonder because the Maya interface has a fairly intuitive organization and an extremely customizable toolbox from which to grab the tools to create your masterpiece.

Part of what makes the initial Maya interface so powerful is that it packs so much into so little space. This efficiency can be incredibly intimidating at first but don't lose hope. In all actuality, the interface is well organized and once you understand the organization, it becomes much easier to grab the tool you need (Figure 1.1).

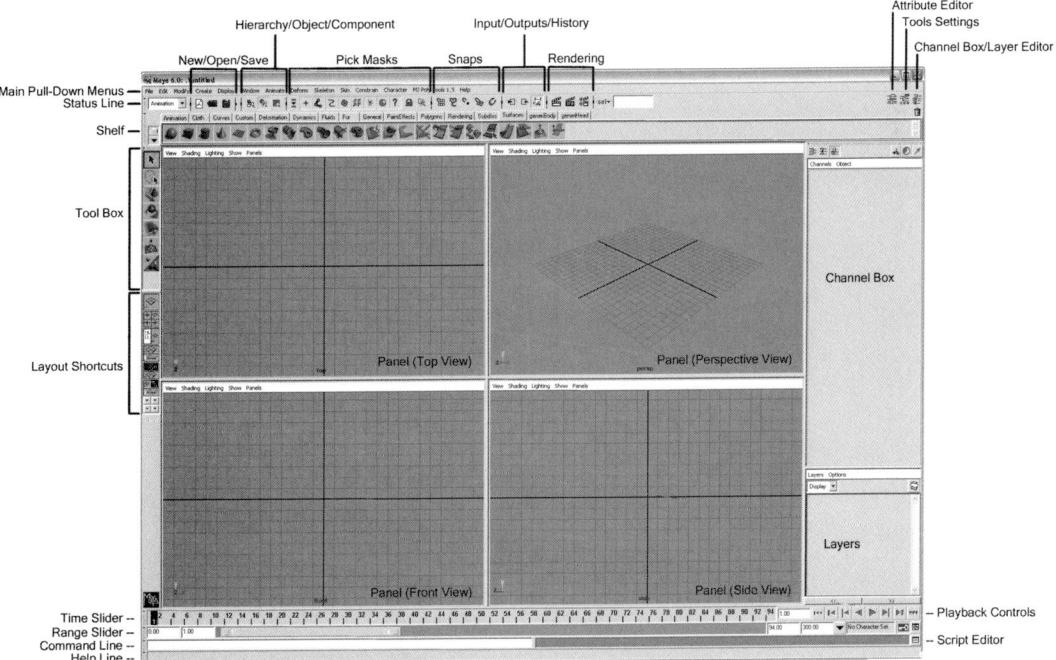

FIGURE 1.1   A general overview and breakdown of the Maya default user interface.

Modules

Maya is so deep that it "hides" many of its tools so that the user isn't overwhelmed by the incredible options it provides. There are several ways that Maya organizes tools but the broadest method is through modules. Modules are general collections of tools and pull-down menus that are organized specifically for one aspect of Maya. To access or change modules, use the first Menu Set pop-up menu on the Status Line (Figure 1.2).

In Maya Complete, the modules are Animation, Modeling, Dynamics, and Rendering. In Maya Unlimited, the modules include Animation, Modeling, Dynamics, Rendering, Live, and Cloth.

As discussed in the Preface, varying collections of tools and pull-down menus are available depending on what module is active. Be sure to take note of which module you're in when working.

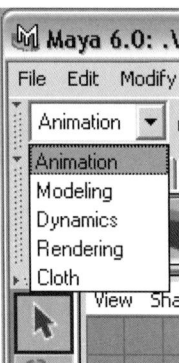

FIGURE 1.2 Shift modules through the Menu Set in the Status Line.

Menu Bar

Like most any application in the Mac or Windows worlds, the menu bar includes the main pull-down menus in Maya. Unlike most applications, there are so many pull-down menus that they aren't all displayed at once. The File, Edit, Modify, Create, Display, and Window pull-down menus are always visible, regardless of which module you're in. However, to the right of these six pull-down menus are others that will change depending on your module (Figure 1.3).

Converting Pull-down Menus to Floating Menus and Palettes

The Menu Bar, with its pull-down menus, also has some user-friendly options of note. First, notice that pull-down menus need not remain pull-

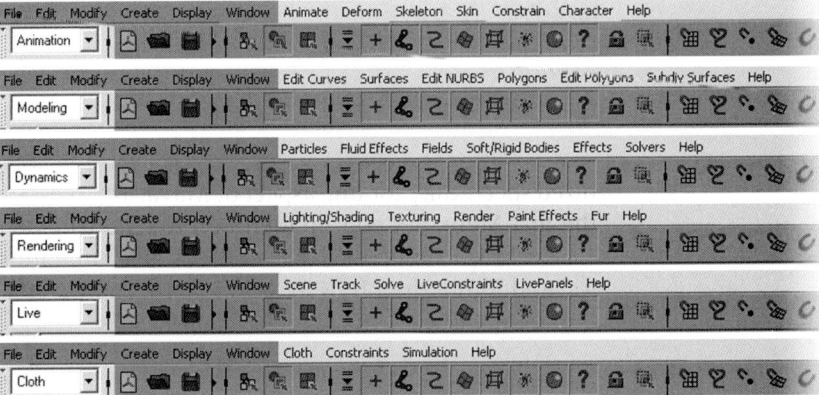

FIGURE 1.3   A brief overview of the various pull-down menus available with different modules.

down menus. When a pull-down menu is first activated, a set of double lines is highlighted (Figure 1.4a). When these double lines are selected, the pull-down menu becomes a floating palette of sorts (Figure 1.4b). This is a nice temporary modification to the interface that allows you to have a collection of tools you're going to be using repeatedly in your process.

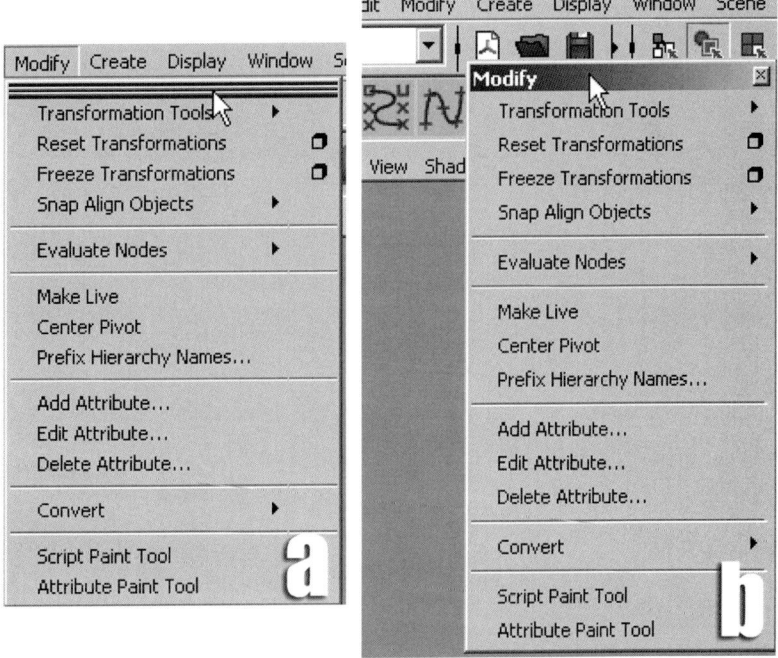

FIGURE 1.4 (a–b)   Change pull-down menus into floating palettes.

Appendix B, "Customizing the Maya User Interface," is all about modifying the interface to adjust to your work flow. As you work and become more familiar with Maya, be sure to take a look at that appendix for tips on putting together Maya's user interface just the way you want it.

Option Boxes

Notice that within many of the pull-down menus, items have a small square to their right (Figure 1.5). This is referred to as the option box.

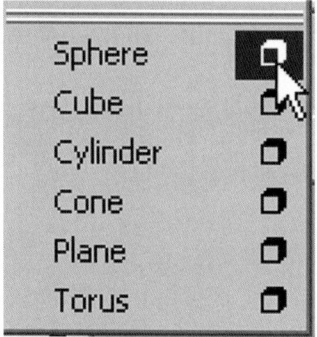

FIGURE 1.5   Select an option box to specify aspects of the tool.

The presence of the option box signifies that this particular tool has some customizable options that you may want to adjust before using the tool. Simply move your mouse over the box before releasing the LMB to open the option dialog box.

Be aware that when you change the settings in an option dialog box, Maya remembers those changes. So, if you choose that tool again, all the altered options remain in effect. In general, if you are using a shared machine, such as in a lab, be sure to open the options for tools the first time you use them to reset the options (Figure 1.6).

We will talk much more about manipulating dialog boxes in the tutorials of later chapters.

Status Line

Moving straight down the interface, the next collection of tools below the pull-down menus makes up the Status Line (Figure 1.7). The Status Line is an interesting collection of tools. We will not talk in great detail here about each tool individually; rather, we will cover broad collections of

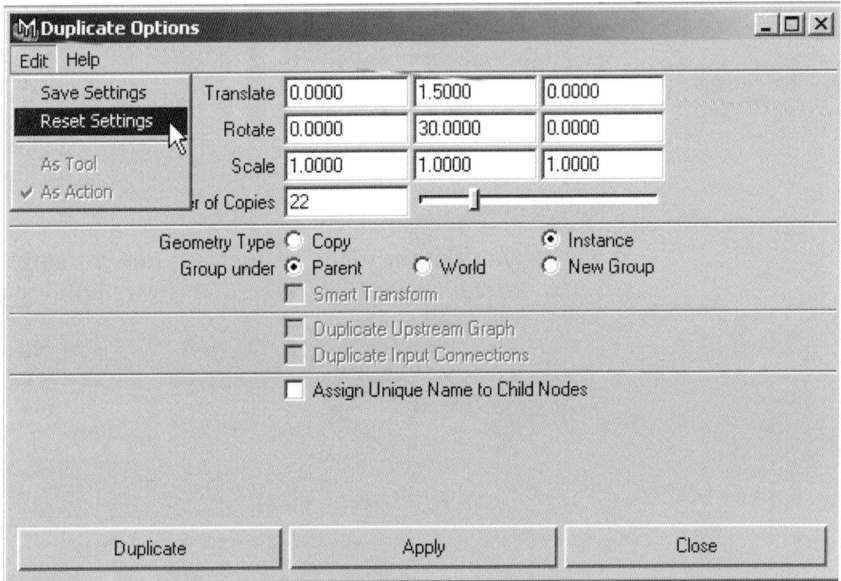

FIGURE 1.6   This option dialog box allows you to reset the settings for this tool.

tools. Because of this, notice the circled elements that are called collapsers. You can click them to hide or show the tools to their right. We will talk about tools in the context of collections between collapsers.

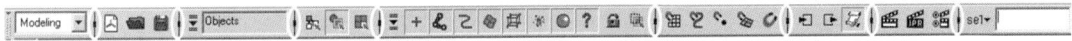

FIGURE 1.7   The collapsers in the Status Line are circled.

As we talk about collections of tools within the Status Line, we will start with a completely "collapsed" Status Line. We will uncollapse the collections as we go.

Module Menu Set

The first part of the Status Line consists of the previously discussed module menu sets. Remember, you get an entirely new collection of pull-down menus when these are changed (Figure 1.8).

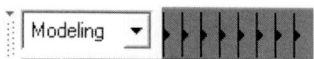

FIGURE 1.8   The Menu Set module allows you to bring up new collections of tools depending on the point in your creation process.

New, Open, and Save

The New, Open, and Save tools are fairly standard options for many applications (Figure 1.9). They are just visual representations of File > New Scene . . . , File > Open Scene . . ., and File > Save Scene . . . . Remember that **Ctrl-N** (New), **Ctrl-O** (Open), and **Ctrl-S** (Save) are still faster ways to create, open, or save scenes.

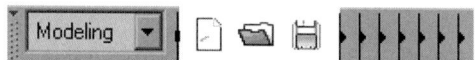

FIGURE 1.9   The New, Open, and Save tools are available within the Status Line.

Selection Masks

As your projects become more complex, the number of objects, lights, or animation tools will begin to increase dramatically. As time goes on, it can become nearly impossible to select the object you want as you work. This Selection Mask (Figure 1.10) allows you to define which objects are selectable.

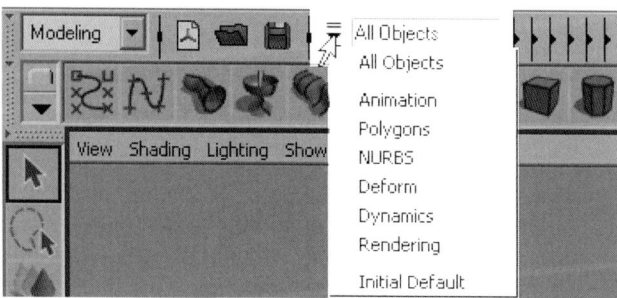

FIGURE 1.10   The Selection Mask allows you to define what items may be selected within your Workspace.

When the time comes for animation, being able to select the right object in your Workspace becomes especially important. It is important to have an eye for this tool and remember that it is there. Often, problems that students have when working with a complex scene can be solved by simply taking time to hone in on the types of objects they wish to select.

The setting listed in the Selection Mask is linked to the next two collections of tools:

- Hierarchy, Object, and Component modes
- Select by Object or Component Types

Hierarchy, Object, and Component Modes

The Hierarchy, Object, and Component modes (Figure 1.11) affect what part or parts of the scene you are able to select and alter. All three of these modes refer to a level of organization within your scene.

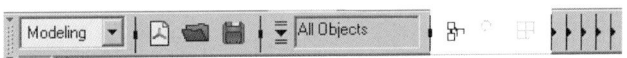

FIGURE 1.11   Hierarchy, Object, and Component mode items.

The ability to alter and control which mode you are in is an incredibly important part of working effectively in Maya. We will explore this aspect much more in depth in the course of the tutorials, but it is important to understand a bit about the theory behind them.

When you create a primitive form or a surface in Maya, you have created an object. This object consists of sub-parts called components. A polygon object is made of vertex, face, and edge components. Non-uniform Rational B-Splines (NURBS) objects contain components such as control vertices, isoparms, and hulls. When objects are grouped, they become part of hierarchies.

Consider Figure 1.12, which shows three spheres (objects) grouped into a group (a hierarchy) called Spheres, which is displayed in the Outliner to the left.

If the Hierarchy button is pressed, notice that the Selection Mask changes to Hierarchy, meaning of course that if we click anywhere in the scene, we're limited to selecting hierarchies. Indeed, if any of the spheres in the scene are clicked, Maya does not select the sphere but the hierarchy that sphere resides in (Figure 1.13).

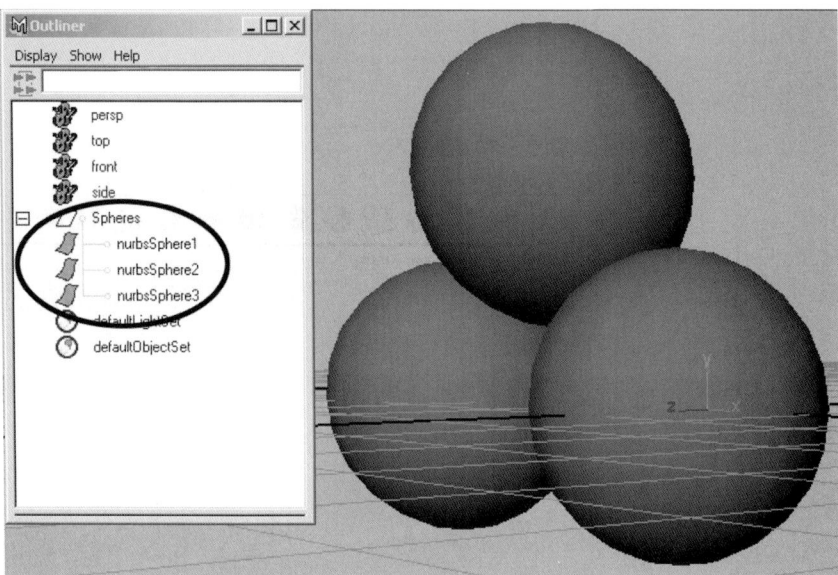

FIGURE 1.12   Three spheres (NURBS) are collected into the group.

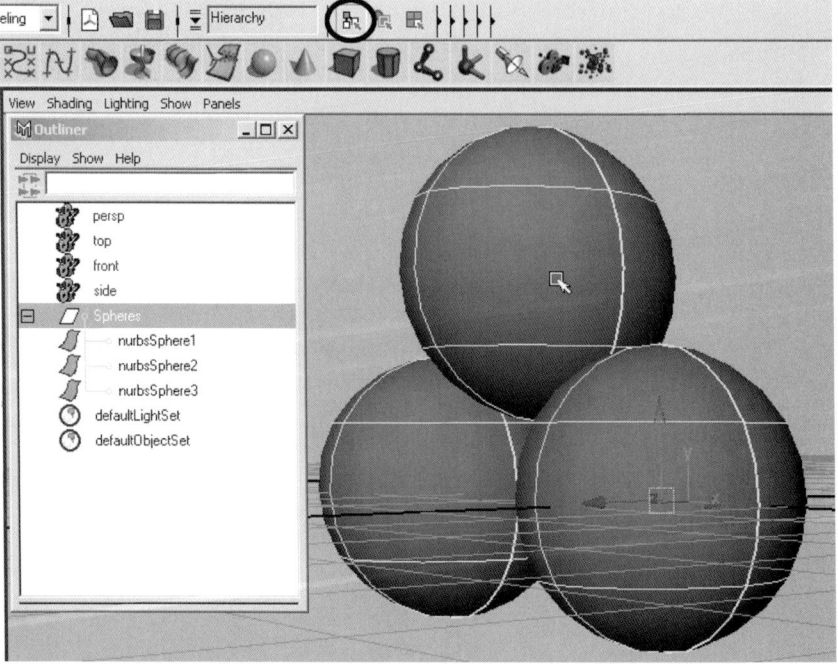

FIGURE 1.13   When the Hierarchy mode is activated, clicking on an object in the scene selects the hierarchy that object is in.

Similarly, if the Object mode is selected, the Selection Mask accordingly changes to Objects and we can select individual objects within the scene by clicking on them (Figure 1.14).

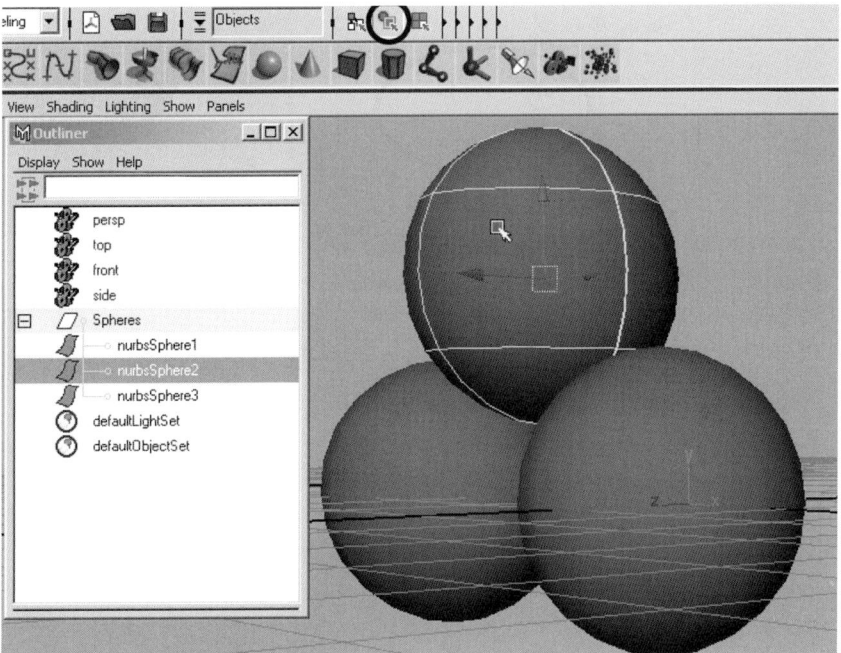

FIGURE 1.14   Object mode allows us to select objects directly.

Finally, if Components mode is chosen, we can select components that are parts of objects. In the case shown in Figure 1.15, we're selecting Control Vertices that are part of the first object, NURBS Sphere.

This may seem rather simple and redundant, because you could do much the same thing by simply altering the Selection Mask. It would be redundant if not for the next collection of tools.

Select by Hierarchy:Type, Select by Object:Type, and Select by Component:Type

In the last section, we looked at a collection of tools that would allow for the specification of what part of a hierarchy is to be selected when clicked in the Workspace. This next collection of tools works as a subset to the Hierarchy (Figure 1.16a), Objects (Figure 1.16b), and Components (Figure 1.16c) modes. This means there are several collections of tools that all occupy the same space. Depending on which mode you are in, the tools that relate to it are displayed. Figure 1.16 shows each collection of Select by: and the particular mode to which the collection is attached.

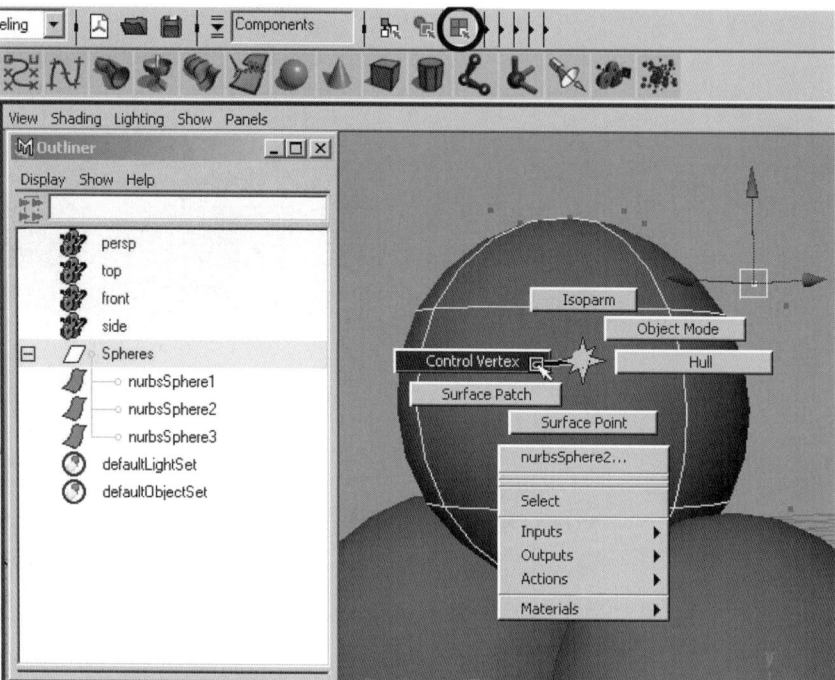

FIGURE 1.15 Components mode allows you to select a part or building component tool of an object.

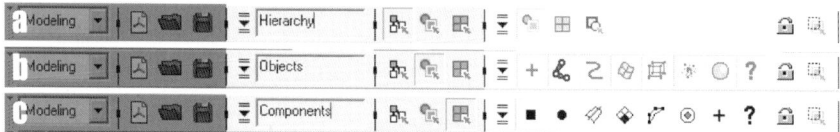

FIGURE 1.16 (a–c) Select by Hierarchy, Object, or Component type.

This particular collection of tools is extremely important as you work in Maya. In the next chapter, we will look closely at these tools in action but we will go over a quick theoretical discussion of them here. Before we get too deep, notice that the iconography of these tools (or any tool within Maya) can be deciphered quickly in two ways. The first is to move your mouse over any tool and leave it there for a bit. A screen hint will pop up (Figure 1.17) to identify the tool for you. The second is by keeping an eye out for the Help Line at the bottom-left corner of your default interface. When you mouse over a particular tool, the name of the tool will appear in the Help Line (Figure 1.17).

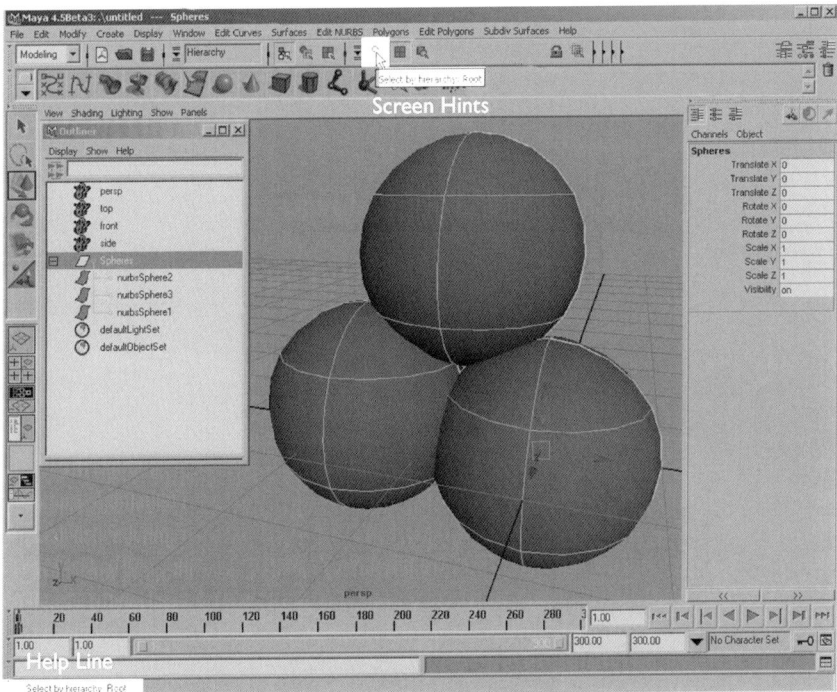

FIGURE 1.17   If you ever get confused over which tool is which, let Maya tell you with screen hints or in the help line.

Select by Hierarchy: Type

This small collection of options (Figure 1.16a) is tied to the Hierarchy mode. The default tool is Select by Hierarchy:Root. This means when you click on any object that exists within a group or other hierarchy, the hierarchy to which it belongs will be selected. Note that besides the default, the other two tools include Select by Hierarchy:Leaf and Select by Hierarchy:Template. These allow you to select parts, or leaves, of a hierarchy rather than the entire hierarchy or you may select Template objects.

We'll talk much more about templates later, but the basic idea is that any object can be temporarily made into a Template object that doesn't render and usually isn't selectable. Template objects can be great as guides for animation or size reference. In any other mode, templates are not selectable.

In Figure 1.18a, you can see that the top sphere is shaded differently than the others. This wireframe, gray representation indicates that the object is a template. When Hierarchy mode is active and Select by Hierarchy:Template is activated, templates can be selected as shown in Figure 1.18b.

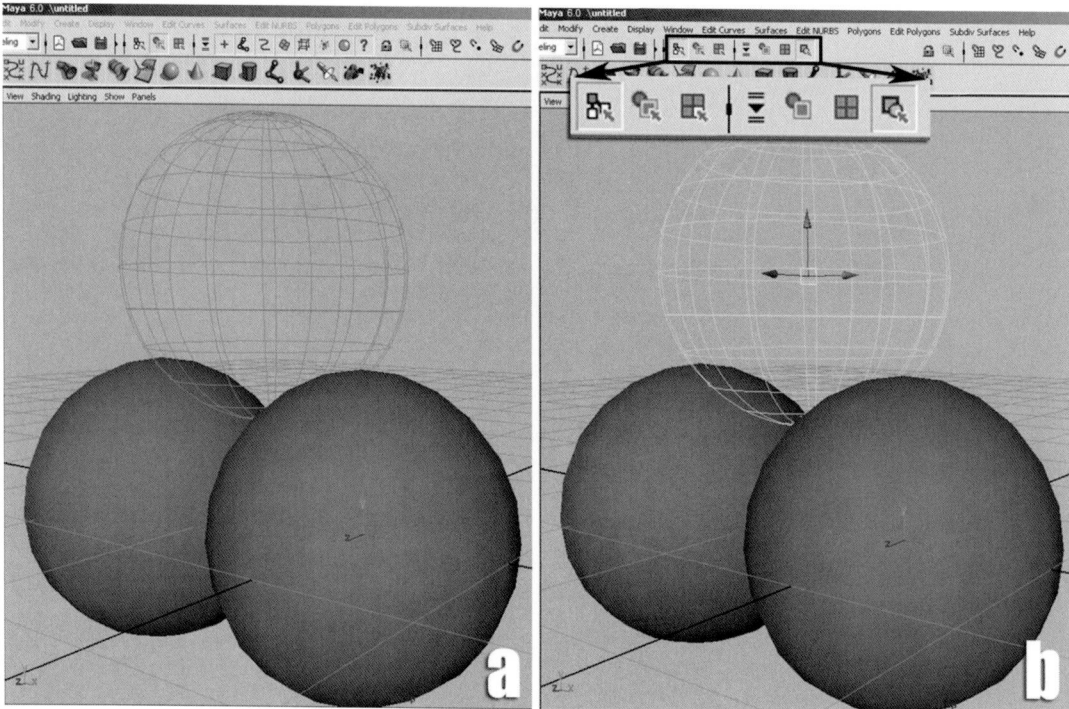

FIGURE 1.18 (a–b) Templates cannot be selected except with the Select by Hierarchy:Template tool.

Select by Object:Type

This is a much broader collection of tools, as you can see back in Figure 1.16b. This collection allows you to decide what sorts of objects will be selectable. The options are Handles, Joints, Curves, Surfaces, Deformations, Dynamics, Rendering, and Miscellaneous. Notice that these are all activated by default, meaning that unless you deactivate items, when in Object mode, you can select any type of object within your Workspace. To turn off an item, simply click on it.

There are too many specifics for each option to go into depth in this chapter. However, as we work, we'll occasionally turn them off and on to help us in different parts of our work process.

One important thing to note about this collection of tools before we move on: there are actually nested tools within these items. If you rest your mouse on any of the Select by Object: items, the screen hint (Figure 1.19a) will indicate "RMB for more info." Indeed, if you RMB-click on any of these items, there will be a collection of sub-items that you can turn on or off (Figure 1.19b).

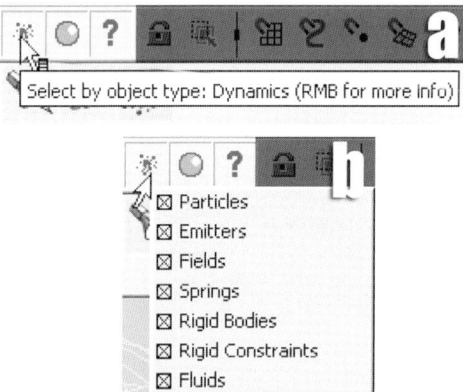

FIGURE 1.19 (a–b)   Many of the Select by Object:Type items are actually categories. The items within these categories are accessed with an RMB-click.

Select by Component:Type

As discussed earlier, objects are made up of, or can be edited by, various components. Of course, the specific components vary depending on the type of object. In general, if all the components were visible at one time in the Workspace, it would be difficult to see what you needed to find. The Select by Component:Type collection of items allows you to decide what types of components will be selectable (Figure 1.19b).

The components are grouped into the Points, Parm Points, Lines, Faces, Hulls, Pivots, Handles, and Miscellaneous buttons. Again, these are general categories of components and most have a collection of specific components nested within them that are accessible through an RMB-click.

One note about this collection of tools: as with many aspects of Maya, there is more than one way to skin this virtual cat. You can also access specific components of a given object while in Object mode. By RMB-clicking on an object (while in Object mode) you'll be given a marking menu that allows you to select a component of that object directly (Figure 1.20). Generally, I find that this method is preferable in most cases.

Lock Current Selection and Highlight Selection Mode

Lastly, before we move onto other parts of the Status Line, it is important to notice the two tools shown in Figure 1.21.

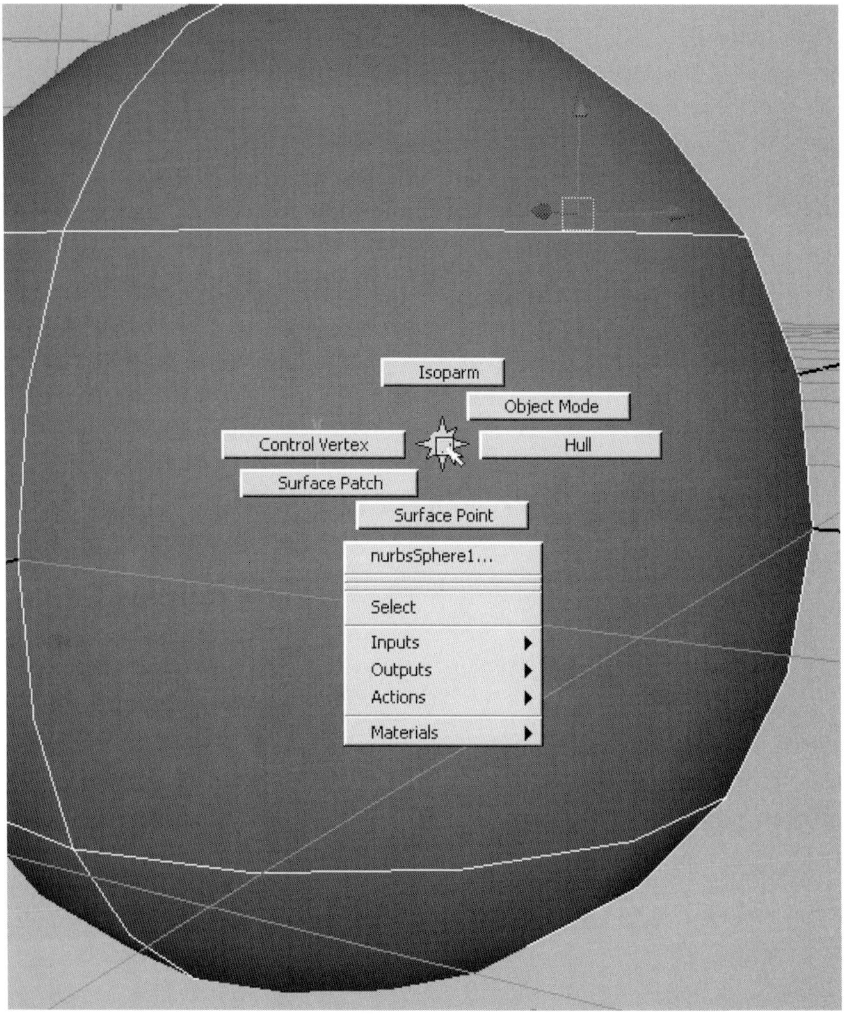

Isoparm

Object Mode

Control Vertex   Hull

Surface Patch

Surface Point

nurbsSphere1...

Select

Inputs   ▶
Outputs   ▶
Actions   ▶

Materials   ▶

FIGURE 1.20   Select components while in Objects mode.

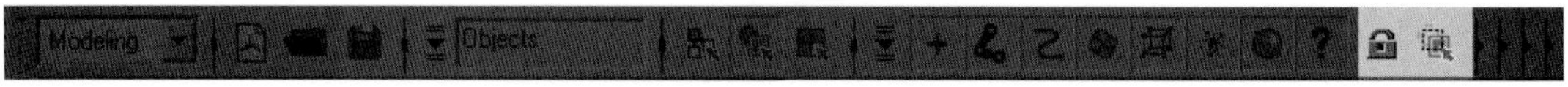

FIGURE 1.21   The Lock Current Selection and Highlight Selection mode tools.

If you have selected a particular hierarchy, object, or component and you know that you wish to work with it for a prolonged period of time, you can lock it with the Lock Current Selection tool. Although this does prevent unintentional deselecting, it also prohibits you from selecting other objects, which can become very bothersome very quickly. In general, this tool is not of tremendous use, so leave it alone.

By default, when you select a hierarchy, object, or component in the Workspace, the item is highlighted. However, you may toggle this off with the Highlight Selection Mode button. Why exactly you would need to do this is a mystery, unless you have an incredibly large amount of items selected (more than you would ever want to have selected at once). However, if you want to remove highlighting from the items you select, this is where you toggle off that option.

Snap to Grids, Curves, Points, View Planes, and Make the Selected Object Live

The next collection of tools (Figure 1.22) is great when you are interested in exact objects, component movements, or curve creation. The next four tools when toggled on allow you to snap the selected object or component to the active grid, curve, point, or view planes. We will be looking specifically at how to use these tools in later tutorials, but the general idea is illustrated in the following figure.

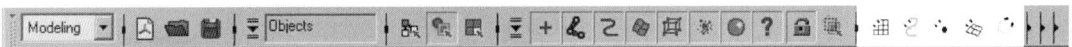

FIGURE 1.22   The Snap to Grids, Snap to Curves, Snap to Points, Snap to View Planes, and Make the Selected Object Live tools.

Figure 1.23 illustrates a very general example of how these tools work. Figure 1.23a shows a scene that includes a sphere and a curve. By selecting the sphere and moving it so that it sits at the end of the curve, we are telling Maya that there's going to be a relationship here (Figure 1.23b). Now, when Snap to Curves is toggled on (Figure 1.23c), the yellow box that was at the middle of the sphere's manipulator changes to a circle. When it is LMB-clicked and dragged, the sphere snaps to the curve (Figure 1.23d).

The notable variation of these tools is the last tool: Make the Selected Object Live. A live object is the object to which other objects or components will snap. So, if we wanted to create a curve that matched a particular surface, we would select the surface and click the Make the Selected Object Live tool (Figure 1.24a). The live object would then appear as a green wireframe (Figure 1.24b). At this point, when a curve is created (Figure 1.24c), all the points of the curve will snap to this live surface. When the curve is complete, and the Make the Selected Object Live tool is clicked once (which makes the live object "unlive" again), the curve lays completely along the previously live surface (Figure 1.24d).

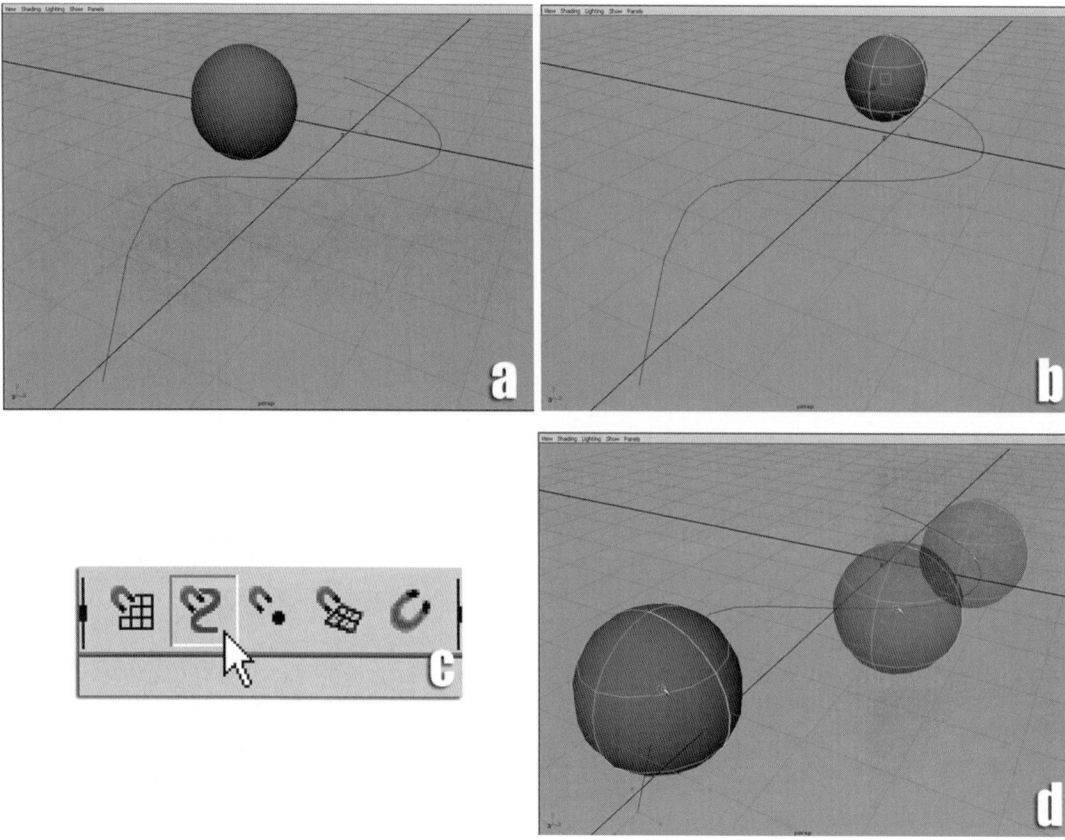

FIGURE 1.23 (a–d)   An illustration of the Snap to Curve tool. The process is similar for all the Snap tools.

Similarly, when an object is live, any objects that are moved in the Workspace will snap to that surface automatically.

Operation Lists and Construction History

The next collection of tools (Figure 1.25) is part of Maya's use of the concept of Construction History. Construction History is an important part of the flexibility that Maya affords and is a vital part of understanding the concept of nodes. You can think of Construction History in a general sense as recorded Undos that are nested within each object of your scene. More accurately, Construction History keeps track of the Inputs and Outputs objects.

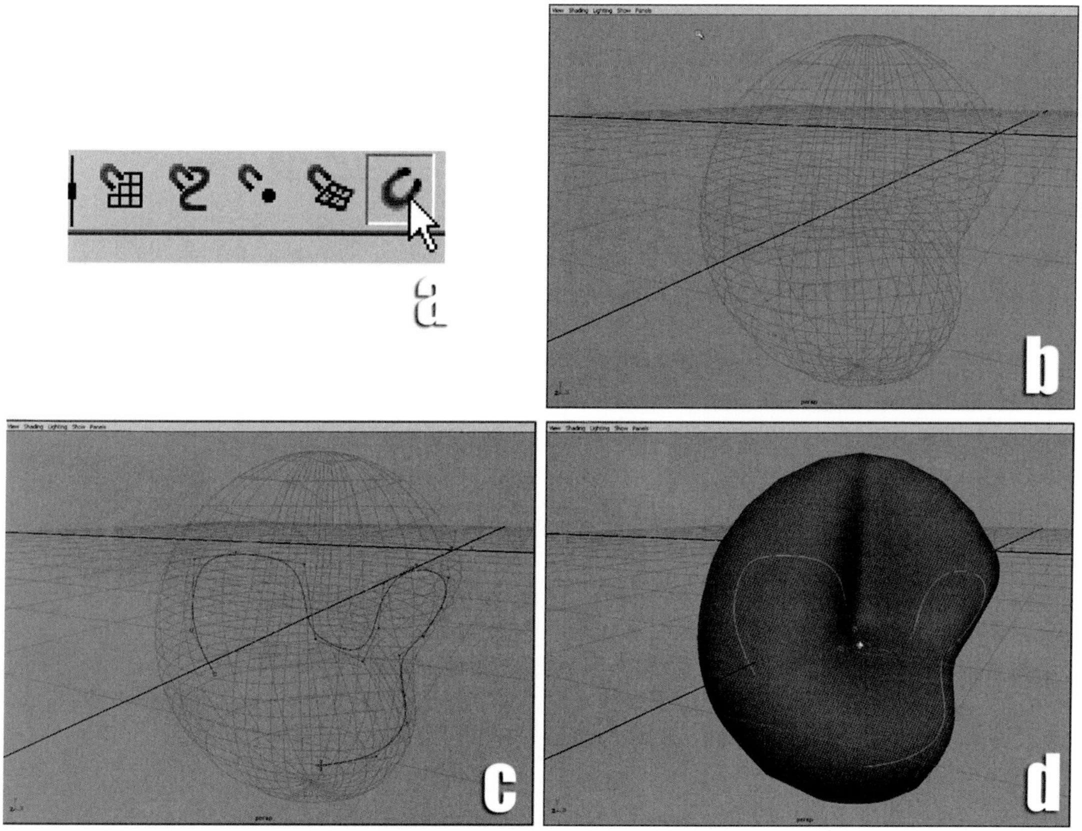

FIGURE 1.24   You can use the Make the Selected Object Live tool to create curves on a surface.

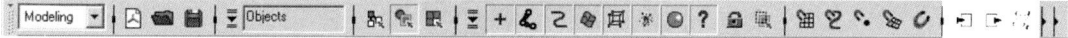

FIGURE 1.25   The Operation Lists tools and Construction History toggle.

Many objects in Maya are created from other objects. NURBS are a great example of this. A NURBS surface can be created from a collection of curves that provide some preliminary information on the desired 3D shape. For instance, Figure 1.26 shows a collection of circles that were used to make the three-dimensional, lofted surface next to it. The 3D shape was created by selecting the four circles and choosing Modeling > Surfaces > Loft. In this simple example, the four curves are the inputs, and the lofted surface is the output. The curves and the surface are linked via the Construction History stored in the surface.

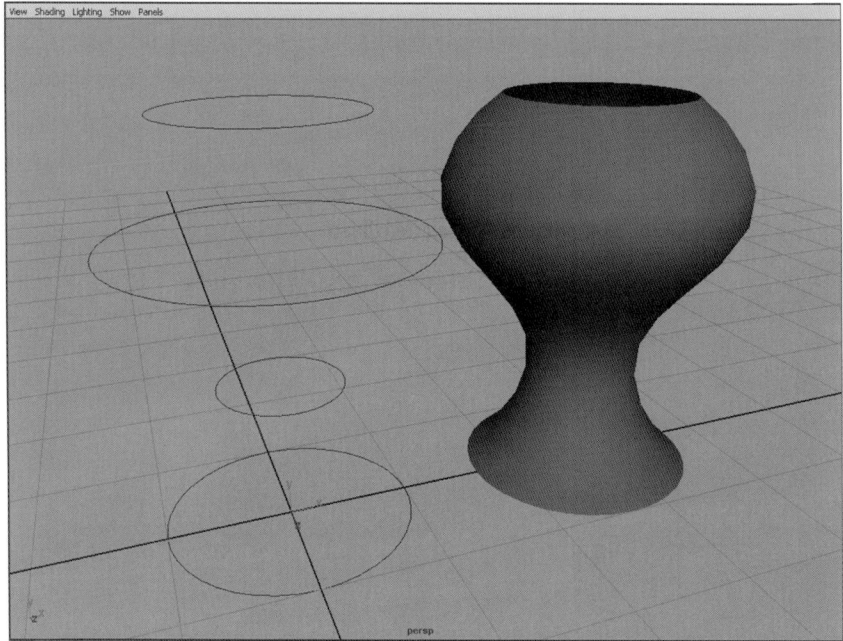

FIGURE 1.26 A Lofted Surface is created from a collection of curves. The curves at the right are the input that allows for the surface at the right (the output).

The collection of tools shown in Figure 1.27 are used to help control and alter Construction History, inputs, and outputs.

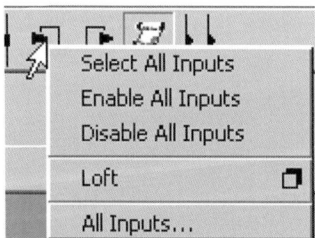

FIGURE 1.27 Select, Enable, and Disable All Inputs. This allows you to make changes to the setting of any node used to create a shape.

Inputs to the Selected Object

The first tool is actually a collection of nested tools. When an object is selected in your Workspace, LMB-click and hold on to this tool, and a collection of pop-up menus will appear (Figure 1.27). These allow you to select, enable, or disable inputs for a particular object. Figure 1.27 is for the lofted surface shown in Figure 1.26. As such, you can see that this also shows the node (loft) that was used to create the surface. You can select this node again here and make changes to the parameters that were set up to create the surface.

Outputs from the Selected Object

Next is the sister tool that allows you to Select, Enable, and Disable Outputs that might have been created using the element that is active (Figure 1.28). Again, be sure to LMB-click and hold to get this pop-up menu to appear.

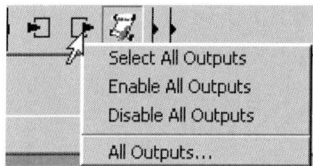

FIGURE 1.28   Select, Enable, and Disable All Outputs.

Construction History On/Off

Although Construction History can be a tremendous help in modeling (we will look at how in Chapters 4 and 5), it can become a nuisance when it's time to animate. There are also other situations in which having a history attached to an object can cause some interesting problems. Although you can delete any objects of the Construction History manually, some folks prefer to turn it off all together as they are performing certain functions.

This tool allows you to turn off or on the recording of Construction History. In general, you want to leave Construction History on, which is its default. Then, when you are sure your modeling is beautiful and complete, you can get rid of the history so you have a no-strings-attached form.

Now, this is probably the quickest discussion of inputs, outputs, nodes, and Construction History on record and it probably does not make a lot of sense at this point. Not to worry; these concepts are best explained when they are seen in action. We will illustrate again and again the benefits of these concepts through the course of the book. By the end of this volume, inputs, outputs, nodes, and Construction History will be second nature.

Render the Current Frame, IPR Render the Current Frame, and Display Render Globals Window

As discussed earlier, rendering is an important part of the 3D creation process. These next three tools give you access to Maya's rendering functions (Figure 1.29).

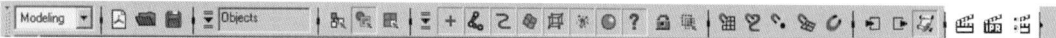

FIGURE 1.29   Maya's rendering functions can be activated and altered with these tools in the status line.

The first tool, Render the Current Frame, does just that using the settings defined by clicking on the last of the three buttons in this set. The second, IPR Render the Current Frame, makes use of a technology Maya uses called Interactive Photorealistic Renderer (IPR). We will talk much more of IPR in Chapters 8 and 9, but the basic idea is that IPR allows for quick adjustments in the rendering process at the expense of a little extra time up front. When you use IPR to render a scene, the render time is longer. However, then you can select interactive regions that automatically refresh as you make changes in your scene. There will be much more on this later.

The last tool of this set brings up the Render Global Settings window (Figure 1.30). This allows you to define the parameters that Maya will use to render your scene. We will be looking at most of these options in Chapter 9, "Lighting and Rendering," so we won't spend much time on them here.

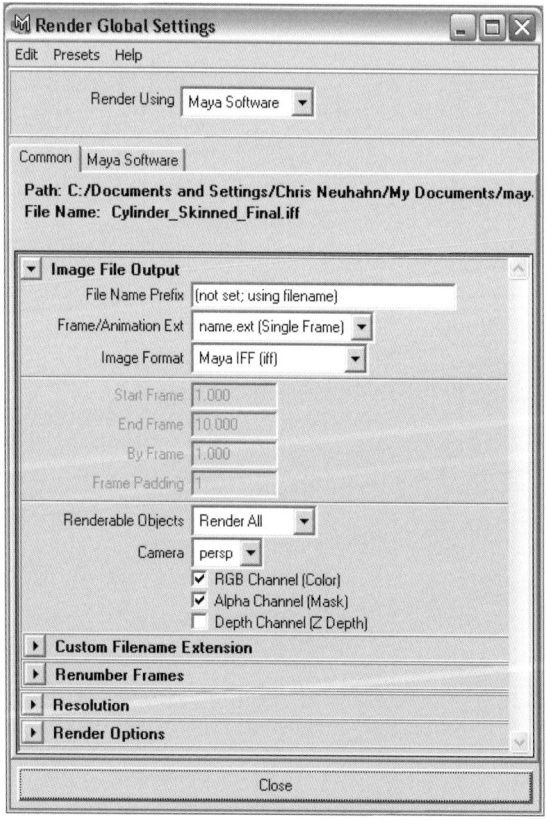

FIGURE 1.30   Render Global Settings window.

Numeric Input Tool

This tool is the last part of the Status Line and it contains two parts: a mode selection and an input field. It allows for quick direct entry of values and names (Figure 1.31).

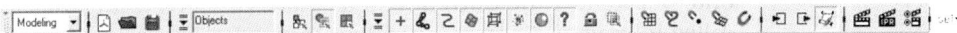

FIGURE 1.31   Numeric Input tools.

Again, like many other tools, this is a collection of several others. LMB-click and hold where it says sel to see the Quick Selection, Quick Rename, Numeric Input: Absolute, and Numeric Input: Relative modes (Figure 1.32).

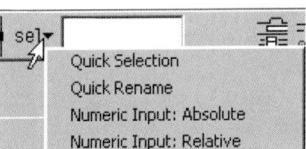

FIGURE 1.32   These nested tools are within the Numeric Input tool.

Quick Selection

This allows you to enter a name in the input field and have Maya search all objects in the scene to find the name you have typed. Note that you may use wildcards. For instance *Loft searches for any objects that end in Loft; Loft* searches for objects whose name begins with Loft; and *Loft* searches for objects with Loft anywhere in them and selects it or them.

Quick Rename

Once you have selected objects, using Quick Rename a new name can be given to entire collections of objects or individual objects.

Numeric Input: Absolute

This allows you to enter values for any Translate, Rotate, or Scale value manually. For instance, Figure 1.33 shows the lofted surface that we've been looking at. It's currently at X = 2.5 (Figure 1.33a). If we wish to center the lofted object back to X = 0, we would follow these steps:

1. Select the surface.
2. Click on the X handle of the manipulator so that it appears yellow (Figure 1.33b).
3. In Numeric Input: Absolute mode, enter 0 in the input field (Figure 1.33c) and the lofted surface will be immediately moved to this absolute location (Figure 1.33d).

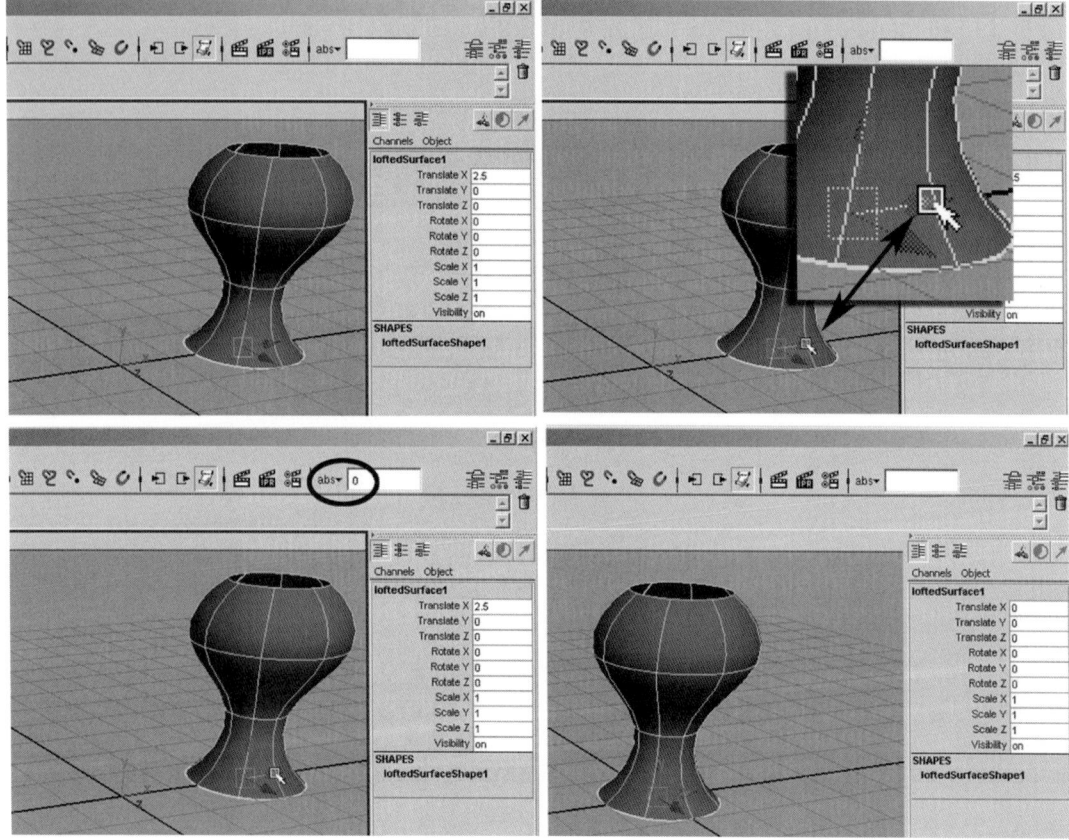

FIGURE 1.33 (a–d) Numeric Imputs: Absolute allows you to enter values quickly where objects are to be placed, scaled, or rotated.

Numeric Input: Relative

This works exactly as do the previous tools except that the value entered in the input field is added or subtracted from the current value.

SHELF

The Shelf is a handy place for frequently used tools. Maya has created by default a collection shown in Figure 1.34.

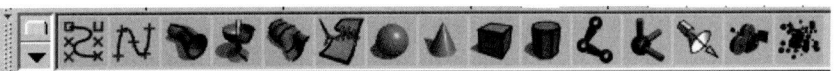

FIGURE 1.34 The Shelf is where Maya has placed tools that it thinks you will need. You can also create and customize your own.

To activate any of the items on the Shelf, simply LMB-click them. Of course, the Shelf can be organized any way you wish. See Appendix B, "Customizing the Maya User Interface," for details on how to organize this space to fit your work flow.

TOOLBOX

The Toolbox contains two main collections of tools: the QWERTY tools and a collection of tools that allow for quick customization of your interface (Figure 1.35).

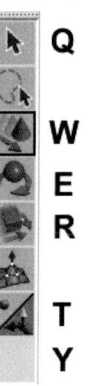

FIGURE 1.35 The Toolbox.

QWERTY

QWERTY is often used as a label for these tools, because they are accessed using the hotkeys **Q**, **W**, **E**, **R**, **T**, and **Y**.

- **Q** pulls up the top tool, the Select tool. This allows you to select a hierarchy, object, or component without altering it by clicking directly on the desired item or marqueeing (clicking and dragging) around the desired item(s). The second tool down, the Lasso tool, has no default hotkey, but it can be used to draw a custom shape around the items you want to select.
- **W** brings up the Move tool, which allows you to move hierarchies, objects, or components.
- **E** launches the Rotate tool, allowing you to rotate items.
- **R** activates the Scale tool, which allows you to scale hierarchies, objects, or components.
- **T** pulls up the Show Manipulator tool. This tool displays the manipulator (we will talk much more of this tool later) if it's hidden or gets hidden between tools.
- Finally, the **Y** hotkey brings up the last tool used, which occupies the last space of the Toolbox shown in Figure 1.35.

QUICK SETUP

The bottom half of the Toolbox contains a collection of quick setup options. One click and your interface is transformed with new collections of tools in new panels. The default setups are nice but remember you can create your own. Be sure to see Appendix B, "Customizing the Maya User Interface," when you're ready to begin customizing these sorts of tools. For most of what we will do in this volume, the default setups are sufficient.

WORKSPACE

We've been referring to the Workspace throughout this chapter. Basically, the Workspace that Maya first shows is a sort of virtual window through which we're viewing the 3D world that we will alter (Figure 1.36).

Understandably, the Workspace is the largest chunk of screen real estate. It's so important that it has its own collection of pull-down menus to allow for quick alteration of the space. In upcoming chapters, we'll look at the details of how to maneuver within this space, and how to optimize and customize the Workspace for different steps in the production process.

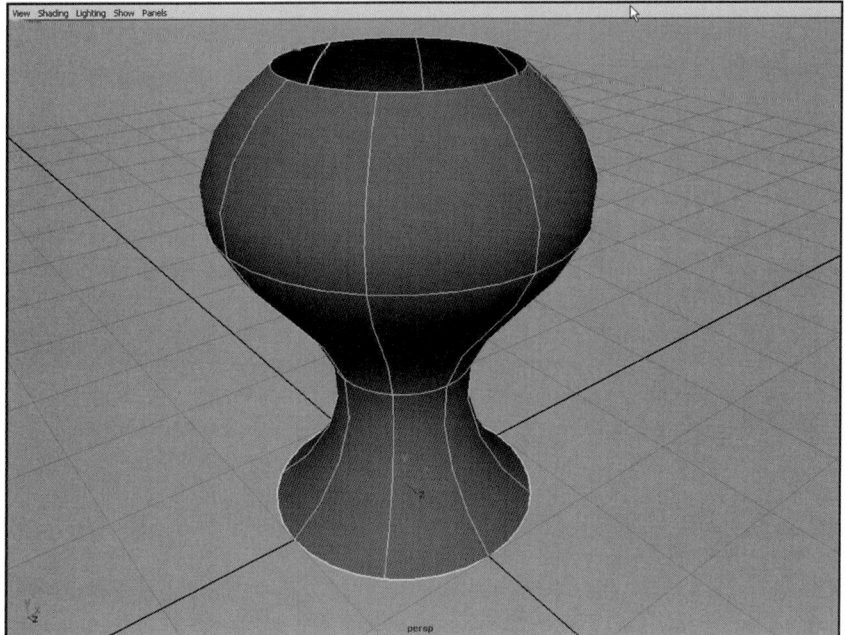

FIGURE 1.36   The Workspace.

CHANNEL/LAYER BOX, TOOL SETTINGS, AND ATTRIBUTE EDITOR

To the right of the Workspace is an area that can be used for a variety of purposes. The default setup uses this space to display the Channel box. The Channel box allows for the viewing and altering of many parameters of items within the scene (Figure 1.37a).

At the top of the Channel box is a collection of three small buttons that allow you to alter the default Channel box, to show the Layer box instead (Figure 1.37b), or both (Figure 1.37c). The Layer box allows you to create and alter layers that can contain collections of your scene. Later, the Layer box can allow you to render complex scenes by rendering chunks of data in your scene, rather than rendering everything at once.

Up at the top-right corner of the interface are three buttons (Figure 1.38a) that allow you to commandeer the space that the Channel/Layer boxes take up. This space can be used to display the Attribute Editor, which allows you to, well, edit the attributes of items within your scene

(Figure 1.38b). You can also choose to see the active tool's settings (Figure 1.38c). The third button is the standard Channel/Layer box's use of the space.

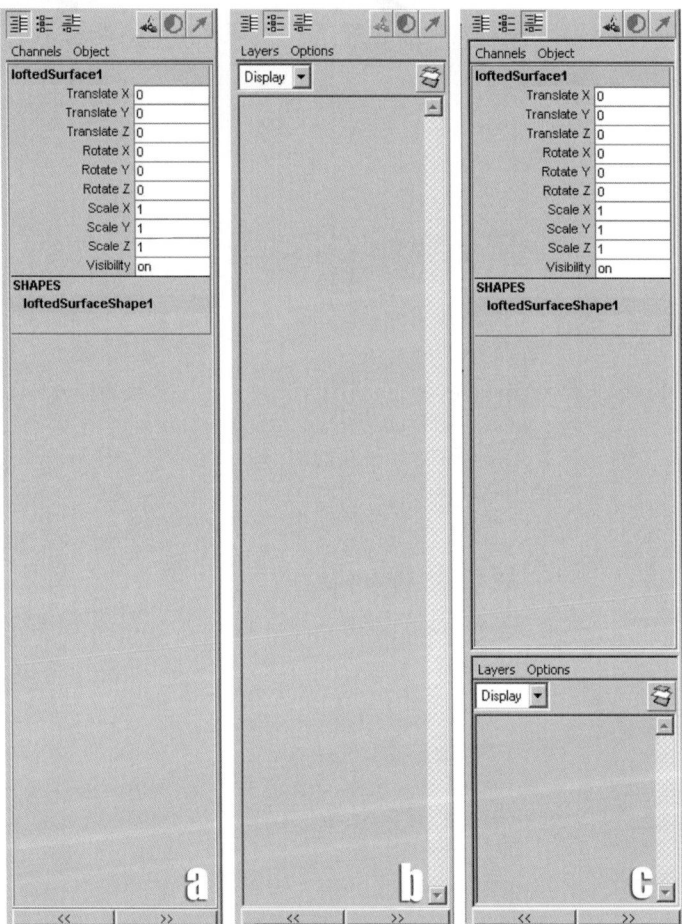

FIGURE 1.37 (a–c) The Channel and Layer boxes.

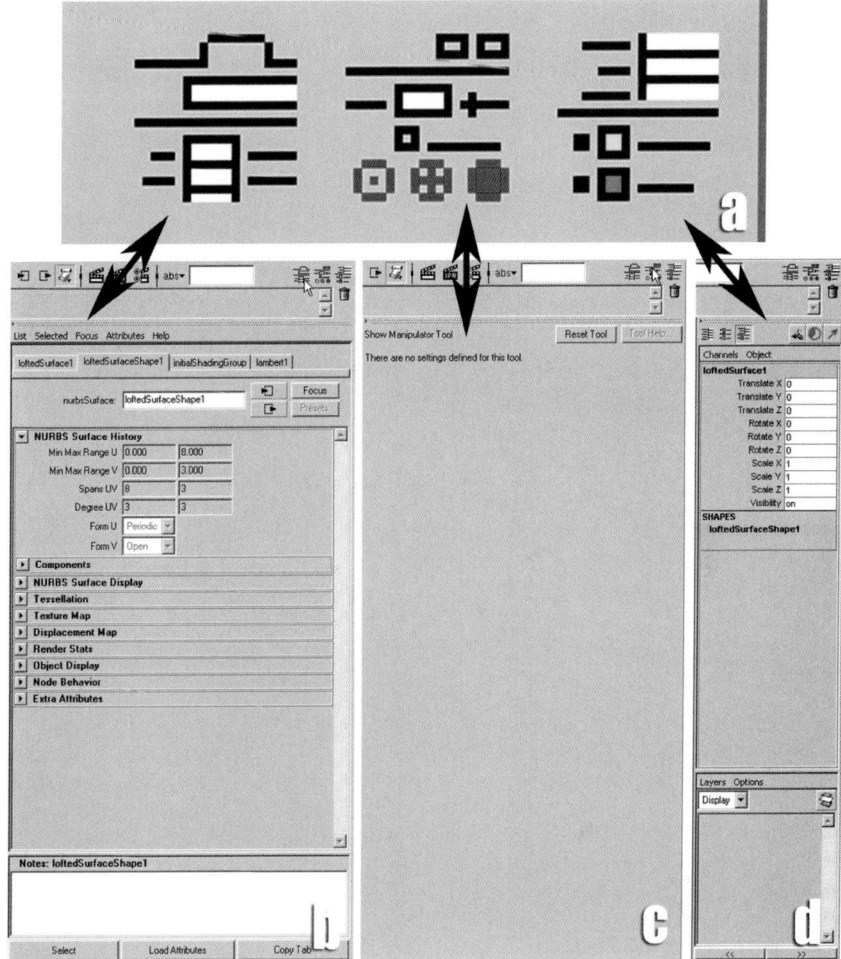

FIGURE 1.38   Shift (a–d) The Attribute Editor, Tool Settings, and Channel/Layer box.

TIME AND RANGE SLIDERS

Below the Workspace and running the length of the interface are Time and Range sliders (Figure 1.39). There are also some other animation tools that sit at the right edge of these two sliders. These are exclusively animation tools, and because we'll explore them so extensively in Chapter 11, "Animation," we won't discuss them areas further here.

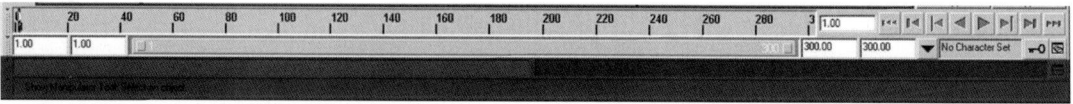

FIGURE 1.39 Time and Range sliders-+.

COMMAND LINE AND HELP LINE

Below the Time and Range sliders is the command line. In this volume, we won't get to use much Mel Script or other high-end functions that would require the Command Line. However, the line below that, the Help Line, is very useful. The left half of the Help Line can provide invaluable information on tools that you are unfamiliar with. The Help Line lists information indicating what tool your mouse is over, and then when a tool is active, the Help Line will provide details on what to do next within that tool. Watch this space closely when you are first learning Maya—it is a great aid (Figure 1.40).

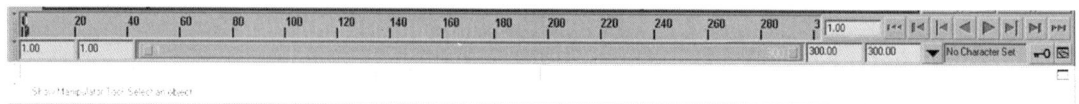

FIGURE 1.40 The Command and Help Lines.

CONCLUSION

This may seem a bit overwhelming thus far, but keep in mind, mastery of tools often depends on repetition of use or exposure to concepts. This chapter provides the first taste of where to find most collections of tools.

Remember that Maya allows for tremendous flexibility in how this interface is displayed and organized. Make sure that when you get comfortable with Maya and are at the point of streamlining your creation process, read Appendix B, "Customizing the Maya User Interface," to see how to make the Maya user interface a custom tool.

Throughout the rest of the book, we will explore how to use the collections that we have been introduced to in this chapter. That's where the fun begins.

We will now advance from overviews of collections to the specifics: the creation process.

GETTING STARTED WITH MODELING

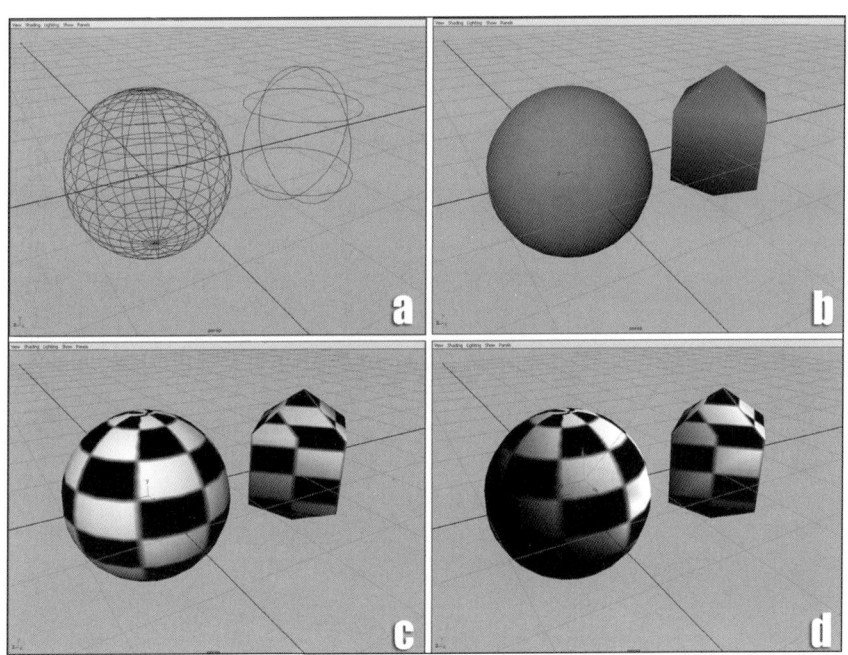

o, we looked at where tools are organized within the Maya interface in Chapter 1. We've looked at a general sense of how projects are realized with a rough idea of a work flow. This chapter will start that work flow journey with modeling. Each chapter in the rest of the book will begin with a bit of theory or general techniques. Then, we will get to the good things and look at all the details: the specifics of how projects get created. We will look at a wide variety of tools and how to bend them to your creative will. At the end of this modeling chapter, we will have created the room shown in Figure 2.1.

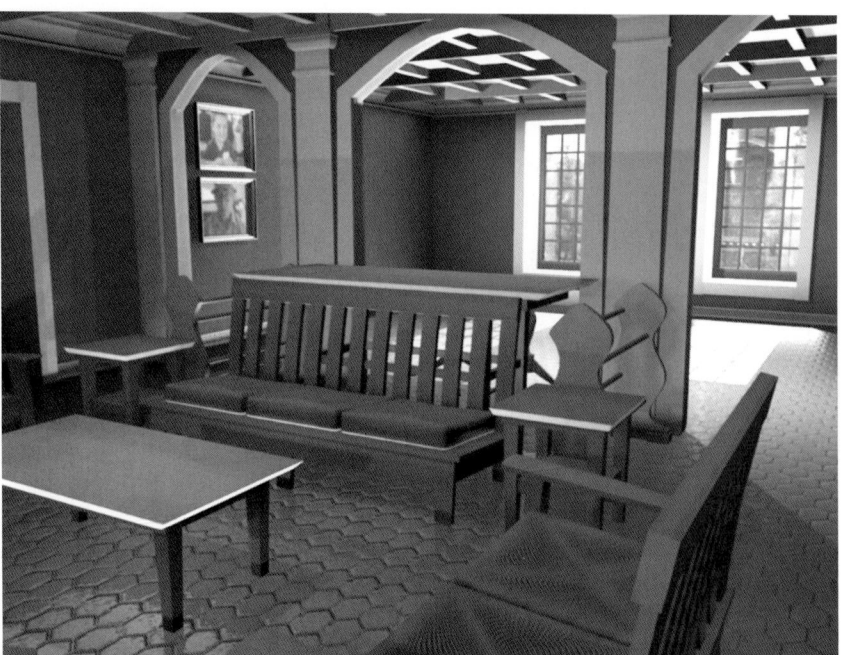

FIGURE 2.1   The completed room model created in this chapter.

SETTING UP YOUR PROJECT

Before we start building or even maneuvering, we need to set up a project in which we can store our Maya information. Follow these steps to do this:

1. With Maya open, select File > Project > New.
2. In the New Project window that pops up, enter Room_Tutorial in the Name input field and then choose a location where you'd like to save all the related files. Remember that Maya is very particular with its

naming conventions: spaces and special characters are not accept-able. Be sure to have the underscore in the Name input field.

3. Click on the Use Defaults button at the bottom of the screen and then click the Accept button.

You are ready to start creating a project in Maya. Make sure you remem-ber that any changes you make to preferences or to the interface will be stored in this project.

Maneuvering in Maya

Before we begin building our room, it is important to know how to move around in our digital world. The default view of our virtual world shows us a grid that lies along the X, Z plane. In the middle of the plane is an indicator to let us know which directions Maya understands as the X, Y, and Z directions. Also notice the small axis at the bottom-left corner of the screen. This small axis always stays there so you can get your bearings.

The **Alt** (the **Command** key on a Mac) key is critical to all move-ment. The other vital part of movement is a three-buttoned mouse. All movement through our virtual world will take place through some com-bination of these two elements.

Maneuvering through your space assumes that the Workspace is the view through a type of virtual camera. To move through the scene, you are moving the virtual camera to a new location. As such, all the names for different types of movement are traditional camera terms. Take a mo-ment to try these combinations:

Tumble (Alt-LMB):   Tumbling can also be referred to as rotating your camera around the object; you'll use it often. Hold down the **Alt** key, then click and drag the LMB to tumble around the scene. Notice that you always tumble around the center of the Workspace.

Track (Alt-RMB):   Tracking is similar to moving your camera from side to side without turning it. This allows you to move what your camera is looking at and brings into play a new center of your Workspace. Once you've tracked to a new location, when you tumble, you'll tumble around the current center of the screen.

Dolly (Alt-LMMB—that's left and middle mouse button):   A dolly move is the equivalent of moving your camera closer to the center of the Workspace. It is important to notice that the camera's focal length doesn't change (we don't get any more telephoto or fish eye), but the camera does get closer to the scene, and conse-quently, the objects look bigger.

Get familiar with these combinations. Maya is amazingly snappy in its OpenGL implementation, and you'll find yourself doing much more work in a perspective view than you may have done in your previous 3D experience. So it is important that you feel comfortable and in control of movement within the 3D perspective view.

Much modification of any item within Maya takes place via a manipulator. To better understand the manipulator, consider the following mini-tutorial.

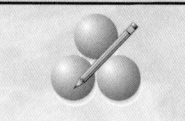

TUTORIAL 2.1   **EXPLORING THE MANIPULATOR**

Step 1: Select Modeling | Create > NURBS Primitives > Sphere.

Step 2: Dolly into the scene until the sphere appears a bit larger in the Workspace (Figure 2.2a).

Step 3: Hit 3 and then 5 on your keyboard. We will talk more about this in a minute. For now, suffice it to say it makes the geometry more intuitive (Figure 2.2b).

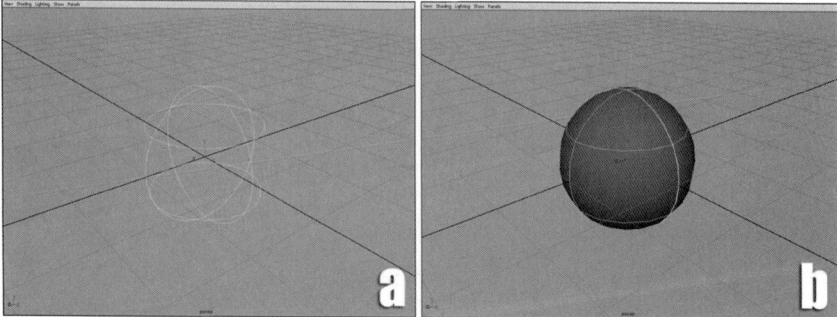

FIGURE 2.2 (a–b)   Create a sphere, dolly in to see it closer, and have it display as a solid object.

Step 4: Activate the Move Tool from the Toolbox. You can also hit **w** (make sure it is lowercase) on your keyboard to activate it. Immediately, you'll notice that in the middle of the sphere is a new icon for the manipulator (Figure 2.3a).

Step 5: Switch to the Rotate tool (e) (Figure 2.3b) and then to the Scale tool (r) (Figure 2.3c). Notice how the manipulator changes to match.

When you wish to move, rotate, or scale any element within your scene, the manipulator is the visual tool that allows you to do so. The ma-

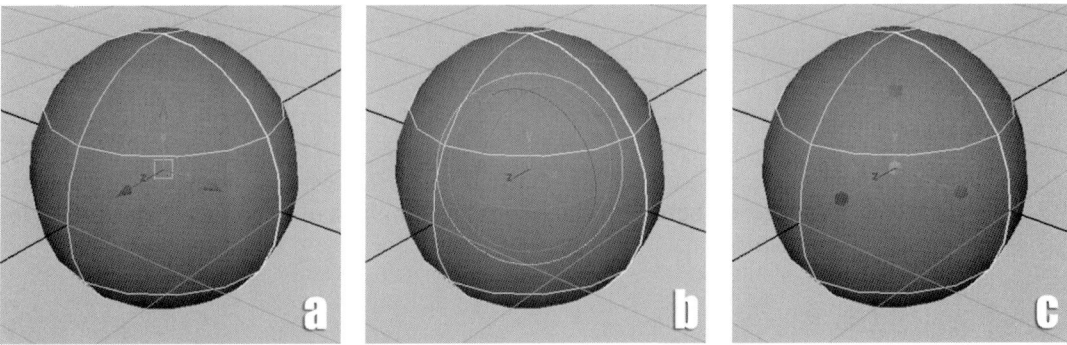

FIGURE 2.3   The manipulator appears at the geometric center of the selected object. (a) The Move manipulator. (b) The Rotate Manipulator. (c) The Scale manipulator.

nipulator is essentially a collection of handles that you can grab to make changes. The Move manipulator, for example, consists of four handles: X, Y, Z, and center (Figure 2.4a).

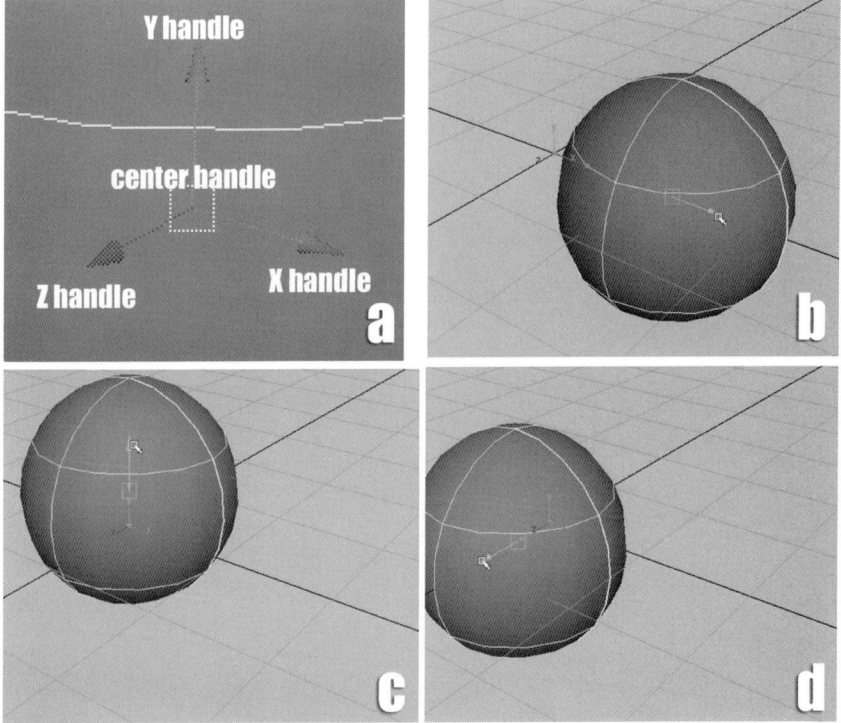

FIGURE 2.4   (a) Handle breakdown. (b) Moving object in X direction with the X handle. (c) Moving object in Y direction with the Y handle. (d) Moving object in Z direction with the Z handle.

The way these handles work is simple. Just LMB drag any of the handles to move the selected item in the direction of the handle. So, to move the sphere in the X direction, simply grab the red X handle and drag (Figure 2.4b). Do the same for the Y and Z directions and handles (Figures 2.4c and 2.4d). The handle you are manipulating will turn yellow.

The center handle allows you to LMB drag the element in all directions. The center handle for the Move manipulator does have some other important qualities. Look closely at the center handle and you'll notice that it is a square (Figure 2.5a). No matter which direction you look at the manipulator from, that center handle remains a square. This square represents the view plane. The view plane is the imaginary plane that runs perpendicular to you, the viewer. This means that when you grab this center handle and move the object (although it is moving absolutely in three dimensions), it is always sitting on the current view plane.

If you **Ctrl**-LMB any one of the X, Y, or Z handles, it turns off that direction handle. The center handle (previously a box) then becomes a plane that corresponds to the two directions in which you can still move the object (Figure 2.5 b, c, and d).

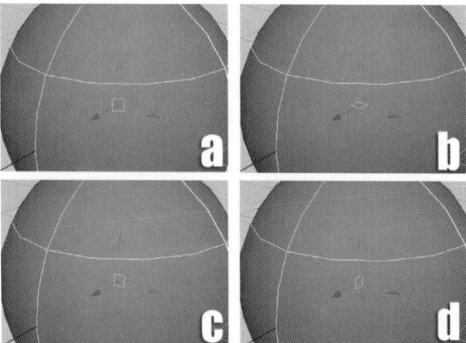

FIGURE 2.5 (a–d) The center handle indicates the directions in which you can move an item in the Workspace. You can turn off potential directions by **Ctrl**-LMB-clicking them.

To return the Move manipulator's center handle to move along the view plane, simply **Ctrl**-LMB-click the center handle again.

The Rotate manipulator and Scale manipulator aren't quite as complicated. In each, LMB-dragging any of the directional handles rotates or scales exclusively in that one direction. LMB-dragging the center of the rotation handles, or the center scale handle, rotates or scales in all directions.

UNDERSTANDING STATES OF OBJECT DISPLAY

When we first created the sphere, it didn't look much like a sphere—it kind of looked like four circles that intersected each other at their poles. In the early days of 3D, the actual visual representation of your model wasn't much more than this view of the isoparms that made up the shape. Isoparms are one of the components that make up NURBS shapes (more on what exactly NURBS are later in Chapters 4 and 5).

By default, Maya shows objects to you as simply as it can. In the case of a NURBS object, it does this by showing these circles that help define the shape. If we look at a polygonal sphere, the default view shows us a transparent view of all the polygons that make up that shape (Figure 2.6a). This view of objects that allows us to see through the objects as though we were looking at a papier-mâché piñata before the papier-mâché is placed over the frame is called a *wireframe*.

Wireframe is a mode that your computer with its video card is able to draw quickly. It doesn't have to spend a lot of energy deciding which surfaces aren't going to be seen or thinking about how those surfaces react to the virtual light around them. However, wireframes can be a bit distracting. For one thing, when displayed as a wireframe, your model doesn't look much like the actual object.

As computers have increased in power and complexity, they've become better equipped to show 3D objects in increasingly lifelike fashions. OpenGL is the technology that allows your video card to take the 3D information and process it into increasingly lifelike representations in real time. This means that instead of having to work with collections of lines, we can work with visual forms. Maya has one of the best OpenGL implementations in the industry.

To display your model as a smooth object, simply hit **5** on your keyboard. This brings up Smooth Shade (Figure 2.6b), which attempts to create a solid version of your model. Something to note about Smooth Shade is that it functions with the assumption that there's a flood light sitting atop your virtual camera. That is, no matter how you tumble, you'll never see the dark side of your object. Also, it doesn't show any textures or shaders that may have been applied.

To get a better idea of how light in a scene actually functions, hit **6** on your keyboard to bring up Smooth Shade with Hardware Texturing (Figure 2.6c). This tells Maya not only to show you the objects as solid shapes but also to show an approximation of any textures that may have been applied to the surface.

Hitting **7** on your keyboard adds the extra burden and help of attempting to calculate how the light in the scene would look, approximately (Figure 2.6d). Now of course, this quick hardware shading (the hardware refers primarily to your video card) isn't tremendously accurate.

However, it can give you a very rough idea of where your lights are pointing and how the colors of the lights and the colors of the surfaces will interact.

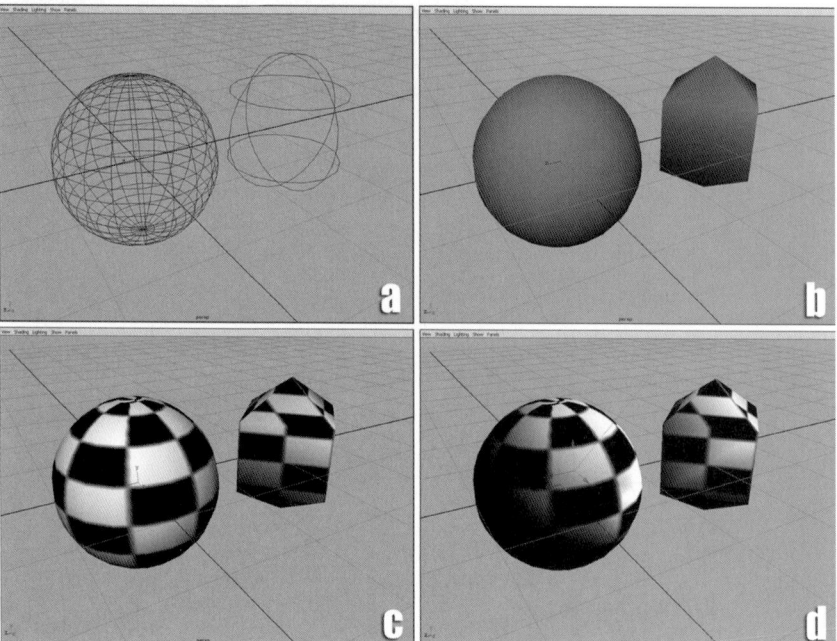

FIGURE 2.6   (a) Compare Polygonal Sphere (left) and NURBS Sphere (right) using Wireframe. (b) Smooth Shade. (c) Smooth Shade with Hardware Texturing. (d) Smooth Shade with Hardware Texturing and Lighting.

Now, you'll notice that the NURBS sphere to the right in each example in Figure 2.6 doesn't look much like a sphere. This is because NURBS can be displayed as rough, medium, or fine within the Workspace. To change the level of smoothness, simply hit **1**, **2**, or **3** for rough, medium, or fine, respectively (Figure 2.7).

In general, when you first start a scene, it is a habit to hit **3** and **5** or **6** quickly to get a vision of the 3D space you are working with that has solid shapes. Later, if things get complex and the interface begins to slow down, you can always reduce the smoothing, choose not to show textures, and so on. However, up front, it is nice to take advantage of that expensive video card in your machine and give it a bit of a workout for your benefit.

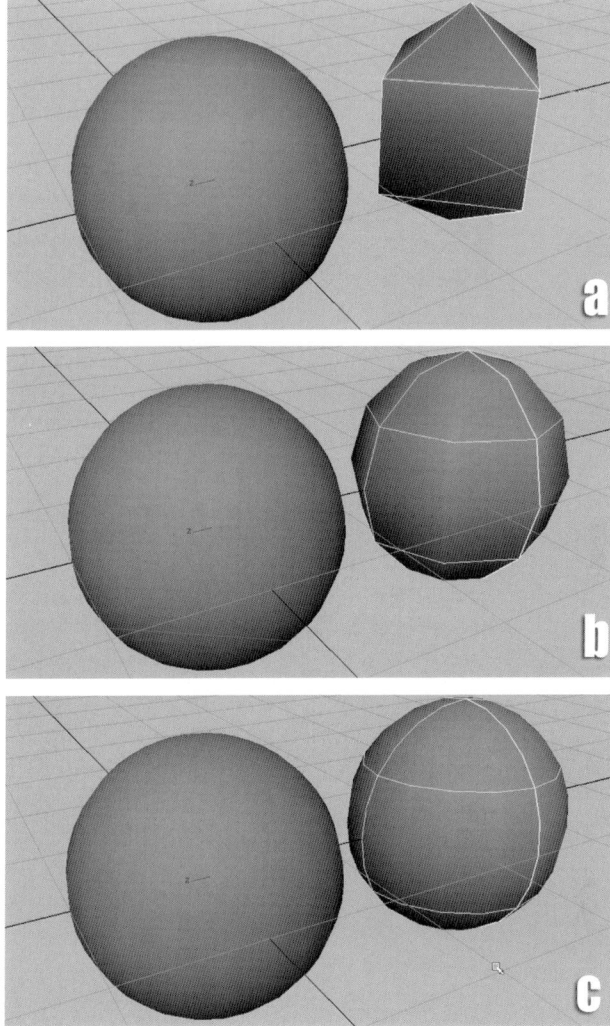

FIGURE 2.7   (a) Change the Rough, (b) Medium, and (c) Fine display of NURBS. Note that the change has no effect on the polygonal sphere on the left.

MOVING ON

So now we've talked about the manipulators and know how to do basic move, rotate, and scale functions; how to move around within our scene; and how to can control how Maya displays our scene. Now it is time to start creating the scene. LMB-click on the sphere used for these examples to select it. Then delete it from your scene by hitting the **Backspace** or **Delete** key and start on the next tutorial.

TUTORIAL 2.2   PRIMITIVE ROOM FORMS

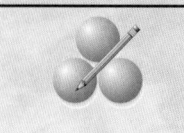

To start modeling this room, we're going to begin with 3D shapes that Maya makes automatically. Although you can make just about any shape imaginable in Maya, there's a small collection of shapes that Maya has built in that are readily accessible through the Modeling module pull-down menus.

In this tutorial, we will look at how to create, scale, and position these primitives into position to rough out our room. At the end of this chapter, you should be comfortable with maneuvering within Maya's Workspace and feel confident in your knowledge of basic object manipulation.

Step 1: Activate the Modeling module.

Step 2: Create a floor with a NURBS plane. To begin, we will work with both NURBS and polygonal objects. We will talk much more about when to use which later, but for this project, we will explore the placement and alteration of both.

Go to Modeling | Create > NURBS Primitives > Plane (Option) to bring up the NURBS Plane Options window. To be sure that you are not inheriting any earlier settings, use Edit > Reset Settings (within the NURBS Plane Options window) to clear out everything. For now, simply hit the Create button to place the plane in the scene.

Step 3: Resize to 20 units by 35 units. Although we could just eyeball the size of this floor, since it will help define the shape of the entire rest of the room, it will be important that we create it with accurate dimensions.

In the Channel Box, enter 25 in the Scale X input field and hit **Enter**. Then, enter 40 in the Scale Z input field and again hit **Enter**. This tells the previous 1 unit by 1 unit plane to become 25 by 40. For the sake of this tutorial, we will assume that the units here are feet.

Hit **3** and **5** on your keyboard to give yourself a solid look at the floor (Figure 2.8).

There are a few things to notice about this NURBS plane. First, it is truly two-dimensional. It has depth in the X and Z directions but it has no actual thickness. It is like a piece of paper lying in space though it is infinitely thinner.

The next thing that's important to notice about this step is that we re-sized the plane, but left it in place. This means that the plane's center is sitting at 0,0,0. The benefit of this is that the floor is indeed on the default ground plane.

Step 4: Create the first wall with a Polygon Cube primitive. Choose Modeling | Create > Polygon Primitives > Cube (Option). Again, this will open the options box for the Cube. Make sure you reset the settings to clear out any random settings that may already exist. Hit the Create button.

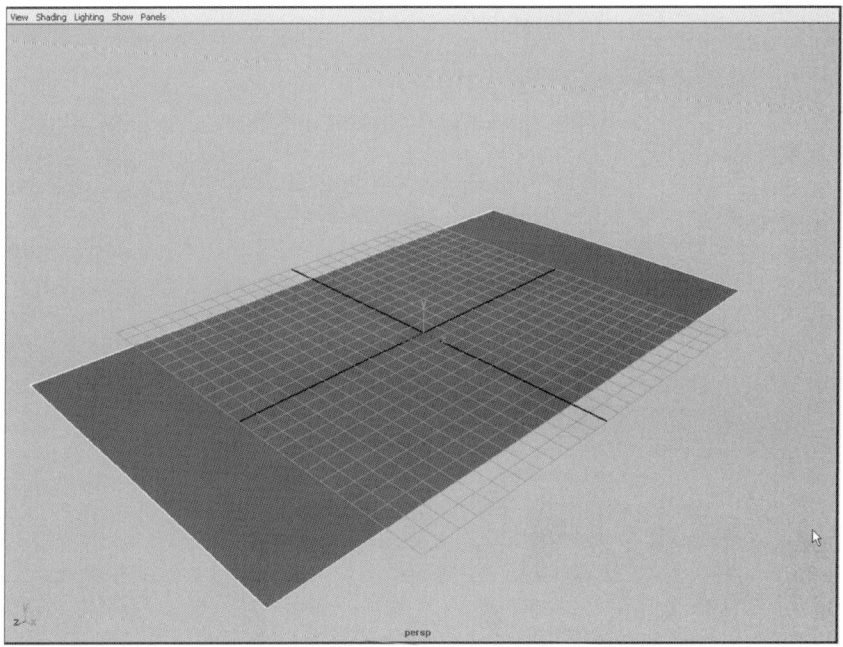

FIGURE 2.8   Our 25 by 40 floor is made from a NURBS plane.

The newly created cube will be small and sitting in the middle of your room. We will resize and position this cube using the Channel Box.

Without clicking anywhere in the Workspace, enter 40 in the Scale Z input field in the Channel Box. We know that the floor is 40 feet long, so a side wall would also need to be this long. Also enter 2 in the Scale X input field to give this wall some extra thickness. Finally, enter 9 in the Scale Y input field.

The wall will be halfway into the floor. We need to place it so it rests on the floor. We know that the wall is 9 feet tall, and that the wall expanded up and down from the middle. So, we need to move the floor up 4.5 feet (half of the height of the wall). In the Channel Box, enter 4.5 into the Translate Y input field. This will move the wall up so that it sits on the floor.

Continuing with the Channel Box method, we know that the wall's center is sitting halfway across the room (in the X direction). From the current position to the edge of the floor is 12.5 feet (half of the floor's 25 feet). But, the wall is 2 feet thick. If we enter 12.5 in the Translate X input field, the wall will hang halfway off the floor. So, we need to subtract 1 foot (half of the 2 foot thickness of the wall) from the direction it needs to move. Enter 11.5 feet into the Translate X input field to move the wall so that the outer edge of the wall lines up perfectly with the edge of the floor (Figure 2.9).

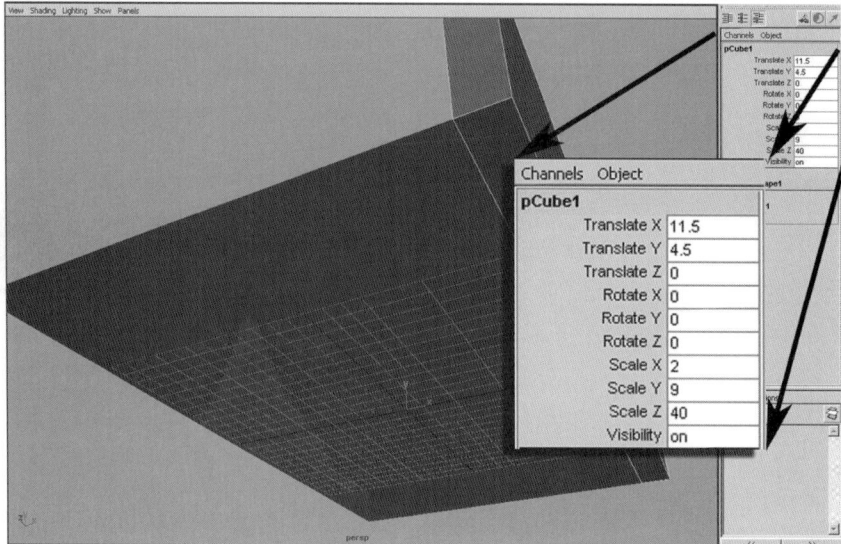

FIGURE 2.9   Placed wall and resulting Channel Box with defined values.

Step 5: Create a second wall through duplication. To create the wall on the opposite side of the room, we could simply repeat the process outlined in Step 4. However, to save time, we will take this perfectly good wall and make a duplicate of it.

Select Edit > Duplicate (Option). Again, because this is the first time we've used the tool, select Edit > Reset Settings in the Duplicate Options window to clear any past settings. Hit the Duplicate button.

In the Workspace, there won't seem to be change. This is because the new duplicated wall is sitting in exactly the same space as the original one. Open the Outliner (Window > Outliner) and see for yourself that there are two pCube objects in the scene.

Step 6: Use Maya's Align tool to align the new wall to the opposite end of the room. We could simply work with another collection of values in the Channel Box to position this wall on the opposite end. However, though that method is exact, it isn't necessarily the most wieldy or intuitive. For this step, we will use a function introduced in Maya 4.5: the Align tool.

Select Modify > Snap Align Objects > Align Tool. This will make your mouse change from an arrow to a small cross, and some small grayed out icons will appear around your wall. They are grayed out because the Align tool needs at least two objects to work with. So, hold down the **Shift** key and click on the floor. All of a sudden, you'll get a collection of gray and blue icons surrounding objects in your scene (Figure 2.10).

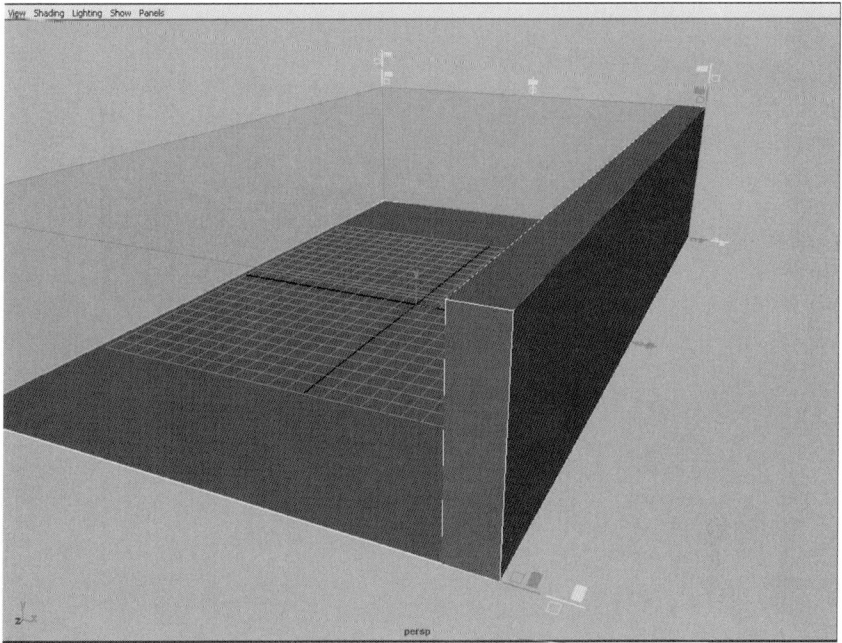

FIGURE 2.10   When two objects are selected, the Align tool will present icons that allow you to align your objects.

These icons are fairly intuitive, but let's look at a few for just a minute (Figure 2.11). There are some conventions that are important to know. The first is that the initial object that you select (of the two that must be selected to align) will be the object that moves. Further, this first object (the one that moves) is represented by the hollowed-out box. The solid blue box is the second object selected and it remains stationary. So, in this case, the wall was selected first, so it will be doing the moving and is represented in the Align tool by the hollow box. So, if the middle icon shown in Figure 2.11 is pressed, the wall will be moved so that its horizontal (X) center matches the center of our floor.

Similarly, on the far left are two icons. The top icon represents moving the wall so that it is inner edge lines up with the outer edge of the floor. The bottom icon is the one we want, because we want the outer edge of the wall to match the outer edge of the floor (Figure 2.11b).

To exit the Align tool, simply select any other tool.

Step 7: Rename the elements created thus far. Before we get too far, it is important that we take control of the scene in terms of nomenclature. Terms such as pCube1, pCube2, and nurbsPlane1 do nothing for us

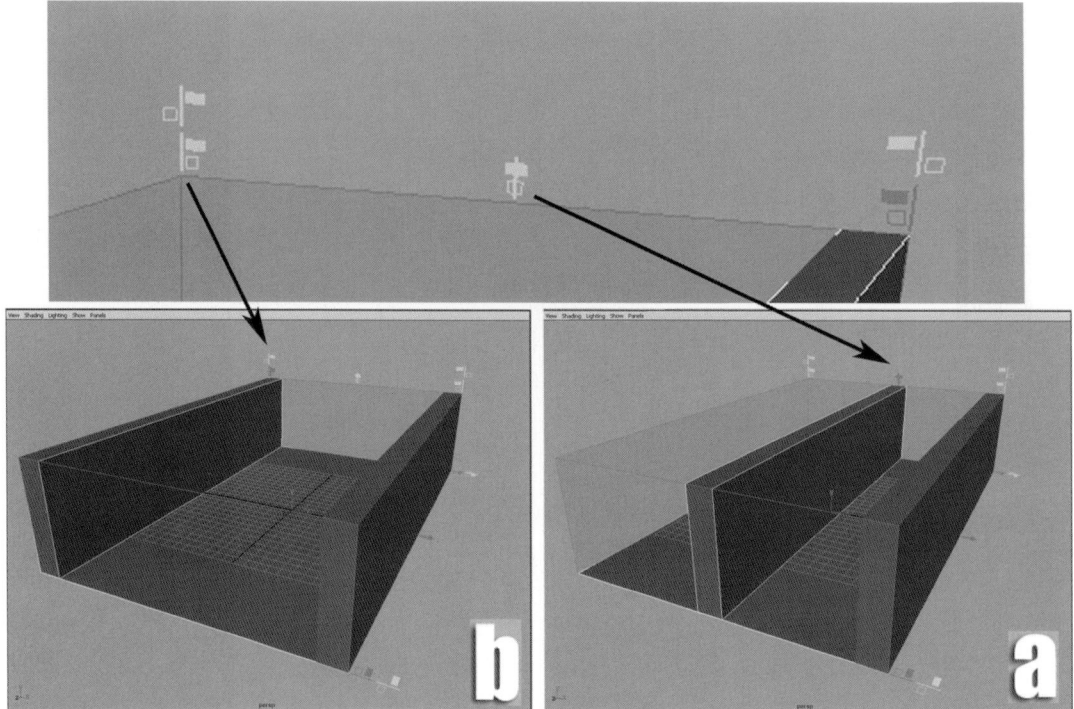

FIGURE 2.11 (a–b)   Take a quick look at the Align tool. Remember that the first object selected will move and that it is represented by the hollow blue boxes.

as we try to organize our scene. For now, it may not seem like a big deal that we are not giving objects more indicative names, but when there are 200 or 300 objects and hierarchies in a scene, it is vitally important.

There are a few ways to name objects or rename objects that have already been created. The easiest is through the Outliner, which is a window that outlines objects within your scene. It can be pulled up through the Window > Outliner pull-down menu, or viewed by pulling up one of the premade panel organizations.

In the Toolbox at the left edge of the UI (user interface), select the Persp/Outliner preset (Figure 2.12). This will change your interface to look like Figure 2.12.

The Outliner, of course, is the new box on the left of the Workspace with a list of objects. Some of these objects are invisible to you presently (such as the defaultLightSet, defaultObjectSet, and the four cameras), but don't worry about them for now. What's important is that we've created the three objects now. To rename an object, double-LMB-click its name in the Outliner. This highlights the name so you can change it to whatever you wish.

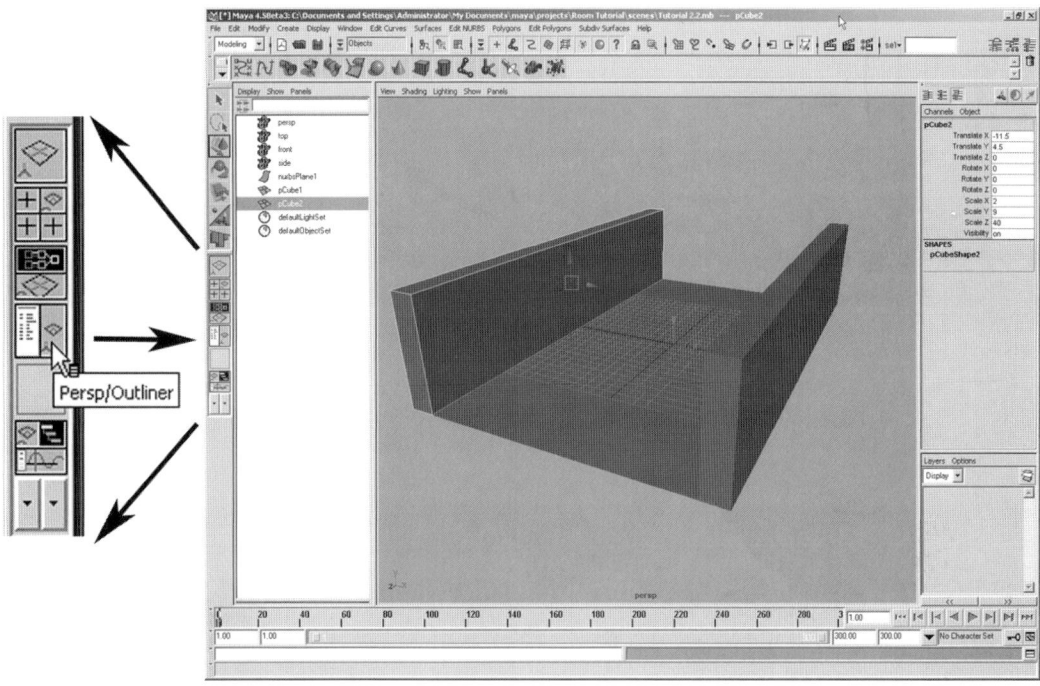

FIGURE 2.12   Take some time to bring Outliner into your panel layout. The premade Persp/Outliner setting will do the trick.

Rename nurbsPlane1 to Floor; rename the wall that's to the left (–X) direction WallNorth; and rename the wall to the right (+X) WallSouth. The directions aren't arbitrary, because the final image will make use of lights coming in through the window and we want to make sure that's facing east. Plus, it becomes easier to refer to walls by their north, south, east, and west bearings.

Step 8: Create WallEast and WallWest by duplicating existing walls and put them into position with the Align tool. Select Wall-North and hit **Ctrl-D** (the keyboard shortcut for Duplicate). We can just use the keyboard shortcut, because we can remember that the settings are all clear since we reset them earlier.

A new wall called WallNorth1 will appear in the Outliner. Again, there will be little visible difference as the new wall is in the same space as the old one. We want to rotate this wall 90 degrees off its present heading. The easiest way to keep track of how Maya rotates objects is to decide along which axis the object would need to turn. In this case, to rotate the wall so that it is at a right angle to the other walls, we would need to rotate the wall around its Y axis. So, enter 90 into the Rotate Y input field (Figure 2.13a).

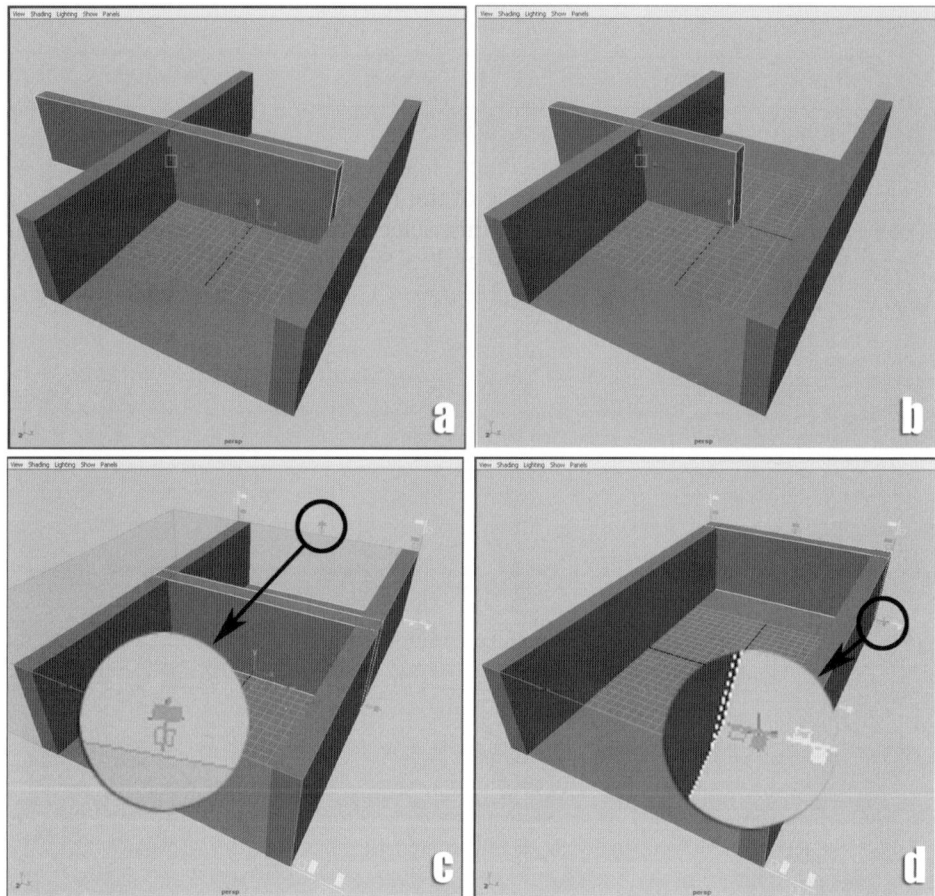

FIGURE 2.13 (a–d)   Duplicate an existent wall, rotate it, and resize it to match the floor. Figures c and d show the results of the Align tool and which icons to use.

We know that the floor is 25 feet wide. For the floor, this is the X measurement. However, because we've rotated the wall, remember that the length of the wall is its Z scale measurement. Change the existing setting (40) to the new 25 in the Scale Z input field of the Channel Box (Figure 2.13b).

Now, activate the Align tool (Modify > Snap Align Objects > Align Tool) and first align the wall to the middle of the floor in the X direction (Figure 2.13c). Then align it so that its outer edge matches the inner edge of the floor (Figure 2.13d). Notice that to do this, we used icons that resided along different planes of the gray align box that the Align tool creates to assist us.

Rename this new wall WallEast.

Duplicate WallEast and use the Align tool to place it on the opposite end of the room. Rename this new wall WallWest.

Step 9: Create a placeholder wall. Later, in Chapter 4, we're going to create the arched wall seen in the final rendering of this room. But for now, to help with spacing, we're going to just place a primitive polygonal cube in the middle of the room to help us as we create the beamwork in the ceiling. To do this, select WallEast, duplicate it (**Ctrl-D**), and change its Translate Z to 0 and its Scale X to .3. This puts a wall in the middle of the room with a thickness of about 4 inches. Again, this will go away but it will be important for us in future steps. Rename this wall WallMiddlePH.

Step 10: Create and position the first beam. The first beam we're going to create will rest right up against the placeholder wall that we've created. Although you could copy and paste walls that exist, for practice, create a new cube polygon primitive. Resize this polygon primitive so that it is 25 units in X (Scale X = 25), .5 units in Y (Scale Y = 0.5), and .1 units in Z (Scale Z = 0.1). This makes a beam that's 25 feet long, 6 inches tall, and a bit over 1 inch thick.

Use the Align tool to place this new beam at the top of the placeholder wall. Now activate the Move tool (hot key **w**) and move this beam along its Z axis just far enough so that you can see it without it being inside the placeholder wall (Figure 2.14). We will place this beam much more accurately later but for now, we just need to see it.

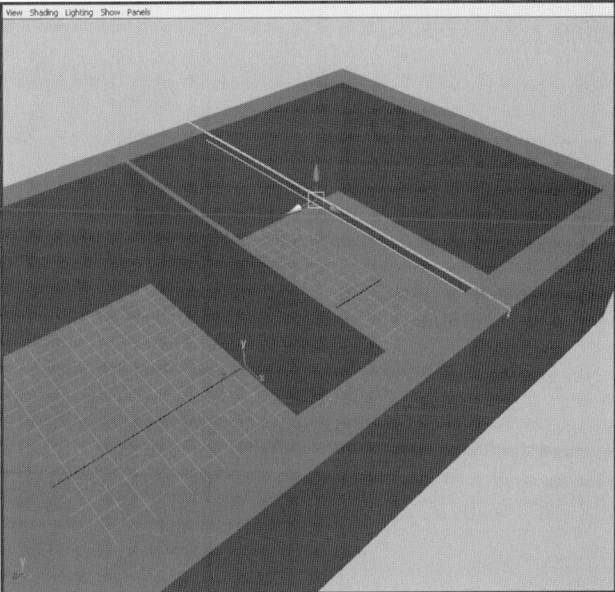

FIGURE 2.14   The beam is aligned with the tops of the walls and offset from the middle placeholder wall.

Now we could figure out mathematically where this beam would need to be so that it butts up against the middle wall, but let's take a minute to examine some other methods of moving and aligning objects.

While your mouse is inside the Workspace, press and hold the **Spacebar** until you get the Marking menu shown in Figure 2.15. Click in the middle of the Marking menu and select Top View. The Workspace will shift into an orthographic Top view. Orthographic means that you can only see and manipulate two dimensions. In this Top view, you can see and alter objects in the X and Z direction.

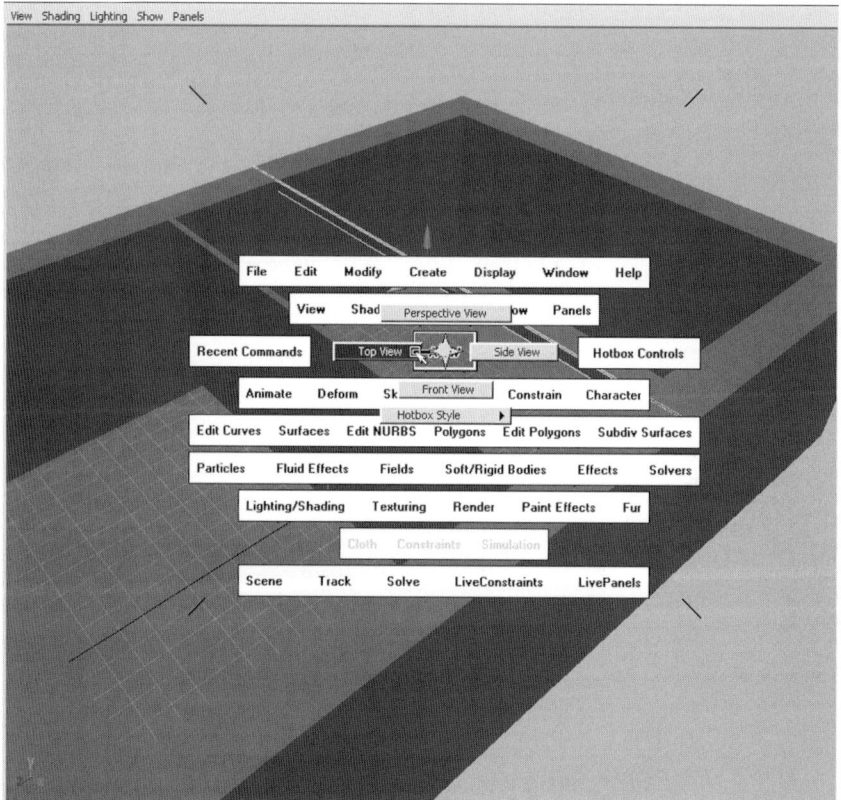

FIGURE 2.15   Changing the Workspace to the Top view with the Spacebar Marking menu.

Hit **4** on your keyboard to display the scene as a wireframe. Otherwise, everything is a flat gray and it is impossible to differentiate where one shape ends and the next one begins. Assuming that the Move tool is still active, you'll see the manipulator for the beam sitting in the middle of the beam in both the X and Z directions (Figure 2.16a). We're going to shift this manipulator so that it rests on one of the corners of the beam. Then, once it is sitting right on the corner, we can snap that corner to other parts of our model.

To do this, hit the **Insert** button on your keyboard. The manipulator will change immediately to an icon similar to the one shown in Figure 2.16b. Be sure to notice the inset image in Figure 2.16b to get a better idea of what this looks like.

This new manipulator allows us to change the position of the manipulator for the Move, Scale, and Rotate tools. In situations where you are rotating an object, this is especially important, as the geometric middle of an object such as a door isn't the place where you want the door to rotate. You can move this manipulator by LMB-clicking and dragging in the middle of the yellow box or by dragging any of the manipulator handles represented by simple lines.

In this case, we want to get the manipulator to be right at the corner of the beam. To do this, we will snap the manipulator to the point (or vertex) that exists at the corner of the beam. You can activate Snap to Points in the Status Line, or hold down the **v** hotkey. Either way, the manipulator's yellow square will change to a yellow circle. LMB-click and drag the manipulator to the bottom-right corner of the beam (Figure 2.16c).

Release the mouse before releasing the **v** on your keyboard. You may need to dolly in to see closer where the manipulator is sitting. You should be able to feel it snap into position. Hit the **Insert** button again to tell Maya that you are done changing the position of the manipulator.

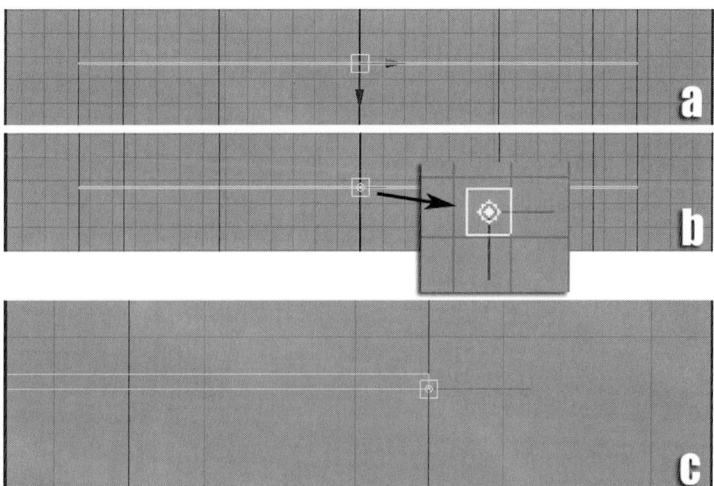

FIGURE 2.16 (a–c) Manipulate the position of manipulator. In this case, there's special care to make sure that the manipulator is snapped to the corner of the beam.

Still in Top view, take a moment to dolly out until you can see both the beam and the box that represents the placeholder wall. Again, using the Move tool, we can snap this beam right up against the placeholder wall by holding down the **v** hotkey and LMB-dragging the blue (Z) manipulator handle down until it snaps into place against the wall.

Press and hold the **Spacebar** and select Perspective view again by clicking in the middle of the marking menu. In Perspective view, tumble around so that you can see how the beam lines up against the placeholder wall (Figure 2.17). Rename the beam Beam.

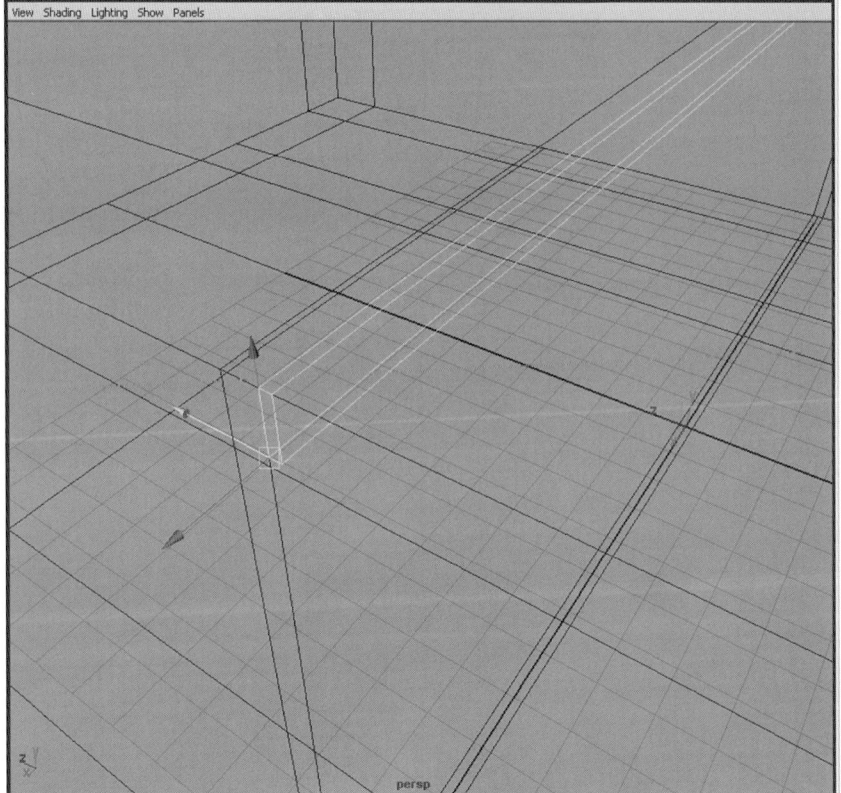

FIGURE 2.17 View of the beam snapped up against the placeholder wall.

Step 11: Duplicate and place another beam against WallEast. Hit **Ctrl-D** to duplicate Beam. This will create a new object called Beam1 automatically. To get it butted up against WallEast, we could change the position of the manipulator as we did earlier. But in the interest of exploring various methods, we will make use of the Numeric Input tool in the Status Line (far right).

Using the Move tool, hold down the **v** key to indicate that you wish to Snap to Points. Then LMB-click and drag the Z handle of Beam1's manipulator so that it snaps against the inside vertex of WallEast (Figure 2.18). Now, remember that because the manipulator is on the inside corner of the beam, this newly placed beam is inside the wall.

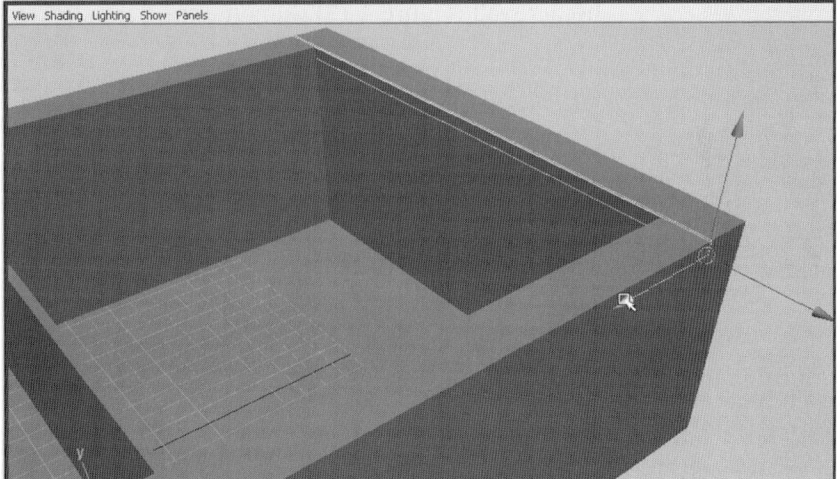

FIGURE 2.18   The newly placed Beam1 is actually .01 feet inside the wall.

However, we know that this beam is exactly .1 units thick. So, you can double-check this in the Channel Box while Beam1 is selected. This is important, because it means that the beam is exactly 0.1 foot into the wall.

In the Status Line, at the far right, change the Numeric Input tool to Numeric Input: Relative (Figure 2.19a). To refresh your memory from the last chapter, this change allows us to enter a value that will be added to the active value. Right now, by default, there's no active value; we need to activate one in the Channel Box. Because we want to move Beam1 out of the wall, we need to make the adjustment in the Z direction. So, click on Translate Z in the Channel Box (not the input field). It should highlight.

Now, in the Numeric Input tool's input field, enter 0.1 (Figure 2.19b). When you hit Enter, Beam1 will shift in the Z direction 0.1 units. The new value for Translate Z, 17.95, should be reflected in the Channel Box.

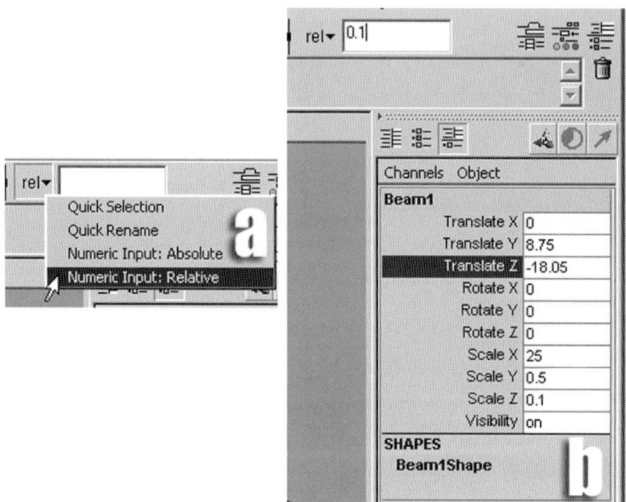

FIGURE 2.19 (a–b)   Alter the Numeric Input tool to allow for a value that adds to the one in the Channel Box.

Step 12: Hide extraneous objects and measure the distance between Beam and Beam1. We will need to put some additional beams between Beam and Beam1. To make sure that they are appropriately spaced, it is important that we know exactly how far apart the extant beams are from each other.

Maya has some nice measuring tools, but if there are too many objects in the scene, it can become tricky to indicate which distances you really want to measure. So, we will hide objects that would be in the way. Select Floor, and then hold down the **Shift** key, and add all the walls to the selection. You can do this in either the Workspace or in the Outliner (the Outliner is probably slightly easier).

Once all these objects are selected, hit **Ctrl-H**. The pull-down menu for this command is Display > Hide > Hide Selection. This should make Beam and Beam1 visible in the Workspace.

Change the Workspace to Top view (**Spacebar**, Marking menu, click in the center, Top view). This will give you a clear view of the distance between the beams.

Select Create > Measure Tool > Distance Tool. Your mouse will change to crosshairs. These crosshairs allow you to plot points between which Maya will measure the distance. In our case, we want to know the distance from the inside corner of Beam to the inside corner of Beam1 (or in this view, the bottom corners of each). To get exact measurements, we also want to make sure that as we're plotting these points to measure between, we snap right to the corner. So, hold **v** down and LMB-click on the bottom corner of Beam in the Workspace.

A large green cross should appear and a new object called locator1 will appear in the Outliner. Now, while still holding down the **v** key, click on the bottom corner of Beam1. A whole slew of things happen at this point. Two new objects appear in the Outliner: the second locator (locator2) and the actual distance (distanceDimension1). In the Workspace, the measurement should read 17.75 (Figure 2.20).

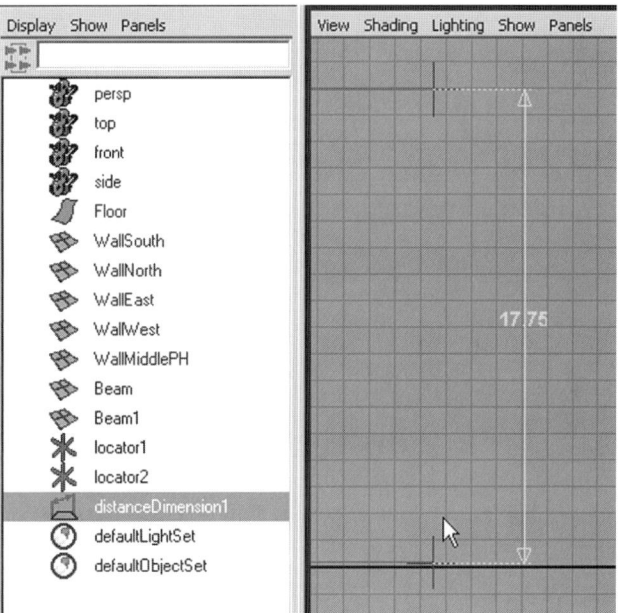

FIGURE 2.20   The result of taking a measurement.

Step 13: Duplicate three new beams directly into place. Because the design calls for five beams, we will have four spaces between beams. A quick calculation (one-fourth of 17.75 = 4.4375) gives us the distance the next three beams should be from each other to give us five beams that are equal distances apart. However, instead of duplicating and placing each beam individually, we will have Maya do it with the Duplicate function.

Select Beam in the Workspace and choose Edit > Duplicate (Option). Figure 2.21 shows the Duplicate Options dialog box. The three columns connected to the rows—Translate, Rotate, and Scale—although unlabeled, represent X, Y, and Z values, respectively. This window allows us to do things such as move (Translate), rotate, and scale duplicates. So in our case, we know that we want each duplicate to be 4.4375 feet from the beam before it. Specifically, we need the duplicate beams to be moving in the –Z direction. So, by entering this value in the Z column of the Translate row, we're telling Maya to move each duplicate –4.375 units from the original object or the last duplicate. Up to now, we've been making single duplicates but notice that there's an area to define the number of copies. In our case, we would like three.

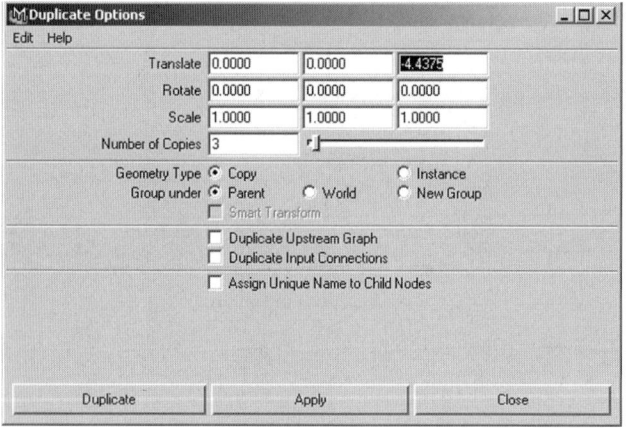

FIGURE 2.21   The Duplicate Options window with altered Z Translate input field and Number of Copies.

Click the Duplicate button, and voilà! Three new beams called Beam2, Beam3, and Beam4 appear and they are each 4.375 feet from the last beam and right in between the two beams created and positioned earlier (Figure 2.22).

One caveat to remember: because we changed the values in the Duplicate Options window, if we now hit **Ctrl-D**, whatever object is selected will be duplicated three times and moved –4.375 units from its present location. Be sure to remember that the settings have been changed and reset them before duplicating again.

Step 14: Clean up. Cleaning as you go is important as your projects increase in complexity. In this case, we will clean in a couple ways. First of all, in the Outliner, select locator1, locator2, and distanceDimension1,

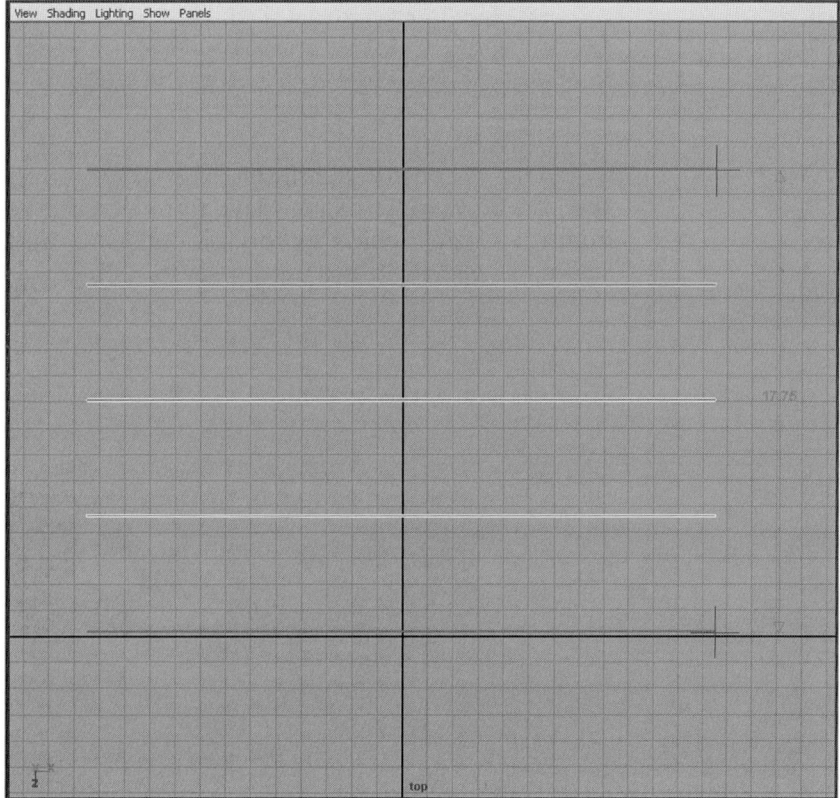

FIGURE 2.22   Results of duplication.

and delete them. The measurement is important to remember for a few steps in the future but it's nice to clean out those things as you go.

Second, select all the beams in either the Workspace or the Outliner (marquee around them or hold down the **Shift** key to add to selections) and hit **Ctrl-G** to group them together. In the Outliner, you'll notice that a new hierarchy called group will have appeared. If you expand the hierarchy, you'll see all the beams sitting within it. Rename the group BeamsNS (for beams north and south).

Step 15: Duplicate BeamsNS to the other side of the room. To do this, first we need to see the rest of the room. Select Display > Show > All to bring back all the objects you had hidden before. Or, if you haven't hidden anything since we hid the walls, you could use the hotkey combination **Ctrl-Shift-H** to Show Last Hidden.

Hit **4** on your keyboard to make sure you are viewing the scene as a wireframe. For an exercise, click anywhere in your scene where there's not an object. This effectively selects nothing and deselects any active objects. Now, click on any of the beams in the Workspace. Notice that the beam will highlight in both the Workspace and the Outliner. But what if you wish to select the entire group of beams? Well, you could try and marquee around them in the Workspace, but that would also likely select a bunch of other elements in the scene that you didn't mean to select. Some better methods include directly selecting the group BeamsNS in the Outliner or choosing any one beam in the Workspace and hitting the **Up Arrow** key. Doing this selects up in any hierarchy to the next parent level. Now, the group BeamsNS is selected and highlighted in both the Outliner and Workspace.

Your manipulator for the group BeamsNS is likely to be in the geometric middle of the group of beams. To get a duplicated group of beams into the other side of the room, we could figure it out mathematically or simply move the manipulator so that it rested on one of the outer corners of the outer beams.

Figure 2.23a shows the manipulator snapped onto the bottom corner of the bottom beam. As a quick review, remember to move the manipulator, hit **Insert**, and then activate the Move tool (**w**). Hold down **v** (to snap to point/vertex) and then click and drag the manipulator into the desired position. You may need to dolly in close enough to make sure you snap to the edge of the beam and not some other vertex that might be close by. Finally, hit **Insert** again to lock the manipulator into position.

Now, select Edit > Duplicate (Option) and reset the settings (Edit > Reset Settings) before hitting the Duplicate button. This will create a new group in the Outliner, called BeamsNS1, and a new collection of beams that is sitting at the same place in space.

Still with the Move tool active, hold **v** down and click and drag the group BeamNS1's Z manipulator handle down so that it snaps into place on the west wall (WallWest) as shown in Figure 2.23b.

Step 16: Create new beams that run the length of the room. As the final rendering shows, this room includes another set of beams that run the length of the room. To do this, use the same sorts of methods to start out. Create a new polygonal primitive cube (Modeling | Create > Polygon Primitives > Cube). We know that the room is 40 feet long (Z), so change the Scale Z in the Channel Box to read 40. These beams also happen to be 0.3 foot by 0.3 foot, so change the values in the Scale X and Scale Y to 0.3.

Now, use the Align tool to get it aligned to the tops of the walls: select the new cube then **Shift**-select one of the walls and choose Modify > Snap Align Objects > Align Tool. After aligning, hit **Enter** to exit out of the Align tool. The results should look close to Figure 2.24. Be sure to rename this beam CrossBeam in the Outliner.

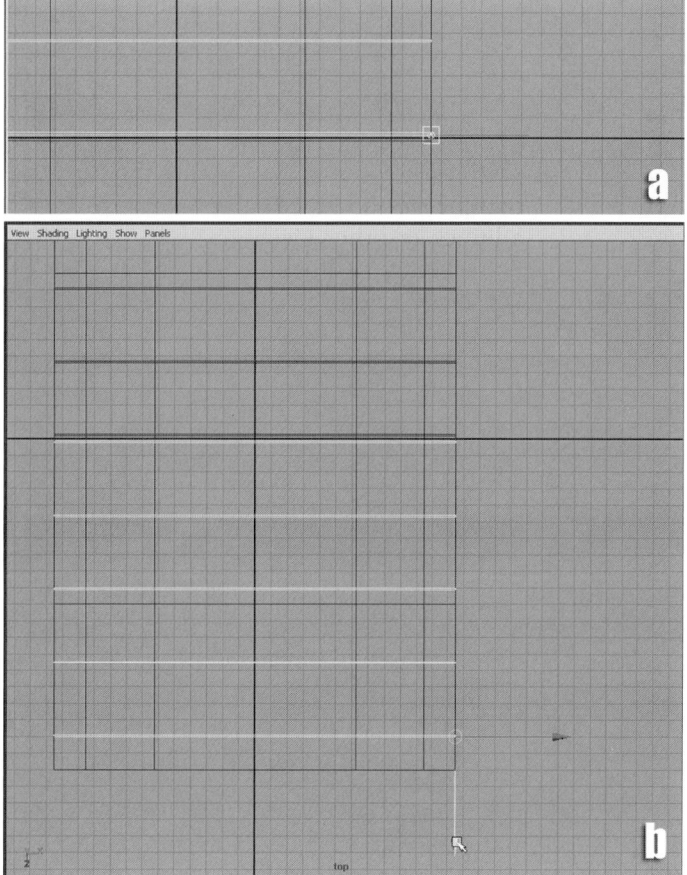

FIGURE 2.23 (a–b)   Adjust the manipulator for the newly created BeamNS1 and move the new group into position (snapped to the WestWall).

Click anywhere in the scene where there's no object to deselect both your new CrossBeam and whatever wall you used to align it and then select CrossBeam. Make four duplicates of the CrossBeam, each two feet in the positive X direction (Edit > Duplicate (Option). Be sure to enter **2** in the X column of Translate and change the number of copies to 4.

Again, select CrossBeam and duplicate four copies, only this time make them all –2 feet from the last. Select all the CrossBeams in the Outliner and group them together (**Ctrl-G**). Rename the group CrossBeams. The result should look like Figure 2.25.

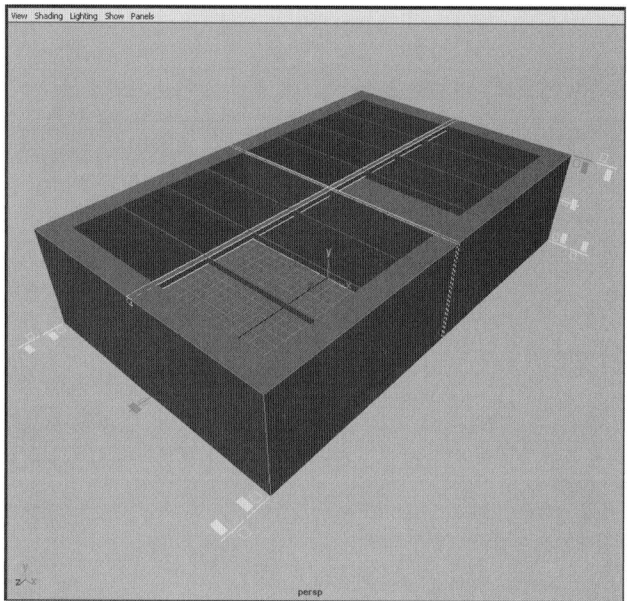

FIGURE 2.24 Newly created and aligned CrossBeam.

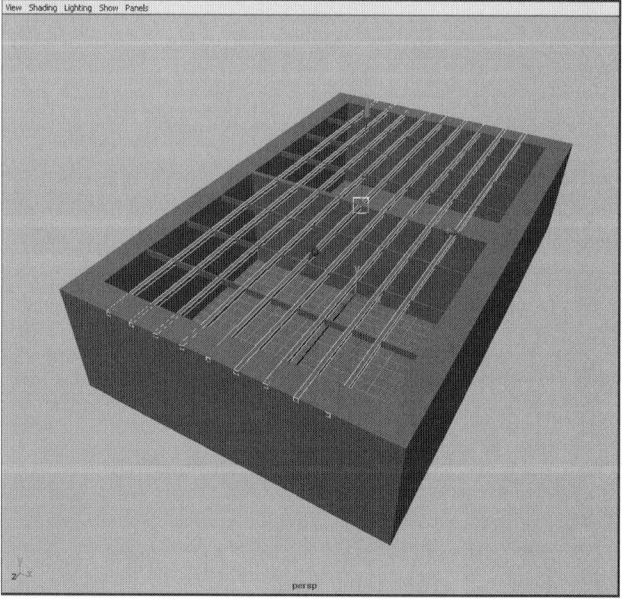

FIGURE 2.25 Completed new CrossBeams.

Step 17: Create a ceiling. You can create the ceiling either by creating another NURBS plane (Modeling | Create > NURBS Primitives > Plane) and changing the Channel Box's Scale X and Scale Z to 25 and 40, respectively, or by selecting the Floor and duplicating it (be sure to reset the Duplicate Options settings). Either way, be sure to either enter 9 for the Translate Y setting or snap the new plane to the top of the walls. Rename the object Ceiling.

Step 18: Organize the layers. In the never-ending battle of properly organizing your project, let's take a minute to organize parts of the creation into layers. Layers in Maya aren't like layers in Photoshop®, Illustrator®, or other 2D-based applications. Don't think of layers as resting one on top of another but rather as collections of objects. Part of the reason we want to do this is to be able to hide collections of objects quickly. Right now, we're looking at an entirely enclosed box that makes it fairly awkward to do anything inside the room.

At the top of the Channel Box are three buttons (Show Channel Box, Show Layer Editor, and Show Channel Box and Layer Editor). Click the one to the far right that will show both the Channel Box and the Layer Editor in this space to the right.

The Layer Editor will appear below the Channels Box (Figure 2.26). There are several ways to create a new layer but the quickest is to click the button that the mouse is resting on in Figure 2.26.

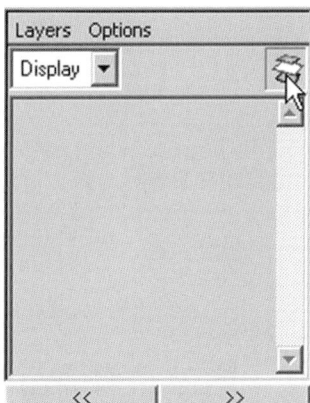

FIGURE 2.26   Display the Layer Editor and create a new layer.

Once you've created a new layer (Figure 2.27a), double-LMB-click the name to rename it. The dialog box that appears will allow you both to rename a layer and assign colors to it. For now, simply rename this layer Ceiling_Floor and click the Save button (Figure 2.27b).

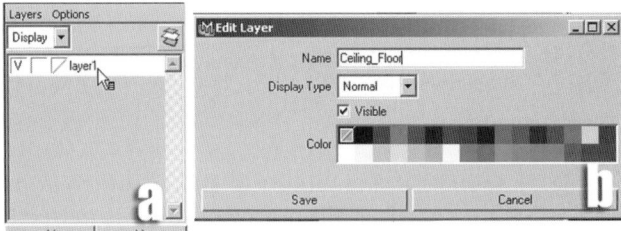

FIGURE 2.27 (a–b)   Rename layers.

Now, in the Outliner, select the groups BeamsNS, BeamsNS1, and CrossBeams and the objects, Floor and Ceiling. Remember that holding down the **Shift** button will add to a selection in much the same way as it does in Microsoft Explorer, including selecting everything between two selections. **Ctrl** will allow you to add to the selection without choosing objects in between on the list. Once all these groups and objects are selected, RMB-click the layer Ceiling_Floor in the Layer Editor and select Add Selected Objects from the pop-up menu. Notice that the Ceiling_Floor layer has three boxes to the left of the layer's name. We will discuss other uses of these boxes but for now, the box of interest is the one to the far left with a V in it. The V stands for visible and once you've added objects to a layer, you can click the V to make that layer invisible in the display. For now, click this V, and you should be able to see the room with just the walls.

Step 19: Save and take a break. If you haven't done so already be sure to save your scene (File > Save Scene). You may want to name it something like Room. Then take a break; we've covered a lot of different methods and have the basic shape of our room to show for it. However, we still have lots more to do to make this room the beautiful creation as it is designed.

CONCLUSION

We've covered in this chapter how to create some basic primitive shapes. We've discussed how to scale them, move them, place them, and rotate them. We've looked at how to align objects so that they butt up exactly against one another. We've looked at how to measure objects and distances so that we can make exact calculations in our creations. In projects of the future, we won't get so precise in all our measurements; most of the time we will simply eyeball the shapes to get them about right. However, in areas such as architecture, being this exact is important.

ON THE CD

Remember that if you want to check your work against this tutorial, you can open the results on the CD-ROM (Tutorials/Chapter02). Also remember that if there are slight variations—no sweat. Feel free to improvise and change things as you see aesthetically fit.

In the next chapter, we will learn how to begin cutting holes in objects and changing the shapes of these primitives that we've begun to create. After all, not everything is perfectly square or flat. Being able to tweak shapes is what makes Maya a powerful modeling tool. So read on; the modeling that's most fun is yet to come.

Although we cover things step by step in the tutorials of this and later chapters, if you ever want to see the finished project, be sure and take a look at the included CD-ROM. In the Tutorials folder, you will find folders for each chapter. Contained in those folders will be the Maya scene files for the tutorials with scene files in that chapter.

3

NURBS AND COMPONENT-LEVEL EDITING

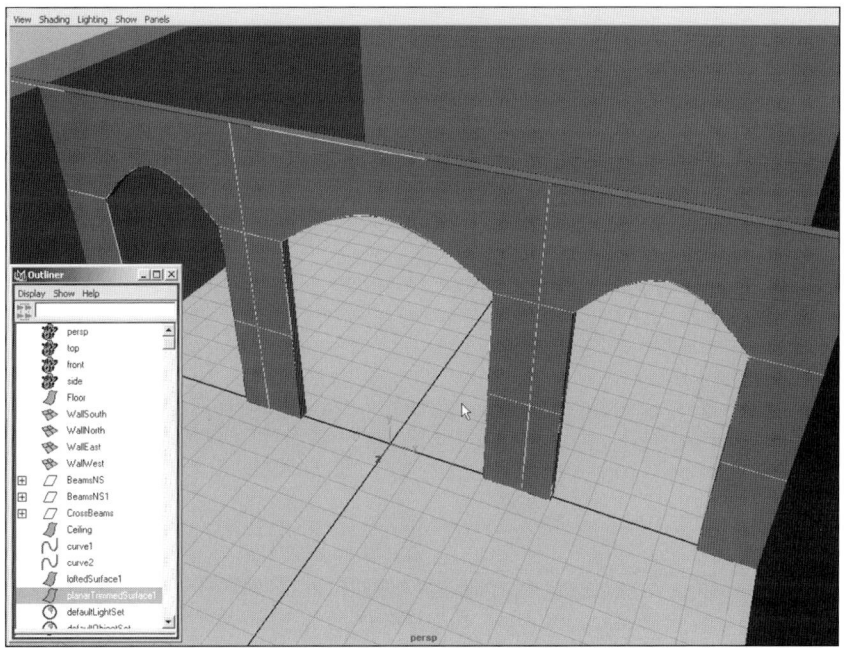

In the last chapter, we looked very quickly at how to create, scale, rotate, and move basic shapes. Primarily, we dealt with polygonal cubes. Polygons are one of the various ways to model within Maya; however, for most forms, it is not the most effective.

NURBS (non-uniform rational b-splines) represent a very dynamic method of modeling almost any shape imaginable. NURBS are especially good for smooth surfaces and organic forms. Now before we go too far, it is important to point out that while you can use NURBS to create forms in Maya, eventually Maya must convert those NURBS into polygons to render. This process is called tessellation, and we will talk much more about it later. So, you may ask, why bother modeling in NURBS when they end up as polygons anyway? Well, for several reasons, the first of which is the complications of tessellation. When Maya takes the nice, curved surfaces possible with NURBS and creates collections of polygons to simulate that curve, it has to do so with quite a few triangles. Without enough triangles, the model looks blocky. If you were building your shape with polygons, it would be incredibly painful and a waste of time to have to go in and modify all the thousands of polygons.

Figure 3.1a shows a section of a NURBS surface. Figure 3.1b shows the same surface with the tessellation visible. Notice the sheer volume of polygons needed to create this type of surface.

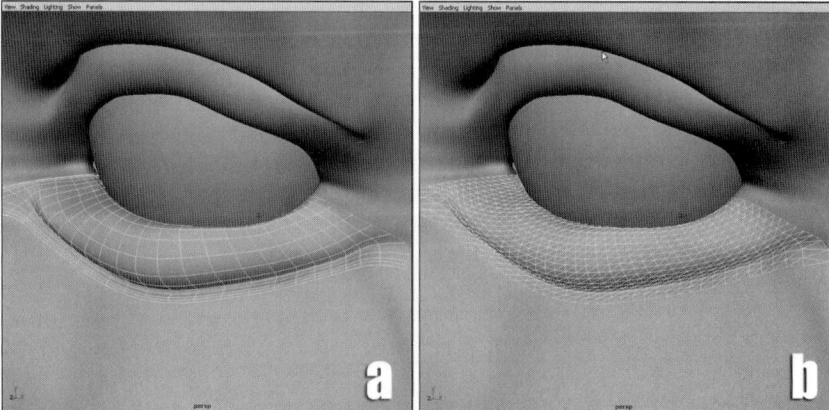

FIGURE 3.1 (a–b)   Tessellation of NURBS surface.

It is usually easier to allow Maya to take the information you have provided in NURBS and do all the hard work by determining how the polygons need to be arranged.

Now, there are some cases in which pure old grab-a-polygon-and-move-it is the method to use. Games, for instance, are typically limited in the number of polygons that can be displayed at one time. So, economical use of polygons is key; thus, being able to control each polygon becomes tremendously important.

SubD (subdivision) surfaces are another place where being able to control the polygons directly is important. Although we will talk much more about subD surfaces later, the basic idea is that you make a low-poly proxy of a particular shape. There are comparatively few polygons to have to deal with on this proxy, thus, you can quickly get general shapes roughed out. Maya then takes every polygon, subdivides it into smaller polygons, and rotates each polygon to create a smoother, rounder, and more complex shape.

Because these two instances are both important situations in which modeling with polygons is important, we will be talking more about polygon modeling in Chapters 4 and 5.

But for now, NURBS will rule this chapter. NURBS are great tools and offer some flexibility that polygonal modeling does not. Although many shapes that we will create in this chapter could be created with either NURBS or polygons, we will be using NURBS in an effort to understand this powerful modeling tool.

CURVES

Before we can really get into effective NURBS creation and editing, we need to talk for a second about how to create and manipulate curves. Curves are the splines that NURBS surfaces use to define the three-dimensional shape. Although ultimately, NURBS surfaces can exist completely independent of the curves that create them, effectively manipulating curves before creating the surfaces can get you started on the right foot and make your modeling job much easier.

Before we get started, note that there are two main types of curves in Maya: EP (Edit Point) curves and CV (Control Vertex) curves. Both have their uses, and some folks prefer different curves for different situations. In general, CV curves provide a more easily controlled and predictable method of creating curves. However, we will still look at how EP curves work before taking an in-depth look at CV curves.

TUTORIAL 3.1   **GETTING STARTED WITH CURVES**

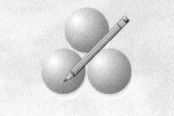

Step 1: Start with a clean slate. To explore curves, we want to start off with an empty scene without having to worry about messing up the boxy room we created in the last chapter. So, save the work you have done on the room and exit out of Maya (File > Exit).

Start Maya up again, and you will have an empty scene. You should have an interface where you are back to a single panel for your Workspace with a Perspective view. If you do not, be sure to select Single Perspective View from the Toolbox.

Move your mouse over the Workspace and quickly click the **Spacebar**. This will swap the view into the four-paneled view.

Step 2: Create a curvilinear (Cubic) EP curve. Select Modeling | Create > EP Curve Tool (Options). Unlike other tools' options, the EP curve's options may appear at the right where the Channel Box was. There are a couple of things to notice here before tearing into creating curves with the EP Curve tool (Figure 3.2).

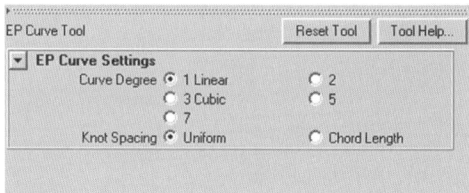

FIGURE 3.2   The EP Curve Tool Options box.

The first is the Curve Degree setting. This value indicates how smooth the curve will be between the Edit Points that you will define. The default, 3 Cubic, is usually a pretty good setting for curvy curves while 1 Linear works great for more straight curves.

For now, leave the default 3 Cubic as the setting for Curve Degree. In the Top view, LMB-click and place the first Edit Point. Move to another space (still in Top view, of course) and LMB-click again. Technically, you could end this curve right now, as an EP curve only needs two Edit Points to define it. But for now, move to another place and LMB to create a third Edit Point; here is where you begin to see the curve part of EP curve emerge.

Click in several other places and play with how the position of each Edit Point controls how the curve develops. Notice that if you LMB-click and hold, you can create a new Edit Point and drag it around the space to see how the curve is affected.

When you are done, or have created enough Edit Points to get the idea, hit Enter to tell Maya that you are done creating this curve (Figure 3.3).

Select this curve and delete it.

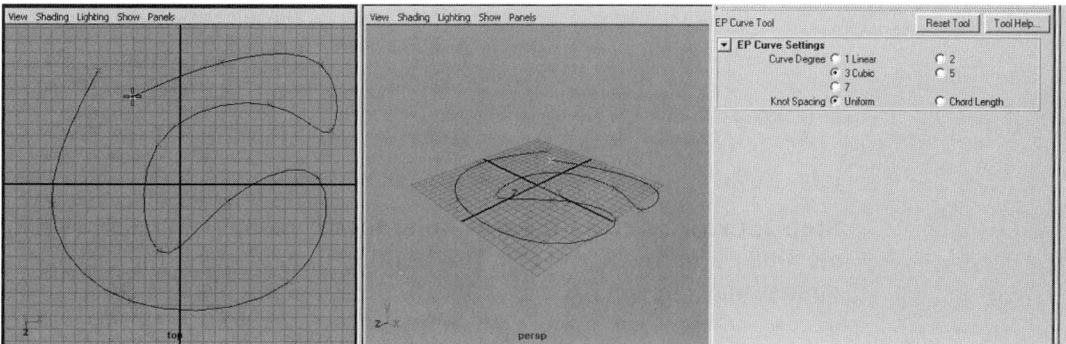

FIGURE 3.3   Completed EP curve.

Step 3: Create a curvilinear (Cubic) EP curve in three dimensions.
The curve we created in the last step was all drawn in the Top view. This
means that the curve and all its Edit Points laid flat along the XZ plane.
However, you can also create 3D curves on the fly.

Select the EP Curve tool again but this time, simply select the tool on
the Shelf (Figure 3.4).

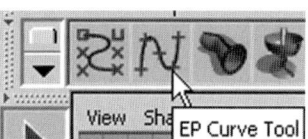

FIGURE 3.4   Activating the EP
Curve tool on the Shelf.

Now, create three or four Edit Points in the Top view. When you get
ready to place the next Edit Point, instead of placing it in the Top view, do
so in the Front view. Notice that this new Edit Point now brings the curve
into a new dimension other than the XZ plane. Place a couple more Edit
Points in the Front view and then place a few in the Side view. Next, go
up to the Perspective view and place still more Edit Points. Finally, hit
Enter to finish off with the EP Curve tool.

Notice that you probably have a very bizarre curve that exists in all
three dimensions (Figure 3.5). The point of this little exercise is that
curves can be built in any view or any combinations of views to create
any sort of shape you wish.

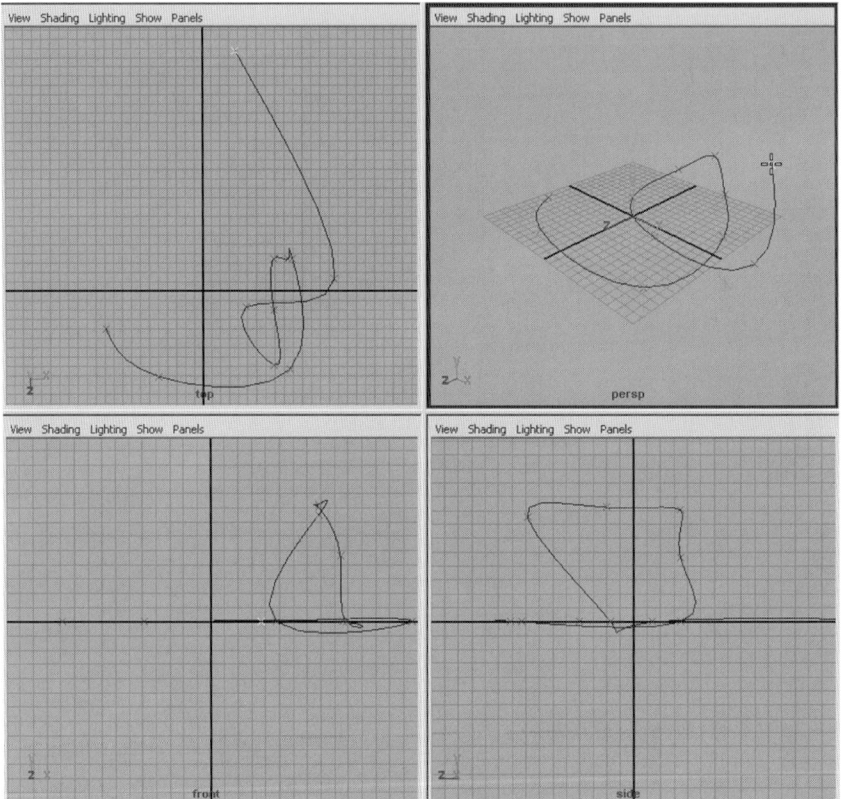

FIGURE 3.5   EP Curve created by placing Edit Points in all four views.

Select this crazy curve and delete it.

Step 4: Create a straight (linear) EP curve. Select Modeling | Create > EP Curve Tool (Option). In the Options for the tool (shown at the right of the UI), change the Curve Degree to 1 Linear. Again, in any view you please, LMB-click several Edit Points into place. Notice that the result is a curve that is straight: linear. This works well for creating profiles of stairs or other manmade shapes. Remember that holding down the **x**, **c**, or **v** keys while creating a curve will snap the Edit Points to the grid, curve, or vertex (Figure 3.6).

Delete this linear curve.

Step 5: Create a curvilinear CV curve. When we created EP curves, we created Edit Points through which the curve ran. When we create CV curves, we are creating control vertices that act like magnets on a wire. With EP curves, we only needed two Edit Points to create a complete curve, whereas with CV curves, you must have at least four.

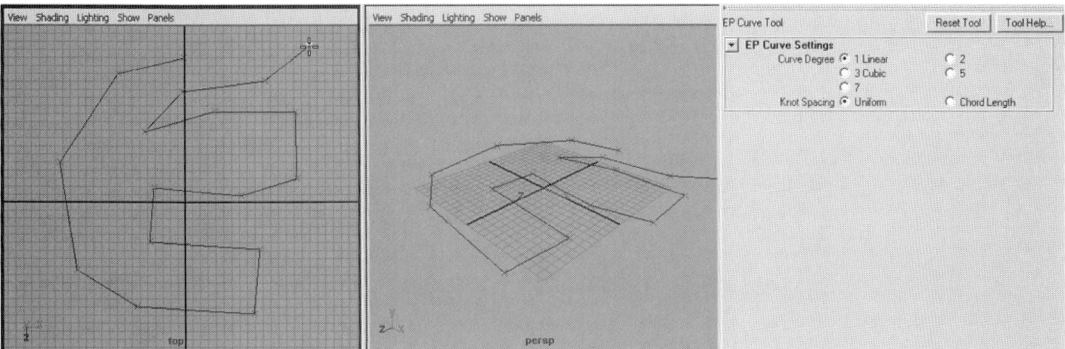

FIGURE 3.6   Creating an EP curve with a 1 Linear Curve Degree setting.

The first- and the last-placed CVs will indicate where the curve is to begin and end. The other points help to define the general curvature. The CV Curve tool takes a bit of getting used to before you can control curves exactly like you want them. However, once you get the hang of it, you can truly make any shaped curve you can imagine.

To get started, select Create > CV Curve Tool (Option). This will display the options for the tools on the right of the UI. Because we have already talked about Curve Degrees, we will not cover them again for the CV Curve tool, but do notice that you can change the degree to include things like linear lines. Also, note that like the EP Curve tool 3 Cubic is usually just right for most curves.

In the Top view, create four CVs by LMB-clicking and releasing at any four points (Figure 3.7a). Notice that the only points that the CV curve actually touches are the first and last. Hit **Enter** to complete the curve and exit the CV Curve tool.

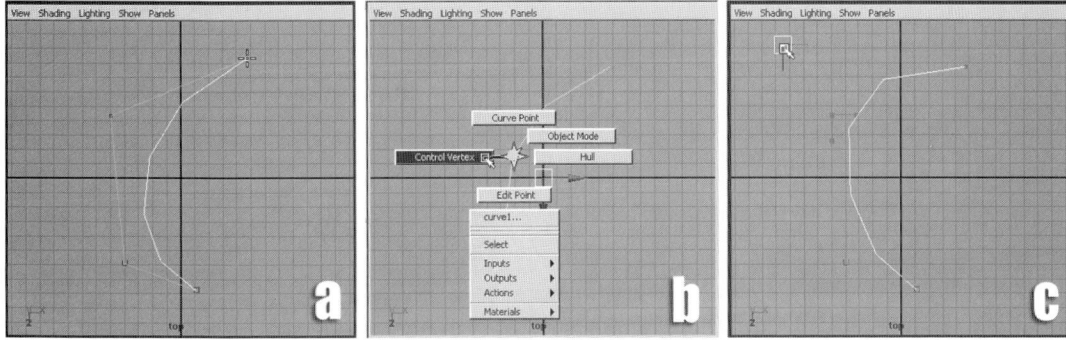

FIGURE 3.7 (a–c)   Creating and editing a basic curvilinear CV curve.

To understand this a bit better, select the Move tool. RMB-click-and-hold on the curve in the Top view and select Control Vertex from the Marking menu that pops up (Figure 3.7b). This will show the CVs that you created earlier as little purple dots. Using the Move tool, select one and LMB-click-drag the point to a new location and see how the curve changes (Figure 3.7c).

Remember also that, like the EP Curve tool, this tool can be used to create CVs for a curve in any window. Delete this curve before moving onto the next step (RMB-click-and-hold off the curve and select Select All from the marking menu. Then hit **Delete**).

Step 6: Create curvilinear/linear combinations. If we continue with the idea of CVs as magnets that control the curve that is a wire, it makes sense that if you cluster magnets (CVs), the wire (curve) will hug tighter to that cluster.

Consider the following examples. Figure 3.8 shows four examples of CVs or clusters of CVs in the exact same locations. The difference between each sub-figure is that some curves include two CVs placed at the exact same place. The result of this mini-cluster is a line that hugs the CVs closer or determines the path of the curve as it moves away from the cluster.

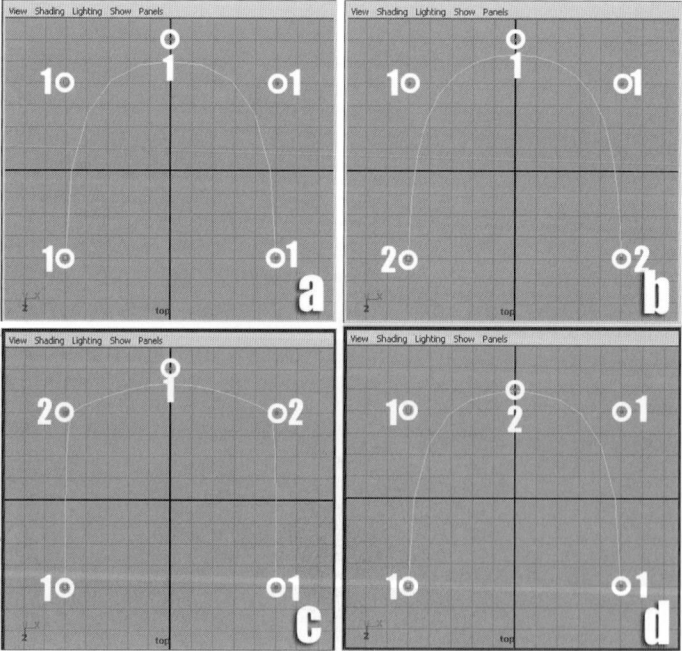

FIGURE 3.8 (a–d)   Results of clustering CVs.

Increasing the number of CVs causes the curve to hug that cluster even closer. In most cases, three CVs in the same place make for a sharp corner (Figure 3.9). This can make for combinations of linear and curvilinear curves.

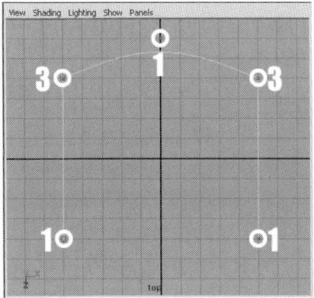

FIGURE 3.9   By placing three CVs in one location, there is no "pulling away" of the curve from the placed CVs.

The caveat to this is that you want to make sure the CVs are in exactly the same place. Often, the best strategy to do this is by snapping to the grid (**x** hotkey) so that as you place subsequent CVs, you know that they are all snapping to the same spot.

Step 7: Close a curve. Up to now, we have been creating curves that are open. That is, the curves are lines that do not encompass a shape. It will be important as we work in the future that we know the difference between open (Figure 3.10a) and closed (Figure 3.10b) curves, and that we can close off open curves.

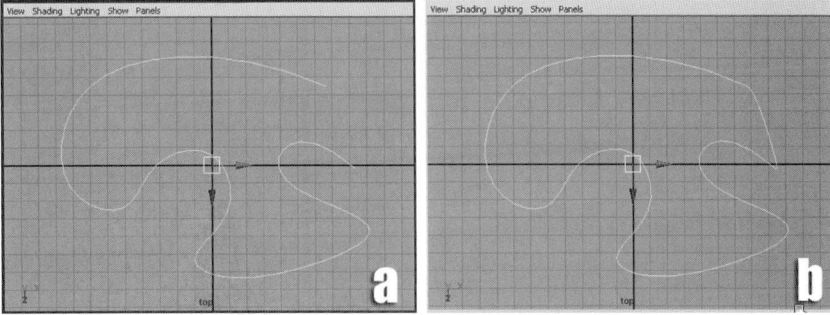

FIGURE 3.10   (a) Shows an open curve: one that does not completely encompass a shape. (b) Shows a closed curve.

Many 3D applications allow you to create closed curves on the fly. Maya does not. However, it is fairly easy to create an open curve and then close it off. Begin by using the CV Curve tool to create an open curve (Figure 3.11a); the exact shape does not matter. Hit **Enter** to exit the CV Curve tool.

To close the curve, select Modeling | Edit Curves > Open/Close Curve (Option). The Options window (shown in Figure 3.11 b, c, and d) allows you to determine how Maya will close the selected curve. The Shape option tells Maya what sort of shape it is to create as it attempts to create the needed CVs or weld together the extant CVs to create the closed shape. We will not go into too much depth here on these options as it is beyond the scope of the book; however, note that in most cases, the Preserve option is a good setting. Delete this closed curve, when you are done exploring this tool.

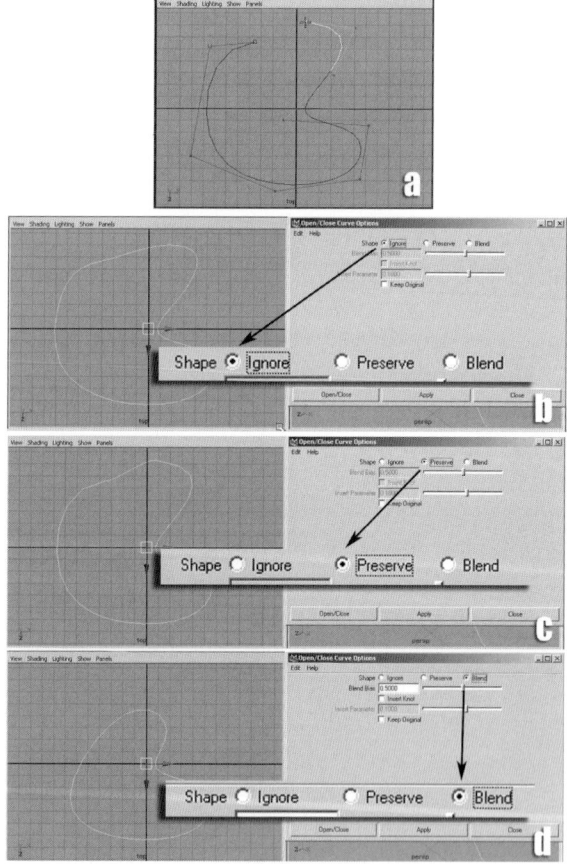

FIGURE 3.11 (a–d) Closing curves.

Step 8: Edit existing curves. Use the CV Curve tool to create a new open curve (Figure 3.12a). Hit **Enter** to exit the tool.

There are several things that we can do with this curve:

- Select the entire curve and move, rotate, or scale it similar to any other 3D shape.
- In Component mode, or by RMB-clicking and holding (Figure 3.12b), you can tell Maya to display the control vertices of the curve. You can then select a CV and move it to adjust the shape of the curve (Figure 3.12c). Remember that you can select more than one CV at a time.

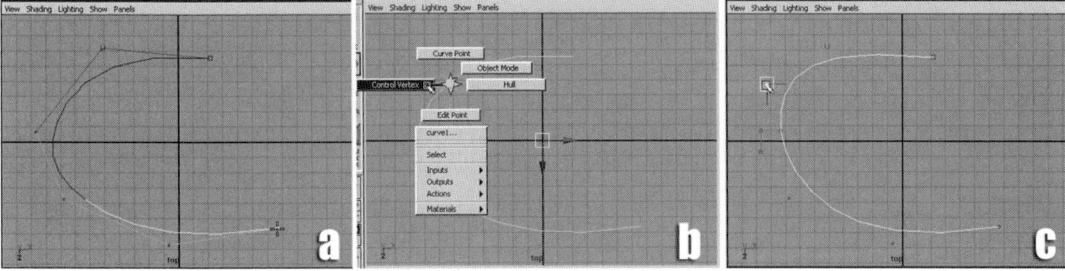

FIGURE 3.12   (a) Creating an open curve. (b) Telling Maya to show you a curve's control vertices. (c) Moving the position of a CV.

- Extend a curve with Modeling | Edit Curves > Add Points Tool. This will display your curve as though you were creating it with the CV Curve tool. Your mouse will also turn to the thick white cross. Just LMB-click where you would like to add new CVs to the end of your existing curve. Hit Enter to exit the Add Points tool.
- Change the shape of the curve through the Curve Editing tool. Access this tool through Modeling | Edit Curves > Curve Editing Tool. This tool will appear on the surface of the selected curve (Figure 3.13a). There are several different tools all nested within this tool. The first is the blue box that sits on the curve itself. LMB-click-drag that box to move that particular point of the curve to a new location (Figure 3.13b). The little blue diamond immediately above it (that turns yellow when clicked) allows you to shift the tool to a new point on the curve (Figure 3.13c). Off of these tools is a black line that represents a tangent to the curve. The blue box along this line allows you to change the tangent (and thus the shape of the curve) as shown in Figure 3.13d. The blue diamond at the end of the line allows you to shorten the tangent (Figure 3.13e).

Notice that in the Modeling | Edit Curves pull-down menu, there are many more options that we have not covered. Later, we will look more

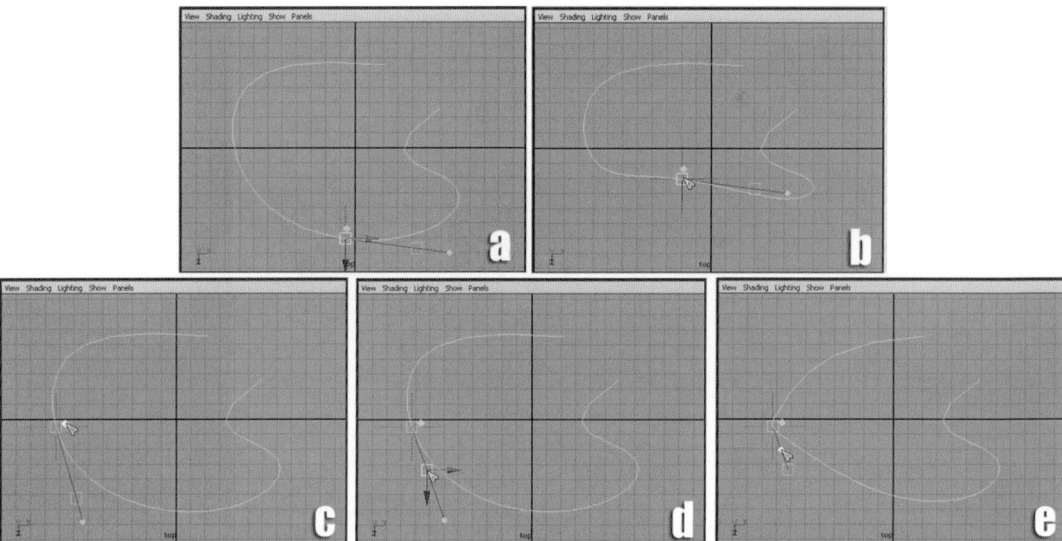

FIGURE 3.13   (a–e) The Edit Curve tool.

closely at some of the other tools here. Unfortunately, we don't have the room to cover everything in this volume. However, if you have the control covered earlier in this chapter when creating the curves, many of the Edit Curves options will not be necessary.

NURBS

Non-uniform rational b-splines (NURBS), despite the name, are actually best thought of as surfaces. We have looked briefly at creating NURBS primitives in the last chapter's tutorials. The Sphere, Cube, Cylinder, Cone, Plane, Torus, Circle, and Square are all NURBS primitives. These are NURBS surfaces that Maya creates for you. As our tutorials progress, we will be creating custom surfaces. For now, let's look a bit at the anatomy of a NURBS surface.

Figure 3.14 shows a primitive NURBS sphere. By RMB-clicking-and-holding, we are presented with a Marking menu that allows us to select components of this surface object. These are some of the basic anatomical parts of a NURBS surface.

Control Vertices (CVs):   These are represented in the Workspace as small purple dots that can be selected by marqueeing around a collection of them or by selecting and **Shift**-clicking to add to the selection. Once a collection of CVs is selected, it can be moved (Figure 3.15b), rotated (Figure 3.15c), or scaled (Figure 3.15d). We will do much more work with manipulating CVs as we go along.

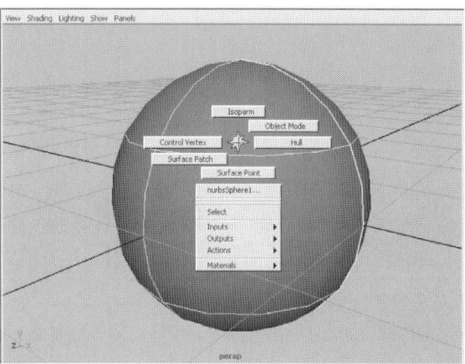

FIGURE 3.14   A NURBS surface with its selectable components.

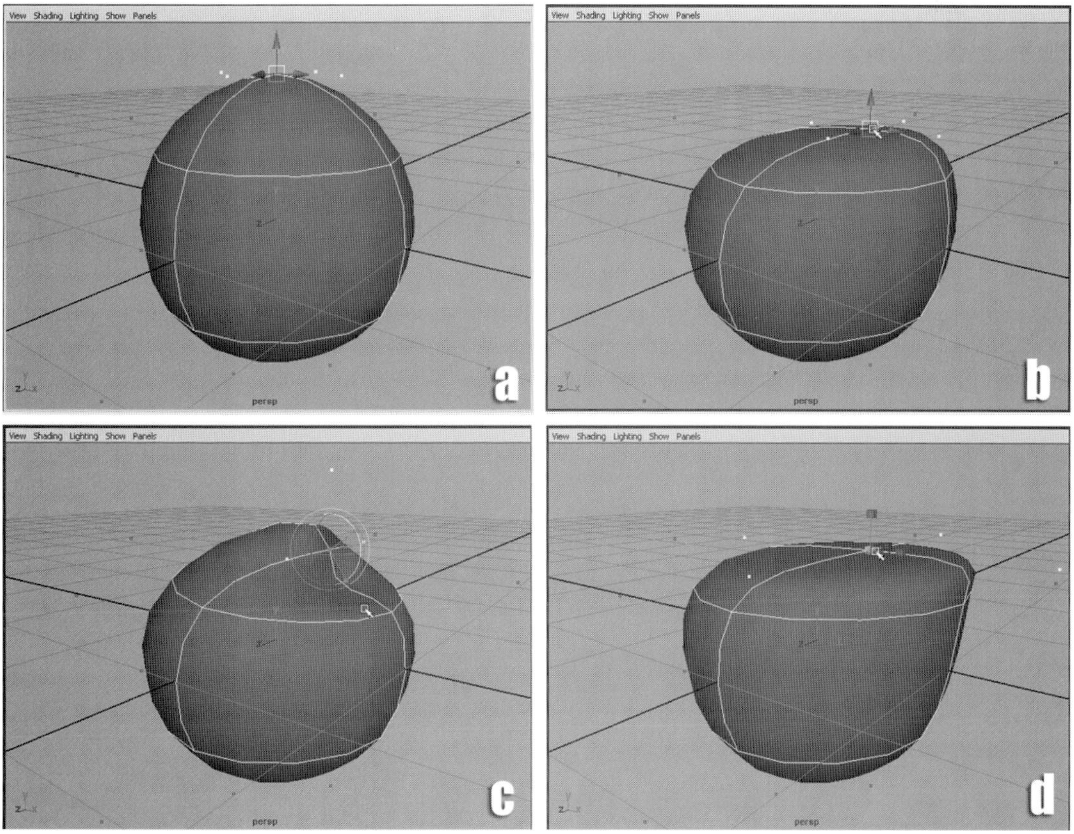

FIGURE 3.15 (a–d)   Control Vertices (CVs) are the magnets of a NURBS surface that are analogous to the CVs discussed in curves.

Isoparms: These are visual lines across a NURBS surface that indicate the organization of the NURBS topology (Figure 3.16). By adding isoparms to a surface (more on how to do this later), you add CVs as well. Although you cannot move or otherwise alter isoparms, the accompanying CVs and hulls related to an isoparm can be edited.

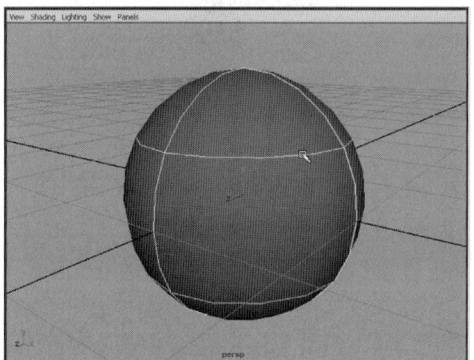

FIGURE 3.16 Isoparms are a visual indication of a surface topology. Although they themselves are not editable, they accompany CVs and hulls, which are.

Hulls: If you take some CVs and connect them in rows (both horizontally and vertically), you get hulls. You can move, rotate, or scale a selected hull. This works well for manipulating a surface in multiple directions at once (Figure 3.17).

Surface Points and Surface Patches: We will look more at these later in more detail. For now, suffice it to say that these are visual representations of points along the surface (Figure 3.18a) or patches between collections of isoparms (Figure 3.18b). Neither may be directly moved, rotated, or scaled.

That's enough theory. To get to know how to build NURBS from curves that we have created, we are going to get right into a tutorial to continue working on our room. Over the course of the next tutorial or two we will be creating a multitude of NURBS surfaces to add new visual interest to our room.

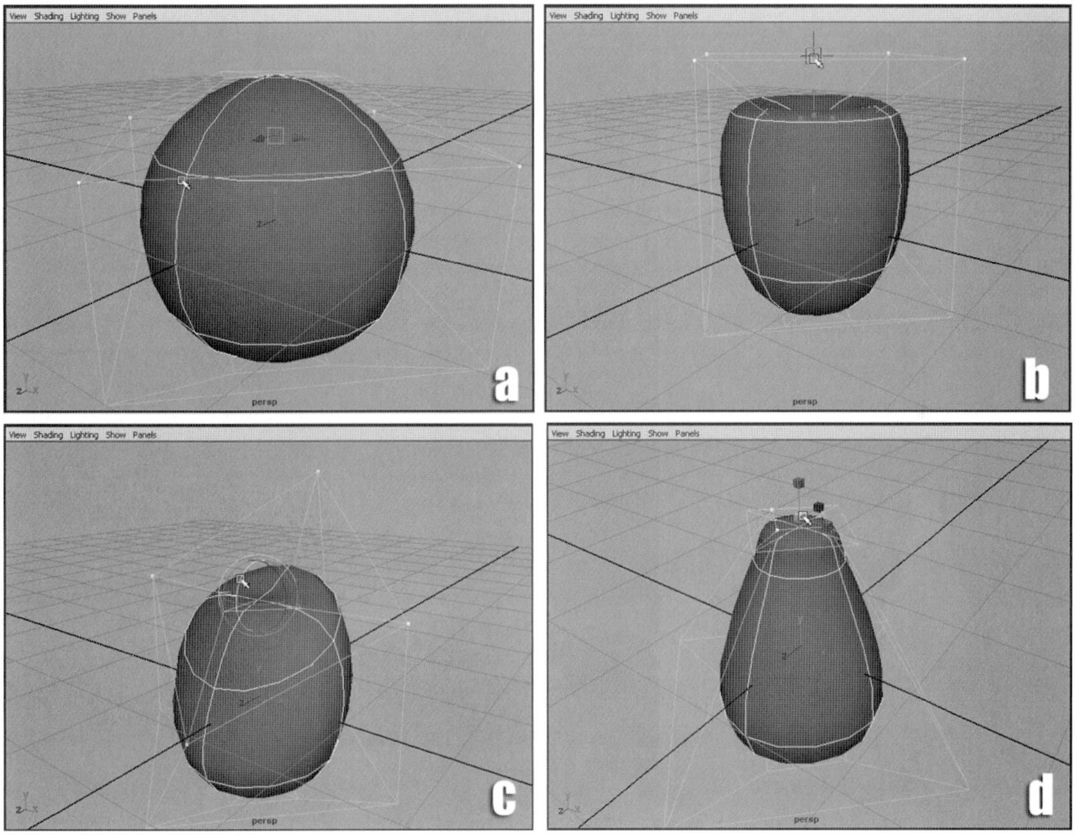

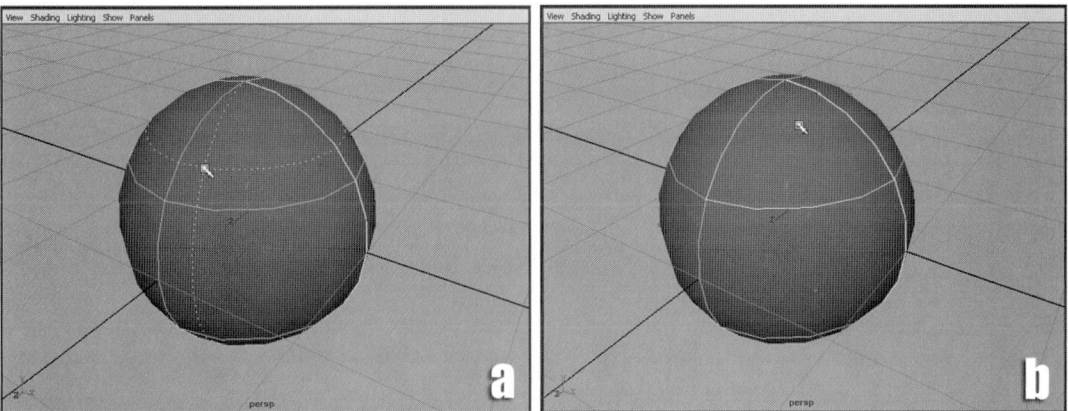

FIGURE 3.17 (a–d)   Hulls are like connecting rows or columns of CVs into one selectable collection.

FIGURE 3.18 (a–b)   Surface Points and Patches.

TUTORIAL 3.2   NURBS MODELING IN "THE ROOM"

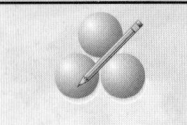

ON THE CD

To continue building the room, make sure you open the room that we were using in the last chapter—it is probably named Room. You can do this by either selecting File > Open Scene or going to wherever you saved the Room_Tutorial project. Open the Scenes folder and double-click the scene Room. Remember that you can see the results of this tutorial on the CD-ROM (Tutorials/Chapter03/).

Step 1: Make sure you have your Workspace set up similar to Figure 3.19. It probably is already. However, it will be important for our modeling steps for a while that you have the standard four-view panel layout with the Outliner available as a separate floating window.

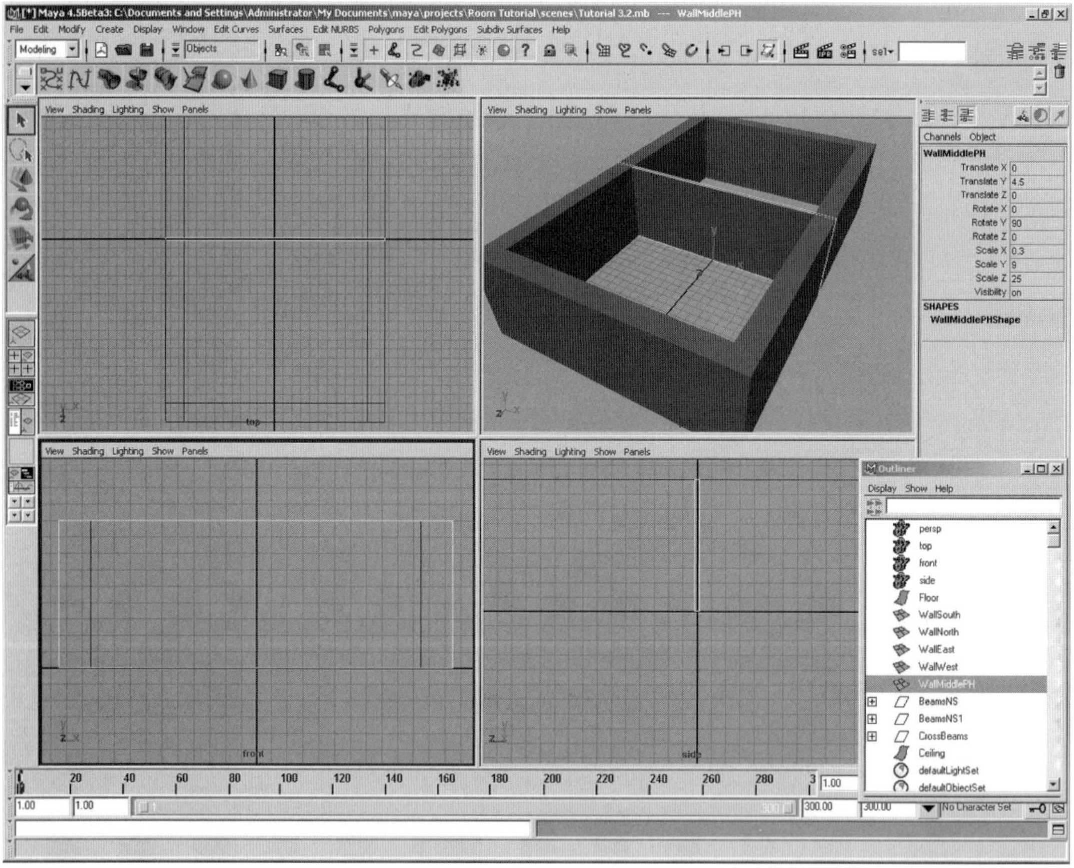

FIGURE 3.19   Layout needed for the modeling in this tutorial.

Creating Arched Walls

Step 2: Create center arched wall curve. In our earlier tutorials, we created a wall called WallMiddlePH with the PH standing for placeholder. In this step, we will replace this wall. To do this, we will create two curves and create two types of NURBS surfaces: Loft and Planar.

Before we can create the NURBS surfaces, we need to create the curves that will be used to compose them. Move your mouse over the Front view and hit your **Spacebar**. This will maximize this view in your Workspace.

Select Modeling | Create > CV Curves Tool (Options). Make sure that your Curve Degree is set to 3 Cubic.

Now in the Workspace, we want to make sure we are using a combination of the grid and the WallMiddlePH to act as guides in creating this curve. Hold **v** (to snap to points, or in this case, vertices) and click three times on the vertex at the bottom-left corner of the WallMiddlePH (Figure 3.20a). Still holding down the **v** key, move up and click three times on the top-left corner (Figure 3.20b). Continue holding down the **v** and click three times on the top-right corner (Figure 3.20c). Because we have carefully put three CVs right atop one another at every point, we should have nice crisp corners so far. Continue down to the bottom-right corner and again, holding down the **v**, LMB-click three times to create another corner (Figure 3.20d).

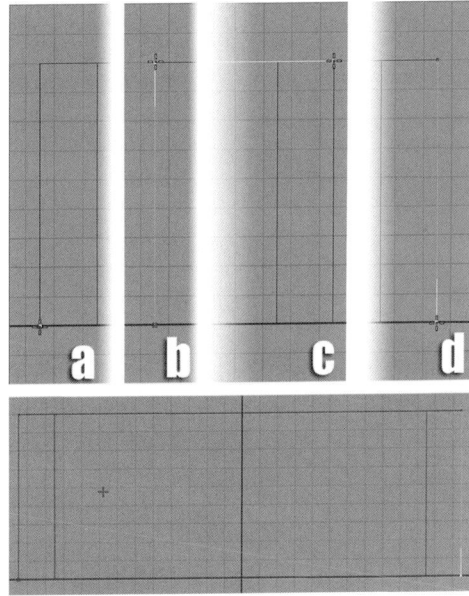

FIGURE 3.20 (a–d)   Creating the hard corners for the bottom and tops of the wall. No arches have been created yet. Each corner was snapped to point (**v**).

This is where things get interesting. For the arches in the middle of the wall, we really do not want to snap to any point on the wall itself. We have already snapped to all the vertices we can see from the Front view. However, snapping is still an important thing to do because we want to be able to place multiple CVs atop one another.

The solution will be to snap to the grid. Hold down **x** and LMB-click on a grid point about three-and-a-half units from the outside of the wall (Figure 3.21a). Still holding down the **x**, place two more points on the same spot so that we get a crisp corner here.

Still holding down the **x**, move up six feet (or six units, each represented with a box on the grid) and place three more CVs in that spot (Figure 3.21b). Now, move over two units and up one (still with the **x** down) and place one CV here (Figure 3.21c). We want this CV to define a gentle curve, so one will suffice. Do not worry that it is looking awfully linear here; it will round off in a bit. Continuing (still with the **x** button depressed), move over two units and down one and place three CVs here (Figure 3.21d). Finally, place three more CVs straight down from the last at ground level (Figure 3.21e).

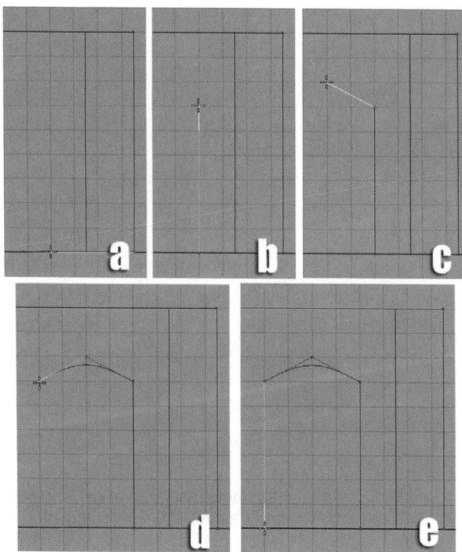

FIGURE 3.21 (a–e)   Creating our first arch.

Move over two units and place three CVs; up six units, place three more CVs; and then for this middle arch, move over three units and up one to place one CV. Continue over three units and down one, and place three CVs. Now, move down to the floor level and place three more (Figure 3.22).

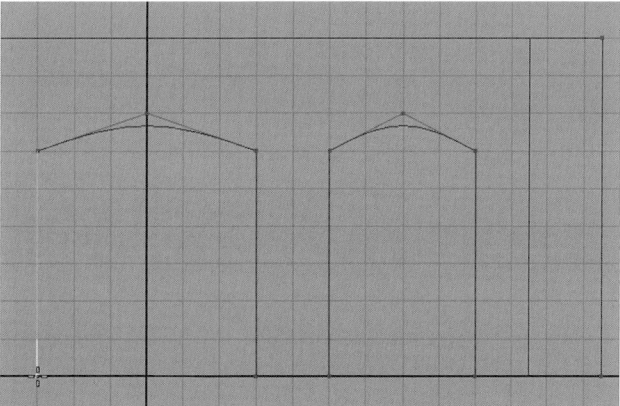

FIGURE 3.22   Creating the middle arch in much the same way.

Move over two units and repeat the first arch created (Figure 3.23). When you get to the bottom of the arch (where you will have created three CVs), do not attempt to close the curve by going back to the very first CV we created. Instead, hit **Enter** to finish the CV creation process and exit out of the CV Curve tool.

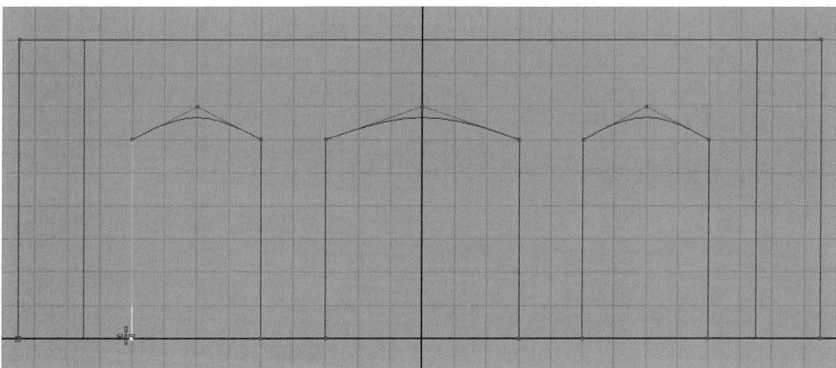

FIGURE 3.23   Completed arches.

To close the curve, select Modeling | Edit Curves > Open/Close Curves. This should close the curve off so you have the completed curve.

Step 3: Adjust the manipulator to the bottom corner of the curve.
Hit the **Spacebar** quickly so that you can see a four-view panel. Notice

that the curve you have just created is sitting flush against the west wall while your manipulator is sitting back at 0,0,0 (Figure 3.24). This happened because as we were snapping in the Front view, Maya assumed we were snapping to the nearest object in the view plane (which was the west wall). This could have been prevented by hiding all the walls except the middle one, but because we want to adjust the location of the manipulator, there was no need.

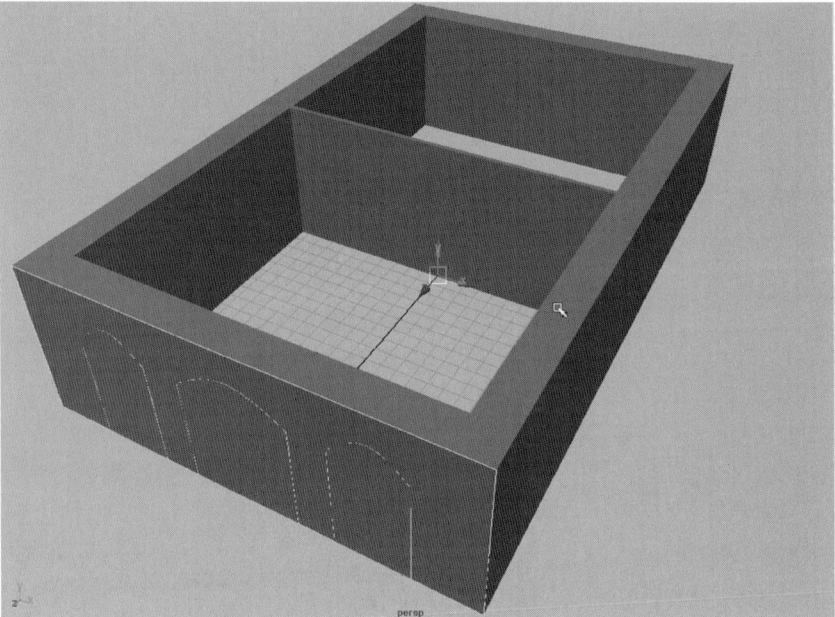

FIGURE 3.24   Curve exists on the west wall, but manipulator is back at 0,0,0.

We want to be able to snap this curve (and a copy of this curve) to the front and back of the middle wall. Because we will be snapping to the wall, we want to be able to snap to the wall's vertices, which sit on the corners of the wall. So, on the curve, we want the manipulator to be sitting on its corner also.

Hit the **Insert** key to indicate to Maya that you wish to reposition the manipulator. Press the **v** key to tell Maya you want to snap to points and then move the manipulator so that it snaps into the bottom-right corner of the curve (Figure 3.25).

Hit **Insert** again to lock the manipulator into place in this new location.

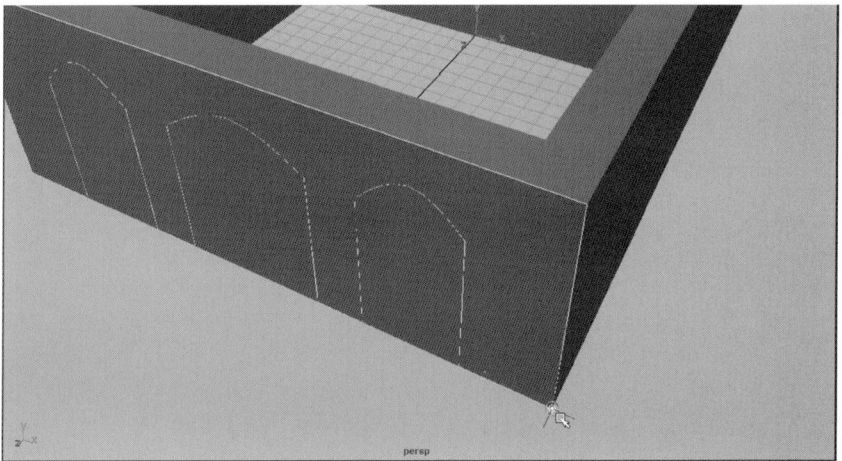

FIGURE 3.25   Repositioned manipulator.

Step 4: Position curve1 at the front of WallMiddlePH. We will now use WallMiddlePH as it was meant to be used. With the Move tool and the **v** key held down (to snap to point/vertex), move our curve (curve1 in the Outliner) so that it snaps back to the front of WallMiddlePH by LMB-click-dragging the Z (blue) manipulator handle (Figure 3.26).

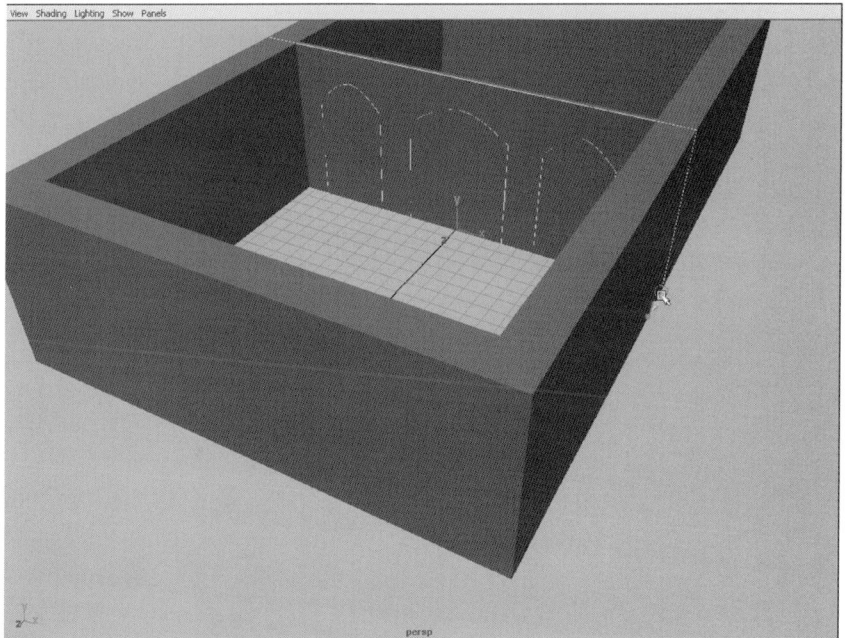

FIGURE 3.26   Placed curve1 at front of WallMiddlePH.

Step 5: Duplicate and place another curve on the opposite side of WallMiddlePH. Remember to reset your Duplicate settings if you cannot remember exactly what they are and then duplicate our curve. You should now have two curves listed in your Outliner (curve1 and curve2). With curve2 still selected, snap to points (**v**) and move this new curve so that it snaps to the back end of the WallMiddlePH (Figure 3.27).

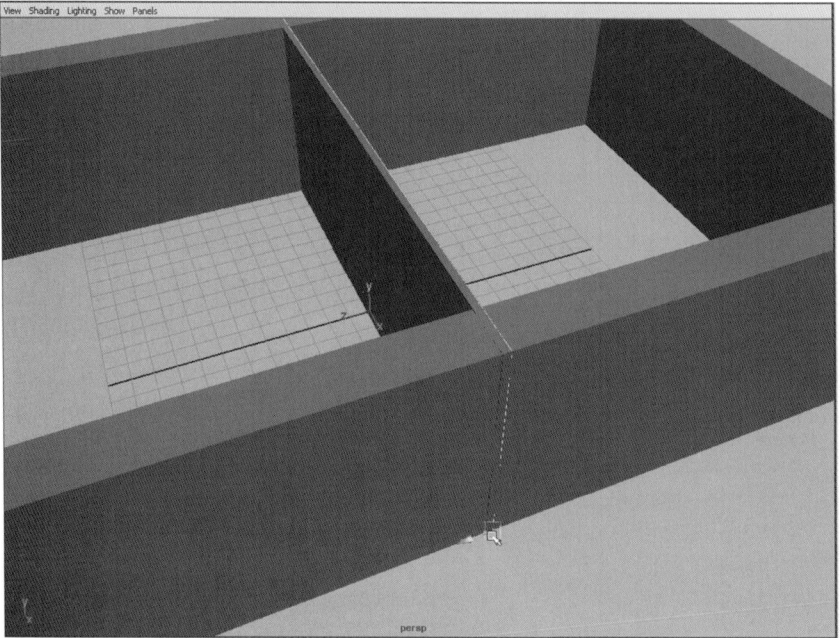

FIGURE 3.27   Duplicated and placed second curve.

Step 6: Delete WallMiddlePH. Now that our curves are created and placed, WallMiddlePH is no longer needed. Select it in the Workspace or Outliner and delete it.

Step 7: Loft curve1 and curve2 to create a NURBS surface. As we discussed in theory earlier in this chapter, NURBS surfaces can be created through primitives, or we can create them ourselves through curves. In earlier steps, we have created two curves that we will use to create a wall.

To create a NURBS surface, you must first select the curves that will be involved in its creation. The order in which you select these curves is often very important, especially if there are more than two curves involved. In this case, because there are only two, it is less important.

Select curve1 and then hold down the **Shift** key and select curve2. Both will appear highlighted in the Outliner and Workspace. In the

Workspace, one will appear white (the first one selected) and the other will appear green.

With both curves selected, go to Modeling | Surfaces > Loft (Option). Once you have the Loft Options window open, make sure you reset the settings. Notice however, that among the options here (Figure 3.28) is the ability to choose things like the Section Spans (how many spans, and thus isoparms will be created on the new surface) and the Output Geometry (allowing you to choose to create a NURBS surface, Polygonal, Subdivision, or Bezier). We will not be delving too deeply now into each option, because the default setting works just great. Hit the Loft button.

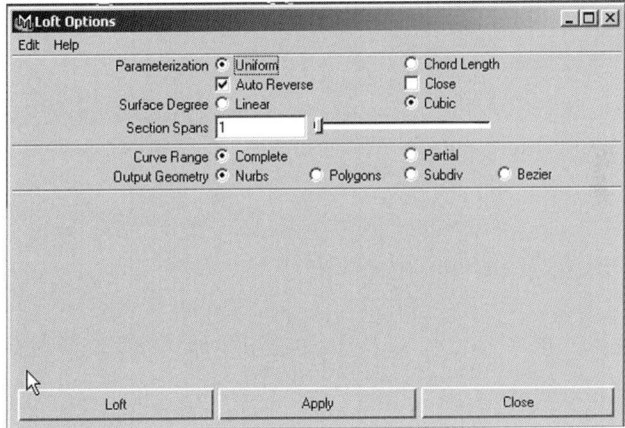

FIGURE 3.28   The Loft Options window.

The results of the Loft function displayed in Figure 3.29 show that a new surface has been created between the two curves. Notice also that in the Outliner a new object called loftedSurface1 has been created. If the surface seems to "pull away" from the curves, it is because this new surface is being displayed at too low a resolution. Make sure you hit **3** to display it smoothly.

Now, this is a nice start, but it is obvious that there is something missing in this wall. To make this wall so that it actually appears solid, we will be creating another NURBS surface.

Step 8: Create a new planar NURBS surface from each of the two curves, curve1 and curve2. When we created the lofted surface in the last step, the two curves we used to create the surface remained intact. This is important, as we will need these to create the solid part of the wall. Planar NURBS surfaces can be created from just one curve.

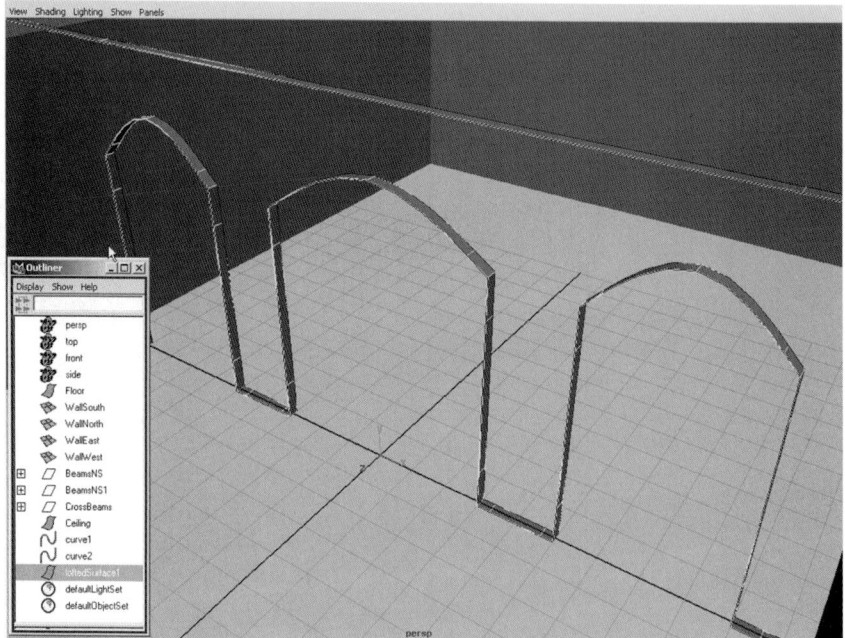

FIGURE 3.29 Lofted surface lofted between the two curves.

First, select curve1 and go to Modeling | Surfaces > Planar (Option). Again, make sure and reset the settings for this tool and hit the Planar Trim button. The result should be a new surface seen both in the Outliner (planarTrimmedSurface1) and in the Workspace (Figure 3.30).

Tumble around to see the other side of this wall, and you will see that you are still missing another planar surface. Select curve2 and again select Modeling > Surfaces > Planar. This will create a new surface that completes the wall.

Step 9: Clean up. Through these last few steps, we have not taken time to rename objects or get rid of objects that we no longer needed. Now would be a good time to do so. First, select loftedSurface1, planarTrimmedSurface1, and planarTrimmedSurface2 in the Outliner and hit **Ctrl-G** to group them together. The Outliner will show a new object called group1. Rename this group WallCenter_Group.

Right now, curve1 and curve2 are linked to all three of the NURBS surfaces contained in the group WallCenter_Group. As an example of the benefits of this, select WallCenter_Group and hit **Ctrl-H** to hide this group. This will leave just the curves visible. Move your mouse over the Front view and hit your **Spacebar** to maximize that view in your Workspace.

Select both curve1 and curve2 in the Outliner (Figure 3.31a). Then in the Status Line, change to Component mode and make sure the Points

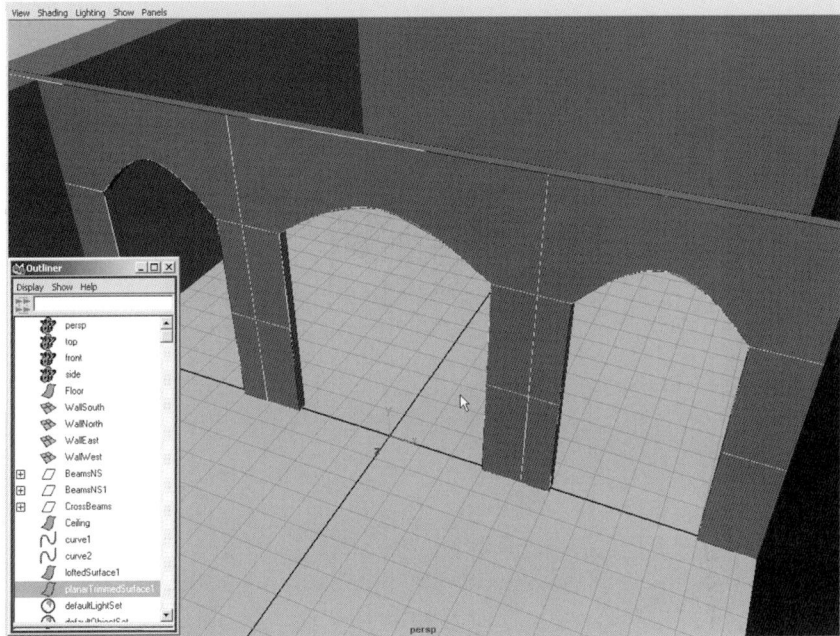

FIGURE 3.30   Planar surface.

mask is on (Figure 3.31b). This will display the CVs of those two curves in the Workspace. Select the points that make up the top of the curves by marqueeing around them, and with the Move tool and snapping to grid (**x**), move them up a couple units (Figure 3.31c). You may choose to do some further reshaping of the curves.

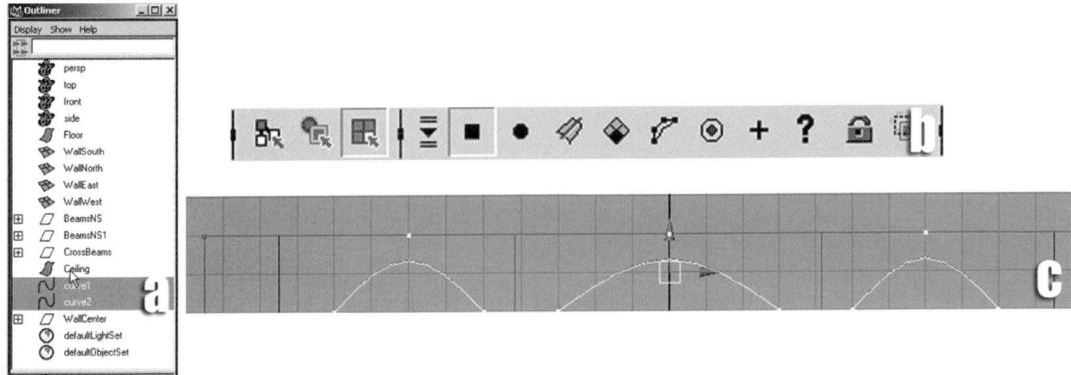

FIGURE 3.31 (a–c)   Because Construction History has been active, if we now choose to reshape the curves, the surfaces that were created from them will be updated.

Hit **Ctrl-Shift-H** to unhide the last hidden (which in this case is WallCenter_Group). You can see that the changes we made in the curves have translated into the surfaces (Figure 3.32).

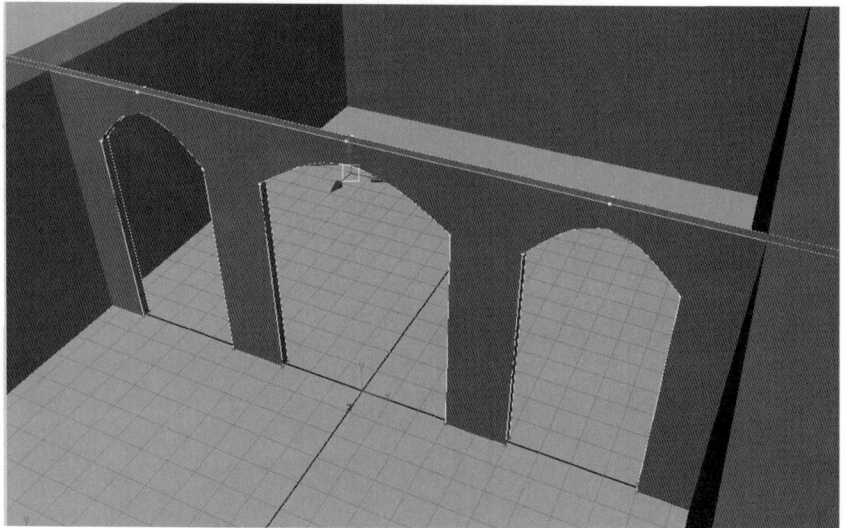

FIGURE 3.32 Altered surfaces.

Because we are sure we like this wall, we will further clean up some things. Make sure to return to Object mode in the Status Line. Next, select curve1 and curve2 (in the Outliner is probably easiest) and delete them as they are no longer needed.

Step 10: Repeat this process (Steps 2–9) for a new WallSouth. The idea here is to create a new wall like that shown in Figure 3.34 that has two arched doorways into the room. Remember to position both curves on the front and back of the old WallSouth so that the thickness of the wall is correct.

In this case, you probably will find that creating the curve from the Side view is a better method than the Front view. Remember to create the curve with the CV Curve tool and place the appropriate amount of CVs (three on each corner) to create sharp corners where they should be (Figure 3.33a). Close the curve (Modeling > Edit Curves > Open/Close Curves and move the manipulator so that it sits on a corner of the curve (Figure 3.33b).

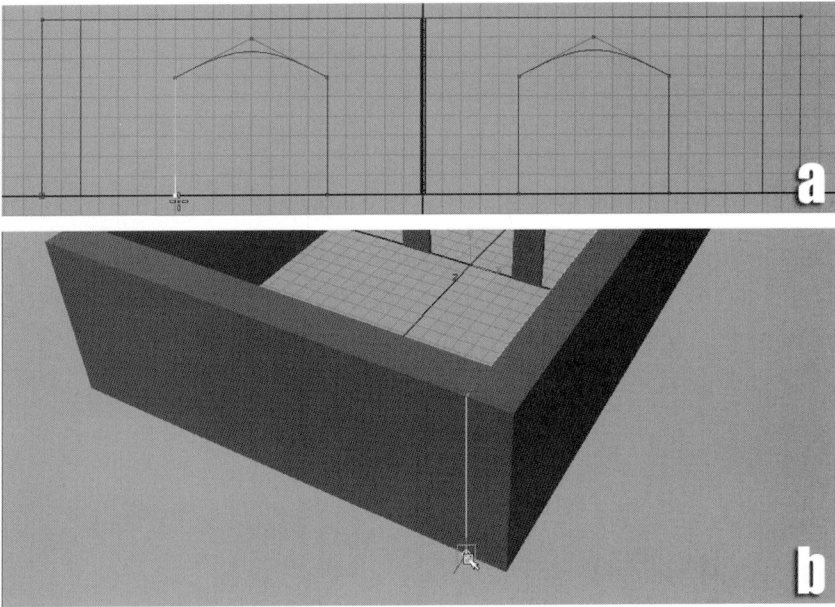

FIGURE 3.33 (a–b)   Creating the curve and aligning the manipulator into place.

Duplicate the curve and make sure that it sits on the other side of WallSouth (Figure 3.34a). Select WallSouth and delete it as it is no longer needed (Figure 3.34b).

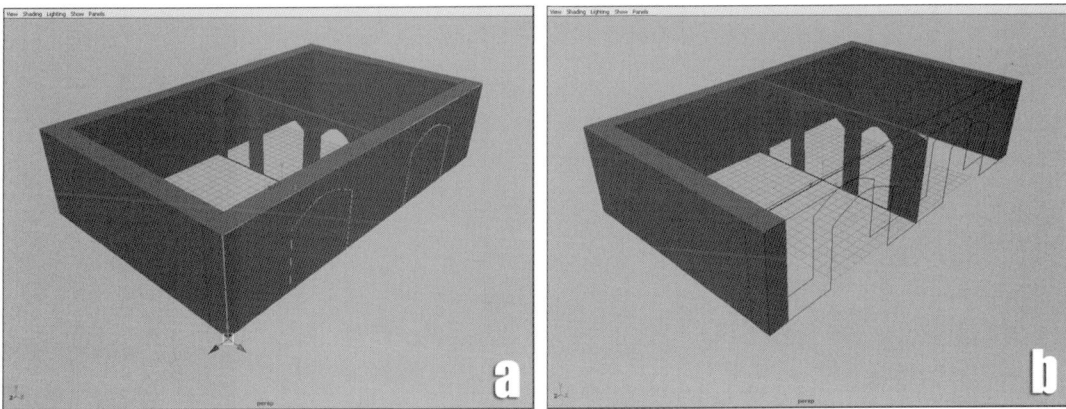

FIGURE 3.34 (a–b)   Duplicating curve and placing in new location. Deleted unnecessary wall.

Now, create the Loft NURBS surface between the two curves and create Planar surfaces from each curve (Figure 3.35).

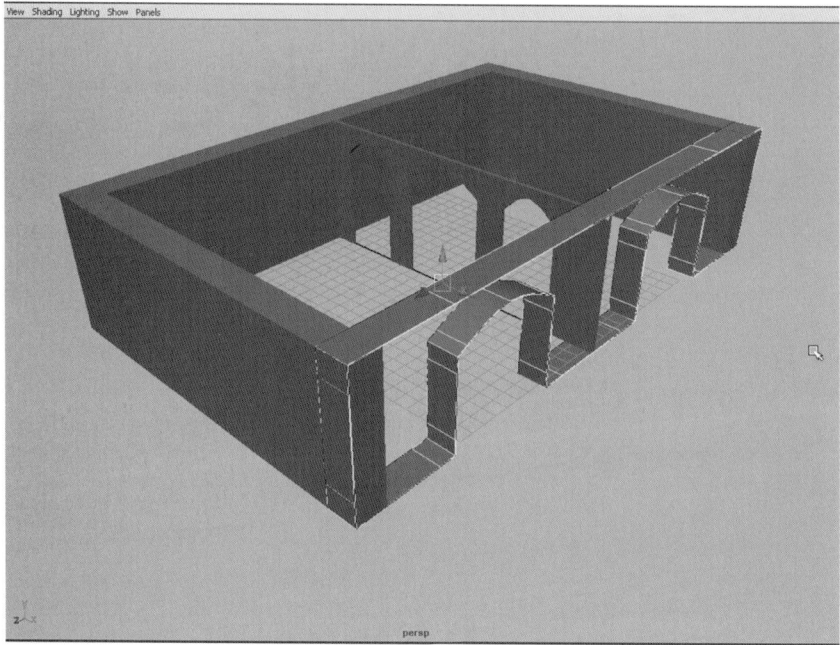

FIGURE 3.35 Lofted surface from two curves. Two Planar surfaces created from each curve.

Finally, group the newly created surfaces into a new group called WallSouth_Group. The results of all this hard work should look like Figure 3.36.

Creating Trim for Doorways

To do this, we will be creating an Extrude NURBS surface. An Extrude NURBS surface requires two curves. One curve is the shape that is to be extruded—think of this as the profile. The second is the curve along which this profile is to be extruded.

Because we want to create trim around a doorway, we will need to create a curve that is the shape of the doorway. Because we created the wall with two arches very carefully by snapping to the grid, we can use this to our advantage in creating our new curve.

Step 11: Create curve for the profile to follow. View your model from the Side view. Zoom in on one of the arches in WallSouth_Group.

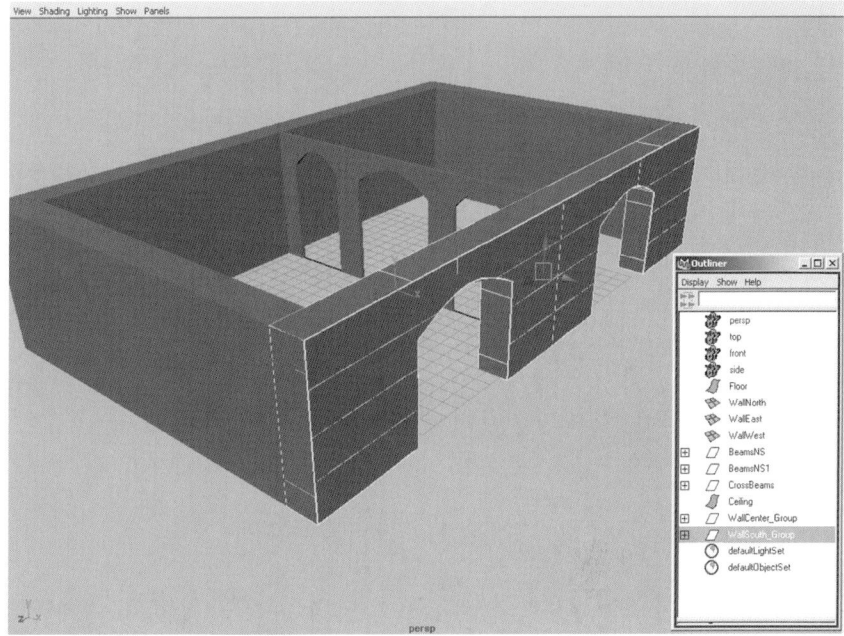

FIGURE 3.36   Newly created WallSouth_Group.

Modeling | Create > CV Curve tool activates the tool we need. Snap to grid (**x**) and create a new curve by placing CVs (and clusters of CVs) where we did when creating the curve that made this wall (Figure 3.37). Make sure to hit **Enter** to exit the CV Curve tool.

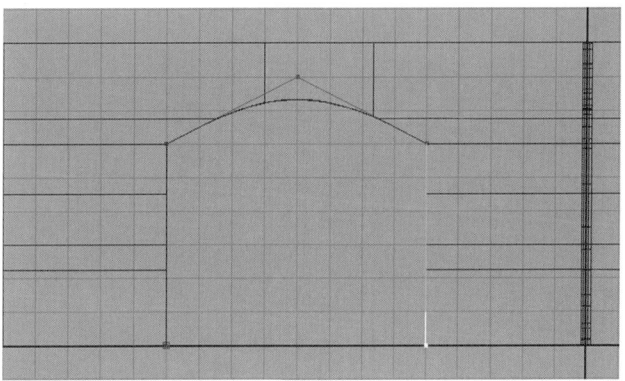

FIGURE 3.37   Creating a new curve for use with an Extrude NURBS surface.

Step 12: Center the pivot point. Notice that as soon as you exit from creating this new curve, the curve will appear green in the Workspace. However, as soon as you select the Move tool, the manipulator will be back at 0,0,0. In the past, we have moved the manipulator manually so that it was closer to the actual object it represented. Maya actually has a function that helps make this a bit easier. Select Modify > Center Pivot. Your manipulator for this newly created curve will now be in the middle of the curve.

Step 13: Create the profile to be extruded. Now that we have the curve along which our profile will be created, we need to create the profile itself. We will want to create this from the Top view.

The profile we wish to create will be in an L shape that has two sides that are four inches long, each about one inch thick. To do this, we will first create it first four feet long by one foot thick. This makes it easy to create nice straight lines as we snap to grid from the Top view.

Because this shape is going to have all straight edges, there is no need to create three CVs on each corner. Instead, select Modeling | Create > CV Curve Tool (Options) and change the Curve Degree setting to 1 Linear. Hold down the **x** key to snap to grid and make a shape similar to that in Figure 3.38. Remember to leave the curve open and close it with the Open/Close Curve command. Also make sure you move the manipulator so that it matches Figure 3.38.

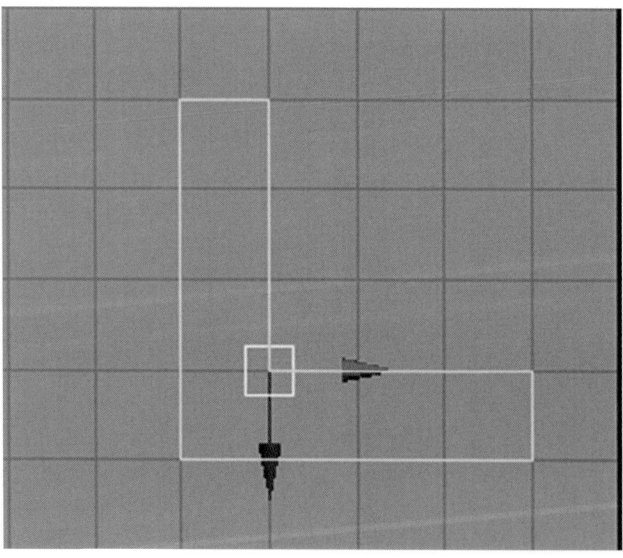

FIGURE 3.38   Large profile made with a linear CV Curve tool while snapping to grid.

Step 14: Arrange our two newly created curves. The two curves just created in Perspective view will look something like Figure 3.39a. Move curve2 (our profile shape) so that it snaps to the bottom of curve1 (our path to follow) as in Figure 3.39b.

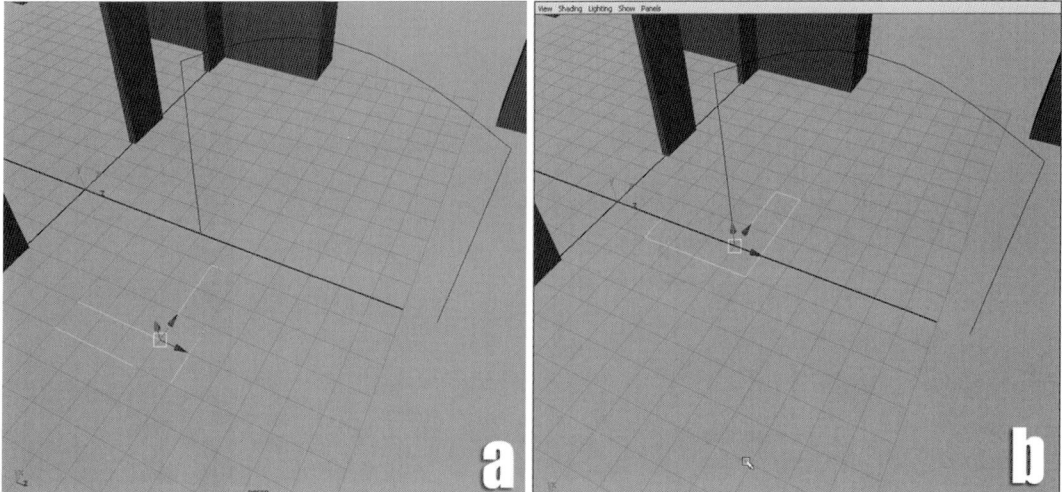

FIGURE 3.39 (a–b)   Arranged curves.

Step 15: Resize the profile to around the actual size. Now resize curve2 (our profile shape) to about 1/10th its current size. The easiest way to do this is to activate your Channel Box (with the rightmost button at the top-right of the UI) and enter 0.1 in the Scale X and Scale Z input fields.

Step 16: Extrude curve2 along curve1 to create a new surface. Extrude NURBS surfaces is one of those cases where the order in which you select curves makes a big difference. The way to think of Extrude surfaces is: "Take this curve (the profile curve, in this case, curve2) and extrude it along this curve (the path curve, in this case, curve1)." So, in this case, select curve2 first, then hold down the **Shift** key, and add to the selection curve1.

Now, select Modeling | Surfaces > Extrude (Option). As this is the first time we have used this tool, make sure you reset the settings and hit the Extrude button. The default settings have all the things set as we need them. The results should look like Figure 3.40. To finish this off, move the manipulator (pivot) so that it sits in a more appropriate place. Then move this newly created extrudedSurface1 (as it appears in the Outliner) into place (Figure 3.41). Finally, rename extrudedSurface1 WallSouthTrim.

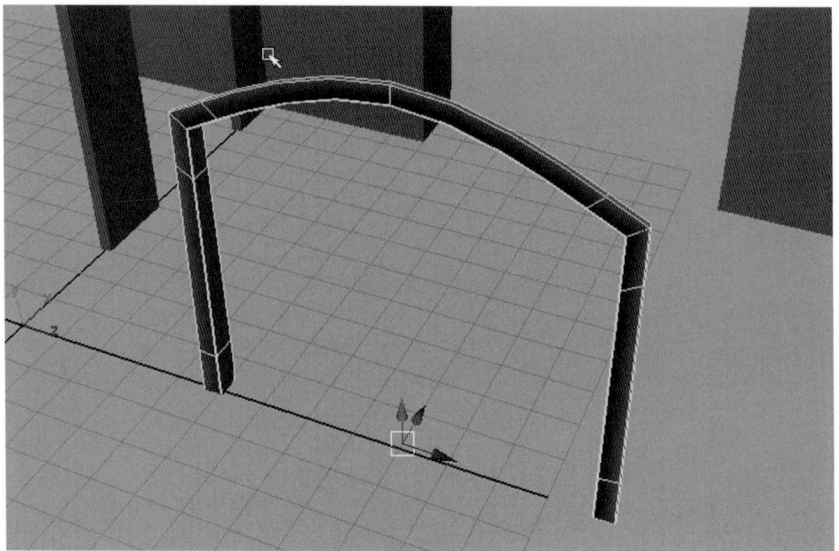

FIGURE 3.40   Newly created Extrude NURBS surface.

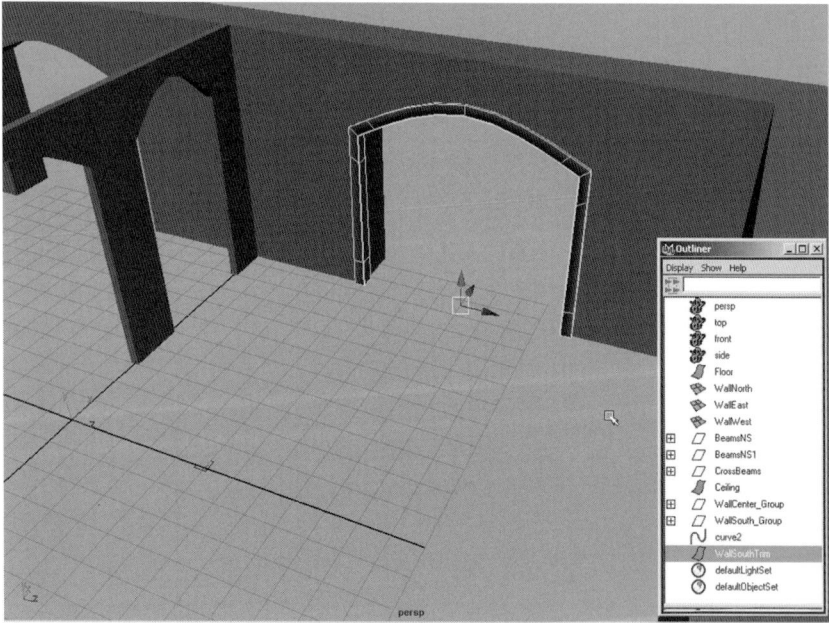

FIGURE 3.41   Placed and renamed WallSouthTrim.

Step 17: Clean up by deleting curve1. Curve1, which is the curve that defined the shape of the archway, is no longer needed, so delete it. However, the profile will be useful for the other arches in the room, so leave curve2 alone.

Step 18: Duplicate WallSouthTrim and place the new WallSouthTrim1. Edit > Duplicate will create a new piece of trim in the same spot as the old one. Use the Move tool and move the new WallSouthTrim1 along its Z axis (use the blue manipulator handle) so that it sits in the second hole on WallSouth. You can eyeball this or hold down the **x** key to find the exact center (Figure 3.42).

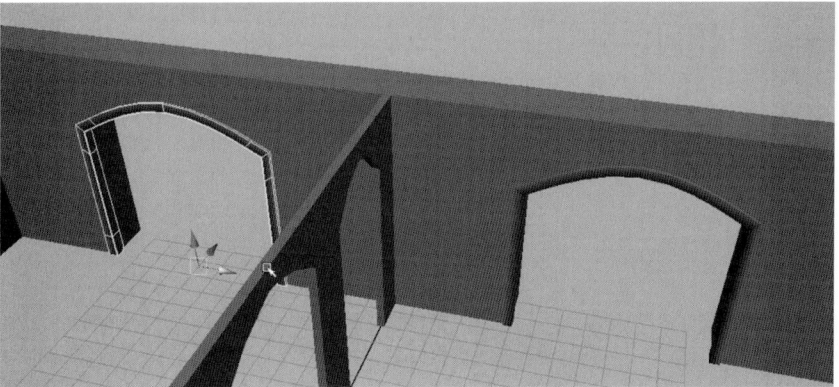

FIGURE 3.42   Creating a duplicate and finding the exact center.

Step 19: Organize. We already have a WallSouth_Group. Currently, this group only includes the surfaces that make up the wall. Select WallSouthTrim and WallSouthTrim1 in the Outliner and MMB-drag them onto WallSouth_Group. This will add these two surfaces as children to the group, WallSouth_Group.

Step 20: Repeat the process for the arches in WallCenter. From the Front view, create a new CV curve (remember to set the Curve Degree back to 3 Cubic) that matches one of the arches (Figure 3.43a). This curve will be listed in the Outliner as curve3. Center the pivot (Modify > Center Pivot) and move it away from the wall (snapping to grid) to get a better look at it. Because you snapped this surface, you can now move the profile shape (curve2) while snapping to grid so that it aligns perfectly with the bottom of curve3 (Figure 3.43b).

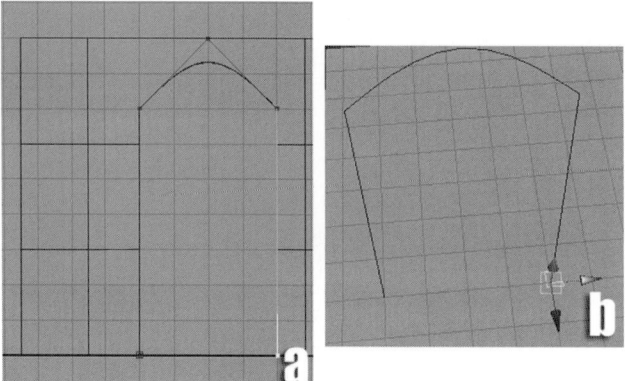

FIGURE 3.43 (a–b) Creating curve and arranging curves in preparation of Extrude surfaces.

Again, select curve2 first (the profile) and then **Shift**-select curve3 (the curve to be extruded along), and select Modeling | Surfaces > Extrude. Center the pivot and move this new extrudedSurface1 back into position (Figure 3.44). Rename it WallCenterTrim.

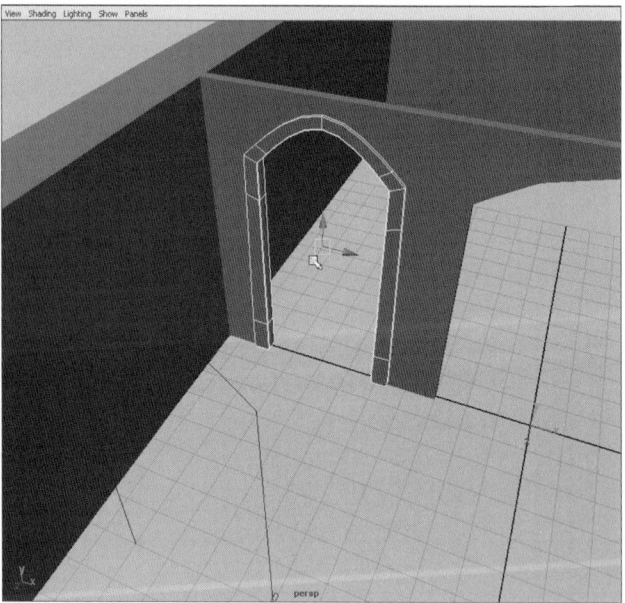

FIGURE 3.44 Newly placed WallCenterTrim.

Duplicate this WallCenterTrim and place the new WallCenterTrim1 into the other arch. Again, delete curve3 (our path that the profile curve2 was extruded along) as it is no longer needed.

From the Front view, create another CV curve for the center arch. Again, organize the new curve3 and the old curve2, create the new Extruded surface, and place the new surface into place. Rename it WallCenterTrimCenter. Now, delete curve2 and curve3.

Finally, select all three and group them (**Ctrl-G**). Rename the group WallCenterTrim_Group. Select this group and duplicate it. In the Channel Box, enter 180 in the Rotate Y input field so that you can place this group of trim on the other side as well. Adjust the position of this new WallCenterTrim_Group1 as appropriate.

The room should look like Figure 3.45.

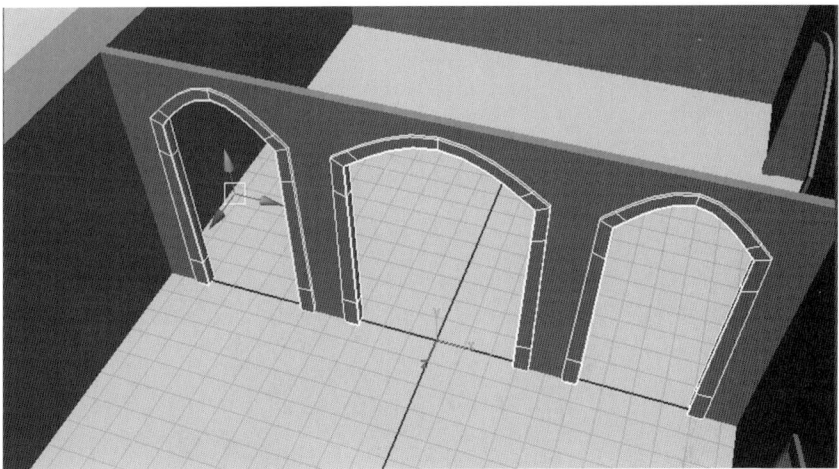

FIGURE 3.45   All the trim in place.

Step 21: Make WallCenterTrim_Group and WallCenterTrim_Group1 children of WallCenter_Group. Do this by selecting them and MMB-dragging them onto the group, WallCenter_Group.

CONCLUSION

Hopefully, through the course of this chapter, you have gotten a good idea of the theory behind NURBS surfaces and the technique of building them. There are still more NURBS surfaces yet to come. In the next chapter, we will continue with NURBS surfaces and build the furniture that will live in this room. We will explore other surfaces and how they are created and modified.

ON THE CD

Remember to take a look at the completed file on the CD-ROM in the Tutorials folder if you have any questions over what things should look like at the end of Tutorial 3.2.

After that, we will look at some methods of creating complex forms through Boolean functions. Finally, we will look at how to use the ever-powerful subdivision surfaces.

NURBS CONTINUED

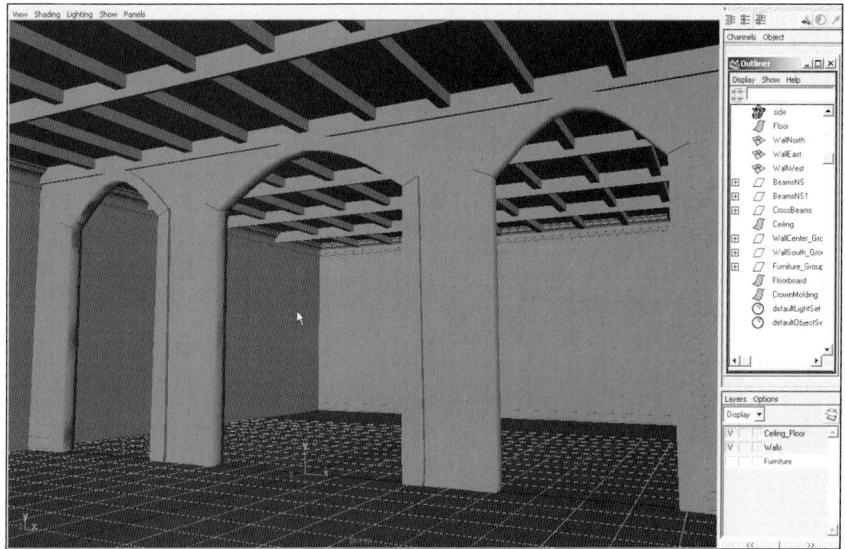

By now, hopefully, you have the general gist of how NURBS surfaces are created. In this chapter, we will continue looking at new surfaces and how to create them. By the end of this chapter, you will be a NURBS creation master.

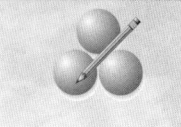

TUTORIAL 4.1   NURBS SURFACES CONTINUED

In this tutorial, we will continue our work from the last chapter. Our room will continue to take shape as we begin to add things like furniture, lamps, doors, and windows. We will use a variety of surface creation techniques and do some basic editing of these surfaces.

As always, the results of this tutorial can be found on the included CD-ROM. So, take a look if you are having problems getting any of the results you are looking for.

ON THE CD

Step 1: Open the Room tutorial that you have created to this point.

Step 2: Create a new layer and name it Walls. Make sure you can see the Layer Editor beneath the Channel Box and select Layers > Create Layer from the pull-down menu within the Layer Editor. Double-click the layer and name this new layer Walls. Hit the Save button.

Step 3: Add all the walls (except WallCenter_Group) to this layer and hide the layer. In the Outliner, select WallNorth, WallEast, WallWest, and the WallSouth_Group (**Ctrl**-LMB). RMB-click on the Walls layer within the Layer Editor and select Add Selected Objects from the pop-up menu. Lastly, in the Visibility column, click the v to turn off the visibility of this layer. This will hide all the walls except for the group, WallCenter_Group. We are leaving this wall so that you have an idea of scale.

Step 4: Begin making a vase by creating a profile curve. We are going to create a vase using a Revolve surface. This is much like a Lathe surface in most other 3D applications and is based on the old idea of a wooden lathe. Basically, a wood lathe takes a block of wood and spins it very quickly. The craftsman then can use a blade that, when held up to the block of spinning wood, cuts in nice round curves. Lathes or Revolves are surfaces that are made by creating the desired profile of the object and then spinning the curve around to create a three-dimensional surface.

To create the curve we want, first take a minute to organize your Workspace. For now, we will create the lamp on the floor. Again, to make sure that we create a clean surface, we are going to make use of the grid for snapping and create a lamp that is too big. Later we will scale the lamp to size.

Maximize the Front view and zoom in on 0,0,0 in 3D space (Figure 4.1).

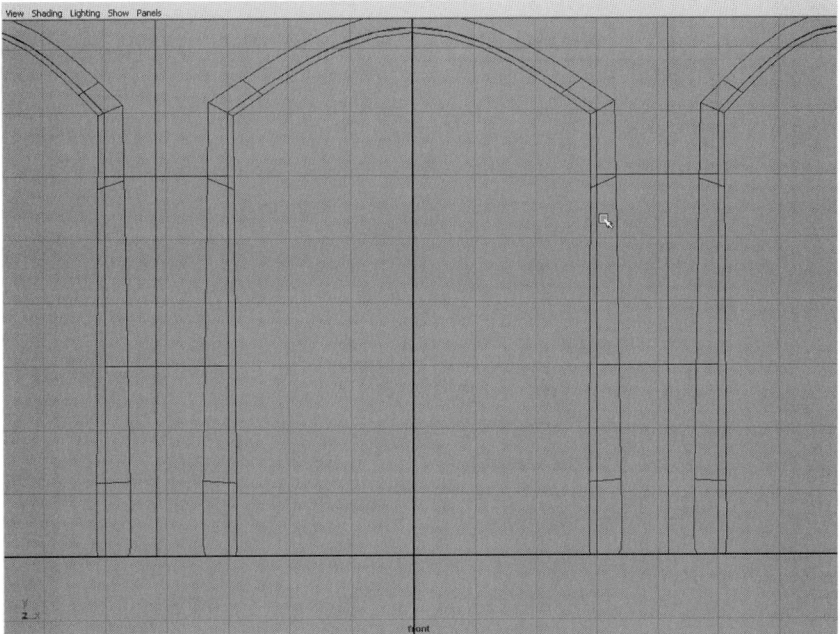

FIGURE 4.1   Zooming in to about the center of the 3D space allows for quick creation of curves and shapes without having to worry about adjusting manipulators/pivots later.

Create a CV curve using the CV Curve tool with a Curve Degree of 3 Cubic that approximately matches Figure 4.2. Notice in Figure 4.2 that the number of CVs are listed to show how the curve was created on the fly. There is no need for this curve to match exactly; make adjustments as you see fit.

A couple of things are important to note. The revolved surface is going to be revolved around the Y axis. So, to make sure this lamp base is closed at the bottom and the top and make sure that those two points are snapped to grid (**x**).

Hit **Enter** to exit the CV Curve tool. Remember that as you are creating the curve, if you place a CV that you dislike, immediately hit **Ctrl-Z** and the CV will be undone, while still leaving you in the CV Curve tool. Also remember that when all is done and you have exited the CV Curve

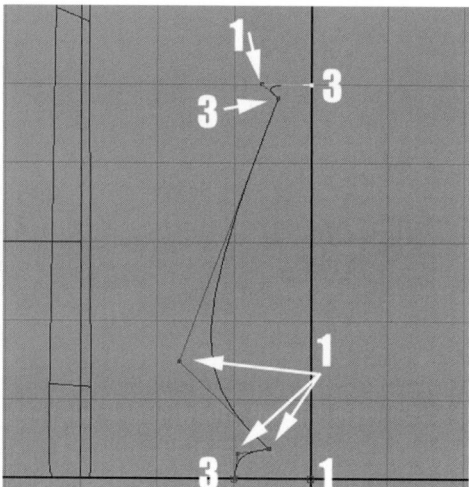

FIGURE 4.2 CV curve listing the number of CVs.

tool, you can use the Move tool and RMB-click on the curve, select Control Vertex from the Marking menu, and then select the CVs you have created and adjust them.

Step 5: Create the three-dimensional lamp from this CV curve. Make sure that this newly created curve is selected and then go to Modeling | Surfaces > Revolve (Options). For now, make sure you reset the settings, because the defaults are great for what we are doing. Before moving on, notice that within this Revolve Options window, you can choose which axis to revolve the curve around, you can choose to revolve in straight segments with the Surface Degree setting, and you can even choose not to revolve all the way around. Using the Start and End Sweep Angle settings, you can create half a form, a quarter of a form, or whatever you would like. Notice that you can decide how many segments to create as Maya revolves this curve around. The default (8) is usually sufficient for basic shapes such as lamp bases. Finally, notice that you can choose to make the surface you are going to create NURBS, polygons, subdivision surfaces, or Bezier.

For now, just hit the Revolve button and get back to Perspective view to see the results (Figure 4.3).

Rename the new revolved Surface1 to LampBase.

Step 6: Use Construction History to your advantage to change the shape of the lamp base. This new surface, LampBase, has some linkages. Because we used curve1 in the Outliner to create this surface, this is the primary linkage. This is important because of how Maya uses Construction History.

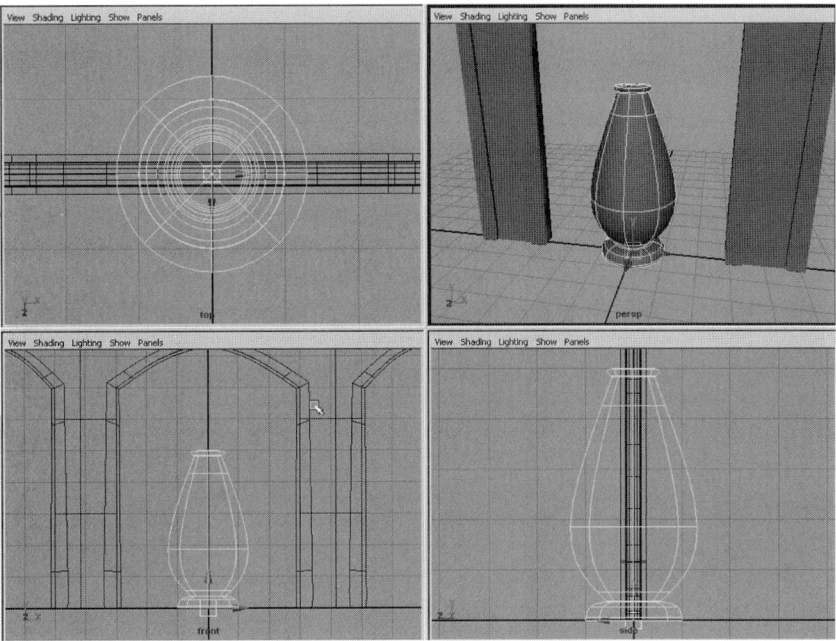

FIGURE 4.3   Revolved lamp base.

Select curve1 in the Outliner. This is the CV curve we created to define the curvature of LampBase. This will highlight the curve in green that is clearly seen in the Front view. RMB-click and hold the curve (in the Front view) and select Control Vertex from the resulting Marking menu (Figure 4.4a). Select any one of the control vertices and use the Move tool to change the position of that vertex; do this from the Front view (Figure 4.4b). Notice that as you change the position of the control vertex of the curve, the revolved surface that the curve created is updated in real time to match (Figure 4.4c).

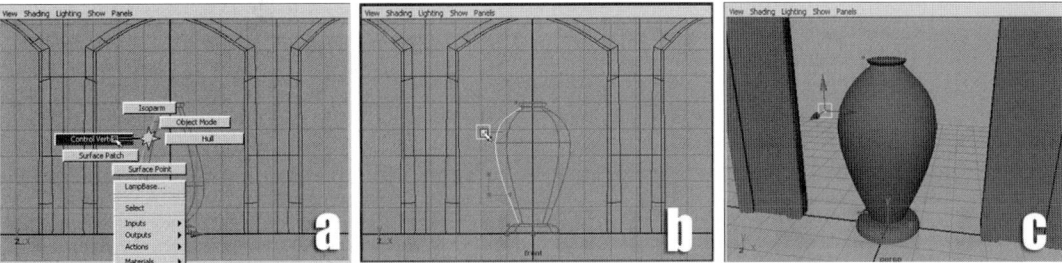

FIGURE 4.4 (a–c)   Because Construction History is active, when the curve is adjusted, the surface updates as well.

Now, this is not to say that the surface cannot be altered without the curve that created it. It is quite easy to edit a NURBS surface, and we will talk more about it later. So, keeping a curve around is not necessary. Further, a huge collection of curves can become visually distracting in the Workspace and confusing in the Outliner.

In general, when creating a surface and making the general adjustments, the curve is great to have around. However, once you are fairly comfortable with the shape, go ahead and delete the curve. Of course with complex surfaces (like some of the faces we are going to create in later tutorials), you might want to keep these curves around a lot longer and simply hide them. Deciding when to get rid of what will become easier as your comfort level with your own work flow increases.

For now and for this tutorial, go ahead and delete curve1.

Step 7: Create the lamp shade using a Revolve surface. Repeat the process outlined earlier by creating a CV curve in the shape of the lamp shade you would like (Figure 4.5a). With the curve selected, create a new revolved surface (Modeling | Surfaces >Revolve) (Figure 4.5b). Make any adjustments to the shape via the curve used to create the Revolve surface (Figure 4.5c) and then delete the curve. Rename this new surface LampShade.

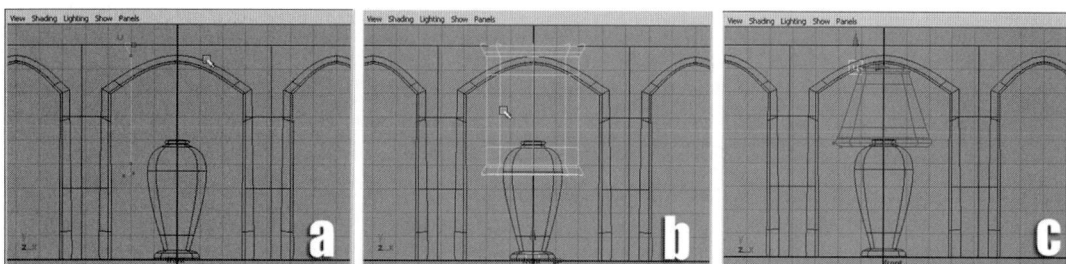

FIGURE 4.5 (a–c)   Creating the lampshade with a revolve surface.

Step 8: Do some organizing. First, select LampShade in the Outliner and **Ctrl**-LMB-click LampBase. Hit **Ctrl-G** to group them together. Name the new group Lamp. Now, for a simple but effective trick: with the group Lamp selected, hit **Ctrl-G** again. It will appear that you just relabeled Lamp to group1. Not to fear. Expand the group group1 and you will see that the group Lamp has just been placed as a child to a new group— group1. Rename group1 Furniture_Group. We will be placing other furniture in this group later.

Finally, in the Layer Editor, create a new layer called Furniture, add Furniture_Group to it and make the layer invisible. While you are there, make the layer Walls visible again.

Step 9: Create curves for the floorboard. The plan here is to create a lofted surface for the floorboards that is able to turn corners. To get started on this process, we need to create a curve that is a profile section of the floorboard. Rather than trying to create this at exactly the right size to begin with, we will make it larger than necessary then resize it to the right scale.

In the Front view, move off to the left of your walls and create a curve that matches either Figure 4.6a or the floorboard in the room where you are now working. Make sure you close the curve. Also, as you create, make sure you snap the CVs at the bottom of the curve to the ground plane.

Center the pivot to get it in the general region of your curve and then snap it into position at the bottom corner (Figure 4.6b). We want to make sure we are snapping with this point to get these curves right into the corners of the room, and we want to resize from here so that we make sure that the curve stays sitting on the ground.

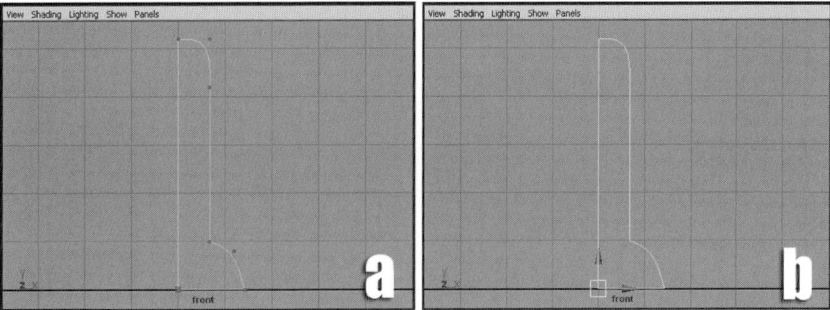

FIGURE 4.6 (a–b)   Create the floorboard curve and position its pivot to the bottom corner.

Step 10: Using snap to points, move this curve into the northwest corner of the room. An easy way to do this is hold down the **v** hotkey and in the Front view, slide the curve into position for the inside of the wall (Figure 4.7a), then still with the **v** hotkey down, in the Side view, slide the curve back into place from the center of the room (Figure 4.7b). The result in the Perspective view (after you have tumbled around to see the northwest corner) will look like Figure 4.7c.

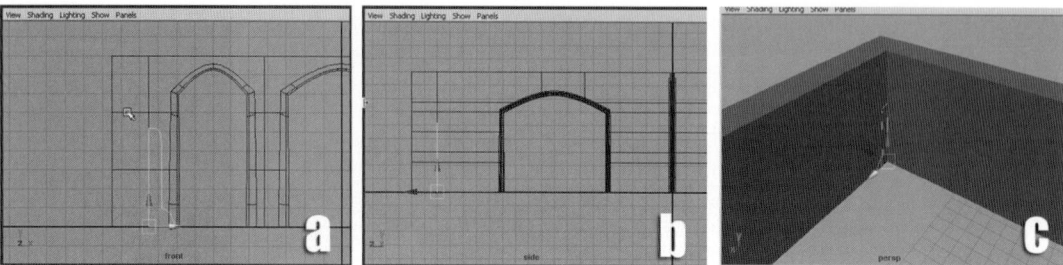

FIGURE 4.7 (a–c)   Placed floorboard curve.

Step 11: Resize and rotate this curve into place. Because this curve was not created with any particular attention to size, we will just eyeball the resizing process. Using the Scale tool, LMB-drag the center of the manipulator (the yellow box) to resize the curve in all directions at once. Resize it so that it is about one-third the height of one of the grid units (Figure 4.8a). This will make the floorboard about four inches tall.

We also want to make sure this floorboard is a consistent width all through the room, so we want it turned in 45 degrees. In the Channel Box, enter 45 in the Rotate Y input field (Figure 4.8b).

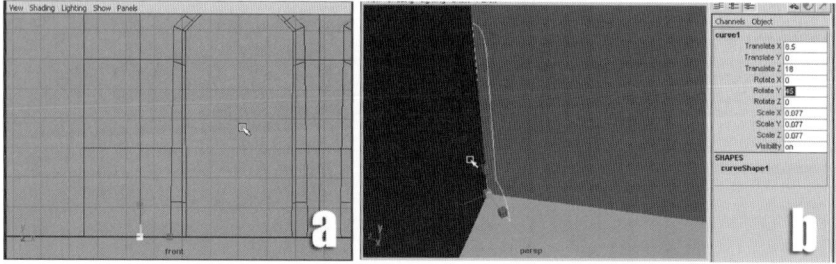

FIGURE 4.8 (a–b)   Resized and rotated curve.

Step 12: Duplicate and place the new curve2 into the next corner. Duplicate curve1 (**Ctrl-D**). Then in the Top view with the Move tool, move the curve along the Z axis to the corner of WallNorth and Wall-Center_Group. Be sure to dolly in so that you can see that the curve is really sitting in the corner. We want the curve facing into the room, so change the Rotate Y input field of the Channel Box to –45. The approximate placement is shown in Figure 4.9.

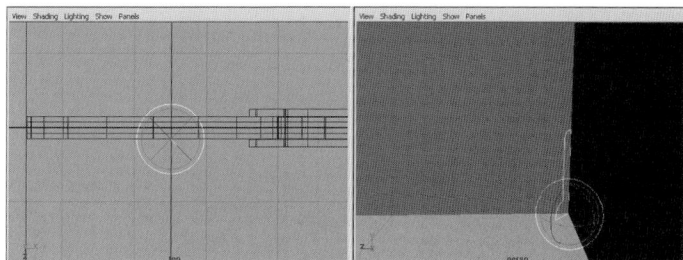

FIGURE 4.9   Second curve placed in the next corner and rotated to face the center of the room.

Step 13: Duplicate and place the next three curves to go around the center wall. Again, duplicate, move, and change the Rotate Y values so that you have curves at each corner of the center wall archway. Curve3 should remain at –45 degrees, curve4 will be at 45, and curve5 will also be at 45 degrees. The curves should approximately match Figure 4.10.

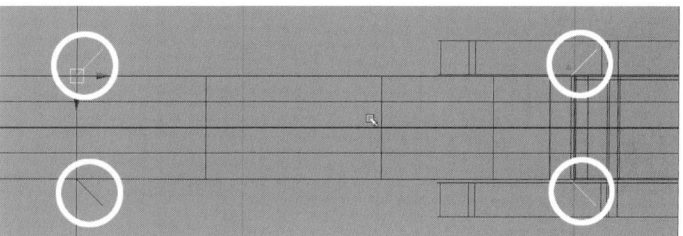

FIGURE 4.10   Duplicated and placed curves to allow the floorboard to go around the inset wall.

Step 14: Continue to duplicate and place curves for all corners of the room. Continue to duplicate, move, and rotate each curve for each corner of the room. For now, do not worry about the archways in the WallSouth_Group. Figure 4.11 shows a breakdown of the location of the needed curves.

Step 15: Loft curve1 through curve2 into a new surface. Select curve1 through curve12 in the Outliner. Select Modeling | Surfaces > Loft (Options). By default, the settings for the Loft Options window are set to create a nice, organic-looking lofted surface. However in this case, we want to have crisp corners and straight lines—very inorganic.

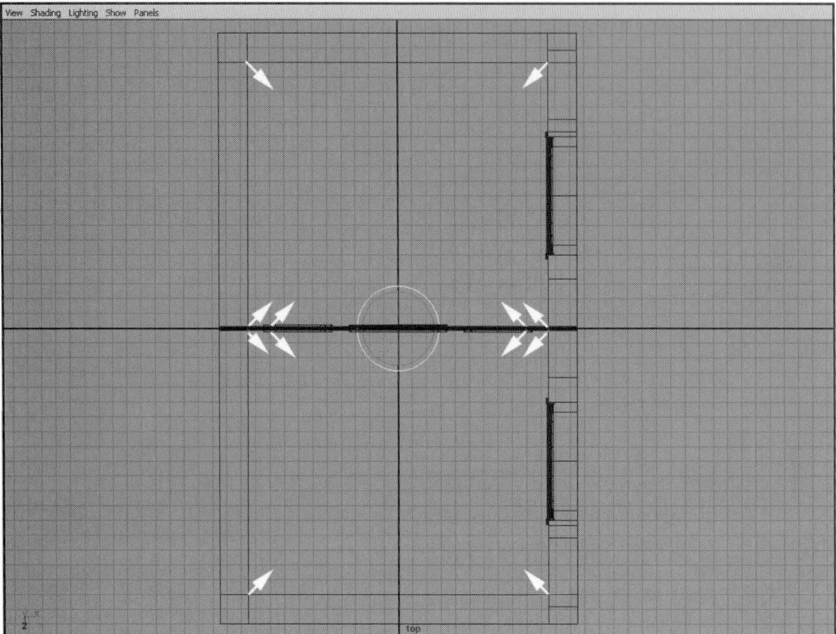

FIGURE 4.11 Breakdown of needed curves for floorboard using a lofted surface. Each arrow represents a curve in the direction it should be facing.

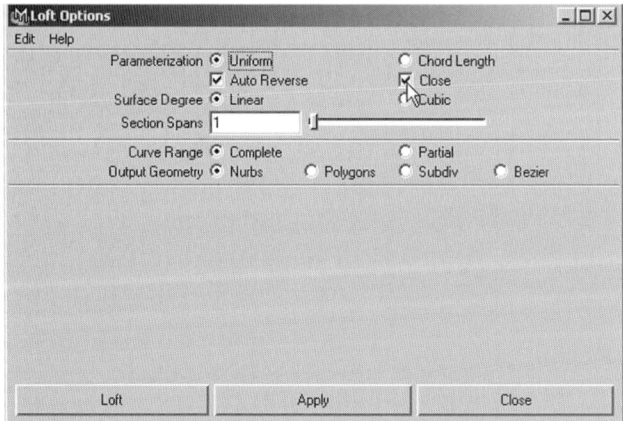

FIGURE 4.12 The Loft Options window with appropriate settings for our clean, crisp floorboard.

To fix this, change the Surface Degree from Cubic to Linear. This will give us the straight surface we are looking for. Also, because we want this floorboard to go all the way around the room—including the last curve back to the first—click on the Close option. Maya will then close the surface by extending it from curve12 back to the first curve1. Hit the Loft button.

Take a minute to inspect the new surface that runs all around the room. Check to make sure it really squeezes into every corner and does the things you need it to. If not, remember that this surface is tied to all those curves you place. If you need to adjust things, you can do so quickly with the curves.

Once you are happy with this new surface, rename it Floorboard and delete curve1 through curve12.

Step 16: Build crown molding using an extruded surface. We are now going to add crown molding to the room. Although we could certainly do this using a lofted surface, we will instead use an extruded surface. As a review, this will consist of two surfaces: the profile we are going to extrude and the path along which we will extrude it.

Start by creating a curve that represents the profile of the crown molding. A suggested shape is shown in Figure 4.13a. Make sure you close the curve (Figure 4.13b) and place the pivot/manipulator at the top corner of the curve. Move the curve to the top corner in the Front view and then, in the Top view, make sure that it is in the northwest corner of the room (Figure 4.13c). Finally, resize the curve so that it matches the size it should be for the room (the exact size is not important—eyeball it).

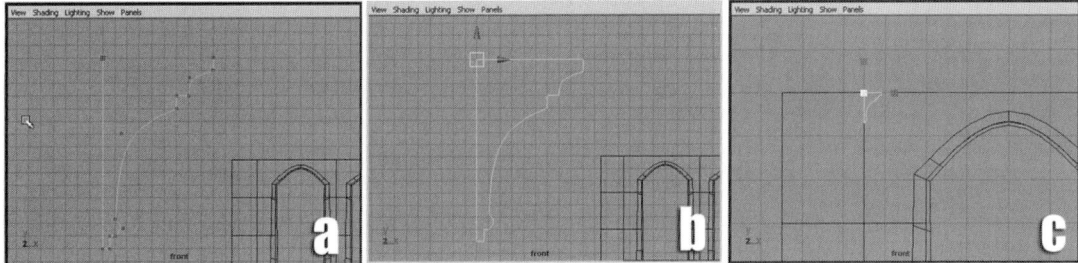

FIGURE 4.13   (a) Create the curve using the CV Curve tool. (b) Close the curve and place the pivot at the top corner. (c) Place and scale this curve into the northwest corner of the room.

Now, in the Top view, select Modeling | Create > CV Curve Tool (Options). Within the CV curve settings, change the Curve Degree to 1 Linear. We are creating a curve that will represent the overall shape of the room, so we need sharp corners. Create a curve with CVs in each corner. Remember to leave the curve open and use Edit Modeling | Curves > Close Curves to close off the shape (Figure 4.14).

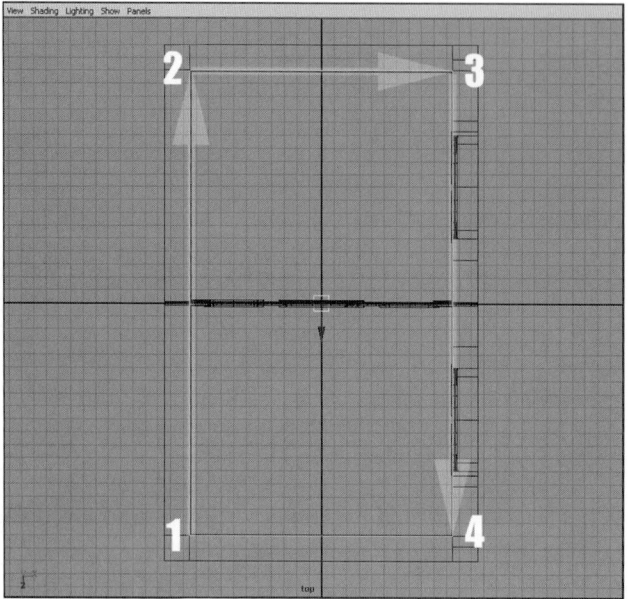

FIGURE 4.14 Creating the curve that the profile will follow.

Snap to grid and snap this curve to the top of the room. You will need to switch to Front, Side, or Perspective view to do this (Figure 4.15).

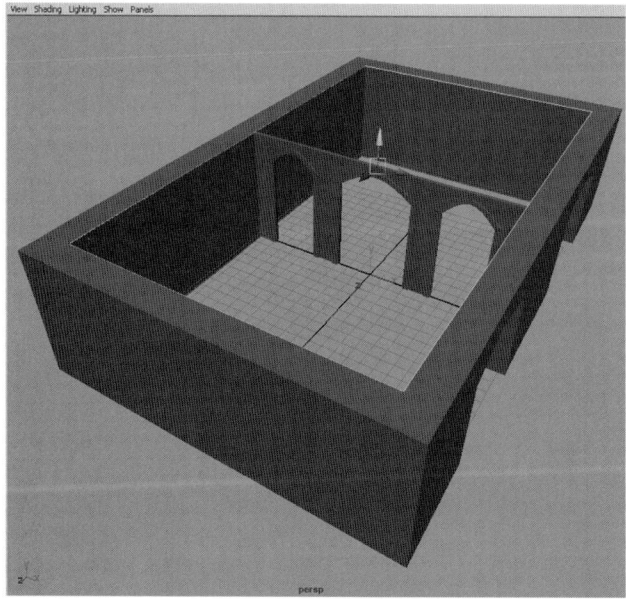

FIGURE 4.15 Curve snapped to top of the walls.

Now, select curve1 in the Outliner and **Shift**-select curve2 (select the profile first and then select the curve along which to extrude the profile). Select Modeling | Surfaces > Extrude. Violà! Your new crown molding is created (Figure 4.16). Rename the new extrudedSurface1 CrownMolding, then delete curve1 and curve2.

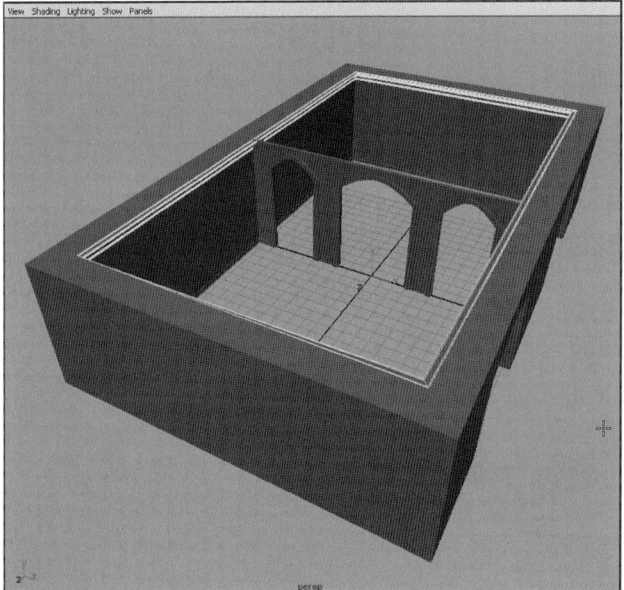

FIGURE 4.16   Finished CrownMolding.

With CrownMolding selected, RMB-click the layer Ceiling_Floor in the Layer Editor and select Add Selected Objects from the pop-up menu. Because the layer Ceiling_Floor is not visible, CrownMolding will immediately disappear.

For fun, make the Ceiling_Floor visible again by clicking on the Visibility column. If your view from the Perspective view is outside the room, this will close off your view of the room. Dolly into the inside of the room and take a bit of a look around to get a feel for what you have created. Hopefully, it all looks like Figure 4.17.

Step 17: Make a lofted surface to create a picture frame. Again, in the Front view, create a profile for the frame using the CV Curve tool. Make sure that the Curve Degree is set to 3 Cubic. Figure 4.18a shows a suggested shape.

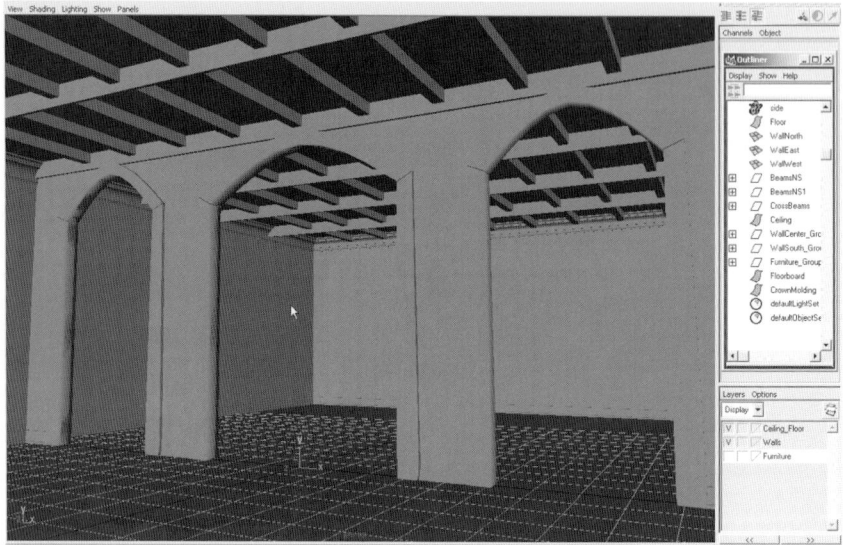

FIGURE 4.17 The room so far.

Center the pivot and then snap it to the bottom corner (Figure 4.18b). Enter 45 into the Rotate Y input field of the Channel Box. In the Top view, duplicate and rotate three more so that you have a setup similar to Figure 4.18c.

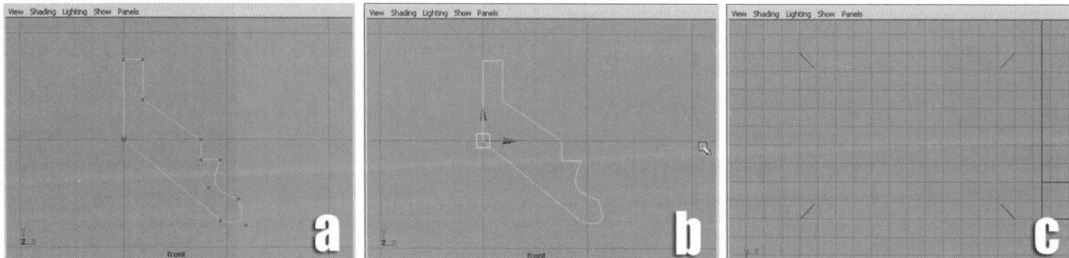

FIGURE 4.18 (a–c) Preparing a lofted surface for a picture frame.

Again, do not worry much about the scale of this frame. Use the grid to make sure you are snapping each curve into position so that they are really straight across from the necessary curves. We will resize this frame when it is all done.

Now, select all the curves one at a time to define the order in which Maya is to loft together these curves. Select Modeling | Surfaces > Loft (Options). Make sure the Surface Degree is set to 1 Linear. Hit the Loft button and you should have a frame similar to Figure 4.19a. Rename it Frame.

This time, do not delete the curves. We are going to use these same curves to create some other frames. However, because we are going to use the curves on other frames, we want to make sure we break the connection between the surface and the curves. With Frame selected, choose Edit > Delete by Type > History. This will erase all the Construction History for the frame, thus freeing it from any ties to the curves.

Create a new NURBS plane Modeling | Create > NURBS Primitives > Plane (Figure 4.19a). Then, scale and move it into position on the bottom of the frame (Figure 4.19b). Finally, group together this new plane and frame and rename the group Picture. With this picture selected, move, scale, and rotate into position on one of the walls in your room. Which wall is up to you.

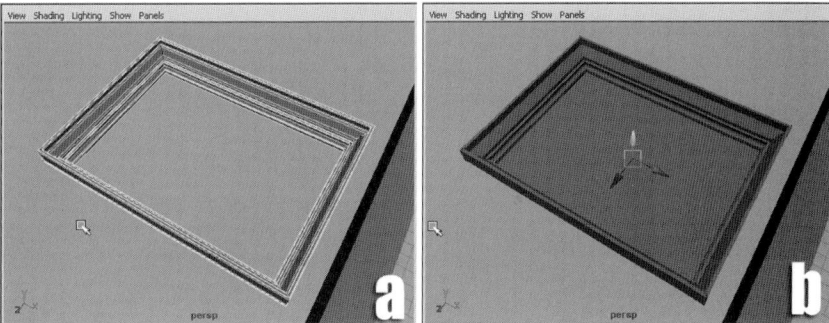

FIGURE 4.19 (a–b)   Creating the surface and final frame for a picture.

Step 18: Use curves to create an alternately proportioned frame.
So, if we want to make a frame that is square, or very long, why not just take the old frame and use the Scale tool to lengthen it? Well, Figure 4.20 shows the frame created in the last step that has been rescaled. Notice that the thickness of the frame at the top and bottom becomes incredibly large, while the width along the sides remains constant.

Clearly, rescaling this type of surface is not the key. Instead, we will create a new surface from the curves created earlier, but first we will reposition the curves. Select curve1, curve2, curve3, and curve4 in the Outliner. Make sure you have a standard Four View panel setup, move your mouse over the Perspective view and hit **f** on your keyboard. This

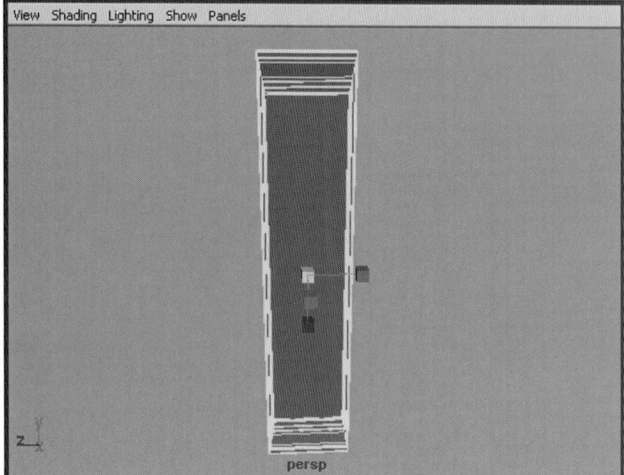

FIGURE 4.20   Rescaled frame. Notice the thick tops and bottoms with the thin sides.

frames the selected curves in the middle of the panel. Now move your mouse over the Top view and hit **f** again. Now, we can see the four curves and alter them easily.

Select the top two curves by marqueeing around them in the Top view. Activate the Move tool, hold down **x** to snap to grid, and move them in the Z direction (blue manipulator handle) until you have set up a fairly square configuration (Figure 4.21a).

Again, select curve1, then curve2, curve3, and finally, curve4. Create a lofted surface by clicking on the Loft button in the Shelf or by selecting Modeling | Surfaces > Loft (Figure 4.21b). Because we will continue to create shapes, select this new surface and delete its history (Edit > Delete by Type > History). Create a new NURBS plane primitive and put it on the back of this new frame. Group together the plane and surface and name the group PictureSquare. Rotate, scale, and place this new frame into your room.

Step 19: Using these same curves or new combinations of curves, create various other frames. Figure 4.22 shows a variety of frames created from variations of the original frame curve. Some frames use different curve placements, while others use more than the standard four curves. Notice the last example is round. This was accomplished by laying out the curves in a diamond shape and selecting Modeling | Surfaces > Loft (Options) and changing the Surface Degree setting to Cubic.

When you have explored the lofted surface enough, be sure to delete the curves.

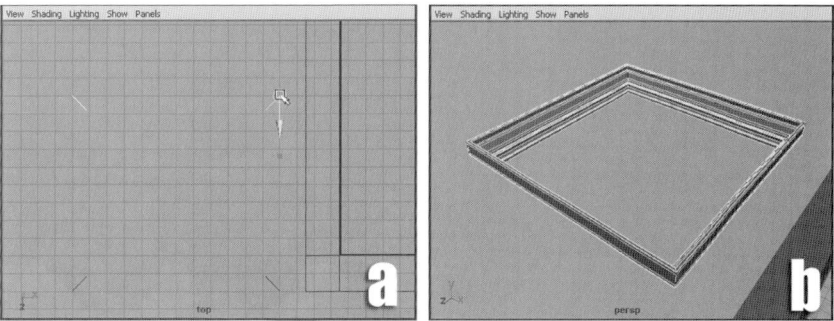

FIGURE 4.21 (a–b)   New square frame created from the same curves used in Step 17.

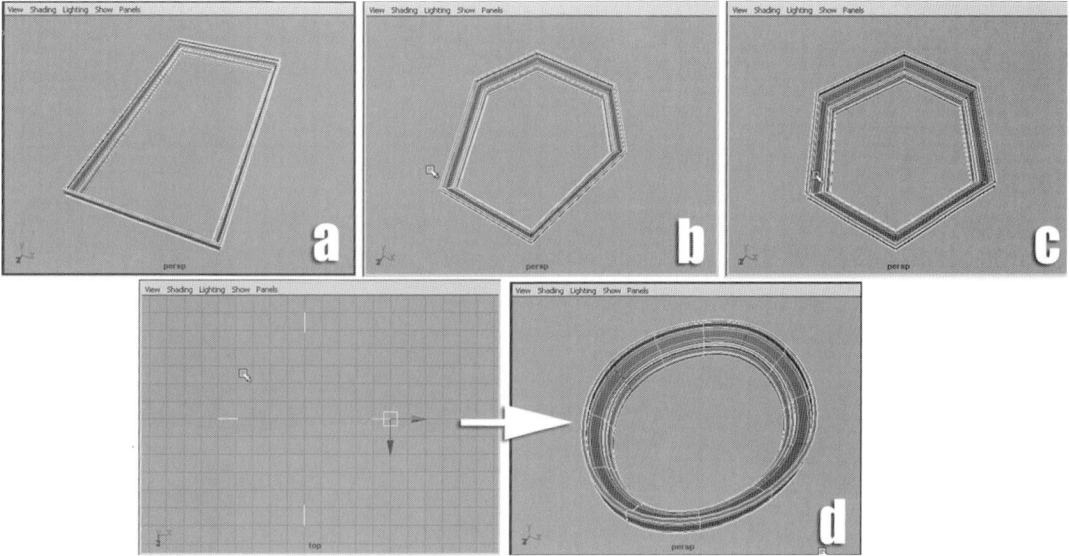

FIGURE 4.22 (a–d)   Variety of lofted surfaces for frames.

Step 20: Duplicate, place, and organize (in the Layer Editor and Outliner) a variety of frames into your room. Scale, move, and rotate away until you have a load of pictures and frames placed throughout your room. When you are happy with your placements, create a new layer in the Layer Editor called WallHangings. Add all the Picture objects to this layer. This will allow you to hide them when necessary.

Finally, you will notice that with a lot of duplicated frames, your Outliner is getting a bit unwieldy with all the objects in it. Select all your pictures in the Outliner and hit **Ctrl-G** to place them all into a group that you will name Pictures_Group. This keeps your Outliner tidy as well.

Step 21: Create windows through a collection of loft and extrude surfaces. Figure 4.23 (a–c) shows the lofted surface created from two CV curves. Make sure you organize the curves from the Top view (assuming that the curve was created in the Front view) so you ensure that they remain straight. After you have lofted the two surfaces, go ahead and delete the curves.

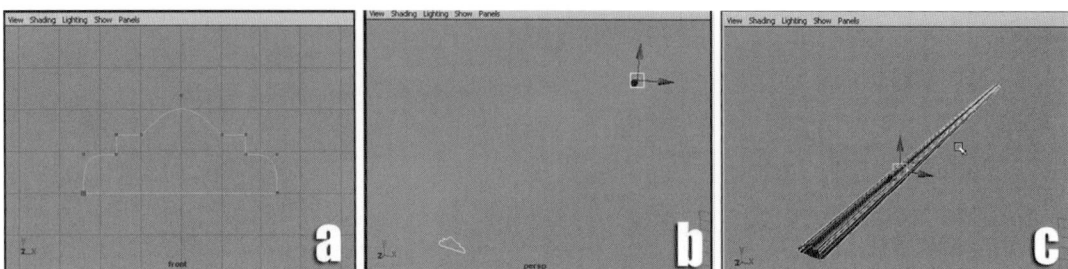

FIGURE 4.23 (a–c)   The beginnings of the transoms and mullions of the window.

Figure 4.24 (a–b) shows the lofted surface being duplicated and rotated into place to create the woodwork that will lie between the glass. Remember to use the Channel Box to rotate things exactly 90 degrees. You may find it helpful to snap to grid and simply count the units you snap to make sure each unit remains a constant distance from the unit just duplicated.

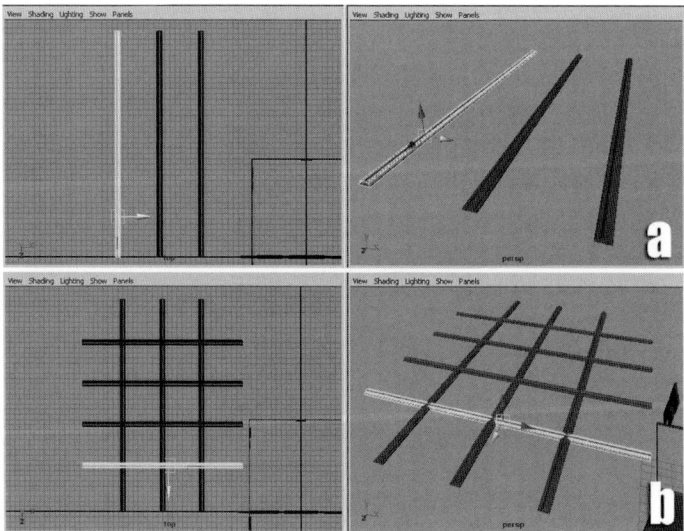

FIGURE 4.24 (a–b)   Creating all the inner transoms and mullions. All are duplicates of the original lofted surface.

When all the transoms and mullions are created, group them together and name the new group Transoms.

When you are comfortable with this woodwork, it will be time to make the frame for the window. To do this, we will also use a lofted surface. Create a CV curve and be sure to rotate each curve to point toward the center (45-degree angles). Make sure you change the options for the loft back to linear for the Surface Degree and then loft together these curves (Figure 4.25a–c).

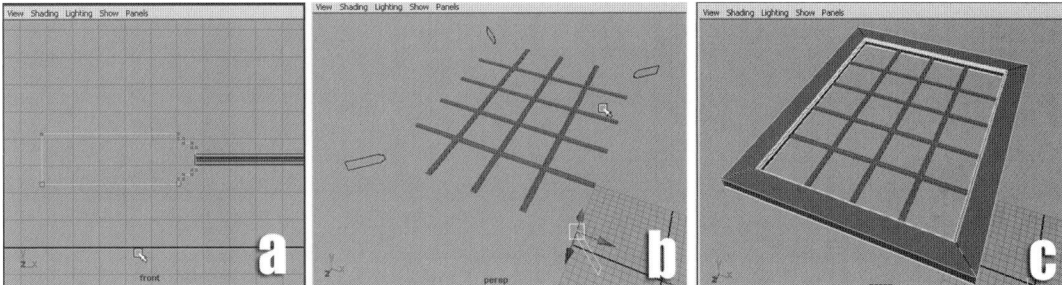

FIGURE 4.25 (a–c)   Creating the lofted surface that is the window frame.

At this point, the window looks too stumpy. So, select the two curves that are the top of the window and use the Move tool to move them up to a new location. The lofted surface that is the window frame will reshape to match. Resize the vertical units of the Transoms group to fit and add new units as necessary.

Figure 4.26 shows the completed window that includes a new NURBS plane placed in the window. Later, this plane will be textured to represent glass and will become transparent, but we must have the geography there to do that.

Finally, make sure you group all the elements for the window into a group that you rename Window_Group.

Step 22: Place windows in the room and organize. If your window matches the preceding figures, it is probably entirely too large. Resize the window, rotate it, and place it into position in the room on WallEast. Duplicate the window and place the new duplicated window a bit to the south.

Duplicate and place three more windows so that they match Figure 4.27(a–b). Notice that these windows are placed about flush with the outside of the walls. Although this seems a little strange, it will make more sense in a bit when we cut the holes for these windows to sit in.

Now, to keep our scene clean, select all the windows and group them into a new group called Windows_All. Also, create a new layer called Windows and add all the windows to it.

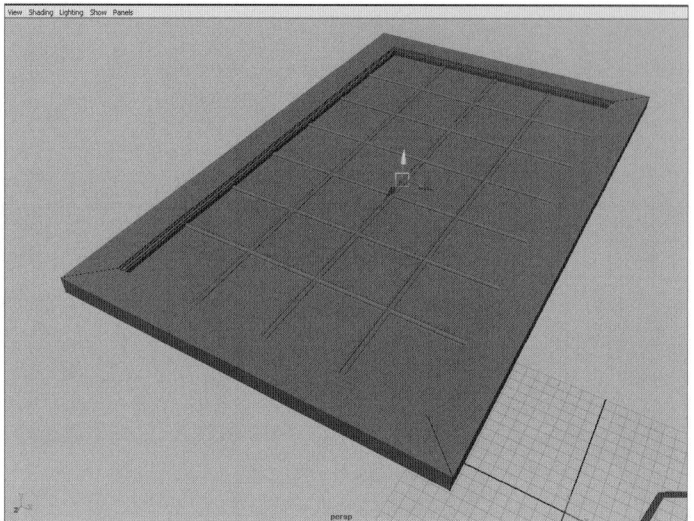

FIGURE 4.26   Finished window.

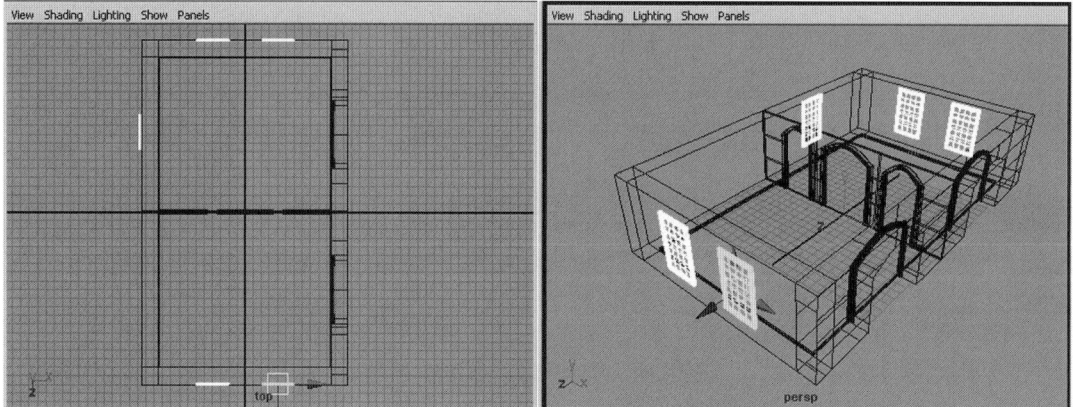

FIGURE 4.27 (a–b)   Placed windows. Notice in b that we have changed the view to Wireframe to see the positions of the windows.

Step 23: Add columns (polygonal cubes) with ornate tops (lofted surfaces). Create a polygonal cube and resize it so that it is positioned between the arches of the center wall. Figure 4.28 (a–b) shows the curves and how they are organized atop the cube to create the trim. Be sure to get close so that these curves are placed appropriately. Loft the trim on top then get rid of the curves. Then, group the polygonal cube and both lofted surfaces into a new group called Column. Duplicate the column and place it between the other arch and between the two side arches and the wall. Finally, select all the columns and group them into a new group called Column_Group (Figure 4.29).

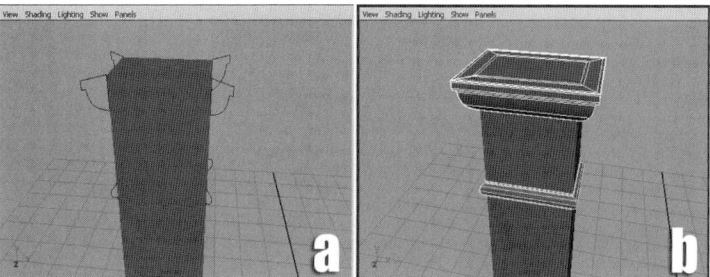

FIGURE 4.28 (a–b)   Creating the tops of columns.

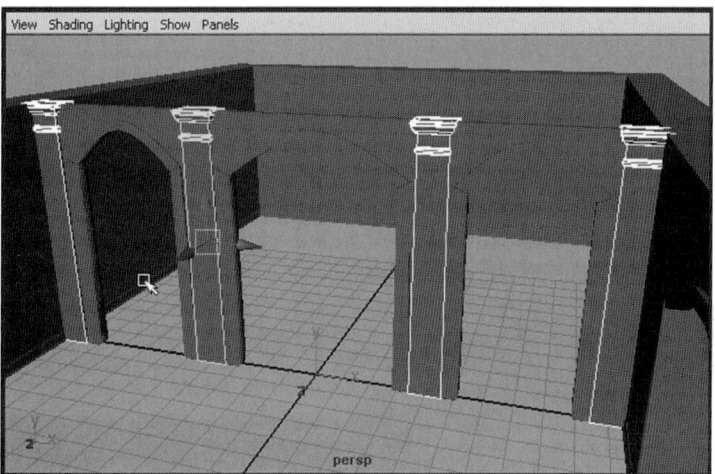

FIGURE 4.29   Final placed duplicated columns.

Step 24: Make the layer Ceiling_Floor active and make adjustments to accommodate it. Click the Visibility column in the Layer Editor and dolly into the room so that you can see how the columns look with the room in place. It probably looks like Figure 4.30 with the beams smacking right into the middle of the columns. This will never do.

In the Outliner, expand the group Column_Group and expand each column so you can see the objects in each group. **Ctrl**-LMB-click each lofted surface in all the columns (Figure 4.31a). This selects all the trim for the columns without selecting the center part of the column. Now, with the Move tool, move these down their Y axes (green manipulator

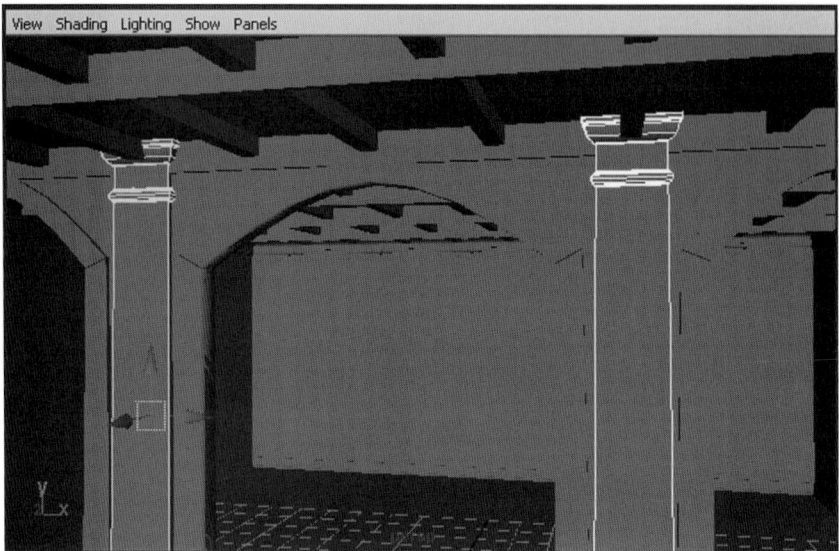

FIGURE 4.30   Because we built the columns without the ceiling visible, we can see that there are problems with how the beams intersect the tops of the columns.

handle) so that the trim lines up with the bottom of the beam sitting at WallMiddle_Group (Figure 4.31b). When you are satisfied with the new placement, make sure you collapse all the groups in the Outliner to keep that space clean.

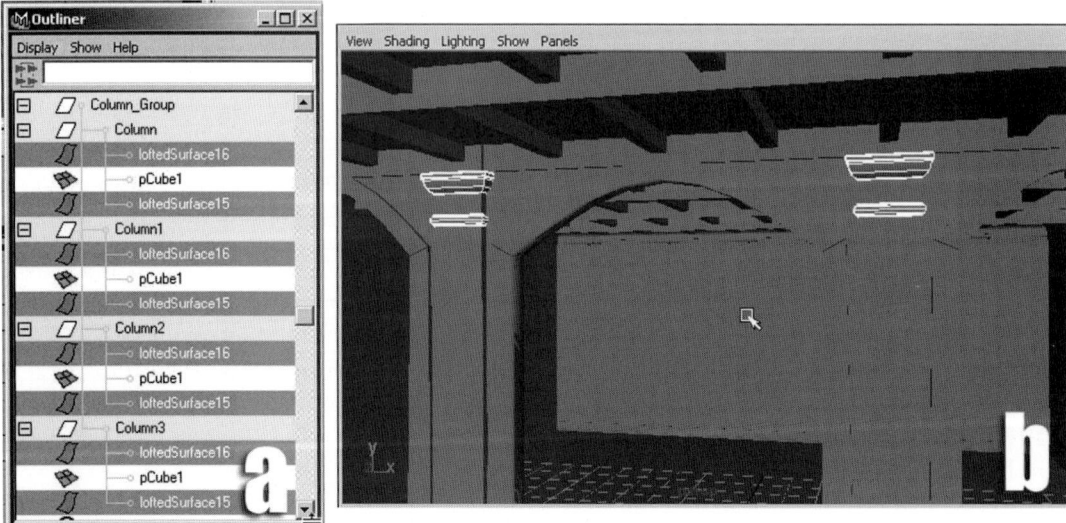

FIGURE 4.31 (a–b)   Fixing the tops of the columns to be appropriate to the ceiling.

Step 25: Save and take a break before moving onto the next step.
The next step includes a lot of things that we will not cover step by step as
it is mostly information that we have covered already. However, it is all
quite a bit of work and could be frustrating if you need to go back and review some steps.

Step 26: Create and place all the tables in the room. The furniture
in the room is not particularly complex. However, there is a lot, so take
some time to create the tables and objects on them using primitives or
make surfaces to create the forms you need. This will undoubtedly include resizing the lamp you made earlier. Remember to hide different
parts of your room if they are in your way as you work. You can do this
through the Layer Editor or through **Ctrl-H**.

Do not worry about too many "props" right now—just create the
major pieces. The tables should look something like Figure 4.32.

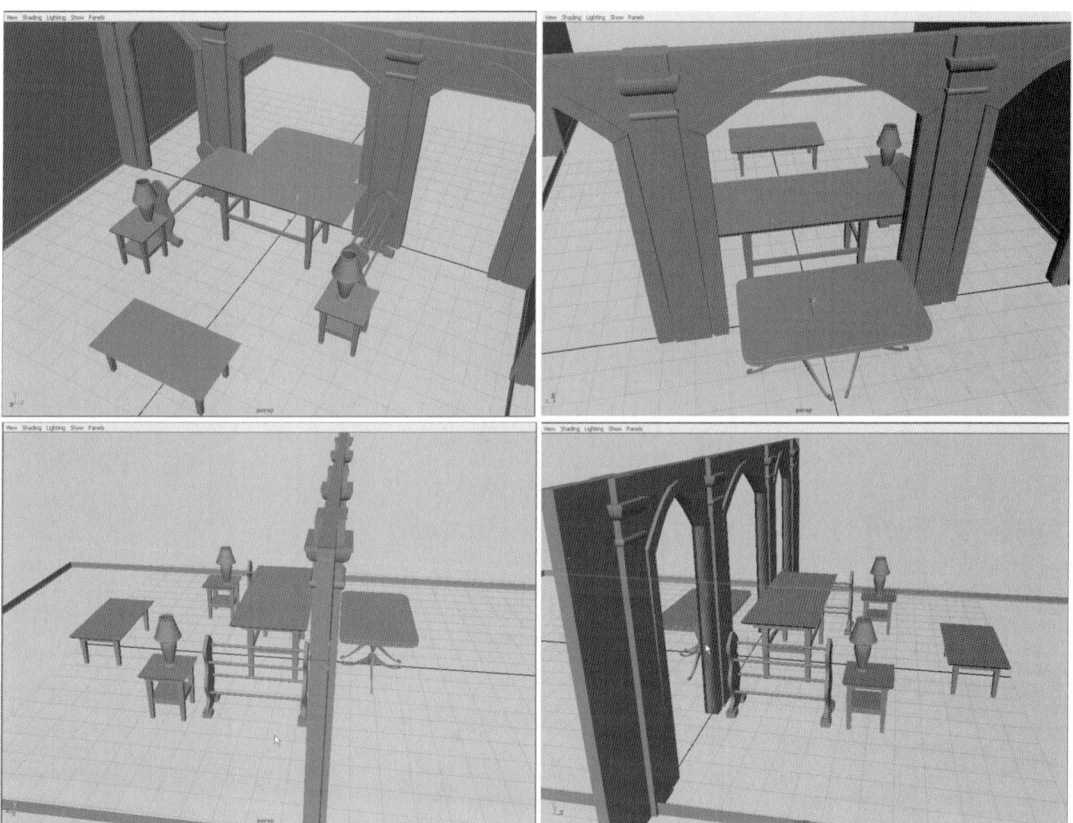

FIGURE 4.32   The room with the tables and odds and ends created and placed.

Make sure you place all these tables in the Furniture layer. Be sure to also group as you go within the Outliner in ways that will make sense to you.

CONCLUSION

We are getting ever so close. By now, you should feel comfortable with moving objects around, creating and modifying curves, and creating and modifying surfaces. We have looked at creating loft, extrude, revolve, and planar surfaces. These are not all, and we have not really explored how to edit those surfaces. Not to worry—much more on that later.

Coming up in the next chapter, we are going to be wrapping up a lot of loose modeling ends. We will look at how to edit on a component level, including altering extant surfaces. We will look at other ways to take control of the Duplicate tool, and finally, we will look at the powerful tool of Boolean operations to cut out the holes for our windows.

At the end of the next chapter, our room will be completely modeled. After that, we will look at some methods of subdivision modeling and do a bit of organic work. Next, we get to move on to making our room not quite so—well, gray. We get to work on creating textures, colors, and lights.

COMPONENT-LEVEL
EDITING AND BOOLEANS

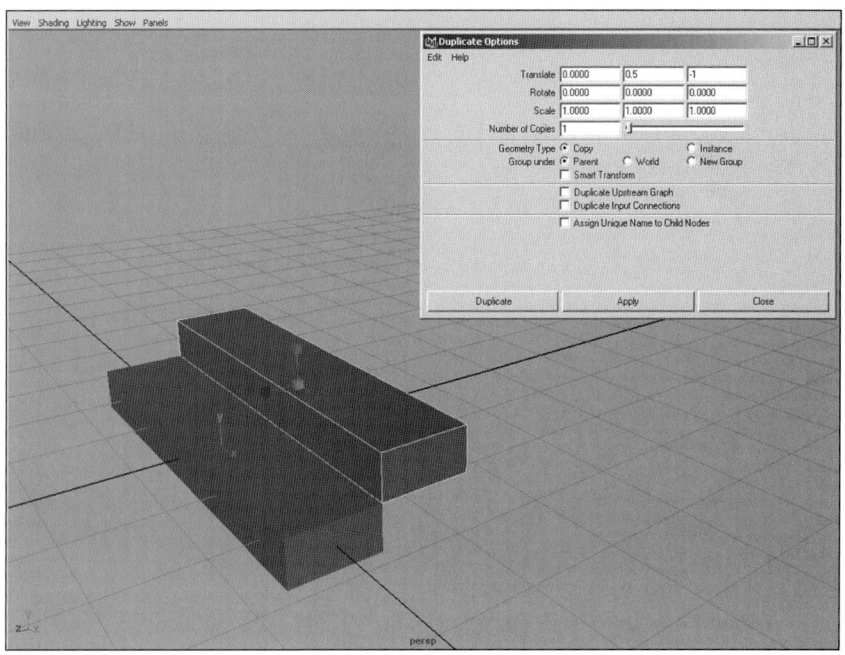

We can start to see the room really coming together now. It is starting to feel like we might even know a bit of what we are doing. In this chapter, we will solidify that feeling by getting down into the minutiae of the editing process. Up to now, we have been focusing generally on creating and editing objects—entire objects. In this chapter, we will look at taking these objects and making the tweaks that turn basic shapes into dynamic and sophisticated forms.

We will discuss how to subtract shapes from each other. We will demonstrate how to add shapes. We will discover ways to break up surfaces that we have already constructed. Finally, we will learn how to "glue" together surfaces.

Although this is by no means an exhaustive treatment of Maya modeling techniques, at the end of this chapter, you will have had a good look at a wide variety of the core tools. In Chapter 6, we will look at the specialty subdivision surface editing and then move on to texturing.

ON THE CD

Again, be sure to note that the results from Tutorial 5.2 can be found and referenced on the included CD-ROM. There is a lot to learn from a finished file, so feel free to pull the file out and dig into it.

POWER OF THE DUPLICATION TOOL

Up to now, we have been looking at duplication as just a shortcut for the ol' Copy and Paste routine. It turns out that there is quite a bit more to this tool. To understand this tool, consider the following tutorial.

| TUTORIAL 5.1 | **EXPLORING THE DUPLICATE TOOL** |

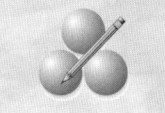

Step 1: Create a new scene. Select File > New Scene. Do not worry about where this file is in terms of projects—you won't save it.

Step 2: Create and resize a polygon cube primitive so that it is 5 units in X, .5 units in Y, and 1 unit in Z. Selecting Modeling | Create > Polygon Primitives Cube will create the cube. Then, enter 5, 0.5, and 1 on the Scale X, Scale Y, and Scale Z input fields. The cube should look something like Figure 5.1.

Step 3: Duplicate a translated cube. Open the Duplicate Options window by selecting the Edit > Duplicate (Options) pull-down menu. Assuming that all settings are set at the default, all the values in the Translate, Rotate, and Scale input fields should read 0. Because of this, when we

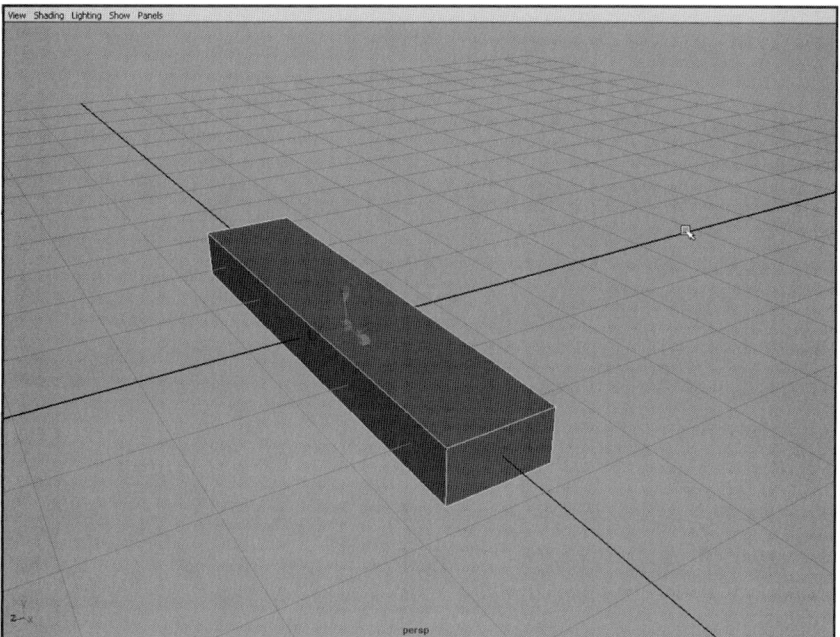

FIGURE 5.1   Cube to be duplicated.

have been duplicating objects, the new object is resting at exactly the same position as the original. However, we can have Maya move, rotate, or scale each duplicate.

For instance, we know that this cube is one unit deep in the Z direction. Enter 1 in the Z column of the Translate row (Z is the third column over). Click the Apply button. Notice that your Duplicate Options window stays around. Second, notice that the new pCube2 (as it appears in the Outliner) is created and translated one unit in the positive Z direction from the original (Figure 5.2).

LMB-click anywhere in the Workspace and hit **Ctrl-Z** to undo the duplicate.

Step 4: Create a set of stairs. If we want to create some basic stairs from this block, we just need each duplicate to be translated 1 unit in the Z direction, and up 0.5 units in the Y direction. To make sure we can see things a bit better, enter 0.5 in the Y column and –1 in the Z column so that the new duplicate is moved up 0.5 units, but back 1 unit. Hit the Apply button (Figure 5.3).

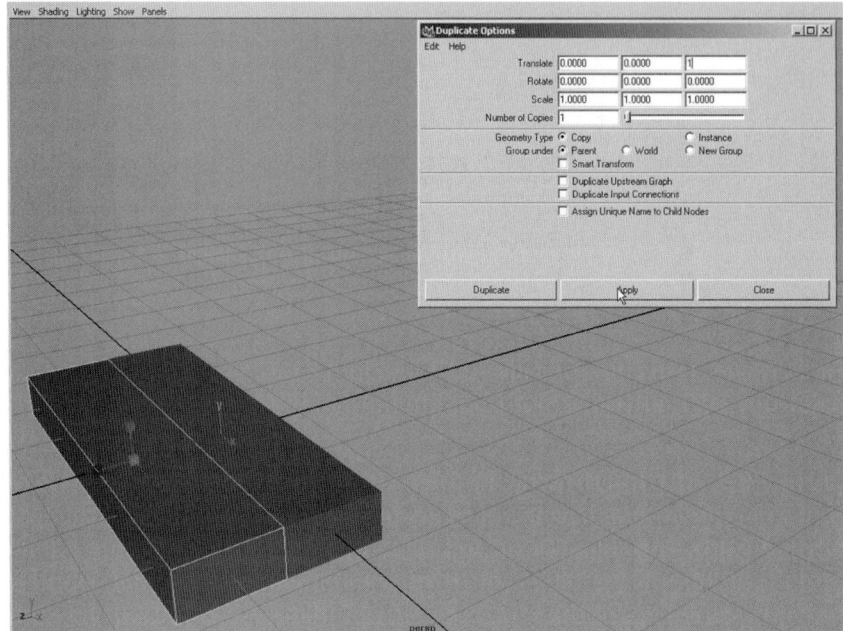

FIGURE 5.2 Duplicated cube translated one unit in the positive Z direction.

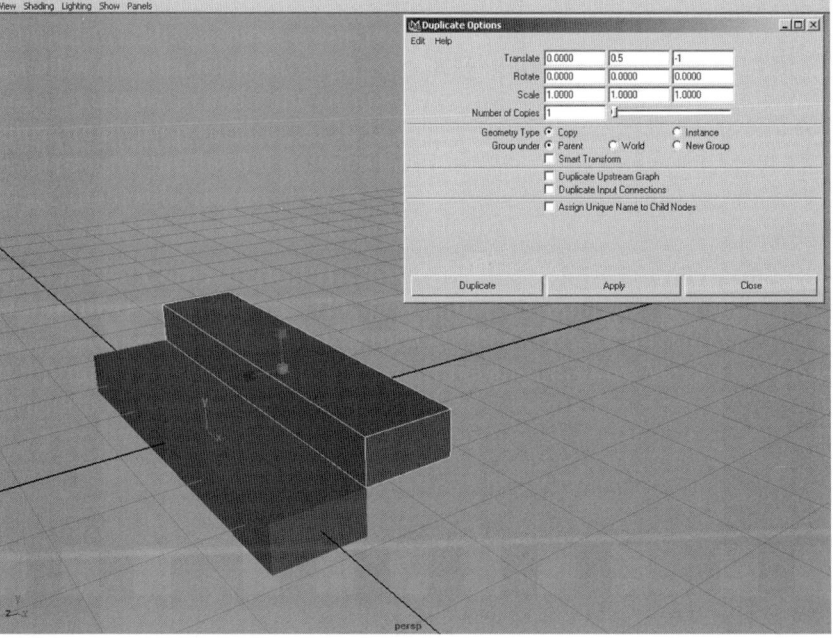

FIGURE 5.3 Duplicated step translated back and up.

Click in the Workspace and undo the duplication.

This is a good start, but it would require multiple duplications to create a lot of steps. One of the nice things about the Duplicate Option window is the Number of Copies slider. Change this to 10. So, now you are telling Maya, "Create 10 duplicates and move each successive duplicated shape up 0.5 units and back 1 unit." Hit the Apply button. The result should look like Figure 5.4.

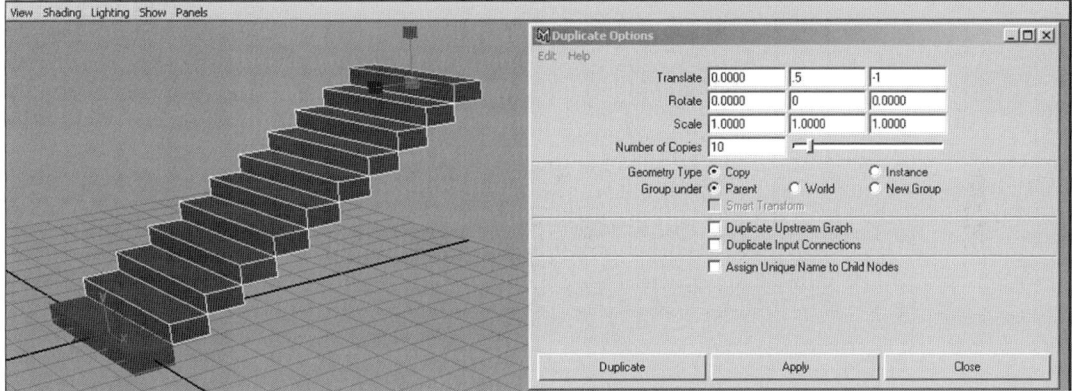

FIGURE 5.4   Duplicating multiple copies.

Undo this duplication.

Step 5: Create a spiral staircase. This time, we do not only want to duplicate and move (translate) many duplicates, but we also want each of the duplicates to be slightly rotated. For this one, let's put a little bit more space between duplicates; change the Translate Y column to 1 and the Z column to –1.5. In the Rotate row, change the Y column to 15, meaning that each duplicate will be rotated 15 degrees on the Y axis from the duplicate before. Lastly, change the number of copies to 50 and hit the Apply button (Figure 5.5).

Step 6: Create spiral stalk. So, it always makes for a nifty demo to show an insta-spiral staircase, but you really do not make a spiral staircase all that often. In this step, we will look at a quick alternate use.

Start by creating a primitive NURBS circle (Modeling | Create > NURBS Primitives > Circle). Select it and open the Duplicate Options window. We want to create a spiral of these circle curves. Enter 2 in Y Translate and –5 in Z Translate. Enter 30 in the Y Rotate and .95 in the

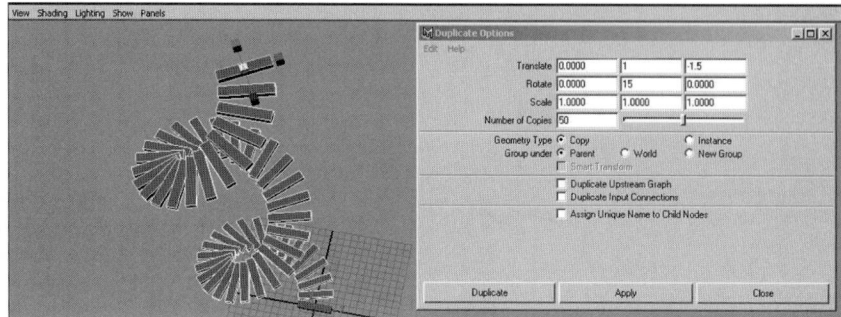

FIGURE 5.5   Spiral staircase created by manipulating the Duplicate Options window.

X and Z Scale. Change the Number of Copies to 50. This will create 50 copies of this circle; each will be .95 the size of the last and each will be moved up 2 units, back 5 units, and rotated 30 degrees. Hit the Duplicate button (Figure 5.6).

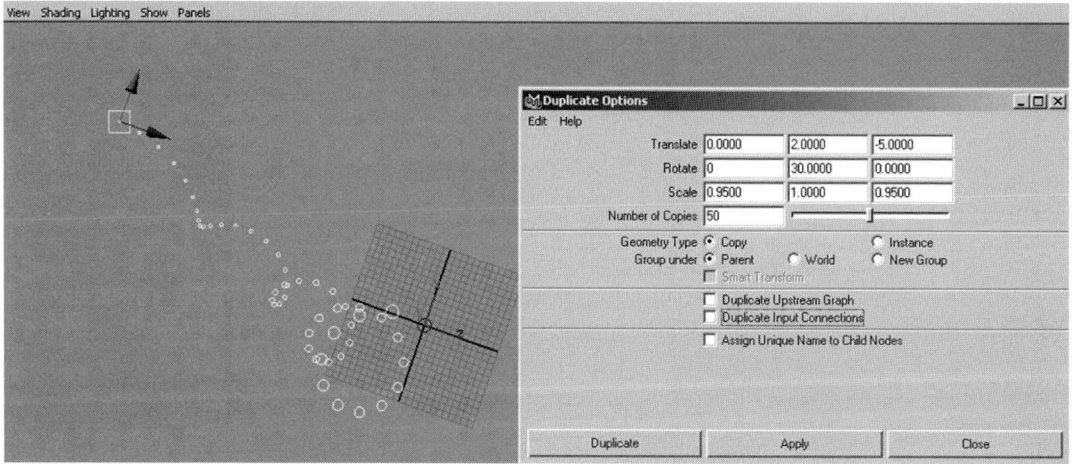

FIGURE 5.6   Duplicated curves. Each curve is also scaled to be slightly smaller than the last.

Now, in the Outliner, select nurbsCircle1 and **Shift**-select nurbsCircle51. This will select all the circle curves in the scene. Loft them together, and the result will be something like Figure 5.7—a spiraling surface that becomes smaller as it rises.

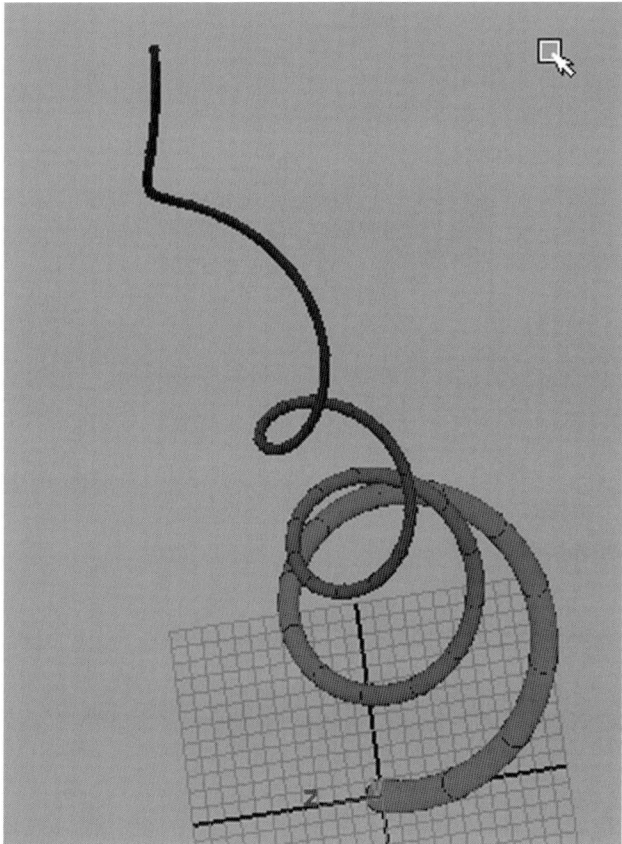

FIGURE 5.7   Lofted duplicated circles.

The Duplicate tool can be used for an incredible variety of things. In fact, in future tutorials, we will use it to help us quickly create the backs of furniture.

TUTORIAL 5.2   FINISHING THE ROOM

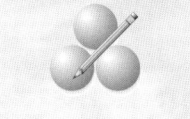

In this tutorial, we will finish up this room by creating the missing furniture pieces and cutting holes in the walls for windows. When we are done, we will be ready to add texture.

Step 1: Open the project. Make sure you have the room file open from wherever you have saved it. Assuming you have not changed projects, the project setting should be intact. If not, make sure you set the project so Maya knows where to save things as you work.

Step 2: Hide all layers. Turn off all the Vs in the Layer Editor. This should leave you with the middle wall (because it has not been assigned to any layer) and perhaps a few extraneous things like floorboards.

As we build the furniture, it can become rather dicey when there are just too many other things in the scene.

Step 3: Create the frame for the couch from anything you would like (primitive polygon cubes work well). The exact size is not really important; just eyeball what you think works well proportionally. The piece in Figure 5.8 is about two feet deep and six feet long. From the floor to the top of the backrest is about three feet. When this example was constructed, the grid was relied upon heavily to give a good estimate of what size the piece would become. One thing to notice is that the two end pieces of the back are made as lofted surfaces to give them a bit of a curve. This was done by creating curves (that were 0.25 feet, or 3 inches, wide in the X direction) on the ground plane, one at the level of the seat, and a third above and behind the seat.

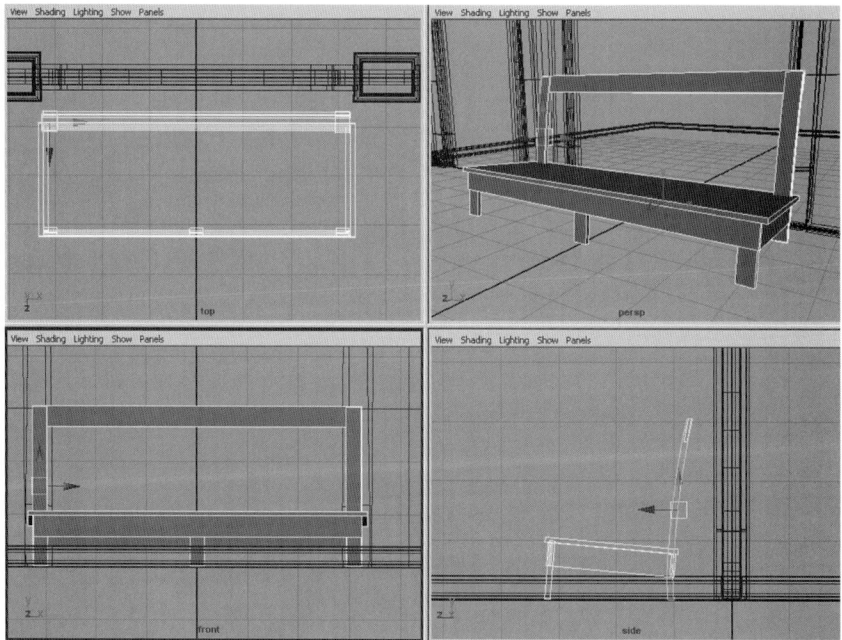

FIGURE 5.8 Framework of the couch.

Step 4: Organize your Workspace to begin duplication. To create the back slats of the couch, we will begin by using one of the back frame ends. As discussed in the last step, this was created with a lofted surface. To get a better visual handle, we will alter the Workspace a bit.

In Figure 5.9, you can see the loftedSurface fairly easily. To view your scene like this in the Workspace window, first hit **4** to display the window as wireframe and then select the Shading > Smooth Shade Selected Items pull-down menu in the Workspace panel.

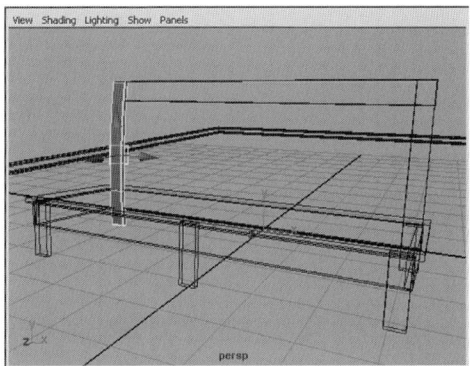

FIGURE 5.9   Displaying the scene as a wireframe with Smooth Shade Selected Items.

Step 5: Duplicate one of the back ends to create one of the middle slats. Select one of the back frame ends. Choose Edit > Duplicate (Options). To make sure you are starting with a clean slate and not the crazy stuff we did in earlier tutorials, reset the settings.

This sample slat is about 3 inches thick or 0.25 feet. If you do not know how thick your slat is, use the measurement tool to find out (Modeling | Create > Measure Tool > Distance Tool). The thickness of the slat is important so we know how far to distance each duplicate.

If your slat is indeed 0.25 feet thick, 6 inches will provide a nice spacing between (3 inches). So, in the Translate row in the X column, change the value to 0.5. Hit the Apply button (Figure 5.10) to leave the Duplicate Options window open, because we will need to keep using it.

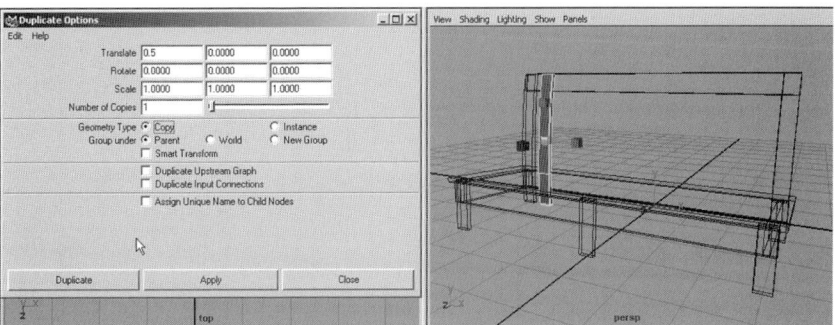

FIGURE 5.10   Duplicated frame to be used as a slat.

Step 6: Duplicate the slat to create all the middle slats. As the images show, and as discussed earlier, the couch is about 6 feet long. So, if we have 3-inch slats with 3 inches between each, 10 copies of this original slat will do the trick. Change the Number of Copies input field to 10.

Finally, do one other thing. Change the Geometry Type to Instance. By default, this is set as Copy, meaning that when you duplicate, it creates an unrelated copy of the geometry. An instance is an entirely separate beast.

When Maya creates 10 instances, what it is actually doing is showing you the original object 10 times. There are not really 10 copies of the slat but rather Maya is showing the same slat 10 times just in different places. The real benefit of this is if you change anything about the original slat, all the instances are instantly updated. Hit the Duplicate button (Figure 5.11).

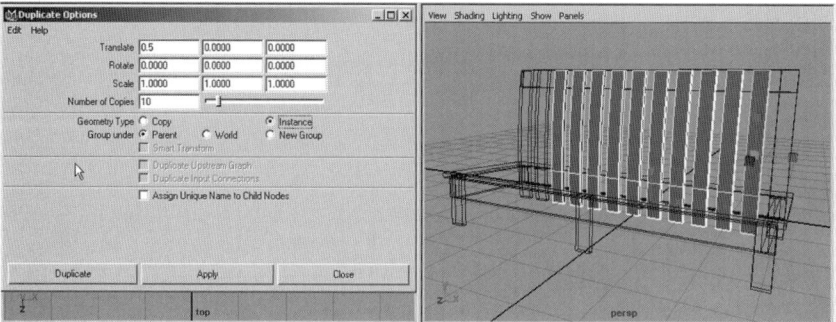

FIGURE 5.11   The settings and results of creating duplicated slats.

Step 7: Alter the original back slat and watch the instance magic unfold. Right now, all the back slats go clear to the floor. Although this is an interesting design choice, it is not the choice for this project. What we want to do is quickly make them all so that they end at the base of the couch.

Select the original back slat (not the original frame but the slat) (Figure 5.12a). We will edit this object at a component level by moving the control vertices (CVs) that make up this surface. To make the CVs visible and selectable, RMB-click and hold the slat (Figure 5.12b). Then, select Control Vertex from the Marking menu. You will then be able to see the purple CVs of the surface (Figure 5.12c).

Marquee around the bottom four sets of CVs (5.13a). Do this in any view that makes these CVs easy to see (Figure 5.13a shows the front view). As soon as you do this, the selected CVs will change from purple to yellow (Figure 5.13b). But not only do they change to yellow on the original back slat, but all the bottom four CVs are also selected on all the instances as well. Now, with the Move tool, move these selected CVs up in

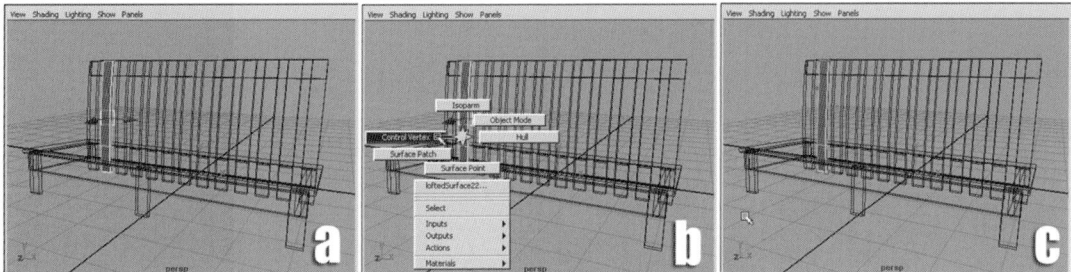

FIGURE 5.12 (a–c)   Getting to the component level of the original back slat.

the Y direction (green manipulator handle) so that the bottom of the slat is within the seat slat (Figure 5.13c). Make sure you take a look at views like the Side view as you do this to get a good idea of where you are actually placing these.

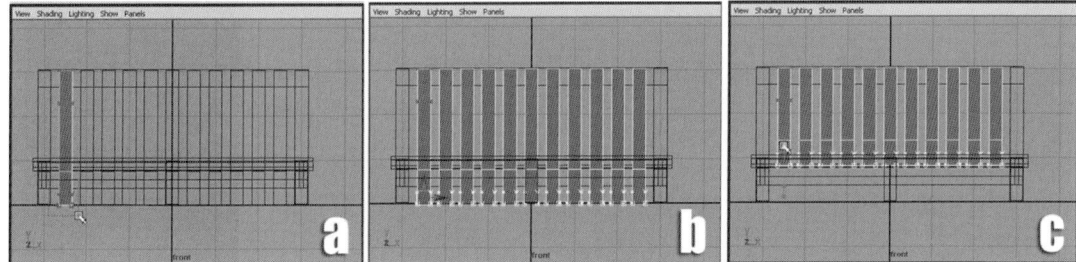

FIGURE 5.13 (a–c)   Selecting and moving the CVs of one object with dynamically updated instances.

When all is said and done, your couch should appear something like Figure 5.14.

When you are happy with the shape, be sure to group all the objects that were used to make the couch into one group and call it Couch.

Step 8: Follow a similar process to create two loveseats and two chairs of similar styles. Again, the exact sizes are unimportant here but do repeat the same sorts of techniques so that your new loveseats and chairs are similar in style (Figure 5.15). Make sure you group and label all the furniture pieces appropriately so that they are easy to work with and find.

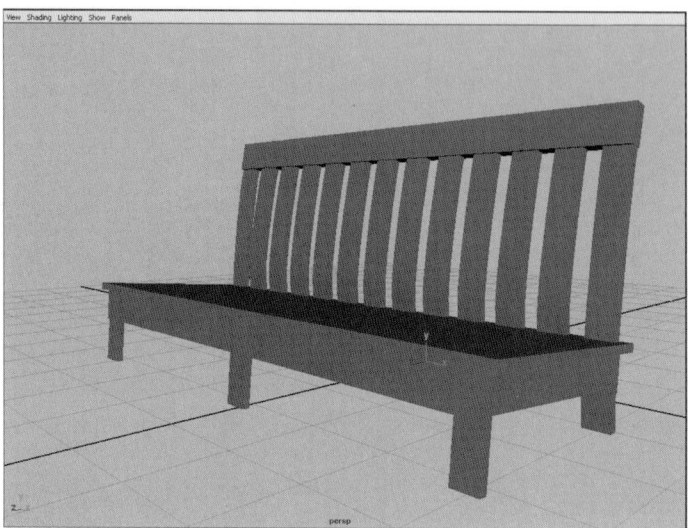

FIGURE 5.14 Completed couch woodwork.

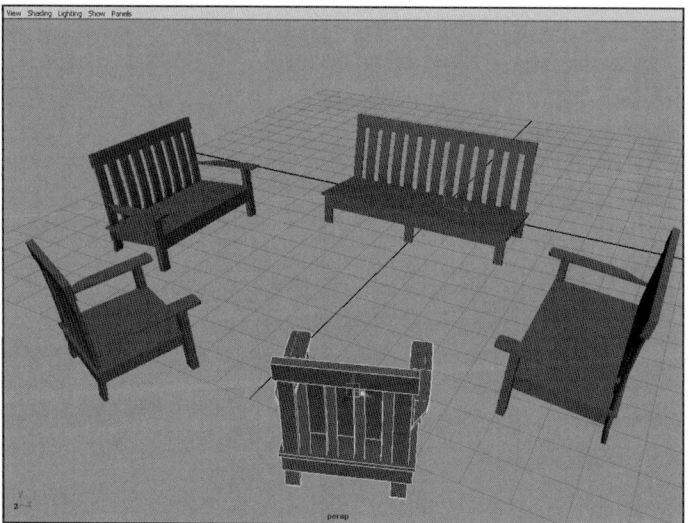

FIGURE 5.15 Completed furniture woodwork.

Notice that the loveseats and chairs have arms. These arms were created using simple lofts and planar surfaces. To give the correct visual weight, the front legs were beefed up a bit (Figure 5.16a–b).

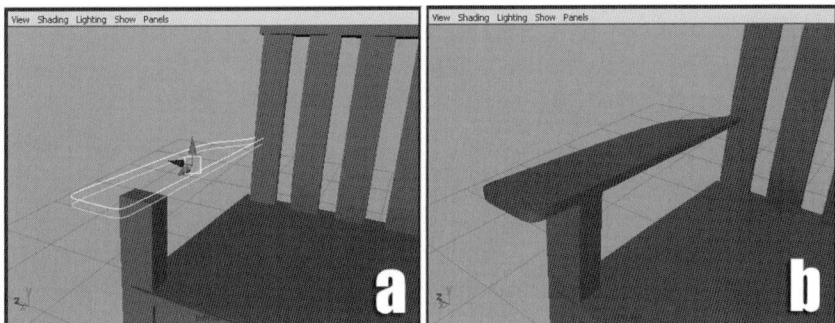

FIGURE 5.16 (a–b)   Creating arms with custom curves lofted and then created with a planar surface.

Here's a trick to modeling symmetrical objects (like the arms): first, model one arm. Duplicate the arm and then in the Channel Box, enter –1 in the Scale input field in the direction you want Maya to create the mirrored duplicate. Even quicker is to change the Scale row in the Duplicate Options window to –1 in the appropriate column.

Step 9: Take a minute to organize. Take all the chairs, loveseats, and the sofa and in the Outliner, MMB-click and drag them into the Furniture_Group. Because Furniture_Group is part of the layer Furniture (which is not visible), when new objects become part of Furniture_Group, they will immediately become invisible as well.

Component-Level Editing

Step 10: Create curves for cushions. A common complaint about Maya is how it is impossible to create a cube with filleted edges. Filleted edges are just rounded off corners.

For the cushions in this room, filleted cubes would indeed be of value. So, we will look at how to create such a shape and how to really get down and dirty on a component level to make the shape what we need.

Begin by hiding any extraneous objects that are visible in the scene. This frees up the middle of the Workspace where we can create the curves we need. Figure 5.17 shows a CV curve created with the CV Curve tool with one CV at each point shown. Snapping to grid helps keep lines straight.

Make sure the first and last CVs are placed on the Y axis, because this is the axis around which we will have this curve revolve. So be sure you snap to grid when you place these two CVs.

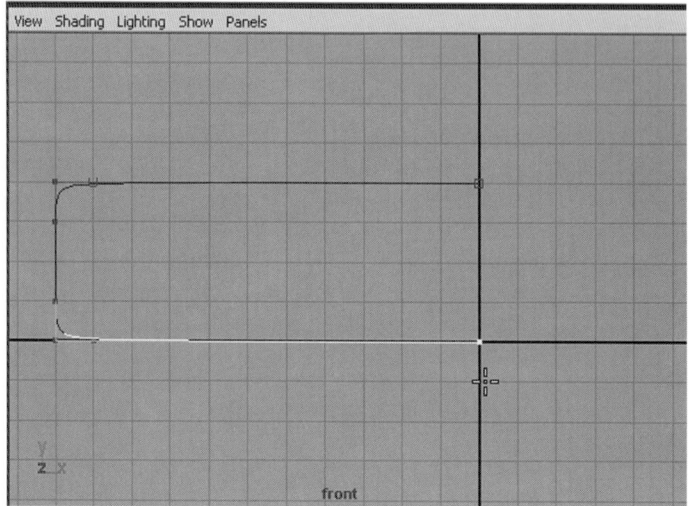

FIGURE 5.17   Creating curve for cushions.

Step 11: Revolve the curve. With just a curve, we have no surface. To create a surface from our curve, select Modeling | Surfaces > Revolve (Options). The only option we really need to change is the Segment input field. We want to have enough segments to be able to construct "corners" from the cylindrical shape that is going to be created. We want three rows of CVs for each corner for a total of 12, plus a row of CVs for each edge. So, we need 16, total. Enter 16 in the Segments input field and hit the Revolve button. (Figure 5.18).

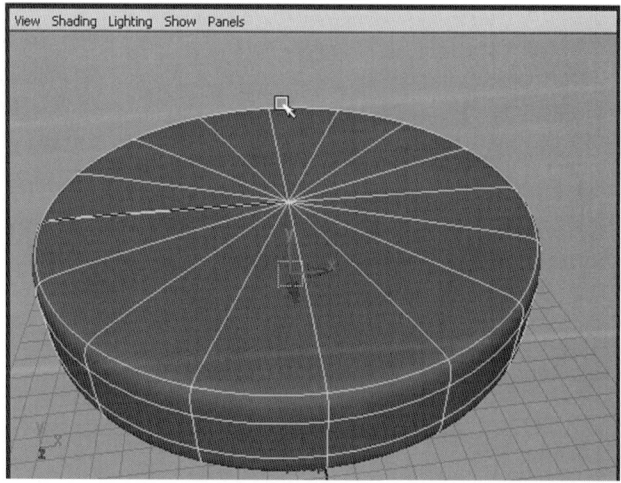

FIGURE 5.18   Revolved curve.

Seems odd and far from a square cushion but do not lose hope.

Step 12: Adjust the Move tool to allow for CVs to maintain their space. Double-click the Move tool in the Toolbox. This will open the settings for the Move tool at the right side of your interface. In the Move Snap Settings area, make sure you check Retain Component Spacing. We are going to snap collections of components to the grid in a second, and with this turned off, when we snap the group to the grid, each individual component would snap together to the same spot. This would destroy the soft edges we are working toward. With this turned on, we will be able to snap the manipulator of a collection of components to the grid, but each component still maintains its relative distance from the others.

Step 13: Rough out the cushion by altering "corner" collections of CVs. In the Top view, we need to alter the component CVs of this surface. To make these visible and selectable, RMB-click and hold on the surface until the Marking menu comes up that allows you to select Control Vertex (Figure 5.19a). When you have done so, you will see all the purple CVs for this surface.

Notice that at each pole (as in north, south, east, and west), the CVs come to rest on a grid intersection, because we snapped the curve as we were building it. What we want to do is take the collection of CVs for all of the corners (which do not exist yet) and snap them up to the same level or corner as the corner of a cube shape would exist.

For instance, Figure 5.19b shows the selection of the desired CVs. Figure 5.19c shows using the Move tool (while snapping to grid: **x**) to move this collection of CVs to the place where the two poles would meet.

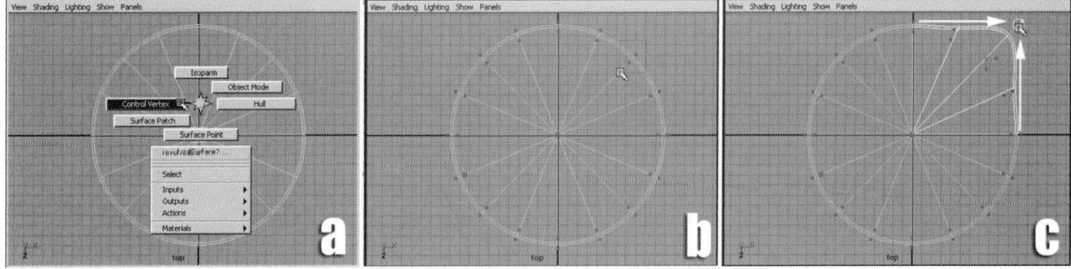

FIGURE 5.19 (a–c)   Roughing out the rounded square shape.

Step 14: Create all the corners. Repeat this process to create all four rough corners (Figure 5.20).

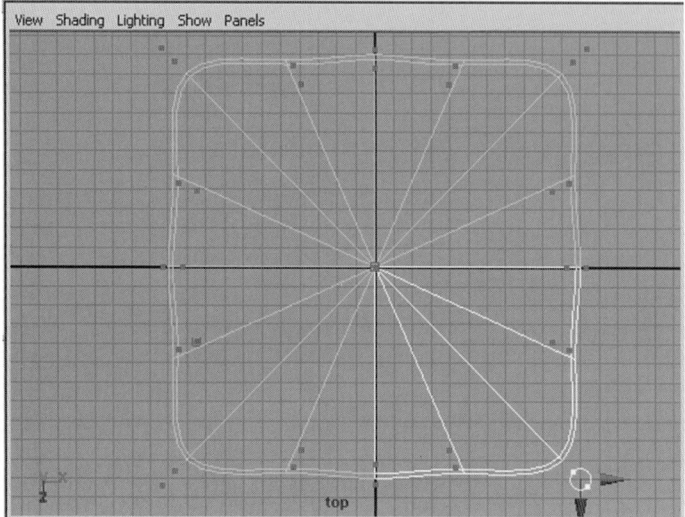

FIGURE 5.20   Created rough corners.

Step 15: Tighten the corners by moving additional collections of CVs closer to the new corners. Do this by again grabbing collections of CVs and snapping them a couple of units over or a couple of units down from the collection of CVs that make a corner. Figure 5.21a shows the breakdown of selecting the next set of CVs down and moving them into place. By Figure 5.21b, you will have all the CVs in position to give nice, soft corners to the shape.

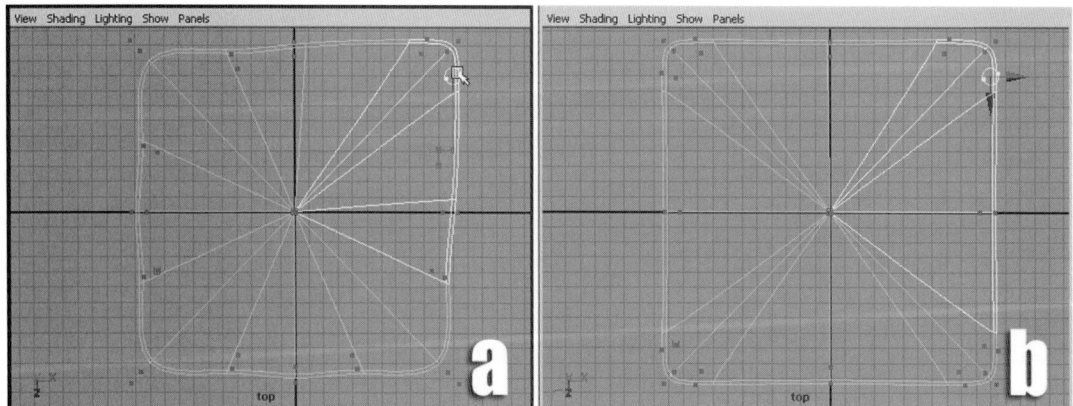

FIGURE 5.21 (a–b)   Creating rounded corners by taking control of CVs.

So, the closer the collections of CVs on the corners, the tighter the corner. Move them farther apart and the corner will be softer.

Step 16: Beat up the cushion a bit. First, take a second and turn off the Retain Component Spacing in the Move tool settings. Then, grab CVs and move them around—bend things up and make things less perfect. Remember that because we have kept our segments reasonably low, some ugly faceting will result if you pull things too far, but you can give things a little more interesting look by manipulating CVs (Figure 5.22).

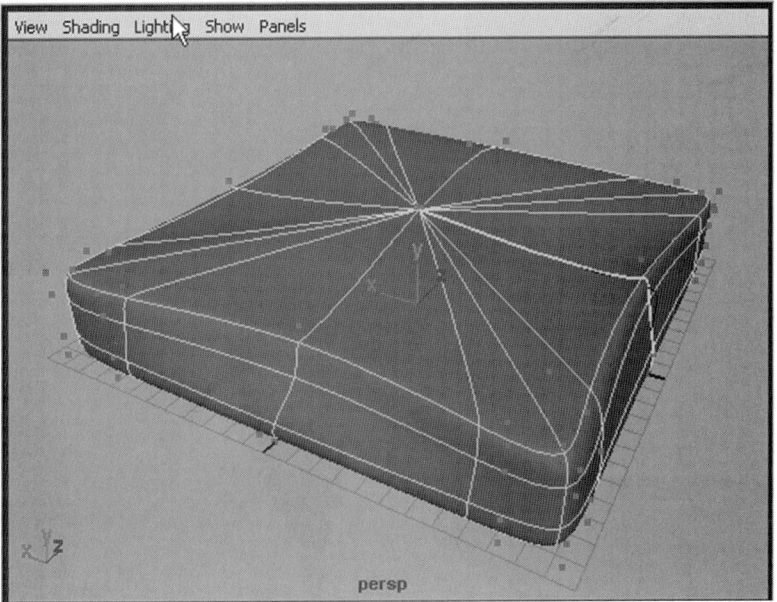

FIGURE 5.22   The "beat up" cushion.

Step 17: Show the furniture and place these new cushions into place. Scale, move, and rotate the cushions into place. If you need to reposition furniture, do so; make it all look something like Figure 5.23. Make sure you group your cushions with the piece of furniture upon which they sit. Remember you can do this by MMB-dragging the cushions onto the group that is the piece of furniture; this makes the cushions children of that group.

Step 18: Take a look at everything in the scene. Make all the layers active to get an idea of where you are (Figure 5.24).

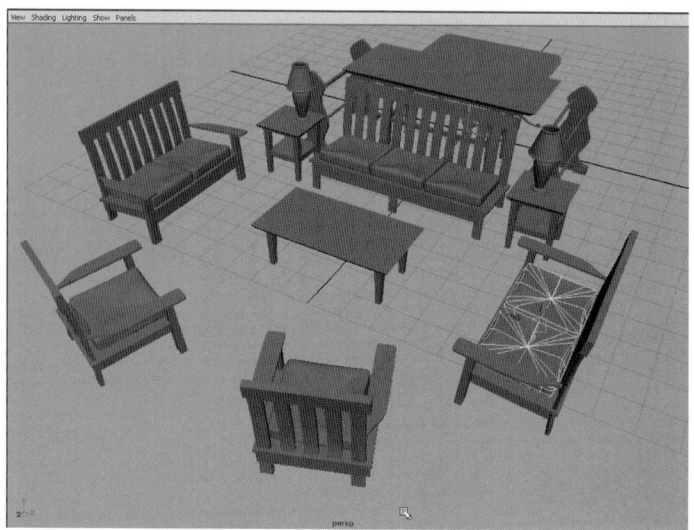

FIGURE 5.23   Placed cushions.

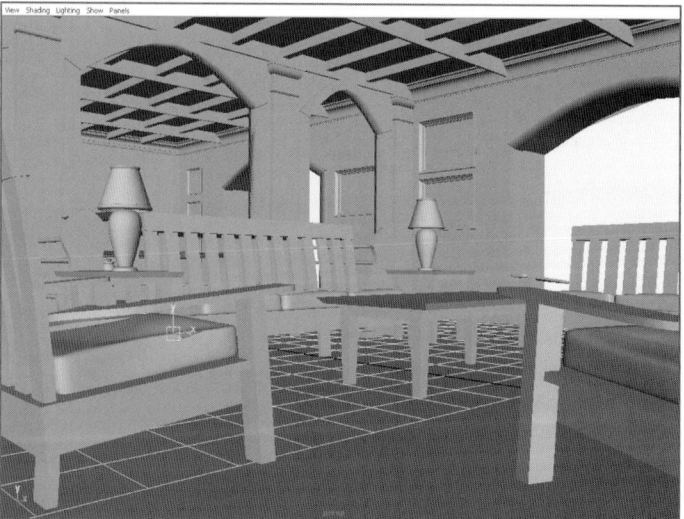

FIGURE 5.24   Scene thus far.

Working with Isoparms

Step 19: Rotate around until you can see the arches that lead you out of the room. Notice that we have a problem here (Figure 5.25). The floorboard that we brilliantly created goes right across the opening. Because this would lead to many tripped visitors, and a house would never really be built this way, we need to clean this up.

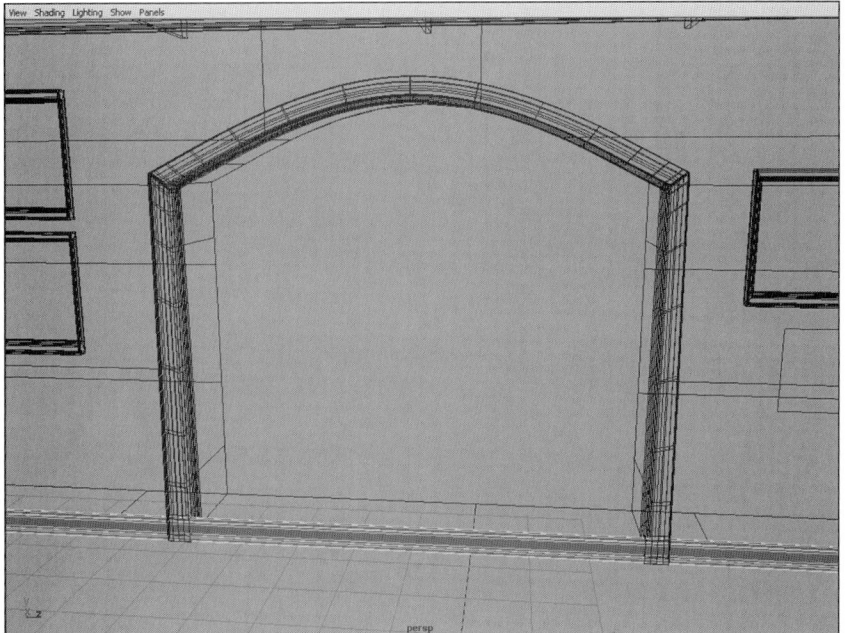

FIGURE 5.25   Problem spot of floorboard across door opening.

Step 20: Add isoparms in places to cut. Display your scene as Wireframe with Smooth Shade Selected Items (both within the Shading pulldown menu of the Workspace panel). Select the floorboard. If you look at the selection, you will see long green lines. These are visual clues as to the organization of the objects. These green lines are called isoparms.

Isoparms themselves are not directly editable. You cannot take an isoparm and move, scale, or rotate it. As such, at first glance, they do not have much use in controlling a surface. However, isoparms are correlated to a lot of things, such as surface patches, CVs (which we have seen are very useful in editing a surface), and hulls, to name a few. However, besides being indicators of where other components are, we can use isoparms to help define where things are going to happen.

In this case, notice that there are lots of isoparms running horizontally but very few running vertically. We basically have isoparms in the corners of the room where the surface makes a turn. We need to get rid of the part of the surface that is sitting across the arch. To do this, we will create isoparms on both sides of the arch to mark where we are going to get rid of surface topology.

First, we need to be able to see and manipulate isoparms. So, RMB-click and hold on the Floorboard object and select Isoparm from the resulting Marking menu. All the green isoparms will now turn blue indicating that you can select them.

Dolly into the corner and, for fun, click on one of the blue lines. When you first begin to click, the isoparm that Maya thinks you are trying to select will turn red. When you release the mouse, it will highlight yellow to indicate that you have selected it. Notice that if you click an existing isoparm and drag, you will get a red line indicating a potential location of an isoparm (Figure 5.26). When you release the mouse after such an action, you get a yellow dotted line. This indicates that an isoparm can be potentially placed here.

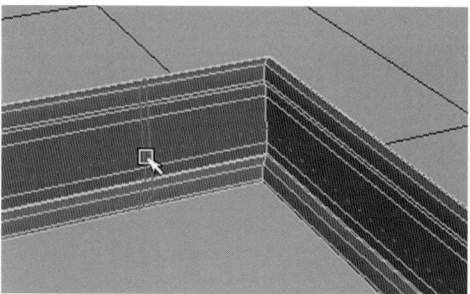

FIGURE 5.26 Clicking and dragging an extant isoparm will show potential placements of new isoparms.

For now, click on the vertical isoparm in the corner and drag the new potential isoparm so that it sits in the middle of the trim around the archway. When you release your mouse, the tell-tale yellow dotted line will appear (Figure 5.27).

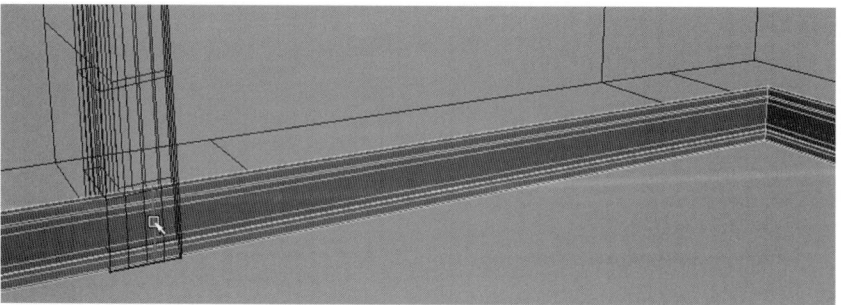

FIGURE 5.27 Mapping out the location where the new isoparm is to be placed.

To add an isoparm here, select Modeling | Edit Nurbs > Insert Isoparms (Options). Notice that within this options window, you can choose to do things like add multiple isoparms by changing the Multiplicity setting. If you have two isoparms selected, you can add isoparms between the selected isoparms. However, in our case, we want to have our Insert Location set to At Selection, because we have just pointed out to Maya exactly where we want an isoparm to be placed. Click the Insert button (Figure 5.28).

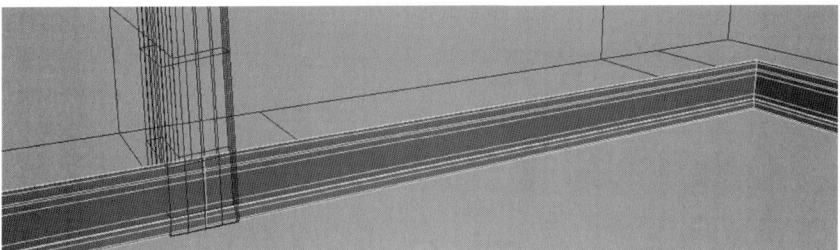

FIGURE 5.28   Newly created isoparm shows up in green at the location we defined earlier.

Repeat this process and place an additional isoparm on the other side of the arch.

Step 21: Detach the surface. Because we have two isoparms newly defined on the surface, we can have Maya think of the space between the isoparms as its own unique surface. This means we can also detach it from the parent surface (the floorboard) and thus delete it.

To do this, select and then **Shift**-select the isoparms on both sides of the arch (Figure 5.29a). Select Modeling | Edit Nurbs > Detach Surfaces. The results (Figure 5.29b) do not look incredibly different than before, but notice the Outliner. There will now be not only the floorboard, but also two new surfaces called FloorboarddetachedSurface.

Now, select the newly created surface in the middle of the arch and delete it (Figure 5.29c).

Step 22: Repeat the detach surface process for the other arch. Mark the isoparms, add the isoparms, and detach the surface so you have two archways that are easy to walk through (Figure 5.30).

Remember that any NURBS surface has isoparms. You can change the shape of these isoparms by altering the CVs or the hull. With any surface, you can use isoparms to detach sections of the surface. You can work these detached sections or delete them altogether. There is a multitude of options to working further with NURBS surfaces that would occupy its

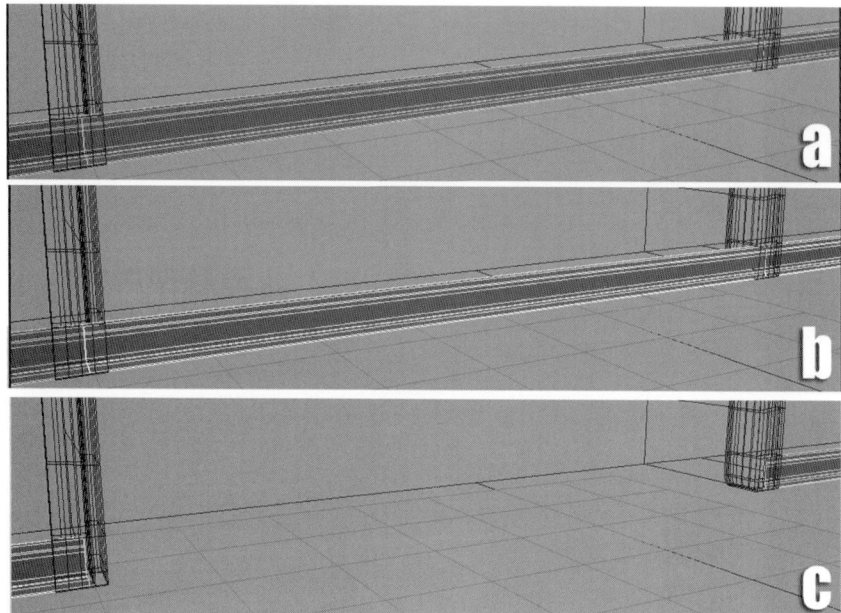

FIGURE 5.29   (a–c) Removing sections of a surface by detaching them and deleting.

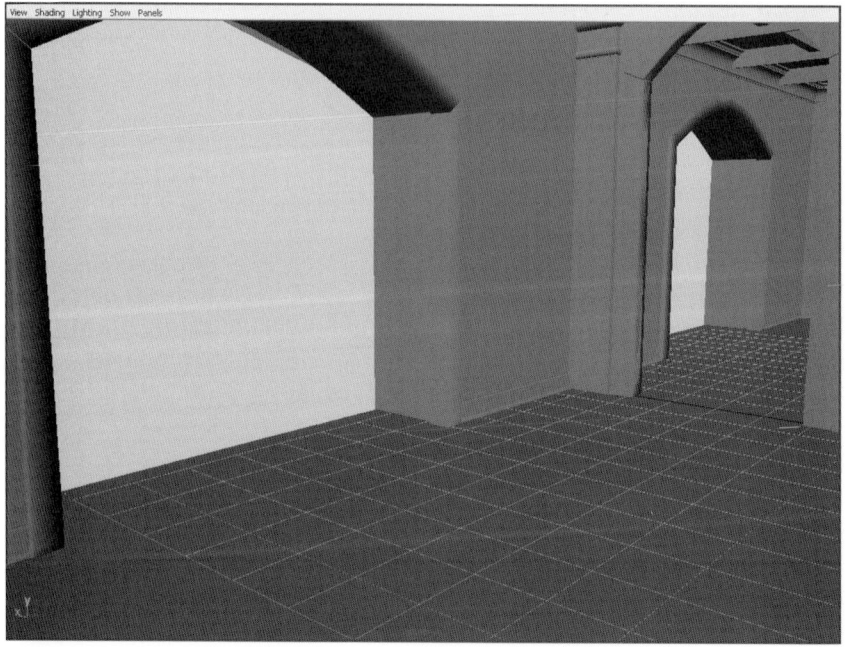

FIGURE 5.30   Cleared archways.

own book, so we cannot cover all those options here. However, take plenty of time to play with them and become the master of NURBS and NURBS surfaces.

Boolean Functions

If you have used a library search engine or even many Internet search engines, you are probably familiar with Boolean functions. If you want pages about black cougars, you could enter "Cougar + black – cars." This would look for sites and books that have both cougar and black in the page but not cars.

In 3D, Boolean functions allow you to subtract shapes from other shapes. They also allow you to add shapes and even find intersections where different forms meet. In these next few steps, we are going to use Boolean functions to cut out the windows and some of the doors in our room.

Step 23: Hide all layers except Walls and Windows.

Step 24: Create the "hole" shape. The first sort of Boolean function we will be performing is a Difference. That is, we will be finding the difference of two shapes, or subtracting one shape from another. We already have the walls from which we will subtract, but we need the shapes that will be subtracted. In this case, the forms will be elongated cubes to make the tall rectangular windows.

The walls are polygonal shapes (not NURBS) so we will want to create the hole forms from polygons as well. Create a new polygonal primitive cube and resize it so that it is about Scale X = 4, Scale Y = 6.5, and Scale Z = 4. The exact size is not overly important; what is important is that this shape looks something like Figure 5.31.

View your scene as Wireframe (**4**), so you can see where exactly you are placing this "hole." Notice in Figure 5.31 that the cube has been positioned so that it is above the ground and completely penetrates WallEast. If this hole object did not go all the way through the wall, the Boolean result would not be a complete hole. Position this hole object (with the Move tool) to about the position of Figure 5.31. Notice that this box sits right where our previously created window sits. Notice also that it should be about the size of the window; if it is not, resize.

Before you get much further, label this cube WindowHole.

Step 25: Duplicate and position other WindowHole objects. Duplicate this WindowHole and, in the Top view, position this new Window-Hole1 into position for the other windows in the room. Moving WindowHole1 from the top ensures that you do not move this hole up or down in the Y direction. Thus, your windows will be the same height on the wall (Figure 5.32).

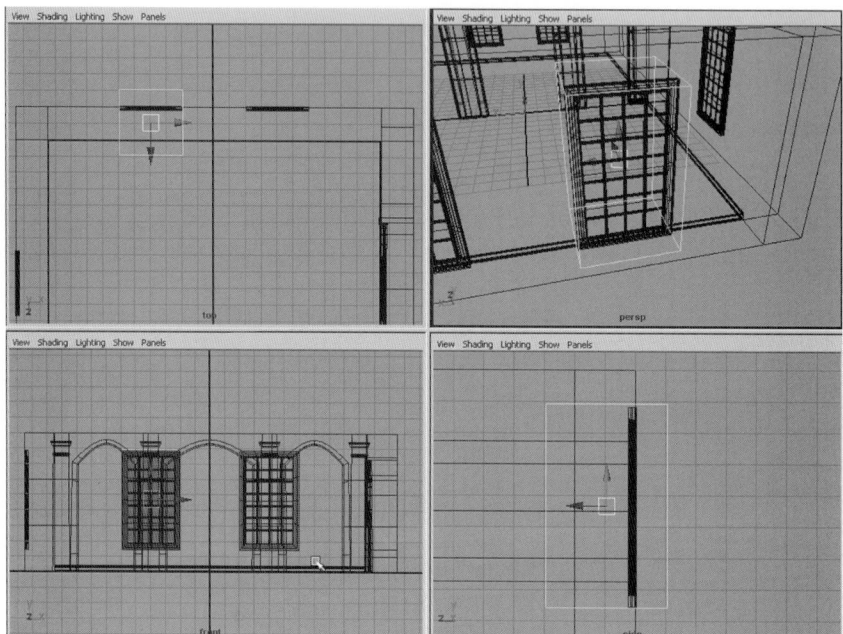

FIGURE 5.31 First "hole" object created, sized, and placed within the wall. Notice that the hold object is big enough and placed in a location to allow for a clean cut to take place through the entire wall.

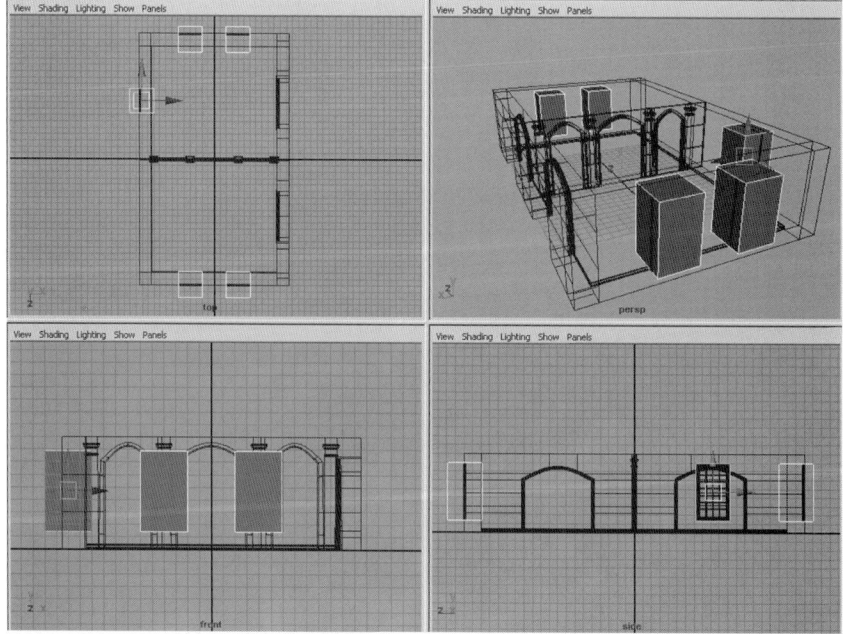

FIGURE 5.32 Duplicated WindowHoles positioned.

Step 26: Create a Boolean Difference from WallNorth and WindowHolex (whichever WindowHole object sits inside WallNorth). Maya decides which shape to subtract from which shape by the order in which you select them. Maya keeps the object that is selected first and subtracts the second object from it. In this case, we want to keep WallNorth, so select WallNorth in the Workspace or Outliner. Hold down the **Shift** key and select the WindowHole in the Workspace (or hold down the **Ctrl** key and select WindowHole2 in the Outliner) that intersects WallNorth. WallNorth will be highlighted white in the Workspace and WindowHole2 will be highlighted green.

Once both are highlighted, select Modeling | Polygons > Boolean > Difference. The result (Figure 5.33) should be fairly quick and should show a nice hole in the middle of the wall.

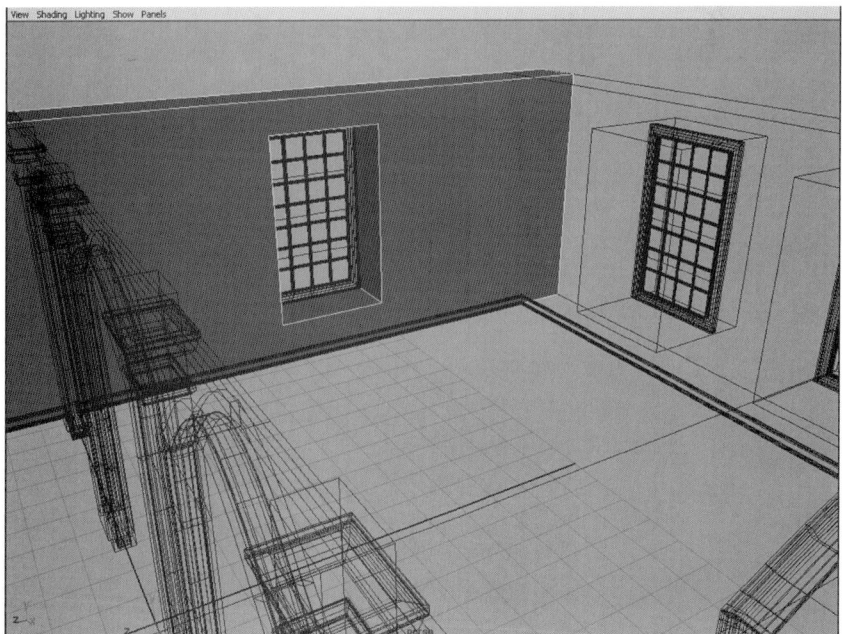

FIGURE 5.33   Result of a polygonal Boolean Difference.

Let's look for a minute at what has happened. Take careful notice of the Outliner. PolySurface1 is the result of the Boolean operation. Notice that the two originally involved parties (WallNorth and WindowHole2) are now actually hierarchies that contain a transform node. It is important to note that you can no longer see these two objects, although they are still integral to the shape, polySurface1. Here's why.

Because Construction History is (by default) turned on, the object polySurface1 is linked to the two objects WallNorth and WindowHolex. To see this relationship, select WindowHolex in the Outliner and activate the Move tool. In the Workspace, the Move manipulator will appear right in the hole of the wall (Figure 5.34a). Grab hold of the Z handle of the manipulator and move it (Figure 5.34b). The "hole" will move!

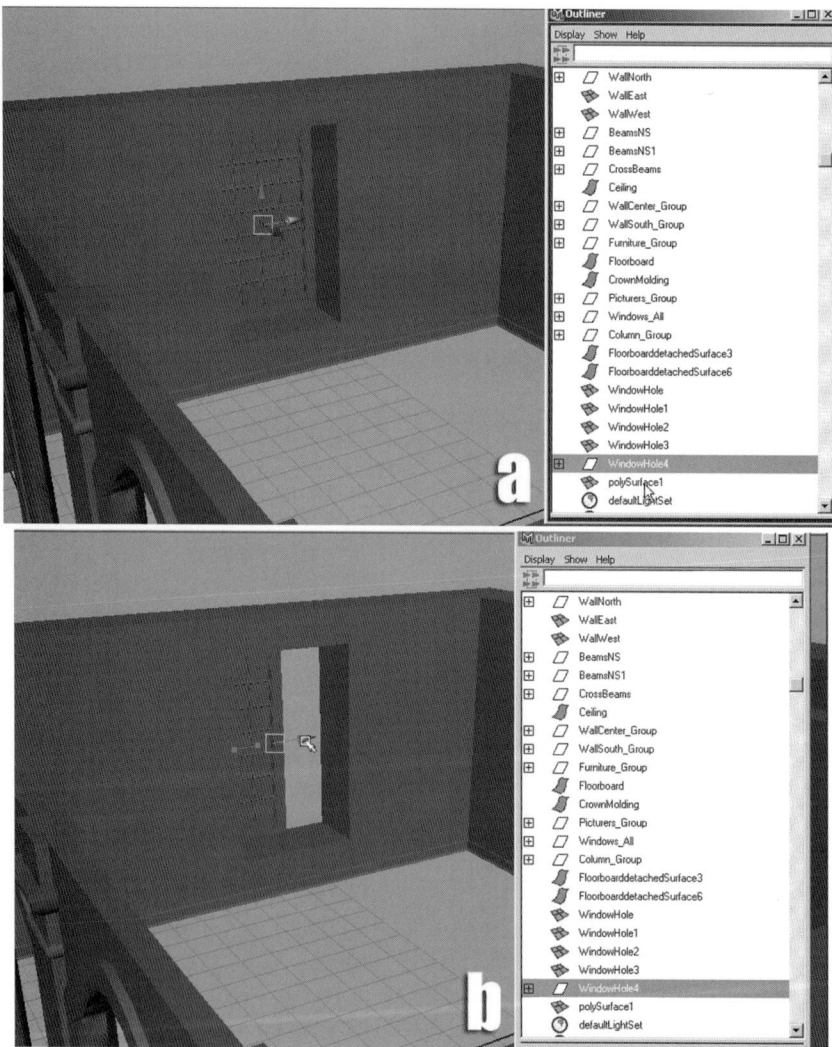

FIGURE 5.34 (a–b)   Because Construction History is active, a Boolean Difference leaves the objects used in the function, which can be adjusted to change dynamically the result of the Boolean Difference.

The benefit is Boolean functions are not irreversible. In fact, 50 steps later, if you decide you want to move the window hole, you can do so by moving WindowHolex. The problem is you increase the number of objects in your Outliner. With a lot of Boolean functions, you can quickly find the number of objects in your Outliner out of control. Also, in certain animation cases, Construction History can cause some funny problems. So, usually, if you know that your hole is where you want it, take a minute to clean out the object's history. To do this, select polySurface1 and choose Edit > Delete by Type > History. This cleans the object from any relations it might have due to construction history. Notice that Wall-North and WindowHole2 are gone from the Outliner.

Finally, rename polySurface1 to WallNorth_Window.

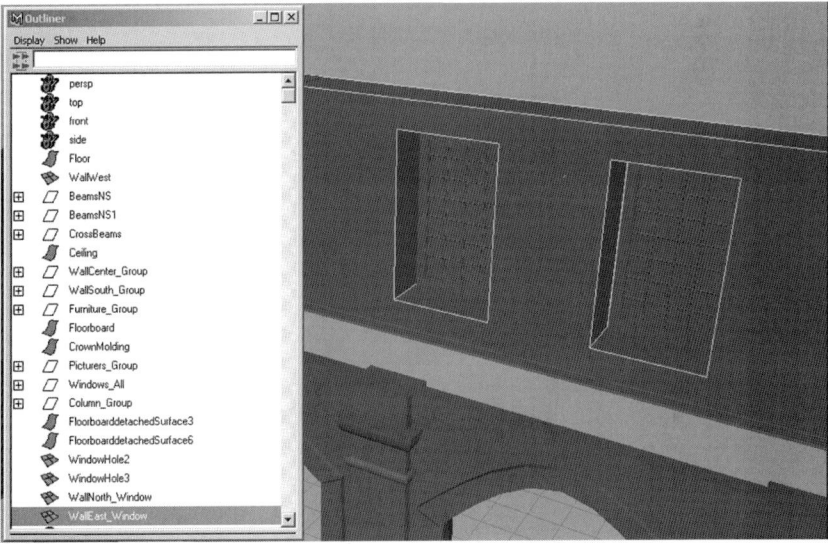

FIGURE 5.35   Results of double Boolean Difference. This gives us two holes in one wall. Each hole has to be subtracted individually.

Step 27: Create a Boolean Difference and subtract WindowHole from WallEast. Select WallEast and add WindowHole to the selection; again, choose Modeling | Polygons > Boolean > Difference. While the new polySurface1 that is created from this function is still selected, go to Edit > Delete by Type > History.

Step 28: Create a Boolean Difference to subtract WindowHole1 from polySurface1. Before we bother renaming the wall, go ahead and **Shift**-LMB-click WindowHole1 in the Workspace (or **Ctrl**-select in the

Outliner) and select Polygons > Boolean > Difference. Again, delete the history for this object. Finally, rename what is now polySurface2 to WallEast_Window. The results should look something like Figure 5.37.

Step 29: Repeat the process for WallWest. Create the Boolean difference shapes and be sure to name the final wall WallWest_Window.

Step 30: Create a hole for a doorway in WallNorth_Window. Do this by creating a new polygon primitive cube. Resize it (Scale tool) so that it looks close to Figure 5.36 (the box here is X = 3, Y = 7, Z = 4). Select WallNorth_Window, then **Shift**-select this new cube and choose Polygons > Boolean > Difference. Delete the history of the new polysurface and rename it WallNorth_Window_Door.

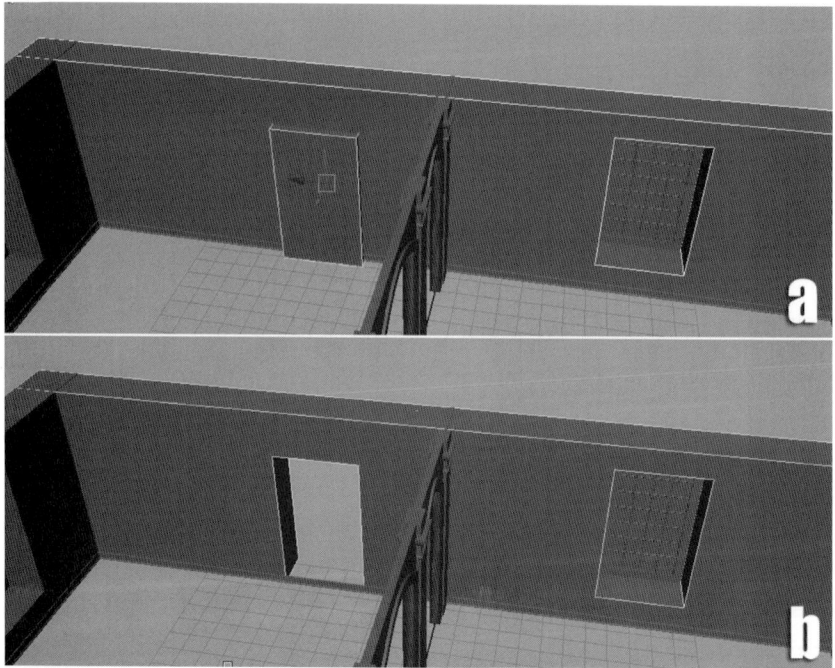

FIGURE 5.36 (a–b)   Creating the hole for the doorway.

Step 31: Do some cleanup. This includes putting trim around all the newly created holes in the walls. It includes getting rid of the floorboard in front of the new doorway. After all that, make sure everything is visible and organize things so that everything fits where it should. All in all, your model should look something like Figure 5.37.

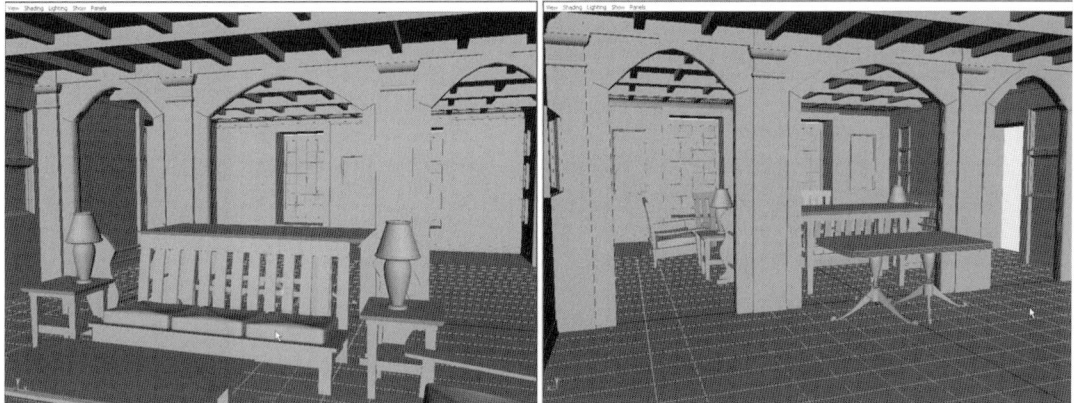

FIGURE 5.37   Room with mostly finished modeling.

CONCLUSION

Thus, we wrap up the modeling of the room. Of course, there are lots of props and other elements that could be added to the room to make it feel more "lived in." You probably will want to create those types of props to practice using all the techniques we have covered so far. But for now, we will leave the tutorial discussion of modeling this room.

In Chapter 6, we will look at subdivision modeling. Then, in Chapter 7, we will return to this room and learn how to bring it to life with color and textures. So hang in there—the best eye candy is still to come.

SUBDIVISION MODELING

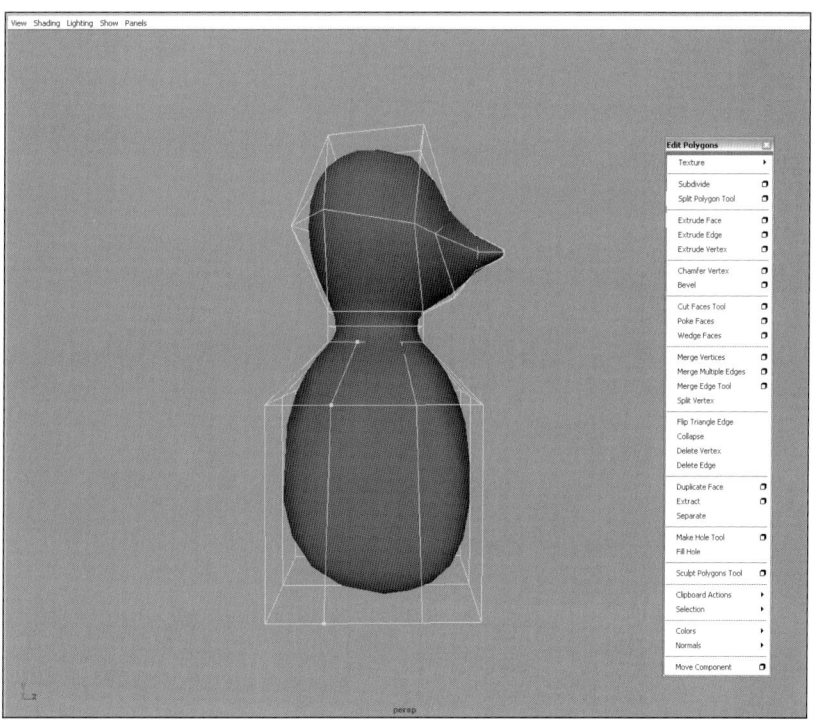

S o, we have looked at some basic polygon modeling and some basic NURBS modeling. Although there is still much to be discussed in those two areas, you have the tools to move in a variety of different directions. The big area we have left to discuss is subdivision surfaces.

Think of subdivision surfaces as an interesting combination of NURBS and polygon modeling. More accurately, think of subdivision surfaces as NURBS surfaces that can be altered like polygonal ones. This is what makes this chapter so valuable. The techniques we will be working with here are somewhat NURBS based and somewhat polygon based, so you will be able to use these techniques and ideas in other realms of modeling.

THE STATES OF A SUBDIVISION SURFACE

To get a better idea of how to work with subdivision surfaces, create one. Select Create > Subdiv Primitives > Cube (Figure 6.1).

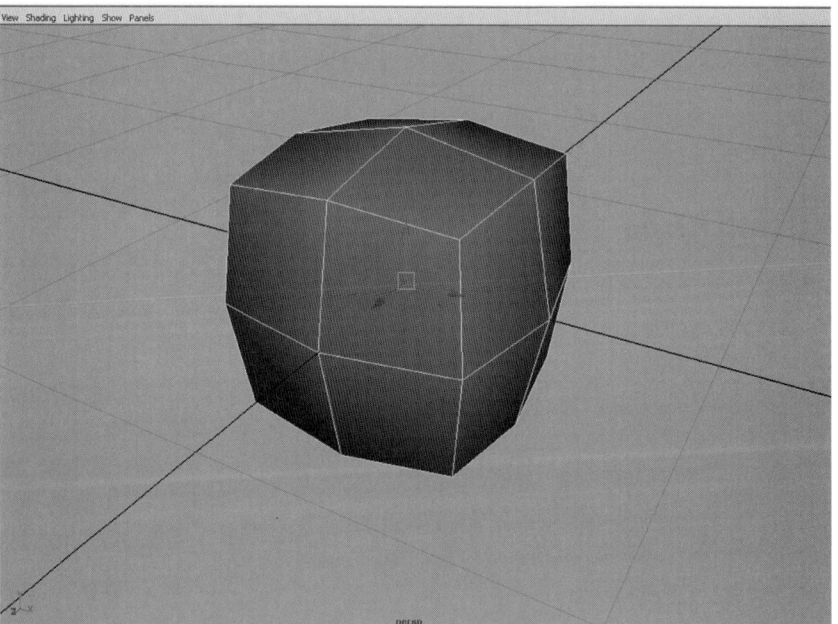

FIGURE 6.1   A subdivision cube.

This cube can be manipulated much like any other object—with the Move, Rotate, and Scale tools, you can manipulate the entire object.

Like other surfaces we have discussed, RMB-holding on an object brings up a hotbox with a collection of components to select from along with other choices (Figure 6.2).

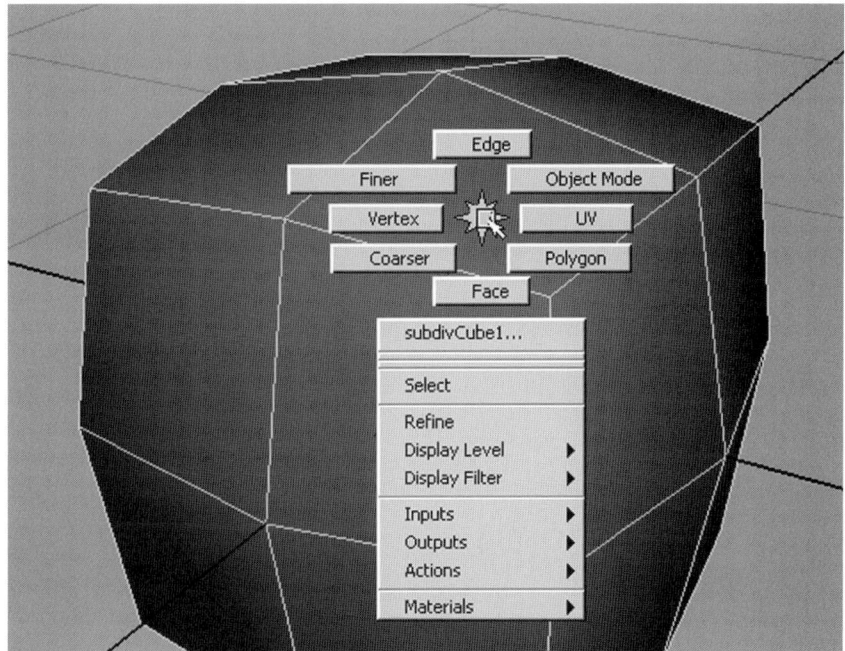

FIGURE 6.2   Subdivision surfaces' components can be selected with a RMB-click-hold.

There are a few important default components to note. First, the subdivision surface is in Standard mode. Notice that at the bottom right, you can change to Polygon (more on this later).

Standard Mode

While in Standard mode, there are some interesting components that can be selected and manipulated. Figure 6.3a shows what happens when a vertex is selected. Vertices are very similar to CVs of a NURBS surface; when they are selected, you can gently pull at the surface to change the shape in very organic ways. Similarly, you can select Face and you will be presented with a sort of cage (Figure 6.3b) that looks much like collections of hulls from a NURBS surface. The only difference is that instead of just being able to select rings of CVs as you do with hulls, you can select the imaginary face that rests between the vertices. These faces can be pulled or pushed, which changes the shape of the subdivision surface.

You can also select an Edge (just one side of a face) to be maneuvered.

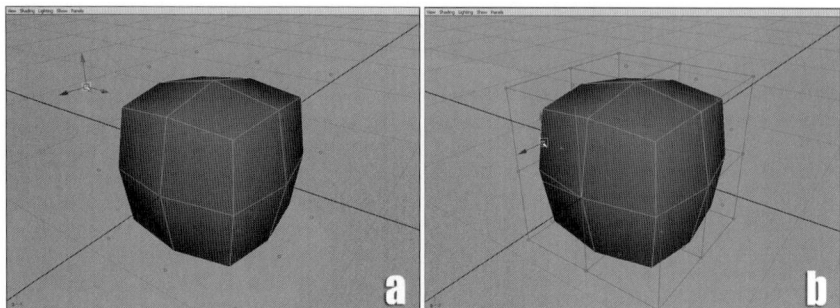

FIGURE 6.3   (a) Selecting Vertex from the hotbox. (b) Selecting Face from the hotbox. In both cases, you can change the shape of the subdivision surface through the manipulation of these components.

Polygon Mode

With all these fancy handles and slightly different ways to change the NURBS-like surface, the real power comes when you are able to maneuver the cage in true polygon-like ways.

To see how this works, RMB-click-hold the subdivision cube and select Polygon from the hotbox. The immediate change may seem rather subtle; the purple/orange color scheme used to indicate NURBS changes to the green of polygonal shapes. You can still see the green cage and the isoparms of the surface.

Just like in standard mode, you can use the hotbox to select a Vertex, Edge, or Face. However, different than standard mode is your ability to manipulate these vertices, edges, and faces like polygons.

RMB-click-hold the subdivision cube and select Face from the hotbox. Now, select any face of the resulting cage (Figure 6.4).

You can move, rotate, or scale this face. More important, you can extrude a new face from it. Select Modeling | Edit Polygons > Extrude Face (Option). When the Extrude Face Options window comes up, make sure you reset the settings. Then hit the Extrude Face button. Figure 6.5 shows the result of this. What has actually happened is that a new face has been created right on the surface of the old face. The new manipulator is interesting in that it allows you to move and scale this new face directly. Notice that with this new face created, the corner of the subdivision surface has become crisper. This is due to the new geometry.

To use this new manipulator, grab the move handle that allows you to pull away from the surface (in the case of Figure 6.6, this is the Z handle) and pull away the newly extruded face.

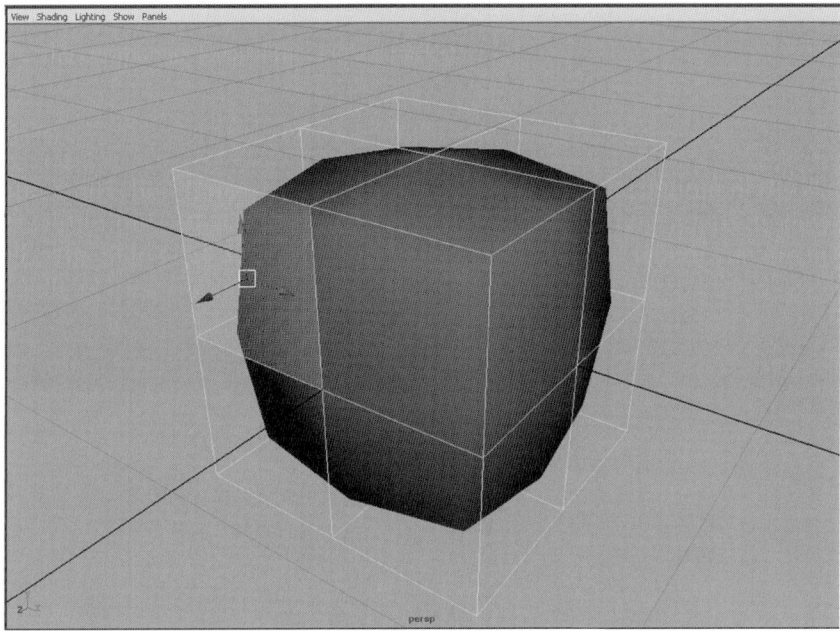

FIGURE 6.4   Selecting a face of the subdivision cage while in Polygon mode.

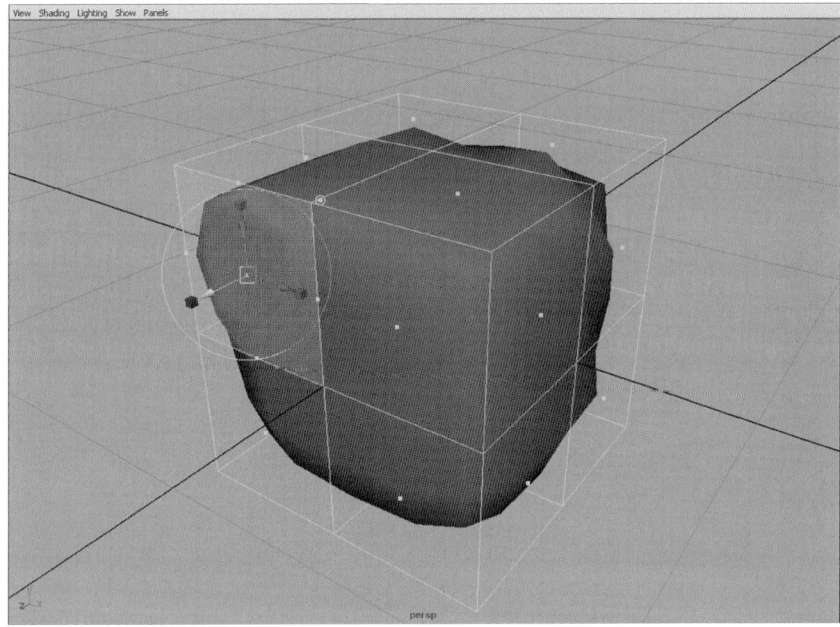

FIGURE 6.5   Extruded face still sitting on the surface of the old face.

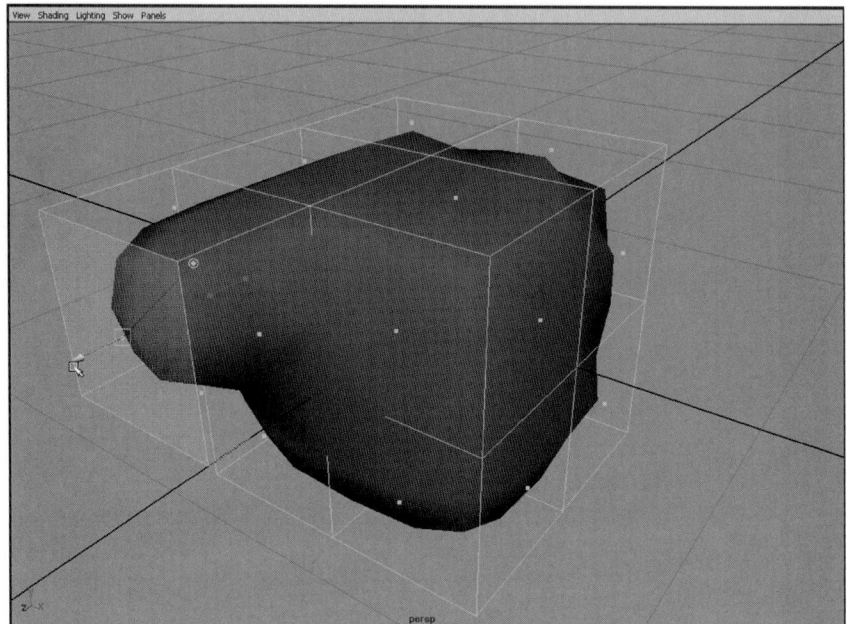

FIGURE 6.6   Pulling the newly created face off the old face to show all the new geometry.

You've now gone beyond adjusting the extant geometry. By creating a new face, you have also created faces on all four sides of that face. When you pull out the new face, you are stretching the new geometry created by adding a new face.

Now, there are several different variations of how to use this tool. For instance, undo back until you have no extruded faces. Now, select two faces that are right next to each other; select one and then **Shift**-select the other (Figure 6.7a). Select Modeling | Edit Polygons > Extrude Face. Use the new manipulator to pull out the new faces that have been created (Figure 6.7b).

Notice that the new face, and the new faces that surround the new face, cause a cleft to appear between the two faces. This is because there is a face running perpendicular to the extruded faces between the new surfaces.

In certain cases, this can be very effective; you can have new faces extruding out in multiple directions, all independent of the faces that are adjacent to them. However, in more cases, when you select more than one face, you want them to extrude as one mass. There are a couple ways to do this. To see how, undo back to the point where two faces are selected but not extruded.

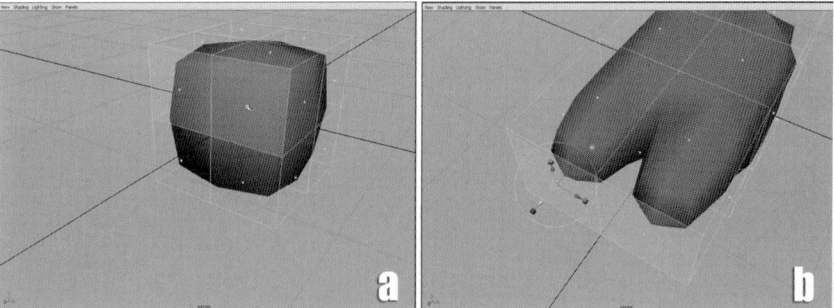

FIGURE 6.7 (a–b)   Extruding two faces.

Go to Modeling Polygons > Tool Options > Keep Faces Together. This is essentially telling Maya that as you make adjustments—such as extruding faces—you don't want it to be creating new faces between collections of extruded faces. Now, select Modeling Edit Polygons > Extrude Faces. Again, use the manipulator to pull out the new faces (Figure 6.8). Notice that now these two faces come out together with no faces between them.

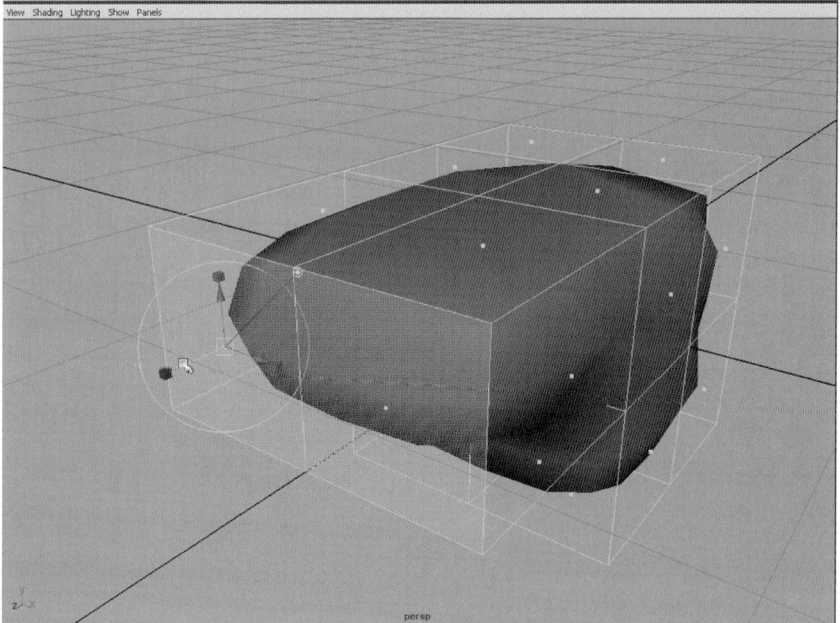

FIGURE 6.8   With Keep Faces Together checked, the new collections of faces extrude together en masse.

So, there are the basics. To get a better feel for the process, let's quickly create a hummingbird that we can use later in the book.

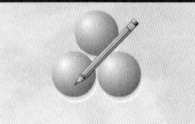

| TUTORIAL 6.1 | **CREATING A CARTOON BIRD** |

The little creature we want to create is shown in Figure 6.9.

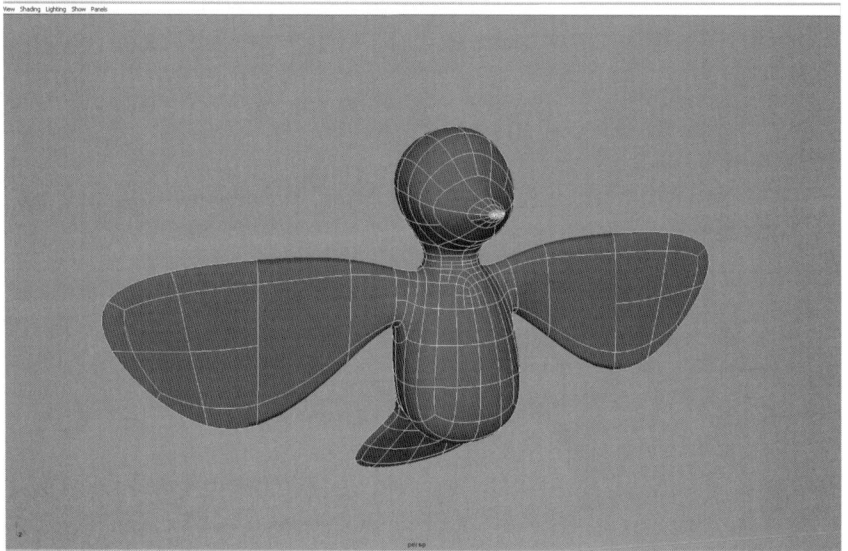

FIGURE 6.9 The cartoon bird created from subdivision methods.

Because it is essentially a round character, we can save ourselves some time by starting out with a round subdivision primitive.

Step 1: Create a subdivision cylinder. Select Create > Subdiv Primitives > Cylinder.

Step 2: Rotate the cylinder so that it is laying down. Select the entire cylinder and rotate it 90 degrees along the X axis. You can do this manually with the Rotate tool or via the Channel Box (Figure 6.10).

Step 3: View the subdiv surface in Polygon mode. RMB-click-hold and select Polygon from the hotbox. This will give you the cage that we can manipulate as polygons.

Step 4: Select the faces on the front of the cylinder. Tumble around to the other side of the cylinder and RMB-click-hold on the cylinder

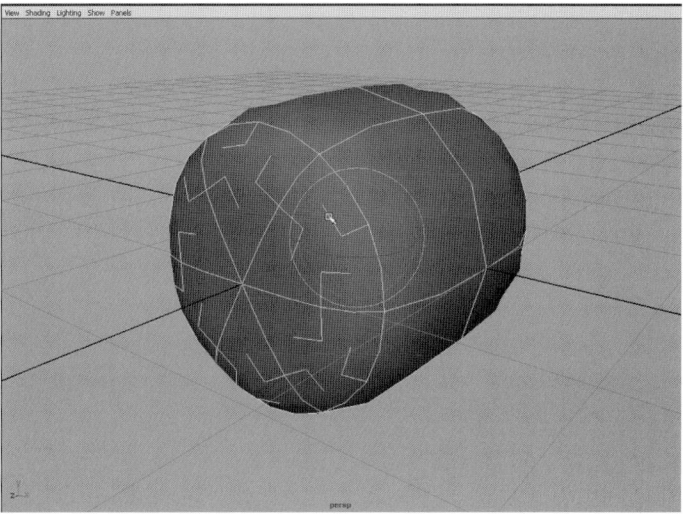

FIGURE 6.10   Rotated subdivision cylinder.

again to bring up the hotbox. Select Face. Now, LMB-click the faces on the front end (**Shift-**LMB to add to the selection). Make sure that as you select, you don't accidentally select faces on the sides (Figure 6.11).

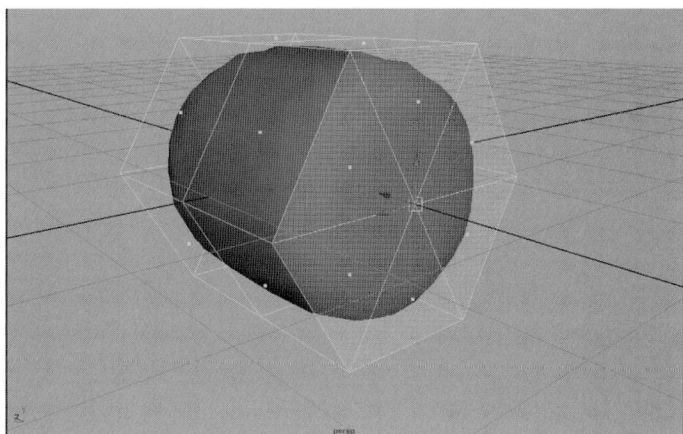

FIGURE 6.11   Select the faces on the front of the cylinder.

Step 5: Resize the faces to match Figure 6.12. This will form the cheeks of our cartoon bird.

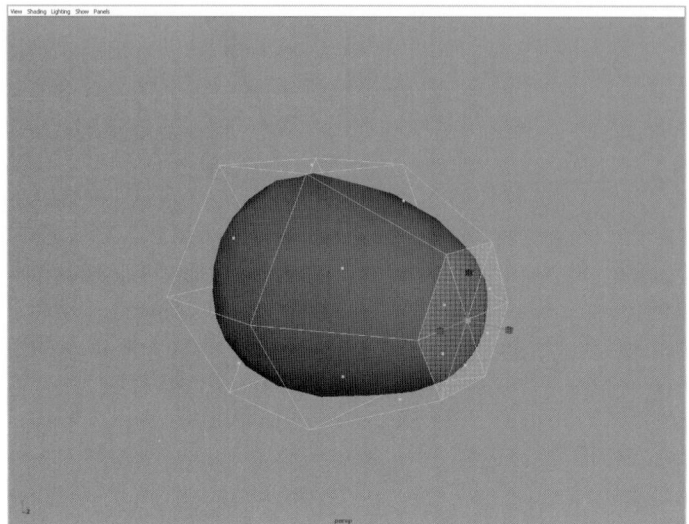

FIGURE 6.12   Resized faces to form cheeks.

Step 6: Move these faces to match Figure 6.13. Use the Move tool to move the already selected faces down and back.

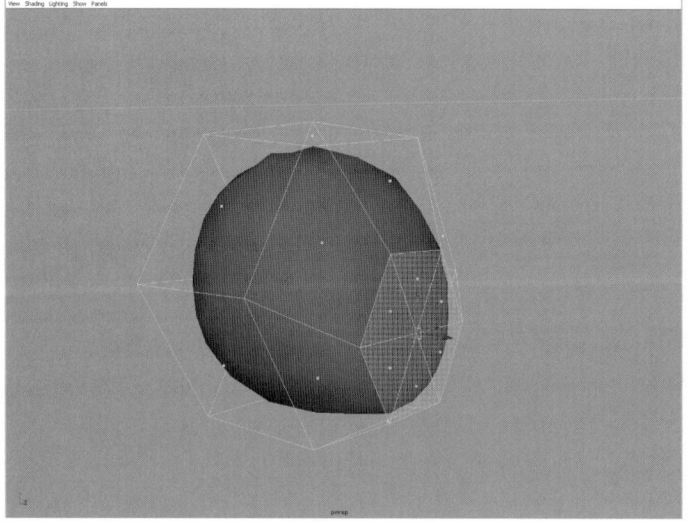

FIGURE 6.13   Selected faces moved down.

Step 7: Extrude the selected faces twice, as in Figure 6.14. Next we will extrude the selected faces twice. The distance of each extrusion is unimportant, because we are just creating geometry for further manipulation.

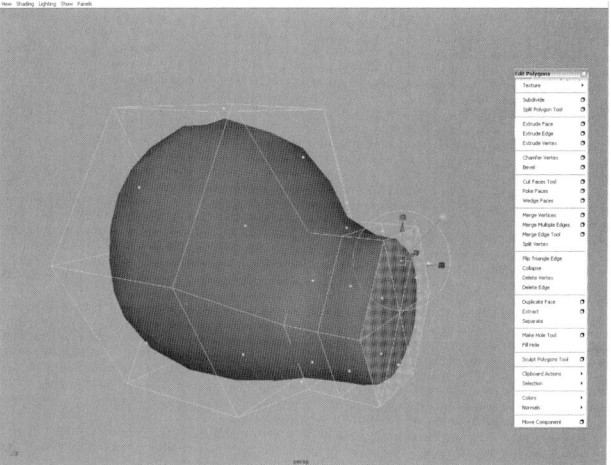

FIGURE 6.14   Face extruded for further manipulation.

Step 8: Form the cheeks and beak. Use the new geometry to form the cheeks and beak of the bird. Since we are not working with an existing design, feel free to play around. Start by selecting the vertex shown in Figure 6.15 and the vertex on the opposite side.

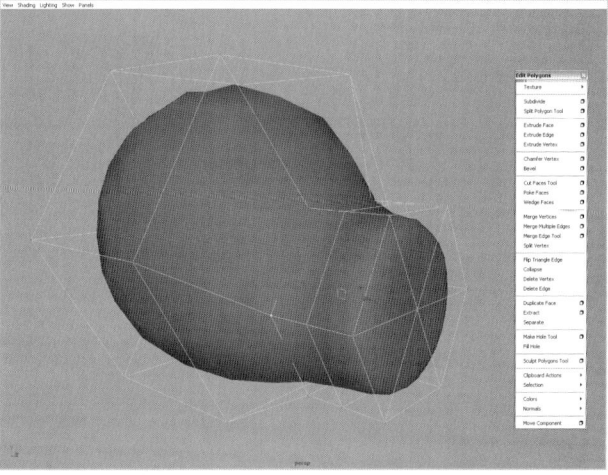

FIGURE 6.15   Select vertices on both sides of the model.

Using the Scale and Move tools together, you can keep everything symmetrical. Scale the two vertices out along the X axis as shown in Figure 6.16a, then move them back and up as in 6.16b.

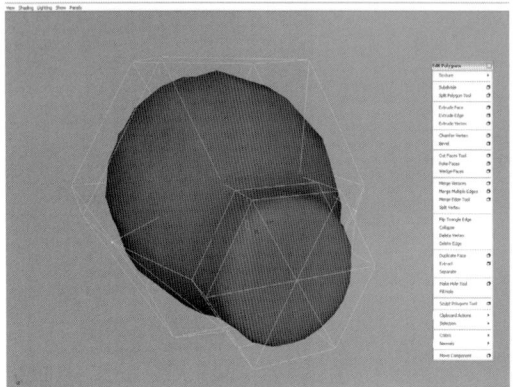 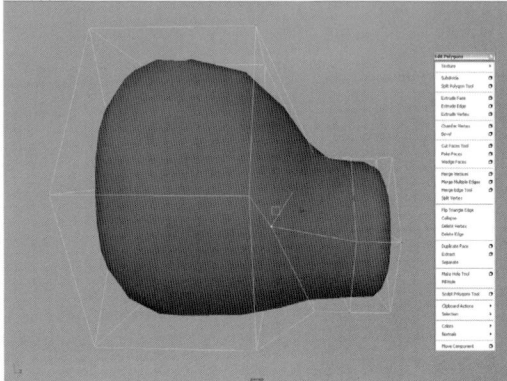

FIGURE 6.16 (a–b)   Vertices scaled wider and moved back and up.

Using the same method, shape the rest of the beak until you get something similar to Figure 6.17.

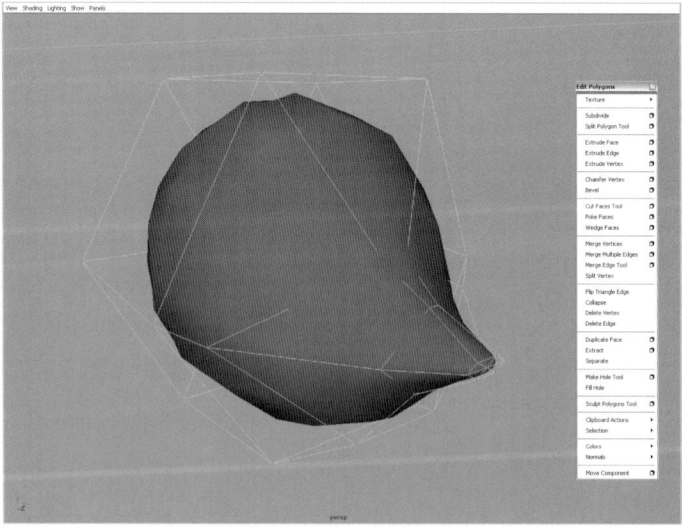

FIGURE 6.17   The beak and cheeks formed by moving and scaling vertices.

Step 9: Round the back of the head as in Figure 6.18. Select the vertex in the back of the bird's head and move it back along the Z axis. Also, move the top two vertices in back down a bit until the bird's head is more aesthetic.

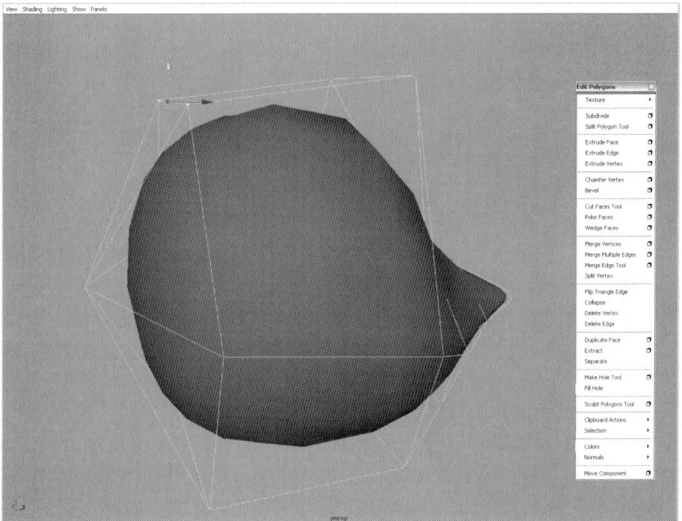

FIGURE 6.18   Shaping the back of the head.

Now we can continue on to the body. We will start by extuding the neck from the bottom of the head and keep extruding to form the body. Since subdivision surfaces allow you to form nice, round shapes from a blocky polygon cage, the temptation is to form the cage with very little detail. As you will see later when we set up the bird for animation, it is better to build the cage close to the shape you are creating. Save your work before continuing.

Step 10: The neck and body. Switch to polygon mode using the hotbox and select the bottom-most polygon, as shown in Figure 6.19.

Extrude the selected face twice (Figure 6.20) and twice more (Figure 6.21).

Select the eight vertices that form the body and scale them on X and Y (Figure 6.22). Now you should have a nice, round belly instead of a well-known candy dispenser.

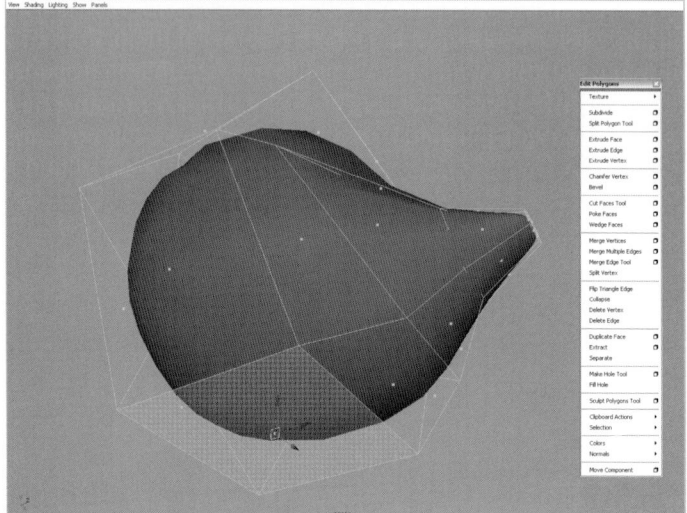

FIGURE 6.19   Select the bottom polygon.

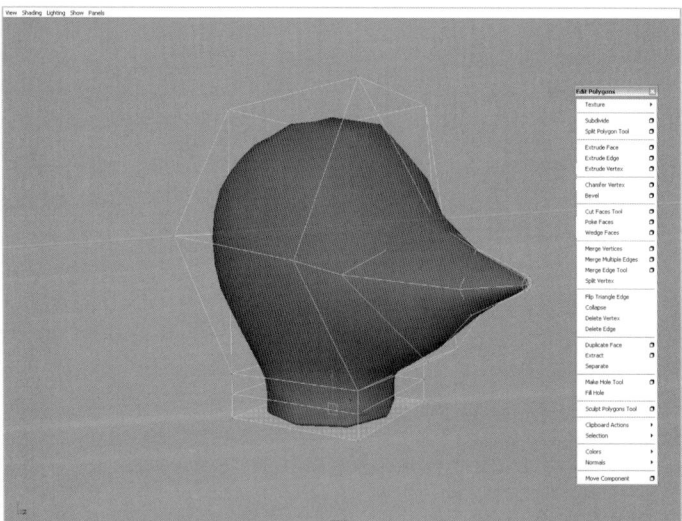

FIGURE 6.20   The extruded neck.

Step 11: Increase the detail in the body. Use the Split Polygon Tool to add detail to the bird's body (Figure 6.23).

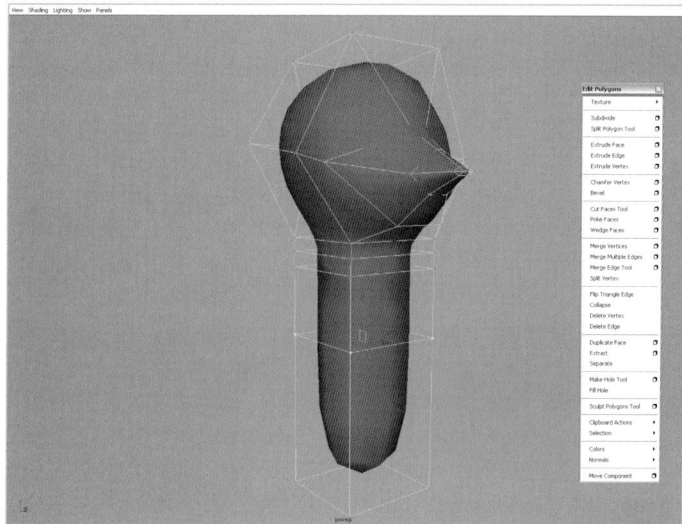

FIGURE 6.21   Continue extrusion for the body.

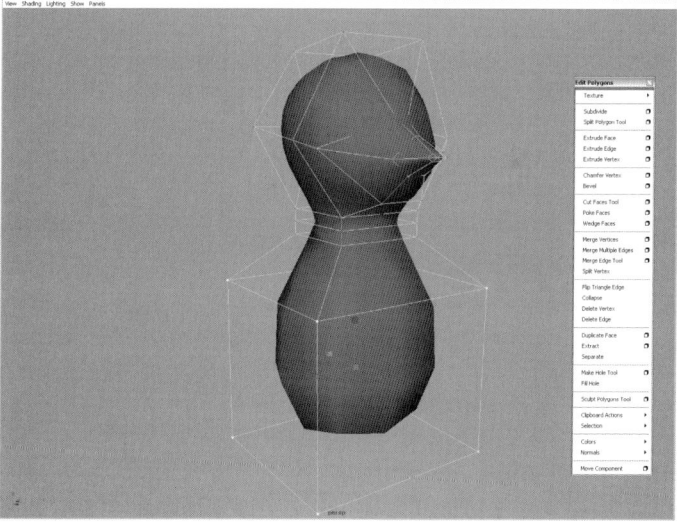

FIGURE 6.22   Risize the body for a nice, round belly.

Before exiting the Split Polygon tool, tumble around to the bottom and back to continue the split up to the back of the neck (Figure 6.24).

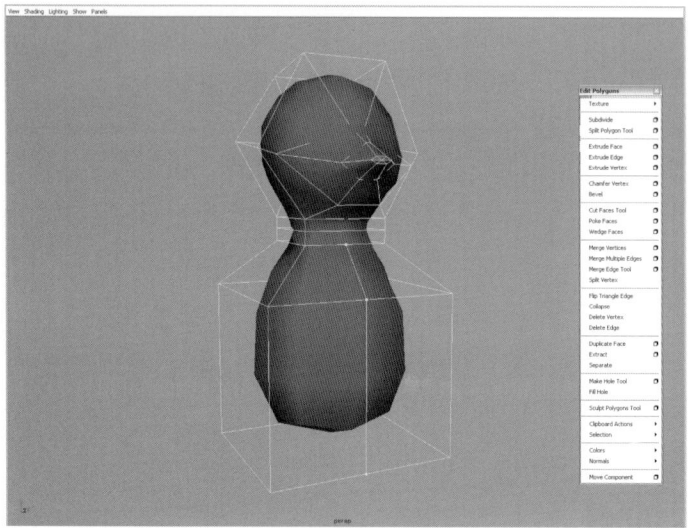

FIGURE 6.23   Use the Split Polygon tool to add detail to the polygon cage.

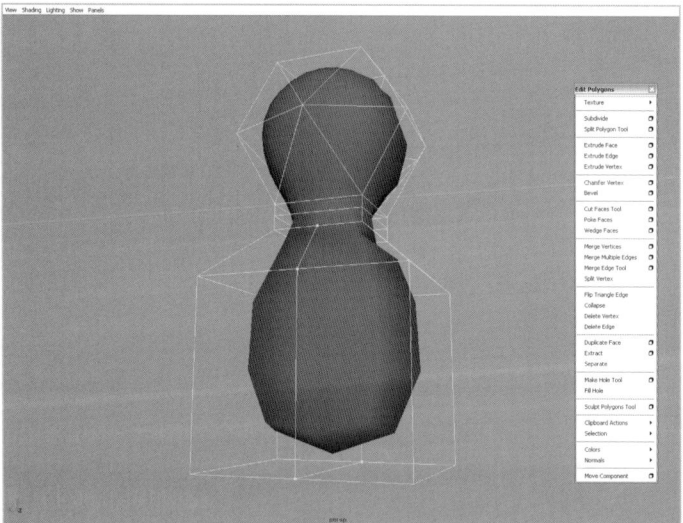

FIGURE 6.24   Continue the line around the back of the bird.

Hit **Enter** to complete the tool. Notice the shape change in the body (Figure 6.25). We will fix this after we add some more detail to the sides. Rest assured, our bird will be back to his round self in no time.

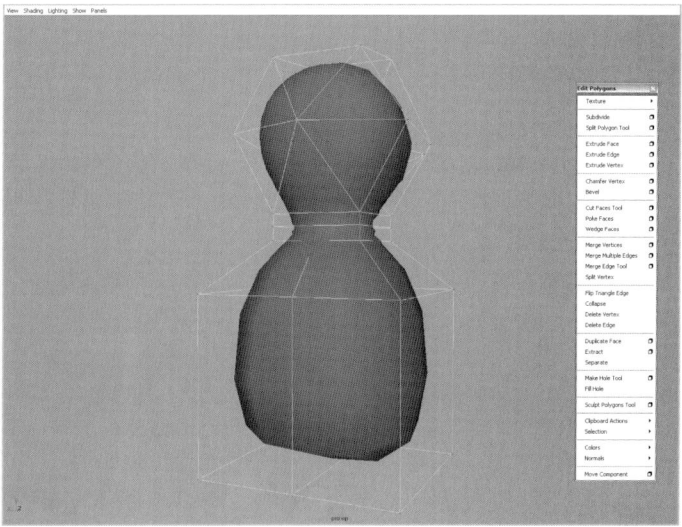

FIGURE 6.25   Result of the new detail.

Step 12: Yet more detail. Again with the Split Polygon tool, add two new edges down the side of the bird's body (Figure 6.26). Press **Enter** to end the tool. Repeat this action on the other side of the bird.

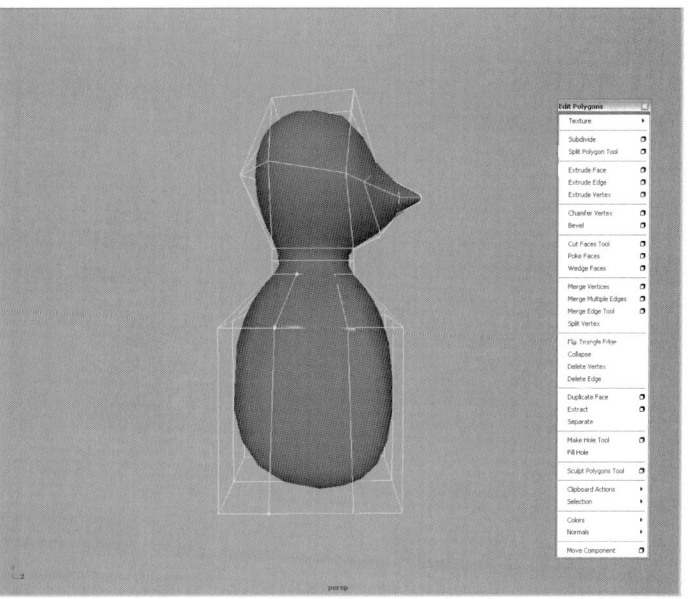

FIGURE 6.26   Additional detail along the side of the bird.

Now, go to the side and make sure the vertices on both sides line up (Figure 6.27).

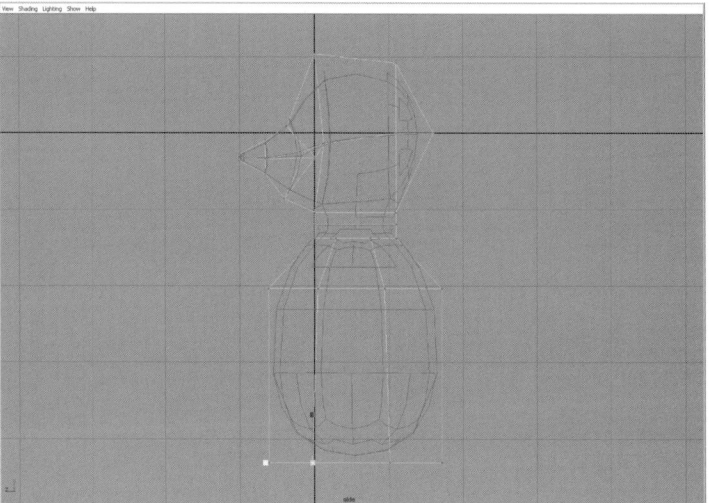

FIGURE 6.27   Lined up vertices on the side.

Step 13: Making the bird round again. In Vertex mode, move the vertices at each corner of the body, as in Figure 6.28.

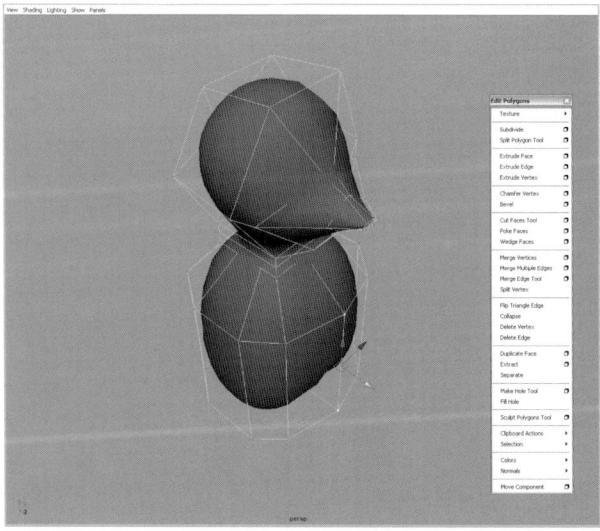

FIGURE 6.28   Reshape the body by moving the vertices.

Step 14: Splitting polygons again. With the Split Polygon tool, add edges to the bottom. Make sure to click where the edges you just created connect. This will create a continuous edge around the whole bird. This is know as an "edge loop" (Figure 6.29).

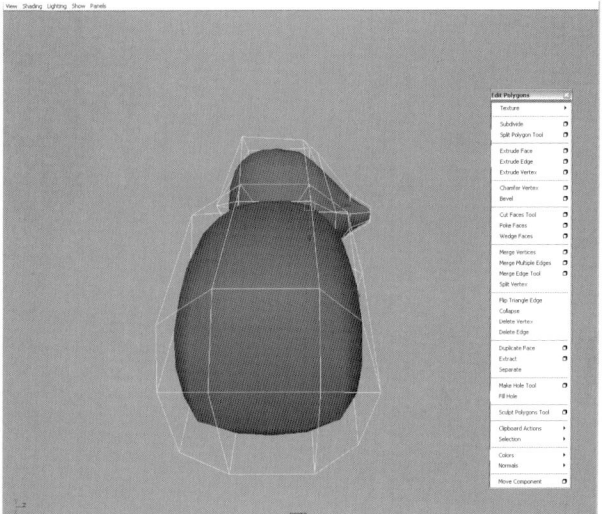

FIGURE 6.29   Continued "edge loops" along the bottom.

Step 15: More shaping. Continue to shape the body by moving vertices until it looks like Figure 6.30.

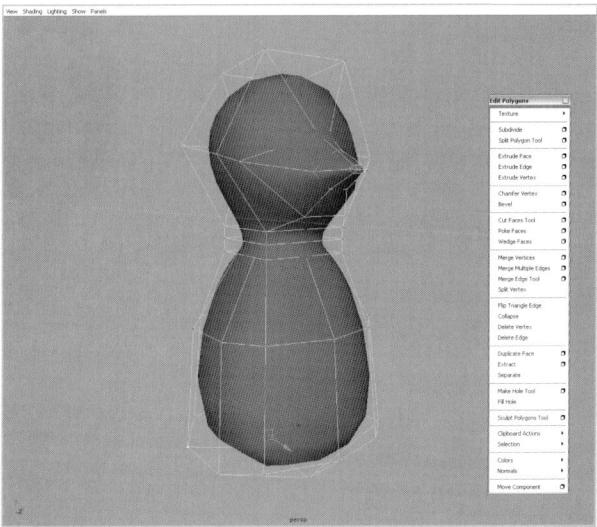

FIGURE 6.30   Continue shaping the body.

Step 16: What's a bird without wings? Switch to Face mode using the hotbox. Select the face shown in Figure 6.31 and the one directly opposite.

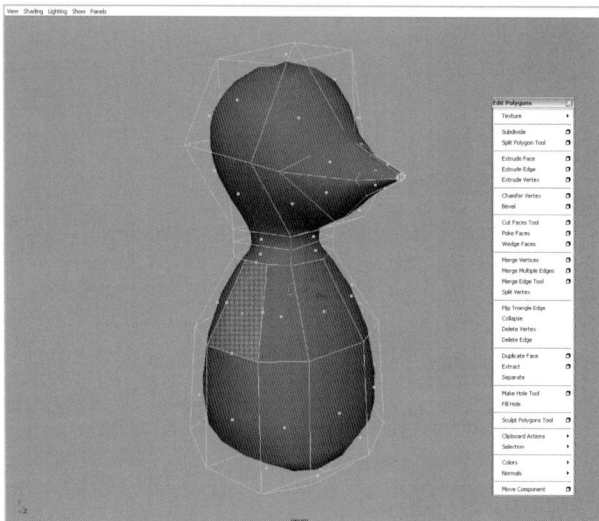

FIGURE 6.31 Select faces to extrude wings.

Using Extrude Face, extrude the selected faces a small amount, as in Figure 6.32.

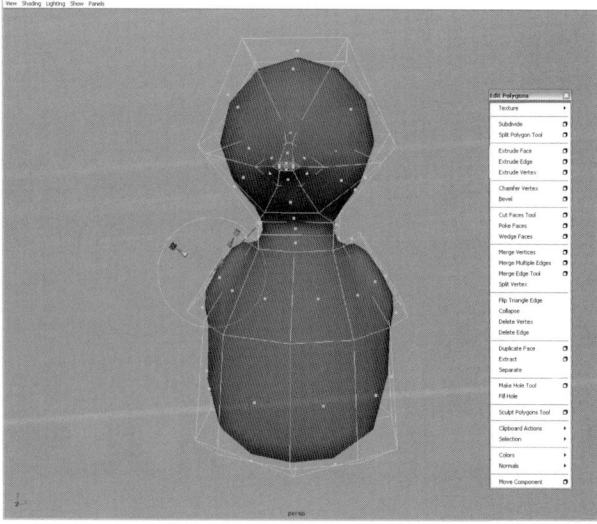

FIGURE 6.32 First extrusion.

As we did earlier, we'll extrude several times and move vertices to shape the wing afterwards. Extrude three more times (Figure 6.33). Now shape the wings using the Move and Scale tools as we did earlier (Figure 6.34).

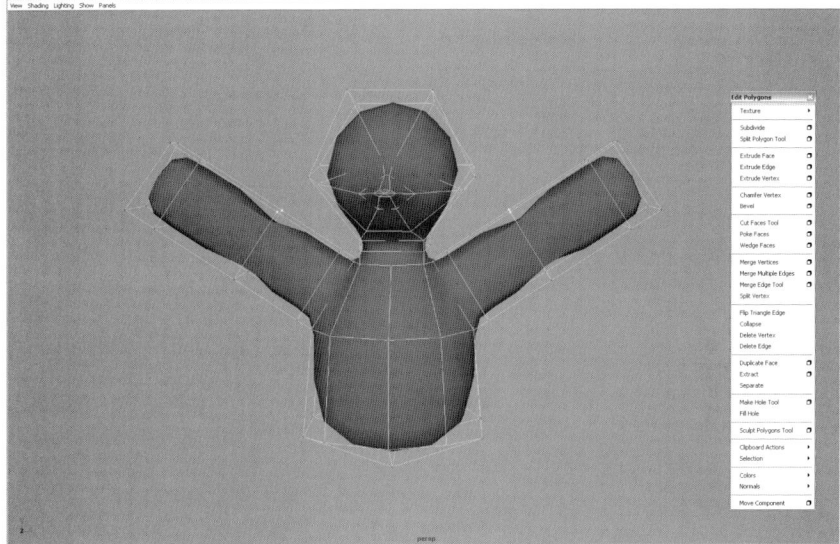

FIGURE 6.33   Three more extrusions to create the start of the wings.

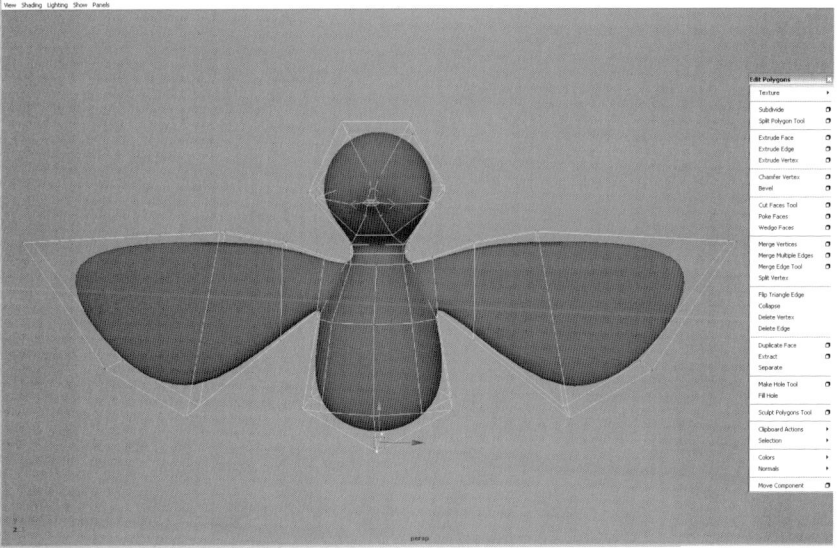

FIGURE 6.34   Reshape the wings from the new geometry.

To make the wing thinner along the bottom, select all the vertices along the lower edge and wing tips (Figure 6.35). Scale these vertices along the Y axis as in Figure 6.36.

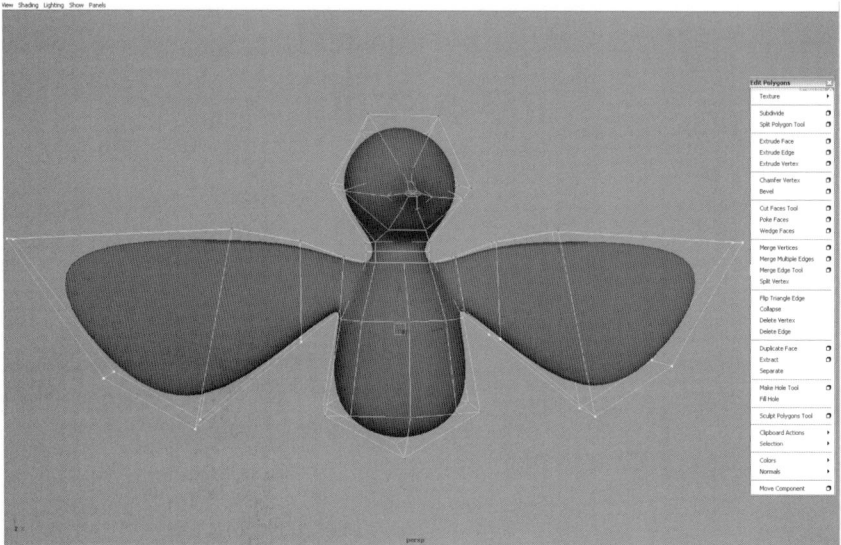

FIGURE 6.35 Select vertices to thin the lower edge and wing tips.

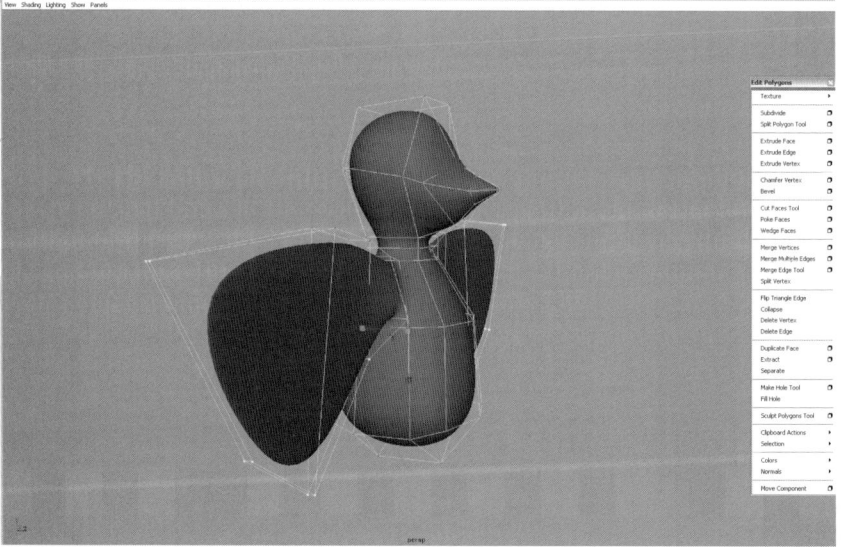

FIGURE 6.36 Scale the selected vertices along the Y axis.

You mave wondered if there is an easier way to keep a model symmetrical. At the end of this chapter, you'll learn a method that will allow you to only build half the model and mirror the other half.

Step 17: Adding some stability. Our bird needs a tail so it can steer a little better. For this, we will extrude the two faces at the bird's caboose (Figure 6.37).

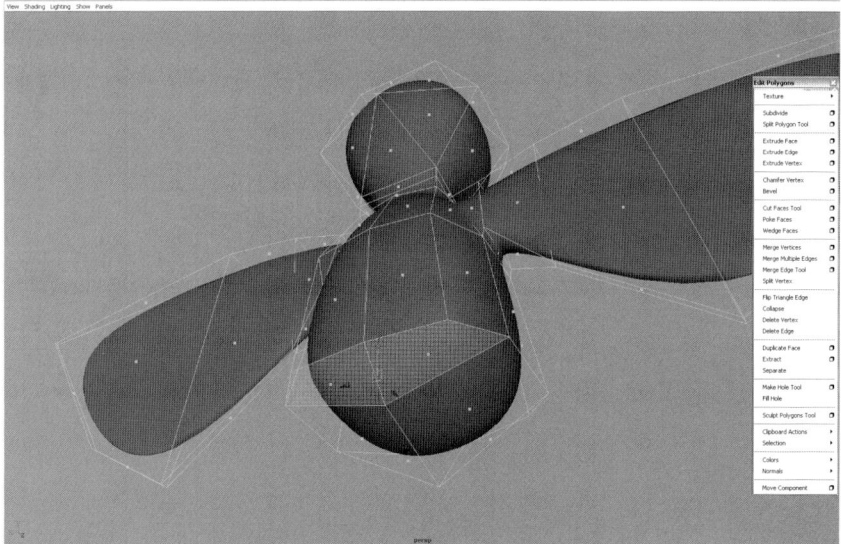

FIGURE 6.37   Faces from which to extrude the tail.

As before, we will extrude twice and then reshape the new geometry (Figure 6.38).

Select the vertices that form the base of the tail—making sure you get the underside as well—and scale them down to make the base more narrow (Figure 6.39).

Reshape the bottom of the tail, as in Figure 6.40.

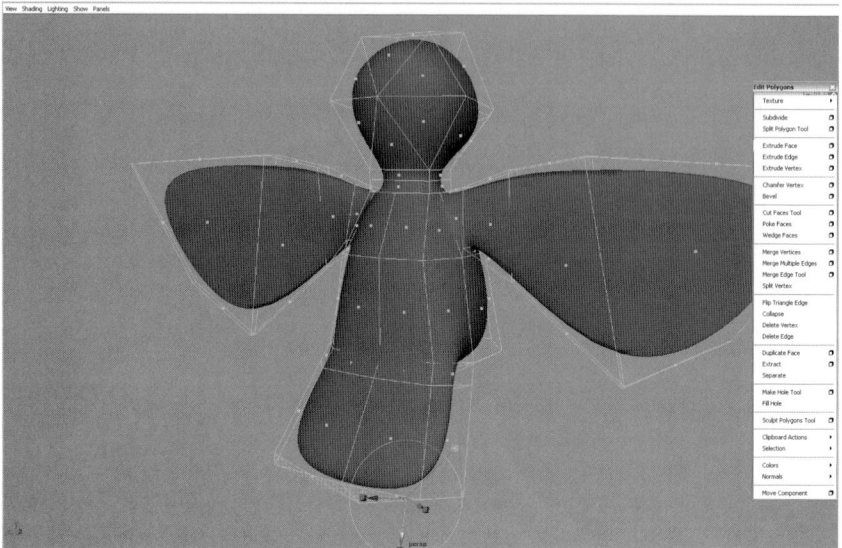

FIGURE 6.38 Extrude the faces twice.

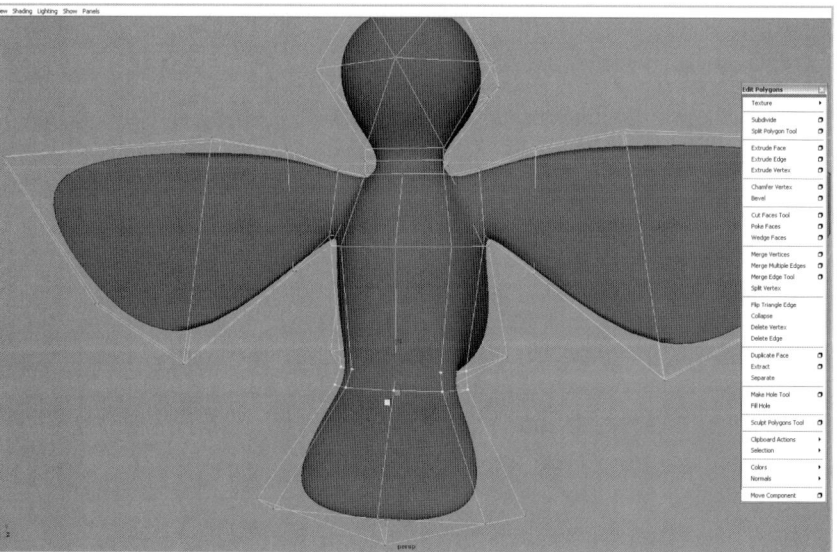

FIGURE 6.39 Scale the base of the tail on X.

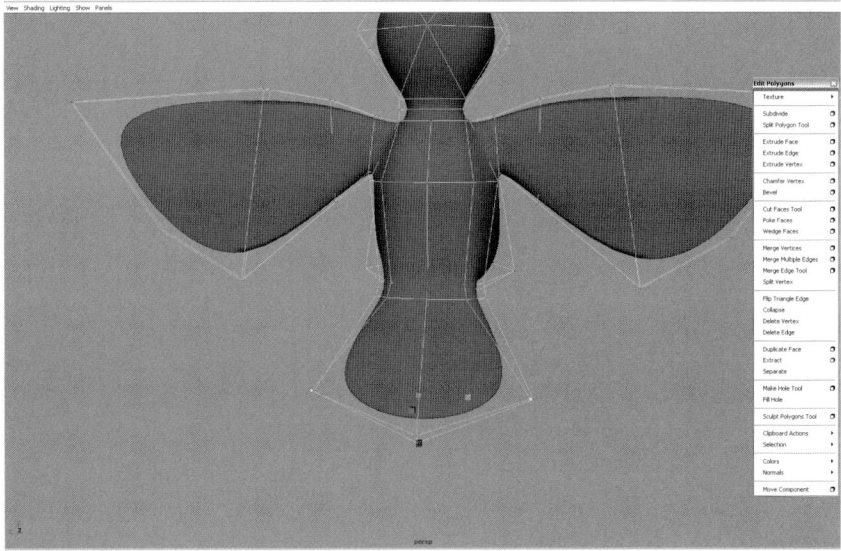

FIGURE 6.40   Reshape the bottom of the tail.

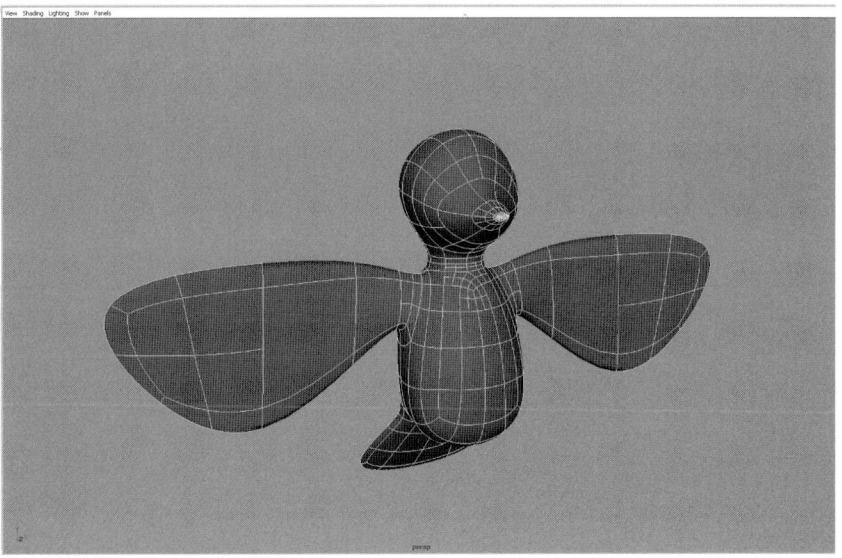

FIGURE 6.41   The finished bird.

Step 18: We're done; it's time to rest. The bird is finished for now. Select Standard mode from the hotbox menu and press **3** on the keyboard to display it more smoothly (Figure 6.41). You may want to add more detail or even find some images of birds and make it more realistic.

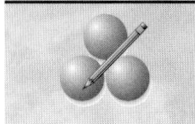

| TUTORIAL 6.2 | **BUILDING HALF A MODEL AND GETTING THE OTHER HALF FOR FREE** |

As promised, here is a way to get a symmetrical model without having to manipulate both sides.

Step 1: Create a box. Create a polygonal cube (Create | Polygon Primitive > Cube). Select Face mode from the hotbox menu and select the face shown in Figure 6.42.

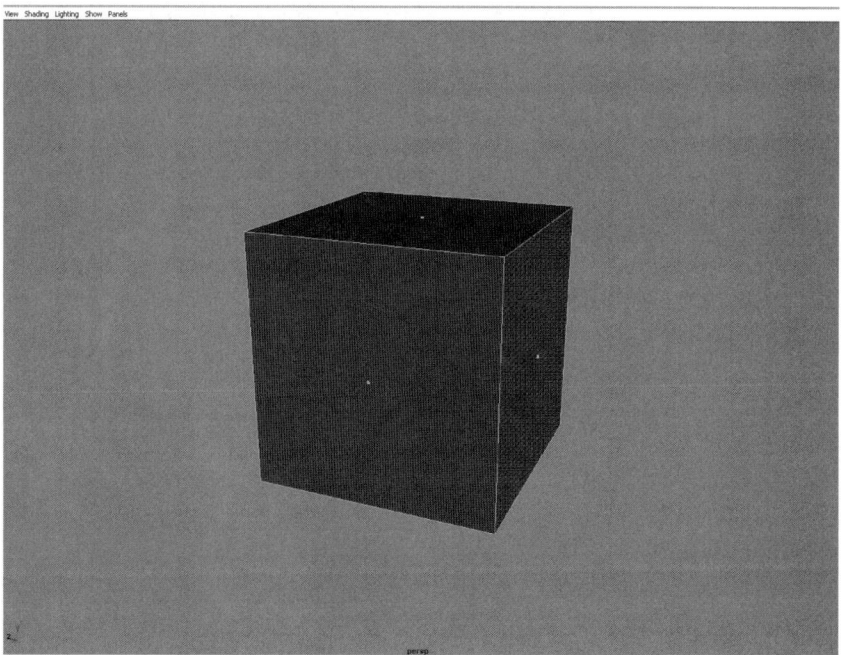

FIGURE 6.42   Select faces to delete.

Because we don't need a face inside the model, we can delete the face along the center. Move the vertices to the center line (Figure 6.43). Use the hotbox to go back to Object mode before the next step.

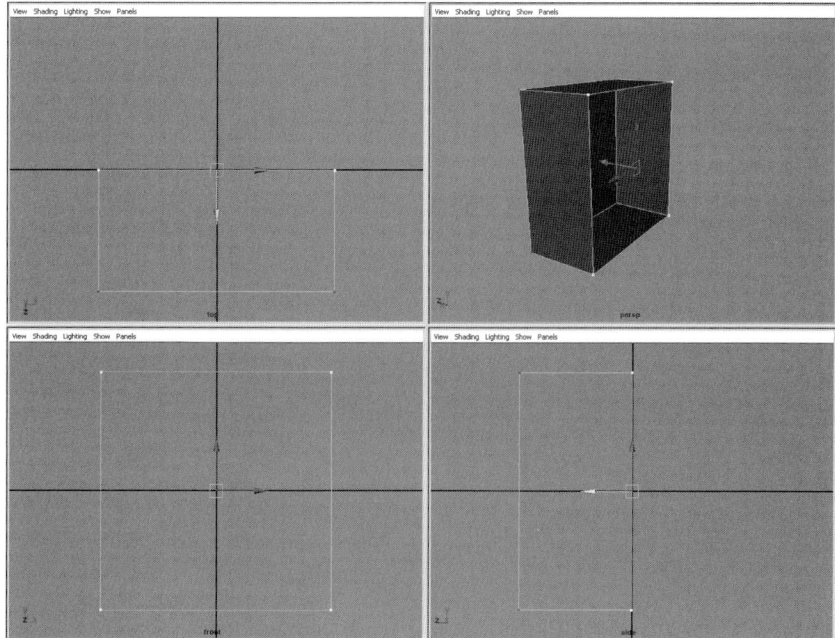

FIGURE 6.43   The box half ready to be duplicated.

Step 2: The Duplicate tool. Bring up the Duplicate tool options: Edit |
Duplicate (Option). Set the Scale Z type-in to –1 and set the Geometery
Type to Instance. After you've done this, press Duplicate. See Figure 6.44.

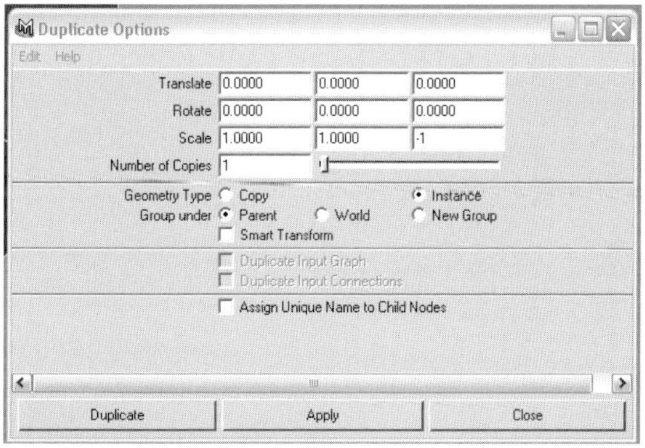

FIGURE 6.44   Duplicate Options Box.

That's it! Now any operation you do to one side will be applied to the other only mirrored. Try moving a vertex around and see the result. 🪓

SUMMARY

Pretty powerful, eh? You can see how quickly we were able to create a single mesh shape that is complex in form and interesting in design. Along the way, we also looked at a variety of methods of altering faces that can be used to change polygons with polygonal modeling.

This technique, though employed to make a simple shape here, is often used very successfully to create complex forms such as faces and bodies. Once you get the hang of what you can do with extruded faces, the possibilities are endless.

MATERIALS AND TEXTURING

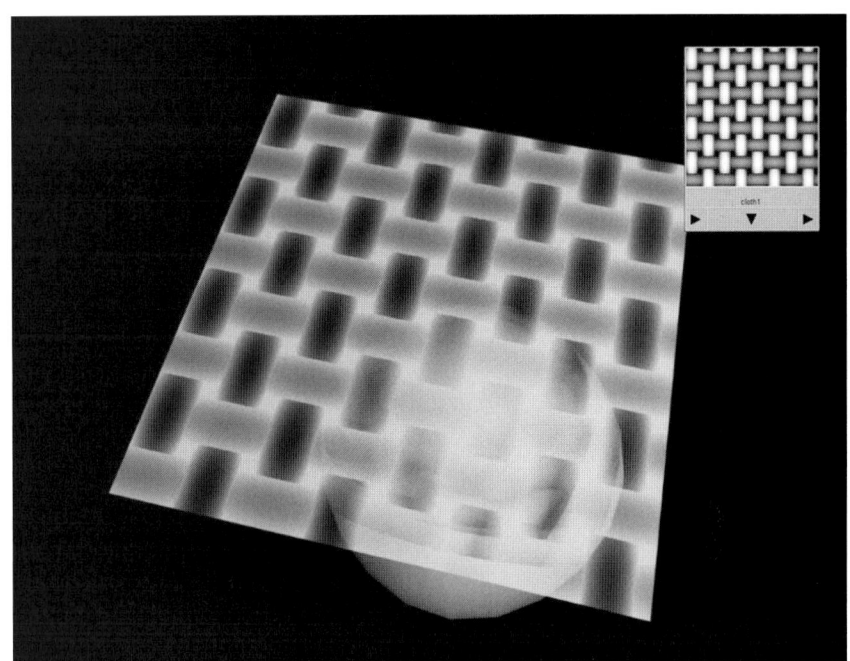

Even though more than half of this book is done and has been dedicated to modeling, that does not mean modeling should take half your time in a 3D project. Although every project is different, most serious 3D artists spend at least as much time on materials and lighting as they do on the modeling process. This chapter presents many techniques for using Maya's texturing tools. Amazingly, these selected techniques will all fit into two chapters—a real departure from the six chapters used to cover modeling. However, these texturing tools take time and require skill and creativity to master, but they produce astounding work when all is said and done.

THE TEXTURING PARADIGM

So, what exactly does it mean to "texture" something? Texture (the verb) in 3D usually refers to the process of giving your models surface characteristics. These characteristics can include color, highlights, bump, and so on. Texturing objects is what makes a marble look different than a basketball, a bowling ball different than a baseball, and a marble floor different than a hardwood one.

In reality, everything within your Maya model is made of, well, nothing—it's all virtual. By default, things are shown in the Workspace as a sort of shiny gray plastic. This is just a default method of helping you visually understand the nature and shapes of the 3D forms you are building. Luckily, objects needn't remain in that gray, fake state. Indeed, making a computer-generated image look not quite so computer generated is largely a combination of effective lighting and cleverly constructed materials on the surface of models.

Texturing is similar to applying decals. If you have ever built a model airplane, you can remember that after constructing the body, the kit usually came with a collection of stickers that could be put on the plane to add color and pizzazz. In 3D, it is much the same, except instead of simple plastic stickers, these 3D "stickers" can make a surface appear shiny, dirty, rough, smooth, metallic, cloth-like, furry, old, or new. Like decals, careful placement makes a big difference. Controlling how the material is placed on the surface of the model can help make a surface appear believable.

TERMS

Before we move on too much further, we should refine the terms we will be using. Although the general 3D market refers to this process of adding surface characteristics as texturing, textures can mean an entirely different thing in Maya.

Objects are either NURBS or polygonal. Often, these surfaces will include UV Coordinates. UV Coordinates constitute a collection of information about the nature of the 3D object. Think of these coordinates as a sort of map so that Maya will know how to attach color, bump, and other information to the surface.

Maya creates visually different surfaces through the assignment of Shaders. Shaders usually include a material. Materials contain various channels that allow you to control different characteristics of the surface. Materials are actually nodes that can be adjusted dynamically and thus dynamically alter the surfaces to which they are assigned. Sometimes, materials may contain textures (sometimes called Texture Maps). Textures are actual images (photographs or otherwise) that help refine or explain the color or bump of a material. They are referred to as maps because they help map out what parts of a surface will be what color or what parts of a surface will appear higher than others. For instance, if you want a floor to look like maple hardwood, you can actually import a photograph of that hardwood to define the color of the material placed on the floor. On that hardwood floor, if you want to be able to define exactly how the planks are laid out, you can create an image in Illustrator to define what parts of the floor should be receded and what parts should rise.

Textures can also be procedural—that is, created mathematically. There are several procedural textures that Maya creates straight out of the box. Often, these procedural textures end up creating materials that look awfully canned, so they usually are not advised. But, on occasion, they can be very helpful in making subtle tweaks to a material created from traditional texture maps.

TYPES OF MATERIALS

If you are coming from most other 3D applications, this delineation of material types may seem a bit foreign. In most 3D applications, you create a new material and define the characteristics of that material to suit your needs. In Maya, there are actually different types of materials from which to choose that contain certain editable characteristics that others may not.

The biggest difference between the material types is how the specular highlight behaves. The specular highlight is the glare or the sheen of a surface. A metal surface has a high, sharp specular highlight, while a piece of felt has a broad, very flat highlight. You can use whichever material is appropriate for the surface you wish to create. You can change a material's type at nearly any time during your work flow, so no need to fret too much over the decision.

The materials available in Maya are Lambert, Blinn, Phong, PhongE, and Anisotropic. Lambert essentially has no specular highlight—it is a matte texture. Chalky surfaces and many fuzzy materials are good candidates for a Lambert material. Blinn, Phong, and PhongE are all quite shiny materials. Most plastics and metals and even some woods are logical choices for these materials. Finally, Anisotropic is also shiny but bends the specular highlights in much more dynamic ways. Often, glass surfaces and brushed metals are best defined with an Anisotropic material.

Because you can switch between material types, and because the names of the material types are far from intuitive, there is no need to worry about memorizing what is what quite yet. As time goes on and you begin to build more materials, you will quickly develop a sense of what to use where. Figure 7.1 shows a quick breakdown of the different materials with the variation of the specular highlight as the primary difference.

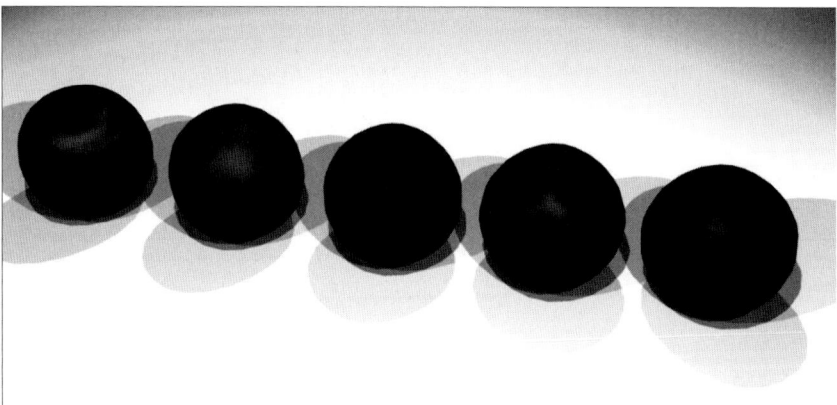

FIGURE 7.1   From left to right the type of materials are: Anisotropic, Blinn, Lambert, Phong, and PhongE. Notice the biggest difference is size, shape, and crispness of highlights.

ANATOMY OF A MATERIAL

Although all the material types discussed in the previous section have differences in the highlight department, they also have some identical attributes. Whenever a material is being edited through the Attribute Editor (more on this in a bit), you will be presented with a collection of editable attributes (Figure 7.2).

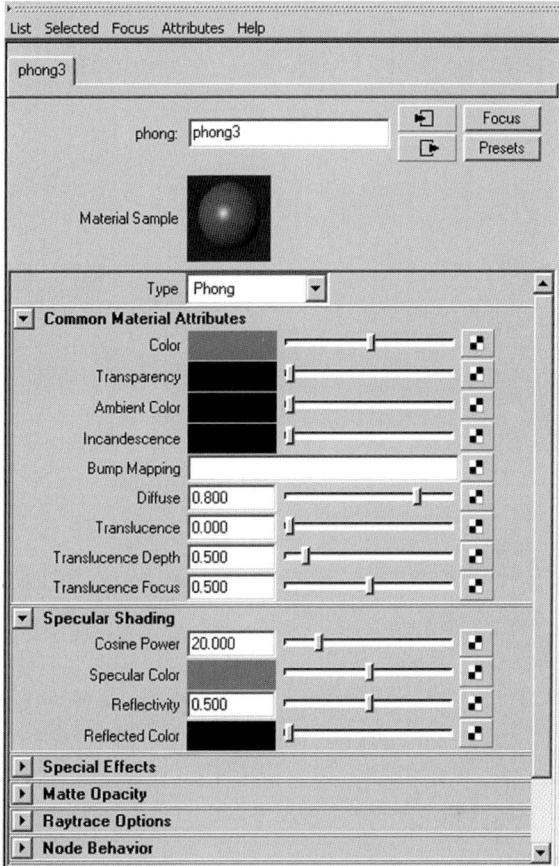

FIGURE 7.2   Attribute Editor. This illustration shows the attributes of a Phong material.

Following is a list of the common attributes seen in all materials and a brief description of what each attribute does:

Color: Determines the color of the surface. You can choose a color using traditional color pickers or you can import a texture. The texture for this attribute can be a procedural texture or a 2D texture image map.

Transparency: Working on a glass surface? Plastic? This is the attribute that allows objects to be transparent or semi-transparent. Interestingly enough, you can use various texture maps here to make certain parts of a surface transparent, while other parts remain opaque. You can even use texture maps to make certain parts of a surface semi-transparent (Figure 7.3).

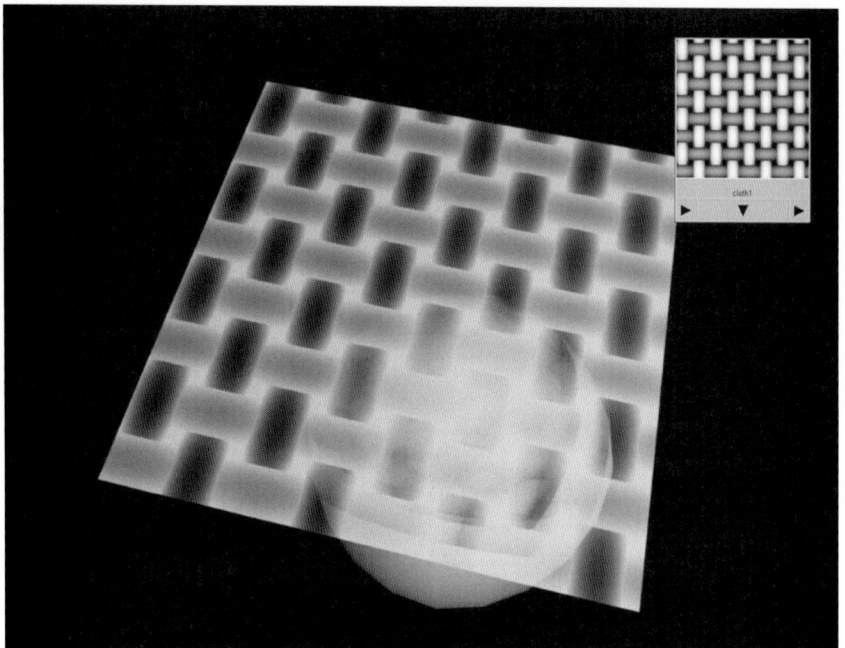

FIGURE 7.3 Using a texture map in the Transparency attribute can make parts of a surface render opaque, transparent, or semi-transparent.

Ambient Color: This is a fairly tricky attribute. Basically, it lets you change the color across all attributes of the material. This allows for quick lightening or tinting of the entire surface.

Incandescence: This is a sort of "inner light." It makes an object look illuminated. The problem is it tends to flatten out any interesting variations of the surface, giving you just the silhouette of the object. Also, this inner light only appears on the surface of the object to which the material is applied—it does not actually cast any light into the scene. It is usually best to stay away from this, unless you are texturing something like a light bulb.

Bump Mapping: This is the idea of painting a faux bump on a surface. When Maya renders the surface, it "paints" the surface to look as though there are bumps in the geometry even though there are none. This is an important distinction. Figure 7.4 shows a sphere that appears to have a mighty bump. However, when the sphere is seen closer, notice that the edge (outline of the shape) is still smooth with no actual change in the geometry.

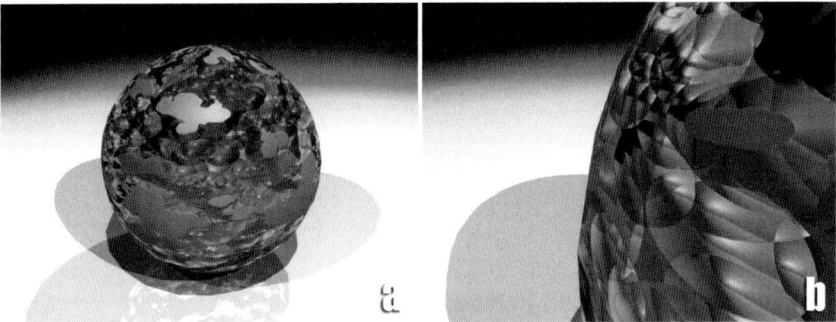

FIGURE 7.4 (a–b)   Bump maps only paint the surface to look bumpy. There is actually no change to the geometry.

Diffuse: Think of this as a dirt layer. Yes, this is over simplified but the idea is sound—you can set up any of the color, incandescence, and other attributes you wish to use and then with an active diffuse attribute with a texture map, you can layer a bit of dirt over everything making computer renderings less "computery." We will cover much more of this later in the chapter.

Translucence: This is fairly new to Maya (Version 4 or so). It is a very nice attribute to have. Think of rice paper in a traditional Japanese room. From the outside, you can see the shadows of the people inside through the paper walls. You cannot see the people—the walls are not transparent—but you can see the shadows. Figure 7.5 shows two planes; the one on the left is transparent and the one on the right is translucent. Notice how the light continues to pass through the translucent plane.

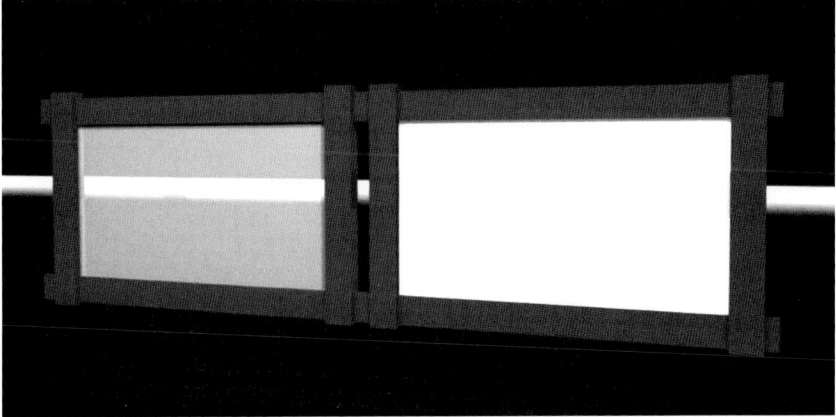

FIGURE 7.5   The plane on the right is using translucency, which allows light to pass through the object without allowing you to see through it.

Glow: It is interesting that this is a common attribute among the different material types, especially for Lambert. It will make any surface glow. Remember that this glow is a post-rendering effect. That means Maya paints it on after it has finished rendering or calculating how the light rays work. That means a glowing object will not appear to glow in reflections (Figure 7.6).

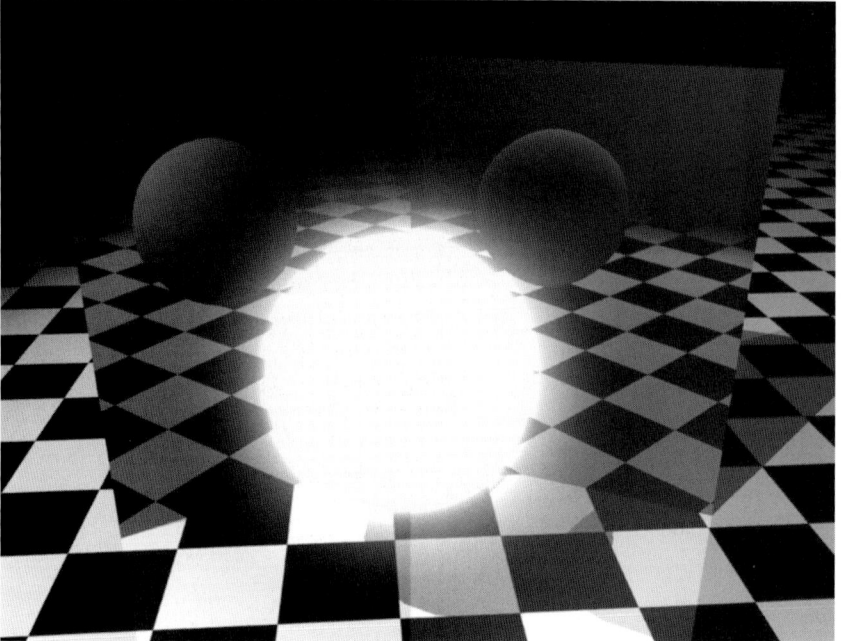

FIGURE 7.6   Because glow is a post-rendering effect, it will not show up in reflected surfaces.

Now, of course there are other attributes for each specific type of material. Some are related to the general common attributes listed earlier in this section and some are very specific to the nature of that material. As we work through the tutorials to follow, we will be looking at how to manipulate and use many of the attributes of all the materials.

TEXTURE CREATION AND EDITING

Like most of Maya, there are multiple ways to work with materials and Shaders. However, most of the core work with materials takes place inside something called the Hypershade, which is kind of like a texture workshop. Within this editor, you can create new materials, decide how materials are organized or interconnected, and change how materials are applied to surfaces.

To pull up the Hypershade editor, select Window > Rendering Editors > _Hypershade. This brings up the Hypershade editor as a floating window. You can also access the Hypershade by selecting the Hypershade/Persp layout (Figure 7.7).

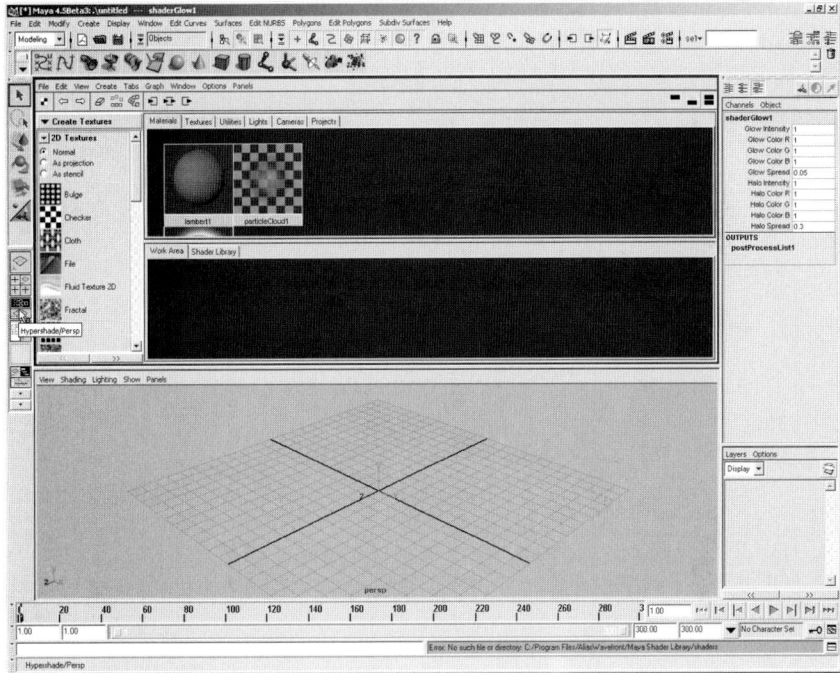

FIGURE 7.7   Bringing up the Hypershade using preset layouts.

Figure 7.8 shows the Hypershade as a free window, which is how most animators like to work with it.

Besides the pull-down menus along the top, the Hypershade essentially has four areas of interest. The first is the row of buttons immediately under the pull-down menus. These buttons primarily are involved with how the Hypershade is shown or organized. We will not go over all these tools here, although we will use them intermittently through the course of the tutorials.

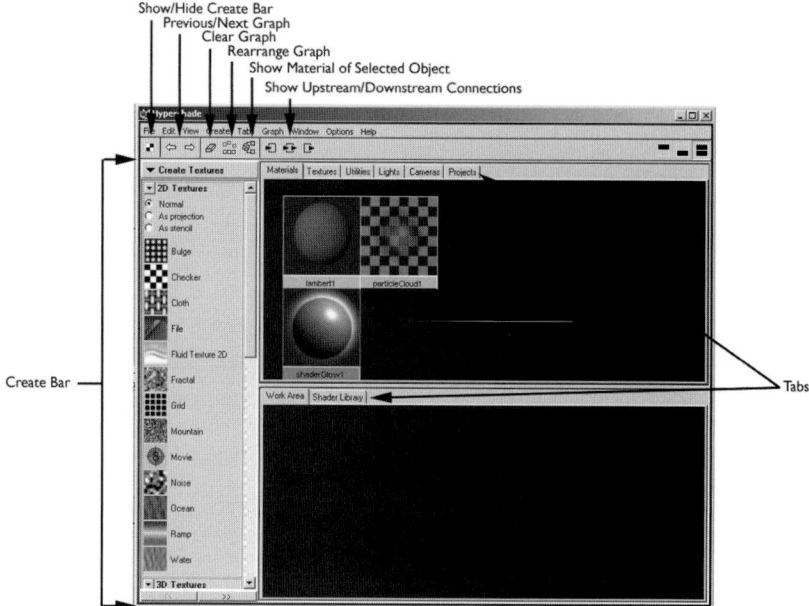

Show/Hide Create Bar
Previous/Next Graph
Clear Graph
Rearrange Graph
Show Material of Selected Object
Show Upstream/Downstream Connections

Create Bar

Tabs

FIGURE 7.8   The Hypershade window.

The second area is the Create Bar (the area to the left) that allows you to create, or (more accurately) activate, textures or materials. To the right of the Create Bar are two areas with tabs along the top. The organization here has always seemed a bit strange, but you can think of the top area as a sort of shelf. Notice that there are several tabs for different types of things (Materials, Textures, Utilities, Lights, Cameras, and Projects). These are different shelves of things that you may use at different times but that stay out of the way until you bring them down onto your workbench. The bottom area also has a library (the Shader library) but more important, it has the Work Area.

The Work Area is the workbench of this texture workshop. You can bring things from the shelf above down to the workbench when you want to use them. Most of what you do in the Hypershade will actually be done here in the Work Area. Keeping control of how this area is organized and its accessibility will greatly enhance your material building experience.

A final note on the Hypershade. One very interesting and effective part of Maya's work flow is the consistency of functions such as moving, rotating, and scaling your view. When you are working within the Workspace, you can use combinations of **Alt**-Mouse button to move, rotate, or dolly in on your scene. **Alt**-LMMB-drag (that is left and middle mouse buttons) will make the swatches in both the top and bottom tab areas smaller or larger. Think of it as moving a camera that is looking at the swatches closer or farther away rather than resizing anything within the Hypershade area.

So, enough talk. Now that we have the metaphor of a workshop worked out, we can actually get to work.

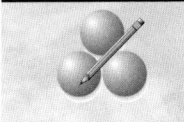

TUTORIAL 7.1   **TEXTURING THE ROOM**

After the brief modeling respite we had in Chapter 6, we are back to working with our room. In the course of this tutorial, we will be laying down the materials on the surfaces we created in earlier tutorials to bring the room out of the drab gray plastic world it is in now. This should be a fun process and one that leaves a lot of room for interpretation. If you do not like the green walls, change the color. Indeed, as we deal with most colors, there will be no call-out for exact numerical values for colors. Green can be almost any green you like.

ON THE CD

Along this same vein, the images in the book are in black and white (as you have undoubtedly noticed). Unfortunately, effective texturing is largely dependent on color. Because of this, make sure you take time to look at the color versions of all the images of this chapter. The images, in full-colored splendor, are on the included CD-ROM in the folder, Images/Chapter07. Also remember that the finished file that makes up this tutorial is included on the CD-ROM and can be a valuable resource if you get stuck.

Step 1: Open the modeled room. Wherever you have set up the room project, go to the scenes folder and open your room thus far. You may or may not have added other props; for this tutorial, we will just texture some of the objects we built through the course of the earlier tutorials. Make sure that as you learn, you expand out to include your newfound skills on other things in the scene.

Step 2: Set up your working space. Make sure that the Hypershade editor is open (Window > Rendering Editors > Hypershade). Or, to mount everything together, which is the view we will use for these tutorials, select Window > Saved Layouts > Hypershade/Persp. The result should look something like Figure 7.9.

Finally, make sure your Outliner is visible (Window > Outliner). It will be an important tool to have when we need to apply materials to surfaces.

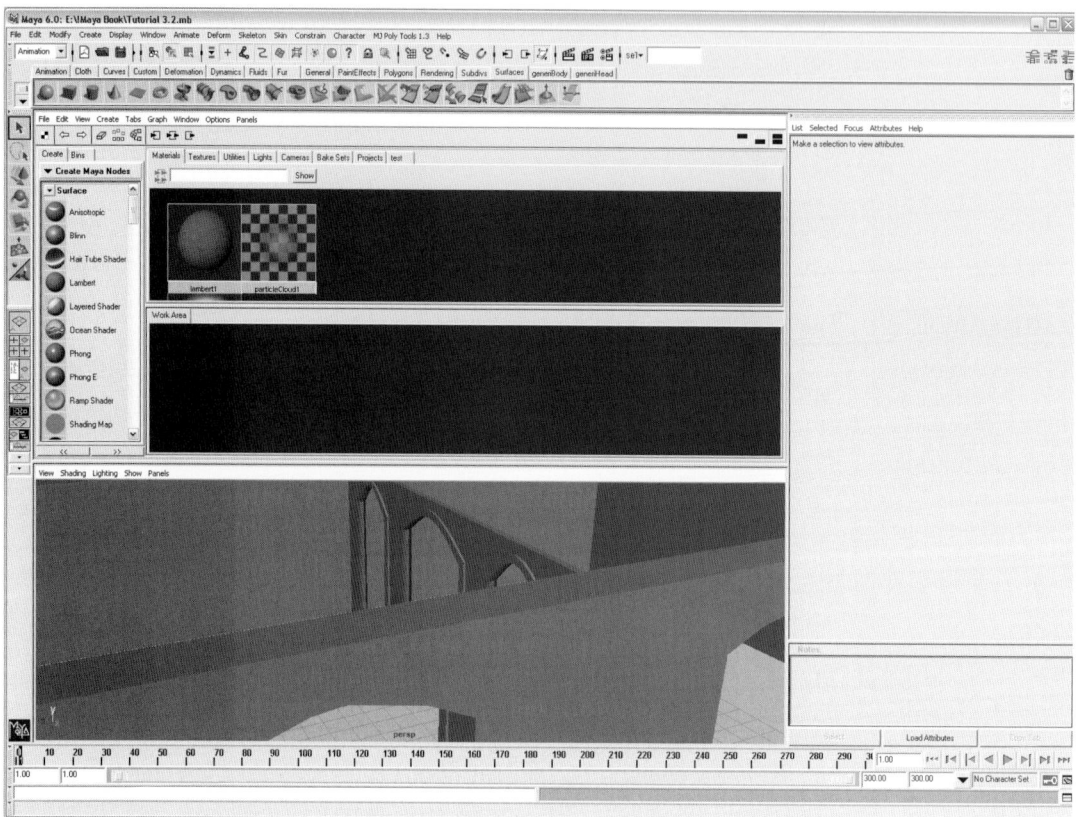

FIGURE 7.9 The Hypershade/Persp gives you the Hypershade, a perspective view, and a space for your Channel Box (or later, your Attribute Editor). All are important for the material creation process.

Step 3: Shift the Hypershade's organization. Your Hypershade's Create Bar probably shows Create Textures at the top, while Figure 7.9 shows Create Materials. LMB-click on Create Textures and choose Create Materials from the pop-down menu. This gives you a quick visual representation of the possible materials that are available.

Next, put your mouse on the top tab area and **Alt**-LMMB-drag to the left so that those swatches are smaller. For now, we want to be able to see all the extant materials.

Step 4: Create a new Lambert material. There are actually several ways to do this. For this step, select Create > Materials > Lambert from the pull-down menus within the Hypershade Editor.

This will do a couple of things. First, a new swatch with the word lambert2 will appear in the Work Area. Also notice that a new swatch (highlighted in yellow) appears in the top Material tab as well. Essentially, creating the new material places it on your Shelf and puts it on your workbench so that you can work with it. At various times, we will clear the workbench, but the materials created there will remain on the Materials tab (Shelf) above, in case you need to take it down and work with it again.

Step 5: Rename the material. Double-click the lambert2 swatch in the Work Area. This indicates to Maya that you want to work with this particular material, so you will be presented with the Attributes Editor on the right (where the Channel Box was). This Attributes Editor is a fairly important window and one that we will be working with quite a bit over the course of this tutorial. For this step, there is an input field at the top called lambert. Change the name from lambert2 to Walls_Material (Figure 7.10).

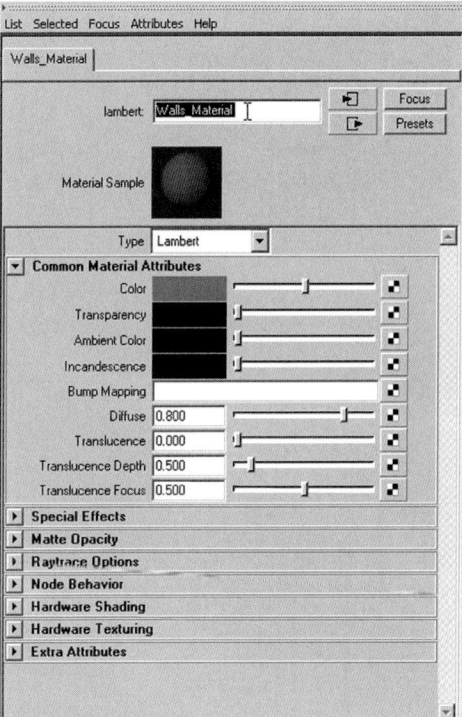

FIGURE 7.10   Opening the Attributes Editor and renaming the new texture to Walls_Material.

Although the name is largely arbitrary, it is always helpful to be as indicative as you can. Name objects and materials as you go along so that you can find them again quickly when the need arises.

Step 6: Change the color of Walls_Material to green. In the Attributes Editor, there are several areas that allow you to define the attributes of this material. By default, the Common Material Attributes area should be expanded revealing a collection of sliders, swatches, and buttons.

The first will be Color followed by a gray box. Click once on this gray box, and a color picker window will open (a slightly different color picker for the Mac and PC). Use the picker to choose a green color (the example uses kind of an olive) as shown in Figure 7.11. Hit Accept (or OK).

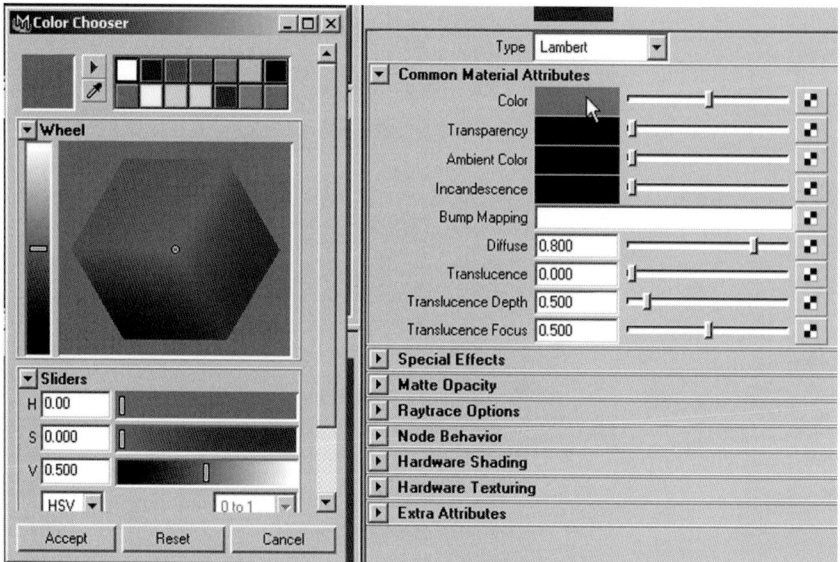

FIGURE 7.11   Choosing a new color for the Color attribute. (This screenshot shows the interface on a PC.)

Now, your Attribute Editor should have a different color than gray next to the word Color. In addition, the swatch in both the Materials area (top tab) and the Work Area (bottom tab) should reflect this new alteration in the Color attribute.

Step 7: Hide the layer Ceiling_Floor. Show the Channel Box/Layer Editor (using the button shown in Figure 7.12). This hides the Attribute Editor, but not to worry; we will get it back when we need it. Hit the visibility button for the layer, Ceiling_Floor, to hide those objects. This will make it much easier for us to see what we do.

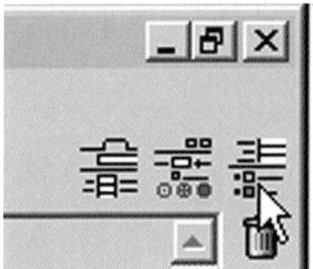

FIGURE 7.12   The Show Channel
Box/Layer Editor button.

Step 8: Apply the material, Walls_Material, to the south wall. In
the Outliner should be a group called WallSouth_Group. Select Wall-
South_Group in the Outliner, and then in the Work Area of the Hypershade editor, RMB-click-hold on the Walls_Material and select Assign
Material to Selection.

Tumble your view in the Perspective view so you can see the wall.
This will place this material on the entire group—wall, trim, and everything (Figure 7.13). It is important to notice that when a material is
placed on an object or group, the children of that group also inherit the
material. We will look at how to override this in a bit.

Your Perspective view should appear something like Figure 7.13. Hit
3 and **6** to make sure that you are seeing things shaded with the materials applied to them.

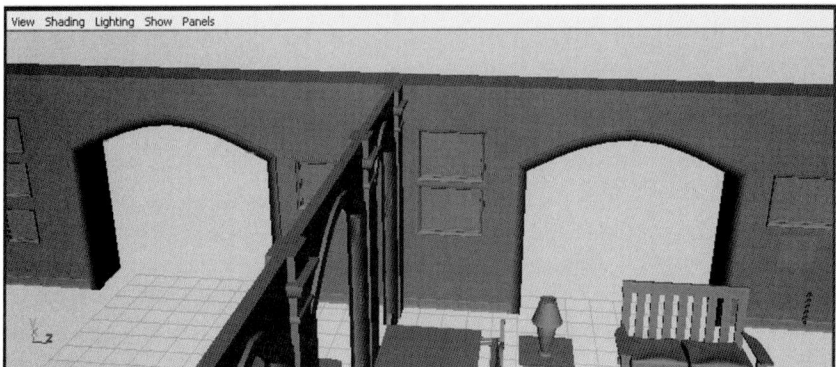

FIGURE 7.13   Results of applying a material to a group.

Step 9: Apply the material, Walls_Material, to the east wall. Besides the method described earlier, you can assign materials to objects or groups by MMB-dragging. Tumble your view around so that you can see the wall on the east side. This time, MMB-drag Walls_Material from the Work Area onto the wall. The mouse will change to include a small plus sign (+). As soon as you release the MMB, the entire group of the east wall will be green as well.

Step 10: Apply Walls_Material to the rest of the walls. Using whichever method you prefer, apply the material to all the other walls in the scene, including the wall in the middle of the room.

Step 11: Adjust Render Settings to allow for useful, targeted renderings. We are going to cover much, much more about rendering in the next chapters; however, as we work with materials, it will be important to be able to render on occasion. So, we are going to set up things briefly to give us a chance to perform some occasional renderings.

Figure 7.14 shows the three rendering buttons on the Status Line. The one on the far right, Display Render Globals window, allows you to change the settings for how Maya renders your scene. Click this button. When the Render Globals window opens, we will change just one thing for now. Expand the Resolution section. By default, Maya renders out to a small, nearly unusable 320x240 image. For now, change these setting to Width = 800 and Height = 300. You may need to adjust this if you have a smaller monitor. Hit the Close button to save the new settings. This will render the scene out into long thin images that are big enough to actually see what is going on.

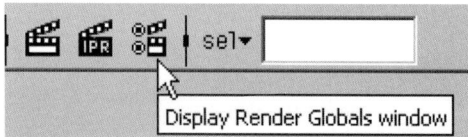

FIGURE 7.14   The Rendering buttons of the Status Line.

Step 12: Tumble and dolly into position and take a quick rendering. Figure 7.15 shows a close-up of the southwest corner of the room. Move your camera in the Perspective view to match roughly and hit the Render the Current Frame button (the left button shown in Figure 7.14).

A new window will pop up called the Render view. Within this window, Maya will render or draw the scene with the materials created so far. Notice that because we have not created any light sources, Maya is

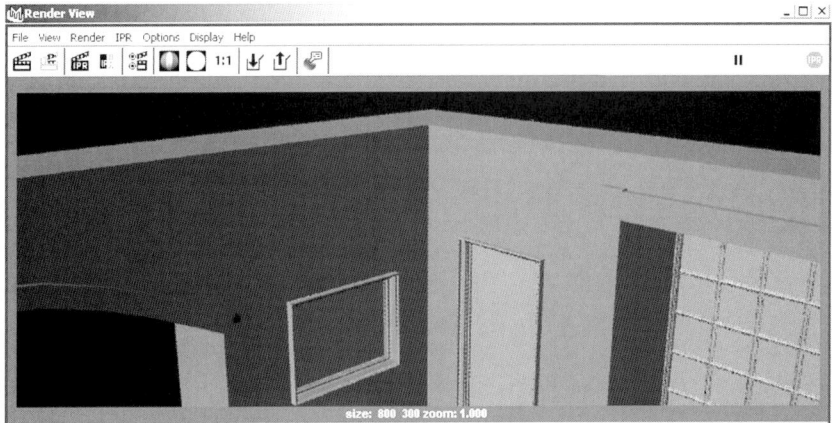

FIGURE 7.15   Close-up of the southwest corner of the room in the Render view.

functioning with the assumption that there is a large floodlight immediately above the virtual camera through which you are looking.

At this point, the rendered view looks very similar to what is seen in the Workspace. However, as we begin to alter attributes further, the difference between the two will increase fairly dramatically.

Step 13: Add bump to the Wall_Material. Well, the walls are currently definitely green, but that's about it. To give these walls a bit more interest, we will be working with a few more of the attributes to spice things up, dirty things down, and make things look a bit more "real."

Double-click Walls_Material again in the Work Area; this will open the Attribute Editor. The fifth attribute down is Bump Mapping. This is noticeably different than the other attributes as it has no slider. This is because a bump map will only work if it has a map to work with.

Basically, the way Bump Mapping works is Maya looks at an image and renders the parts closest to white as raised and those closest to black as flat (or they can be receded). Although color images can also be used as bump maps, grayscale images are usually the most effective.

To tell Walls_Material what to use for its bump map, hit the checkered button on the far right. This will open a new window called the Create Render Node. What we are doing here is adding a node to the material. This node will change the appearance of the material and will remain very flexible. As we edit the node (in this case, the bump map), the material will update as well.

Notice that the Textures tab is highlighted within this window. Maya understands that you will need to place a texture as the bump map. For these walls, we will use Brownian located under the 3D Textures area. Click on Brownian and the Create Render Node will automatically close.

The Work Area will suddenly contain many new swatches. These swatches represent nodes and texture maps that are attached to the material, Walls_Material. Notice that there are a variety of arrows drawn between all the swatches.

The problem is that often when a new map/node is created, the organization of the Work Area becomes hectic at best (Figure 7.16a). To fix up things a bit, hit the Rearrange Graph button at the top of the Hypershade window (Figure 7.16b).

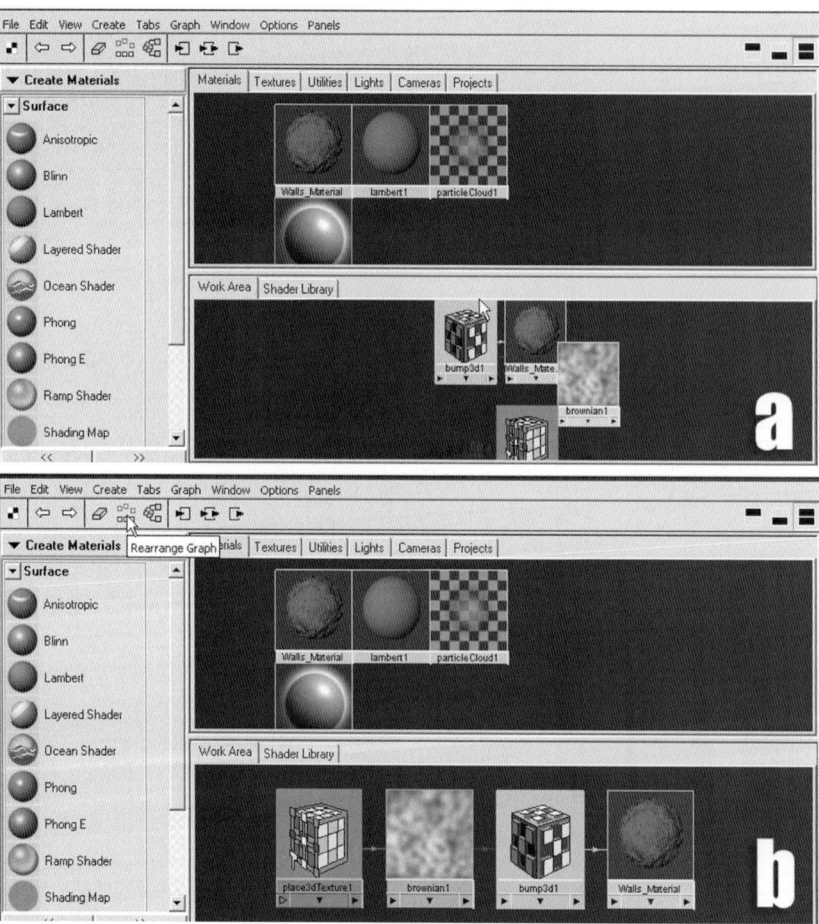

FIGURE 7.16   (a) Newly created nodes and textures can leave a messy Work Area. (b) Using the Rearrange Graph button puts things back into place.

Let's take a second to discuss what each node/texture means.

Notice that at the far right is the final output (Walls_Material) of a collection of inputs. The first input (place3dtexture1) has to do with how the texture is going to be placed on the object. If you click the place3Dtexture1 swatch, the Attributes Editor will change to match Figure 7.17a. This window allows you to adjust the position, size, or rotation of the texture.

Similarly, if you click the brownian1 swatch, Figure 7.17c will appear in the Attributes Editor. This allows you to change things about the procedural (mathematically generated, not an image) texture. This will be slightly different for each procedural texture and different still when the texture is actually an image.

The next swatch, bump3d1, will produce an Attributes Editor window similar to Figure 7.17b and will allow you to do things such as control how high the bump will be.

Don't worry too much about the details of each node for now. We will cover many of them in steps to come. It is important to notice that they are all related and that they feed linearly into the final material, Walls_Material.

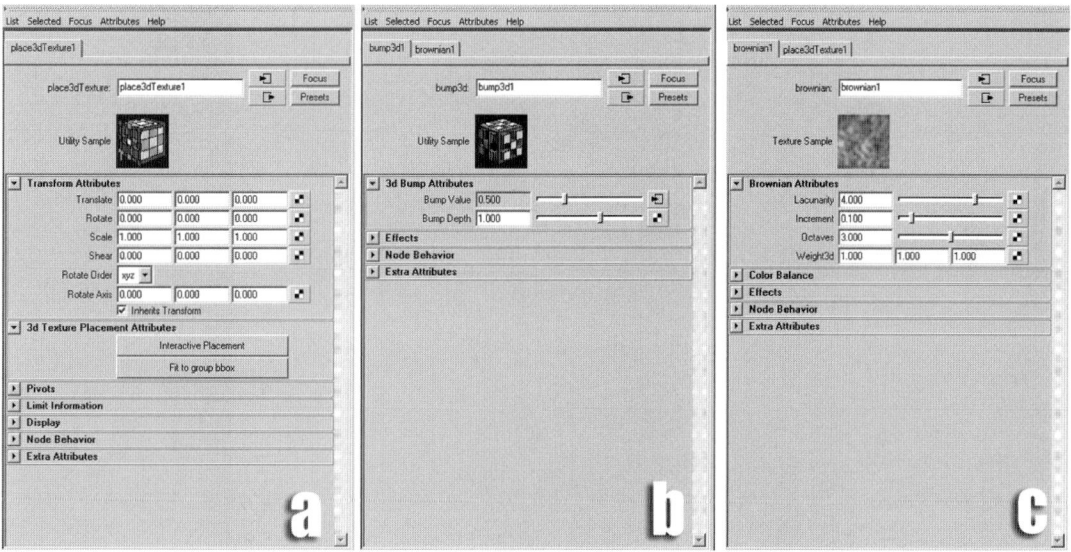

FIGURE 7.17 (a–c)   The nodes created by adding a bump map to the material, Walls_Materials, are all editable and allow you to control various parts of how a material will ultimately look by affecting the textures that make up the material.

Step 14: Render to see the effects of the new bump. Hit the Render the Current Frame button to render out the corner (Figure 7.18). Bump seems a bit too intense, no?

The important thing to notice here is that when we adjusted the material in the Hypershade, all the places where the material had been applied were updated automatically to reflect the changes.

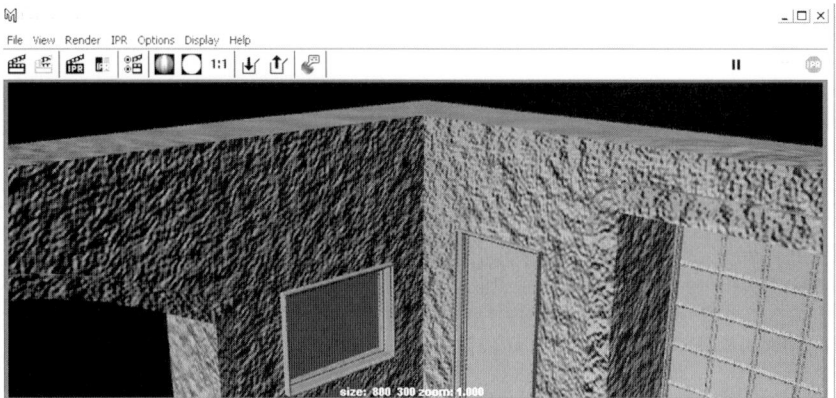

FIGURE 7.18   Rendered corner with new bump map applied.

Step 15: Adjust the height of the bump. The bump is a bit too intense. So, we need to reduce the depth of the bump map. To do this, click on the bump3d1 swatch in the Work Area. In the attributes window, change the Bump Depth to 0.100. You can do this with the slider or by entering the value numerically. Figure 7.19 shows the results.

Now we're getting closer. But still, the bump seems a bit too big on the surface.

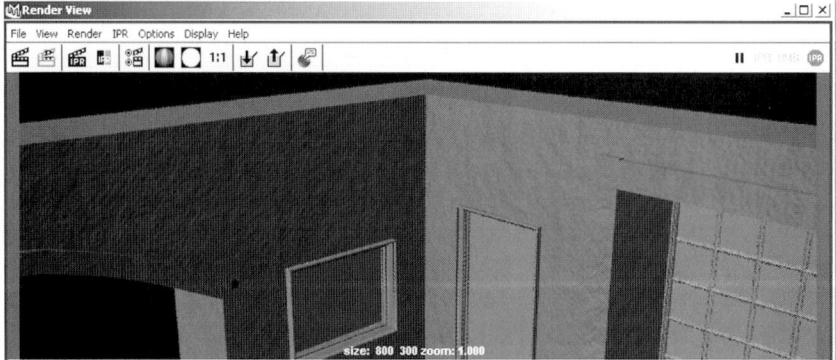

FIGURE 7.19   Reduced Bump Depth provides a more gentle bump.

Step 16: Adjust the size of the placement. To make the size of the bump a bit smaller, we will edit the place3dTexture1 node. Click its swatch in the Work Area. In the Attributes Manager, we now have control over how the texture is to be placed on the surface. As usual, there are three columns represented by the X, Y, and Z. Change the settings for Scale in the X, Y, and Z columns to 0.600.

Take another render (Figure 7.20) to see how close you are getting. If you still feel like the bump needs adjusting, go ahead and do so to taste.

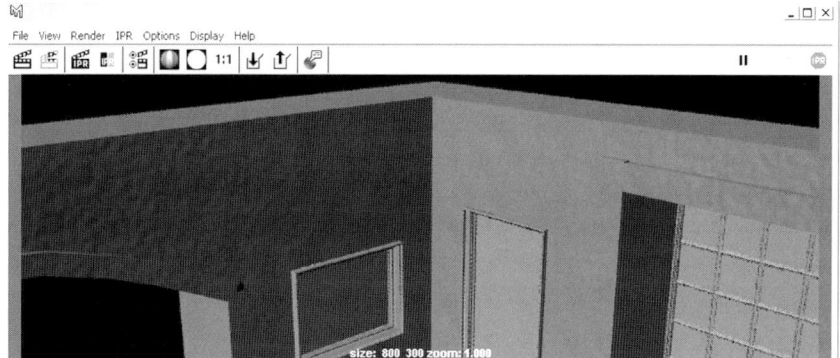

FIGURE 7.20   Bump adjusted in size through the placement node (place3dTexture1).

Step 17: Create a white painted wood material for trim. Last time, we created a new material through the Create pull-down menu in the Hypershade. This time, we will do it by MMB-dragging the Blinn icon from the Create Bar area into the Work Area. The benefit of doing this is you can choose where to place this new material. Select it in the Work Area and rename it WoodTrim_Material.

Change the color to a white shade by moving the slider to the right in the Attribute Editor on the Color attribute.

We will assume that this wood was a satin paint. This means that the specular highlight will be broad but not too shiny. We used a Blinn material because it allows us to work with the specular highlights.

Make sure that the Specular Shading area of the Attributes Editor is open. The Eccentricity setting has to do with how small the highlight is. Smaller values make for smaller highlights. The Specular Roll Off allows you to define how bright the highlight is. For now, change the Eccentricity setting to 0.500 and the Specular Roll Off to 0.300.

Notice that you can also define things such as the color of that highlight. We will change this setting later when we are working with metallic surfaces.

Step 18: Apply this material to floorboards, crown molding, trim, window trims, columns, ceiling, and crossbeams. This step will take a while. There are an awful lot of objects in the scene that need this white wood trim. Basically, everything but the walls, floor, furniture, and pictures on the wall should have this white material applied to it.

You can select many objects directly in the Workspace, then RMB-click-hold WoodTrim_Material, and select Assign Material to Selection. Remember that you can select an object in the Workspace and then hit the **Up Arrow** to move your selection up a hierarchical chain. So, for instance, you could make the Ceiling_Floor layer visible and select one crossbeam. Then, hit the **Up Arrow** key and your selection will expand to include the group that the crossbeam is in. You can then apply the material to the entire group.

You can also search out the needed objects in the Outliner, select them there, and then choose Assign Material to Selection in the Hypershade. Lastly, you can MMB-drag the material, WoodTrim_Material, to an object in the Workspace to apply it.

Notice that previously green trim changes to white when a new material is applied to it, thus overwriting the material that was applied to the group or parent of which the trim is a child.

Figure 7.21 illustrates the Workspace with the appropriate material applied in all the needed places. Notice that there are some problems—namely, the windows (including the glass) are painted white. Not to fear; we will fix that in a bit.

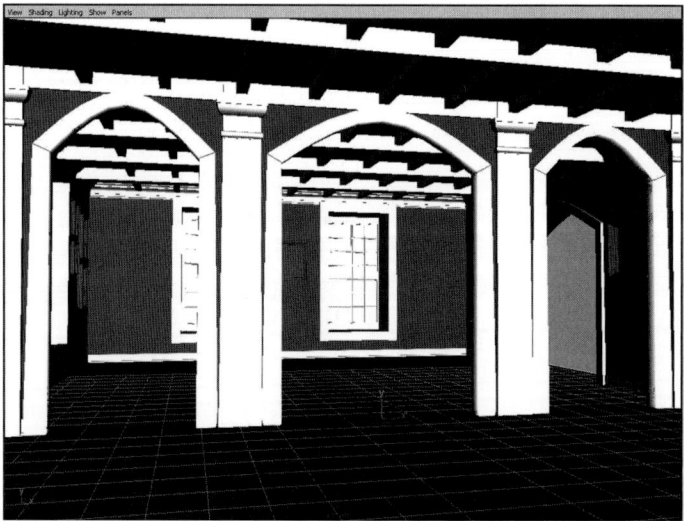

FIGURE 7.21   White applied to all the trim in the room.

Step 19: Create a new painted wood texture by duplicating the existing the WoodTrim_Material. That's right, duplicating works with materials, too. Select WoodTrim_Material in the Work Area and hit **Ctrl-D**. If you get an error, make sure you reset the settings for the duplicate.

Notice that this new material is called WoodTrim_Material1 (make sure you double-click the material in the Work Area). Rename it FrameTrim_Material.

Step 20: Change the color and highlights of FrameTrim_Material. The frames in the room are a dark red. Click on the wide box next to the Color attribute and select a new dark red color.

For this wood, we want it to look like high-gloss paint. So, in the Specular Shading section of the Attributes Editor, change the Eccentricity setting to 0.200 and the Specular Roll Off to 3.00. This will make a small, bright highlight. Notice that by default the Specular Roll Off slider will only slide to 1. By entering 3.00 in the input field, we hyper-extend the value. This trick works often for textures to give you a bit of a boost.

Finally, you may wish to change the Specular Color to a light brown so that the gloss is not quite so intense (Figure 7.22).

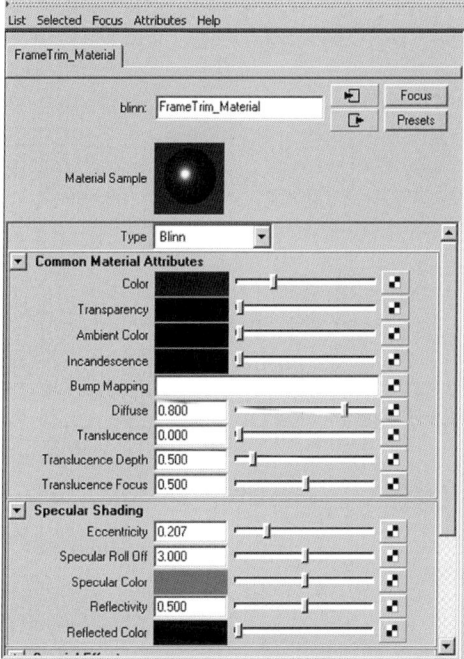

FIGURE 7.22   The Attributes Editor for FrameTrim_Material.

Step 21: Apply this new material to all the frames in the room. If you have all the frames grouped together, you can select the frames group in the Outliner and assign FrameTrim_Material to everything in one swoop. Do not worry that the pictures in the frames are also dark red; we will fix that later (Figure 7.23).

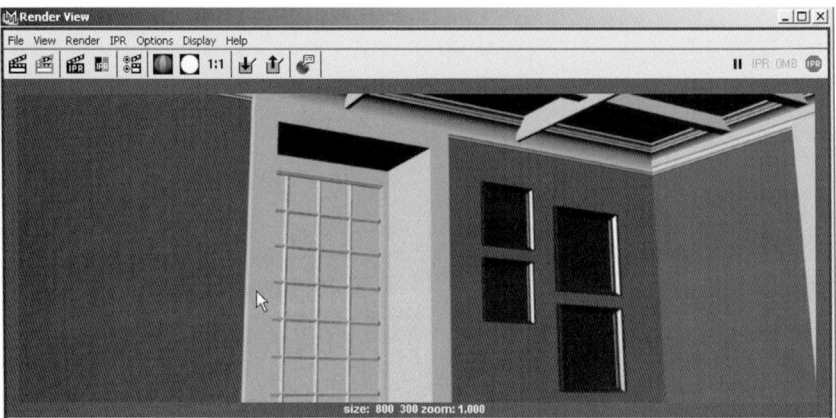

FIGURE 7.23   Frames with the newly duplicated FrameTrim_Material.

Step 22: Create a glass material for the windows. Create a new material by dragging Phong from the Create Bar area into the Work Area. You may want to hit the Rearrange Graph button at the top of the Hypershade to clean up your Work Area.

Double-click the new Phong material in the Work Area to open it in the Attribute Editor. The key to glass is creating a material that has no color, high transparency, and some reflectivity.

To do this, use the sliders for Color and slide it completely to the right, making the color box black. Next, slide the Transparency slider completely to the right. This will change the preview box at the top of the Attribute Editor so that there is a checkered background behind the material. This is there to help you visualize the new characteristics of the material.

Now, to cheat a little bit, we are going to apply just a bit of a tint to things seen through the glass. Although true glass has no color, for illustration purposes, we will view the world through blue-tinted glass. To do this, click on the Transparency color box and select a very, very light blue. This will help us see the glass a bit better.

Finally, in the Specular Shading area, Change the Reflectivity to 0.700.

Step 23: Apply this WindowGlass_Material to all the glass panes. Remember that you do not want to apply this material to the entire window, just the pane. It is easiest to just tumble around your scene to see each window and MMB-drag WindowGlass_Material onto the pane.

Step 24: Render the scene. You will notice that when the scene is rendered, you can suddenly see through the windows to the black outside (Figure 7.24). However, there is no reflection even though we told the glass to reflect its surrounding. This has to do with how Maya is rendering the scene.

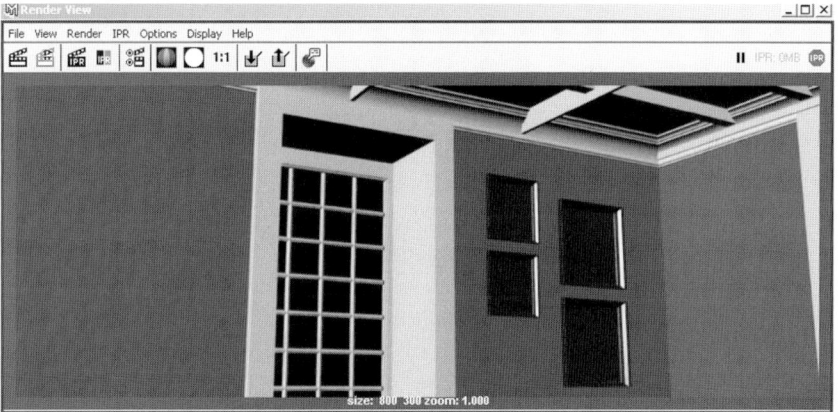

FIGURE 7.24   Rendered scene shows transparent glass but no reflections.

To get reflections, you must use Raytracing for the rendering engine. Raytracing is a more accurate rendering algorithm than the default Maya renderer, but it is also quite a bit slower. We will be talking much more about specifics of Raytracing later. For now, suffice it to say, we need to turn on Raytracing.

Step 25: Activate Raytracing. Open the Render Globals window (click the far-right button of the bank of rendering buttons in the Status Line). There are a lot of different sections of this window, so look carefully for Raytracing Quality. Expand this and, for now, check the Raytracing option.

Do not worry about any of the sliders contained in this section; for now, having Raytracing on is enough. Hit Close to save the changes.

Step 26: Render the scene. Again, hit the Render the Current Frame button. Take a quick break and come back because Raytracing can be a slow process.

The results in Figure 7.25 show reflections alright. The problem is that although the window with the material, WindowGlass_Material, is reflecting, so are all the woods in the room.

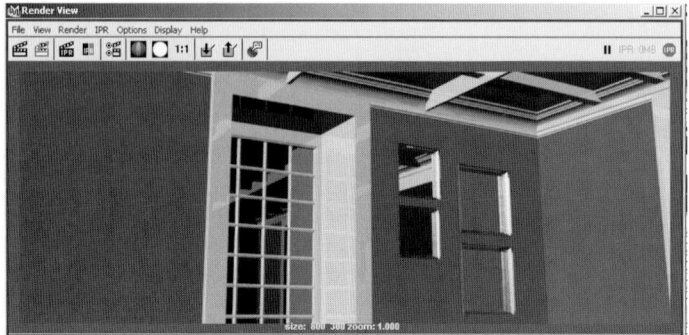

FIGURE 7.25 Raytracing activates reflection; unfortunately, things are reflecting that should not be.

This is happening because Blinn, Phong, and PhongE all have Reflectivity active automatically. Select WoodTrim_Material in the Work Area and in the Attribute Editor, notice that within the Specular Shading section, Reflectivity is set at 0.500 even though we never activated it.

Step 27: Deactivate reflectivity for WoodTrim_Material and FrameTrim_Material. Simply select each material (one at a time) and in the Attribute Editor, pull the Reflectivity slider to 0.

Step 28: Render again. This time when you render, the window will show the reflection of the trim around it in a more believable fashion. Additionally, the wood trim and frames no longer reflect (Figure 7.26).

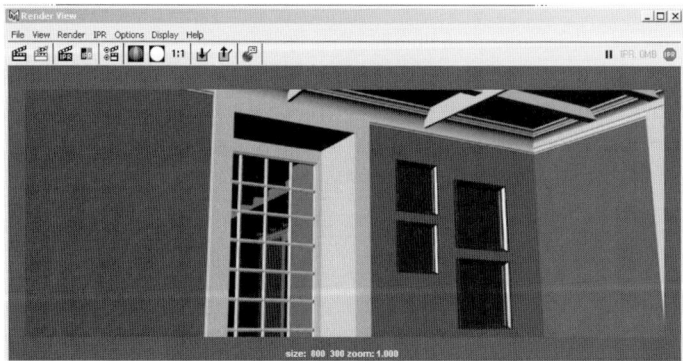

FIGURE 7.26 After adjusting the Reflectivity settings, the glass panes reflect but the wood does not.

Step 29: Turn off Raytracing. For now, open the Render Globals window again and deactivate Raytracing. For the kind of construction that we are going to be doing in the next chapter, we will want a speedier rendering than what Raytracing will provide. Remember, ultimately, we will want to raytrace the room, so keep a careful eye open that the Reflectivity setting is indeed at 0 as we create new materials.

CONCLUSION

We just barely got started on the powerful tools of textures in Maya, but in the next chapter we will be going over how to create custom texture maps. We will further detail how to control how a material is applied to a surface, and we will get to move into the artistry of materials more specifically by making our stale models works of art.

CUSTOM TEXTURE MAPS IN MATERIALS

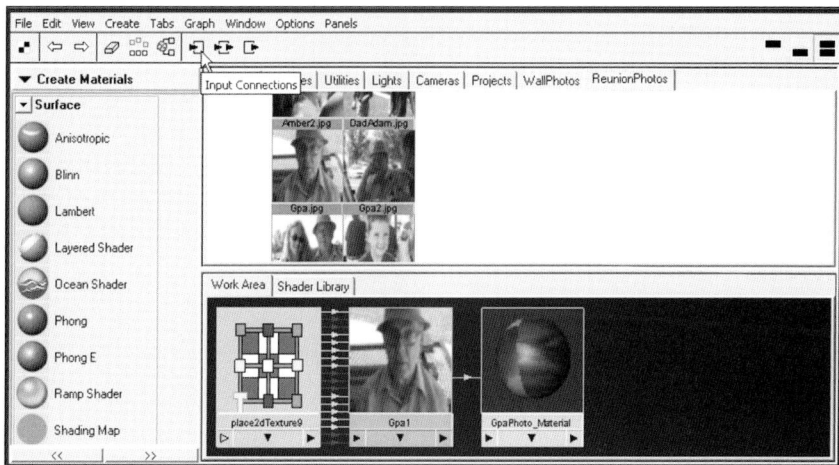

In the last chapter, we got a brief overview of how materials were created and a look at how they were edited. We talked about the Hypershade and how the workshop was organized. We looked at how to use sliders and solid colors to affect a material's color, bump, and transparency. We even looked at how to use a procedural texture to determine how the bump map was supposed to look.

In this chapter, we get away from simply moving around sliders and choosing default options. In this chapter, we get to construct materials that are based on photographs. We get to create materials that are much closer to photorealism than any canned material would ever be.

Because so much of the work done here will be using photographs, there is quite a bit of Photoshop work to do. As outlined in the Preface, we assume that you are fairly familiar with this tool as covering many details is really beyond the scope of this book. However, there are a few places where we will actually delve into the Adobe wonder and look at how to prepare texture maps for use in Maya.

After we have the texture maps prepared, we will import them into our materials and apply these materials to create believable woods, metals, hanging pictures, and other items.

| TUTORIAL 8.1 | **TEXTURING THE ROOM** |

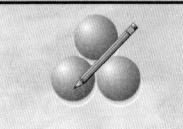

In this tutorial, we are going to continue to texture the room, as we left off in Chapter 7. We will put pictures in the frames and make the wood floor look like a floor. We will add texture to the furniture and make this room really look like it is part of the color age.

ON THE CD

Step 1: Move the folders within Tutorials/Chapter08/Textures into your own Textures directory. On the CD-ROM, we have been placing files that are finished steps of the tutorials. The CD-ROM also includes some image files that you can use for textures in this tutorial. Within the folder Tutorials/Chapter08/Textures, you will see several sub-folders. All these sub-folders contain some images.

Although you could access them within Maya directly from the CD-ROM, this is unadvisable. When Maya imports a texture into a material, it links only to where that texture is located. It does not import the actual file. So, if you are working on your room and you have been saving your scene files to your hard drive, and then you start pulling textures off a CD-ROM, that means that the CD-ROM must always be in its drive when you are working on the room. If not, when Maya gets ready to render and tries to collect the textures it needs, it will not be able to find the necesssary images.

So, you want to copy these textures to your hard drive where Maya will be able to consistently find them (at least as long as you are working with the room tutorials).

When you set up your project at the beginning of the whole room tutorial sequence, Maya created a large collection of folders for you. By default, when you tell Maya to save a new file, it tries to save it into the Scenes folder within the Project directory, although you can tell Maya to save elsewhere.

ON THE CD

Figure 8.1 shows the Project directory we have been using while constructing this tutorial. All the different versions of the room are housed within the scenes folder. However, the important part of that figure is the highlighted textures folder. When you can see all the folders of textures on the CD-ROM (in the directory Tutorials/ Chapter08/Textures/), drag all the folders into the folder called textures on your hard drive.

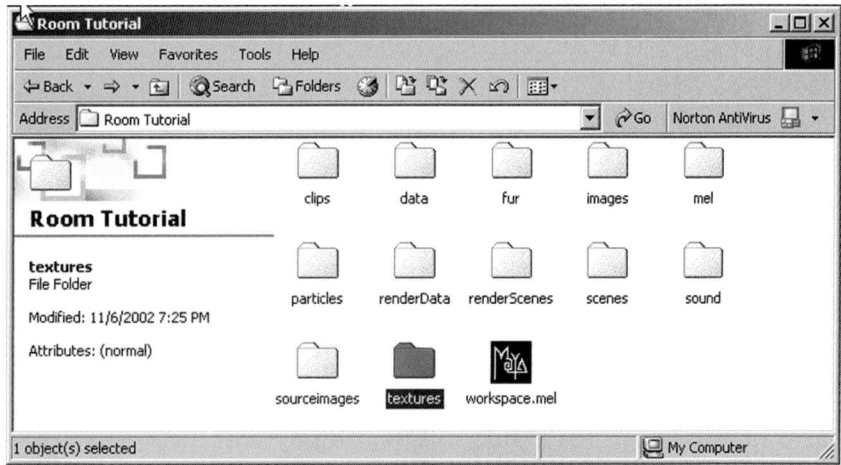

FIGURE 8.1   Project directory with the important textures folder.

You do not have to store textures in the textures folder. Doing so just keeps all the relevant files together, if you take the time to organize and save things in the folders Maya created for you when you first defined your project.

Step 2: Begin by opening the room you have built and textured so far.

Step 3: Organize your UI. Again, we will be doing a lot of work with the Hypershade, so make sure you are using the UI layout Hypershade/ Persp (Window > Saved Layouts > Hypershade/Persp).

Step 4: Clear out the Work Area. We will talk much more about the details of this a little later in the chapter and you might not need to do this step at all. If you did not exit Maya since the last time we worked, your Work Area is probably getting to be pretty messy. We could re-arrange things or even clean them up, but for now, let's clear it. RMB-click-hold on any black part of the Work Area and select Graph > Clear Graph from the pop-down menu. You will be left with a clear, black Work Area.

If you have closed your room and come back to it at the beginning of this tutorial, when you open the room scene again, the Work Area will be clean automatically; Maya cleans off your workbench between sessions.

Step 5: Tumble around your room until you are focused in on any one frame. The exact frame is unimportant; if your room is like the one shown in Figure 8.2, you probably have a lot of frames so you will have plenty of practice placing the needed textures.

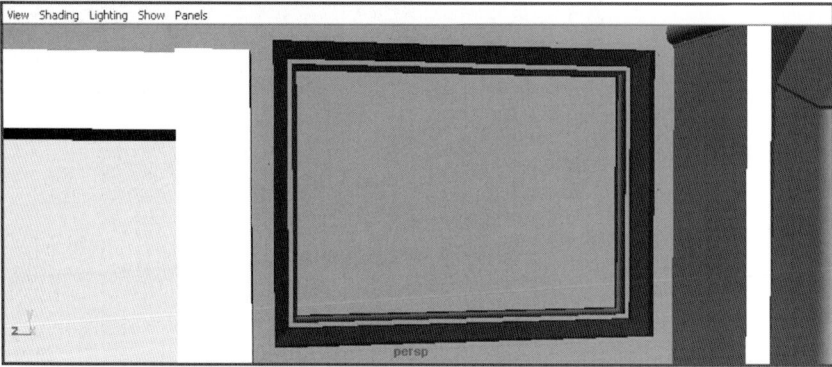

FIGURE 8.2 Focused on one frame so we can see our work clearly.

For this first frame, use a frame that is horizontal in format. We will do some vertically formatted frames later.

Step 6: Import ReunionPhotos textures. Among the items you copied to your Textures directory is a folder called ReunionPhotos. These are the photos we will put on the walls of the room. Before we can use these images, we need Maya to recognize that we are going to use the images as textures. There are several ways to do this. We will look at a few of them here.

In the top tab area, we have been working primarily with the Materials tab. However, there are other tabs there, some of which we will discuss and some that are beyond the scope of this volume. The one of present importance is the Textures tab. Click that tab to activate it. Within an area beneath the tab should be the brownian1 texture that we used for the walls. All the tabs you use for your various materials will be stored here. So, we can also import materials into this space.

Interestingly enough, if you use File > Import (pull-down menu within the Hypershade) or RMB-click-hold and select Import, the result will simply show you the image. For instance, Figure 8.3 shows the image, Jake.jpg, that was selected through File > Import (Hypershade pull-down menu). Rather than importing the file into the Textures tab area, it just opens it in the Fcheck (an image/movie viewer within Maya). So, the most intuitive choice does not work.

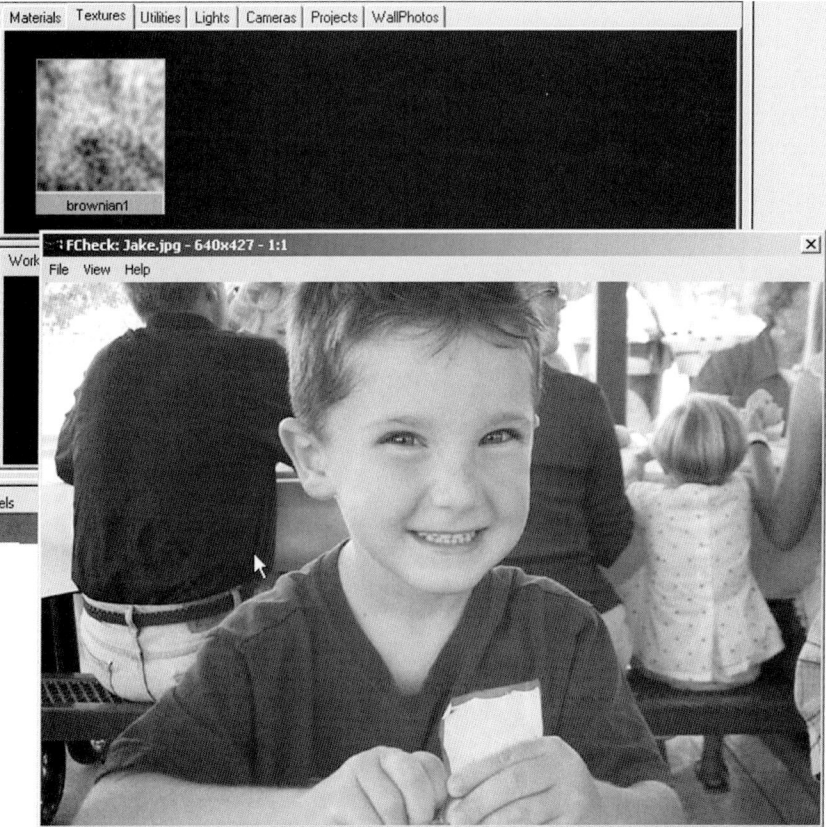

FIGURE 8.3   Using File > Import does not work. It simply opens an image into the Fcheck application.

However, Maya will interact with the Explorer (or Finder if you're on a Mac). Simply open the folder ReunionPhotos (from your own Textures folder) and LMB-drag the file Jake.jpg into the Textures tab area (Figure 8.4a). As soon as you do this, the image Jake.jpg will appear in a new swatch within the Textures tab area (Figure 8.4b).

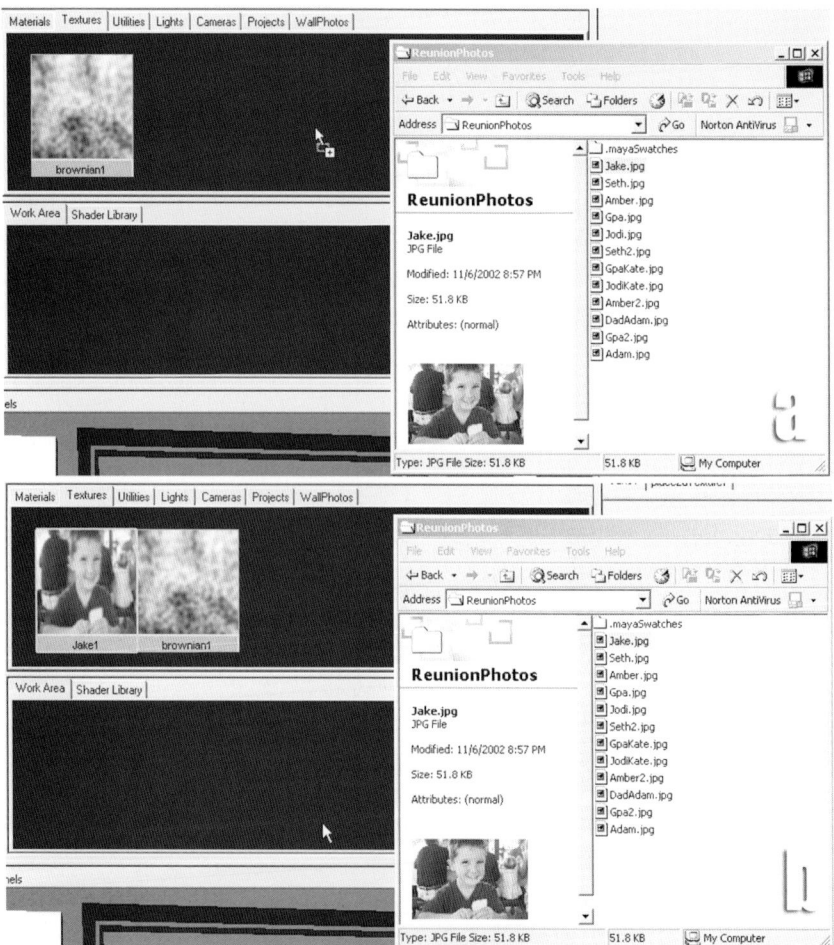

FIGURE 8.4 (a–b) One way to import images for use as textures is to drag them from their locations on your disk into the Textures tab area.

Dragging files to the Textures tab area is an effective method. You can even drag multiple files at once and they will all be imported as textures. But this can leave you with a huge amount of texture swatches all bunched up together in the Textures tab, thus making that Shelf kind of junky.

Instead, wouldn't it be nicer to create new shelves where we could store textures? Turns out, we can.

1. Within the Hypershade, go to Tabs > Create New Tabs to open a dialog box similar to the one shown in Figure 8.5a. There are many options available in this window, but let's stay focused on our task.

2. Change the New Tab Name to read ReunionPhotos. Although you can place a new tab in the Top or Bottom tab areas, it is often easiest to keep your Shelves above the workbench (the Work Area), so leave the Initial Placement at Top.

3. The Tab Type we want is Disk. This tells Maya we are going to create a new tab and that it will place the contents of a directory from a disk. You will notice that as soon as you do this, the bottom part of the dialog box changes to ask you where the Root Directory is (Figure 8.5b).

4. Click on the folder icon to tell Maya what directory to import. Find the folder ReunionPhotos within the Textures folder of your Project directory and hit **OK** (Figure 8.5c). Finally, click on the Only Show Files (Hide Directory Tree) option. This will keep our new shelf (tab) clean. Hit **Create** and you will have a new tab (Figure 8.6) with all the contents of the ReunionPhotos already imported into swatches.

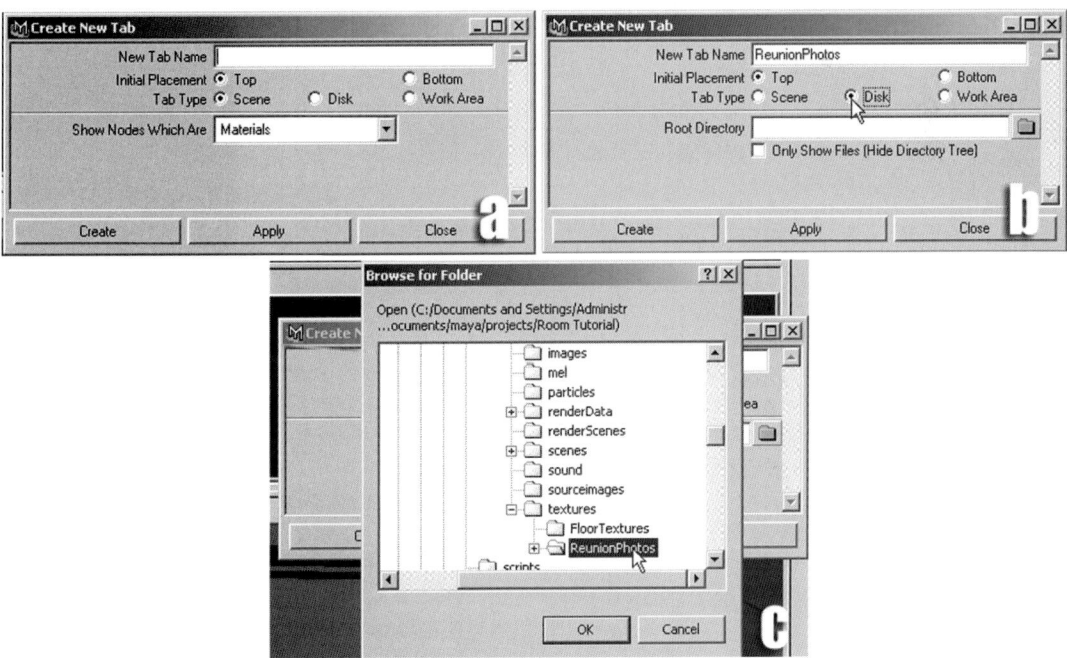

FIGURE 8.5 (a–c)   Creating a new tab with all the images we need for textures.

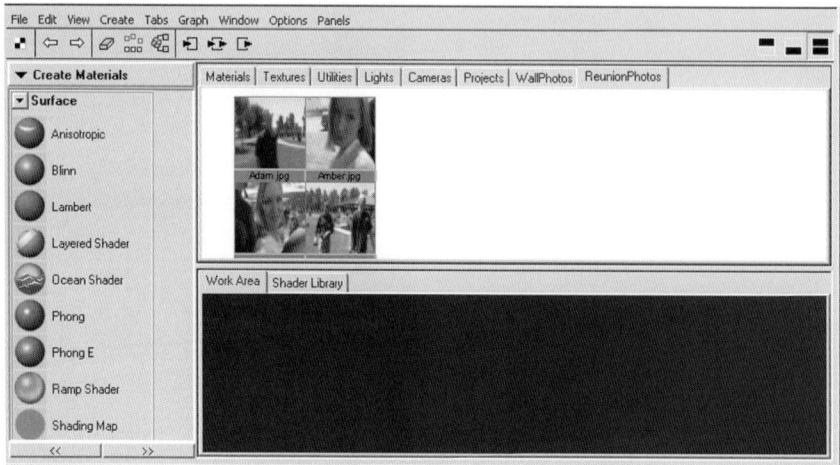

FIGURE 8.6 The newly created tab gives us an easy way to organize large collections of textures.

This is quite a convenient way to import everything in one swoop while keeping things organized.

Step 7: Create a new PhongE material. As a review, you can do this by selecting the Hypershades Create > Materials > PhongE or by MMB-dragging the materials from the Create Bar area into the Work Area. Rename this material JakePhoto_Material.

Step 8: Place Jake.jpg into the Color attribute. In past tutorials, we have altered the color channel by changing the actual hue and brightening and darkening the color. However, now it is time to bring in an actual photograph to define how the color of the material that we are going to place on the plane in the frame will look. Again, there are a couple of ways to do this. For this step, we will use one method and another in the next step.

In the Attribute Editor, click the checkered button at the right of the Color attribute. In the Create Render Node window that pops up there, you can select what file will be used to define the color. A number of procedural textures that Maya creates mathematically are listed in this window. However, in this case, we want to use an image. So, click the File button.

In the Work Area, a couple of new swatches/nodes will pop up. You will see a swatch called file1 and another yellow one called place2dTexture8. To see a little clearer what is going on here, RMB-click-hold within the Work Area on a black area (not on any swatch) and select Graph > Rearrange Graph from the pop-down menu that appears.

The yellow swatch (place2dTexture8) is the node that allows us to define how the Color attribute will be placed on the surface. The swatch called file1 will be Jake—the photo or texture that place2dTexture8 will be placing. Finally, JakePhoto_Material is the last swatch there (in green), which represents the material.

To get Jake.jpg into the file1 swatch, make sure it is selected in the Work Area, and the Attribute Editor will appear asking you to define (in the File Attributes) what image is to be used. In the Image Name input field, you can do the following:

1. Type in the path of the image you wish to use.
2. Hit the folder button and then guide Maya to the image you wish to use.
3. MMB-drag the file Jake.jpg from the ReunionPhotos tab area (you may have to move down within the tab area to find Jake.jpg) into the Image Name input field. Choice c is the easiest for us here.

As soon as you do that, the path will appear immediately in the Image Name input field. More important, the file1 swatch in the work area will show Jake grinning. The green swatch representing the material, JakePhoto_Material, will also show the results of the new texture that was imported into its Color attribute (Figure 8.7).

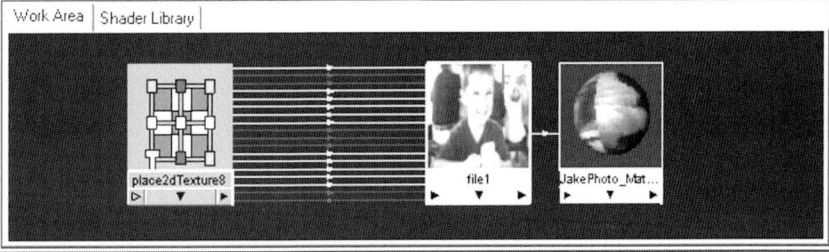

FIGURE 8.7   Rearranged Graph after importing Jake.jpg into the Color attribute.

Step 9: Place JakePhoto_Material on the plane inside the frame.
As we discussed in the last chapter, do this by MMB-dragging the material (JakePhoto_Material) from the Work Area onto the plane at the center of the frame. Hit **6** on your keyboard to tell Maya to show you textures, and you should have something like Figure 8.8.

Now, depending on how you built your frames, there could be some funny things happening. For instance, your image might look something like Figure 8.9. If it does, not to worry—we can fix this.

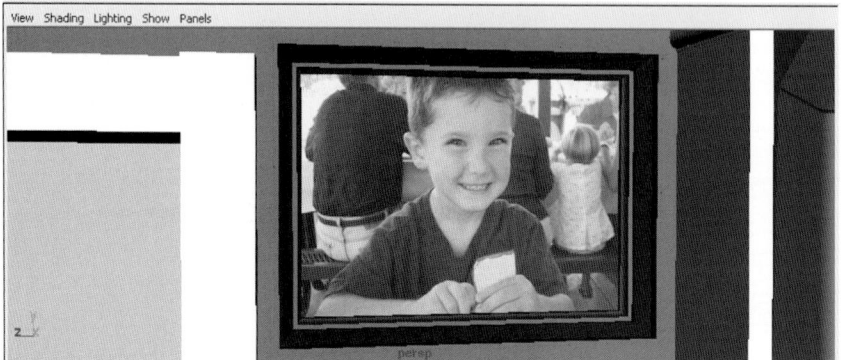

FIGURE 8.8   Placed JakePhoto_Material.

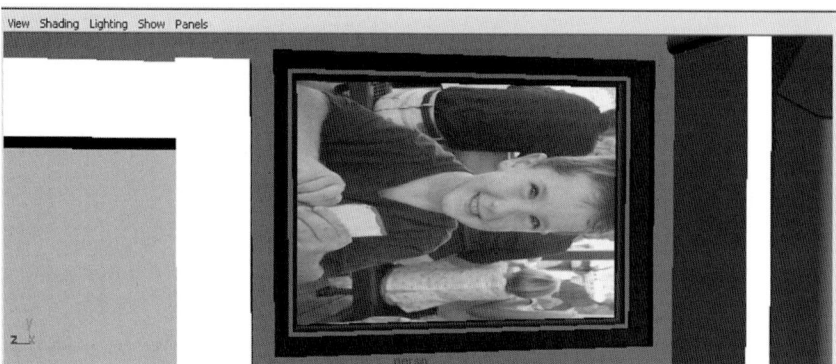

FIGURE 8.9   Material placed but by default, rotated incorrectly.

The problem here is that the Color attribute is placed on the surface incorrectly. To adjust this, click on the place2dTexture yellow swatch. Your Attribute Editor will look like Figure 8.10. Because we need to rotate the placement, just enter 90.00 (or it may need to be −90.00) into the Rotate Frame option. Immediately, the Workspace will show the results, and your photo will look right.

Step 10: Adjust other material attributes for the material, JakePhoto_Material. To do this, click on JakePhoto_Material in the Work Area. This will bring up the material's attributes in the Attribute Editor. Scroll down to the Specular Shading area and change the Highlight Size to 1.00. While you are there, change the Reflectivity to 0.00.

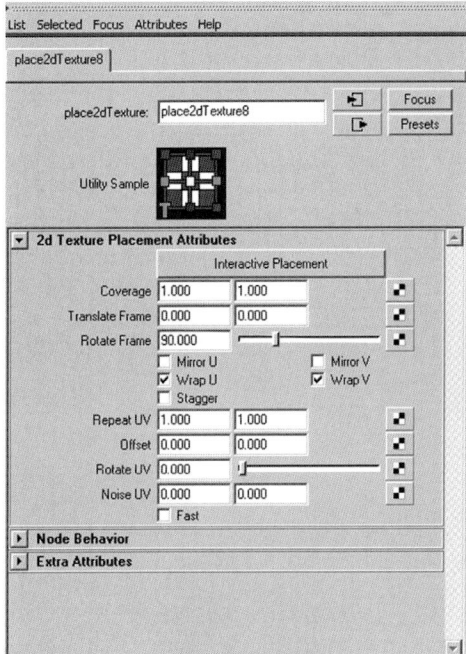

FIGURE 8.10   Attribute Editor for the place2dTexture swatch.

Now, this is really cheating a bit. In reality, the photo would be one plane and a plane of glass would be another. However, because we are not going to be getting very close to any one image, we are going to give a bit of glass characteristics to the one plane that already contains the color information of Jake smiling.

One final note: we are using PhongE because it gives us the option of having Roughness in the Specular Shading area. This gives us a softer specular highlight as though the images were behind a high-quality, no-glare pane of glass.

Step 11: Clean up the Work Area before starting a new material. In the last chapter, we created material after material in the Work Area; this can cause the Work Area to become quite crowded. We can clear the Work Area manually by RMB-click-holding and selecting Graph > Clear Graph from the pop-down menu.

Step 12: Move so that you are focusing on another frame. Again, for this one, find another horizontal frame.

Step 13: Create a new PhongE material and name it GpaPhoto_ Material.

Step 14: Assign a Color texture directly from the ReunionPhotos tab to the new material. We are going to place the Color attribute a bit differently for this one. In the last steps, we used the Attribute Editor to find and place a texture. This time, we will place it by dragging the texture directly onto the material.

In the ReunionPhotos tab area, find the image called Gpa.jpg. MMB-drag this image onto the GpaPhoto_Material swatch in the Work Area. As soon as you release the MMB, a pop-down menu will appear asking you what attribute you wish to assign this texture (Figure 8.11). Choose color.

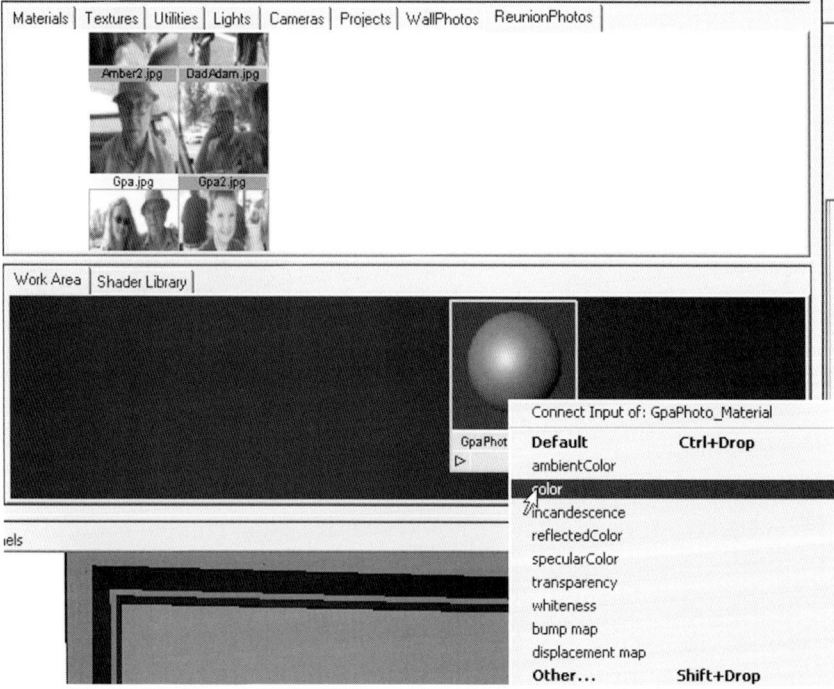

FIGURE 8.11   After releasing the MMB, you can choose directly what attribute to place the texture into.

You might need to rearrange the graph to see a little more clearly what is happening. It may appear odd to you that you are missing the place2Dtexture swatch that you had for the last material. It is actually there, it's just not visible.

The Work Area will display various graphs that show nodes and relationships between textures and materials. Sometimes when editing attributes, relevant nodes will be shown in the Work Area. At other times—as in the method we just used—some nodes are not shown by default.

In this case, place2dTexture is a node that helps the material GpaPhoto_Material know how to place the color information we introduced through the texture, Gpa.jpg. So, to see that node, we need to make sure GpaPhoto_Material is showing all its Input nodes. There are a couple ways to do this but the simplest is to select GpaPhoto_Material in the Work Area using the Input Connections tool at the top of the Hypershade (Figure 8.12). Click that button, and your place2dTexture node will appear.

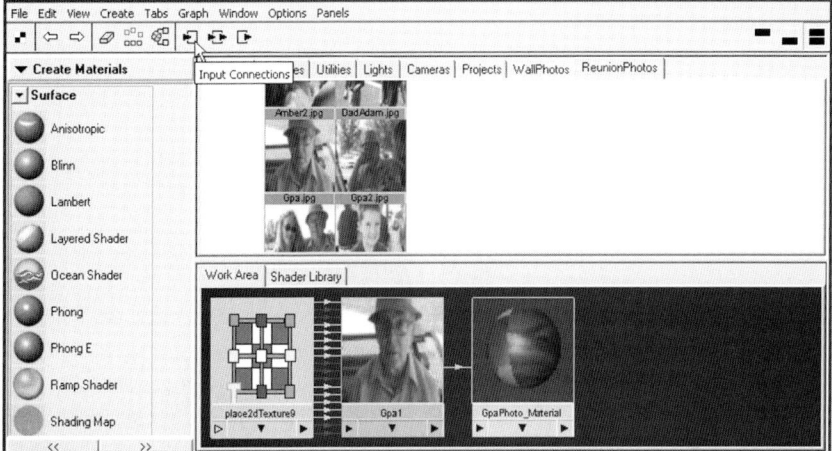

FIGURE 8.12   The Input Connections button will show the inputs to a particular node or material.

Step 15: Adjust the Specular Shading attributes to match those outlined in Step 10.

Step 16: Assign the material GpaPhoto_Material to the plane of the picture frame. The Workspace should look something like Figure 8.13.

Step 17: Prepare to start work on another frame—a vertical one this time. Clear the graph in the Work Area and move around to find a vertically formatted frame in your room. Again, create a new PhongE material named SethPhoto_Material. Change this material's Highlight Size to 1 (in the Specular Shading section of the Attribute Editor) and the Reflectivity to 0 to match earlier materials.

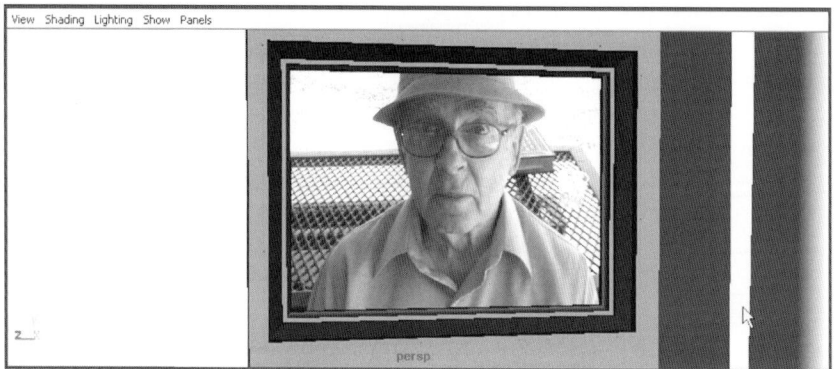

FIGURE 8.13 New photo and frame.

Step 18: Bring in Seth.jpg as the texture for the Color attribute.
You can do this via the Attribute Editor or by dragging directly to the
SethPhoto_Material swatch in the Work Area. Either way, make sure you
can see the place2dTexture node within the Work Area (you might need
to use the Input Connections button). Your Work Area should look
something like Figure 8.14.

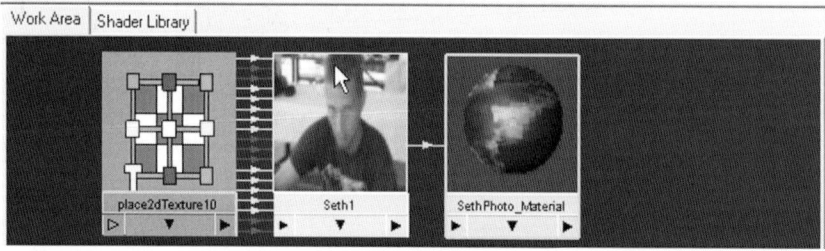

FIGURE 8.14 New SethPhoto_Material with Seth.jpg as the Color attribute.

**Step 19: Assign SethPhoto_Material to the plane in your verti-
cally formatted picture frame.** Remember, a quick way to do this is
MMB-drag the material from the Work Area to the surface itself. Figure
8.15 shows the result. Your outcome may differ slightly in its orientation,
but you will definitely have a "squished" image.

**Step 20: Adjust the Color attribute of SethPhoto_Material using
the place2dTexture node.** If you need to rotate in your file, select
place2dTexture in the Work Area and change the Rotate Frame setting
(in the Attribute Editor) to get the image looking the right way.

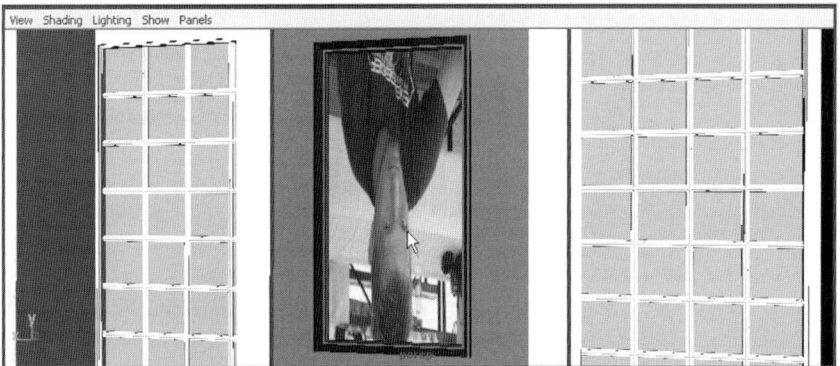

FIGURE 8.15   The squished and upside-down default placement Maya used.

While we are here in the Attribute Editor and we are editing the placement, we can do something about the squished image. Notice that in the input fields such as Coverage, there are two columns. One is for the U coordinate and one is for the V coordinate. A simple way to think of UV is XY.

By default, the Coverage setting is at 1 and 1. This means it takes the texture (Seth.jpg) and covers from edge to edge the assigned surface, and does it exactly once. That is why the image appears squished. To stretch it back out again, we need to change the Coverage settings. Depending on the exact proportions of your frame, this value may be slightly different, but for now, enter 2.50 in the first column. This should stretch out your material (Figure 8.16). Now the problem is we cannot see Seth.

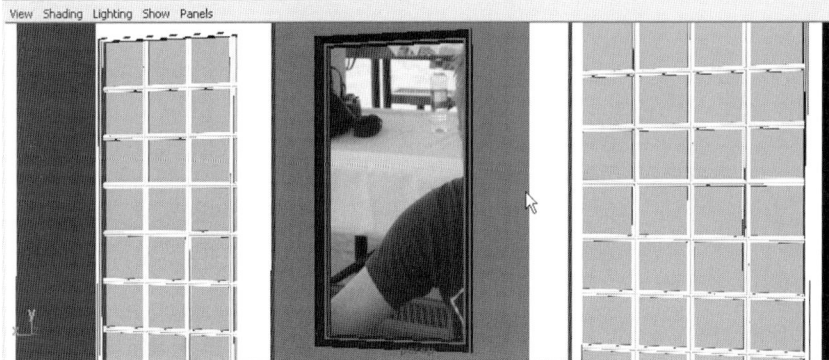

FIGURE 8.16   By increasing the coverage, we stretch out the image to a more appropriate size, but this moves Seth out of the frame.

To get him centered again, we need to move or translate the texture that sits on the surface. In the first column of the Translate Frame input field, enter 1.75. You may need to adjust this value to accommodate your slightly different proportioned frame. The result should look like Figure 8.17.

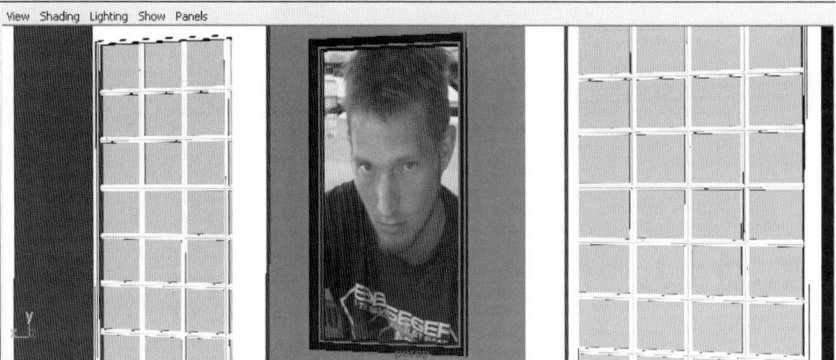

FIGURE 8.17   Translated placement moves the color across the face of the plane to where we can see Seth.

Finally, the texture is placed correctly. However, having to make blind guesses on values is a goofy way to place a texture/material. Read on to find out how to create Interactive Placement.

Step 21: Prepare for a new material and create a new PhongE named AmberPhoto_Material. Clear the graph. Create a new PhongE material and rename it AmberPhoto_Material. Change this material's Highlight Size to 1 (in the Specular Shading section of the Attribute Editor) and the Reflectivity to 0. Finally, move around in your scene so that you are looking at another vertically formatted frame.

Step 22: Bring Amber.jpg into the AmberPhoto_Material's Color attribute and assign the material to the picture plane (Figure 8.18). Notice that in the sample image, the new material's placement is upside down and squished. Yours might not be upside down, but it will definitely be squished.

Step 23: Use the Interactive Placement tool to adjust the texture's placement. Select place2dTexture in the Work Area. This will open this placement node in the Attribute Editor. Notice that above all the input fields we adjusted in earlier steps, there is a button called Interactive Placement. When you click that button, your pointer will look like the

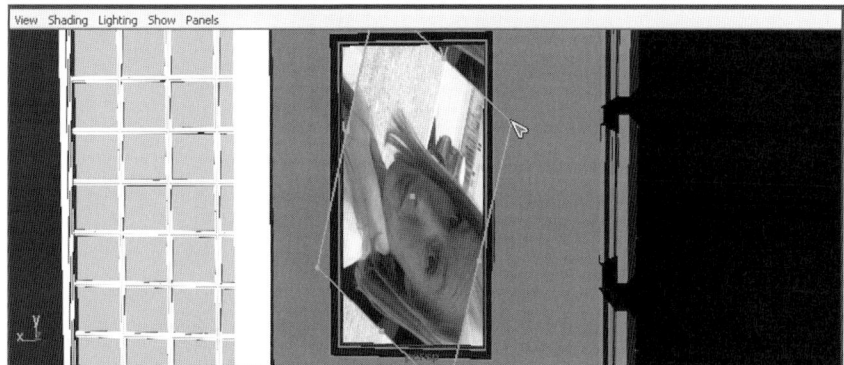

FIGURE 8.18   Rotating a texture using the Interactive Placement tool and MMB-dragging a corner.

one shown in Figure 8.18. When you use this new tool to LMB-click on the plane that has AmberPhoto_Material assigned to it, a red line with several handles will appear.

These handles encompass the texture and its placement. When other handles are MMB-click-dragged, they affect different aspects of the placement. The corner handles allow you to rotate the placement of the texture, while the ones at the top, bottom, and both sides allow you to resize a texture to make it smaller. Notice that you will not be able to stretch the texture larger using the Interactive Placement tool. However, do take a minute to play with rotating the texture by MMB-dragging the corner (Figure 8.18).

Notice that as you rotate or change the texture placement with the Interactive Placement tool, the corresponding numbers in the Attribute Editor change as well.

Change the U Coverage (first column in the Coverage of the Attribute Editor) to 2.5. If you are not in the Interactive Placement tool already, click the Interactive Tool button again. This time, MMB-drag the middle red handle to move the texture along the surface to a new placement (Figure 8.19). This is more intuitive, because it allows you to eyeball the placement. Also, you can use the Interactive Placement tool to MMB-drag the texture thinner if you need to.

Step 24: Use the techniques described earlier in this tutorial to place materials on all the remaining framed picture planes in the room (Figure 8.20).

Step 25: Create a new tab in the top called FloorTextures. Remember, you do this by choosing Tabs > Create New Tab (Figure 8.21). Be

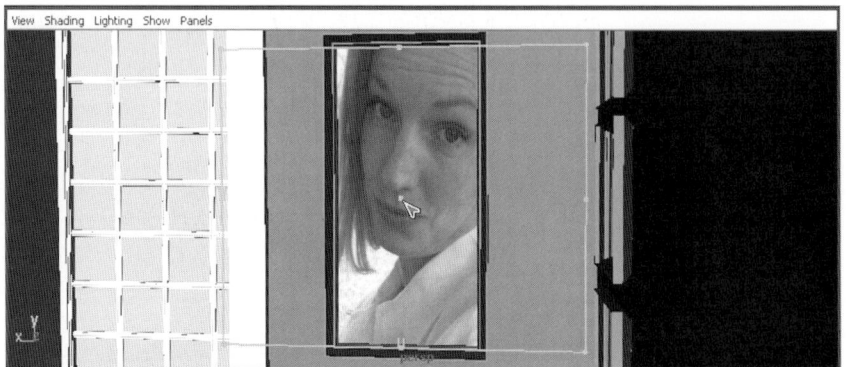

FIGURE 8.19   Using the Interactive Placement tool to place the texture on the surface visually.

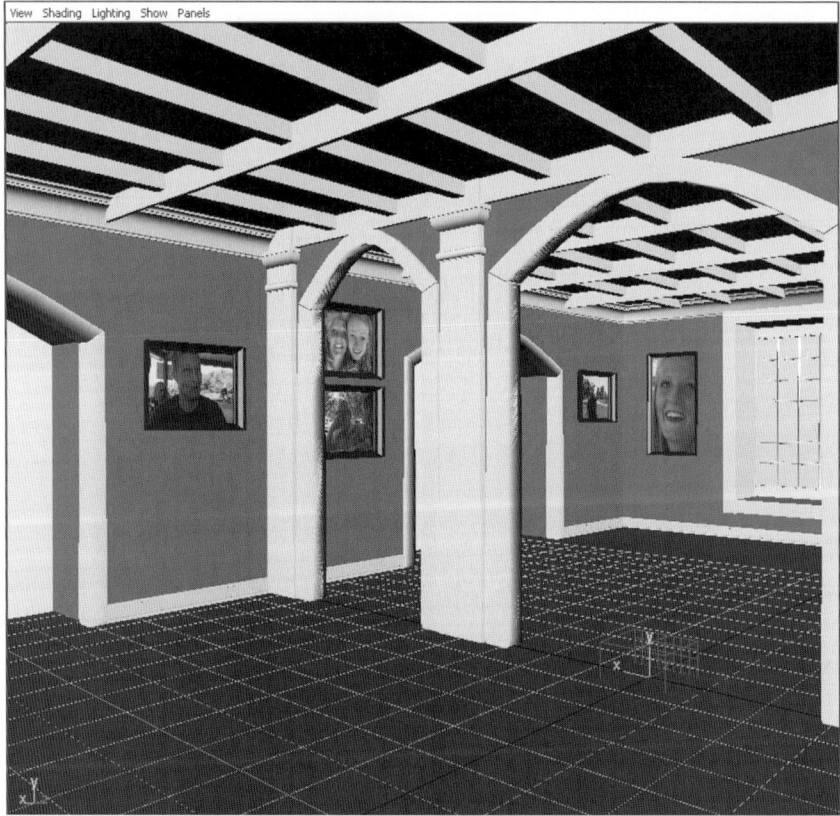

FIGURE 8.20   Lots of placed textures in the room for all the frames.

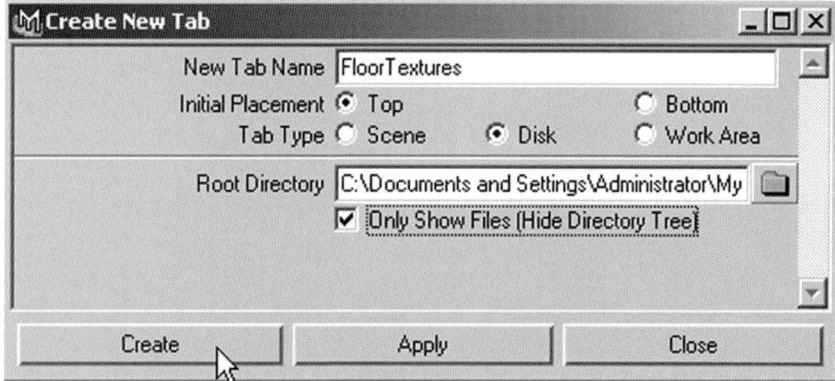

FIGURE 8.21   Creating a new tab with floor textures.

sure to designate the folder FloorTextures as the directory from which to import. This folder was one of those that you copied from the CD-ROM to your hard drive at the beginning of this tutorial.

Now, there are many images for use as textures in this folder. We will not use them all in this tutorial. However, they are provided for your experimentation.

Step 26: Create a new Blinn material and name it Floor_Material.

Step 27: Make TileColor.tif the Color attribute for Floor_Material.

Step 28: Assign the new Floor_Material to the Floor object and render. The result is obviously wrong (Figure 8.22). Taking one copy of our color texture and stretching it over the entire floor makes for huge tiles.

However, we know how to resize a texture across a surface. In the Work Area, make sure you can see the Inputs of Floor_Material and open the placement node in the Attribute Editor (double-click place2dTexture).

For our photos, we changed the coverage to make the texture bigger than the surface to which it was assigned. In this case, we want to do the opposite. However, if we reduce the Coverage settings to below 1, parts of the surface will be without any color texture. Instead, we want the texture to have full coverage but repeat itself many times.

To do this, we want to enter new values in the Repeat UV Input Fields. Enter 10 in the U column and, because the room is twice as long as it is wide, enter 20 in the V column. This will produce a floor with the tiles correct (Figure 8.23). Although you can see this in the Workspace, take a quick render.

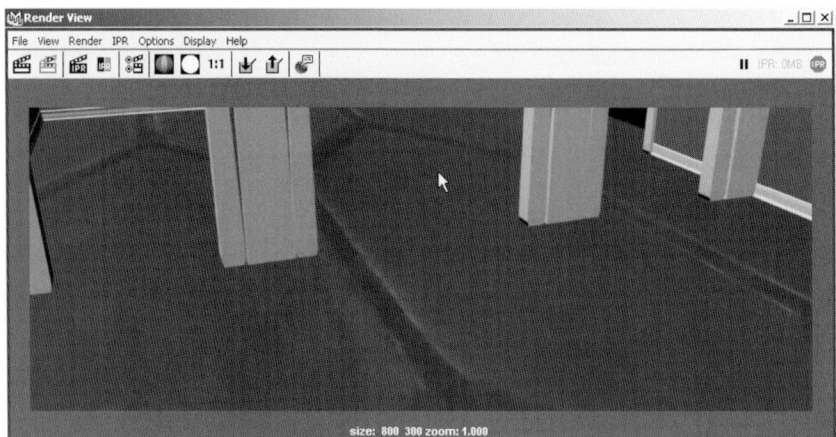

FIGURE 8.22   The default placement of the new color texture leaves much to be desired: it is too big.

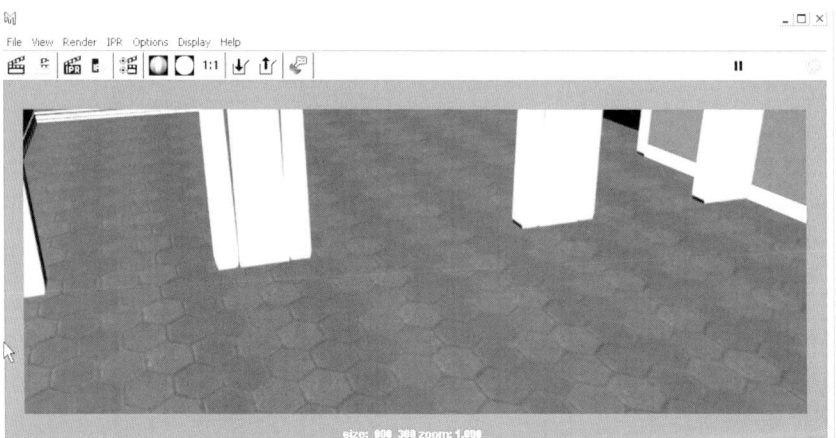

FIGURE 8.23   Correctly shaped and sized tiles.

Step 29: Add a bump map to Floor_Material. The color is a good start for this material, but it looks very flat. To fix this, we will be adding a bump map to give some depth to this surface. Within the FloorTexture tab is another image called TileBump. (For details on how to create these custom maps, see Appendix C).

Assign TileBump.tif to Floor_Material's bump attribute by MMB-dragging it from the FloorTextures tab onto swatch Floor_Material in the

Work Area. Take a minute to clean up the graph and make sure you are seeing all of Floor_Material's inputs. Your Work Area should like Figure 8.24.

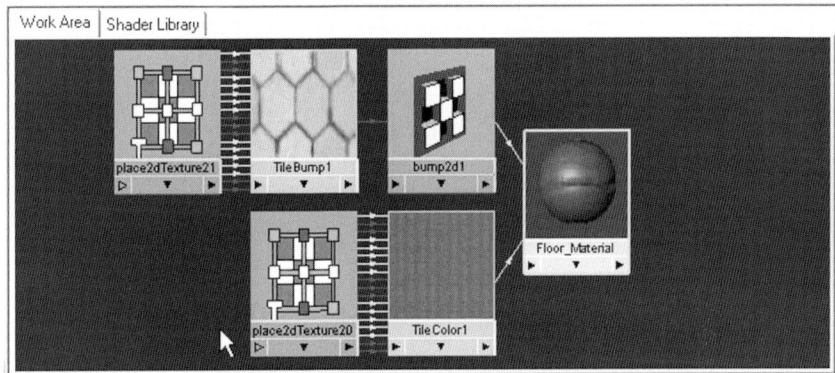

FIGURE 8.24   Work Area with newly placed bump map.

There are some interesting things to note here. There are essentially two branches of information feeding into the final output of Floor_Material: the color and bump. You can see that each input branch has a file that helps define what is happening. However, the biggest issue is that there are two placement nodes. You can actually map the color and bump differently. The problem with this is we have carefully created the tiles' placement with the color. It will be important that our bump texture's placement matches that of our color texture.

Step 30: Make the color's placement node an input for the bump map. Because we have defined the placement for the color, this is the keeper. Select the place2dTexture for the bump map (Figure 8.25a) and delete it (Figure 8.25b) using the **Backspace** or **Delete** key.

Then hold down the **Ctrl** key down and MMB-drag the place2dTexture node (the one associated with the color texture) to the TileBump1 swatch. When you release the mouse (Figure 8.25c), you will see a new connection between the placement node and the bump map.

This makes the placement node the input for both the texture that defines the bump and the texture that defines the color. If you pull the placement node a little ways away, you can see the new arrows emerging from it to both branches of inputs (Figure 8.25d).

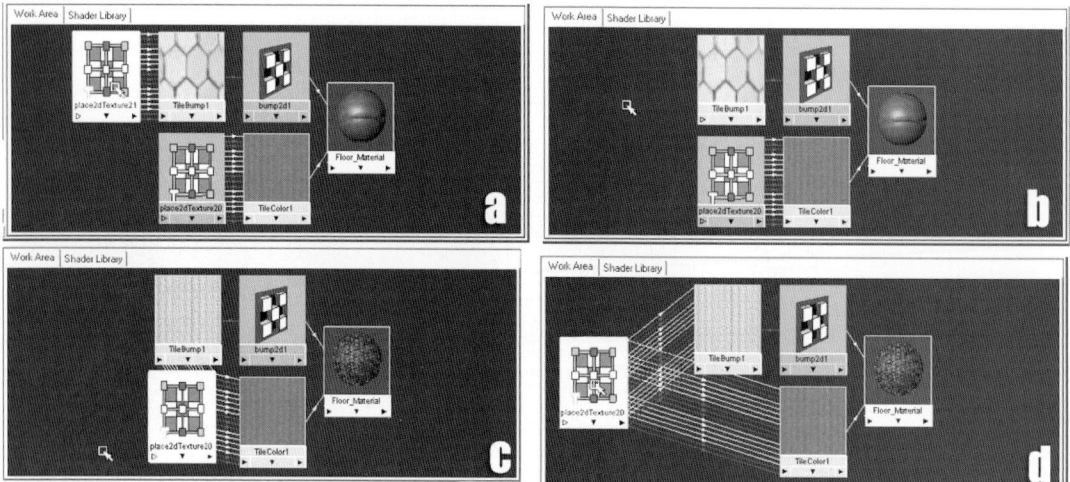

FIGURE 8.25 (a–d) Creating new connections (Inputs) within the Work Area.

Step 31: Tone down the bump height. If you render now, the bump will be a bit severe. To turn this down a bit, select the bump2d1 node in the Work Area. In the Attribute Editor, change the bump depth to 0.10. The result of all this should look similar to Figure 8.26.

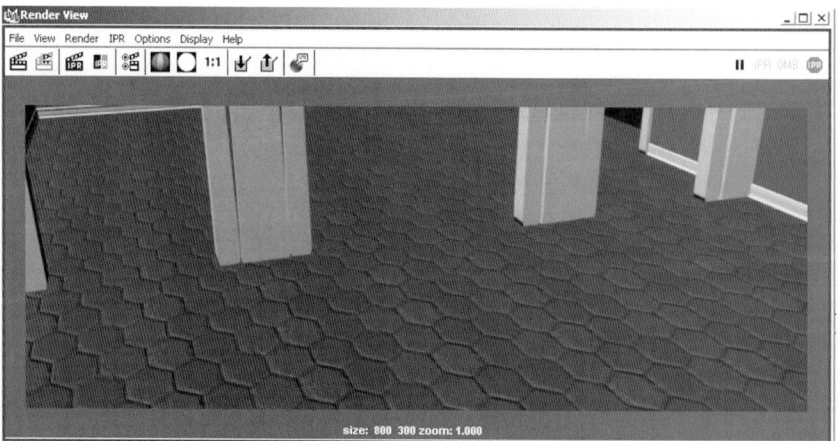

FIGURE 8.26 Final floor with bump and color.

Step 32: Create materials for the rest of the room. A tall order for sure. Remember that there are some extra textures for your use included in the FloorTextures tab. Namely, there is a texture called Furniture-

Wood. In Figure 8.27, this texture was used to create all the materials that went on all the furniture.

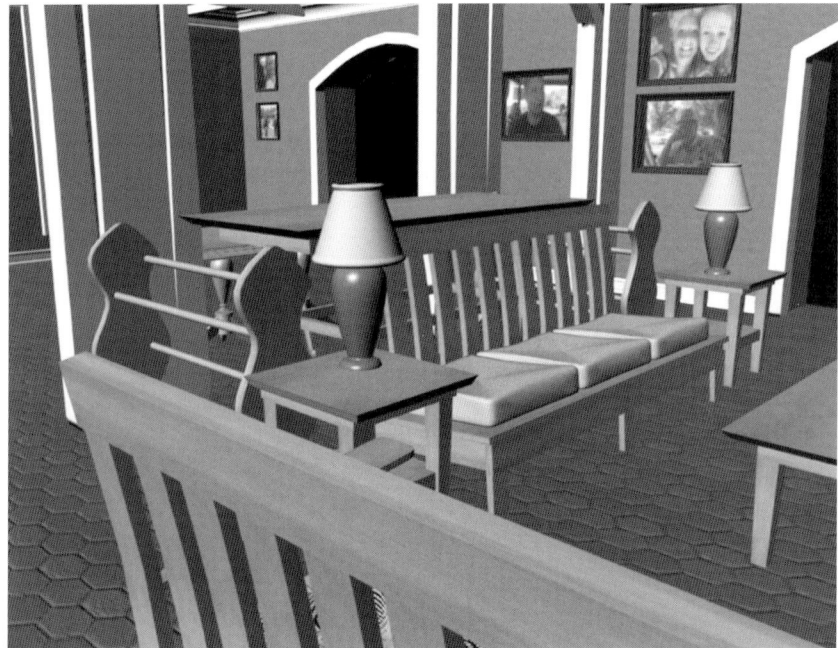

FIGURE 8.27   Finished textures.

Other materials such as the lamp base and the lamp shade were simply done with procedural textures. Even the cushions of the room were done with procedural textures. Play with a variety of things and throw a bunch of colors on everything. There is really no right or wrong—just let it flow.

CONCLUSION

Many pages have gone in the pursuit of texturing excellence. The amazing thing is we have barely scratched the surface. Unfortunately, this book is not big enough to explore all the nooks and crannies of Maya's texturing monolith. However, we have covered most of the general tools and concepts within Maya's paradigm. This probably does not mean you are an expert at texturing at this point, but with the knowledge you have now, you should be able to continue to manipulate and learn new techniques in texturing as you work.

ON THE CD

Remember that the results of this chapter's tutorial are on the CD-ROM. If you would like to take apart any of the materials created to see the details, just open the file and begin ripping. A lot can be learned by looking at someone else's files—it allows you to view a different thought process. Or, if you are comfortable with the things we have covered, you are set to move on.

Texturing is truly an art form. However, as the final figure in this chapter shows, texturing is only half the battle. Even with all our materials created and placed, the room is still stale, unbelievable, and uninteresting.

The other half of effective texture work is lighting. In the next chapter, we will introduce Maya's lighting tools and look at ways to manipulate them to highlight our modeling strengths and even hide weaknesses. So, take a break and then read on. The best eye candy is yet to come.

LIGHTING AND RENDERING

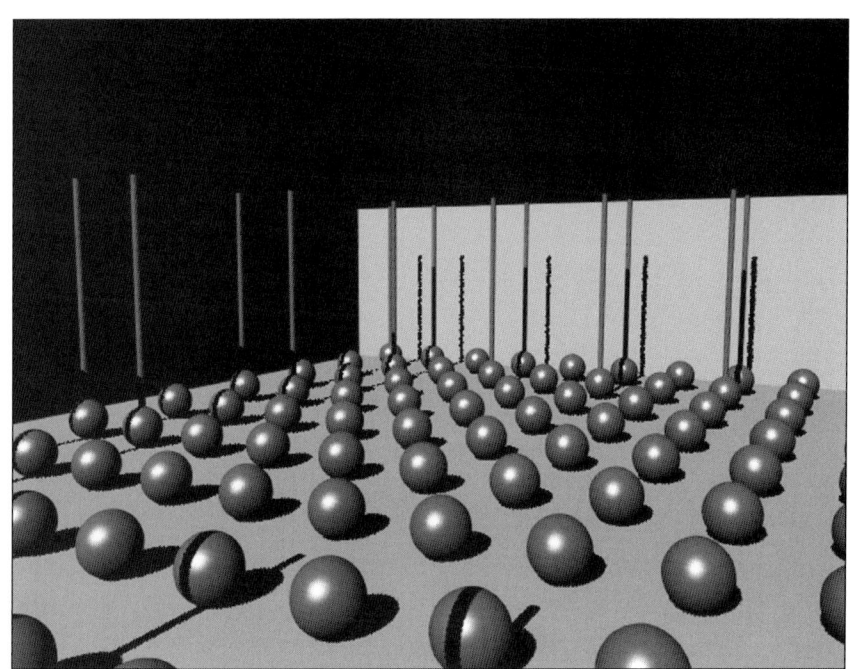

We are getting closer to the image that was our goal in Chapter 2. Although there are many more facets to Maya's texturing capabilities, in the last chapter we built a solid foundation of skills with which to add color and texture to a scene.

Lights are an important part of creating 3D images. They create shadows that help ground objects in the scene. Light can convey moods such as warm and friendly, cold and creepy, or anything in between. Even a simple sphere on a plane, when lit a certain way, can give the impression of the time of day, for example. In this chapter, you will learn how to manipulate lights for the effects you desire.

Also in this chapter, we will cover how Maya renders. In most of the documentation that comes with Maya, lighting and rendering are listed together, because the two are very inextricably linked. Although the Workspace will show you a preview of what your lighting is doing to the scene, rendering is necessary to view shadows, interplay between lights, and real depth. So, we will be covering Maya's default rendering algorithm and some Raytracing.

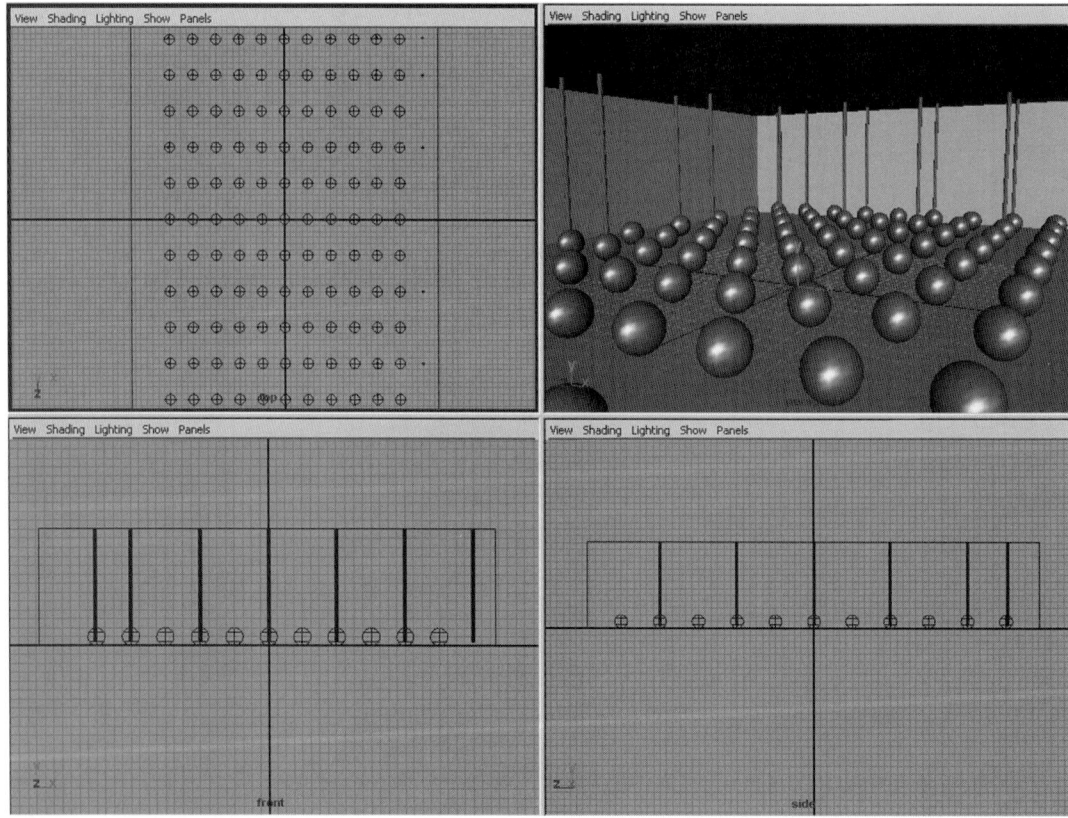

FIGURE 9.1 The lighting lab.

Let's begin by defining the different types of lights and some of their settings. If you are familiar with Maya's lighting basics already, skip forward to the tutorials.

For now, we are going to look at how different types of light affect an area. Figure 9.1 shows our mini lighting laboratory. It contains a box with a bunch of spheres and some strong vertical elements. The spheres have a Phong material on them, and the box that contains it all has a Lambert material.

Note that if there are no lights in the scene, Maya will render the scene as though lights are present. For instance, Figure 9.2a shows the uninteresting screens after hitting **7** on the keyboard. Hitting **7** shows the scene with an estimate of how the lighting in the scene will work. Without light sources in the lighting lab, it looks black. However, upon rendering (Figure 9.2b), you can see that Maya renders the scene as though there is a floodlight sitting right above the camera.

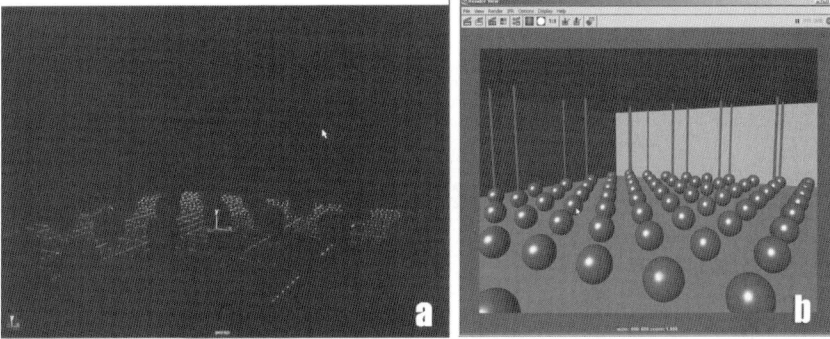

FIGURE 9.2 (a–b)   Even without lighting, Maya will render the scene as though there is a light.

Note that as soon as you place a light in the scene, Maya no longer assumes you want a floodlight. You will never want to leave the default lighting in a scene. That is the quickest way to make your scene scream "CG."

LIGHT ATTRIBUTES

Before we get going on looking at all the different types of lighting instruments, we should talk a bit about which attributes Maya lets you control for lights. With any light, you can select the light and then open the Attribute Editor (**Ctrl-A**) to see and alter the available editable attributes.

Figure 9.3 shows the Attribute Editor of a spotlight. Notice that there are a couple of swatches at the top (Intensity Sample and Light Shape) that give you some visual clues about the light selected.

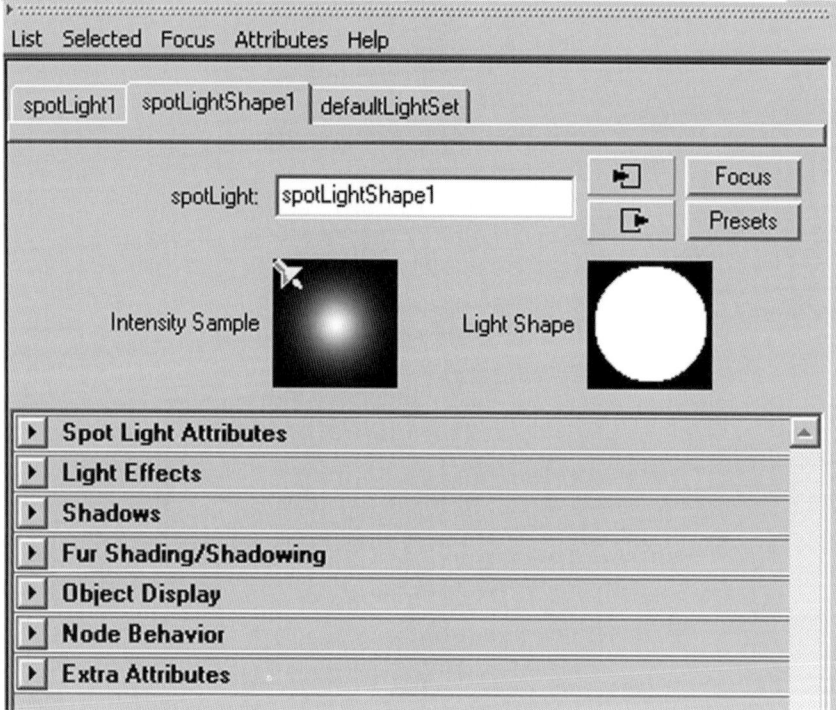

FIGURE 9.3 Spotlight Attribute Editor.

Immediately below that are several expandable sections that contain collections of attributes. There is some variation among the different light types once you get into these areas, but generally, here is how they break down:

X Light Attributes: This area has the largest variation among the different light types. It contains details such as the ability to define or change the type of light that identifies the instrument. You can change the color, intensity, decay (light falloff), and shape here (Figure 9.4).

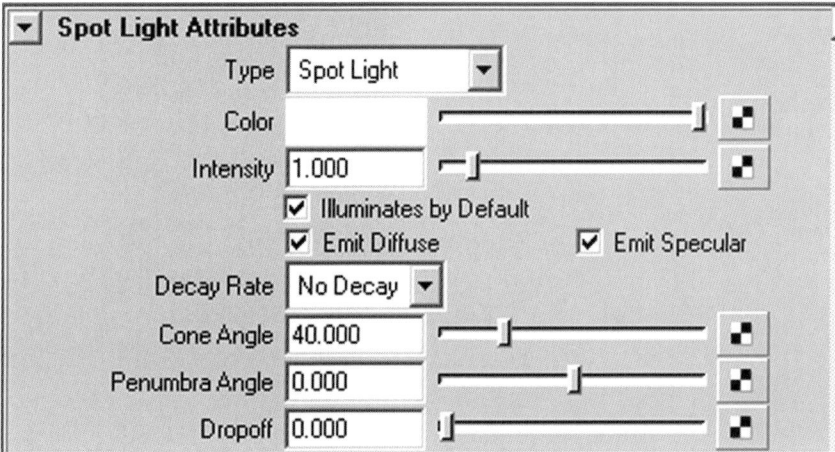

FIGURE 9.4   X Light attributes. These are not specific to Spot Lights; other types of lights also share many of these attributes.

Light Effects: This generally details attributes such as Light Fog, which is similar to volumetric or visible light in other 3D applications. It also allows you to define things such as lens flares (Figure 9.5).

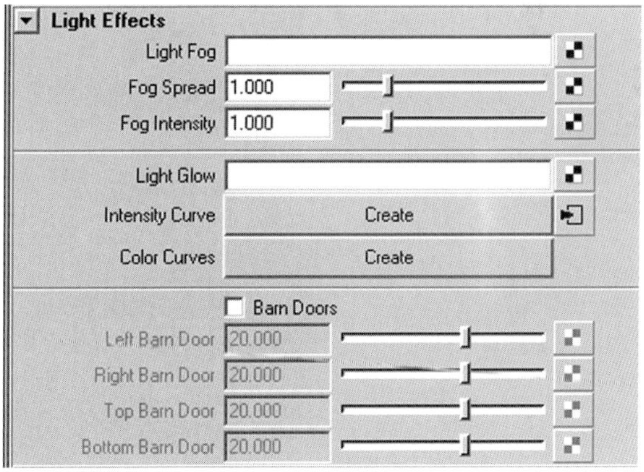

FIGURE 9.5   Light Effects.

Shadows: This is actually a very complex group of tools. Notice that when you expand the Shadows section, two new sections appear beneath it: Depth Map Shadow Attributes and Raytrace

Shadow Attributes (Figure 9.6). The differences here are complex, but simply stated, Depth Map Shadows render faster, are mostly soft edged, have a constant color/transparency, and are typically less realistic (Figure 9.7a). Raytrace Shadows render considerably slower, can be soft, have varying color/transparency, and tend to produce much more realistic results (Figure 9.7b).

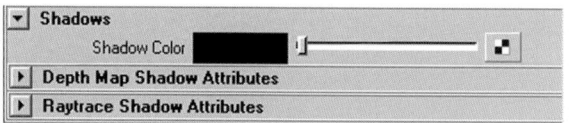

FIGURE 9.6   The Shadow Attributes and sub-attribute sections.

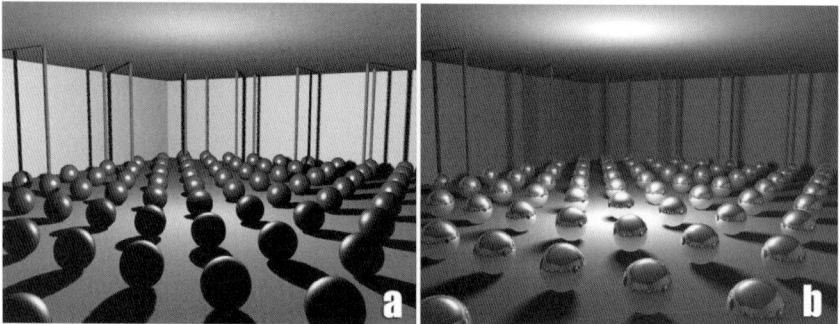

FIGURE 9.7   (a) Depth map shadows. (b) Raytraced soft shadows.

We will talk much more about the difference between Depth Map Shadow and Raytrace Shadow. In general, you should try to make things work with just Depth Map Shadows, but if the need arises, use Raytrace Shadows. Part of the reason for this is that to see Raytrace Shadows, you must activate Raytracing in the Render Globals. Although Raytracing can indeed produce some beautiful renderings, you pay for it in render time.

Fur Shading/Shadowing: Because we are not going to have time or space in this book to get into fur or hair, we will not talk much about this. The core idea though is that when creating hair or fur, there are some specific shortcuts Maya offers to render the fuzzy stuff without sacrificing rendering speed. In this area, you can help define what those shortcuts are and how they work.

Object Display, including the areas of Bounding Box Information, Drawing Overides, Node Behavior, and Extra Attributes: These remaining attributes really affect your work flow when modeling. Here, you can determine if the light is visible, how detailed it displays (LOD—Level of Display visibility), whether it is templated, and so on. This group of attributes is available for most all objects created in Maya but is not very relevant to light. So, no need to be concerned with these (Figure 9.8).

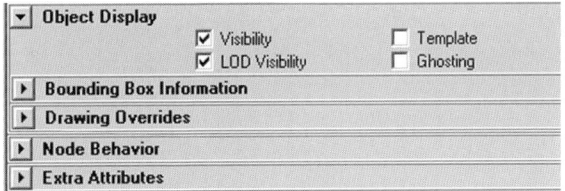

FIGURE 9.8   Remaining general light attributes. Typically, you do not use these much for lights.

We will explore the details of all these attributes as we work through the tutorials.

LIGHT TYPES

Maya creates several different types of lighting instruments. Each has slightly different characteristics, and the light each gives off in your scene has slightly different attributes and editable characteristics. All are available via the Create > Lights pull-down menu. The different light instrument types and some general descriptions are listed in the following sections.

Ambient Light

An Ambient Light is essentially a light that is everywhere. It never falls off, and its light radiation goes forever in all directions. Although an Ambient Light has a source, you have very little control over where the light goes or how it reacts in the scene.

Figure 9.9 shows an Ambient Light placed in our lighting lab. On the left is what the Workspace shows, the middle shows the Attribute Editor with the Ambient Light selected, and the right shows the default rendering result.

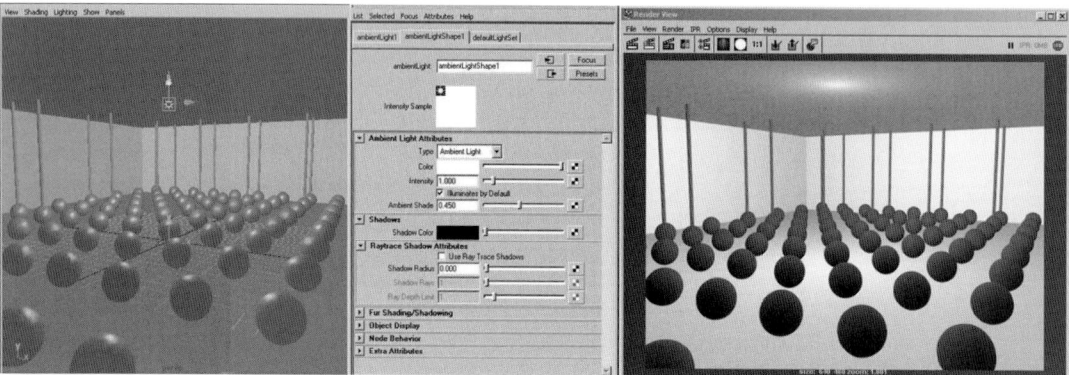

FIGURE 9.9 Ambient Light placed in the lighting lab.

There are several things to notice here. First, despite having a Phong material, the rendering shows no specular highlights. The colors are still extant but there are no highlights. Second, notice that there are no shadows in the scene. In the Attribute Editor there is an area set aside for Shadow Color, but there are no Depth Map shadows available to activate. Creating Raytrace Shadows can solve this. Figure 9.10 shows the same scene shown in Figure 9.9, except this has the Ambient Light's Use Raytrace Shadows attribute checked. The scene is also rendered using Raytracing. Notice that now we have a plethora of shadows, but all the colors are blown out.

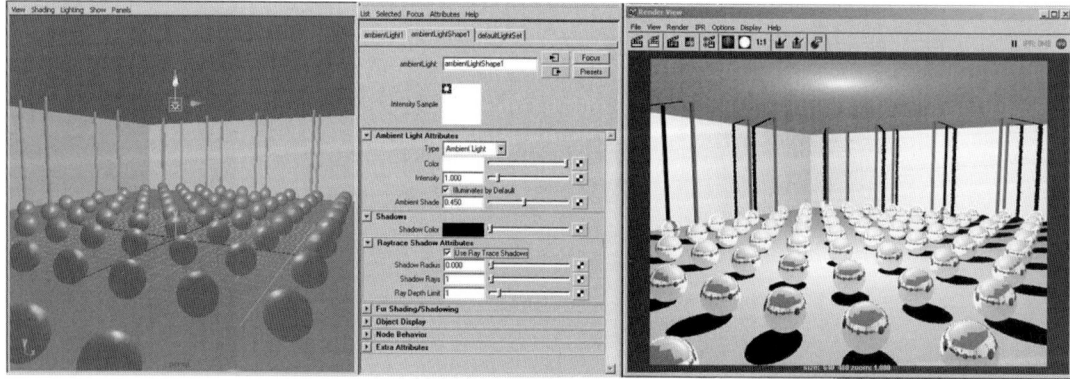

FIGURE 9.10 Raytraced scene with an Ambient Light and Raytrace Shadows.

In general, you will probably want to avoid Ambient Lights. They are seductive as a way to quickly flood the scene with light, but you lose all control when you do so.

Directional Light

The best way to think of this is sunlight. Most of the lights we will be creating in Maya create light rays that emanate from a single point. This gives us angled shadows that can splay or taper. Directional Light consists of many light rays that all run parallel to each other. They come from infinitely far away and throw light to an infinite distance. In fact, in the Directional Light Attributes, there is no option for decay at all; the light keeps going forever and ever.

To better understand this, take a look at Figure 9.11 and that image's inset. This is a Directional Light that has been turned a bit so that it faces downward. The light had its Depth Map shadows activated. Notice that the symbol that represents the Directional Light is sitting in the middle of the room, but the rendering on the far right is completely black! This is because the box of our lighting lab is stopping all the light from entering—in essence, the box is casting a shadow on its own inside. This suggests that even though the symbol is inside the box, the light is actually emanating from a point outside the box.

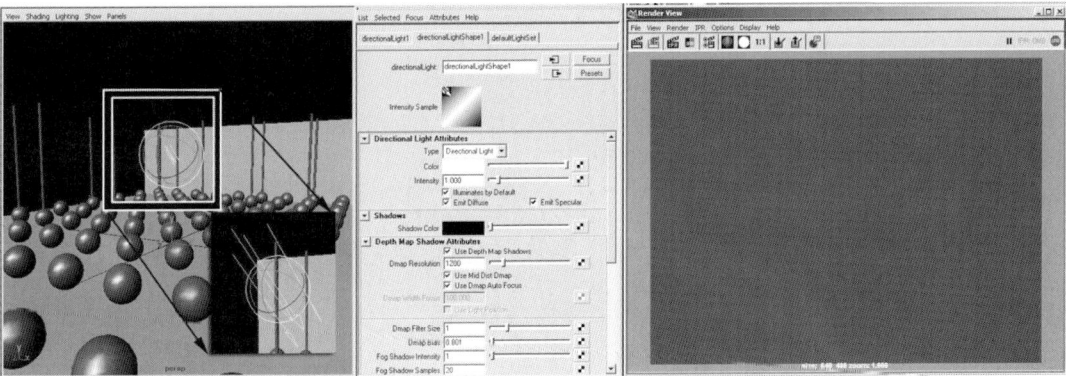

FIGURE 9.11   Directional Light inside the box with light radiation comes from some point outside of the box.

You can imagine Directional Light as similar to sunlight. You can place the actual instrument wherever you wish in your scene. This creates a faraway light source that blasts through the entire scene. For illustration's sake, Figure 9.12 shows our lighting lab, but the box has temporarily been set not to cast shadows. Notice the nature of the light and the shape of the shadows.

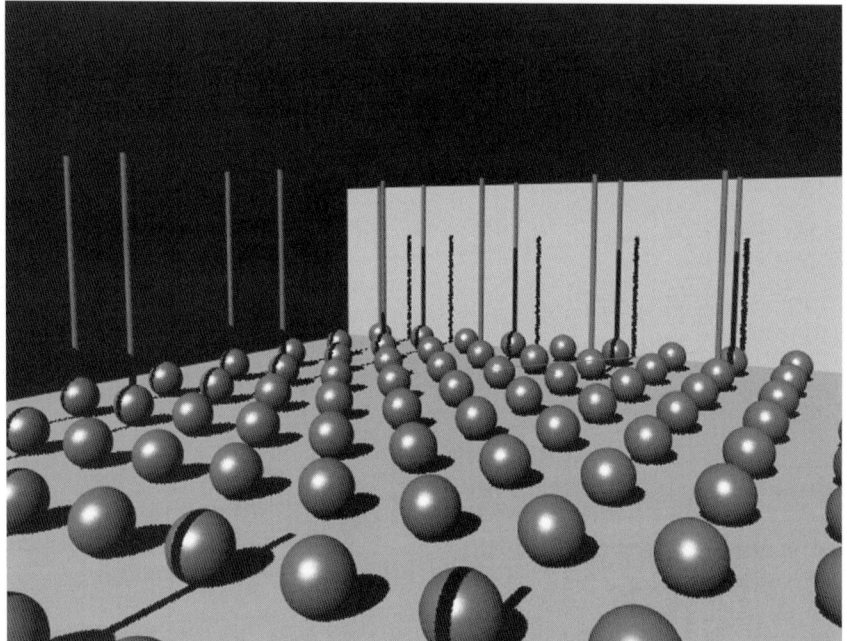

FIGURE 9.12   Directional Light and its shadows.

Point Light

This is a tremendously useful instrument. Point Lights work like light bulbs. That is, there is one point from which the light emits in all directions. This may seem to be similar to the Ambient Light we discussed earlier. However, there are some important differences: you can set decay for the light and you can produce Depth Map shadows.

Figure 9.13 shows our lighting lab with a Point Light set in the middle of the room. Depth Map shadows are turned on, so quickly rendered shadows are present for all our objects. Also notice that the specular highlights of the spheres with a Phong material on them show up well.

Figure 9.14 shows the room using Raytracing as the rendering engine and with Raytrace Shadows activated. Notice the nice shadows and the reflective surface.

Decay

Figure 9.15 makes use of one of the most important parts of creating realistic interior images—decay. Decay refers to how the light loses power

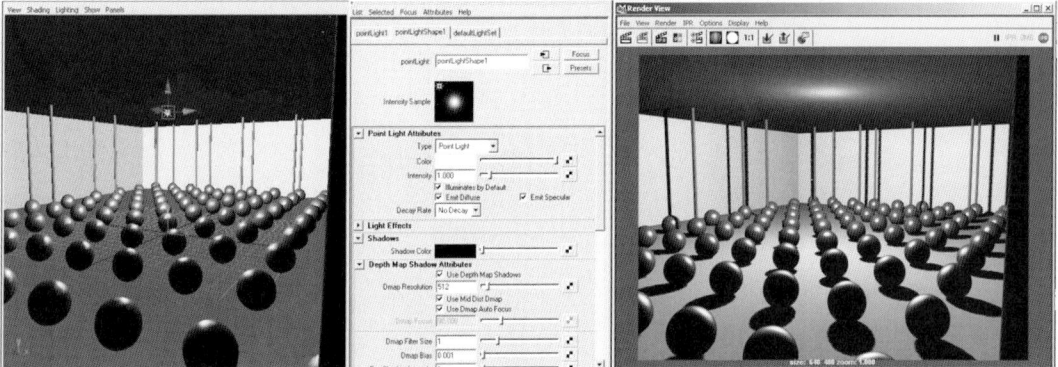

FIGURE 9.13   Point Light with Depth Map shadows activated.

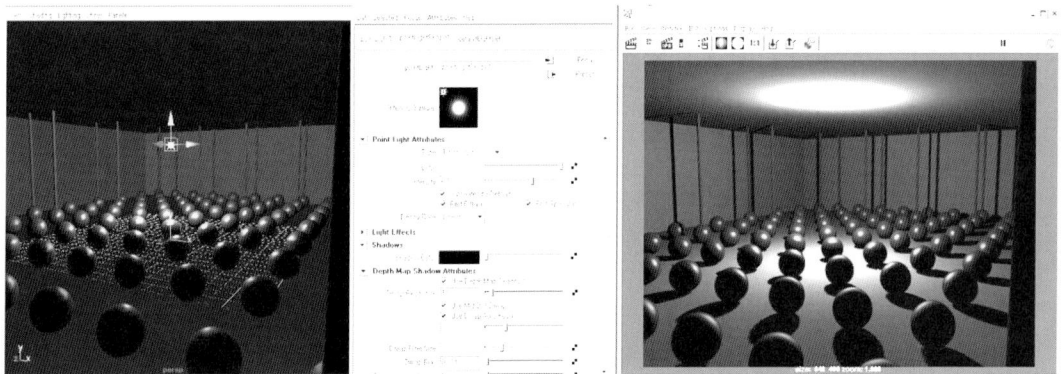

FIGURE 9.14   Raytraced lighting lab with one Point Light.

as it travels farther from the source. A light in a room that is not very bright does not light every corner of the room. Point Lights allow you to set a Decay Rate (Linear, Quadratic, or Cubic) that defines how the light will fall off. The easiest to control, although the least realistic, is Linear Decay.

Maya's implementation of controlling the decay of a light is slightly unintuitive. The only way to control how far a Point Light with decay throws light is to alter the Intensity attribute. To achieve the best effects, play with the Color and Intensity attributes until you reach the intensity and throw you want. We will look a bit more at this in Tutorial 9.1.

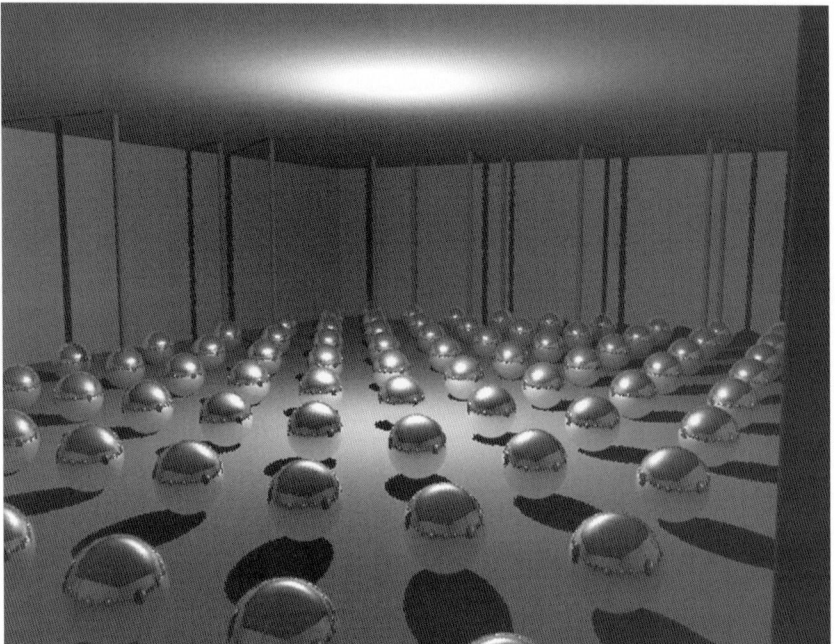

FIGURE 9.15   Point Light with decay renders a room that has dark corners.

Spot Light

The Spot Light offers a lot of control. Spot Lights are lighting instruments whose light rays emit from one point. The path that these rays take is like a cone; they emit outward in the directions you define. Spot Lights allow for decay and all types of shadows.

Figure 9.16 shows a Spot Light pointed (which is an important power of Spot Lights) downward into the light lab. Notice that the light is thrown only in the direction the Spot Light sends it. Specular highlights work well as do Depth Map shadows.

The Attribute Editor for a Spot Light includes sliders for changing the angle of the Spot Light, allowing you to have a broad or tight ring of light. Also in the Attribute Editor, you can change the Penumbra Angle and the Dropoff. These two features help define the sharpness or softness of the light's radiation. In Figure 9.16, the Penumbra Angle is set at 0. Figure 9.17 (a–b) shows the Penumbra Angle at 10 and –10. You can see how this allows the light to spread out gently, or contract, in creating a soft effect.

One final note about Spot Lights is that they work well with Raytracing.

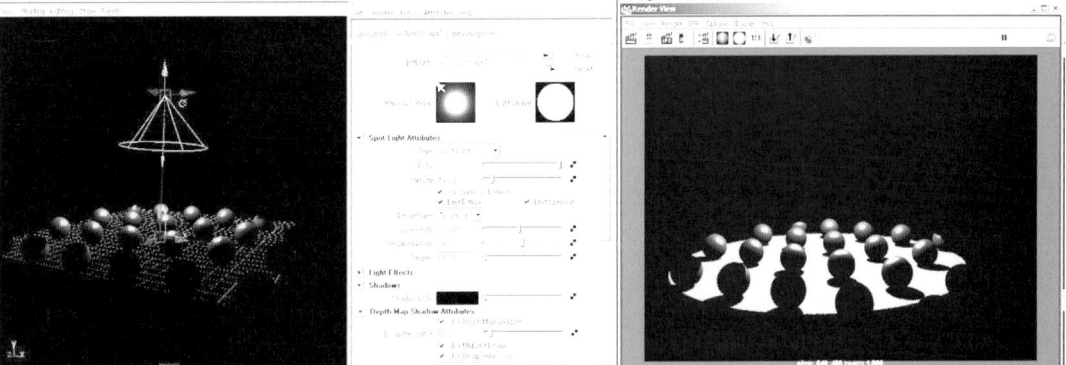

FIGURE 9.16   Spot Light pointed downward.

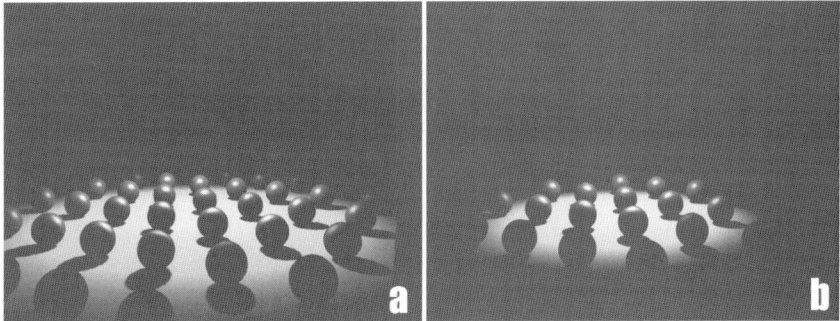

FIGURE 9.17 (a–b)   Altering the Penumbra Angle creates a light with a softer edge.

Area Lights

These are like giant walls of light. Although when they are first created, they are represented by a small square, they can be expanded to the size of a wall or ceiling. They can have a Decay Rate assigned and use Depth Map Shadows and Raytrace Shadows as well (Figure 9.18).

Out of the box, Maya does not include any sort of radiosity renderer. Radiosity is a powerful but slow rendering engine that calculates bounced light in a room. Raytracing does not. However, with strategic placing of Area Lights, you can fake bounced light from any source. Effective use of Area Lights can add a subtle depth that is important for believable scenes. In the tutorials later in this chapter, we will be looking at ways to use these powerful but underused tools.

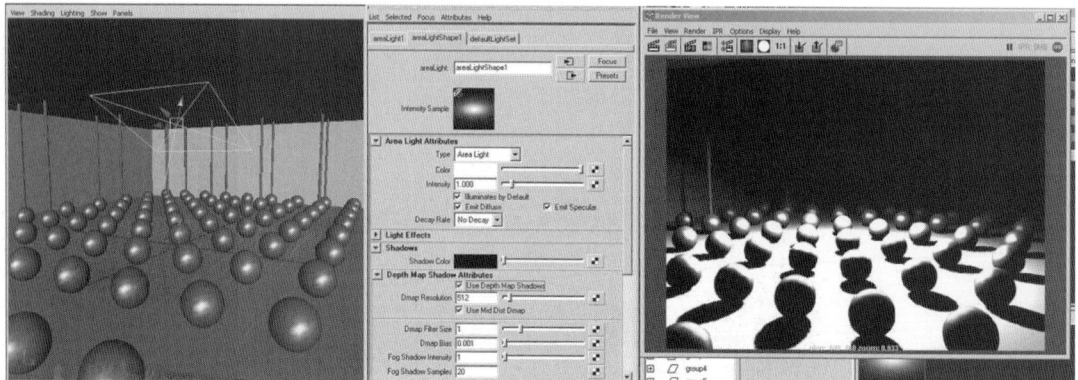

FIGURE 9.18 Area Light. Notice that it is easy to overexpose a scene with this light instrument.

Volume Light

This light is finally what you would expect from a light source if you were coming from another 3D application. Volume Lights give you a geometric 3D shape that is the absolute falloff of the light radiation. This is essentially the outer-limit falloff of other applications. The powerful thing about this tool is that in addition to creating just a spherical shape, you can choose to have the light radiation fill boxes, cylinders, and cone shapes. Additionally, you can alter many of these shapes further into half spheres, and so on. Volume Lights work well with both types of shadow.

Figure 9.19 shows a Volume Light using the Sphere shape. Notice on the left that the Sphere fills the middle of the room but does not reach the corners. The resulting render shows that absolutely no light reaches any of those corners. There is a lot of power and control in this instrument. We will be playing with it in later tutorials in this chapter.

So, that was a brief rundown of the different light types. We will be using many of them in the upcoming tutorials. However, before we do, we have a bit more background information to catch up on. It will be important to know how to manipulate lights and understand the various parts of the light's anatomy.

Light Anatomy

To discuss the different parts of the light, we will use a Spot Light. Each type of light has slightly different characteristics that can be altered in the Workspace or Attribute Editor. However, the Spot Light has quite a few that can be seen in the Workspace, so we will use it for illustration.

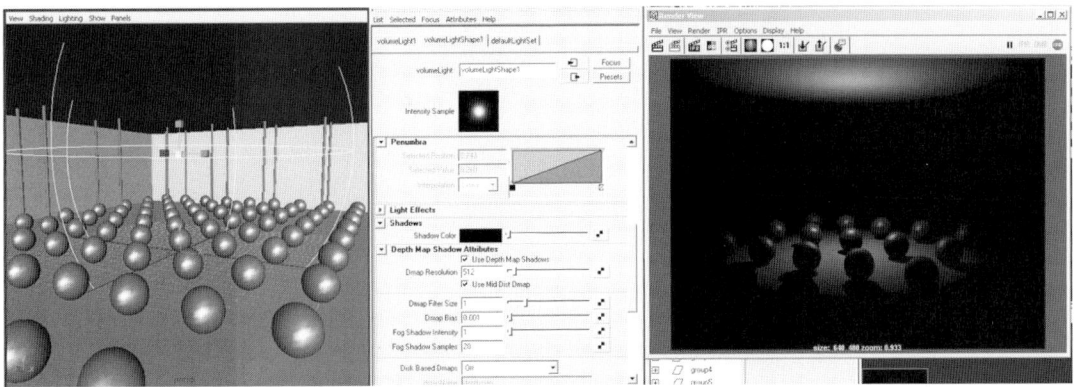

FIGURE 9.19   A Volume Light has definite falloffs. Basically, if an object is within its sphere of influence, it is illuminated; if an object is not, it is in the dark.

Figure 9.20 shows a Spot Light as it appears when it is first created. Notice the large arrow in the middle that indicates the direction of the light's radiation. Directional Lights have a series of similar arrows that become invaluable. Some light sources, such as Area Light, simply have a line to indicate which way they are shooting.

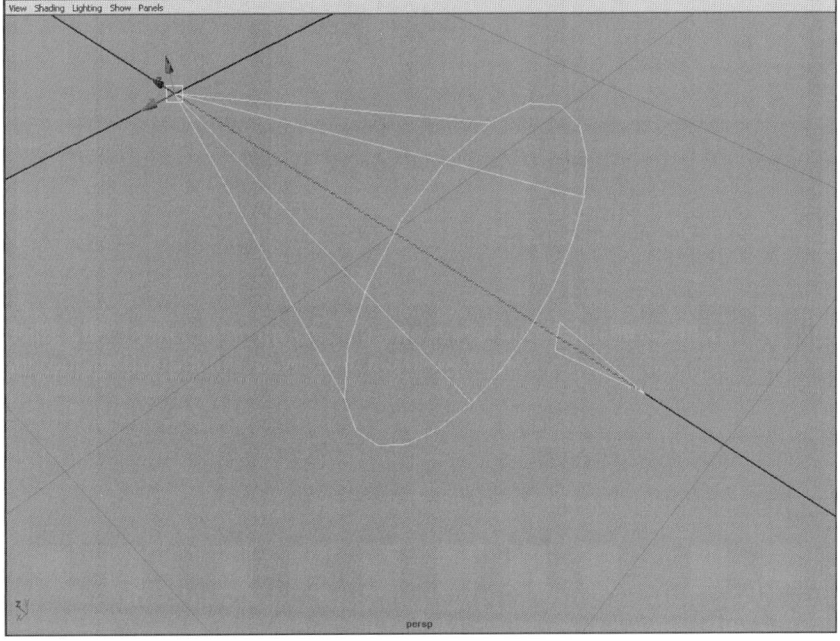

FIGURE 9.20   A Spot Light with manipulator and directional arrow.

The second thing to notice about Figure 9.20 is that the light's manipulator is at the source of the light's radiation. Using the manipulator, you can move, rotate, or scale a light however you need to.

Finally, for a Spot Light, you can see the cone that indicates the width or narrowness of the Spot Light's beam. Not all lights produce a cone of light, but light types such as Volume Lights incorporate other shapes.

Rotating a light into position is certainly one way to get a light to illuminate the desired objects. However, there are more eloquent ways to do this. In the Toolbox on the left of the UI is the Show Manipulator tool (Figure 9.21). When you click this tool, a whole new set of iconography appears on and around the light (Figure 9.22).

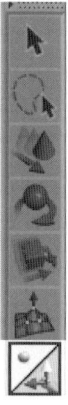

FIGURE 9.21   The Show Manipulator tool.

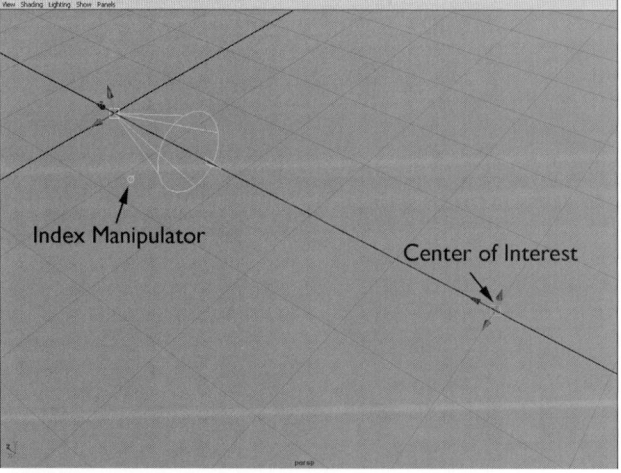

FIGURE 9.22   Once the Show Manipulator tool is activated, new manipulators emerge for a given light.

There are two main manipulators that appear. The first is the Center of Interest (COI) manipulator. Think of this manipulator as a light target. When this is visible, the light will always be pointing at it. Area Lights and Directional Lights also have such a manipulator. They make it easy to point the light at exactly the place or direction you want it. Use the Move tool to reposition the COI, and the light source will rotate to match. You can also simply rotate the light with the Rotate tool.

The second manipulator—the Index Manipulator—is actually just a button to pull up other manipulators. When you click the Index Manipulator, new collections of manipulators that allow you to adjust various aspects of the light visually will appear.

Figure 9.23 shows the manipulators that show up for various positions of the Index Manipulator. The first position simply shows the COI and the manipulator for the light origin (Figure 9.23a). Click the Index Manipulator again (Figure 9.23b), and a new handle emerges that allows you to adjust the center of rotation for the light, just in case you want to rotate a light from another place besides the source.

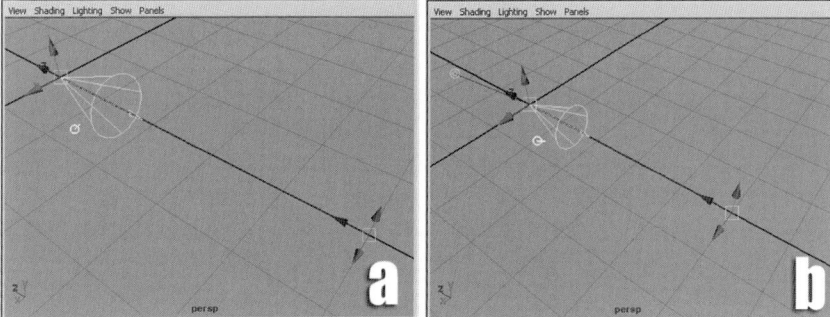

FIGURE 9.23   (a) The COI and source manipulators. (b) This blue-handled manipulator allows you to define a new axis of rotation.

Figure 9.24 shows the next two collections of manipulators that appear if you continue to click the Index Manipulator. Figure 9.24a shows a new handle that appears to let you adjust the width of the angle of the Spot Light interactively. Figure 9.24b gives you a new manipulator that allows you to adjust the penumbra, which changes how hard or soft the edge of the light appears. These are obviously some fairly specific manipulators available only to the Spot Light.

Finally, the last two sets of manipulators are shown in Figure 9.25. Figure 9.25a shows the various levels of decay that the Spot Light calculates. You can actually maneuver these manipulators to adjust the Rate of

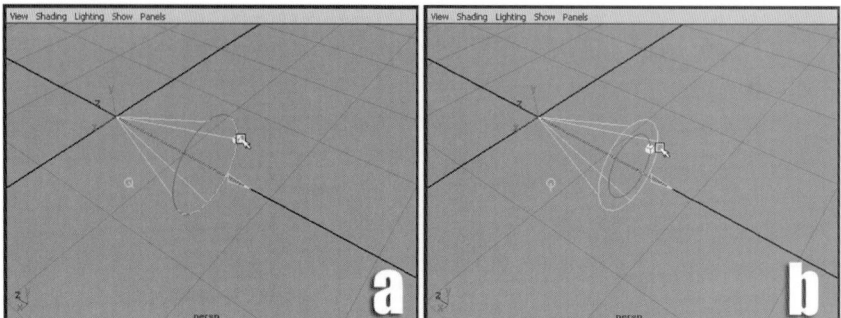

FIGURE 9.24 (a) Adjusting the Spot Light's angle. (b) Adjusting the penumbra.

Decay, although this is very technical and usually requires much more work than it is worth. Figure 9.25b shows the last option, which essentially is a rehash of manipulators seen in the past—the COI, light manipulator, and decay.

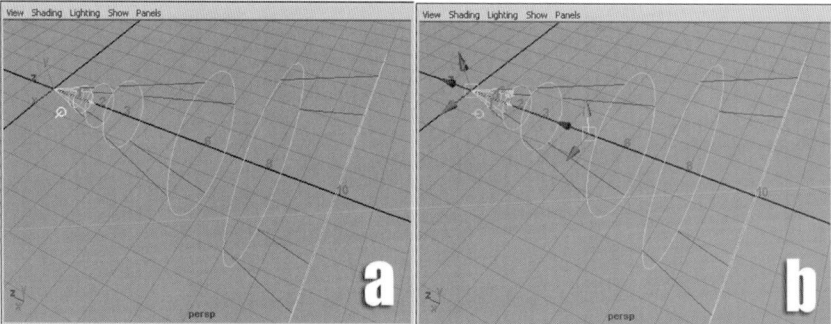

FIGURE 9.25 (a) These manipulators can be used to define Rates of Decay. (b) The final collection shows the COI again, the light's manipulator, and the Rates of Decay.

Once manipulators are shown, they can be altered independently of each other. With a light selected, the first time you hit the Show Manipulator tool, you will have the light's manipulator and the COI. This allows you to move the light quickly and use the COI to point it.

That's enough basics. Let's get on to lighting our room. There are two tutorials here. In the first, we will light the room for nighttime, and in the second, we will light it for day.

TUTORIAL 9.1   NIGHTTIME

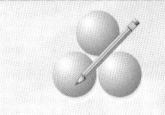

Interestingly enough, creating the lighting for night scenes is easier than for daylight. This is because there is simply less light in the scene. Further, the manmade light that is produced by lamps, sconces, and other electrically driven light sources is much easier to emulate virtually. Natural light, and its play inside a space, requires a bit more thinking.

Step 1: Open your room. Wherever you have been saving your room (which by now is modeled and textured), open it up; the fun is about to begin. Now, because we are going to be lighting this in two different ways, immediately use File > Save Scene As and save the room as Room-Daylight; this file will be used later. Then, again, immediately use File > Save Scene As and save the scene as RoomNightLight; this is the scene we will be lighting right now.

Step 2: Organize your Workspace. For light placement, it will be important at first to be able to see multiple angles of the room. Set up a four-panel layout (Figure 9.26). Also, move your mouse over the Perspective view and hit **7** on your keyboard so you can see what your room looks like with the placed lights. Right now, it should look awfully dark.

Step 3: Set up your Render Globals. We will want to render frequently as we build and adjust our lighting setup. However, as our lights increase, so will the render time. Click the Display Render Globals Window button and change your resolution to either 320×240 or 640×480. Of course, the 320×240 will render quicker but will be a bit harder to see. You might want to start with 640×480 and then downsize to 320×240 if the render times are too long.

Step 4: Create and place a Point Light in a lamp. Create the light with the Create > Lights > Point Light pull-down menu. This will place the light source right at 0,0,0, which of course is in the middle of the floor where it is of no use to anyone. The light is just like any other object, so it can be moved by hitting **w** and then LMB-dragging it into place. Put it in the lamp on the south side of the couch. Render and take a look (Figure 9.27).

Right away, you can see that things are changing. Now there are dark sides to objects, and there are lighter areas on the scene. However, there are also things that are not quite right. For instance, if a surface is facing this light, that surface is bright—artificially well lit. Also, everything seems to be floating; the couch does not quite sit on the ground and the lamps do not quite sit on the tables. We need to adjust the light's attributes.

Step 5: Rename the light. Open the Outliner and double-click on the light. Rename it LampLeft_pointlight. Tumble and dolly around a little closer to the light/lamp.

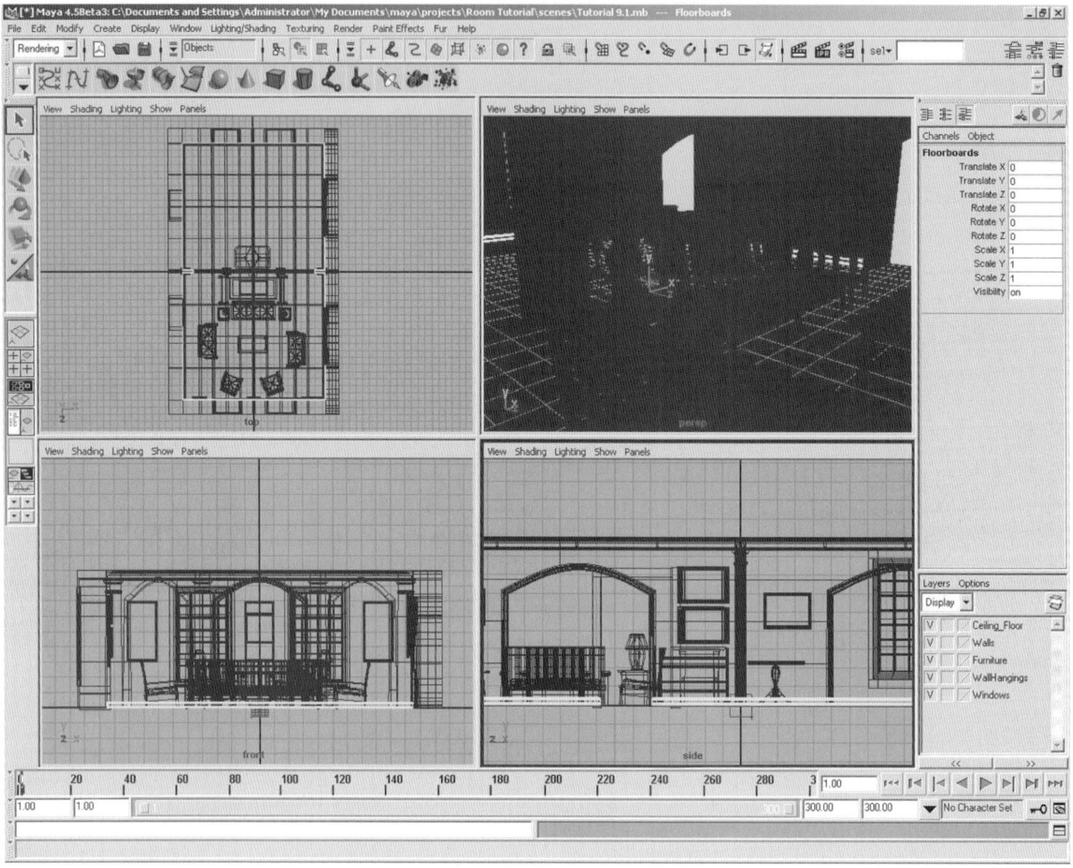

FIGURE 9.26 Setting up your Workspace to light.

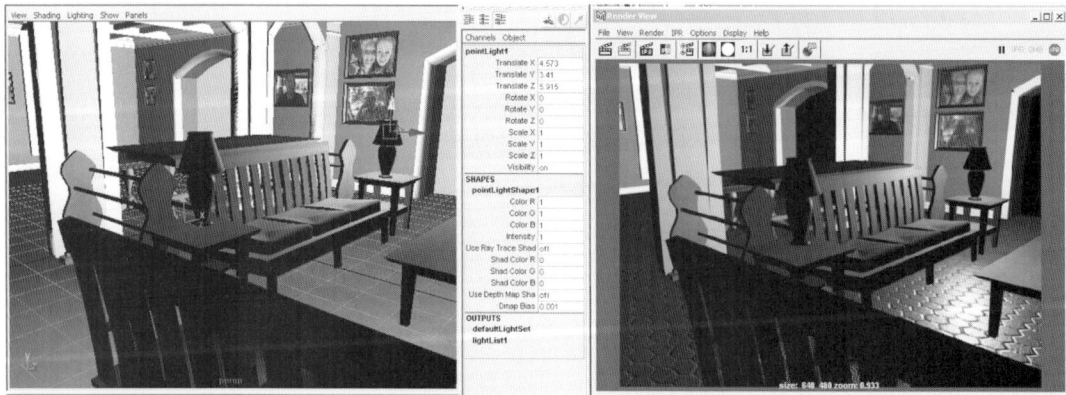

FIGURE 9.27 Placed Spot Light with unchanged attributes.

Step 6: Add the ability to cast shadows to this Point Light. Hit **Ctrl-A** to open the Attribute Editor. As we discussed before, this allows you to define how the light acts. Open the Shadows section and in the Depth Map Shadow Attributes area, check the Use Depth Map Shadows button. Render (Figure 9.28).

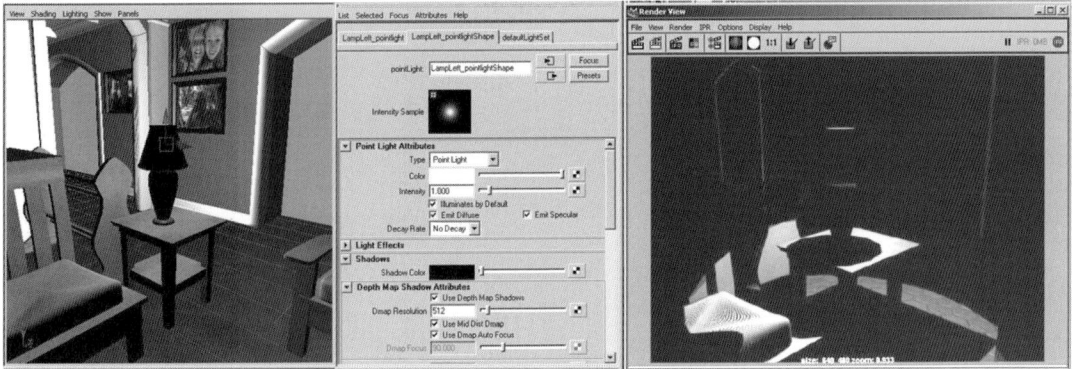

FIGURE 9.28   To make a light cast quick shadows, open the Attribute Editor and activate the Use Depth Map Shadows option.

Some interesting things happen here. In the render, you can see that, indeed, shadows are being cast. A shadow is caused when a surface stops the light from passing through it. In this case, the lamp shade and the lamp below it are stopping most of the light from passing through to anything. As a result, everything is dark but the top of the table.

Step 7: Stop the lamp shade from casting shadows. We don't want the lamp shade to cast shadows into the scene. To prevent this, LMB-click on the lamp shade in your Workspace. Because your Attribute Editor is already open, the attributes for the lamp shade surface will be displayed. Look for the Render Stats section and expand it.

Here are many attributes that define how this particular surface is going to be rendered. The important one for us is the Casts Shadows option, which by default is checked. Deselect it and render (Figure 9.29).

Getting closer but there are still some things that do not quite jive.

Step 8: Adjust the lamp shade's material to "sell" the light source. Part of what makes lighting convincing is not only the light that hits the walls but the object that the light is supposed to come from. There is no need to model a light bulb in this instance, because we will never see inside the shade. However, it is important that the shade looks as though there is a light bulb within it.

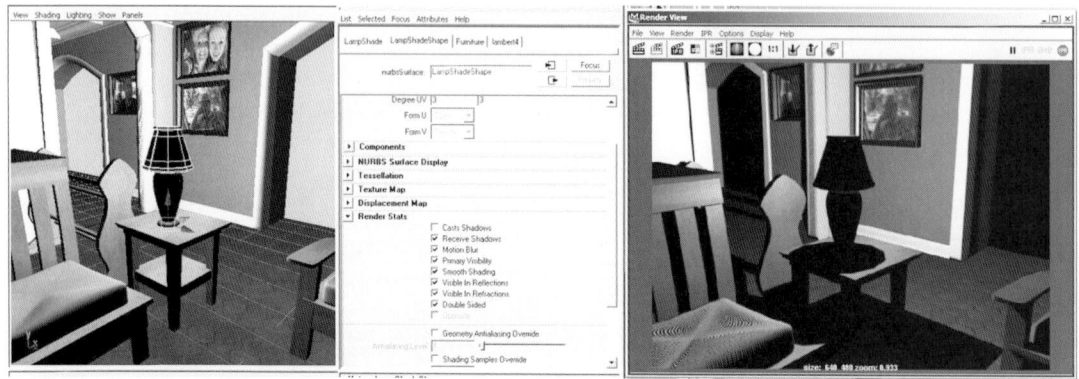

FIGURE 9.29 Deselected Casts Shadows option for the lamp shade allows the Point Light's radiation to pass through it into the room.

To do this, we need to adjust a few of the shade's material's attributes. The lamp shade's material was one that you created on your own at the end of the last chapter. Open the Hypershade, track down in the top Materials tab the material, and LMB-click it. The attributes for that material will appear in the Attribute Editor. In the Common Material Attributes section, change the Translucence setting to 1.00. This will allow the surface to show that there is a light source beneath it.

Open the Special Effects section (still within the Attribute Editor) and enter 0.075 into the Glow Intensity input field. Render (Figure 9.30).

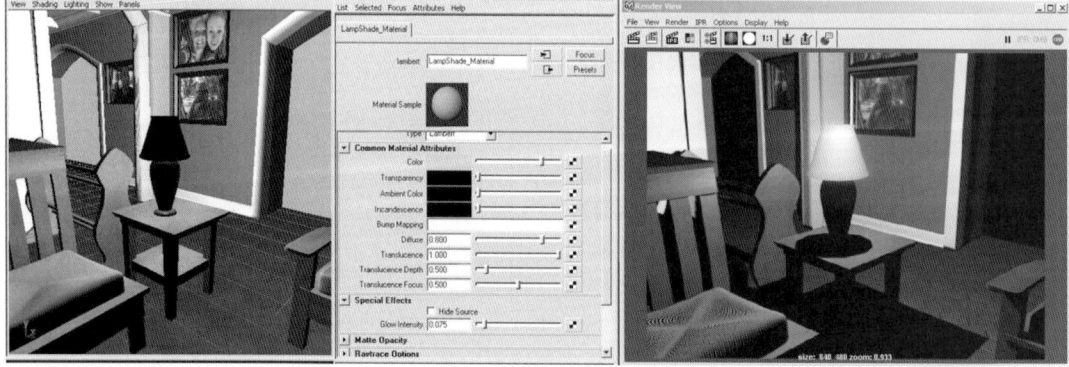

FIGURE 9.30 New lamp shade with Translucence and Glow activated.

Step 9: Activate the LampLeft_pointlight's decay. The problem with the scene right now is that the light from this Point Light is as intense right next to the lamp as it is across the room—clearly not what it would do in reality. We need to tell this light to calm down and not throw its light quite so far.

In the Outliner, find LampLeft_pointlight (probably near the bottom) and select it. Its attributes will appear in the Attribute Editor. In the Point Light Attributes section, change the Decay Rate to Linear. Render and take a look at the results. The decay default for the size room we have is too drastic. The light decays too quickly. To fix this, turn up the Intensity to 2.0. Bringing up the intensity will throw the light a bit farther (Figure 9.31). Render.

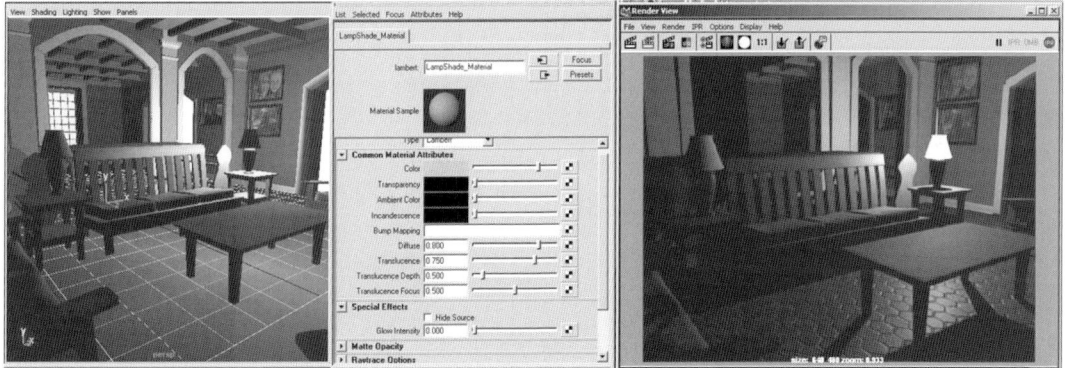

FIGURE 9.31   Decay turned on and Intensity turned up.

You might find that with the higher intensity, the translucency and glow on the lamp appear a bit intense. If need be, go back and alter the Translucence and Glow to lower values until the render makes sense.

Step 10: Duplicate the lamp. Instead of repeating this whole process again, select the lamp on the other side of the couch and delete it. Now, select the lamp (base and shade) and choose the LampLeft_pointlight and group these together. Rename the group Lamp_and_Light.

Select Edit > Duplicate (Options) and reset the settings. Although you may not have needed to reset the settings, because it has been awhile since we used the Duplicate tool, it is always a good idea to do so. Hit the Duplicate button.

Place the new Lamp_and_Light1 group on the other table and render (Figure 9.32).

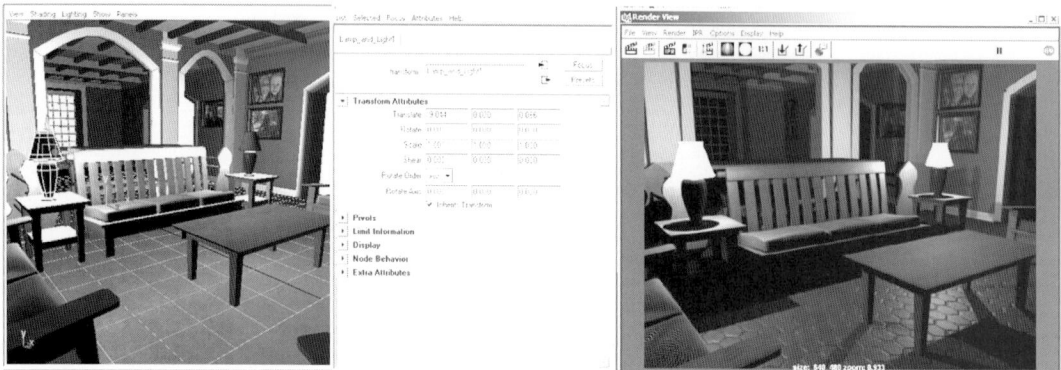

FIGURE 9.32 Duplicated lamp and light.

Our room is starting to look better. To spice it up a bit more, we will add a few more light sources.

Step 11: Create a sconce from a Revolve surface. Create a CV curve and make a Revolve surface from it. Make sure that when you create the Revolve surface you set the End Sweep Angle to only 180. Place the new surface on the pillar so that it approximately matches Figure 9.33. The details are up to you.

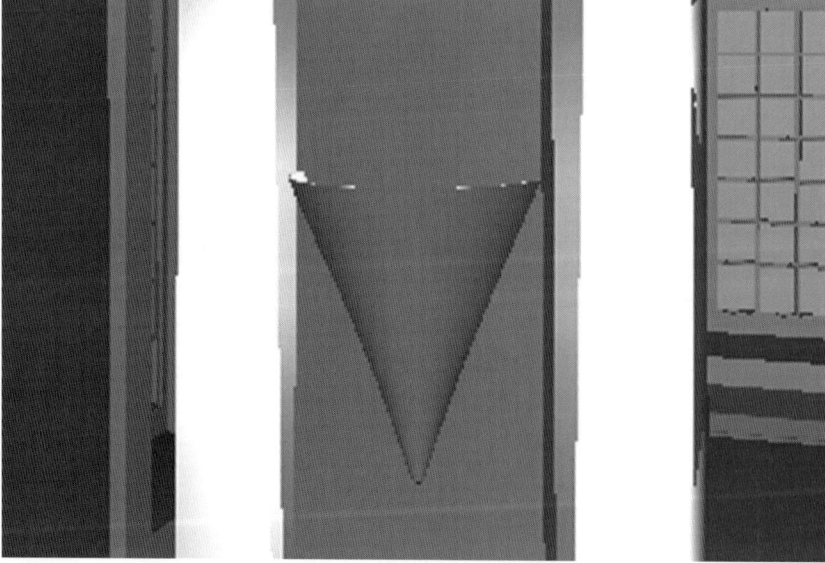

FIGURE 9.33 Sconce created with a Revolve surface and textured with an Anisotropic material.

For this exercise, let's pretend that this sconce is metal (even though it does not really go with the room). Create an Anisotropic (or Blinn or Phong) material and make sure to adjust the Specular Shading attributes so that you have a high, tight specular highlight.

Step 12: Create a new Point Light to place in the sconce. Again, select Create > Lights > Point Light. Move the new light so that it sits in the sconce. Again, activate the Depth Map Shadows, change the Decay Rate to Linear, and render. We need to make sure this sconce overcomes the shadows cast by the other lights in the room, so turn up the Intensity to 2.5, and turn down the color to a gray. This will give us a nice bright light close to the light source but not blast away everything else. Render (Figure 9.34).

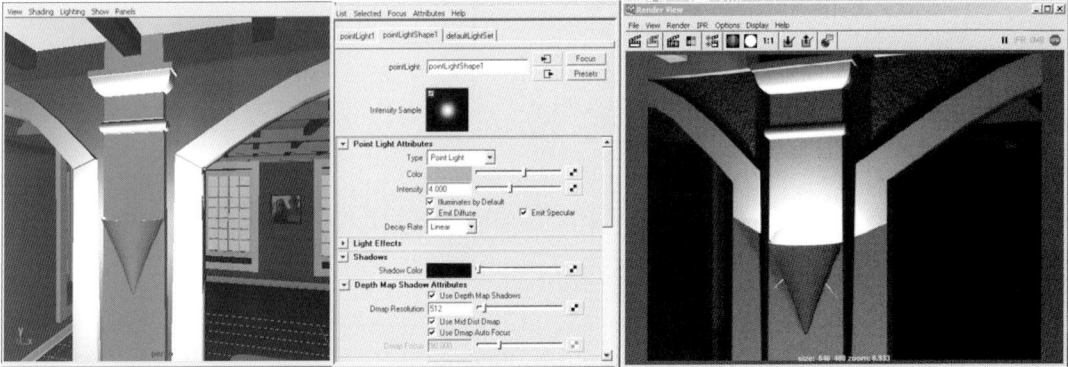

FIGURE 9.34   A sconce created with a new Point Light.

Note that because the sconce is solid and it casts shadows, it helps define the shape of the light. Although that shape would have been made with a Spot Light, it was more accurate by letting the shape of the sconce shade do the work.

Step 13: Create a bit of bounced light. With a high-intensity sconce shooting straight up to a white painted ceiling, we would have some light bounce off of that ceiling, washing objects below with a soft light. To fake this, we will use an Area Light.

Create the Area Light with Create > Lights > Area Light. Use the Move tool to move it up and above the sconce (Figure 9.35a). Now, hit the Show Manipulator tool and move the COI manipulator so that it sits directly below the Area Light, in effect, telling the Area Light to aim its light radiation down (Figure 9.35b).

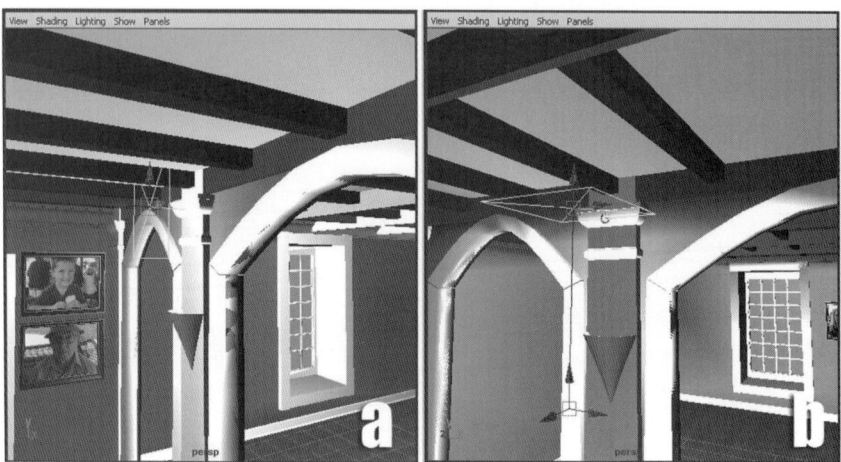

FIGURE 9.35 (a–b)   Creating and aiming the Area Light.

Increase the size of the Area Light so that it roughly matches that of Figure 9.36. In the Attribute Editor, make sure you turn down the Intensity to 0.500, as it is bounced light. Change the Decay Rate to Linear and turn on Depth Map Shadows. Render (Figure 9.36).

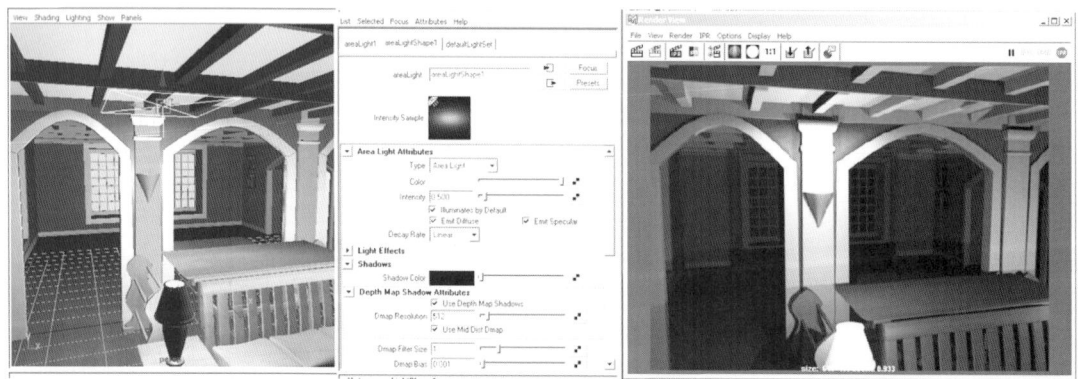

FIGURE 9.36   Sconce with bounced light.

Notice the top of the table behind the couch; this fake bounced light bathes the corner of the table in a soft light.

Step 14: Group together the sconce, pointLight, and areaLight, and place duplicates around the room. Where exactly you place these is up to you. Figure 9.37 shows a suggested output. Because you are copying the bounced light along with the sconce, you create the fake radiosity automatically as you go along.

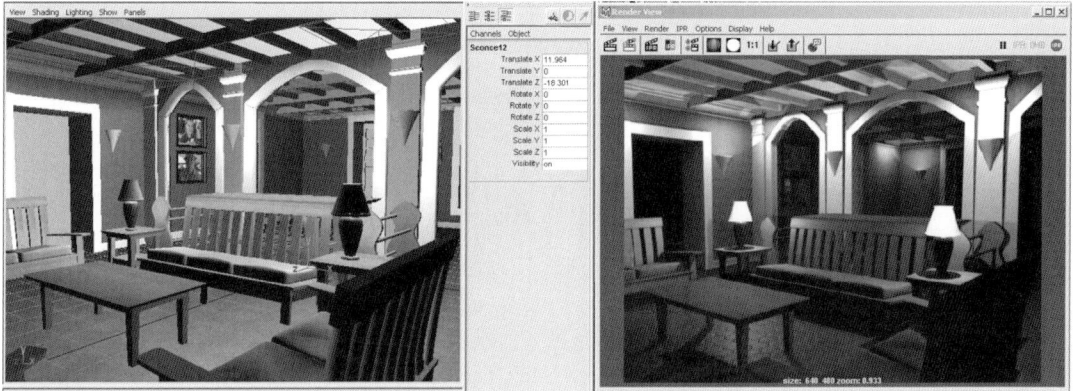

FIGURE 9.37   Duplicated and placed sconces (including the bounced light).

Step 15: Create a small light to light the artwork on the walls. Figure 9.38 shows a close-up of a small lamp that will hang over some of our pictures to illuminate them. Again, this is just the geometry—there is no light source presently in them.

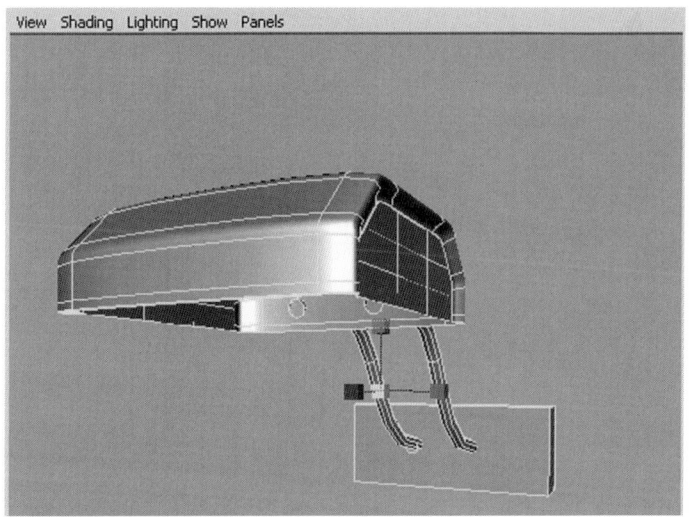

FIGURE 9.38   Geometry of the art lamps.

Step 16: Create a Spot Light to go in the art lamp and position it. Create the Spot Light with Create > Lights > Spot Light. Move the light so that it approximates Figure 9.39a. Show the manipulators and move the COI so that it is toward the bottom of the picture (Figure 9.39b).

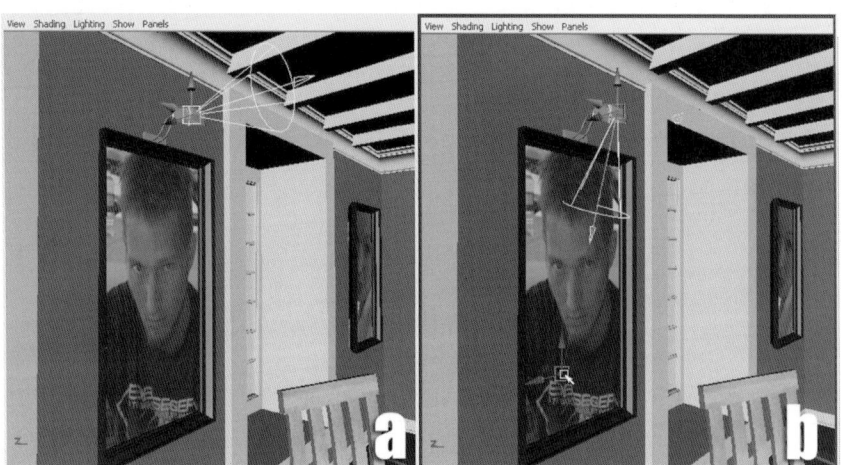

FIGURE 9.39 (a–b)   Positioning and pointing a Spot Light.

Step 17: Adjust Spot Light settings to light the photos appropriately. Right now, the Spot Light is narrow, the light will shoot forever, and it will not cast any shadows. So, we need to adjust a slew of attributes.

Activate Linear Decay: we do not want the light from this small lamp running rampant through the scene. Change the Cone Angle to 85. You can do this with the manipulators if you wish, but it is just as easy and interactive in the Attribute Editor.

To give the light a bit of a soft edge, change the Penumbra Angle to 10. Make sure you activate the Depth Map Shadows. Last are the Color and Intensity settings. These can be rather tough. Because we have decay on, we are definitely trying to control how far the light throws—we do not want too much light emerging. Often, finding the right balance is a matter of reducing the color (closer to a gray) and increasing the Intensity. For Figure 9.40, the Color is about halfway gray (on the slider) and the Intensity is set at 5.00.

Step 18: Finally, add a small light bulb in the lamp and give it some of its own inner light. Of course, this light bulb will not actually be giving off any light—the Spot Light is taking care of that. What the

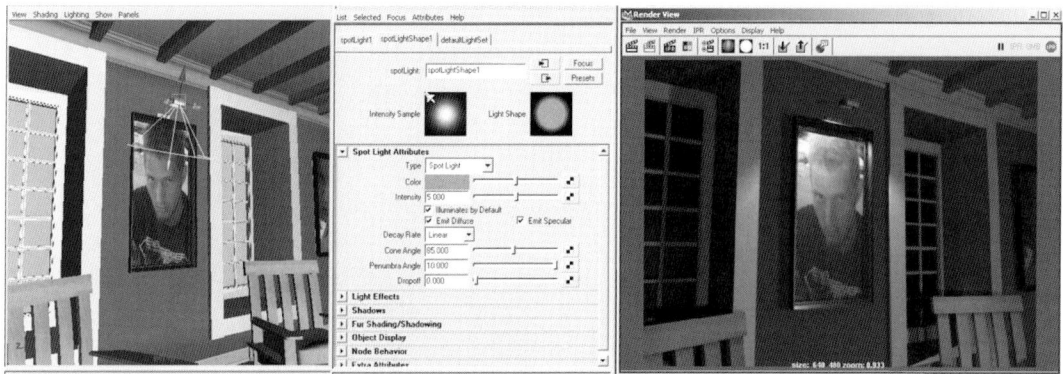

FIGURE 9.40   Adjusted Spot Light to highlight art work.

light bulb will do is make it appear as though there is indeed a hot tungsten source inside the lamp. This can be quickly modeled with a cylinder (NURBS or polygon) with a material (we used Lambert) with a high Incandescence setting. For a little extra pizzazz, open the Special Effects section for the material you are placing on the light bulb and activate the Glow Intensity by increasing the value to 0.25 (Figure 9.41).

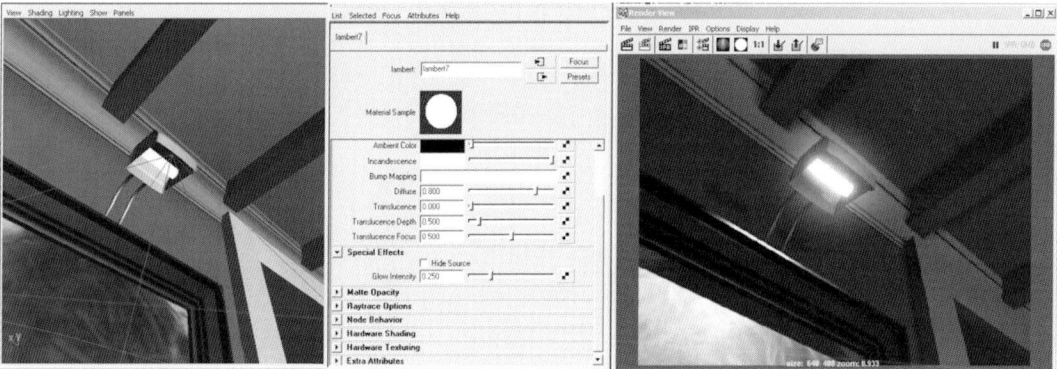

FIGURE 9.41   Light bulb with an incandescent material with Glow activated.

Step 19: Group all the objects related to this artwork lamp, and duplicate the lamp above pieces of artwork you wish to highlight (Figure 9.42).

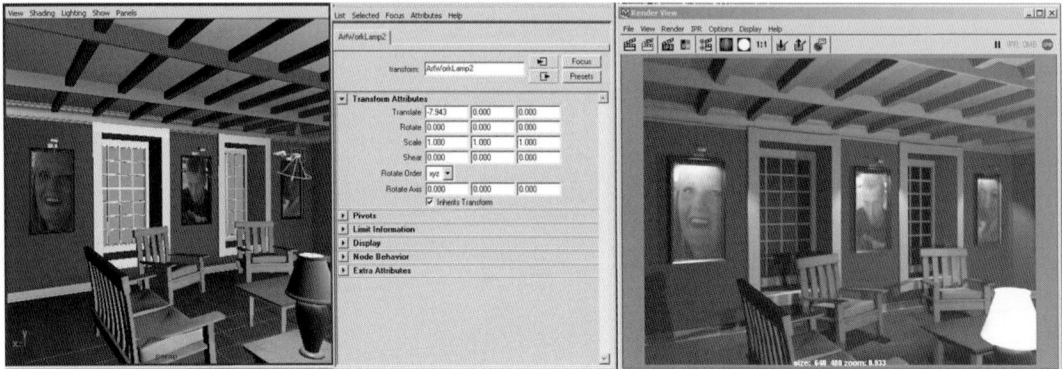

FIGURE 9.42   Placed art lamps.

Step 20: Add lights inside other lamps as you see fit. Remember that believable light comes from a believable source. This means you might need to model some additional objects to get things working like you want them. Remember that the room does not need to be completely bathed in light; often, what you cannot see is almost as interesting as what you can see.

Step 21: Group together your lights and place them on a new layer called NightLights.

Step 22: Create a new layer for just the lights, not the surfaces. In the Top view, choose Show > None (from the Top View panel's pull-down menu). This makes the Top view completely empty. Now again, in the Top View panel, select Show > Lights. The result will look something like Figure 9.43.

Create a new layer in the Layer Editor and name it NightLight_Instruments. Select all the lights in the Top view by marqueeing around them, and add them to the NightLight_Instruments layer (RMB-click-hold on the layer in the Layer Editor and select Add Selected Objects). Finally, hide this layer but make the layer NightLights visible. You now have the geometry of the light objects in the scene, but the actual lights have been made invisible.

Step 23: Save and close the file.

Well, that's it for this tutorial. We have covered Point Lights, Area Lights, and Spot Lights. We certainly did not explore every exhaustive aspect of these light tools but we did use many of them. Remember that if you want to see the exact setting of any of the lights used in this tutorial, the completed Maya file is on the CD-ROM; take a look. Also, many of the figures will simply not make a whole lot of sense unless you look at the color versions; these are also on the CD-ROM.

ON THE CD

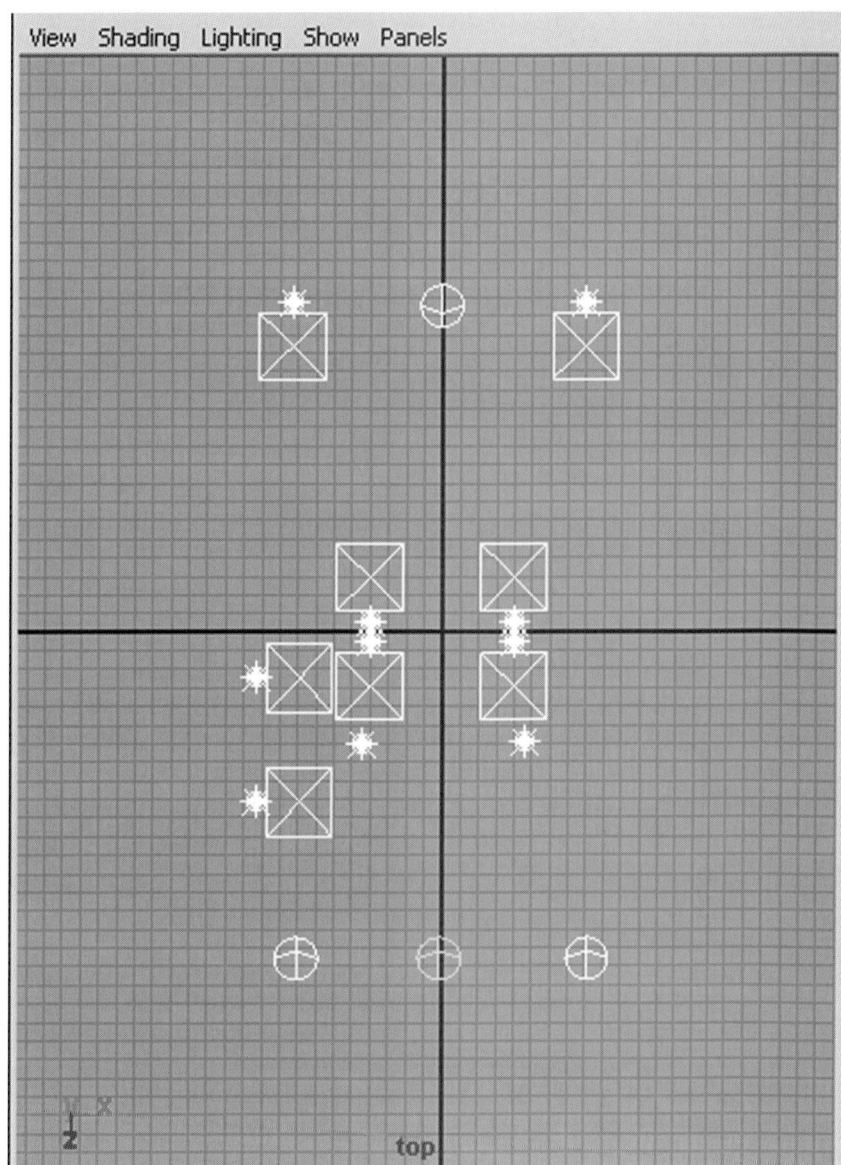

FIGURE 9.43   Showing just the lights in a scene.

In Tutorial 9.2, we will light the scene for daytime. This will require fewer lights, but it will take a bit more finesse to get just right.

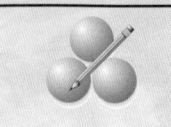

TUTORIAL 9.2 **DAYTIME LIGHTING**

For the daytime lighting setup, we want a clean lighting slate. Remember that at the beginning of the last tutorial we saved a copy of the scene as RoomDaylight. Find this scene now and open it up.

Step 1: Create the sun. As discussed earlier, the best light type for this is a Directional Light. Create this with Create > Lights > Directional Light. We will set the light to come in from the east.

Although we have seen how a Directional Light does not actually need to be outside of a room, it is just more intuitive to set it up that way. Show the manipulators and move the COI so that it is on the floor of the room allowing the Directional Light to come streaming through the windows (Figure 9.44).

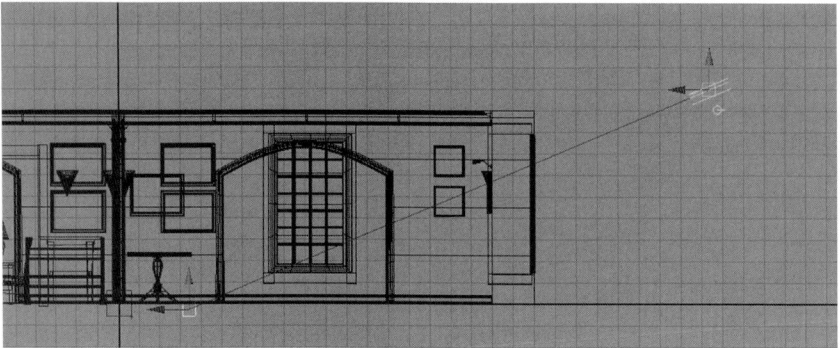

FIGURE 9.44   Setting up the sunlight with a Directional Light and a COI on the floor.

Finally, rename the Directional Light Sun_Light in the Outliner.

Step 2: Adjust the attributes of the Directional Light. Your Attribute Editor may not be open if you were working with the Layer Editor from earlier. So, make sure of this and hit **Ctrl-A** to access the attributes. Turn up the Intensity to 3.00. Turn on the Depth Map Shadows. Render.

This should be a fairly fast render; indeed, the scene will render quickly because it will be completely dark inside of the room. Even though we have transparent glass, the default renderer in Maya does not understand how transparent glass works. So, what is happening is that the glass windows that should be allowing light through are stopping everything up and not letting any light enter the room.

Now, we could get around this in several ways. One way would be to turn on Raytrace Shadows for the Directional Light and then use the Raytracing engine to render, but this adds a lot of rendering time—more than we want to deal with now.

Step 3: Make the glass not cast shadows. A more effective way is to make the glass of the windows so that it does not implement the Cast Shadows feature; in other words, don't let the glass stop the light, so the light can come streaming in unhindered.

Select the glass pane (just the pane—not the whole window) and in the Attribute Editor, expand the Render Stats section and turn off Casts Shadows. Repeat this for all the glass in the room. Render (Figure 9.45).

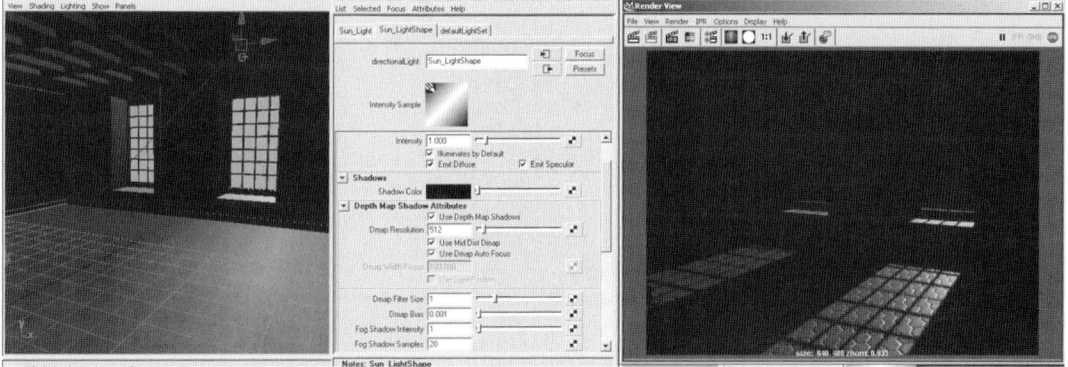

FIGURE 9.45   With the glass not stopping light, the Directional Light comes in to illuminate the room.

Sure enough, the light is streaming in. However, it's not quite right yet. In a real room, if there were sunlight streaming through the windows like that, the entire room would be bathed in a gentle light from all the bounced surfaces. The light would bounce off the floor, the ceiling, all the walls, and so on.

Step 4: Add bounced light. As we did in the previous tutorial, we will employ the ever-useful Area Light. Create a new Area Light (Create > Lights > Area Light) and position it near the ceiling (just below the beams). Use the manipulator (show the manipulators first) to point the Area Light straight down on the ground. Finally, resize the Area Light so that is about the size of the side of the room closest to the east wall (Figure 9.46).

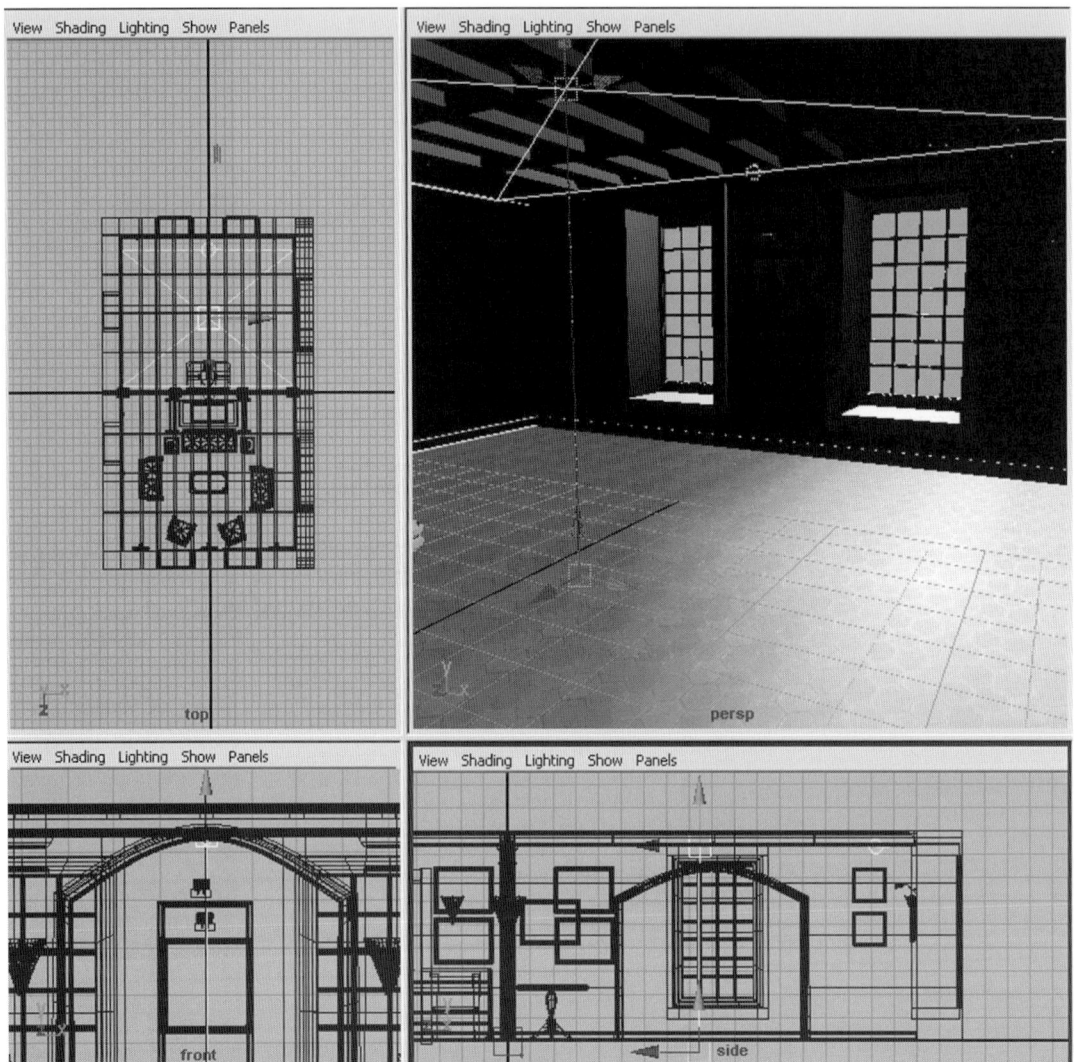

FIGURE 9.46 Placement of the Area Light for the bounced light from the ceiling.

Rename this light in the Outliner BouncedEastCeilingLight.

Step 5: Adjust the attributes for BouncedEastCeilingLight. You might try and adjust these before reading this step. Much of this sort of adjustment starts out as good guesses and then is refined to the correct setting (which is then written here). If you would like to compare your results, change the Intensity to 0.300. Make sure the Decay Rate is set to Linear. Turn on Use Depth Map Shadows.

You were probably able to get all these things right to begin with. There is one more cheat that we will use here. The bounced light that this ceiling will be giving off would be a soft, diffuse light that would also be bouncing off a multitude of other surfaces. So, the shadows that this bounced light would cause would be quickly washed down to a much lighter color. To simulate this, move the Shadow Color slider to about midway—a light gray. This actually creates semi-transparent shadows that do not appear as harsh. Finally, render (Figure 9.47).

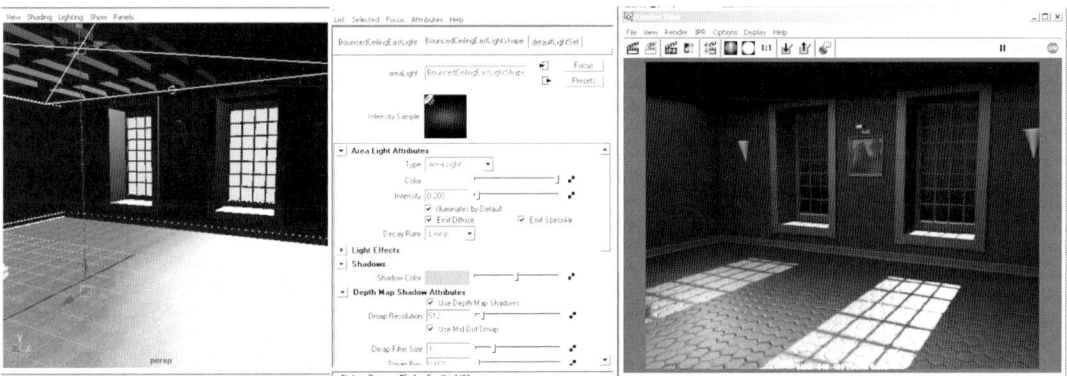

FIGURE 9.47   Bounced ceiling light.

This is starting to look a bit better. We now need to add the light that would bounce off of the floor.

Step 6: Duplicate the light, BouncedCeilingEastLight, and position it on the floor pointing up. Remember to use the manipulators. Rename the light BouncedFloorEastLight. Remember that this bounced light needs to be just above the floor of the room.

Because this bounced light would be the first as the sunlight strikes this surface in the room first, turn up the Intensity to 0.400. Render (Figure 9.48).

We're getting awfully close. While we are working on these two surfaces, let's create the bounced light for the west end of the room.

Step 7: Duplicate BouncedCeilingEastLight and BouncedFloorEastLight and move them to the west end. Rename them BouncedCeilingWestLight and BouncedFloorWestLight. Finally, because the light will have traveled the farthest here, reduce the Intensity of BouncedCeilingWestLight to 0.200 and BouncedFloorWestLight to 0.300. Also, we want the shadows from these bounced lights to be extra light, so turn the Shadow Color to a lighter gray still. Render (Figure 9.49).

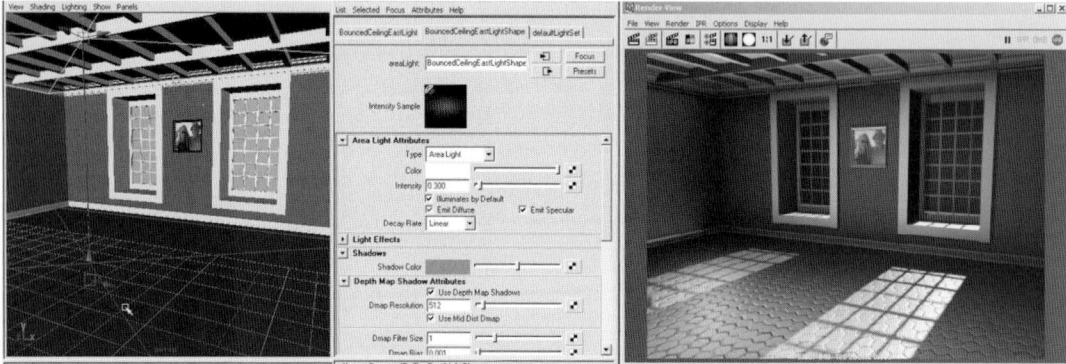

FIGURE 9.48 Bounced light added from the floor.

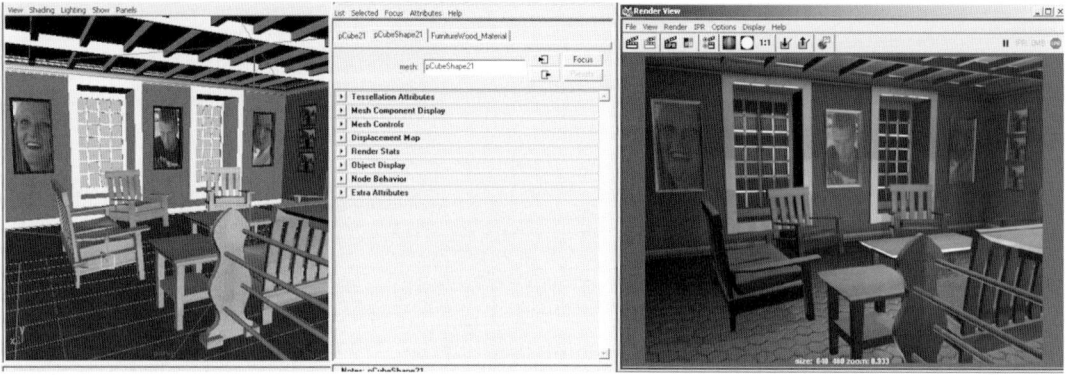

FIGURE 9.49 Bounced light on the other side of the room.

Step 8: Add a sunlight wash from the windows. There are some really nice things happening here now. Figure 9.50 shows some great renderings of what we have thus far. The only problem is that there are still some really dark surfaces on objects that are facing other windows.

On a sunny day, there would be light coming in from all the windows, even though there would be one primary light source. All the other windows in the room would be letting light radiate from the outside in. So, we need to fake this with some extra light sources.

Step 9: Add Area Lights the shape and size of the windows. Create new Area Lights and resize them so that they are the size of a window. Make sure they are pointing into the room. Finally, make sure the intensity is set low (0.100). For these objects, you can choose to turn shadows

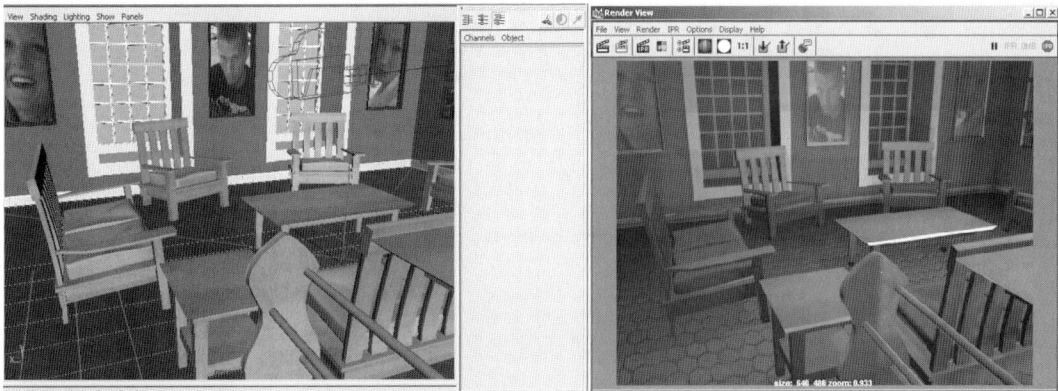

FIGURE 9.50   Room thus far.

on or not. Leaving off the shadows can help give you a nice gentle wash, but it can also create hotspots below the window. Figure 9.51 has the shadows turned off. However, from Figure 9.52 on, the shadows are on. Place one in each window and render (Figure 9.51).

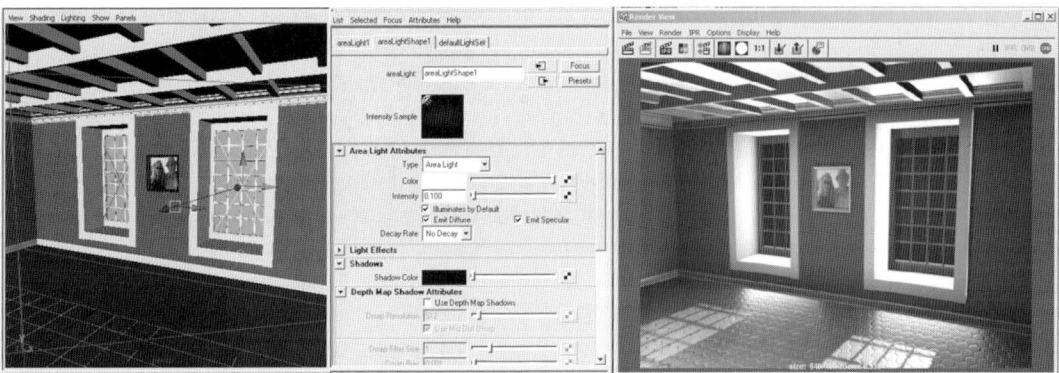

FIGURE 9.51   Added Area Lights for the window radiation.

Step 10: Add a cyc. All this lighting seems to work great. The only problem is regardless of how the lighting looks on the wall and furniture, when you look out the window and it looks black, we do not believe the lighting. To fix this, we will use an old theater trick.

A cyclorama—cyc for short—is a backdrop that sits at the back end of a stage. It is usually just a drop painted to look like a skyline, fields, or whatever is appropriate for the play. What we want to do is create such a cyc for the outside of this room.

Good cycs are actually curved. So, first—for the west end of the house—build your cyc by creating a CV curve in the Top view (Figure 9.52). Duplicate it, move it up, and create a loft surface between the two curves. Rename the lofted surface WestCyc. Once the surface is created, a material needs to be placed on it (Figure 9.53).

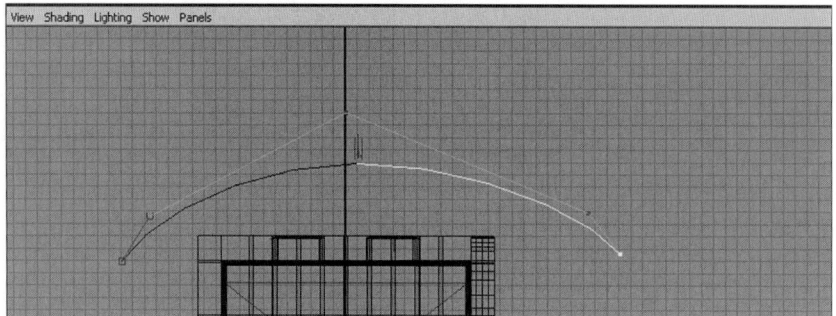

FIGURE 9.52   Create a cyc by starting out with a CV Curve.

ON THE CD

Copy from the CD-ROM Tutorials/Chapter09/Textures the folder called Cycs to your hard drive into the directory in which you are storing your textures. In this folder are a couple of long photographs. In the Hypershade, create a top tab and define it as a Tab Type: Disk. Point Maya to the Cycs folder to use as the directory and hit Create.

Create a new Lambert Material and place the texture, WestSideCyc.tif, in the Color and Ambient Color attributes. We want to make sure that the cyc is not reliant on any light sources to illuminate it. Rename the material WestSideCyc_Material and place it on the lofted surface.

Before rendering, there are a few things we need to do. This cyc should not block any light coming into the room, so select the cyc and, in the Attribute Editor, open the Render Stats section. Turn off the Casts Shadows option.

In addition, we want to make sure the lights in the room do not cast a shadow onto the cyc—it destroys the illusion. So, also uncheck the Receive Shadows button (Figure 9.54).

Tumble and dolly around until you can see out of the windows to the cyc. Figure 9.55 shows the result (be sure to look at this image in color). The problem is that the surface's colors are completely blown out. This is because the light from inside the room is bleeding out through the windows, and the Directional Light is lighting it as well. Too much light is not a good thing, so we need to tell all these overzealous lights to ease off.

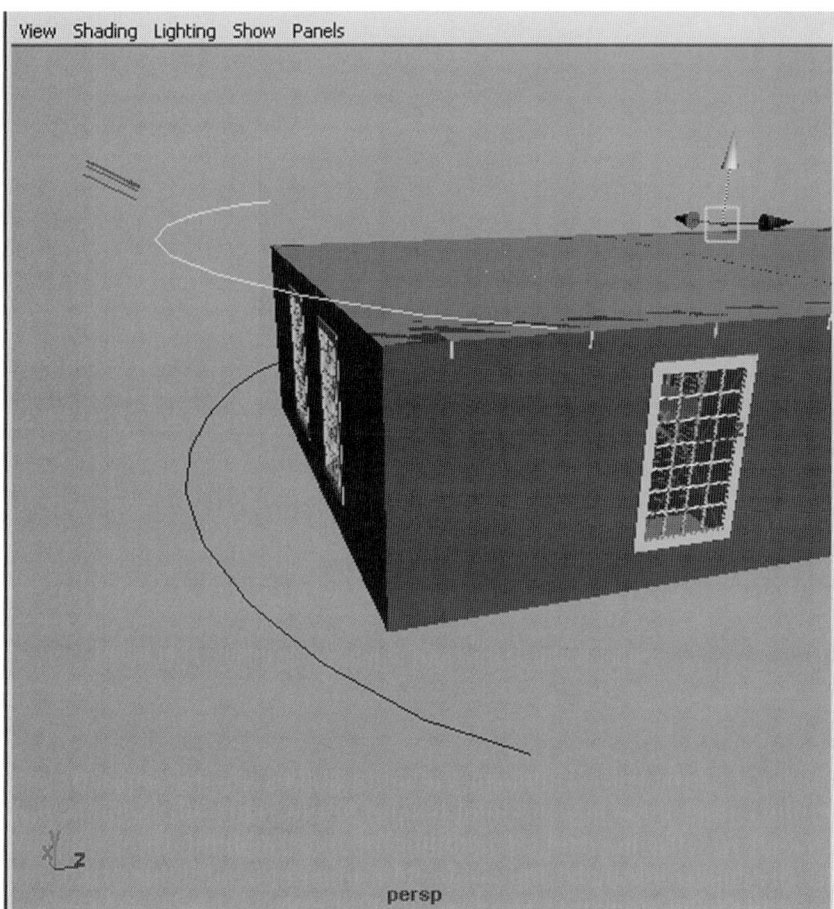

FIGURE 9.53   Create a surface by duplicating the surface.

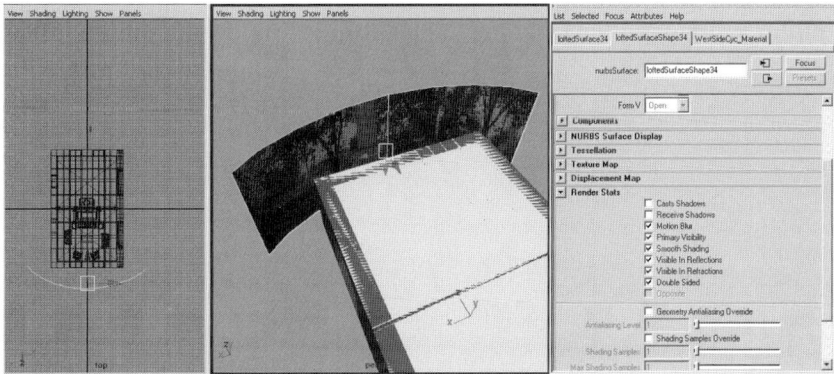

FIGURE 9.54   The cyc setup.

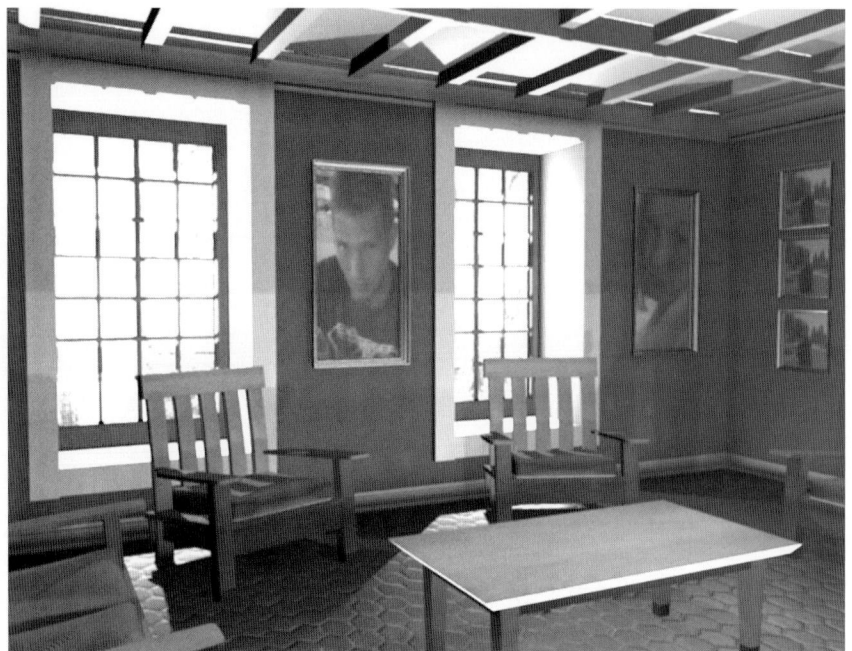

FIGURE 9.55   Overexposed cyc.

Step 11: Refine the relationships of lights and objects. Select any light in your scene and make sure the Attribute Editor is open. Look carefully in the Area Light Attributes section and notice the Illuminates by Default option (Figure 9.56).

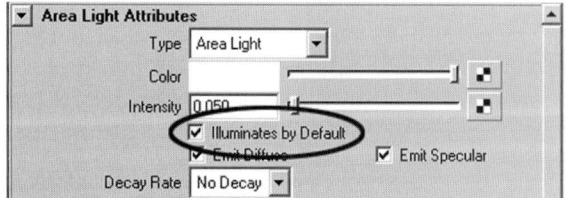

FIGURE 9.56   Illuminates by Default for a light.

What this means is that by default, this light's radiation will be "felt" by all objects in the scene (unless covered by a shadow). This is how real light works, of course. However, because we are in a virtual environment, we can bend certain rules and have lights simply not shine on certain objects.

Managing this sort of trickery is done in the Relationship Editor. There are several types of Relationship options that can control everything from display layers, to render layers, to defining all the objects a light affects, or in this case, defining all the lights that affect an object. Choose Window > Relationship Editors > Light Linking > Object Centric. We want to use Object Centric, because it will allow us to select our WestCyc and tell all the lights not to bother it at once rather than selecting each light, finding WestCyc, deselecting it, and moving on to the next light.

Once the Object Centric Light Linking window is open, click on WestCyc in the left column (Illuminated Objects). In the right column (Light Sources), all the lights in the scene will of course (by default) be highlighted. Simply start at the top and click-drag to the bottom. This will deselect all the lights, meaning that none of them will illuminate the WestCyc object (Figure 9.57).

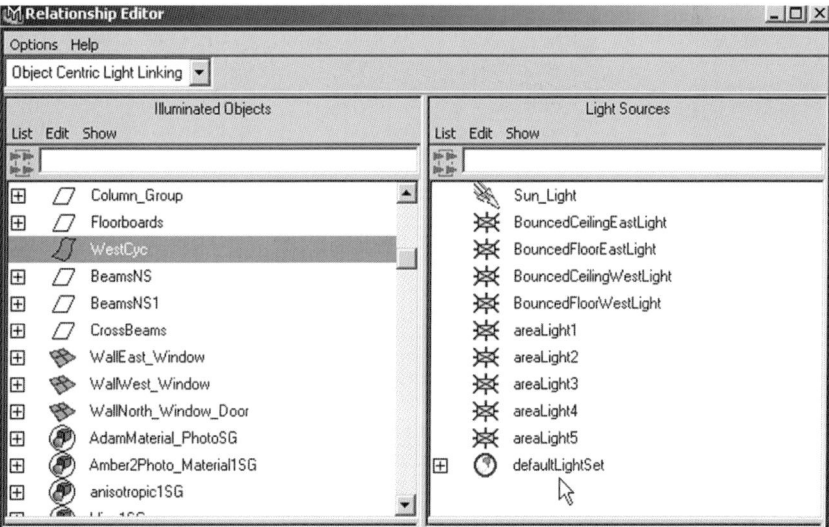

FIGURE 9.57   Removing the light link for all lights on the WestCyc object.

Take another render (Figure 9.58).

Step 12: Repeat Steps 10 and 11 for another cyc for the east side called EastCyc. Simply duplicate WestCyc and rotate it around so that it is curved in the right direction. Rename it EastCyc. Create a new Lambert material and place the image texture EastCyc.tif in the Color and Incandescence (or Ambient Color) attributes. Place the new material (renamed EastSideCyc_Material) on the object EastCyc. Lastly, make sure that in

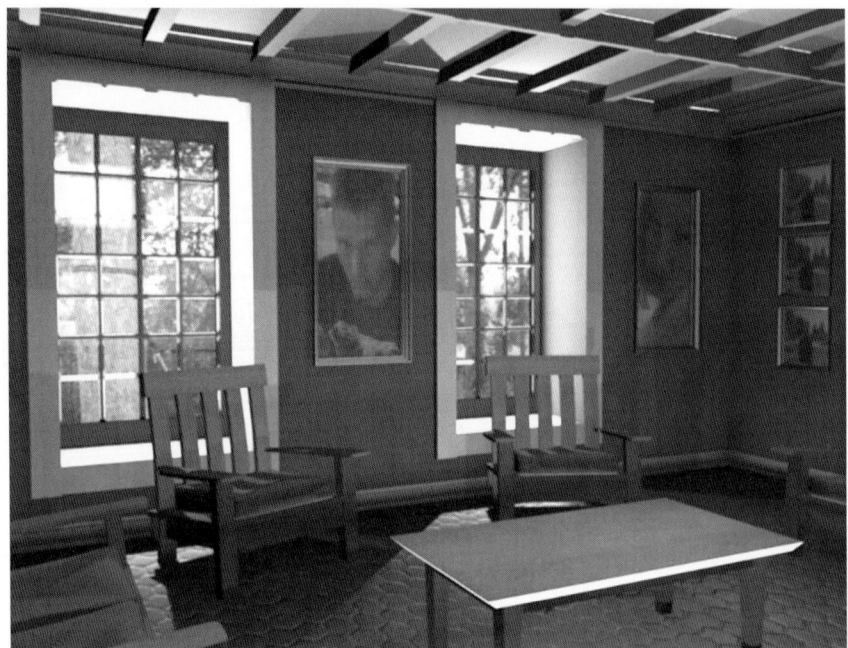

FIGURE 9.58 Rendered cyc with no lights on it. The "illumination" comes from the material only.

the Relationship Editor, the lights in the scene do not affect EastCyc. Finally, render (Figure 9.59).

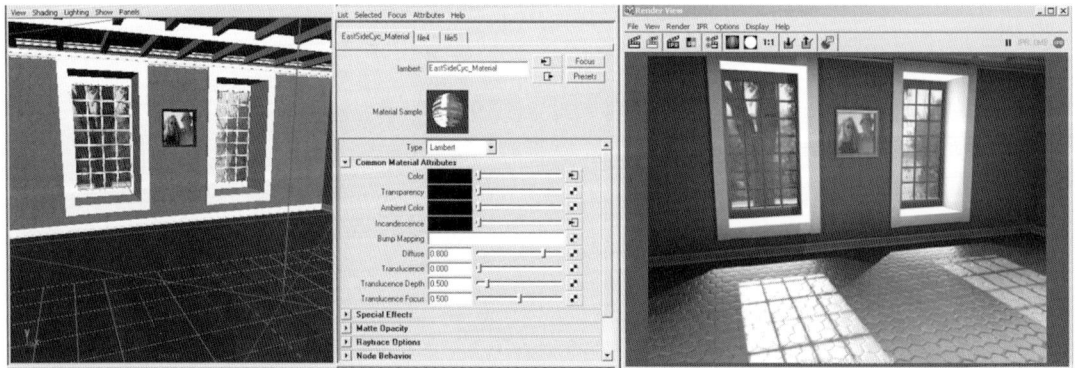

FIGURE 9.59 EastCyc in place and rendered.

Step 13: Save your file and take a break. This is just a start for this room. There could be a lot more fine-tuning to do, and you might find some areas that could be adjusted to match more closely your vision of what the room should look like. Now that you have the tools, you can do anything with the lighting in the room (Figure 9.60).

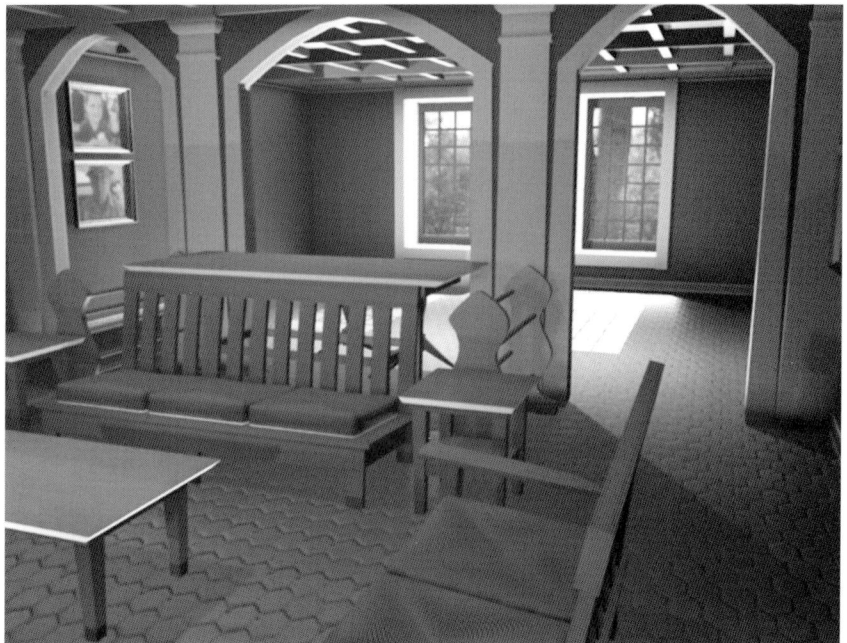

FIGURE 9.60   Final lit room.

RENDERING

Let's discuss the Render Globals windows, looking briefly at the IPR (Interactive Photorealistic Rendering) function.

Figure 9.61 shows an overview of the Render Globals window. We will not be covering every option available here. Those details are available in the Maya documentation and would make for some very dry reading. We will focus on some core ideas and tips.

The Render Using Drop-down List

Maya allows a few options for style of rendering. To select a renderer, you click on the Render Using drop-down list. Since the Maya Software renderer is the most used, we will not explore the other choices other than to give a brief explanation of the differences.

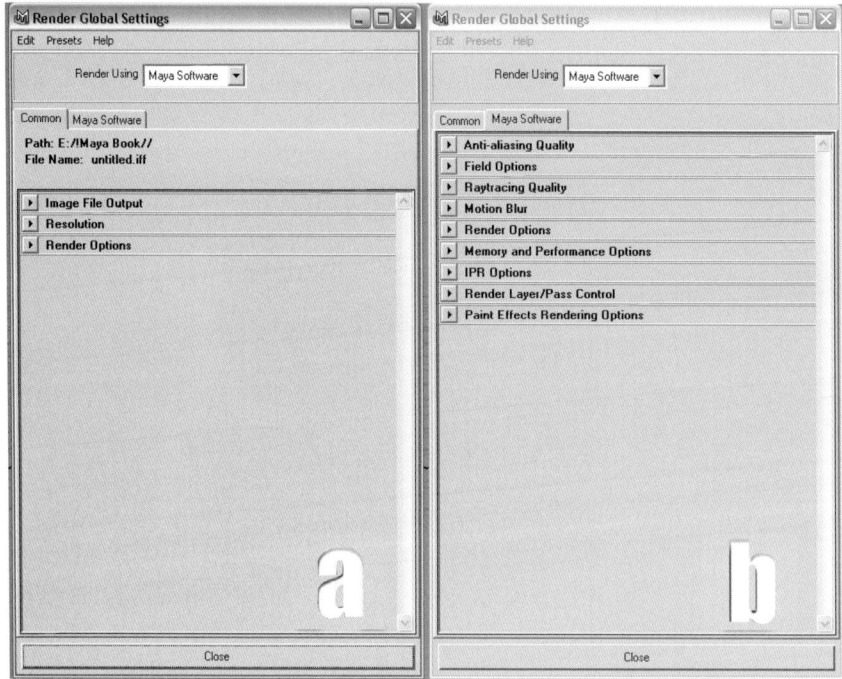

FIGURE 9.61   The Render Globals window. (a) The Common tab. (b) The Maya Software tab.

Software rendering produces the best quality with the most control. It takes longer to render but the results are worth it. Other than some limited cases, you will always use Maya Software to render your scene.

Hardware rendering uses your computer's video card to generate the images. The quality is much lower. It tends to look the way real-time video games do. The advantage is that it is fast

Vector rendering lets you create stylized renderings, such as cartoon-style, in various bitmap image formats and 2D vector formats.

Maya Software and Common Tabs

There are two tabs for access to render globals parameters: Common and Maya Software. These parameters are detailed in the following sections and illustrated in Figure 9.61.

Common Tab

The Common tab includes the following settings that are common to all renderers.

Image File Output: This area (Figure 9.62) allows you to establish general rules about how Maya is going to save the objects it renders. You can define how it is going to save the strings of stills that make up animations (as in, which image format it will use), and you can even determine how it is going to number these frames (by the "File Name Prefix" plus the frame number or by "Frame/Animation Ext" plus the frame number). Within this area, you can also define which camera Maya will use to render when it is rendering things such as animations or batch renderings.

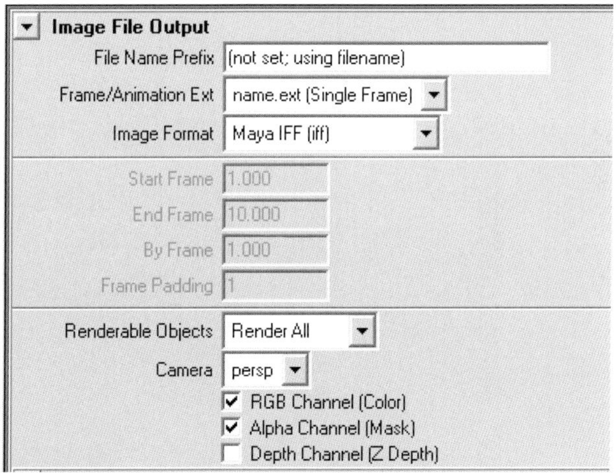

FIGURE 9.62   Image File Output area.

The last important part of this section consists of the Channels options. In general, you need not mess with these, although if you plan to do any sort of compositing, you want to be sure that the Alpha Channel option is active.

Resolution: If you have worked much with digital imagery, this area is fairly straightforward. Remember that Maya is rendering in absolute pixels. So, if you are working in video, you want to render 640x480; DV 720x480. There is a collection of presets here that can set things up for you.

If you are working in print, make sure you do the necessary calculations. If you have an image that an editor wants at 4x3 and she wants it in 600 dpi, make sure you enter 2400 for the

Width and 1800 for the Height. Remember that rendering this large an image will take a long time, so plan ahead.

Render Options: This allows you to define plug-ins or how MEL scripts will be used in the rendering pipeline. The notable exception is the Environment Fog. This is a fairly goofy implementation of the idea of adding fog to your scene. However, for quick and dirty fog effects, you can choose the colors, opacity, and density of the fog via the Channel Box once the fog is activated. Figure 9.63 shows the room with fog added.

This is a section for advanced users.

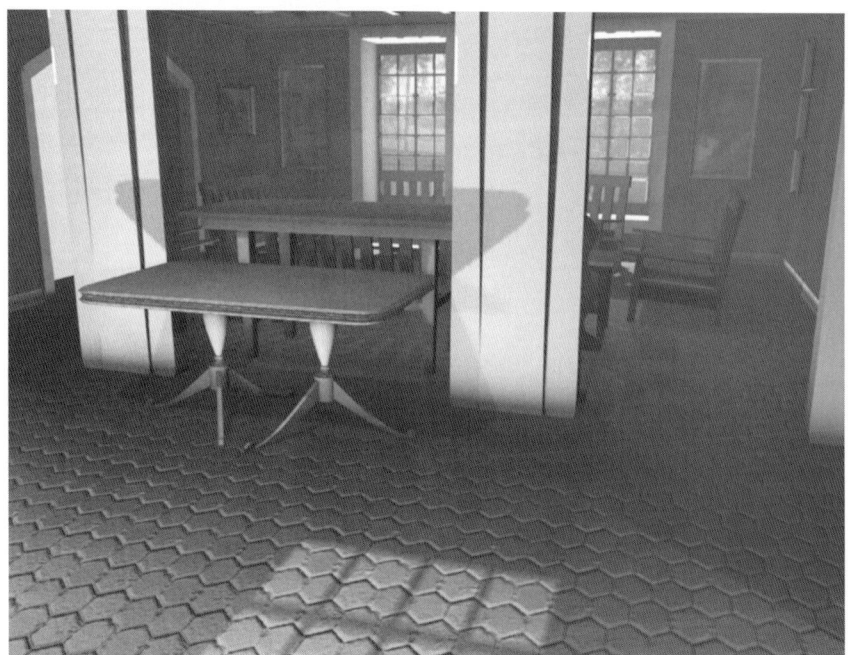

FIGURE 9.63 Adding fog to your scene.

Maya Software Tab

This tab is where you control the look and quality of the software renderer.

Anti-aliasing Quality: Anti-aliasing is the process in image creation of evening out the jaggies that often appear when a program is creating a large collection of pixels. The Anti-aliasing

Quality section allows you to choose how Maya builds the images and how much time it takes to smooth the visual lines of pixels (Figure 9.64).

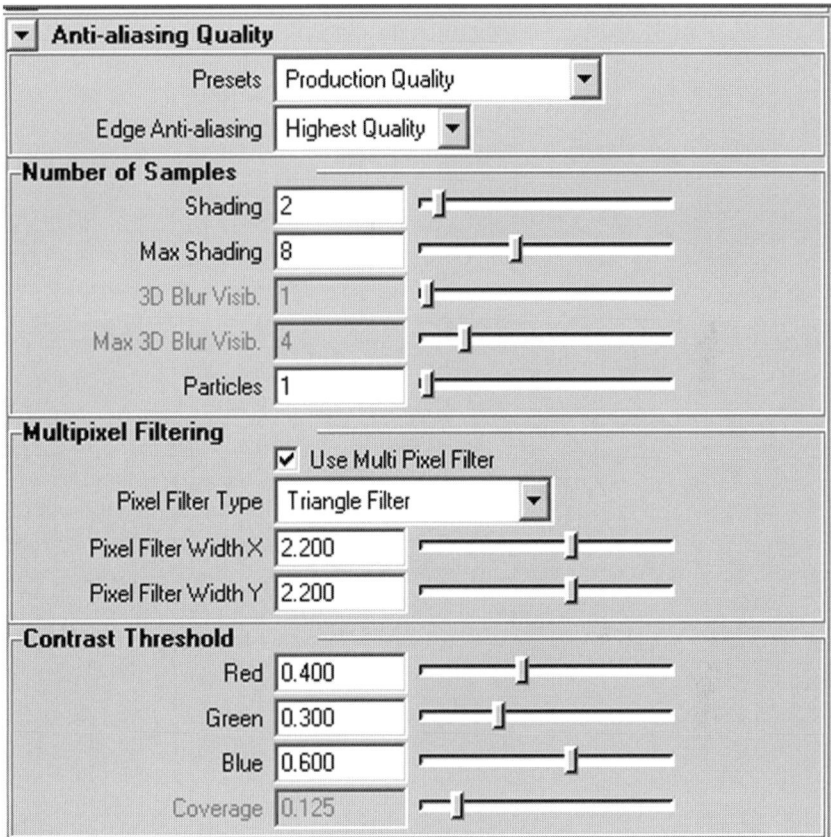

FIGURE 9.64   Anti-aliasing.

If Maya takes a lot of time to work out the anti-aliasing, the rendering slows considerably. However, if Maya does not anti-alias, your image quality can suffer. Like most of Maya, the depth of tools here is fairly intense. In general, the Presets and Edge Anti-aliasing settings are all you need to worry about. The other sections are powerful but technical and more than we want to cover here.

In general, keep the presets set at Preview Quality as you work. When you are happy with your image and you are ready to make that "final" render, come back in and turn up the presets to Production Quality. This preset will kick up all the settings to where they need to be for a great quality image.

Field Options: This has to do with how a television displays an image. This is well beyond the scope of this volume, but when your work is ready for broadcast, there is much written about the theory and implementation of field options.

Raytracing Quality: As we have looked at earlier, this section allows you to decide whether to activate Raytracing. In the tutorials we have been taking on thus far, we have used Maya's plain-Jane, out-of-the-box, fast-as-it-can-go render. There are some definite drawbacks to this rendering engine. It does not handle shadows well and it does not handle reflections at all. Raytracing can help solve some of these problems. As we discussed earlier, Raytraced Shadows look better, and Raytracing can handle reflective surfaces of any type. The drawback is its cost in render time.

The Settings, Reflections, Refractions, and Shadows have to do with how many times the Raytracing engine calculates the surfaces or reflected surfaces. Higher values help produce more accurate images but also slow down the rendering. Keep these as low as you can. For example, if you have an error such as you begin seeing black planes where two reflective objects face each other, then come in and adjust these. In most cases, the default settings are fine. Fooling with them too much without a solid need and understanding can make the usually long rendering process even more excruciating.

If you are serious about rendering a large amount of animation or stills that need heavy reflections or other Raytracing-specific functions, you probably should be considering options such as Maya's implementation of MentalRay. Other functions that renderers such as MentalRay allow you to do include caustics, more accurate refracted light, bounced light, and other radiosity and radiosity-like functions. Although Maya's default renderer has been making strides over the past versions, it is still dog slow and there are just better alternatives available.

Learning MentalRay could take up a book all by itself and is far beyond the scope of this volume.

Motion Blur: When you are playing back a VHS tape or even a DVD and hit the Pause button, often the moving parts of the image are blurred beyond all visible recognition. This is a result of the shutter of the camera only being able to open and close so fast. In 3D, you can fake this effect and often give a bit of realism to animation by activating Motion Blur.

Motion Blur always takes longer to render and, depending on the type of Motion Blur you use, it can dramatically increase the time needed. If you are doing heavy Motion Blur scenes, you are probably not using Maya's renderer—it's just too slow. If you wish to dabble with it, Maya's documentation has a fairly good overview of what it does and how to use it.

Memory and Performance Options: By default, the settings within this area are set to try and optimize the power of your machine. There is usually no need to change them.

IPR Options: IPR stands for Interactive Photorealistic Rendering. It is an interesting idea to allow Maya to take a little longer to render certain parts of a scene so that as you change elements in your Workspace, they are "instantly" updated to reflect the changes. For some things, it really does work remarkably well— for example, light intensity, some texture work, and so on.

The way to use IPR is simple. Along the top Status Line next to the Render Globals Window button is a clapboard with the symbol IPR on it. With the view you wish to render active, hit this button. Render time takes a bit longer.

When this is done, the Render View window will show the scene with a prompt on the bottom of the screen to Select Region to begin Tuning. Right then, you can marquee around a section of the image that you wish to update quickly as you tweak your scene. It is probably not a good idea to marquee around the entire object, but small sections can work out.

You will then get a red box that is the updating region. As you make changes to your scene in the Workspace, Maya will update the area highlighted in red as quickly as it can. For details such as how high a bump map is or how bright a light is, this works great.

In general, IPR is best for those times when you are tweaking settings and only need to see certain parts of the scene updated.

Render Layer/Pass Control: Full exploration of this area is the subject of another volume. Maya has the incredibly powerful option of rendering an image in layers—that is, rendering only parts of the scene in each pass that can be assembled together later. This means Maya needn't deal with the entire scene all at once. It also means that you can separate the walls from the floor, and if you need to adjust the color of the walls, you can do so with just the Wall pass without having to re-render the entire scene.

CONCLUSION

That is really a whirlwind overview of the rendering options. There are lots of options to tweak here—so many that there are entire books written simply on optimizing and working with Maya's rendering engine. This should be enough background so if you run into problems you know where to go to begin tweaking.

Earlier in the chapter, we explored lots of the lighting tools. Despite improvements over the years, Maya's lighting and rendering aren't as refined as some of its competitors, but there have been many fine renderings done with the basic tools. With the recent addition of MentalRay, Maya's power has expanded significantly.

Now we'll leave the room behind and get to the real fun. In the next chapters, we will be looking at how to set up the bird to be animated and at the process of animation itself—the part where we will bring the scene to life. After, we'll revisit some of these tools and try to expand on the look we created. There are lots of props to be added, new materials to be created, and new lighting setups to explore. When you feel more confident, design and build your own room with its own furniture. Look around the room you're in now and see what makes it look the way it does, not just the objects, but the colors and light. Then consider trying to replicate your surroundings.

RIGGING THE BIRD
FOR ANIMATION

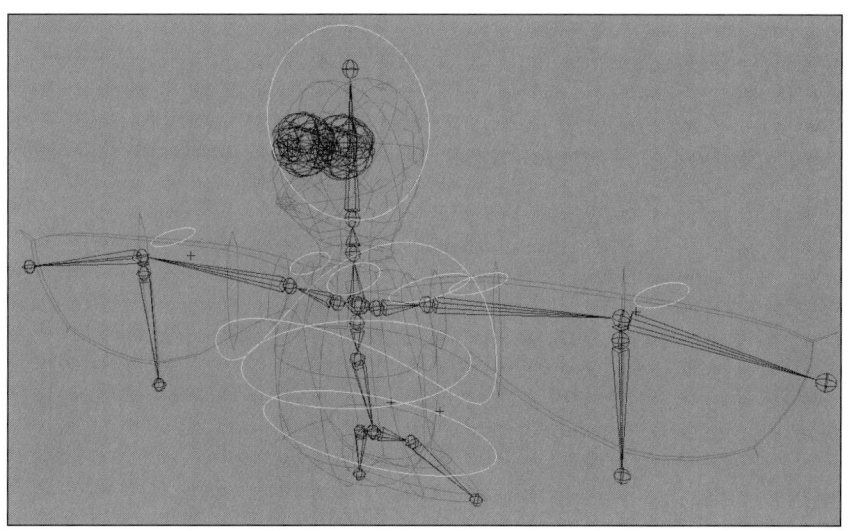

Wₑ have a scene. We have a bird. But for our bird to fly through our scene, it needs a skeleton. This skeleton is made up of joints that Maya uses to deform an object. By the end of this chapter, our bird will be able to flap its wings, look around, and fly around our virtual set.

If you didn't take a break after the last chapter, take one now. There is a lot to cover on this subject, and a tall glass of iced tea or a vacation might go over well just now. Well, it's not really that bad.

We will look at the Joint tool, which makes the skeleton of the bird. Then we will use Smooth Bind to make the skeleton control the bird's mesh

TUTORIAL 10.1	**THE JOINT TOOL**

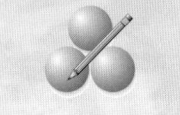

To understand joints before we tackle the bird, we'll use the Joint tool and Smooth Bind to bend a simple cylinder. By covering the basics on this simple object, the work on the more complex bird will go a little easier.

To start with, let's create a cylinder. Go to Create | Polygon Primitives > Cylinder and select the Options box. Set the Height to 10 and the Subdivisions Height to 30.

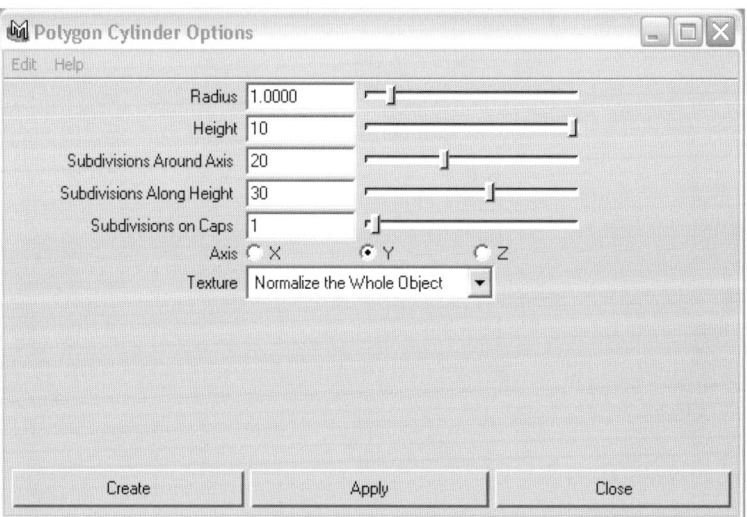

FIGURE 10.1   The Polygon Cylinder Options box with the correct values.

Now we will create the joints that will bend the cylinder. We must first switch Menu Sets (See Chapter 1) to the Animation set. Figure 10.2. Within this Menu Set, we can access the tools for rigging and skinning a character.

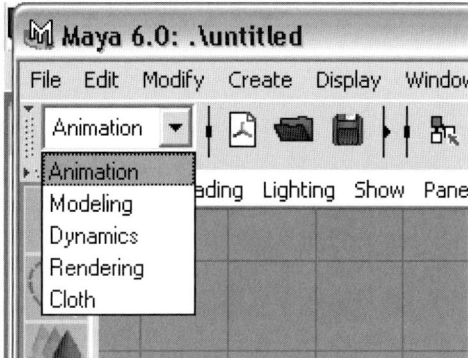

FIGURE 10.2   Selecting the Animation Menu Set.

To start creating joints, go to the Animation | Skeleton > Joint Tool. Your cursor changes to a +, and you can now start creating joints. Create a few for practice. Click where you want a joint to start and then click where you wish to end it. You can keep doing this, creating long chains even, until you hit **Enter** to exit the tool.

Get rid of the Joints you just made by selecting joint01 and pressing **Delete.** Notice that when you delete the root joint of any chain, it deletes the whole chain. This is important to know, because deleting an object from a hierarchy will delete all its children.

Fortunately, Maya has a tool if you need to remove a joint but not its children. Hit **Ctrl-Z** to undo the delete or create a new chain. Select a joint in the middle then from the Skeleton menu, click on Remove Joint (Figure 10.4).

Similarly, we can add a joint into a chain with the Insert Joint tool found under the Skeleton menu. Again, the cursor will change to a +. Click and drag from an existing joint to the spot where you'd like the new joint to end.

If the placement is not perfect, remember that you can press the **Insert** key to move the pivot like other objects in Maya. In fact, hit the **Insert** key now and move the pivot around. Note that the other joints

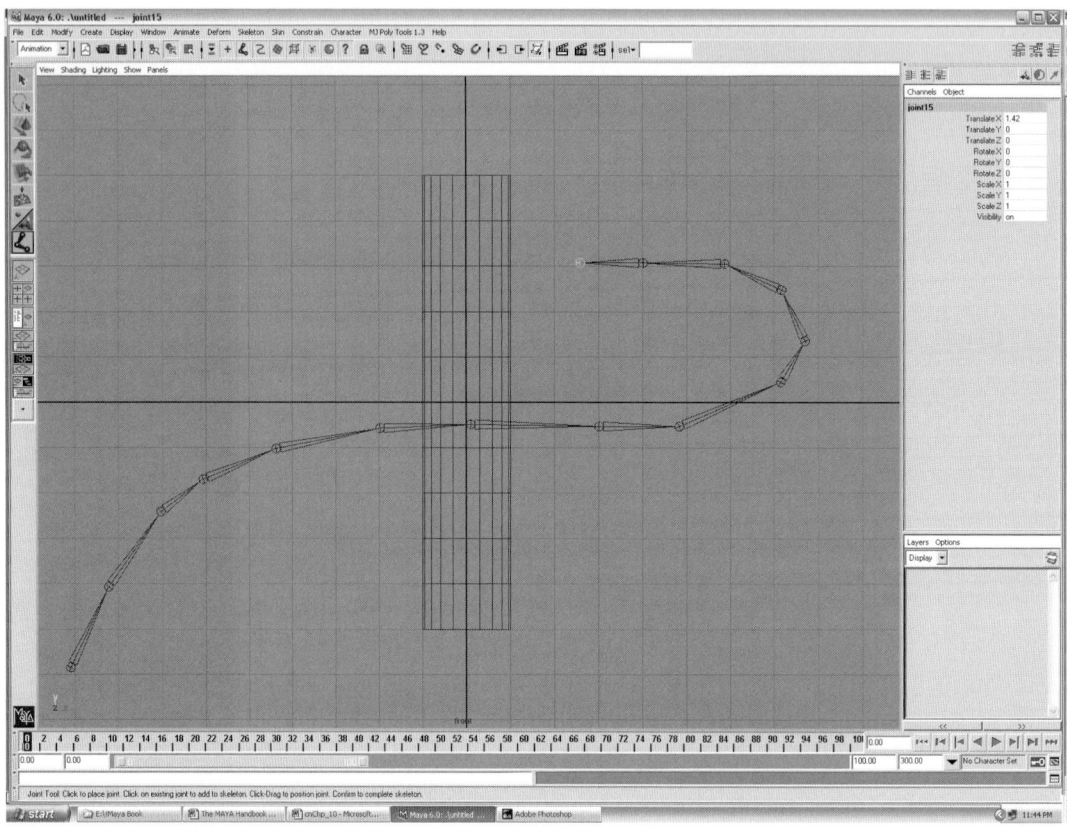

FIGURE 10.3 A long chain of joints created with the Joint tool.

are unaffected (Figure 10.5). This comes in handy if, for example, you must reposition a knee on a character and don't want the foot to move.

We will cover some of the other tools in the Skeleton menu later in this chapter. For now however, enough playing around, let's make our boring cylinder bend so we can get on to more exciting lessons with the bird.

Unhide the cylinder (if you hid it) by selecting it in the Outliner and then going to Display > Show > Show Selection. Delete any joints that you were playing around with and switch to a front view.

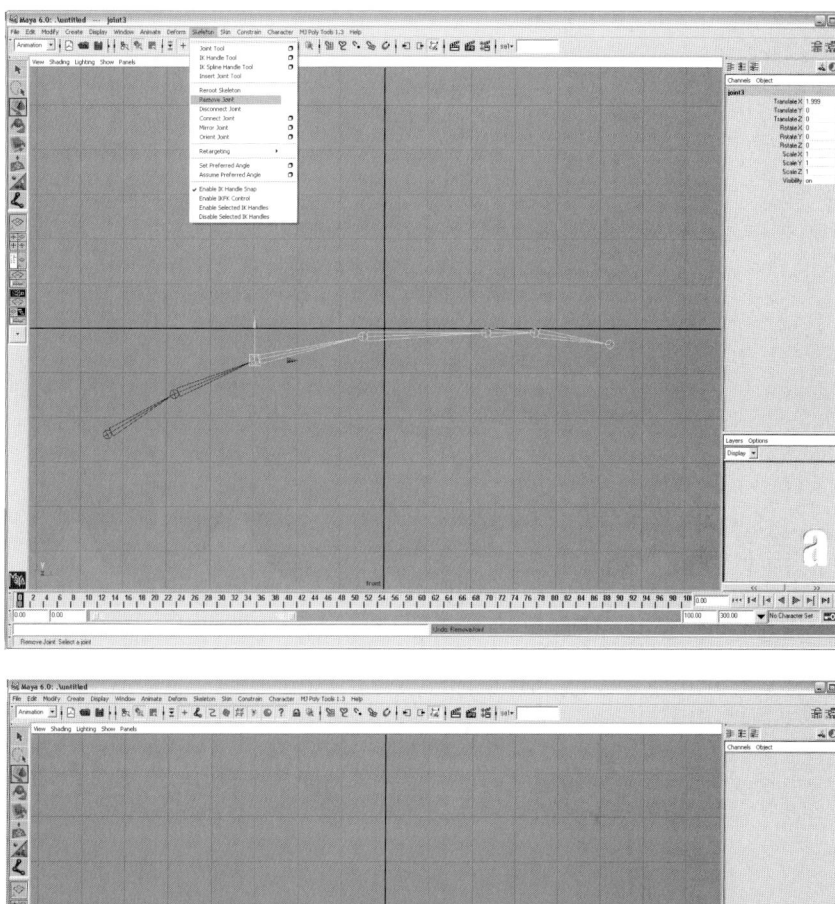

FIGURE 10.4 (a–b)   The chain before and after the Remove Joint tool was used.

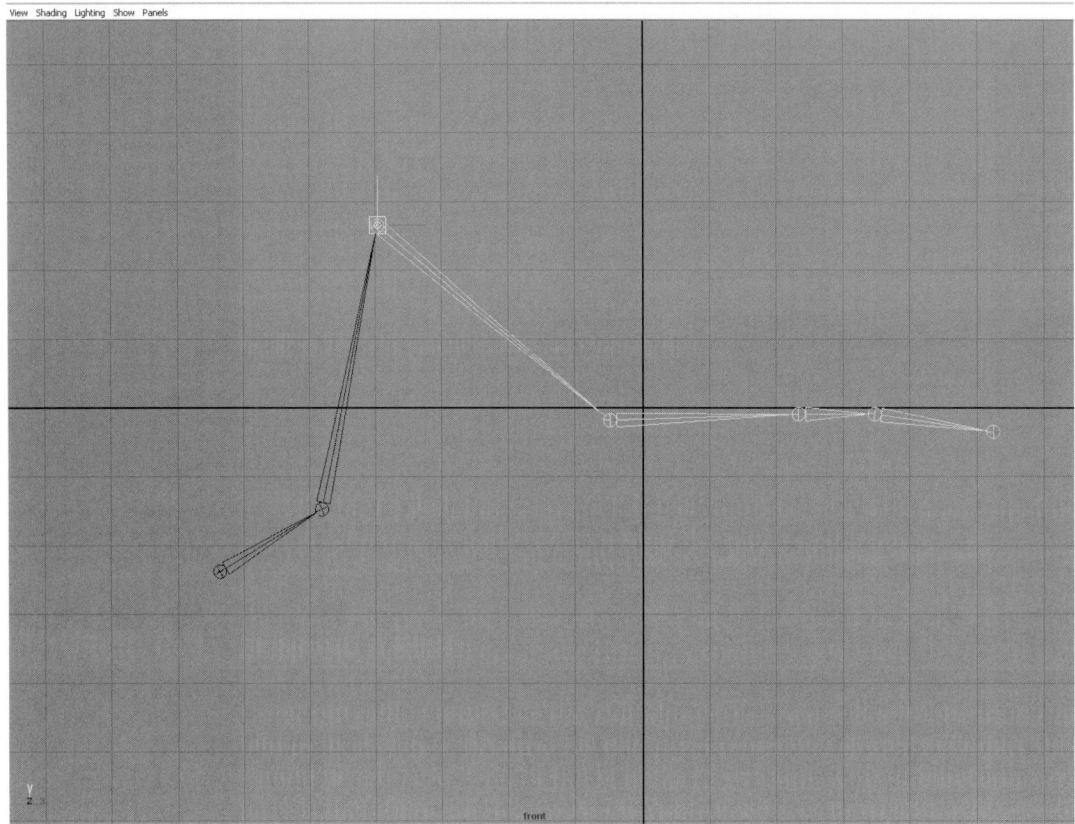

FIGURE 10.5   Use insert key to move pivot without affecting the rest of the hierarchy.

Once again, enable the Joint tool from Animation | Skeleton > Joint Tool. Click once at the center of the base of the cylinder (Figure 10.6a), then once in the center (Figure 10.6b), and one more time at the center of the top (Figure 10.6c). Press **Enter** to complete the tool. The result will look like 10.6d.

If only all skeletons were this simple to create. Sometimes a lot of planning and experimentation goes into creating a skeleton for a character.

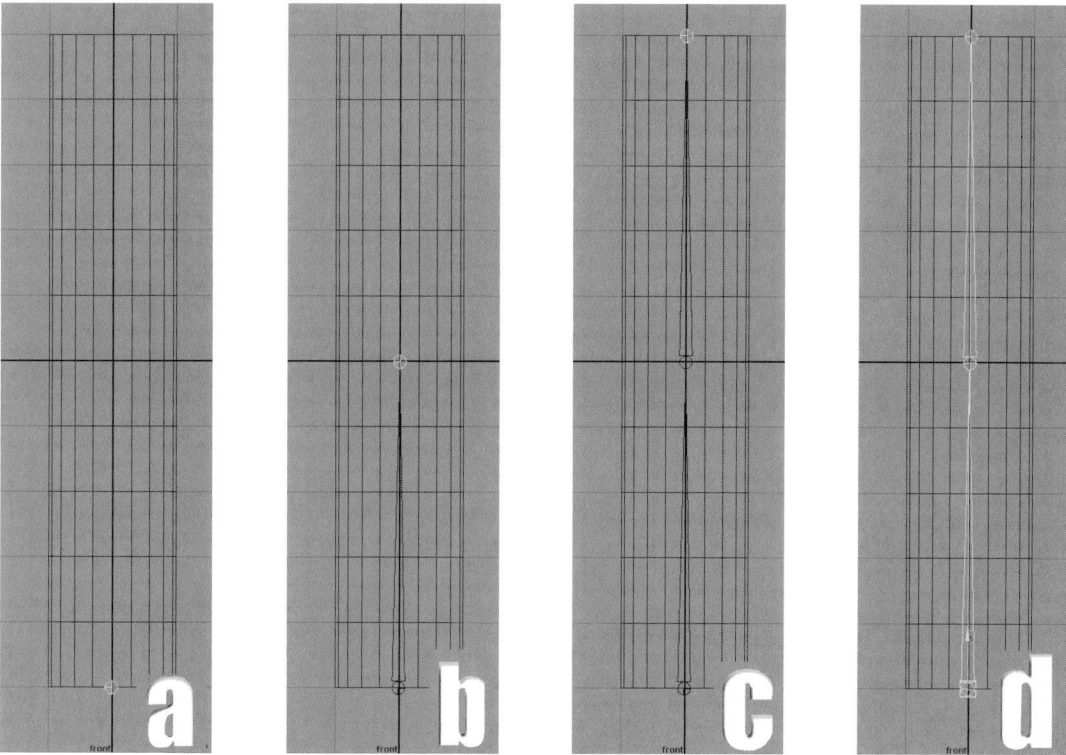

FIGURE 10.6   (a–d) Creating the joints to deform the cylinder.

| TUTORIAL 10.2 | **SMOOTH BIND** |

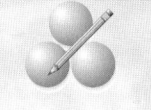

Skinning is the process of making a skeleton deform an object.

The first step in this is to use Bind Skin. To do this we must select the object we want to deform and then the skeleton that will drive the deformation.

Step 1: Apply Smooth Bind to the Cylinder. So, select the cylinder and then select joint01 (use the Outliner if you prefer). Now go to Animation | Skin > Bind Skin > Smooth Bind and click the Option box (Figure 10.7).

Before hitting Bind Skin in the Option box let's explore some of these settings.

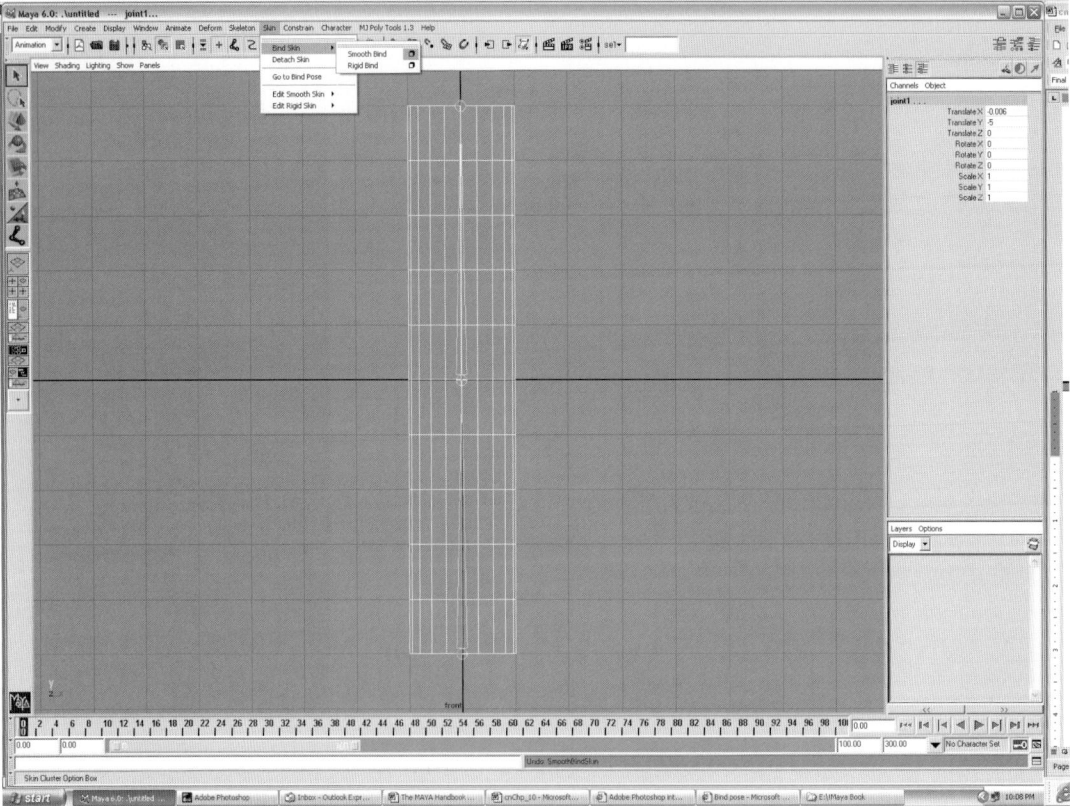

FIGURE 10.7   With the cylinder and joints selected, apply smooth bind.

Bind to: This drop-down list lets you choose whether the entire skeleton will be used or just the currently selected joints.

Bind Method: This is how Maya decides which joint controls the skin. Closest Joint, which decides the influence based on hierarchy, is the choice you'll use most often. Closest Distance decides influence, regardless of hierarchy, on the proximity of the joint to the skin.

Max Influences: This limits the number of joints that can affect a given point on the skin.

Dropoff Rate: This is how far the joint's influence reaches.

For the exercise, we will leave all these values at their defaults, so click Bind Skin. Notice that the cylinder is now magenta colored. This shows you that it is affected by the currently selected object, in this case, joint01. If you click in the viewport to deselect all objects, the cylinder returns to blue. Again, select any of the joints and you see that the cylinder

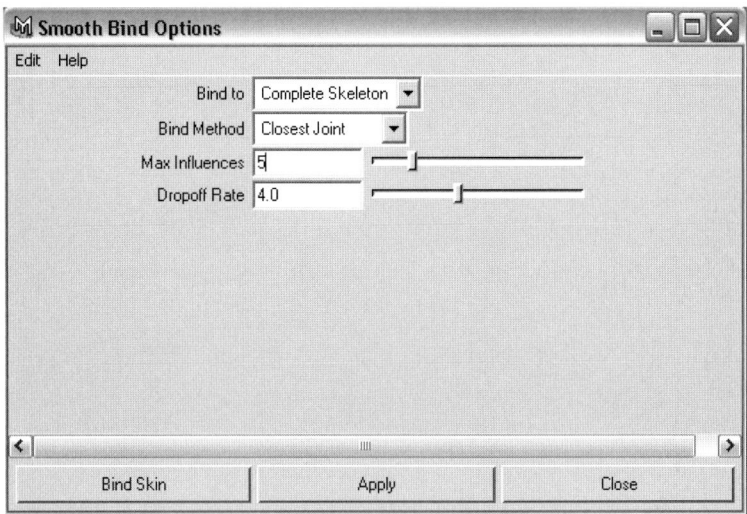

FIGURE 10.8   The Smooth Bind Options dialog box.

turns magenta. This color change that enables you to see when objects are affected in some way also occurs with Constraints (more on this later) as well as other operations.

Step 2: Testing the initial results. To see the results, select joint2 and rotate it about the Z axis. You can see the potential here; legs, arms, and much more.

The area around the "elbow" doesn't bend quite right, but the Paint Skin Weights tool will take care of this.

Before we get to that, undo the rotation on joint2. You can either hit **Ctrl-Z** or type 0 in the Rotate Z channel in the Channel Box.

Step 3: Using animation to test skinning. To edit the skinning, you will often want to bend joints back and forth. To save yourself switching objects and tools, you can animate the joint. Then all you have to do is move through frames to see if you are getting the results you want. Select joint2, click on frame 0 on the Time Slider (Figure 10.9), then press **S** on the keyboard. This will set a key frame for joint2. (Animation will be covered in depth in Chapter 11, so there is no need to absorb how to set keys just yet.) Now click on frame 1, rotate joint2 about 90 degrees, and press **S** again. You can now move between frame 0 and 1 to check your skinning.

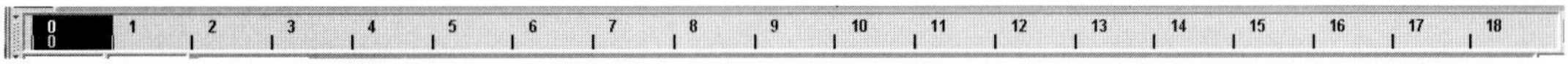

FIGURE 10.9   The Time Slider.

The Paint Skin Weights Tool

The Paint Skin Weights tool, a powerful and intuitive feature, allows you to "paint" the influence that joints have over parts of your mesh. Let's jump in and see what happens when you paint weights.

Step 4: Using the Paint Skin Weights Tool. Select pCylinder1 then choose Animation | Skin > Edit Smooth Skin > Paint Skin Weights Tool and click the Option box (Figure 10.10). You'll notice that in the Perspective view the cylinder turns black and white (Figure 10.11). White means the joint (currently selected in the Influence section of the Paint Skin Weights Tool options; Figure 10.12) has 100% control of this area of the skin, and black means the joint has no control. The level of gray in between shows how much the joint shares influence of the area with other joints.

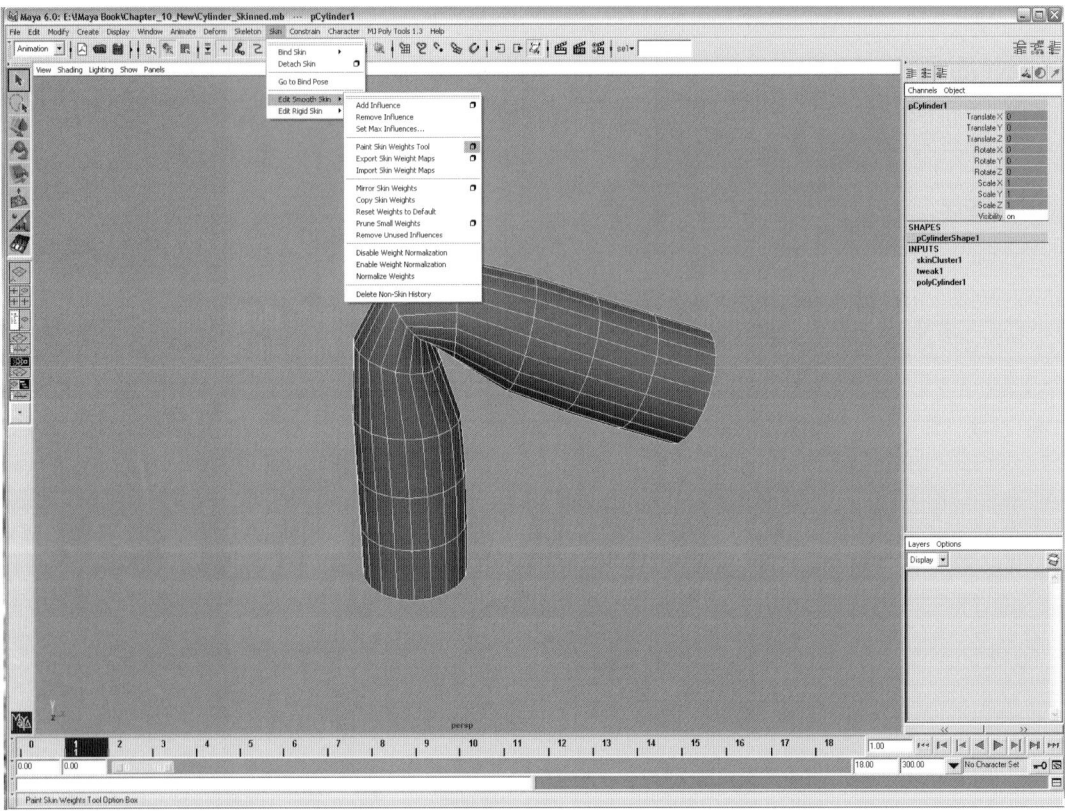

FIGURE 10.10   Opening the Skin Weights Tool Option box.

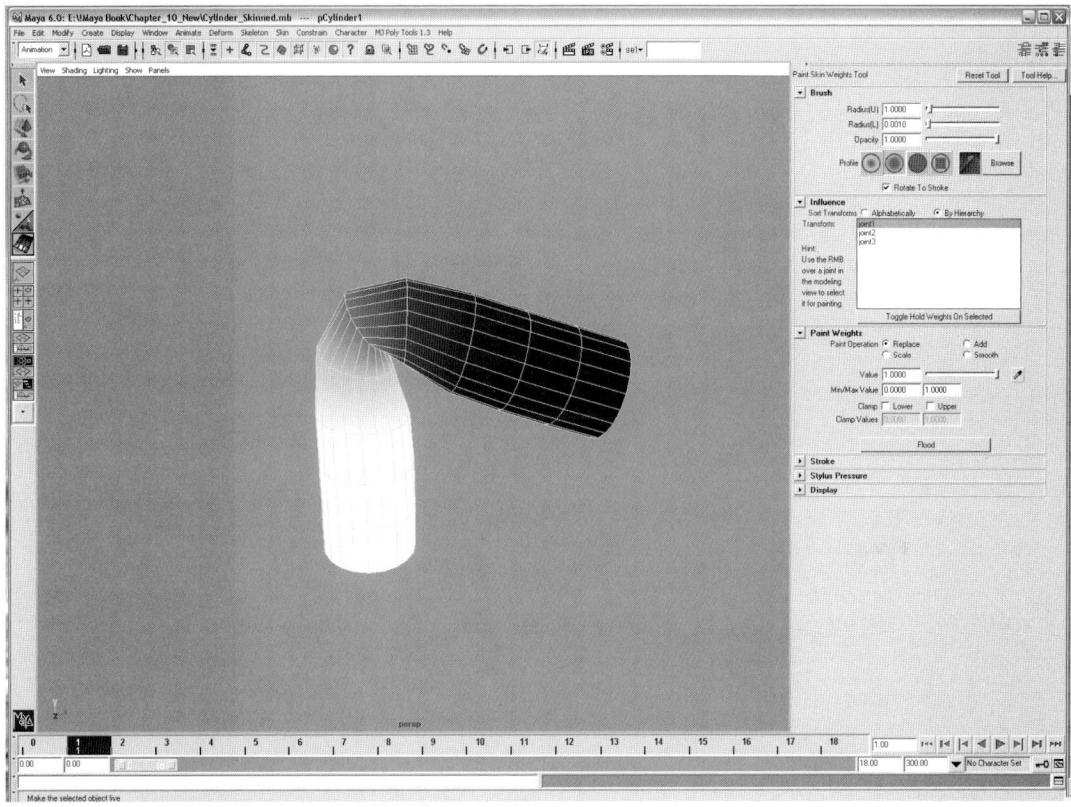

FIGURE 10.11   In the Perspective view, the cylinder turns black and white.

Step 5: Paint a few strokes. Move your cursor over the cylinder and you'll see a red circle on the surface that represents the size of the brush. Click and drag somewhere in the black to see the painting in action. Notice how you are adding white, or influence, to more of the mesh. Each time you click and drag you create a paint stroke. Go to frame 1 of the Time Slider and see that we've created a real mess of it. Hit **Ctrl-Z** to undo any paint strokes you did.

Usually you won't want paint with the settings the way they are. By lowering the Opacity in the Brush section you can gradually build up the influence. If you have a graphics tablet such as a Wacom, you can use the pressure of the stylus to control the level of Opacity, the Size of the brush, or both.

Step 6: More painting. Let's set a few values and paint some more. In Opacity (in the Brush section) set the value to 0.1. You can use the slider but it is a bit sloppy to control. Now in the Paint Weights section next to

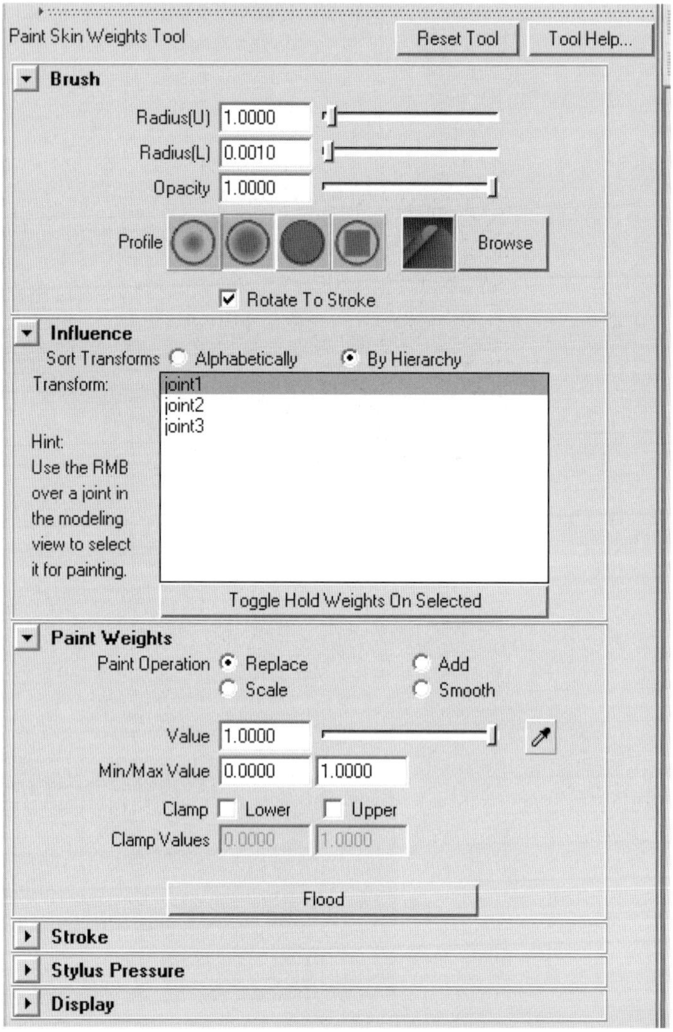

FIGURE 10.12   The joint currently selected in the Options box.

Paint Operation click Add. Add is what allows us to build up influence with each brush stroke. See Figure 10.13.

Click frame 1 on the Time Slider so you can see the cylinder bent. Like this, we will be able to see the results of our paint strokes right away. If you need to paint around the crease, simply go back to frame 0. With joint1 selected in the Influence section, paint along the side of the cylinder toward the elbow and watch how it affects the deformation of the

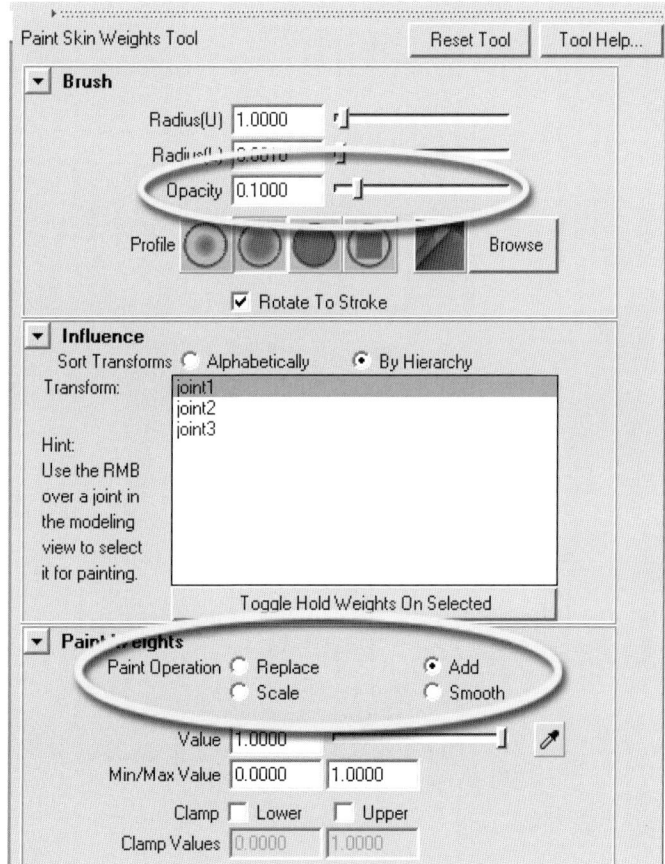

FIGURE 10.13   Paint Skin Weights Tool with changed values.

bend. Because we are adding influence for joint1, each stroke is taking away some of the effect of the rotated joint2. If you want more control over how much influence you are adding, try a lower opacity: try 0.05 or even 0.01. You'll have to paint a lot more, but when the complexity of your models grows, the slow build up will save you many headaches.

Figure 10.14a shows what we're starting with and Figure 10.14b shows our goal. Notice how in 10.14b, the gradation from white to black is much shorter. To get from A to B, you need to paint more white toward the bend for joint1 and joint2. In other words on joint1, you are painting influence up toward the elbow, and on joint2 you are painting down toward the elbow.

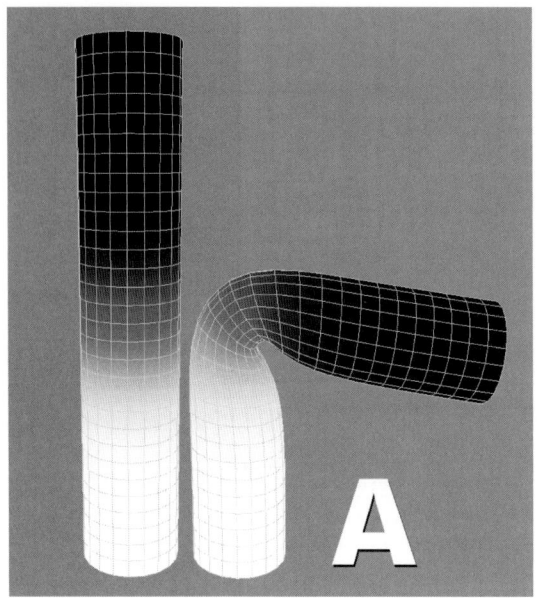 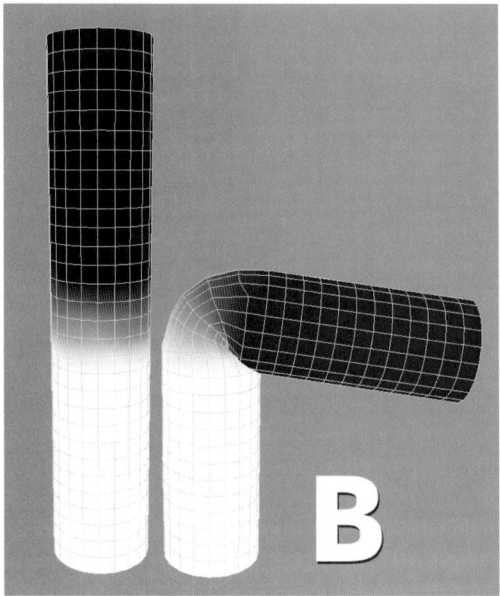

FIGURE 10.14 The cylinder before and after painting skin weights.

That's the basics of skinning. Now that we have that, let's get to the bird.

TUTORIAL 10.3 **BUILDING A SKELETON FOR THE BIRD**

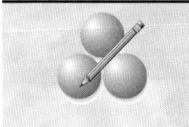

There are many things to consider when creating a skeleton for a character. The first thing to decide is where the root of the character will be. In other words, what will be the main center of rotation and movement? In most cases it will be the hips of you character, as most movement originates there. Since our bird will be flying, however, its center of rotation will be between the wings, or about the middle of the chest. This means all the parts of our skeleton will radiate out from this point.

ON THE CD

Step 1: Open the bird. To start, open the file CartoonBird.mb from the CD-ROM (Tutorial/chapter10/). You'll notice this file includes a little more tweaking to the original model from Chapter 6. Also, eyes created from NURBS spheres and a simple texture have been added.

Step 2: Template the bird for easier joint creation. In the Side view, press **4** to display the model in Wireframe. Within this view, we will begin to create the bird's skeleton. To make it easier to see what we are doing, let's set the bird to display as a Template. Select the object

BirdMesh either in the Workspace or through the Outliner. Then from the Display menu, go to Object Display > Template. The bird will now be displayed as a pink wireframe. This color indicates that the object selected is a template. When it is not selected, it will display as a gray wireframe. You will not be able to select a template object in the Workspace, which makes it easier to work on the skeleton. To reverse the Template setting of an object, you must select the object through the Outliner.

Step 3: Building the chest and head joints. As we did before, we need to go to Animation | Skeleton > Joint Tool to start creating joints. First, we will create the joints that go from the chest through to the head. To do this, click once in the middle of the chest to start the joint, and then click once at the base of the neck, once at the base of the head, and finally just past the top of the head. Press **Enter** to complete the tool. Figure 10.15.

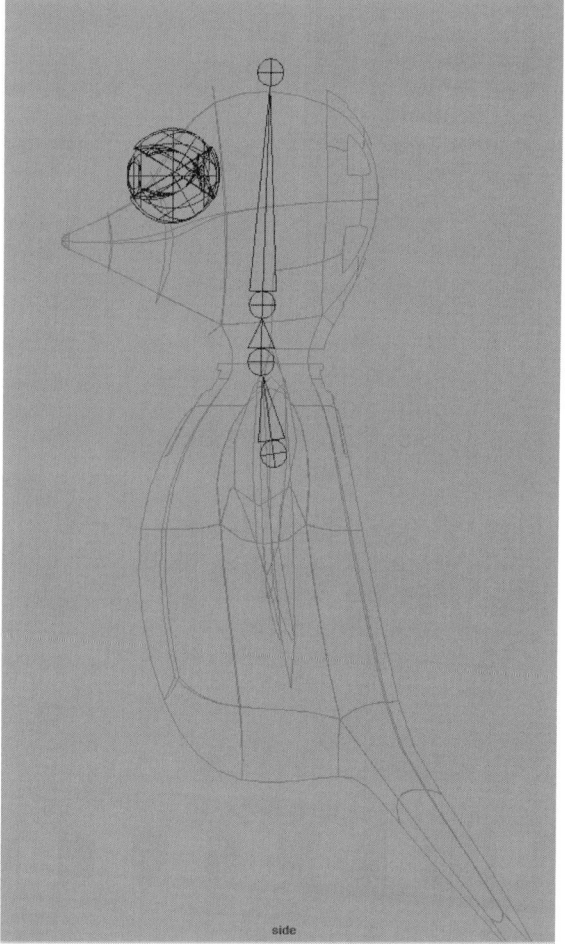

FIGURE 10.15   The first set of joints from the chest to the head.

Step 4: The lower body. Activate the Joint tool again. Remember that you can get the most recently used tool from the bottom of the Toolbox (Figure 10.16). Start from a point just below the set, then click once near the bottom of the chest, and then once near the base of the tail. Press **Enter** to complete the tool. You should have something like Figure 10.17.

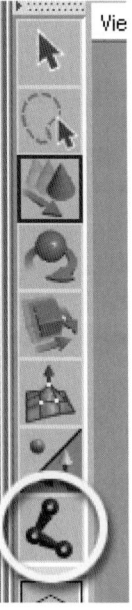

FIGURE 10.16 Access the Joint tool (or your most recently used tool) from the bottom of the Toolbox.

Step 5: Wing joints. To create the joints for the wings, switch to the Front view. Enable the Joint tool again and create joints as indicated in Figure 10.18. So we can have more control over the wing, let's create some joints for the lower part of the wing as in Figure 10.19

Step 6: Connecting the pieces. You probably noticed that we have several separate sets of joints. We will fix this on the wing first; the others we will get to in a few minutes. Select joint12 and then hold down **Shift** and select joint10. Let off the **Shift** key and press **P** to parent the lower wing set to the main part of the wing. You should have a small joint connecting the two sets now (Figure 10.20).

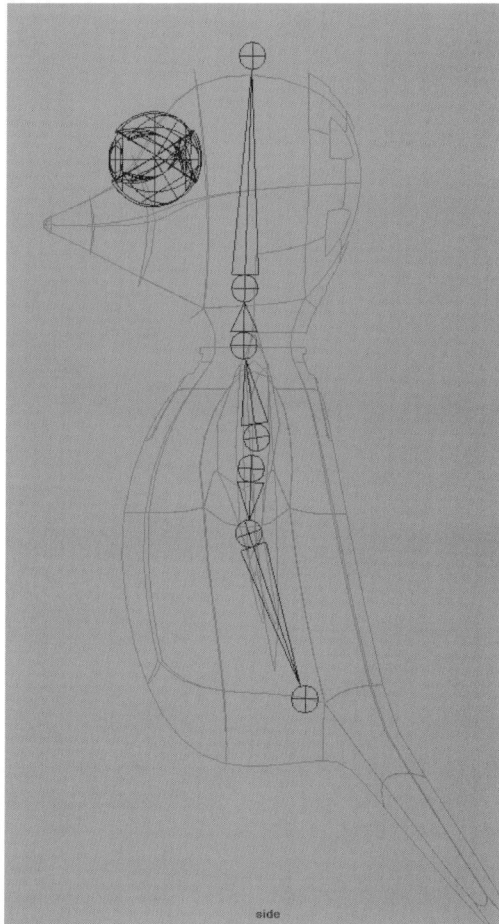

FIGURE 10.17   Joints for the lower half of the bird.

Step 7: Mirroring joints. Before you jump ahead and create the joints for the other wing, let's look at another tool in the Skeleton menu. Select joint8 (the base of the wing) and then go to Animation | Skeleton > Mirror Joint and click the Option box (Figure 10.21). In the Mirror Across section, click on YZ. Leave the other settings as they are and click Mirror. Now you have both wings without having to do the extra work.

Step 8: Organization. Let's rename these joints before we go on. Open the Outliner and expand all the hierarchies of the joints by **Shift**-clicking the + on the left of each name. Start with joint8 and rename it Shoulder_L. Rename joint9 Wing_L. See Figure 10.22 for the rest of the names.

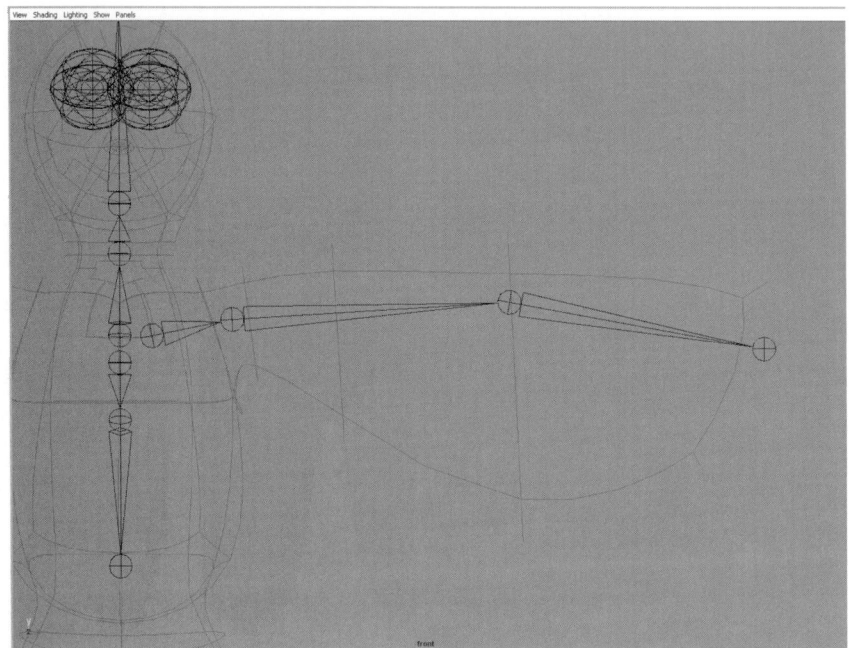

FIGURE 10.18   Enable the Joint tool and create joints.

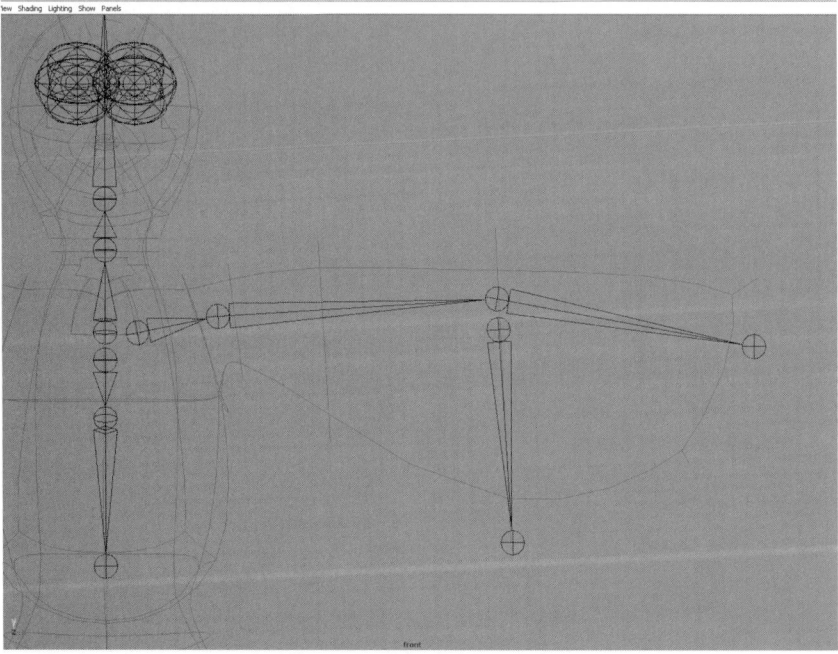

FIGURE 10.19   Create joints for the lower part of the wing.

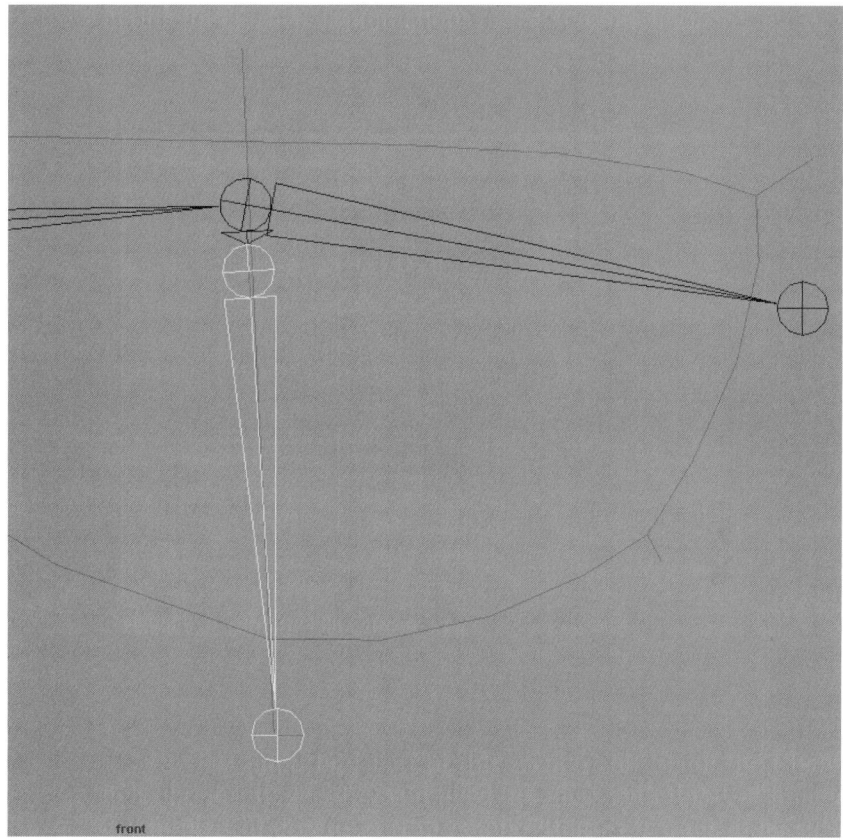

FIGURE 10.20   Two pieces of the wing skeleton now connected.

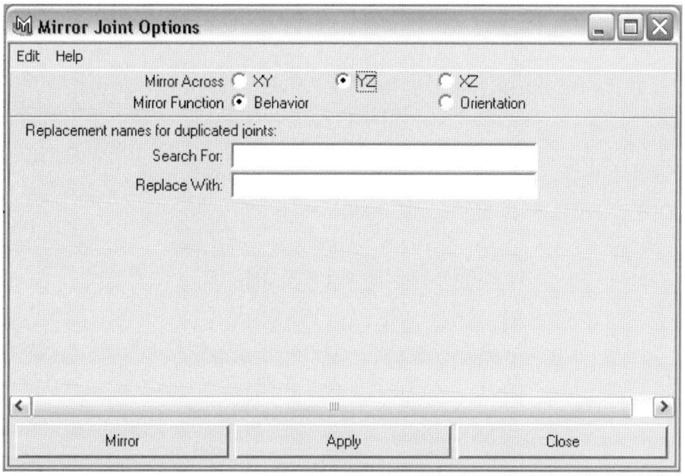

FIGURE 10.21   Mirror Joint Options.

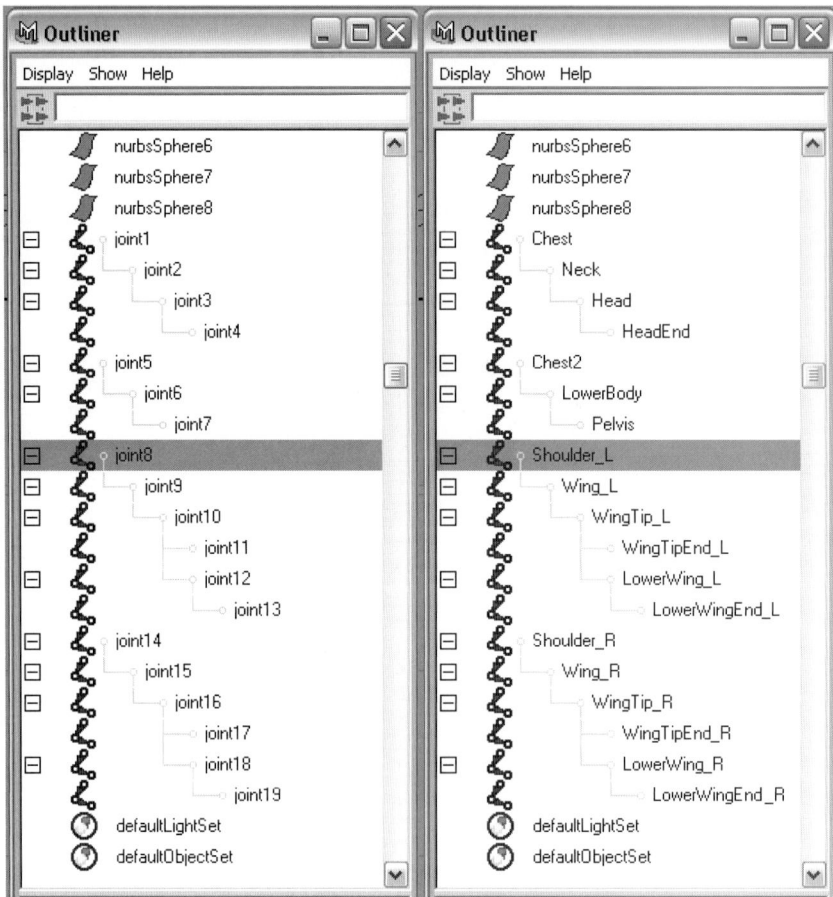

FIGURE10.22   Rename each corresponding joint as shown.

Step 9: Aligning the wing joints to the mesh. Select Shoulder_L and Shoulder_R and switch back to the Side view. You can see that the wing joints don't line up with the wings on the BirdMesh. Move them back along the Z axis to -.155. Then select LowerWingEnd_R and LowerWingEnd_L and move them back to 0.202 along Z. Your Side view should look similar to Figure 10.23.

Step 10: Connecting the wings to the body. Now we can parent the wings to the chest and we'll be nearly complete with the skeleton. The term parent (or parenting) is confusing in 3D. When you parent Object A to Object B, it is Object B that becomes the parent. Unfortunately, this convention is solidly stuck in the world of 3D.

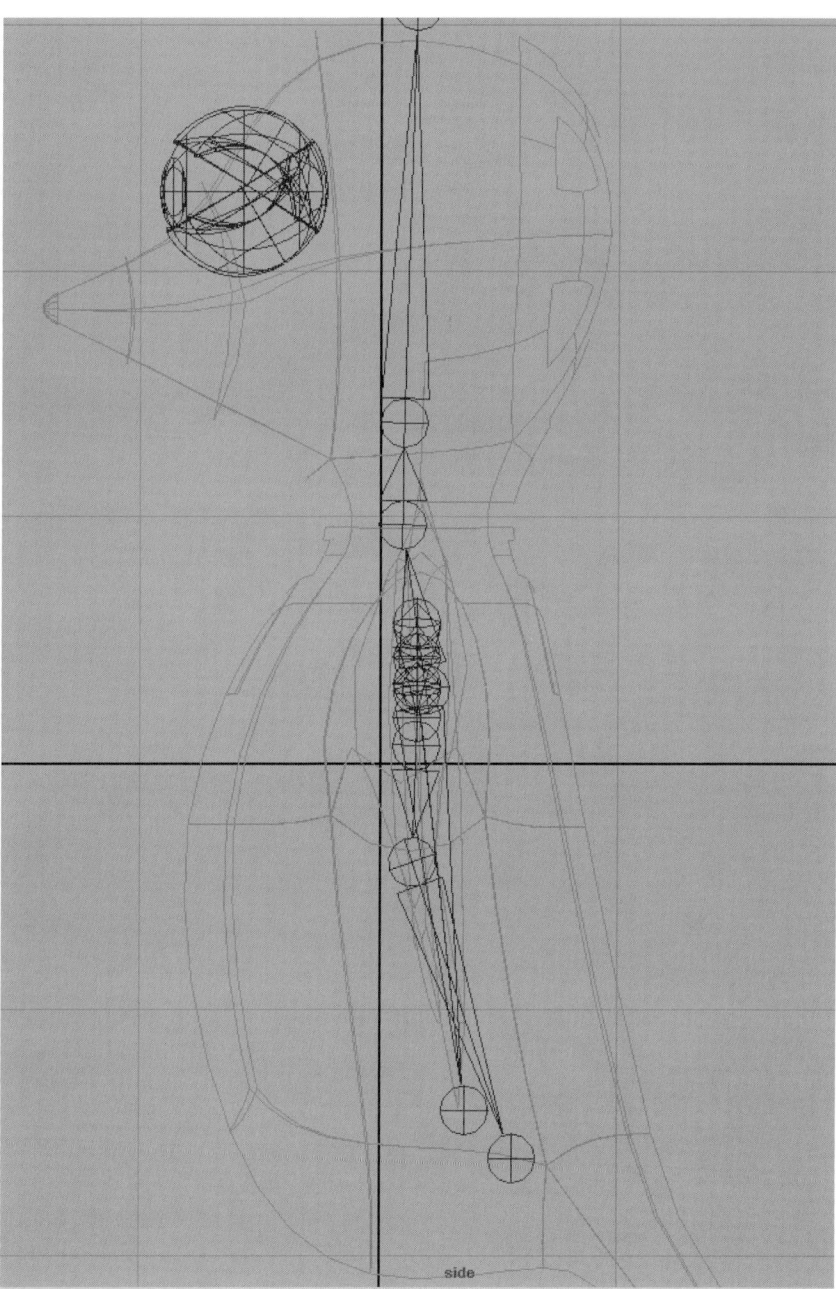

FIGURE 10.23   Side view of the skeleton thus far.

Select Shoulder_L and Shoulder_R and then select Chest. Now press **P** to parent the wings. Using the same method, parent Chest2 to Chest (Figure 10.24).

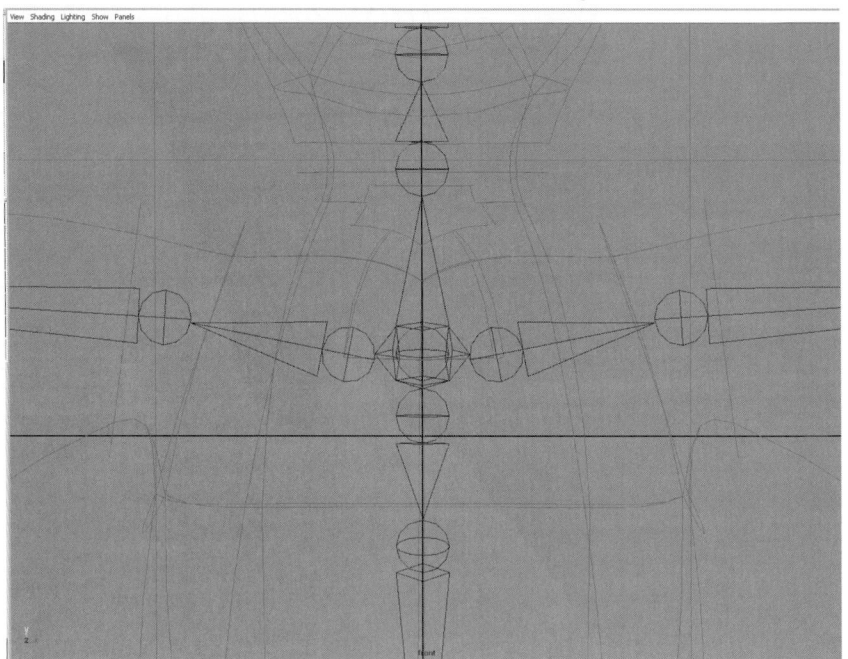

FIGURE 10.24 All the different sets of joints parented to the Chest joint.

Step 11: Creating tail joints. The last part of the skeleton we need to create is the tail. While still in the Front view, create joints as in Figure 10.25a, and then switch to the Side view and arrange these new joints as show in Figure 10.25b.

Step 12: Mirror the tail joints. Like we did with the wings, we will use the Mirror Joint tool to replicate the left tail joint. Go to Animation | Skeleton > Mirror Joint Tool and use the same settings as before.

Step 13: More organization. Now we simply rename the tail joints and parent them to the Pelvis. Name the right tail joints Tail_R and TailEnd_R. Do the same for the other side using L instead of R. Next, select Tail_R and Tail_L then select Pelvis and press **P** to parent. Your perspective view should look like Figure 10.26.

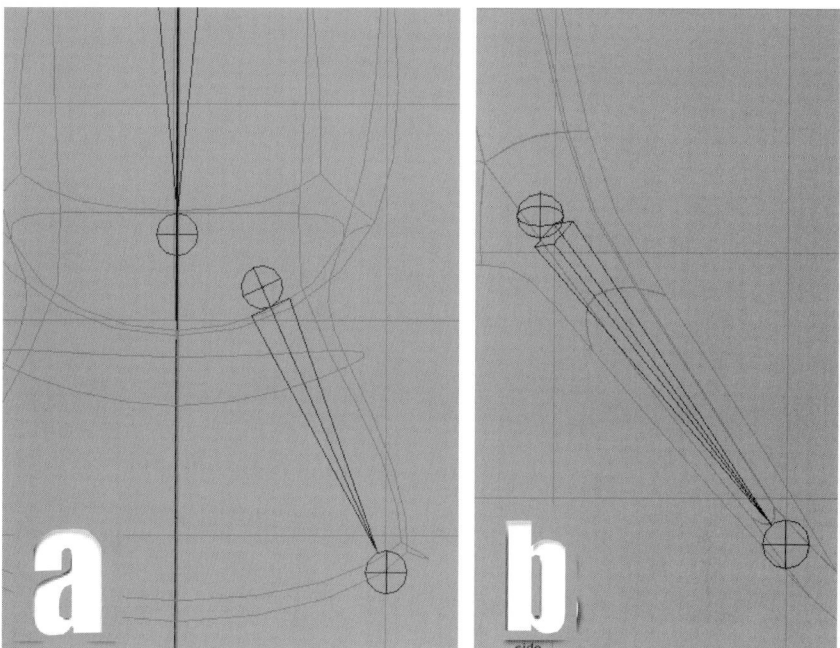

FIGURE 10.25   (a) Tail joint created in the Front view and (b) repositioned in the Side view.

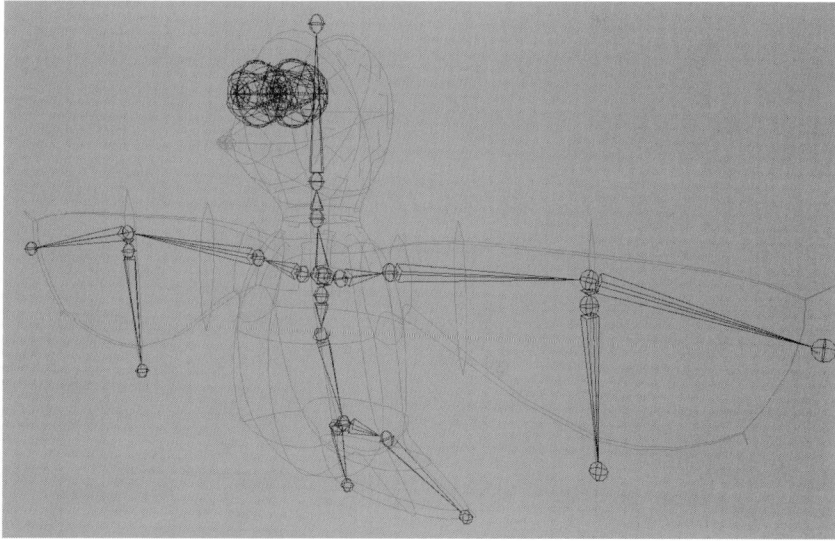

FIGURE 10.26   Perspective view of the completed skeleton.

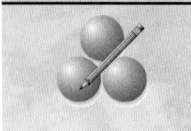

TUTORIAL 10.4	**SETTING UP CONTROLS FOR ANIMATION**

You can use the skeleton to animate as it sits now by grabbing each joint and moving or rotating it. But it is much better to create a set of controls or handles that can be easily seen and manipulated with the BirdMesh visible in Smooth Shaded mode. Most of the time, the pros use NURBS curves to create these handles and have them drive the joints. To put it another way, the handles are rotated or translated and the corresponding joint or joints react.

There are several ways to accomplish this result; the most common are constraints and expressions. For this example, we will use constraints.

ON THE CD

Step 1: Start fresh with Bird from the CD-ROM. From the CD-ROM, open CartoonBird_Skeleton.mb (Tutorials/Chapter10/).

Step 2: Turning on joint handles. If you want to simply select a joint to animate, there is a way to make it easier to see outside the mesh. We will do this on several joints for the sake of illustration. Select the following four joints: LowerWing_R, LowerWing_L, Tail_R, and Tail_L. Now go to Display > Component Display > Selection Handles. There is now a small + at each joint. Next we need to go into Select by Component Type mode and disable every component type except handles. Figure 10.27 shows which buttons should be depressed. This allows us to select the handles without worrying about selecting anything else.

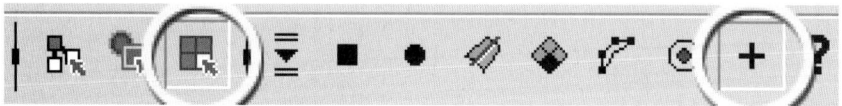

FIGURE 10.27   Component type buttons.

Notice that the selected joints have turned light blue and that there is now a small purple + displayed at each selected joint (Figure 10.28). These are the selection handles for the joints.

Now select the handles at the top of each joint and they will turn yellow as (Figure 10.29). You may want to look at this in color on the CD-ROM if you are confused about which to select.

ON THE CD

You can now translate these on the Z axis to the back of the bird, as in Figure 10.30. Now when you switch back to Select by Object Type, the handles for these joints can be selected by clicking the +.

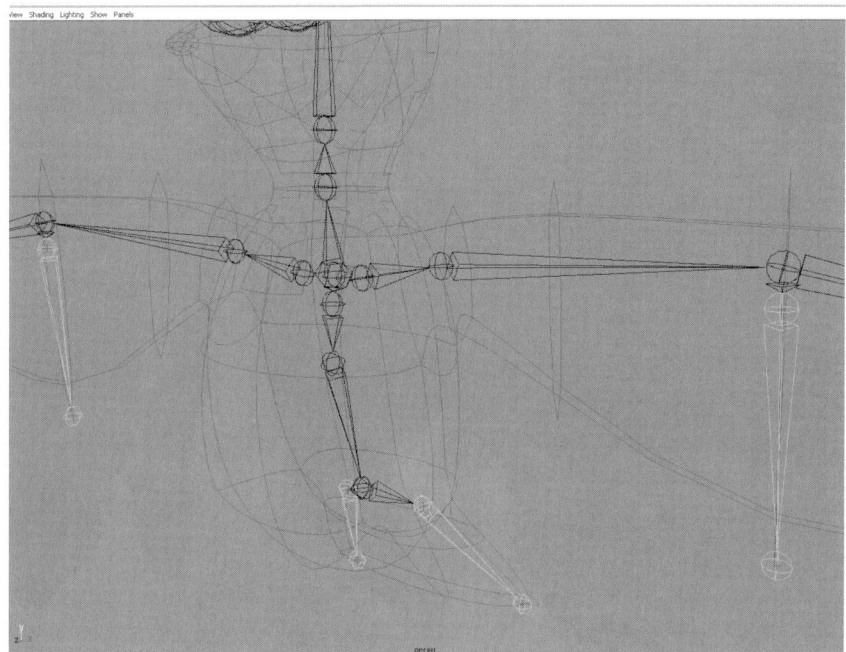

FIGURE 10.28   Selection handles for the joints.

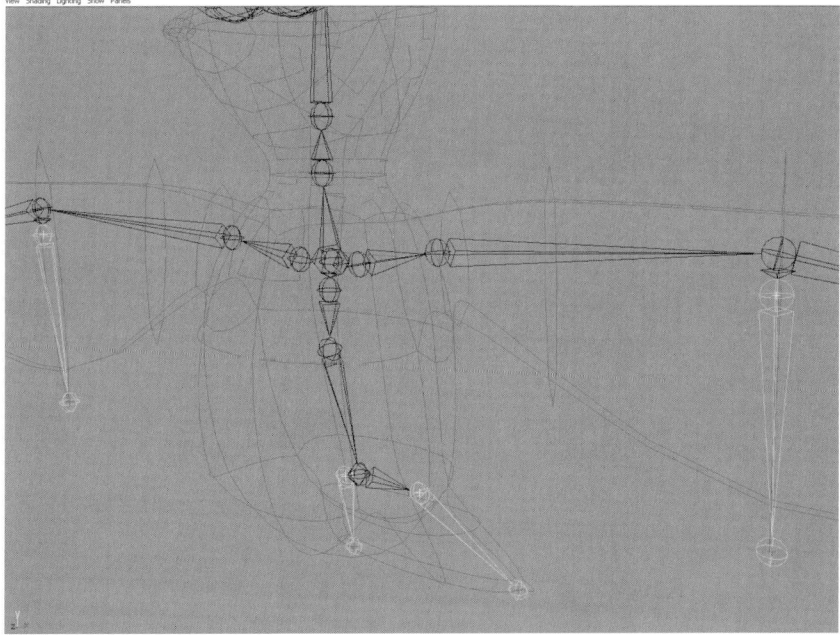

FIGURE 10.29   Select the handles at the top of each joint.

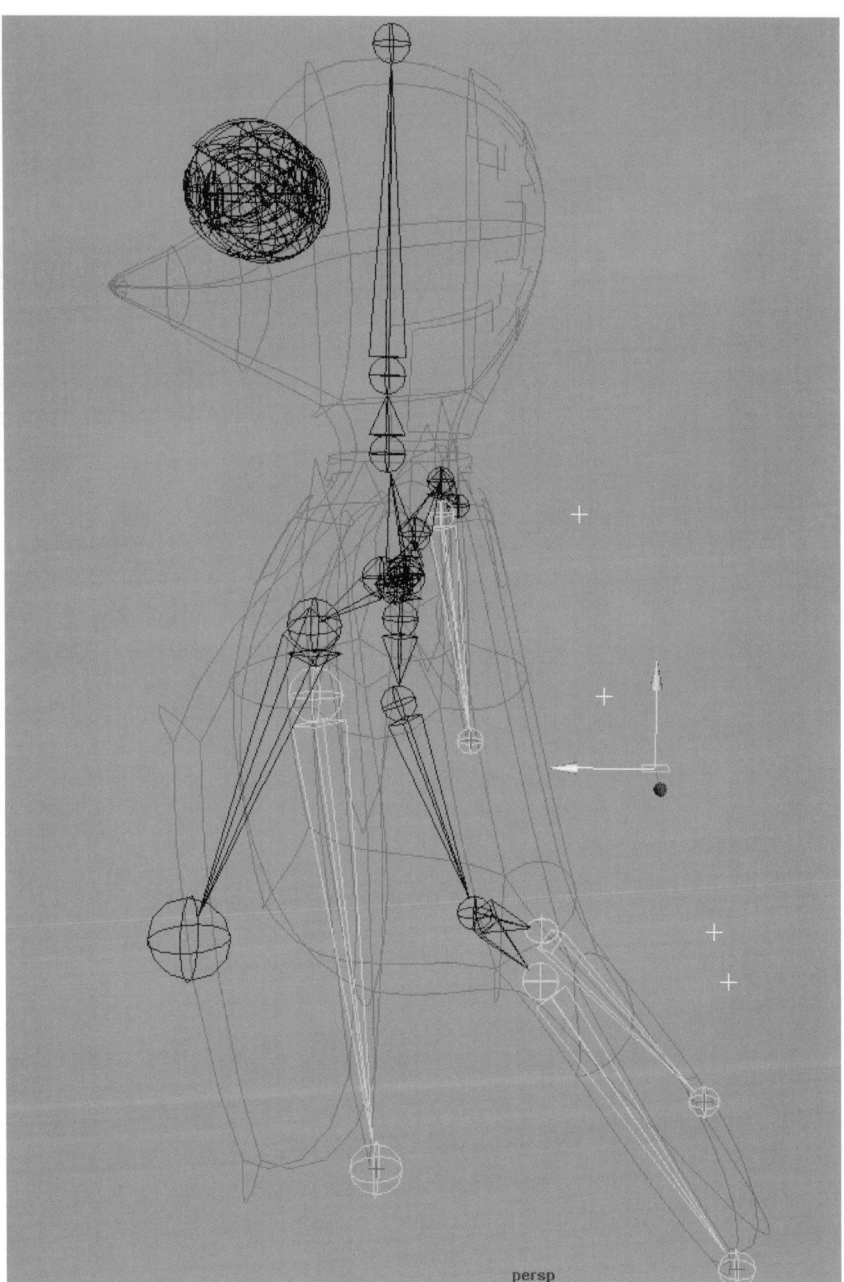

FIGURE 10.30 Translate the handles on the Z axis.

Step 3: Using external handles. An even better way to do this is to import CTRL_Curves from the same directory by clicking File > Import . . . and selecting the file.

You'll now see series of NURBS curves at various points around the bird. They create a NURBS circle that has had its shape tweaked a little. All of them are named with the prefix CTRL_ so they are easy to identify in the Outline. Each one will be used to drive a joint in the skeleton. Figure 10.31.

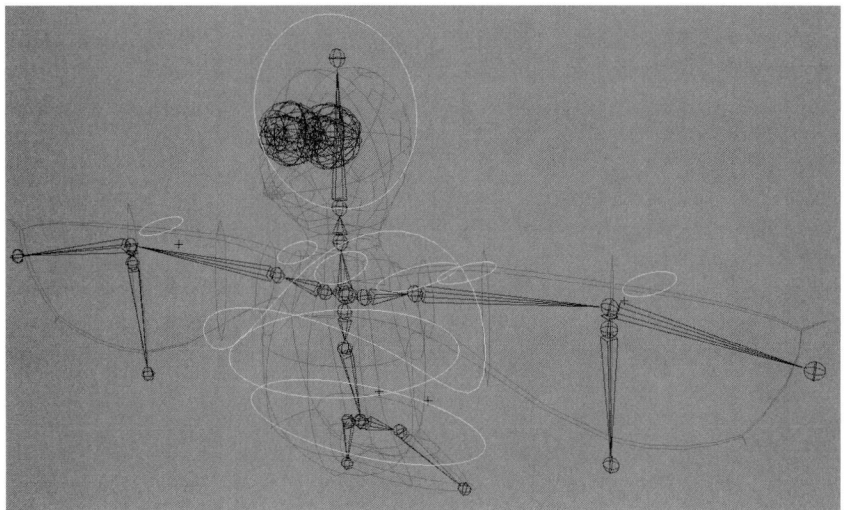

FIGURE 10.31   NURBS curves used to drive the skeleton's joints.

We will be using two types of constraints to control the skeleton: Parent Constraint for the joints that will translate and rotate and Orient Constraint for joints that will only rotate.

Step 4: The master Control. Before we get to the constraints, we are going to parent Chest to BirdMaster. Select Chest and then **Shift**-click BirdMaster and press **P**.

Step 5: The lower body controls. For the lower body of the bird, we want to be able to stretch the bird by pulling down on the controls, so we will use a Parent Constraint on its two joints. Applying a Parent Constraint is just like parenting one object to another but preserves the hierarchy of the skeleton.

For Parent Constraint (and other constraints) you select the parent or controlling object first then the object to be controlled next. This is a bit confusing at first, but it will become second nature soon enough. Select the curve named CTRL_LowerBody and then the joint named Lower-Body. Now go to Animation | Constraint > Parent and click the Option box (Figure 10.32). Make sure that Maintain Offset is checked; also All should be check for both Translate and Rotate. In some cases, you will want to have the constraint work only for certain axes. You can do this by checking only the axis or axes you wish to use. In this instance, we want all axes to be controlled. The Weight parameter is for when you have multiple constraints on the same object. You can use the weight to set one control object to have more influence than another. You can even animate this value to change over time which control object has influence. Leave this value at 1.0000 and click Add.

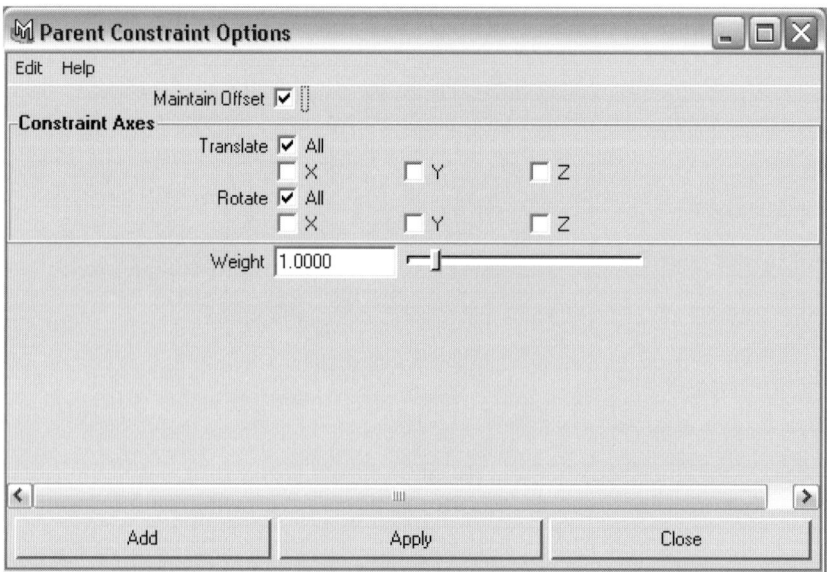

FIGURE 10.32   The Parent Constraint Options dialog.

Now if you rotate or translate CTRL_LowerBody, the lower portion of the bird's skeleton will move with it. Select the joint LowerBody and look at the Channel Box (Figure 10.33). Notice that all the Translate and Rotate channels are highlighted blue. This shows you that there is a constraint controlling these values.

Step 6: Pelvis controls. Continuing with the rest of the lower body, select CTRL_Pelvis and then the joint Pelvis. You can now press **G** to repeat the last command, and the constraint for the pelvis will be set up. Next

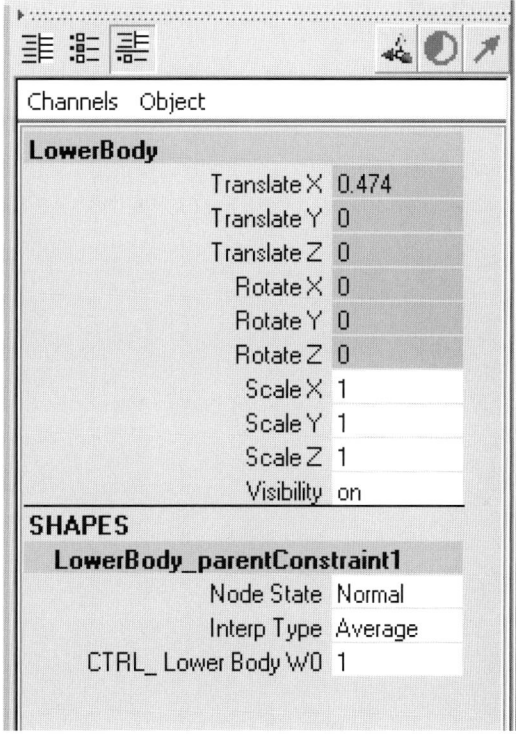

FIGURE 10.33   LowerBody Channel Box.

Select CTRL_Head and then Head and press **G**. Do the same for CTRL_Wing_L and Wing_L; CTRL_WingTip_L and WingTip_L; CTRL_Wing_R and Wing_R; CTRL_WingTip_R.

Step 7: Shoulder controls. The shoulders do not need to stretch the way the other joints do, so for them we will use an Orient Constraint. Orient Constraints work the similar to the Parent Constraint but it only controls the rotation of the constrained object. Like the other constraints, we must select the controlling object first and then the corresponding joint.

Select CTRL_Shldr_L and then the joint Shoulder_L. Now go to Animation | Constrain > Orient and click the Options box (Figure 10.34). Like the Parent Constraint option, you can specify which axes are controlled. We will want to check All next to Constrained Axes and also check Maintain Offset. Click Add to apply the constraint. Next, select CTRL_Shldr_R and then Shoulder_R and press **G** to repeat the command. Save your work.

Orient Constraint Options

Edit   Help

Maintain Offset ☑

Offset [0.0000]   [0.0000]   [0.0000]

Constraint Axes ☑ All
☐ X   ☐ Y   ☐ Z

Weight [1.0000]

| Add | Apply | Close |

FIGURE 10.34   The Orient Constraint Options dialog.

Our bird's skeleton is created, it has controls with which we can animate it, and now, finally, we can bind the mesh to the joints.

TUTORIAL 10.5   SKINNING A BIRD

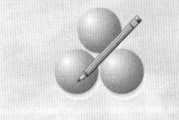

Using the same method as the cylinder earlier, we will Smooth Bind the bird to its skeleton. Because we had practice on that simple example, this should be a breeze. One of the benefits of working with Subdivision surfaces is that there are relatively few control vertices to weight. Also, some neat tools allow us to paint weights for one side and then mirror those results.

Step 1: Smooth Binding the BirdMesh. To start skinning, we need to untemplate BirdMesh. So select BirdMesh from the Outliner then choose Display > Object Display > Untemplate. Hold down **Shift** and select the joint Chest. Remember, there is no need to select every joint as we have the option in Smooth Bind Option to use the entire skeleton.

Go to Animation | Skin > Bind Skin > Smooth Bind and click the Option Box. This time, we will change the Max Influences to 3 and the

Dropoff Rate to 2.5. This will help save work by keeping too many joints from influencing any given part of the mesh. Click Bind Skin. Figure 10.35.

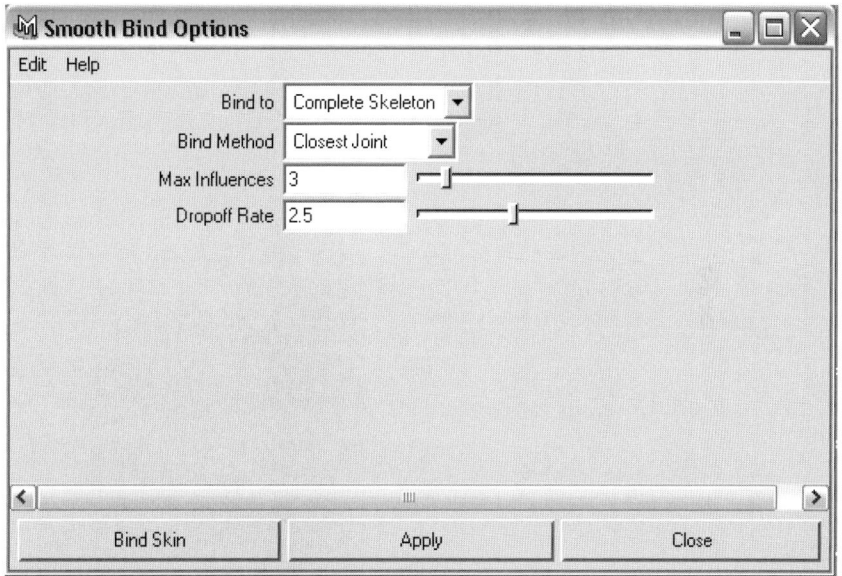

FIGURE 10.35   Smooth Bind Options with correct settings.

Step 2: Test the initial results. Try a couple of the CTRL_ curves; rotate them, move them, and play around. You can see that some of the areas look pretty good as they are. A few, such as the head, need some work. You won't always get this lucky; in fact, it is really rare. Make sure you undo any actions before continuing.

Step 3: Creating a layer of the joints. Because we don't need the joints for this, let's hide them. Better yet, we'll put them on a layer so they can be kept out of the way. Create a new layer and call it Bones and add all the joints of the bird's skeleton to it. You can then turn its visibility off.

Step 4: Using animation to test results. Remember on the cylinder example that we animated one of the joints so we could see the results of our skinning better. We will do that on the bird. First select all the CTRL_ objects and click on frame 0 on the Time Slider. Press **S** to set a key. By doing this, we are locking the bird's pose at frame 0.

In most cases, you want to work on one part of the mesh at a time. We will start with the head, so select CTRL_Head and click on frame 5 on the Time Slider. We use frame 5 so we can see what is going on with the skin from one position to another. Rotate CTRL_Head about 80 degrees in Y and press **S** again. You will see the head distort and lose its volume (Figure 10.36). We will use the Paint Skin Weights Tool to fix this and any other problem areas.

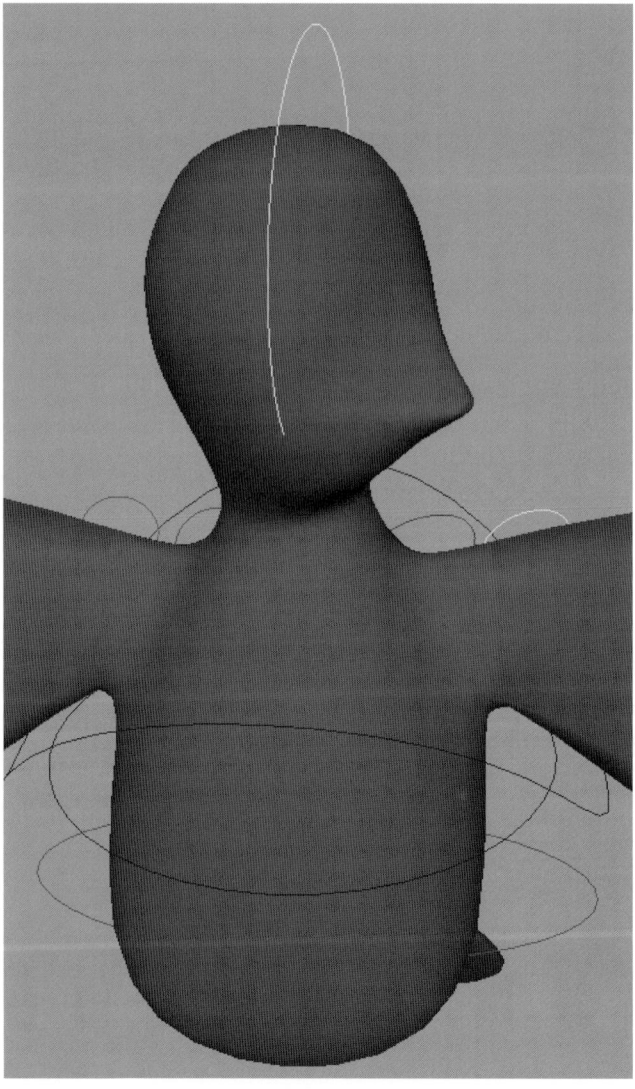

FIGURE 10.36 The head in need of some skin weighting.

Step 5: Fixing the head deformation with the Paint Skin Weights Tool. Select BirdMesh and go to Animation | Skin > Edit Smooth Skin > Paint Skin Weights Tool and click the Options box. In the Influence section of the Paint Skin Weights Tool Options, select Head. You will see that the surface around the head turns dark gray. We need that to be white and fade to black from the base of the head to the shoulders.

As before, set the Opacity to 0.1 or below to gradually build up influence. Set the Radius to 0.5 and start painting. Begin at the top of the head and paint toward the base of the head. You will see it gradually regain its correct shape. Your bird's head should look like Figure 10.37. If you paint too far down, don't worry; you can fix it when you paint for the Chest joint.

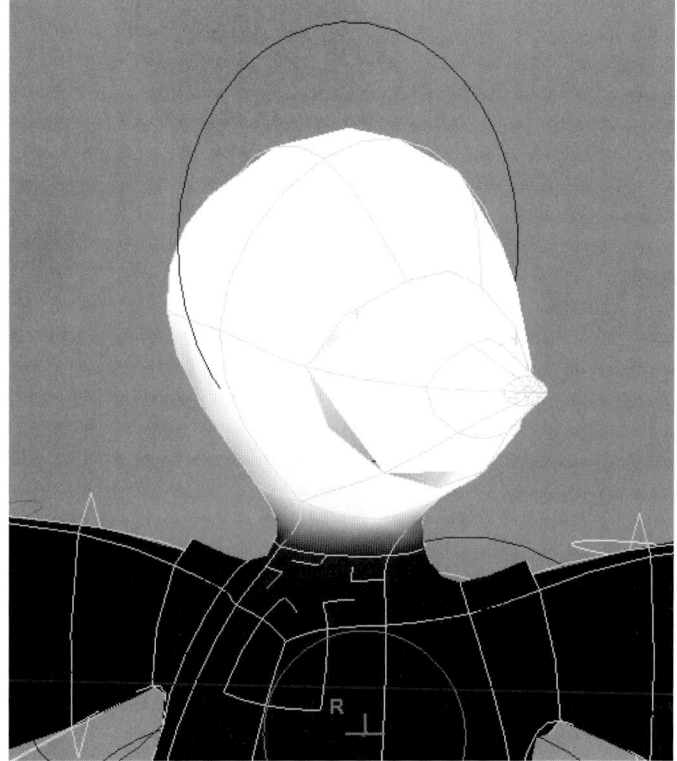

FIGURE 10.37   Correct head weight paint.

Step 6: Now select Chest in the Influence section of the Paint Skin Weight Tool settings. We want it to cover a similar area to what it does now (Figure 10.38), but the influence needs to be much greater. Paint on the chest area of the mesh, concentrating on the left side (right side of the screen, if you are looking at the front of the bird), because we will be mirroring the weights later. Also, if you rotate the wing, you'll see the side of the body being moved. We don't want this to happen, so paint under the wing until you have something like Figure 10.39.

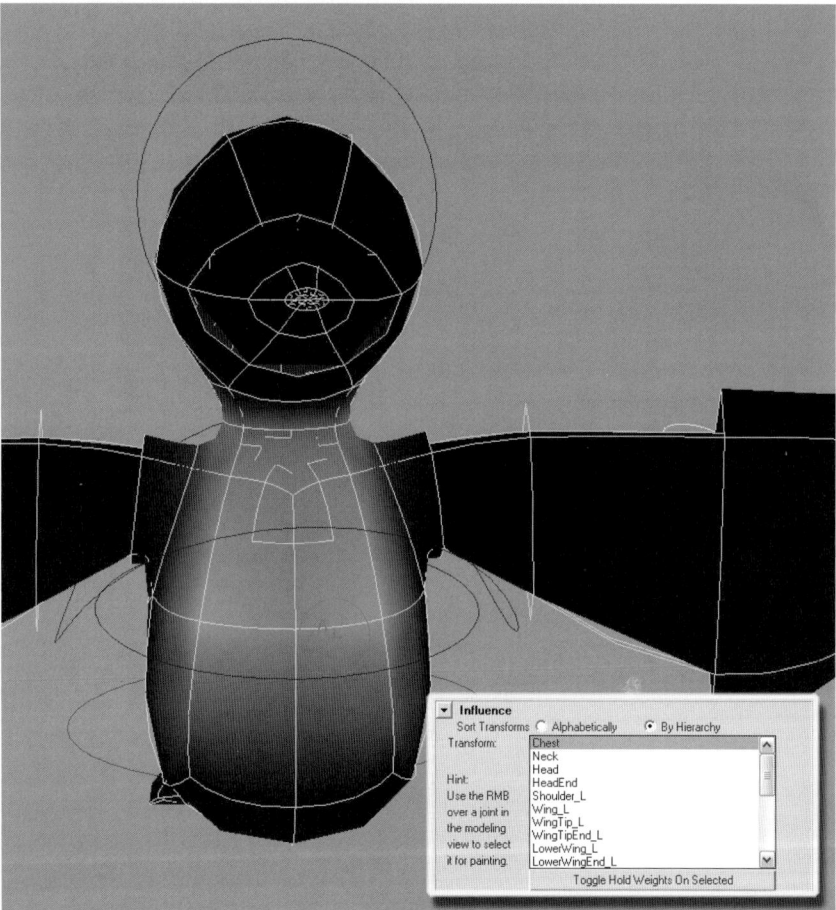

FIGURE 10.38 The skin weights for Chest before editing. (Inset shows Influences section of the Paint Weights Tool settings.)

 When skinning a character, remember that a lot of the results are subjective. In some cases, you may want a joint to have broader influence than these examples show. Skinning also requires a lot of trial and error. Sometimes you will not see a problem until you are actually animating. This can be frustrating but it is normal. It's a good idea to "stress test" a rig and skinning before sending it to be animated. This simply means do some test animations that run the character through its range of motions to spot any errors.

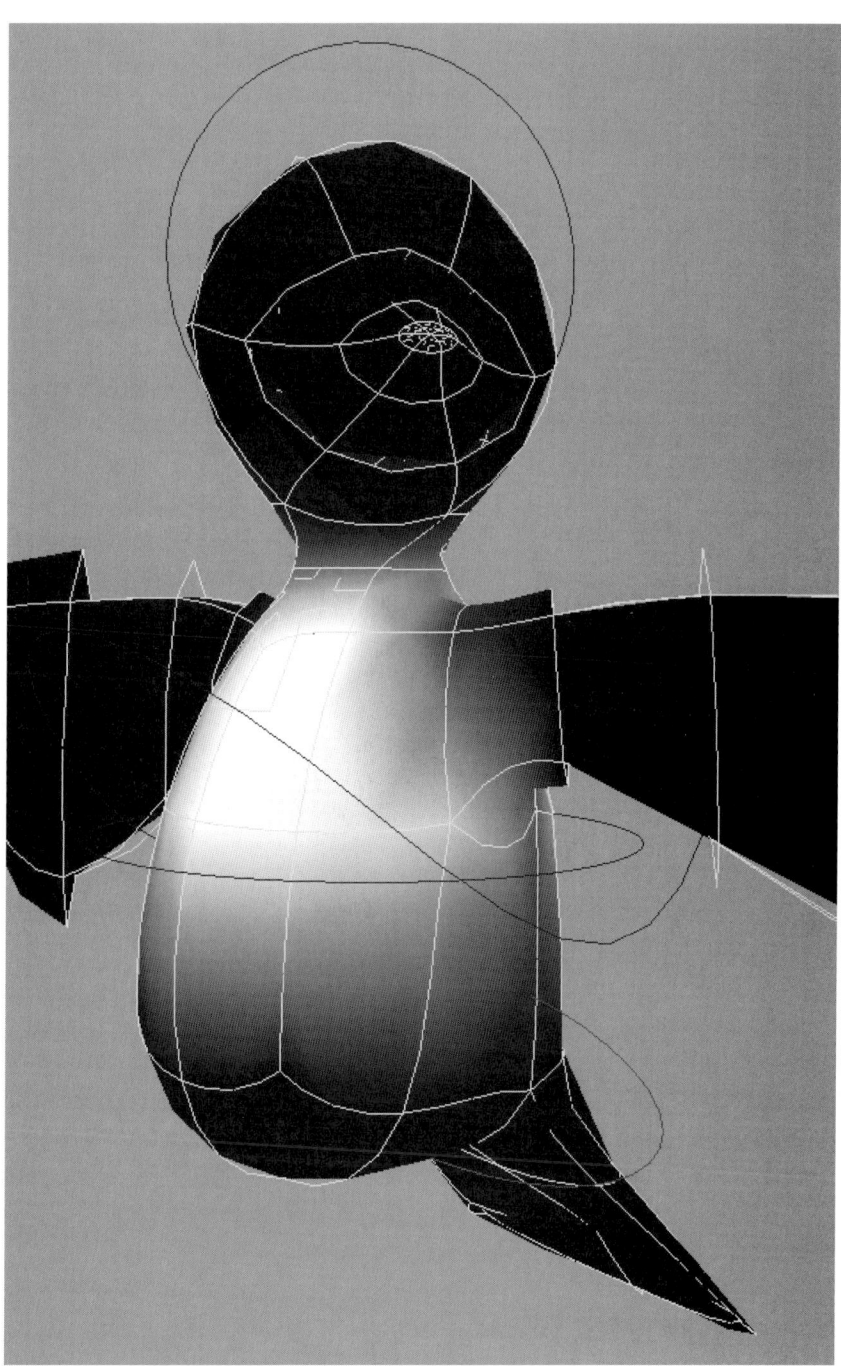

FIGURE 10.39   The skin weights for Chest after painting.

Step 7: The shoulders. Now let's work on the left shoulder. Select Shoulder_L in the Influence section of the Paint Skin Weight tool settings. Figure 10.40. The shoulder only needs a little work. Paint only four or five strokes on the top of the shoulder (front and back). See Figure 10.41.

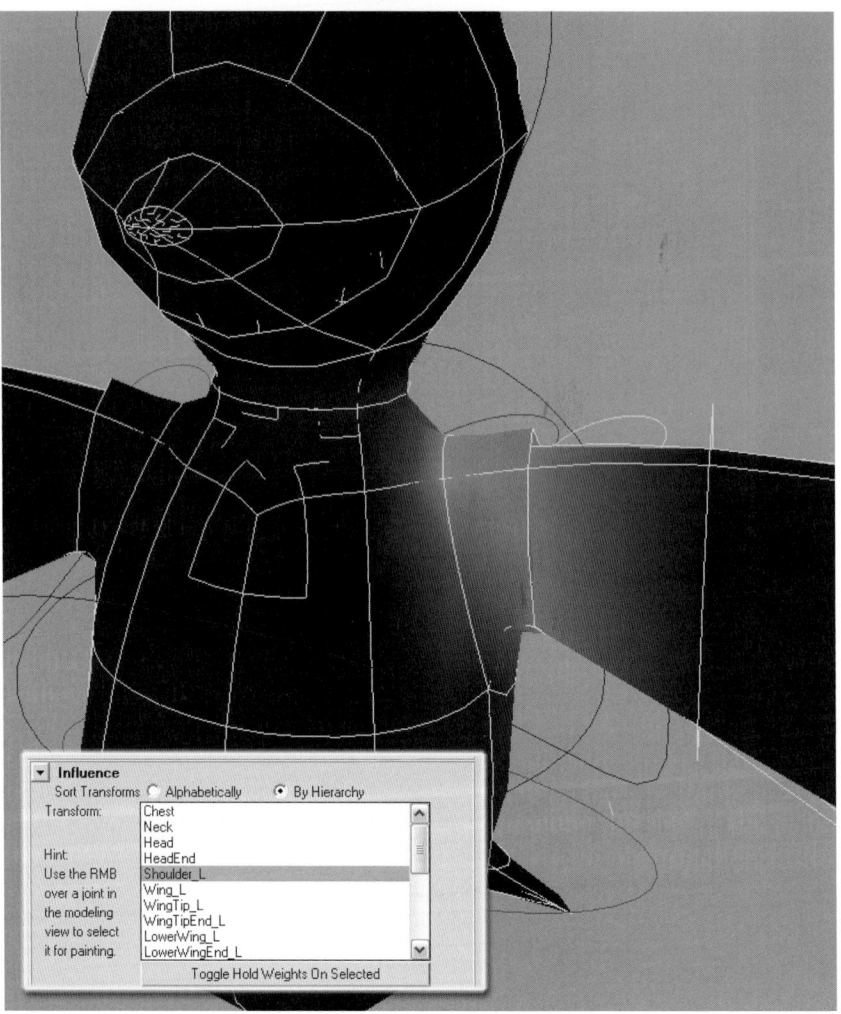

FIGURE 10.40 Shoulder before painting weights.

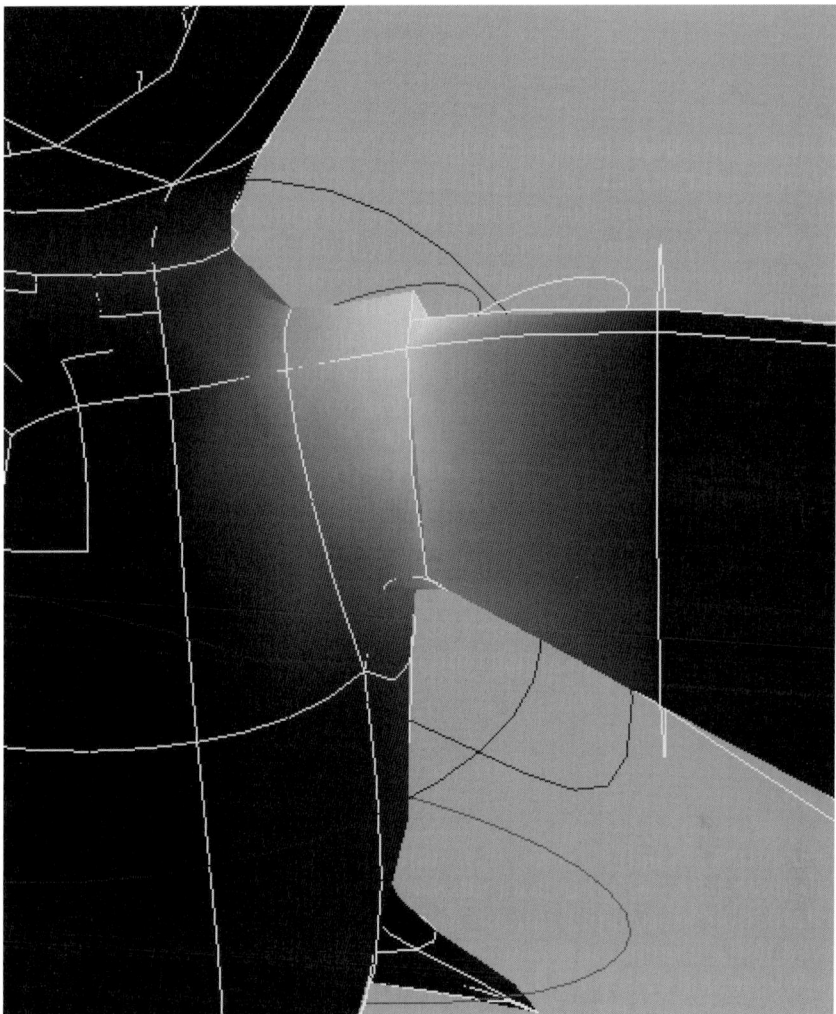

FIGURE 10.41   Shoulder after painting weights.

Step 8: The wings. For the rest of the wing, we want to make nice curves for a flowing shape when flapping. The goal here is not realism. The wing will work as is; if you'd like to change the way something deforms, use what you've learned so far to edit the wing. You can take away influence with the Paint Skin Weights Tool but you might find it quicker to just paint the influence onto the joints that should have control rather than take it away from the ones that shouldn't.

Step 9: And now, the rest of the body. Moving on to the lower body; select Pelvis from the Influence Transform list. Like the chest joint, the influence of the pelvis area is good but needs strengthening. Paint along the bottom of the body until it is nearly white, as in Figure 10.42. Don't paint on the tail, because we want the tail joints to control it.

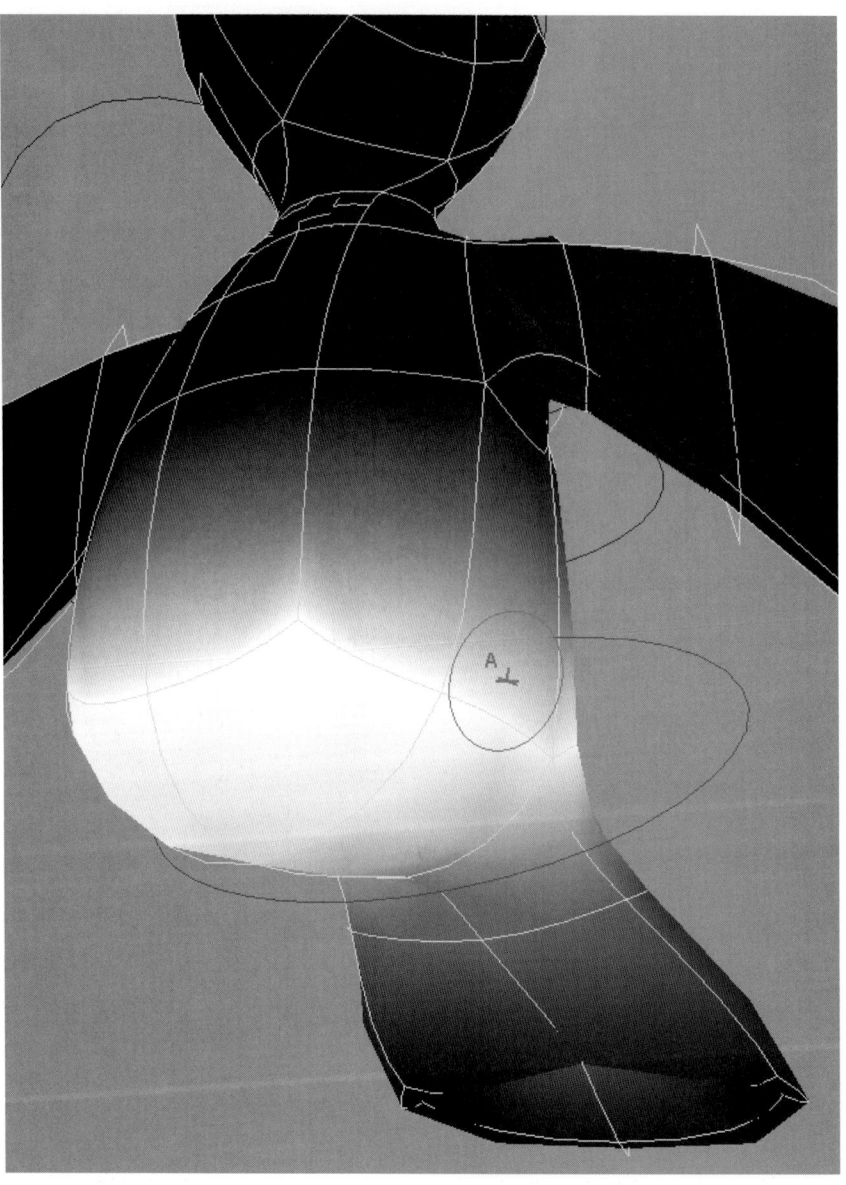

FIGURE 10.42 Paint the bottom of the body until it is white.

When you've done that, press **W** to get the move tool and select CTRL_Pelvis and pull it around. When we get to animating the bird, you will see how this will make the bird lively by having it stretch when it moves quickly. Undo any move you performed before continuing (Figure 10.43).

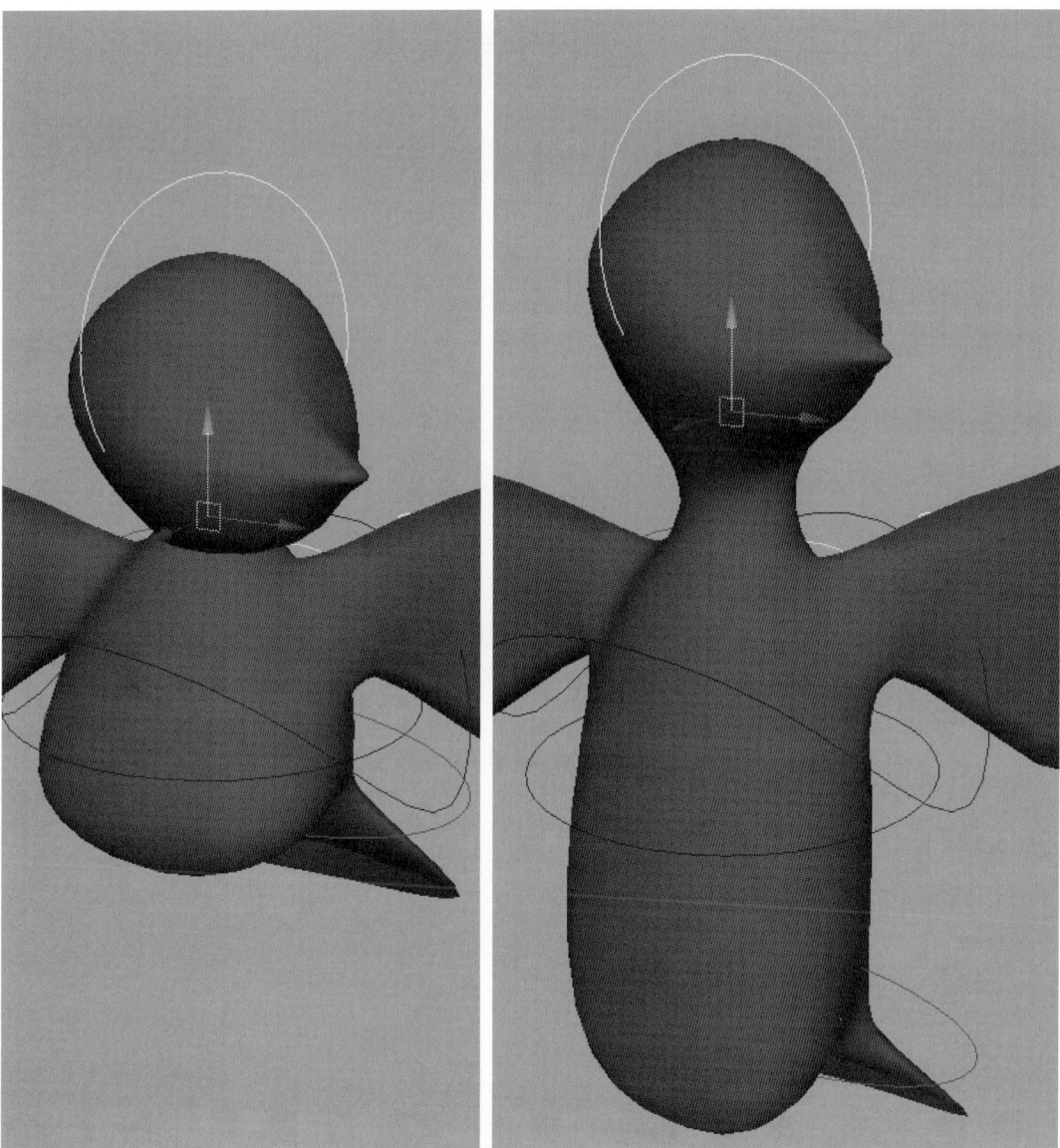

FIGURE 10.43   The bird squashing and stretching by using the controls, and the skinning created earlier.

Step 10: The tail. The only thing left before mirroring the skin weights is the tail. Select BirdMesh and activate the Paint Skin Weights Tool and select Tail_L from the Influences list. Paint the left half of the tail until it is white at the edge with a gradual fade toward the center (Figure 10.44).

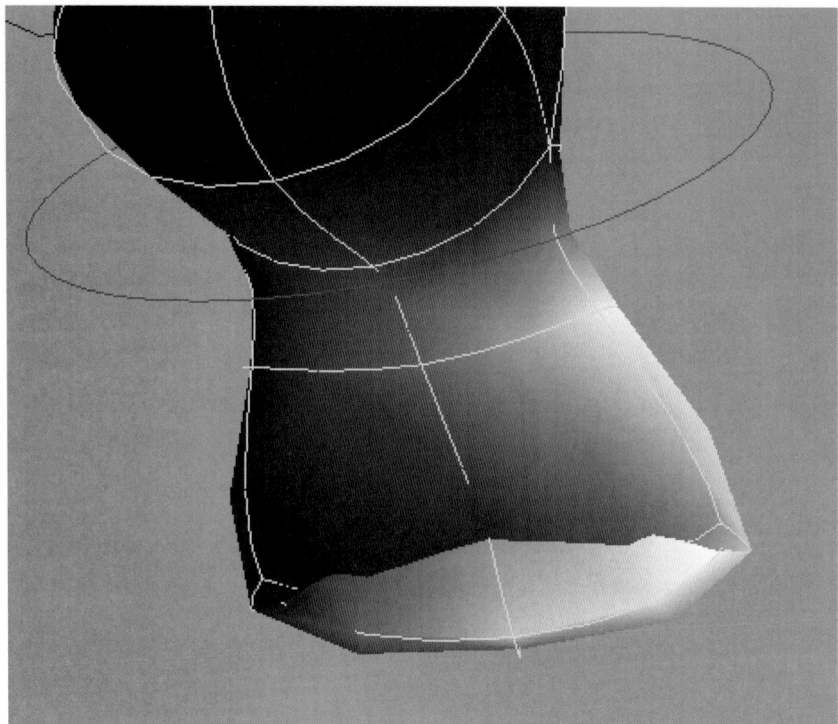

FIGURE 10.44 The skin weighting of the tail.

The Mirror Skin Weights Tool

The Mirror Skin Weights tool will take the weighting from one half of a symmetrical mesh and copy them over the other half. This saves a lot of skinning time. Even if your model is not symmetrical it can get you part way there.

Step 11: Mirroring the bird's skin weights. To access the tool go to Animation | Skin > Edit Smooth Skin > Mirror Skin Weights Tool and click the Option box (Figure 10.45). The simple dialog box can be confusing. If you click on the radio buttons next to Mirror Across, you will notice the word next to the Direction checkbox changes to reflect what is going to be mirrored. Since nearly all characters are built with sides along X, as with our bird, the default settings (Mirror Across: YZ, and the Direction checkbox checked to indicate going from positive X to negative X) will be used. Make sure your settings match Figure 10.45 and click Mirror. Save your work.

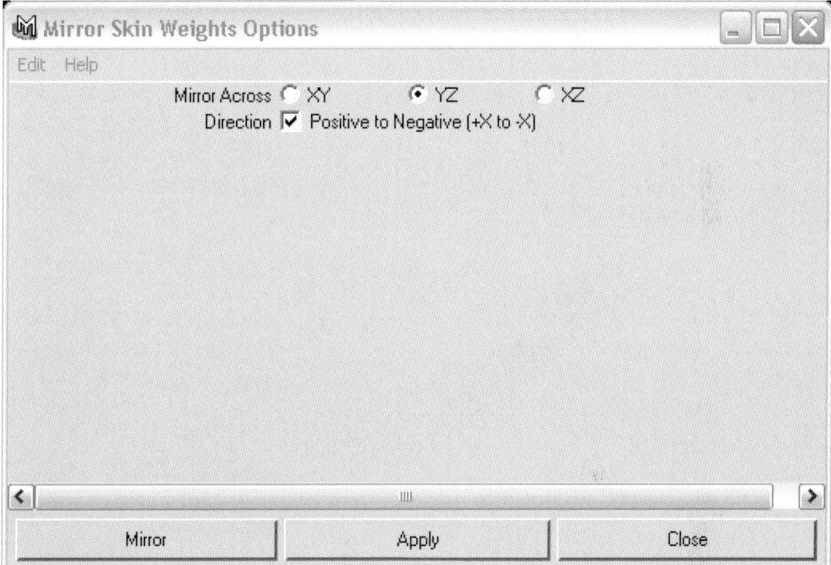

FIGURE 10.45   Use the default settings in the Mirror Skin Weights Options dialog.

CONCLUSION

You have covered the basics of rigging and skinning. Remember that the tools covered in this chapter work the same for NURBS, polygons, and Subdivision surfaces. There are many more features in the tools covered in this chapter that are beyond the scope of this volume, but now you can look into them with a good base of knowledge.

In the next chapter, we will learn the basics of animation and have some fun making the bird fly.

ANIMATION

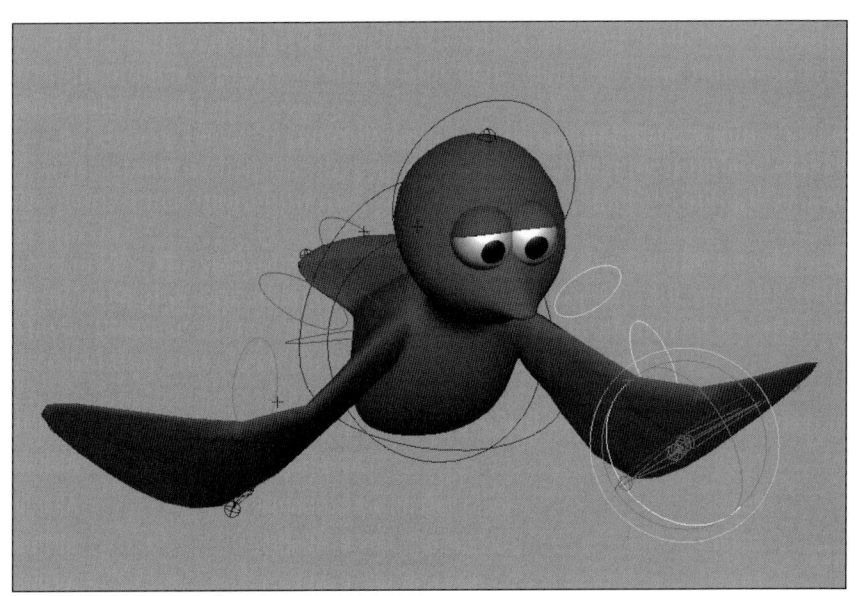

M odeling and texturing can be fun, and are certainly marketable skills, but they are usually just stepping stones on the path to animation.

There are a lot of people who create amazing environments and stills, but animation can really bring it all to life. In fact, to animate means to invoke life.

Because of the complexity of animation, the art of understanding motion, and the techniques for applying that understanding, we are unable teach the whole process. However, we will cover the core of Maya's animation tools, which are widely regarded as the best in the business. We will also brave some of the ideas for creating an aesthetic animation.

WHAT IS ANIMATION?

Before we look at how to animate in Maya, let's look a little at the core ideas of animation in general.

First, *animation* (or any moving picture) is actually a string of still images that, when played quickly enough in succession, create the illusion of movement. Each still image is referred to as a frame. The number of frames played in each second help to determine how smoothly a motion plays. To complicate matters, different formats of media use different frames-per-second (fps).

Movies use 24 fps, which is the default setting for Maya. It will be important to know how to change this, because most of the time beginning animators are not animating for film but for other media such as video or broadcast. In the U.S., NTSC fps rate is 30 (actually 29.97), while in most of Europe, PAL standards dictate 25 fps. The variation never ends.

For the purpose of our discussion here, we will assume that we are dealing with 30 fps. This means the arithmetic is always done with 30 as the core number. If you want to create a three-second animation clip, you will need 90 frames (30 fsp × 3 = 90). If you want to know how long 300 frames will actually take to play out, just divide the number of frames by the fps (30) and you know that it will play for 10 seconds.

It is rather awkward at first to take a linear idea such as time and look at it on a Timeline that is shown in terms of frames, but mastering the idea of timing via frames is important. It will become easier as time goes on when you do more timing/animation work.

So, we now know that we need 30 frames for every second of finished animation. How do we get those frames? There are several ways to do this but the most common is called keyframe animation.

Keyframe Animation

In traditional hand-drawn animation, there are two basic ways of animating; pose to pose and straight ahead. Let's say we have an animation of a character sitting on a chair who stands up and points at something. In pose-to-pose animation, you would draw the character on the chair in one frame and then draw him standing and pointing in the other. These two drawings would be the key drawings, or keyframes. You would then draw the frames in between to get from the chair to the pointing. These frames, called in-betweens, are often drawn by assistants in traditional animation.

In straight ahead animation, you would start with the drawing in the chair and then draw the next frame in succession, and the next one after that, and so on, until you got to the final pose.

On the computer, because it is so flexible, you can choose to work either way or both. The simplest method to understand is pose to pose, and that is what we will discuss later by animating the bird we set up in the previous chapter.

Computer-generated keyframe animation is similar to pose-to-pose animation. The major difference is that you create the key poses for each position at different times and the computer will create the in-betweens for you. When it comes to animating characters, you will never give the computer complete control. In feature films, you will sometimes end up with keys on nearly every frame to make sure every picture on screen is doing exactly what you intended. This sounds daunting, but it is very satisfying to craft animations to this degree.

For the scope of this book, we won't get that severe. There are many books on animation techniques, should you want to delve into this wonderful world.

Setting Up Maya for Animation

Before we get into the tools that allow us to create and modify keyframes, we need to make sure Maya understands the rules of the animation game. To do this, select Window > Settings/Preferences > Preferences.

On the left are the categories of preferences that can be set. The organization of what is where is really odd, so take careful note. First, go to the Settings category. Here, you can define the Working Units of everything, including time. Change the Time setting to NTSC (30 fps) as shown in Figure 11.1.

Next, jump down to the Timeline category. Make sure the Timeline lists 1.00 as the Playback and Animation Start/End value. The End value is irrelevant for now; it can be changed easily later. Also, move down to

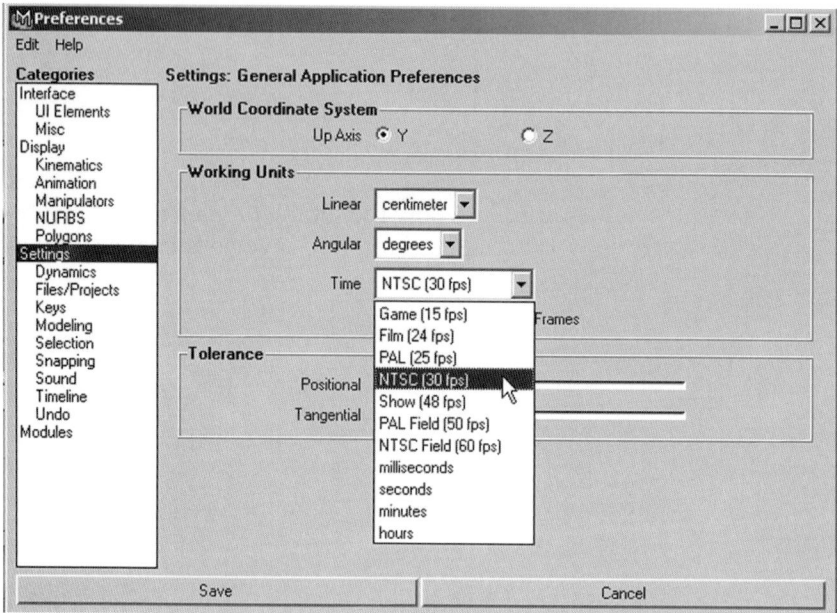

FIGURE 11.1 Changing the animation to work at 30 fps.

the Playback area of the same window and change the Playback Speed to Real-time (30 fps) as shown in Figure 11.2.

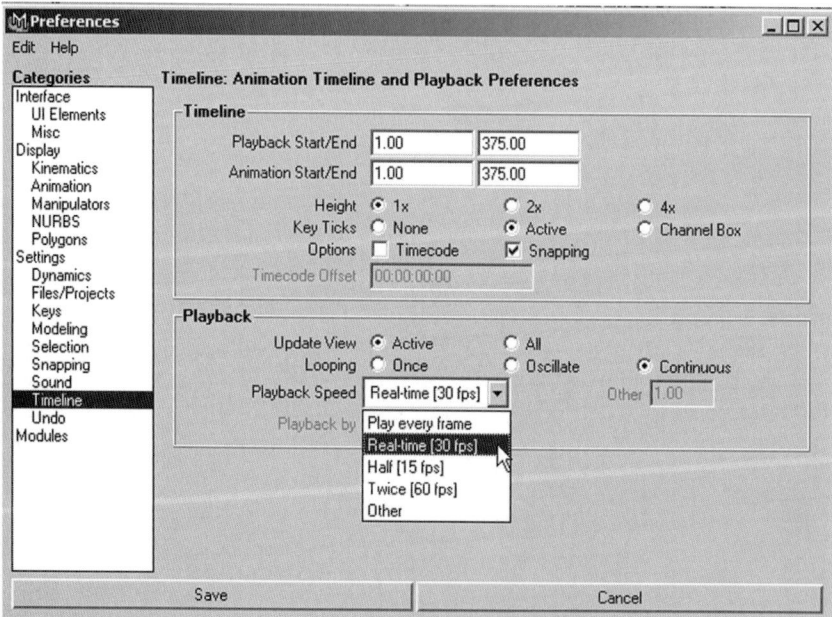

FIGURE 11.2 Changing the Timeline and Playback preferences.

This is actually quite important. Without telling Maya to play in real time, it instead attempts to show you every single frame, as fast as it can, when you are previewing the motion. This means that if nothing is happening, it flies through those frames, while if lots of complex things are going on, it crawls through those frames. With real time selected, Maya will drop frames if necessary to keep up. This actually gives you a much better idea of how the timing of your motion really works.

Hit the Save button to save your changes and exit this window.

THE ANIMATION TOOLS

Maya provides a surprisingly powerful collection of tools in a very small space in the default UI. Right toward the bottom is the Timeline (Figure 11.3). Within these two rows of tools are most of the tools to create most any type of keyframe. Although there is much refining to do within other editors, most of the "blocking-out" of animations can be done solely through this collection of tools.

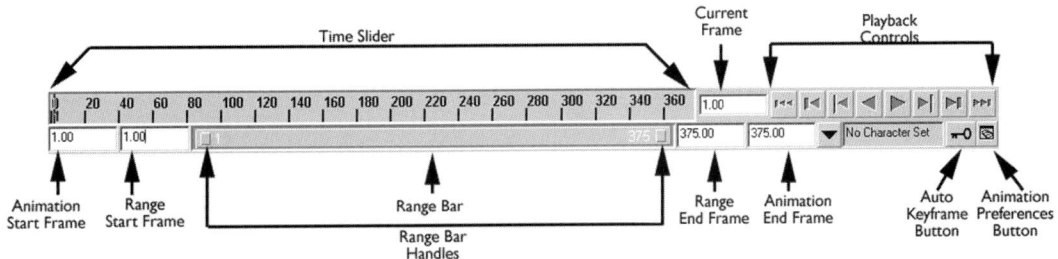

FIGURE 11.3   The Timeline.

Time Slider and Current Time Marker

The actual Time Slider is the collection of numbers and hash marks at the top of this collection of tools. The numbers there represent frames. Notice that Figure 11.3 illustrates one specific black line that goes from the top to the bottom of the Time Slider; this is the current time marker. It lets you know where you are in time. The Workspace will show the state of your 3D universe at the time indicated by the current time marker in the Timeline. If you LMB-click anywhere in the Time Slider, the current time marker will jump to that new time.

Just to the right of the Time Slider is a small input field that shows numerically which frame you are on. You can also enter values there to move the current time marker to a new time manually.

Playback Controls

At the top-right corner of the Timeline are the Playback controls that allow you to navigate or play the animation you have created. Notice that from the far left, the buttons are: Jump to the Beginning of the Animation, Move Back 1 Keyframe, Move Back 1 Frame, Play Backward, Play Forward, Move Forward 1 Keyframe, Move Forward 1 Frame, and Jump to the End of the Animation. These are fairly intuitive and anyone who has worked a VCR will be familiar with the interface paradigm here.

Range Bar

The tool that takes the most space below the Time Slider is the Range Bar. Notice that this bar has two square handles at either end. Next to those handles are numbers that indicate which frames are visible in the Time Slider immediately above it.

If you drag one of the Range Bar handles in or out, you will be able to see less or more of the total frames of the animation. This can help you zoom in on certain keyframes and be more exact in your placement when necessary.

Similarly, on both sides of the Range Bar are pairs of input fields. They indicate both the length of the entire animation (on the outside of both sides) and what frames are visible in the Time Slider (on the inside of both ends of the Range Bar).

Auto Keyframe Button

As we work, we will begin to create keyframes. You can maintain complete control over which keyframes are placed where by defining manually what type of keyframe is to be placed at the current time marker (more on this later). However, you can also set a starting keyframe, and then with the Auto Keyframe button depressed, whenever you change the parameters at a different time of that original keyframe, a new keyframe is placed for you automatically. Be warned though: this is a seductive tool and one that often ends up creating more trouble than it is worth. Maya will be happily placing keyframes while you are working through details of placement or movement even if you do not mean to record any animation. In general, for now, leave this off.

Animation Preferences Button

Click this button to pull up the animation preferences that we changed earlier in this chapter. It is the same as selecting Window > Settings/Preferences > Preferences and then selecting the Timeline category.

ANIMATABLE ELEMENTS

Turns out, in Maya, most everything can be animated. If it has a numerical value, you can record a keyframe for it. Then, change the value later, record another keyframe, and Maya will animate the difference.

For our introduction here, the important ideas will be the ability to animate movement, scaling, and rotation. This is reasonably intuitive if you have gotten used to using the keyboard shortcuts for the Move tool (**w**), Rotate tool (**e**), and Scale tool (**r**). To record a motion keyframe, hit **W** (or **Shift-w**). Similarly, rotation keyframes are **E** (**Shift-e**), and to record a scale keyframe, hit **R** (**Shift-r**).

The core idea of keyframe animation is that any motion is generated by two keyframes. The first dictates where the object is to start, and the second indicates where the object is to end. So, to create an object sliding across a room over 30 frames, you would begin by moving the current time marker to frame 1. Then, select the object, move it to where you want it to start, and hit **Shift-W** to tell it, "Start Here." Next, move the current time marker to frame 30, move the object to the new location, and again hit **Shift-W**. This tells the object, "At frame 30, I need to you be here." Maya then figures out how to get it there in the interim frames.

Enough talking about animation. Let's make some motion. To do this, we are going to animate a little character—a simple cartoon bird—flying through the room you have been creating in previous chapters. (Use the hummingbird we created with subdivision surfaces in Chapter 6.) Through the process, we will be creating several kinds of keyframes and altering how Maya decides to move between them.

TUTORIAL 10.1   **BASIC BIRD ANIMATION**

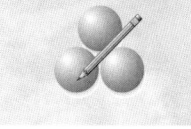

ON THE CD

Step 1: From the CD-ROM, open the file Bird_ReadyToAnimate. mb from the Tutorials/Chapter11/ folder.

Step 2: Set your animation preferences. As we discussed earlier, it's important that Maya knows the parameters that we are going to be using for the animation. Hit the Animation Preferences button at the bottom right of the Timeline. When the Preferences window appears, jump up to

Settings and change the Time to NTSC (30 fps). Then, jump back down to the Timeline category and make sure the Playback Speed is set to Real-time (30 fps). Click Save to save the changes and close the Preferences window.

Step 3: Change the selection mask so only the controls are selectable. Turn off all the selection mask buttons except for curves. By doing this we can easily grab the controls without selecting any other object.

Step 4: Set a key at frame zero. Select all the CTRL_ curves from the Outliner (Figure 11.4). Press **s** with the Time Slider at frame 0. This will set position and rotation keys for all our controls. When doing pose-to-pose animation, it is a good idea to set a key for the entire character at each major pose.

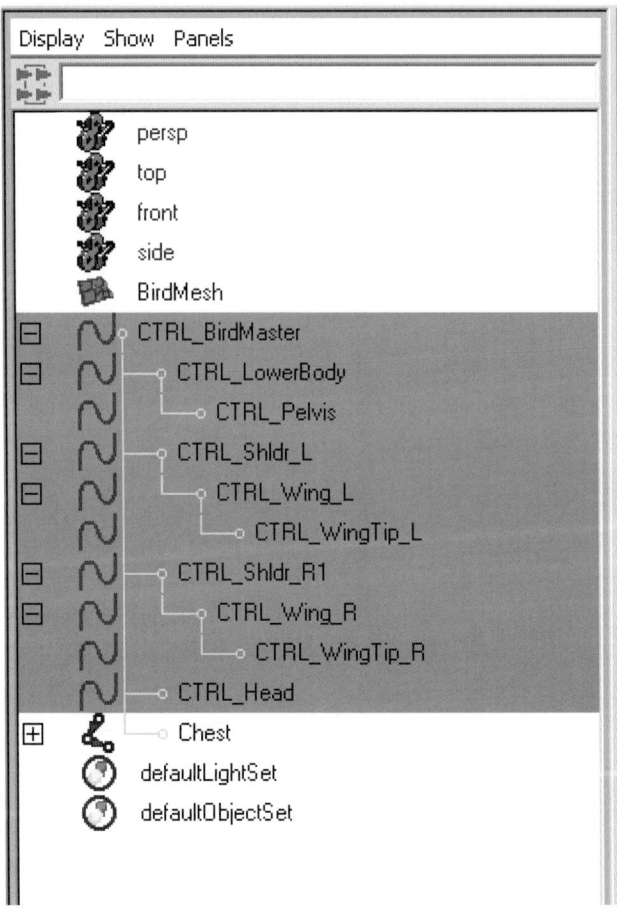

FIGURE 11.4   All the CTRL_ curves selected.

Step 5: Set the playback start time to frame 1.

Step 6: Our first pose. Since this bird has quite a few controls, we will do this with general descriptions and figures for reference. Turn on the Auto keyframe toggle.

Select CTRL_BirdMaster and rotate it so the bird is leaning forward about 45 degrees. We're not making robots, so don't worry about precision. Next, rotate CTRL_Head so the bird continues to look forward and translate the head back a little along Z. Now using the shoulder and wing controls, bend the wings back so they are ready to flap down. Use mostly the Y axis. Figure 11.5.

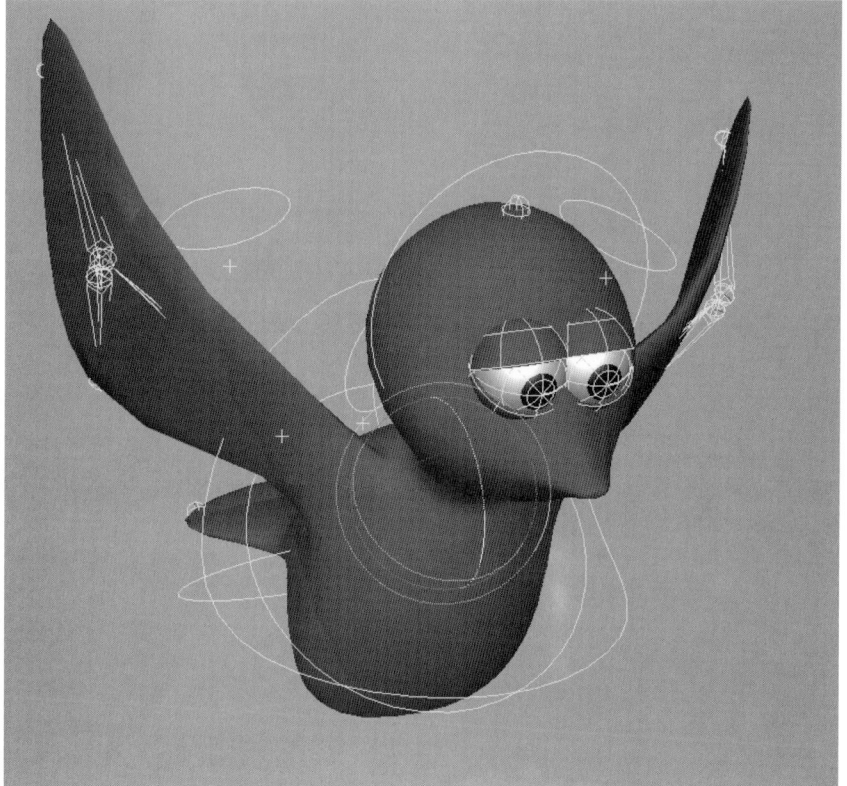

FIGURE 11.5   The bird's first pose.

Again select all the CTRL_ curves and press **s** to set keys for all the controls.

Step 7: Our second pose. Select frame 10 on the Time Slider. Now we will make our next pose with the bird's wings at the bottom of the flap. To keep the bird from looking stiff, we will tweak some other controls as well.

Start again with CTRL_BirdMaster and rotate him forward about 10 degrees. Also this time we will move it up about .5 units in Y axis using World. Nearly always you will start with the master control on a character. Like in drawing, you want to start with the major shapes and then work out to the smaller details.

The head needs to rotate back so the bird looks more forward again. Also, move the head forward a little on Z. This will make the head thrust forward when he flaps his wings.

Now the wings need to be rotated down using the controls as we did before (Figure 11.6).

Set keyframes for the entire bird like we did previously.

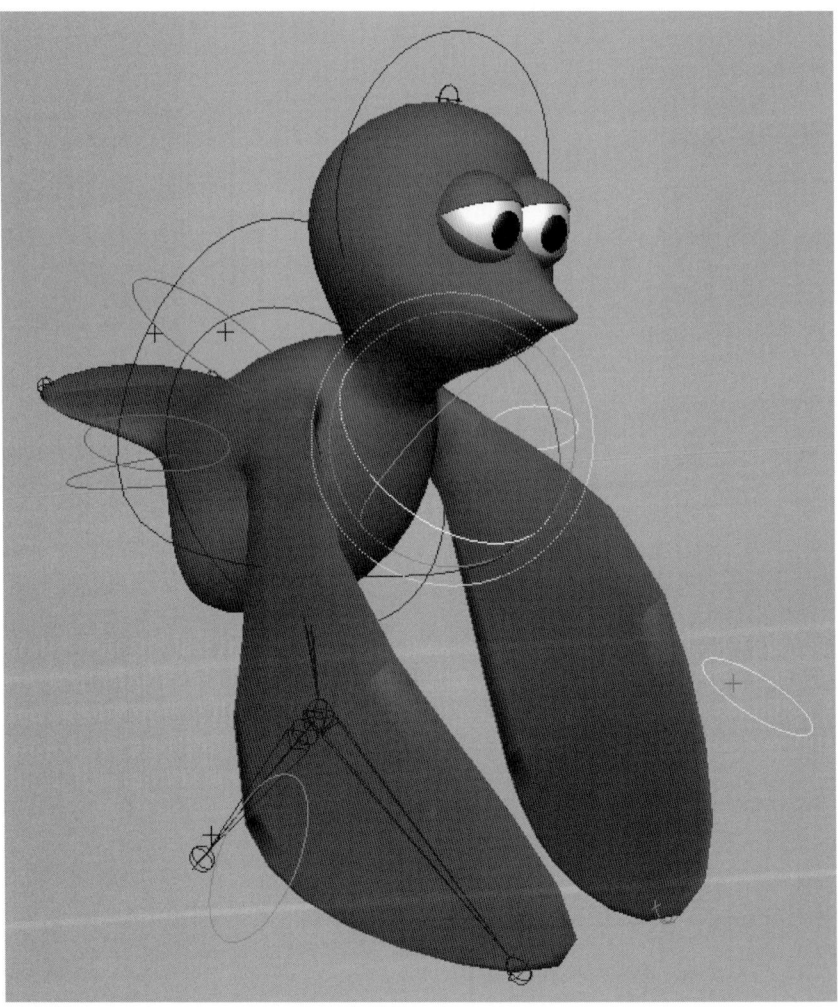

FIGURE 11.6   The bird's second pose.

Step 8: Let the computer do some work for you. Maya lets you copy keyframes and paste them on another frame. So go back to frame 1 and RMB-click to bring up a useful little menu. From this menu select Copy. The keys for any selected object are now ready to be pasted. Now click on frame 20 and RMB-click again but go to Paste > Paste. You should see the wings in the up position now.

Step 9: Flap, flap, flap. Set the Playback End Time to 19.00 and press the Play button on the VCR controls. Our bird is now flapping its wings. You could take this and have it fly through the room we created earlier, but let's make the animation a little better first.

Step 10: Breakdowns; taking some of the computer out of computer animation. As I said earlier, you almost never want to leave the in-betweens completely to Maya. Notice the wings are stiff and a bit lifeless. To fix this we will create a few breakdowns. Breakdowns are tweaks to the action between the poses. Sometimes we even create an entire pose to help guide the action.

Go to frame 5. We are going to tweak the wings to make the animation a tad more dynamic. For this, we will rotate the shoulder and wing down a little closer to the keyframe on frame 10. For the wingtips, we'll rotate them back up (Figure 11.7).

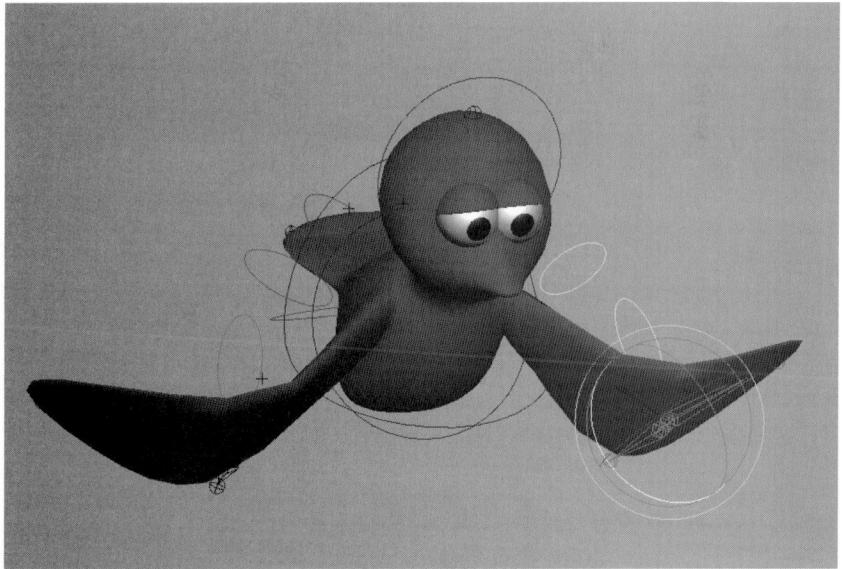

FIGURE 11.7   First breakdown for wings to make the animation less stiff.

Step 11: More breakdowns. The wings need a breakdown for the way back up. We want the opposite of what we did for frame 5. Rotate the shoulders and wings up closer to the keyframe on frame 20 and then rotate the wingtips back down (Figure 11.8).

Press Play on the VCR controls again. Now the wing flap looks much more fluid and interesting.

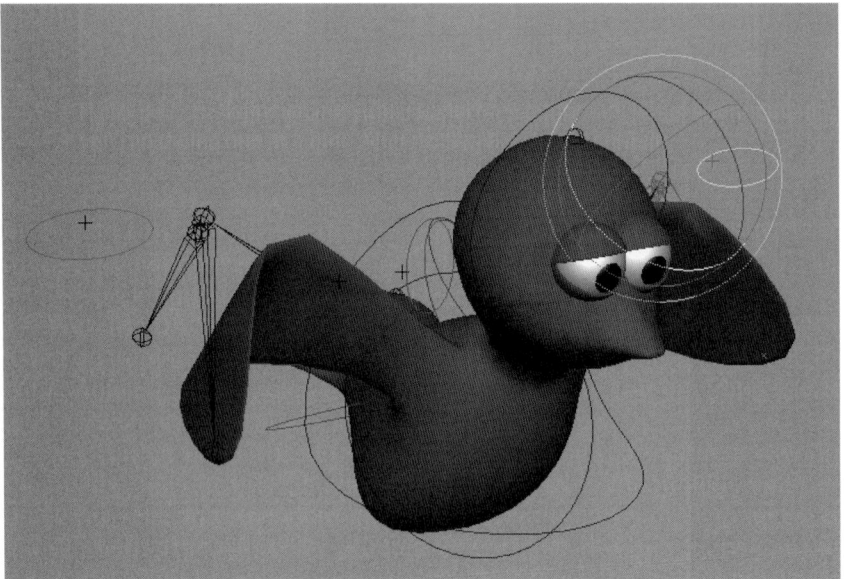

FIGURE 11.8 Second breakdown.

Step 12: Copy the animation to make more flapping. Another way to copy animation is to select a range of animation on the Time Slider. Set the Playback End Time to 50.00 and select all the CTRL_ objects.

To select a range of our animation, hold down **Shift** and then click and drag from frame 20 down to frame 5. As you do you'll see a red highlight showing the frames selected. Before we copy the keyframes let's look at what else we can do with the selected frames.

Notice that there are four black arrows on the red highlight: two in the middle and one at each end. With the arrows in the middle, you can move the selection backward and forward in time by simply dragging it left or right. The arrows at the end can stretch the time between the keyframes. The stretch feature is a nuisance though, because it puts your keyframes on partial frames (Figure 11.9).

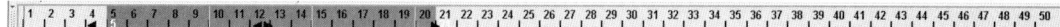

FIGURE 11.9   Selecting a range on the Time Slider.

Back to copying. Just like before, you copy by RMB-Clicking and select-ing Copy from the menu, but this time it will copy only the selected frames. Click on any frame outside the highlight to deselect the frames. We want to paste the animation starting at frame 25. So as before, RMB-Click and go to Paste > Paste. Now paste again at frame 45 and again at 65. You can keep going for as long as you think you'll need.

Congratulations! You just made a bird fly without too much effort. You can import the bird into your room scene and make it fly around. Create a NURBS circle below the bird and parent CTRL_BirdMaster to it. Use it to move the whole bird around the room.

Play around with the animation. The wing flap cycle we created here is slow and tame; you could make the action broader and faster. Exagger-ate all the parts and make something wild. Remember that you can Tum-ble around the animation as it plays.

ON THE CD

You can also see the example animation in the file Bird_Animated. mb on the CD-ROM in the Tutorials/Chapter11 folder.

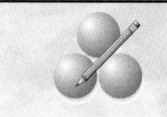

TUTORIAL 10.2   **OUTPUTTING YOUR ANIMATION**

Step 1: Playblast the animation. Now, unless you have a real beast of a machine with a huge video card, you will probably not be able to see a complex animation play in real-time. If you hit the Play Forward button in a heavy scene, there would be no change in the Workspace, although you would see the current time marker jumping across the Time Slider. There is just too much data to deal with.

Rendering would take too long as well. As slow as stills are to render, imagine waiting for that time multiplied by 300. Much too long to just get an idea of what we have done.

Playblasts are Maya's way of letting you do a quick rendering of the Workspace using the OpenGL algorithms. It creates and quickly assem-bles a short animation for you to view. You can choose to Playblast the entire animation or just sections of it.

To tell Maya to Playblast, choose Window > Playblast . . . (Options). Figure 11.10 shows the window. We want to be able to define exactly what it is putting together.

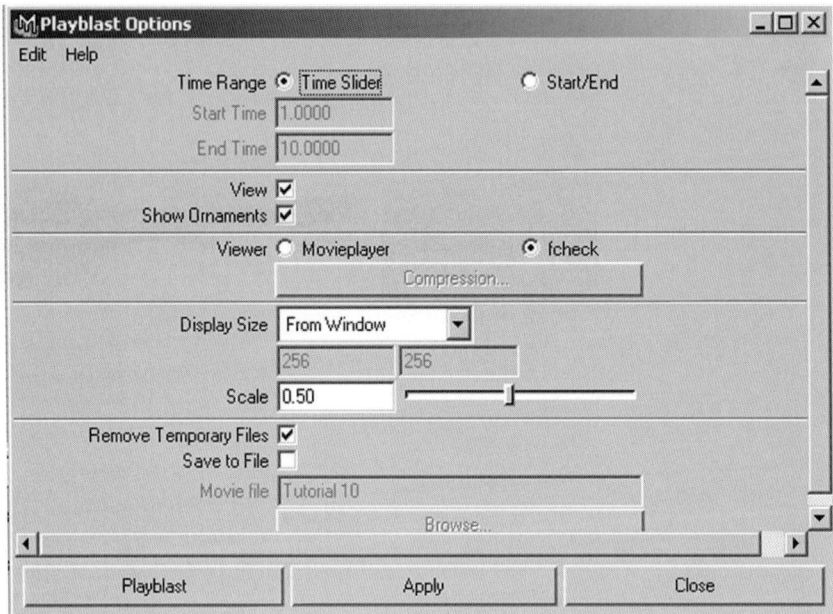

FIGURE 11.10 The Playblast Options window with settings to check out our animation.

Figure 11.10 shows what the settings should be. Using the FCheck, which is a kind of media player inside of Maya is fine. You can define a Display Size but, because the motion is small, just leave the Scale setting at 0.5; this will create the Playblast at half the size of your Perspective view. Leave the last part alone as we only want a temporary file—no need to save the files for this Playblast.

Hit the Playblast button.

Your UI will do some funny things here. You will start to see some motion in the corner of your Perspective view, and you will see the current time marker marching across the Time Slider. When it is all done, a new window called FCheck will pop up playing the animation.

By default, FCheck is playing every frame as fast as it can. If you have a slow machine, this may not be in real time. Hit **t** on your keyboard and FCheck will jump to playing the animation in real time, even if that means dropping frames (Figure 11.11).

Close the FCheck when you are done previewing this animation.

Hopefully, you are excited and pleased with what you see.

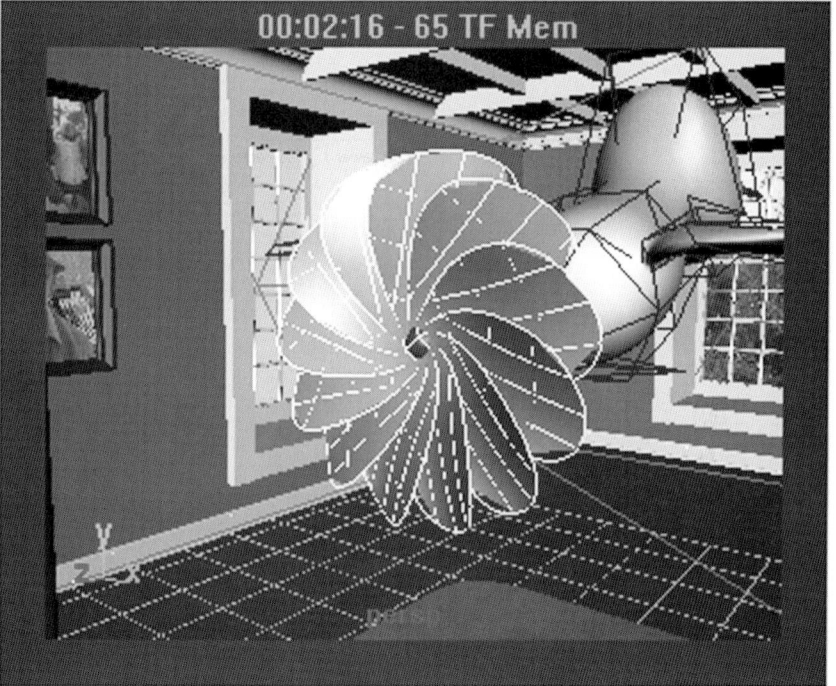

FIGURE 11.11   FCheck in action.

Step 2: Adjust Render Globals to render the project. There are several things that are important to adjust in the Render Globals window when you are ready to render an animation (Figure 11.12):

> **File Name Prefix Chapter11Final:**   This is the name that you want Maya to use as it saves the individual frames or completed clip.
>
> **Frame/Animation Ext name.#.ext:**   If you plan on rendering as anything but an AVI, you want to make sure to select an option with # (pound sign) in it. The # means that Maya will name each sequential still that it renders with a number attached to it. This becomes very important when it comes time to assemble the stills in a video editing system. For our purposes here (because we are rendering to an AVI), this is a less important detail, but it is important to note.

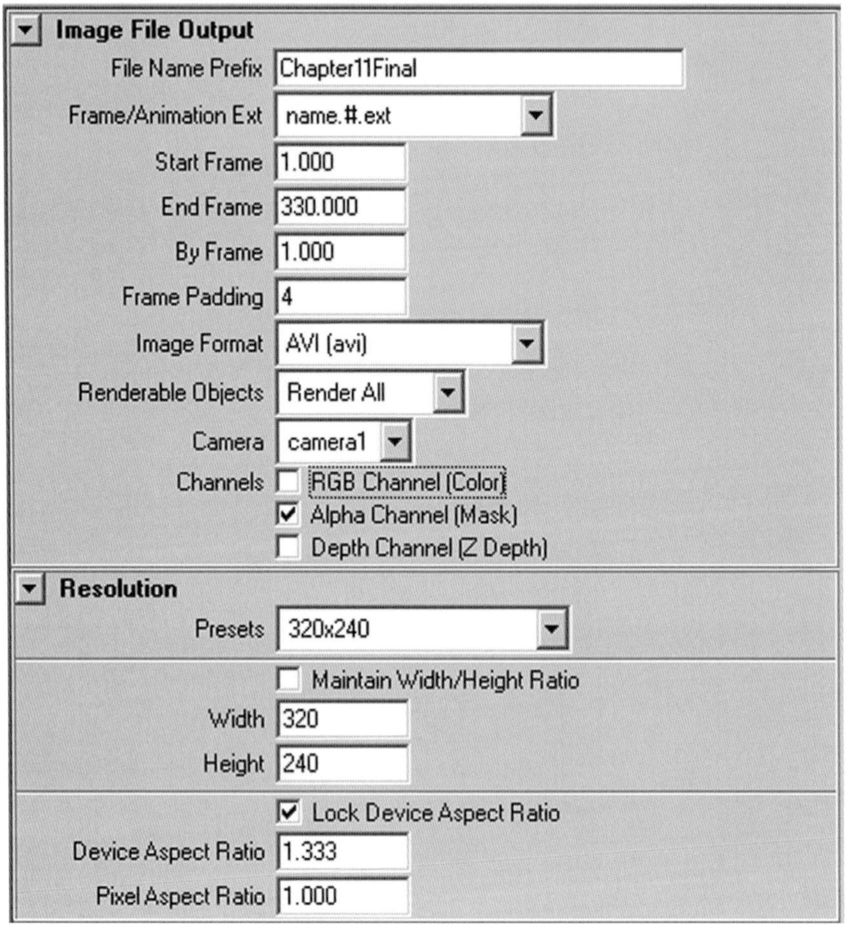

FIGURE 11.12   Consult the Render Globals window to get an early rendered test.

Start Frame 1.000:   This can be set at anything and should be if you only want to render a chunk of an animation. For us, we started our animation at frame 1.

End Frame: Again, this can be set at any value you wish when you want a part of an animated clip.

By Frame 1.000:   We want to render every frame and only one rendered frame per animated frame.

Frame Padding 4:   When Maya gets ready to render animations, it does so as a collection of stills. The frame padding is essentially how many zeros go before the frame number. This makes the numbering of the frames right when you get ready to import the sequential stills (if you are rendering to stills) into a video editing package.

Image Format AVI (avi):   This can be changed to have Maya render to sequential tiffs, jpegs, or a whole slew of other formats. For what we are doing here, we want Maya to render a movie file. AVI files are movie files that will play in a media player or Quicktime player as soon as you are done rendering; no need to import a large collection of sequential stills. When you finally get ready to render a project that is destined for broadcast, sequential tiffs that will be assembled in a nonlinear digital video editing system are a good idea.

Camera: Use the default Persp unless you have created a camera.

Resolution/Presets 320X240:   Although this size will definitely change when you are preparing for final output for initial renderings, 320×240 is a good preview render.

The rest of the settings can remain as they were set for the stills. It is important to notice that when you are ready for final output, you will want to make refinements in the settings such as turning up the Anti-aliasing Quality. You might even choose to use Raytracing. Also, there is a section for Motion Blur that allows Maya to blur shots as it renders to simulate "real" footage. Unfortunately, all these options add significant rendering time, so use them sparingly and only when you know you have what you want.

Finally, when all the Render Globals have been set, it is time to let Maya do its rendering magic. To render the animation, go to Rendering | Render > _Batch Rendering (Options). If you have multiple processors, make sure to check the Use All Available Processors button. Hit Batch Render, and Maya will begin rendering the project. If you look at the bottom-right corner of your screen, you will get updates on where Maya is in the rendering process. It will be slow, but sooner or later, your finished piece will be ready to play.

By default, rendered clips are stored in the Images folder in your Project directory. Watch for your clip there and play it in your media player of choice.

CONCLUSION

We have covered an awful lot through the pages of this book. Through the course of the tutorials, you have looked at basic modeling techniques of NURBS surfaces, polygon objects, and Subdivision surfaces. We looked at how to create visual interest through color, bump, and other attributes assigned to materials that were placed on our surfaces. We explored

Maya's lighting scheme—how to create lights, alter them, and fake complex lighting schemes. Finally, we have taken an overview of how to animate in Maya.

Unfortunately, we have just scratched the surface of all of these areas. The great power of Maya is complex. The techniques and tricks of Maya are wide and varied and must be explored. However, with the information gained in this book, you now have the vocabulary and the theoretical knowledge to understand the discussions and advanced tutorials you will find throughout the Internet and in other volumes.

Although you are probably not a Maya master quite yet, you should feel confident in the skills you have explored in this volume. Like any 3D package, successful mastery of Maya takes constant vigilance in continued practice. Work with Maya often—daily, if possible—to keep the skills gained here and explore new corners of the vast realm called Maya.

A

WHICH HARDWARE TO USE?

Appendix A's title is a complicated question. Without a doubt, Maya is a demanding piece of software not for the faint of heart or weakling hardware setup. Further, different animators will have different levels of need. If you are a hobbyist and are using Maya as an interesting toy to fool around with shapes and basic animation, you probably have no need for the $5,000 super-duper-show-7-trillion-polys-per-second-render-film-resolution-scenes-in-less-than-a-second system. But, if your animation jobs are lined out the door, and quickly realizing projects in Maya is the key to your success, the previously mentioned system is probably a necessity.

Because of this complexity, it's difficult to define what system or type of system you need. In this appendix, we will look at "Qualified Hardware" and break down the basic components of a computer that are necessary for using Maya effectively. Remember that this discussion is by no means exhaustive, and many parts of it will be largely subjective. As with any large purchase, make sure you do your homework, ask trusted experts, read reviews, and research carefully before upgrading your existing system or buying a new one.

MAYA'S QUALIFIED HARDWARE

Alias includes an "official" list of "approved" systems that are certified to run well with Maya. This chart is usually located on the Alias Web site under "Qualified Hardware Chart" or in the Support section under "Qualified Hardware." These lists represent hardware solutions that have been tested successfully by Maya. Now, this definitely does not mean that Maya will not run on other systems; in fact, Maya will run on many systems not mentioned on Maya's Qualified Hardware list, including some that are built from scratch. However, if you have more money than time, purchasing these qualified systems ensures that you are up and running with Maya out of the box.

Mac Systems

If you are among the Apple faithful, or are looking for an alternative to Windows-based machines, the choices are clear and fairly limited. As of this writing, the qualified Macs for running Maya are as follows:

COMPUTER	SYSTEM	GRAPHICS CARD	OSX
Any G3	Any	Any	—
Power Mac G4 (PCI Graphics)	Single 350MHz Single 400MHz	ATI Rage 128 PCI ATI Rage 128	
Power Mac G4 (AGP Graphics)	Single 350MHz Single 400MHz Single 450MHz		
Power Mac G4 (Gigabit Ethernet)	Single 400MHz Dual 450MHz Dual 500MHz	ATI Rage 128 Pro ATI Rage 128 Pro	—
Power Mac G4 (Digital Audio)	Single 466MHz Single 533MHz Single 667MHz Single 733MHz Dual 533MHz	ATI Radeon ATI Rage 128 Pro	—
Power Mac G4 (QuickSilver)	Single 733MHz Single 867MHz Dual 800MHz	NVIDIA GeForce 2 MX ATI Radeon NVIDIA GeForce 2 MX	10.2.4 10.3 10.2.4 10.3
Power Mac G4 (QuickSilver 2002)	Single 800MHz Single 933MHz Dual 1.0 GHz	NVIDIA GeForce 3 ATI Radeon 7500	10.2.4
Power Mac G4 (Mirrored Drive Doors)	Dual 867MHz Dual 1.0 GHz Dual 1.25 GHz	NVIDIA GeForce 4 MX NVIDIA GeForce 4 Titanium NVIDIA GeForce 4 MX	10.2.4 10.2.4 10.3 10.2.4
Power Mac G4 (FW 800)	Single 1.0 GHz Dual 1.25 GHz Dual 1.42 GHz	ATI Radeon 9000 Pro NVIDIA GeForce 4 Titanium NVIDIA GeForce 4 MX	10.2.4 10.3 10.2.4 10.3 10.2.4

COMPUTER	SYSTEM	GRAPHICS CARD	OSX
PowerBook G4	400MHz	NVIDIA GeForce	10.2.4
(Titanium)	500MHz	4 Titanium	10.3
PowerBook G4	550MHz	ATI Radeon 9000 Pro	10.2.4
(Gigabit Ethernet)	667MHz	ATI Radeon 9700 Pro	10.2.4
PowerBook G4	667MHz	ATI Mobility Radeon M3	10.3
(DVI)	800MHz	ATI Mobility Radeon M6	10.2.4
PowerBook G4 12"	867MHz		10.2.4
PowerBook G4 17"	1.0GHz		
iMac	Single 700MHz	ATI Mobility Radeon 7500	10.2.4
(15-inch Flat Panel)	Single 800MHz	NVIDIA	10.2.4
iMac	Single 700MHz	GeForce 4 420 Go	10.2.4
(17-inch Flat Panel)	Single 800MHz	NVIDIA	10.3
		GeForce 4 440 Go	10.2.4
		NVIDIA GeForce 2 MX	10.3
		NVIDIA GeForce 2 MX	10.2.4
		NVIDIA GeForce 4 MX	10.2.4
		NVIDIA GeForce 2 MX	10.3
eMac	Single 700MHz	ATI PCI graphics	—
Xserve	Single 1.0 GHz	ATI Radeon 8500	10.2.4
	Dual 1.0 GHz	NVIDIA GeForce	10.2.8
		FX 5200 Ultra	
Power Mac G5	Single 1.6 GHz	ATI Radeon 9600 Pro	10.3
	Single 1.8 GHz	ATI Radeon 9800 Pro	10.2.8
	Dual 2.0 GHz		10.3
			10.2.8
			10.3

An important thing to note is that everything but the highest-end Macs usually comes with video cards that you will want to replace. The video cards in the machines listed above are full of caveats (make sure to see the Alias Web site for details). If you have the cash after purchasing a good Mac, you should seriously look into upgrading the video card. Although the latest round of Macs include the NVIDIA GeForce FX 5200 (not a shabby card), most Macs still have comparatively weak cards. If you are serious about using Maya on a Mac, consider upgrading to as nice a card as possible. See the video card discussion later in this appendix.

Now, this means that if you have or plan to purchase an iMac or PowerBook, you are stuck (as there are really no video card upgrade options). For this reason, I would really not recommend buying either of these two types of systems for serious Maya work. Although they will seem to be snappy when placing a few quick primitive shapes, they will become entirely too slow for poly-heavy projects down the road. If you are serious about using Mac for Maya, get a robust G5 tower system. With the recent announcement of all dual-processor systems for towers, you can purchase decent horsepower for reasonable prices.

Linux Systems

Ah, the Linux lovers. Folks who know Linux typically know more about hardware than people should. So, besides listing the approved systems here, we will leave the Linux discussion alone.

COMPANY	MODEL	WEB
HP	HP Workstation X1000/X1100/X2000/X2100/X4000	*www.hp.com*
HP	HP Workstation xw4100, XW5000, XW6000, XW8000	*www.hp.com*
IBM	IBM M Pro 6219, 6230	*www.ibm.com*
IBM	IBM Z Pro 6221	*www.ibm.com*
Compaq	W6000/W8000	*www.compaq.com*

A great thing about the Linux community is that they tend to be well connected. Make sure that if you plan to run Maya on Linux, you put out the feelers amongst your Linux contacts to find the ideal system for you.

PC Systems

As of this writing, the "qualified" systems are listed as follows:

COMPANY	MODEL	WEB
Boxx	3DBOXX R1	*www.boxxtech.com*
Compaq	Professional Workstation 6300	*www.compaq.com*
Compaq	Professional Workstation AP 400, 500, 550	*www.compaq.com*
Compaq	Professional Workstation SP700	*www.compaq.com*
Compaq	Professional Workstation 6000	*www.compaq.com*
Compaq	Professional Workstation EVO 6000, 8000	*www.compaq.com*
Compaq	EVO Notebook N800	*www.compaq.com*
Dell 1	Precision Workstation 210, 410, 610	*www.dell.com*
Dell 1	Precision Workstation 220, 420, 620	*www.dell.com*
Dell 1	Precision Workstation 330, 530	*www.dell.com*
Dell 1	Precision Workstation 340, 360	*www.dell.com*

COMPANY	MODEL	WEB
Dell	Precision Workstation 350, 450, 650	www.dell.com
Dell	Precision Workstation m50 with NVIDIA Quadro 4 Go	www.dell.com
Dell	Precision Workstation m60 with NVIDIA Quadro FX 700 Go	www.dell.com
HP	HP Workstation X1000, X1100, X2000, X2100, X4000	www.hp.com
HP	HP Workstation xw5000, xw6000, xw8000, xw4100	www.hp.com
HP	HP Mobile Workstation nw8000 with ATI FireGL T2	www.hp.com
IBM	Intellistation E Pro 6836, 6846	www.ibm.com
IBM	Intellistation M Pro 6868, 6849, 6850, 6229, 6219, 6230	www.ibm.com
IBM	Intellistation Z Pro 6866, 6221	www.ibm.com
IBM	Thinkpad A31p (with ATI FireGL 7800 mobile)	www.ibm.com
IBM	Thinkpad T40p (ATI Mobility FireGL 9000)	www.ibm.com
IBM	Thinkpad R50p (ATI FireGL T2)	www.ibm.com
Intergraph	TDZ 2000 Graphics Workstation	www.intergraph.com

This list will undoubtedly be updated again soon as new systems will continue to be developed and tested. As Maya 6 matures and more folks use it, new systems will look to be certified.

Remember that many times manufacturers have other systems that work great with Maya that they (the manufacturer, not Alias/Wavefront) have tested extensively. For instance, Boxx Technologies has certified their R1 series of Dual-Athlon machines. Indeed, these machines work great (it is the machine this book was written on). However, if you are strictly an Intel computer user, Boxx Technologies also make the S-Series that are Dual-Xeon equipped. Of course, these Dual-Xeon systems also run Maya like a dream—Boxx has tested the setup extensively. Now, just because a manufacturer makes a certified system does not mean that all their systems play well with Maya. However, if you can talk to a living, knowledgeable person at the manufacturing companies, they will be anxious to tell you of other feasible alternatives. So do your research, but make sure you do not limit yourself to the models shown earlier in this section.

IMPORTANT COMPONENTS

If you purchase a system off Maya's Qualified Hardware list, you will receive a machine (minus a monitor, probably) that has all the things you need. However, if you are more adventurous or cannot afford the systems listed on Maya's "official" list, there are some general guidelines of hardware that you must have, and guidelines of hardware that you should have.

Processor(s)

This is definitely a must have, although there is a fairly wide range of possibilities here. As you know, the processor is kind of the like the brain of your 3D station. It makes the calculations necessary for creating complex 3D in real time and especially for rendering your projects. Although there are areas of calculations when you are building a project that make heavy use of the processor (such as dynamics); the biggest difference you will see in different speed processors is in rendering times.

Processors raise an interesting question of want versus need. There are some true needs depending on what platform you are working with. For instance, if you are a Mac 3D artist you need at least a G4 processor. Maya can run fairly smoothly on a 667MHz as well as a dual 1.25GHz machine. The leap in price is substantial, but the leap in performance (except for rendering speed) is not that noticeable.

Similarly, if you are running a PC, you will be surprised at how small a machine will run Maya successfully. A P3 is usually plenty when you are first getting started. Even a Celeron-equipped machine will suffice, although this begins to really push things. Naturally, if you can use a P4 or similar generation AMD chips, you get much better performance, especially with rendering speeds. However, when you are learning Maya, there's no need to drop four grand on the latest and greatest machines. In one of the labs at the University of the Incarnate Word, we run Maya on P3 800MHz machines quite well. These machines do have decent video cards (NVIDIA Quadro 2), and that makes for fairly smooth operation.

Usually, the bleeding edge processors have an inexplicably heavy jump in price over the next fastest processor choice. In general, the absolute fastest processor is rarely worth the price for most Maya users; especially because that same processor will drop by hundreds of dollars in six weeks when the next speed bump occurs. However, most folks cannot buy a new machine very often, so you want to make sure you purchase a machine that stays with you long enough to get your money's worth. So, a general rule that is to find the absolute fastest machine available and then look for its little brother. Typically, the little brother is still a strong machine with good legs that comes at a huge discount over its top-of-the-line counterpart.

A Note on Multiple Processors

Maya is one of several 3D software packages that will actually make use of more than one processor. Although this is never truly a "double-the-speed" situation, there is usually a worthwhile drop in rendering times when you have two processor brains calculating those light rays. Typically, dual processors render 1.6 to 1.7 times faster than a single processor unit. Although you do not see a jump in the speed of the interface, dual processors help a lot if you do not have a render farm at your disposal.

Video Cards

Video cards are responsible for many things, but the most important is how quickly Maya interacts with you, the user. A larger, faster video card can display more polygons at once and refresh the screen more quickly than a smaller one. If you are coming from a 3D package other than Maya and have dealt with large projects, you have undoubtedly experienced the move-your-camera-wait-five-seconds-for-screen-redraw dilemma. Usually, you fix this problem by turning off lights or viewing things as isoparms or wireframes. Maya is much better at providing a great OpenGL accelerated experience when moving models or moving around models. However, this is still dependent on how much muscle your video card has.

As always, bigger is typically better. Putting good money into a video card is usually worth the investment. Having a snappy interface makes the work much more intuitive, and the computer appears to think as fast as you do.

Luckily, the cost of video cards continues to drop as the speed rises. Remember that not all consumer cards are appropriate for working with Maya. Because video cards are constantly being improved it's recommended that you check the Alias Web site for the latest card.

3Dlabs	Wildcat VP560, 760, 870, 970, 990	3.01–0834
NVIDIA	Quadro DCC	60.85
NVIDIA	Quadro 4 Go (in Dell M50)	60.85
NVIDIA	Quadro 4 700, 750, 900 XGL	60.85
NVIDIA	Quadro 4 780, 980 XGL	60.85
NVIDIA	Quadro FX 500	60.85
NVIDIA	Quadro FX 1000, 2000	60.85
NVIDIA	Quadro FX 1100	60.85
NVIDIA	Quadro FX 3000	60.85
NVIDIA	Quadro FX 700 Go	

(in Dell M60)	60.85	
NVIDIA	GeForce 2, GeForce 3, GeForce 4 (ANY GeForce)	NOT QUALIFIED
	NOT QUALIFIED	
ATI	FireGL 7800 mobility	
	(In IBM Thinkpad A31P)	6.13.10.6200
	7.79.6-021213a-007988c-IBM or 7-7.79.6-021019a-006279E-IBM available from IBM	
ATI	FireGL 9000 mobility	
	(In IBM Thinkpad T40P)	6.14.10.6444
	8.011-040427a-015929E-RC1-IBM available from IBM	
ATI	FireGL T2 mobility (In IBM Thinkpad R50P)	6.14.10.6444
|	8.011-040427a-015929E-RC1-IBM available from IBM	
Mobility	ATI	Radeon 8800
	(in Compaq EVO N800)	6.13.10.6206
	7.77.3-021016a-006195E-1.00C	
ATI	FireGL X2-256t, X2-256	8.01
ATI	FireGL T2-64, T2-128	8.01
ATI	FireGL Z1/X1	8.01

A discussion of important details about these graphics cards follows.

This of course does not mean that all consumer level cards are in-compatible. It also does not mean that all these professional cards work without flaw; in fact, when you look at this list on the Alias Web site, you will also find a huge list of issues that exist with each card.

In general, if you can afford a "professional" grade card, buy it. If not, purchase the biggest, fastest card you can afford but keep your receipt. Make sure you experiment with all sorts of objects as well as pull-down menus within Maya and return the card if necessary. An unapproved video card should work fine, but issues do arise.

The process of picking a video card does indeed seem mysterious. There appear to be hardly any cards that are perfect for all aspects of Maya, so do not worry about small issues. The up-front pains are worth it when working with video cards, as once you have the card that is right for your work flow and budget, Maya will feel more smoothly interactive than any 3D applications you have ever worked with.

If you have to choose where to put your money as you built a Maya system, this would be the place. A good video card is vital to effective Maya use.

RAM

Only one piece of advice here: get lots of it. RAM is cheap these days and anything less than 512 MB can get downright painful. As your skills increase and the complexity of your projects rises, your RAM requirements will blossom. Insufficient RAM can really slow you down so if you have the budget, max out your board. Besides the video card, this is the second most important place to put your money as you develop your Maya box.

Monitor

The monitor is the one piece of hardware that you spend the most time looking at. However, many users scrimp on their monitors in an attempt to beef up their central processing units (CPUs). Spend some good money on your monitor. Going into all the dot-pitch, refresh rates, and other issues of the monitor, and whether to go cathode ray tube (CRT) or liquid crystal display (LCD) is beyond the scope of this volume. However, remember that the size of icons remains the same, so if your monitor only does 640X480 or even 800x600, your actual working space is severely limited.

In general, make sure your monitor does 1024X768 with a high refresh rate (75–85 KHz) at the very least. You will be much happier and your eyes and head will thank you when running a nice size (19-inch to 21-inch) monitor running at 1600x1200 at 85KHz. A good monitor can last you through several generations of CPUs. Remember, you will be looking at that piece of machinery for countless hours as you learn and master Maya; get something you are really happy looking at.

Mouse

Three-button, three-button, three-button (and that does not mean two buttons and a scroll wheel). Honestly, the standard two-button mouse or the "luxury" two-button with a middle scroll wheel are just not what you need when using Maya. As was discussed in Chapter 1, Maya uses a very quick, effective method of moving the camera around your digital world. However, it does this by combinations of all three buttons on your mouse. A true three-button mouse is not a huge expense but can really speed along your work process.

CONCLUSION

People get passionate about the computers they build or buy. Everyone has an opinion about what machine/video card/RAM brand/platform/OS is the best. In reality, your Maya box, whether it be an out-of-the-box, ready-to-go Apple, Dell, HP, or Boxx or built from scratch to match the specs of these other boxes, it can and should be a help in your 3D creation process. Make sure you are not cheating yourself in the long run by selling yourself short on the machine as you learn.

B

CUSTOMIZING THE MAYA USER INTERFACE

Throughout the earlier chapters, we looked briefly at various ways to change the user interface (UI) of Maya to accommodate a particular work flow. This appendix serves as the workout gym for your Maya interface. Although it does not cover every single way to modify the Maya UI, it does provide steps on the methods that are most commonly used and most helpful in trimming down the interface fat present in some areas while building up the interface muscle needed in others.

GENERAL OVERVIEW

There is a lot going on when you open Maya. As discussed throughout this volume, there are so many things going on that Maya hides many of the available tools just to keep things cleaned up a bit. Through hotboxes, Marking menus, and other such tricks, Maya allows you to get to those options that are not immediately accessible rather easily. However, sometimes this is just too slow. Sometimes, you want a collection of tools to be right there—easy to grab, easy to use, easy to find.

Additionally, the individual panels that are present and created by default when you first open Maya may not provide you with the spaces and tools that you wish to use. A great thing about Maya is that nearly every panel is customizable; nearly every tool can be organized where you wish it. You can really create the interface you desire.

Windows

When Maya is first opened, all its tools, pull-down menus, and panels are contained within one large customizable window. However, because there is a limited amount of screen real estate, you will find a limited number of the vast types of tools available in Maya. As we discussed throughout this volume, Maya allows you to create and edit a large variety of functions and characteristics of your scene through collections of editors. There are a lot of editors. Because of this, most are hidden until you choose to call them up.

All editors may be called up as floating windows that you can move wherever you wish within the interface. To access any editor, see the Window pull-down menu where all the editors are organized by General, Rendering, Animation, and Relationship options. Figure B.1 shows a quick breakdown of what each sub-menu of the editors presents. Many of these particular editors are used throughout this volume.

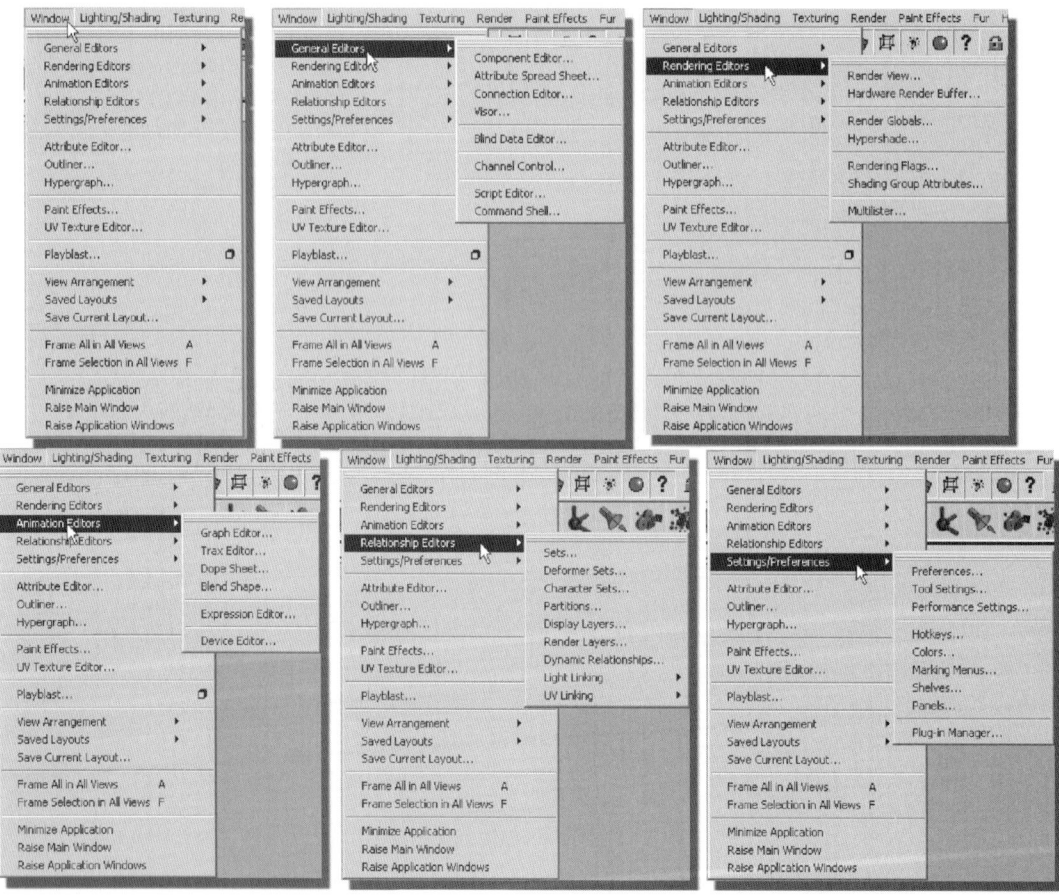

FIGURE B.1 The Window pull-down menu (accessible in any module) allows you to access editors and other important tools such as the Outliner and Hypergraph.

Notice also that within the Window pull-down menu, you can access the Settings/Preferences sub-menu. This is a huge part of customization that we will be looking at exclusively later in this appendix.

Managing Panels

Maya's interface is divided up into easily recognizable panels. Panels are the large sections that contain either editors (Outliner, Hypergraph, Trax Editor, Relationship Editor, and so on) or camera viewpoints. In general, panels are a bit different from the windows we just looked at, because panels are docked into place within the interface. For instance, when you select Window > Outliner, the Outliner that appears is a window—it floats through the interface. These windows have the advantage of being easy to move around when you need them out of the way. However, this also means that this window is always on top of some other part of the interface. You can also view things like the Outliner as a panel—that is, the window gets nestled into the interface occupying its own real estate and is never in the way.

When Maya is first opened, there is one large panel in the middle of the screen generally referred to as the Workspace. Notice that this Workspace has its own collection of pull-down menus (Figure B.2).

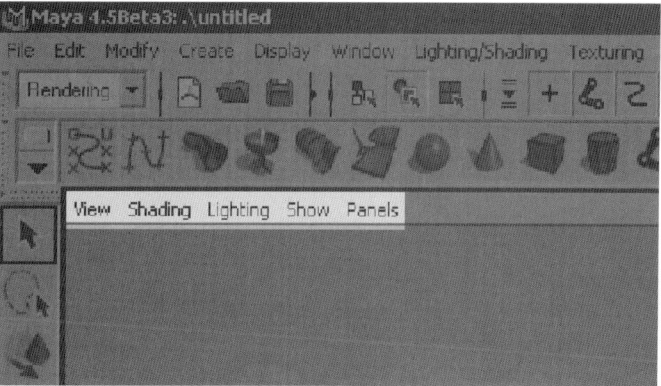

FIGURE B.2   The main Workspace panel has its own collection of pull-down menus. These menus allow for the modification of the content of the panel.

We already looked at and made extensive use of switching from one view to four views by quickly hitting the **Spacebar**. This divides this main Workspace panel into four smaller panels—each with a different view of the scene. An important thing that happens here is that each new panel has its own collection of pull-down menus. Among these is the Panels pull-down menu (Figure B.3). This allows you to control what is contained within each individual panel and how the panels are arranged.

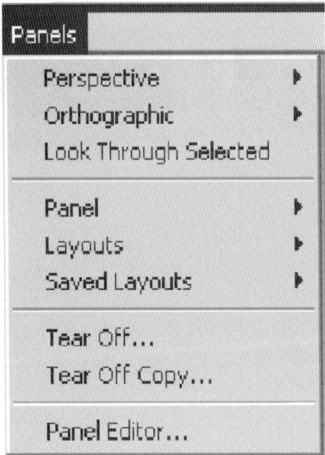

FIGURE B.3   The Panel pull-down menu is the source of rearranging the Workspace.

The most general change you can make is to select Panels > Layouts and then choose one of the many split options that are available. The names of the options are fairly self-explanatory, so we will not detail them here. Suffice it to say they allow for a multitude of organizations for your panels (Figure B.4).

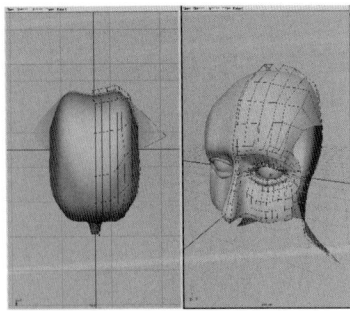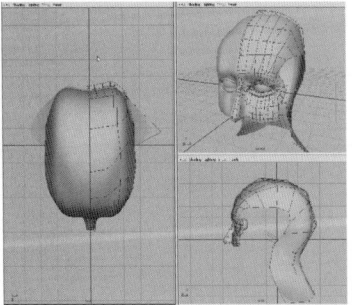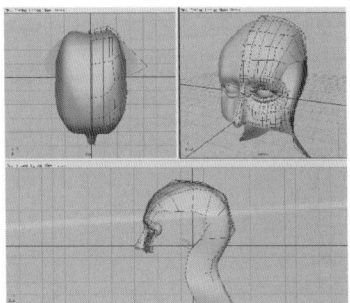

FIGURE B.4   A quick look at a few variations possible through the pull-down menu within each panel, Panel > Layouts.

Still within each panel, and within the Panels pull-down menu, there is Panels > Saved Layouts. Here, you are given several options to select a variety of prepared collections of panels. These collections of layouts will also include various editors. You may find that at different times of your work flow, some of these saved layouts will be just the ticket (Figure B.5).

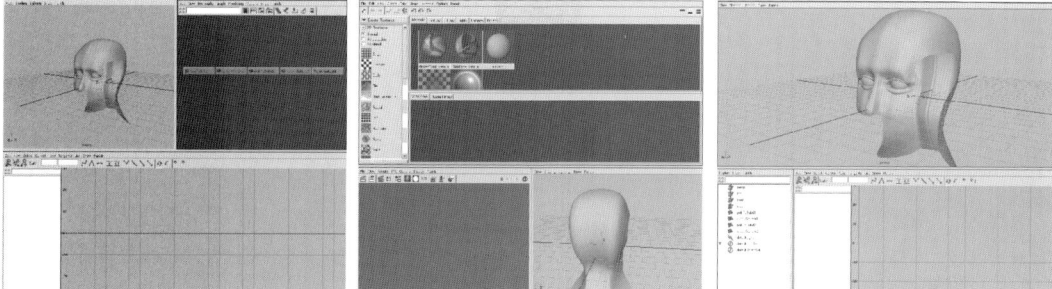

FIGURE B.5   A few examples of some of the Panels > Saved Layouts options. Notice that many of these saved layout combinations include panels containing things like the Hypershade, Outliner, or the Trax Editor.

Maya 4.0 and later include a collection of buttons along the left side of the interface (in the Toolbox) below the QWERTY tools (Figure B.6). These contain collections of saved layouts that can be selected with a quick click.

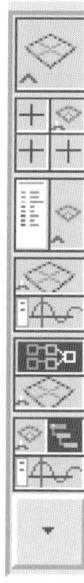

FIGURE B.6   Saved layouts available in the Toolbox.

To change or add new saved layouts to these buttons within the Toolbox, simply RMB-click any of the extant icons for layouts and select the new desired layout (Figure B.7).

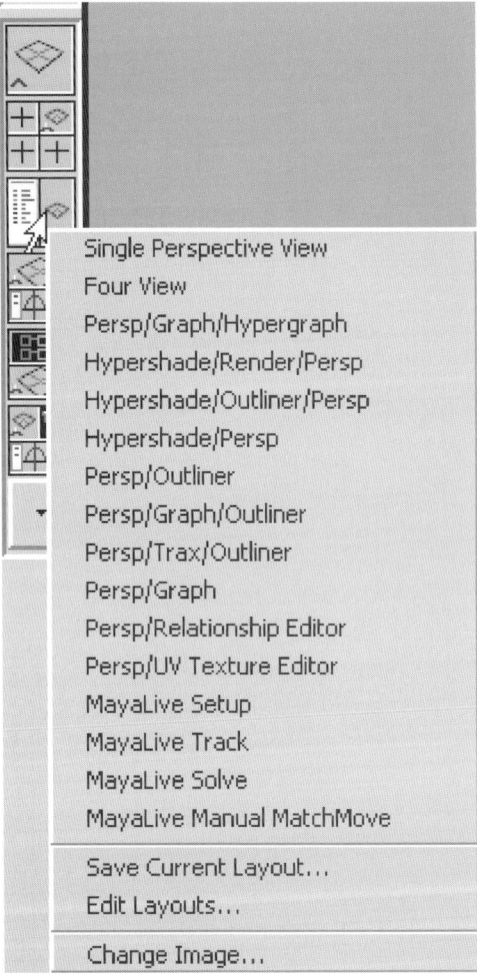

FIGURE B.7 To customize the Toolbox's collection of saved layouts, RMB-click on the tool to change and select the new desired layout.

Notice that the last option within Panels > Saved Layouts is Edit Layouts. The resulting dialog box (Figure B.8) allows you to create custom layouts that can be pulled up again at a later time. Once you begin to establish a work flow and find where you prefer to have each panel for various times, this option becomes very handy.

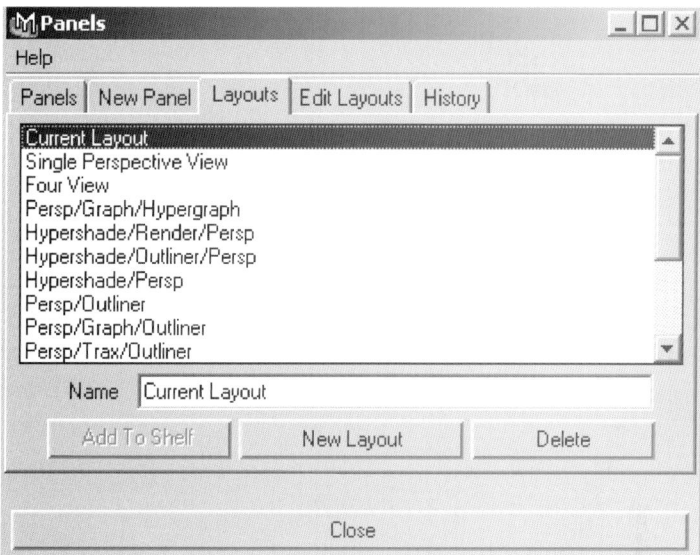

FIGURE B.8   You can create your own saved layouts with Panels > Saved Layouts > Edit Layouts to be called up again at will. Remember that Maya saves these created layouts within the defined project file.

Finally, still within the collection of pull-down menus in each panel, notice the Panels > Panel option (Figure B.9). Here, you can define manually what each individual panel will contain. For temporary setups, this works well.

Showing and Hiding Parts of the Interface

In the first image of this appendix, we looked at a general overview of the Maya UI. Maya works hard to minimize the tools used for visual tool buttons and maximize the Workspace. However, this might not be enough for you. Sometimes, you might want to get rid of (or show) parts or all of the UI.

The standard way to pick and choose what parts of the interface are visible is with the Display > UI Elements pull-down menu, and then by selecting or deselecting the parts of the interface you wish to show or hide (Figure B.10).

Of interest is that the first two options (Status Line and Shelf) are elements of the UI that appear at the top when activated. The next four (Time Slider, Range Slider, Command Line, and Help Line) are all parts of the UI that appear across the bottom. The next one (Tool Box) is for UI

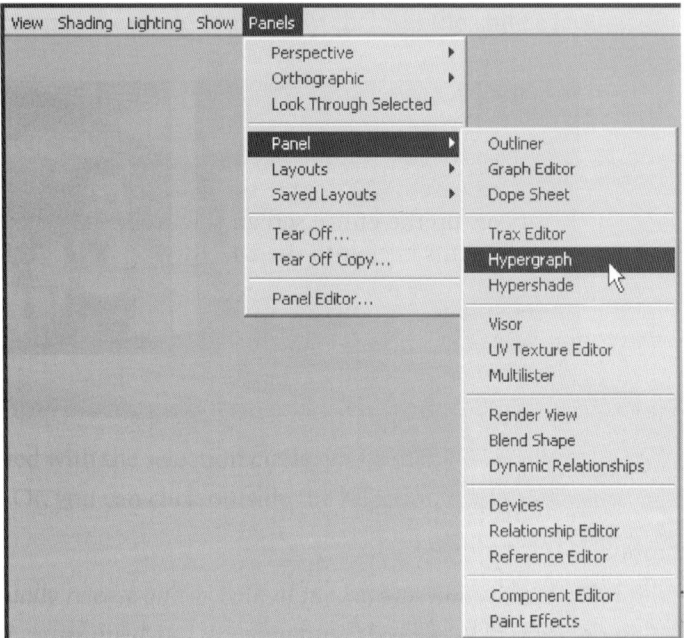

FIGURE B.9 To define an individual panel for a temporary panel arrangement, you can define one at a time what each panel should contain.

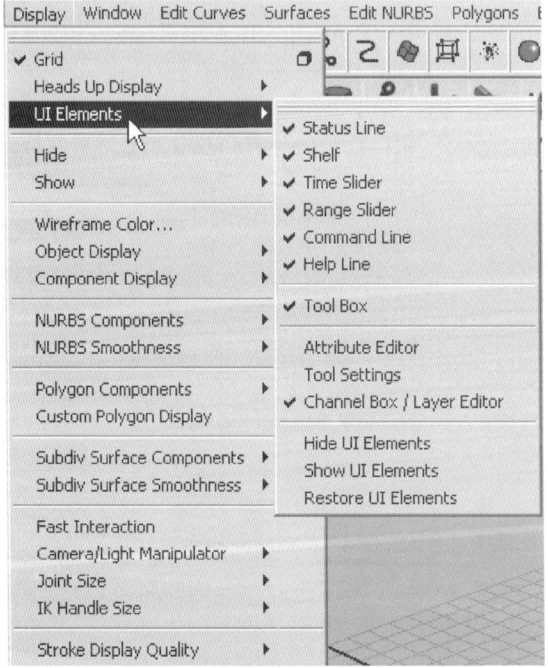

FIGURE B.10 The Display > UI Elements pull-down menu allows you to define what parts of the UI are to be seen and what is to be hidden.

elements on the left, and the last three (Attribute Editor, Tool Settings, and Channel Box/Layer Editor) are for panels that will be nested along the far right edge.

Notice the last three options of Hide UI Elements, Show UI Elements, and Restore UI Elements (which restores all the default elements). Hide UI Elements hides all the elements, leaving you with a Workspace that takes up the entire screen (Figure B.11). Show UI Elements brings all the elements back into the UI.

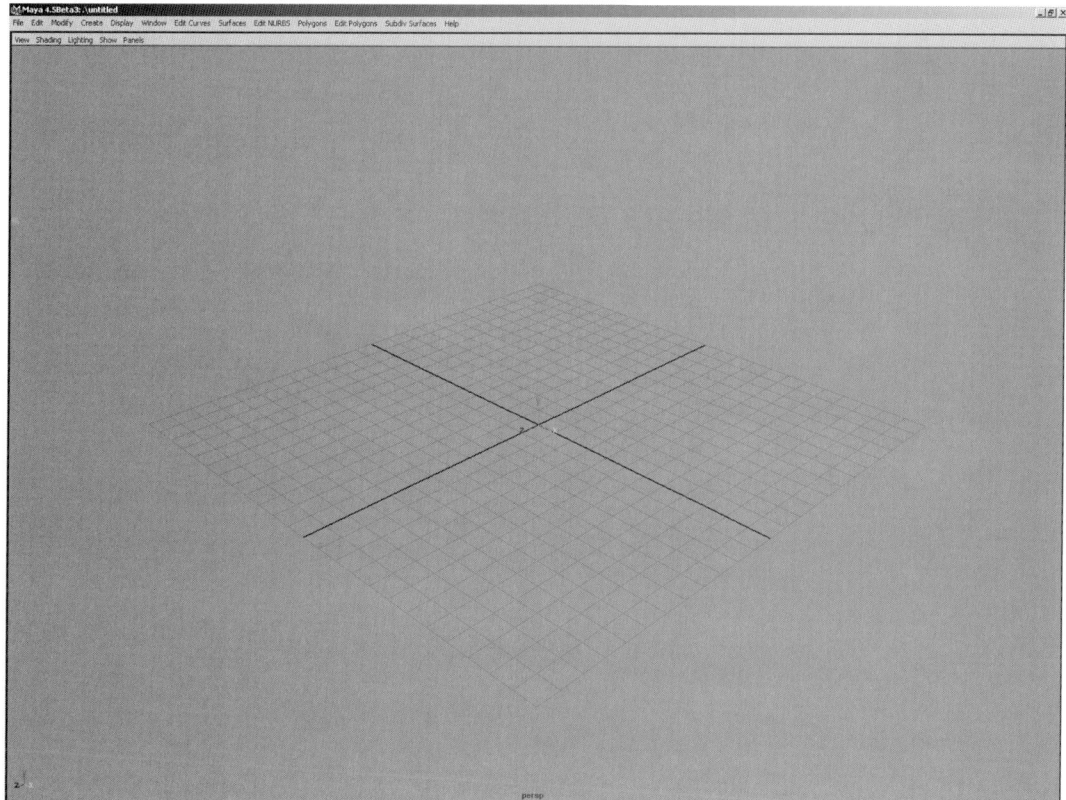

FIGURE B.11   Hide UI.

ADJUSTING UI ELEMENTS THROUGH PREFERENCES

We have looked at a wide variety of interactively altering the user interface to suit our needs. The obvious method of optimizing the interface is through the method you are probably used to in most other 3D applications: editing preferences.

To access Maya's UI Preferences, select Windows > Settings/Preferences > Preferences. Now, this collection of preferences entails more than just the user interface. For this appendix, we will only be discussing the first three sections: Interface, UI Elements, and Misc.

The first set of interface preferences shown in Figure B.12 allows you to define what will be the default module (Modeling, Animation, and so on) when you first open the application. In addition, this Preferences window allows you to gain further screen real estate by choosing to show or hide things like the Menubar (in both the Main window and in Panels) and the Title Bar. If you want to have the main Workspace take up absolutely the entire screen, you can use Display > UI Elements > Hide UI Elements (as we discussed earlier) and then here in the Preferences, you can uncheck the Show Menubar and Show Title Bar options. The result will be an interface devoid of everything but the Workspace.

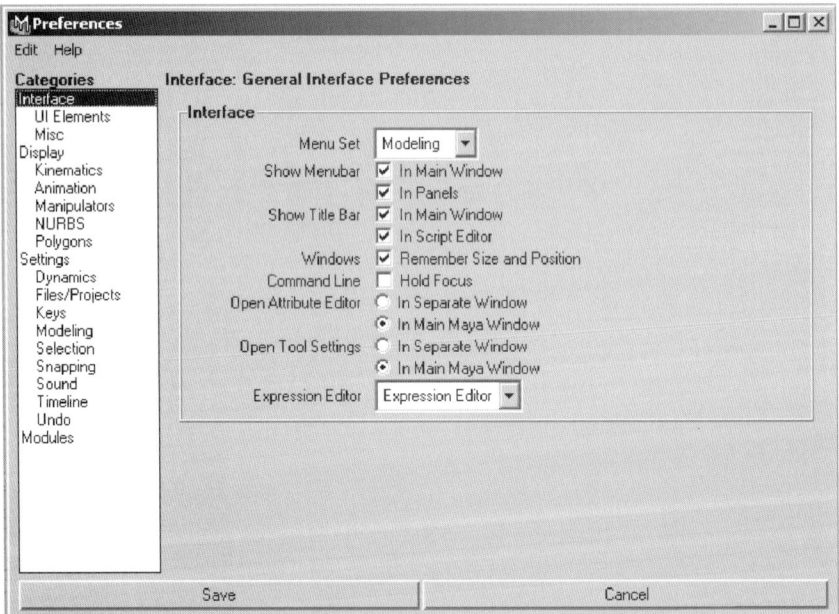

FIGURE B.12 Windows > Settings/Preferences > Preferences allows you to define further issues of how the interface will be displayed and interact with you, the user.

If you indeed hide every bit of the UI, remember that holding the **Spacebar** still allows you to access the various pull-down menus you will need.

Be aware though, that there are sometimes unexplained problems with the hotbox.

Other options in this dialog box are self-explanatory, so we will move on to the second window of this Preferences window—UI Elements (Figure B.13).

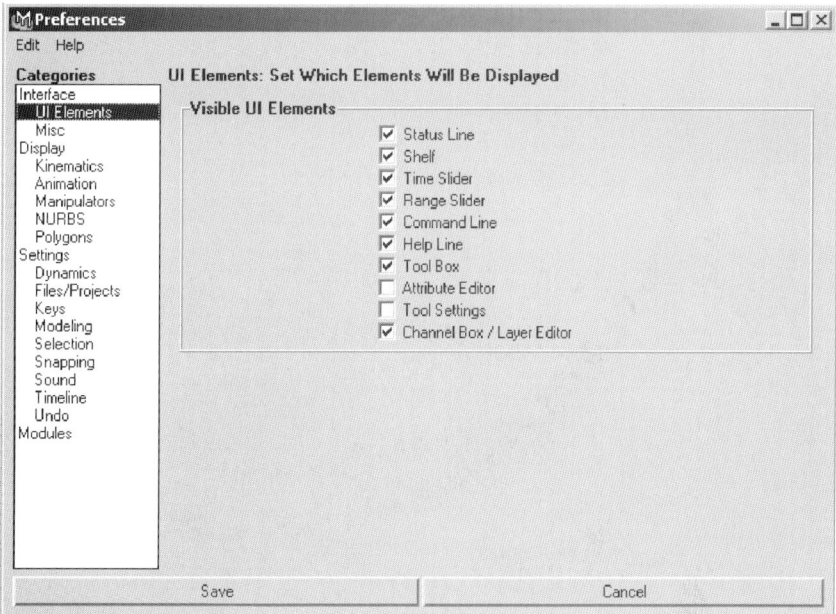

FIGURE B.13   The second pane of the Preferences window.

This window allows you another way to define which UI elements to display. This is just like the Display > UI Elements collection of pull-down menus.

The last part of the UI preferences (Figure B.14) is largely not of note except for the Panel Configurations area. This allows you to define whether your collection of panel organizations created for a specific project will be saved with the file or not. Similarly, you can set the default interface layout to the one you work in most comfortably at early parts of your work flow.

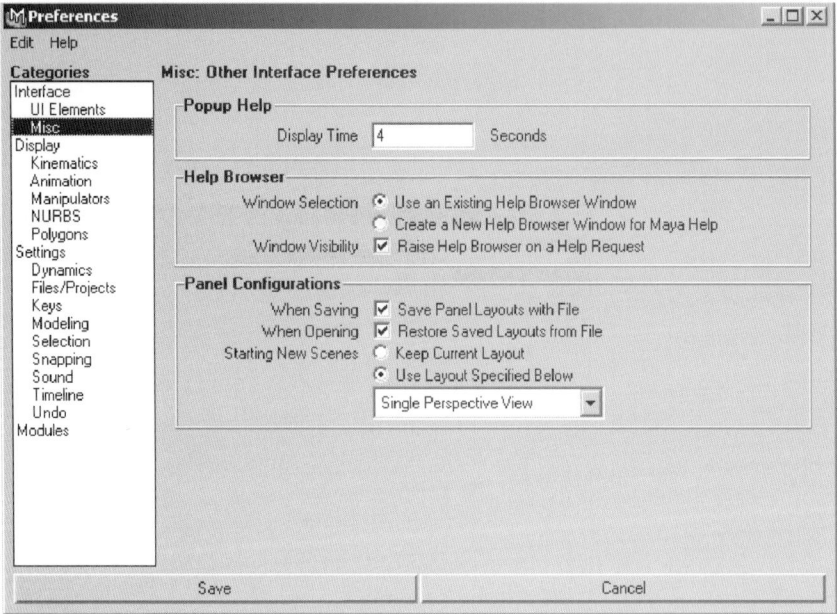

FIGURE B.14   The final UI preferences pane.

EDITING INTERACTION

Up to now, we have been looking at adjusting the visual UI of Maya. The rest of this appendix will address how to optimize the way that Maya interacts with you, the user. Although this is not a visual interface alteration (for the most part), it still can dramatically affect your work flow and consequently, the effectiveness of Maya as a tool for you.

EDITING HOTKEY CONFIGURATIONS

Also within the Window > Settings/Preferences is the Hotkeys option. Selecting this opens the Hotkey Editor (Figure B.15). Simply put, this editor allows you to choose the command you wish to assign a hotkey to by finding the pull-down menu where the command is located in the Categories column. Then, find the command in the Commands column. If the command already has a hotkey assigned to it, this will be displayed in the Current Hotkeys column. If not, you can enter a hotkey in the Assign New Hotkey area of the pane. Notice that you can change the modifier here as well. If the key or key-modifier combination is already in use by some other command, you will be warned within the Assign New Hotkey area. If all is well, or if you are willing to overwrite an extant hotkey setting with a new one, click the Assign button and your new hotkey is ready for use.

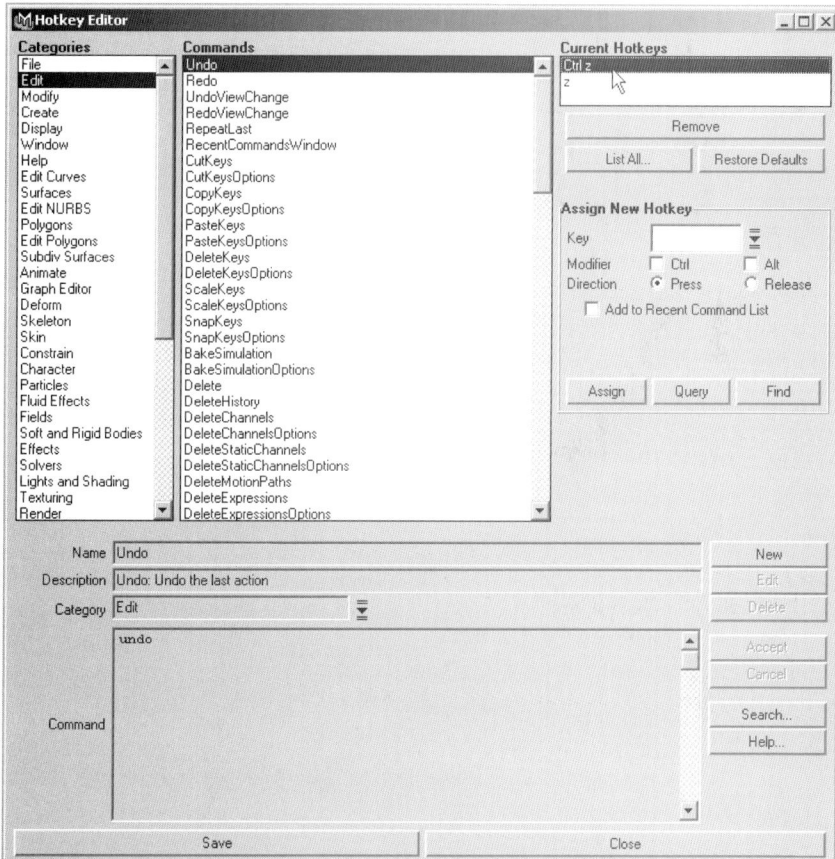

FIGURE B.15   The Hotkey Editor. Of primary use to us is the top part of this window. It allows you to define any command to a hotkey of your choice.

CHANGING INTERFACE COLORS

OK, so we may be getting a bit esoteric here but being able to change colors also has some very legitimate functional issues as well. Depending on the textures you are using within your scene, you may want to have different colors represented on your screen as you work. Or, maybe you are colorblind and the blues and greens just do not work for you; or perhaps you just do not like working in a gray world. No matter what the reason, the Window > Settings/Preferences > Colors option allows you to change the color of just about every single part of the interface. Want a black background as you work? No problem. In the mood for pastel colors on the X, Y, Z transform tools? Again, easy to switch here. Do you find the CV purple annoying or the isoparm blue deceiving? All of this is easy to change within this one window. For this book, we will leave all the colors as their defaults, but be aware that this is the place to colorize your Maya interface world (Figure B.16).

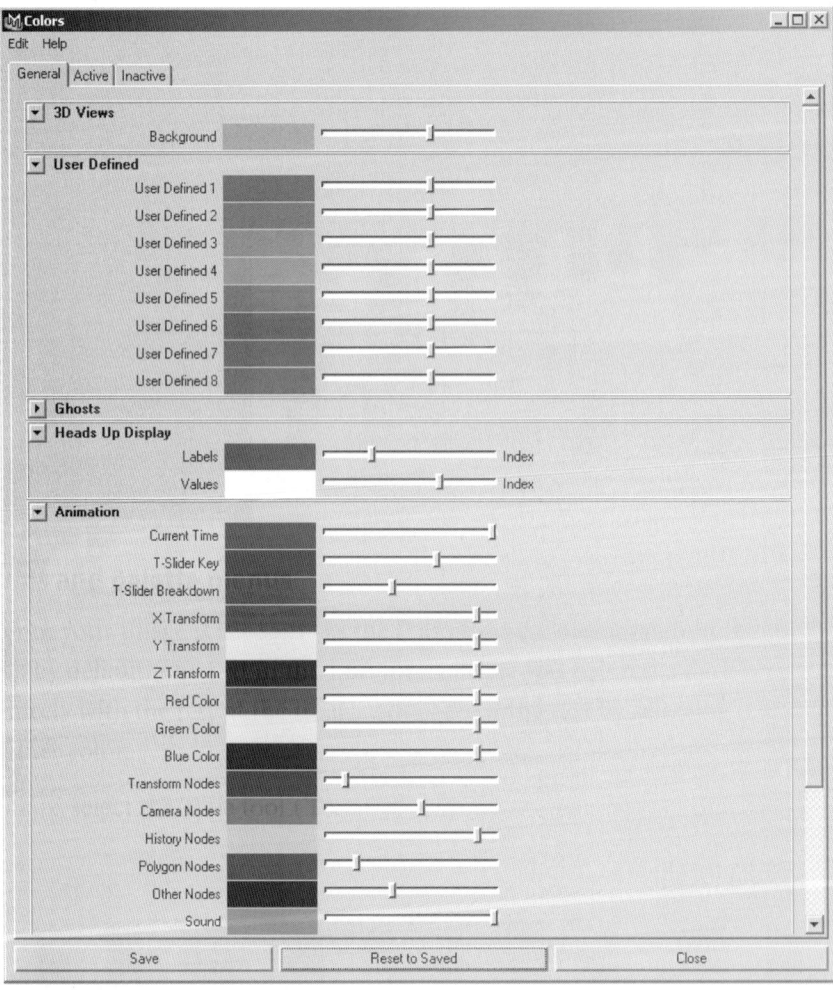

FIGURE B.16 All the colors of the interface—including backgrounds, tools, and components—can be changed through Window > Settings/Preferences > Colors.

Customizing Marking Menus

Marking menus, as discussed earlier, are ways to bring collections of tools, or even pull-down menus, to the visible forefront of your interface upon demand. Marking menus are pulled up by clicking on them and holding down a particular key on your keyboard. For instance, some Marking menus are located within the hotbox (pulled up by pressing and holding the **Spacebar**). These Marking menus are set up around the perimeter of the hotbox itself (Figure B.17).

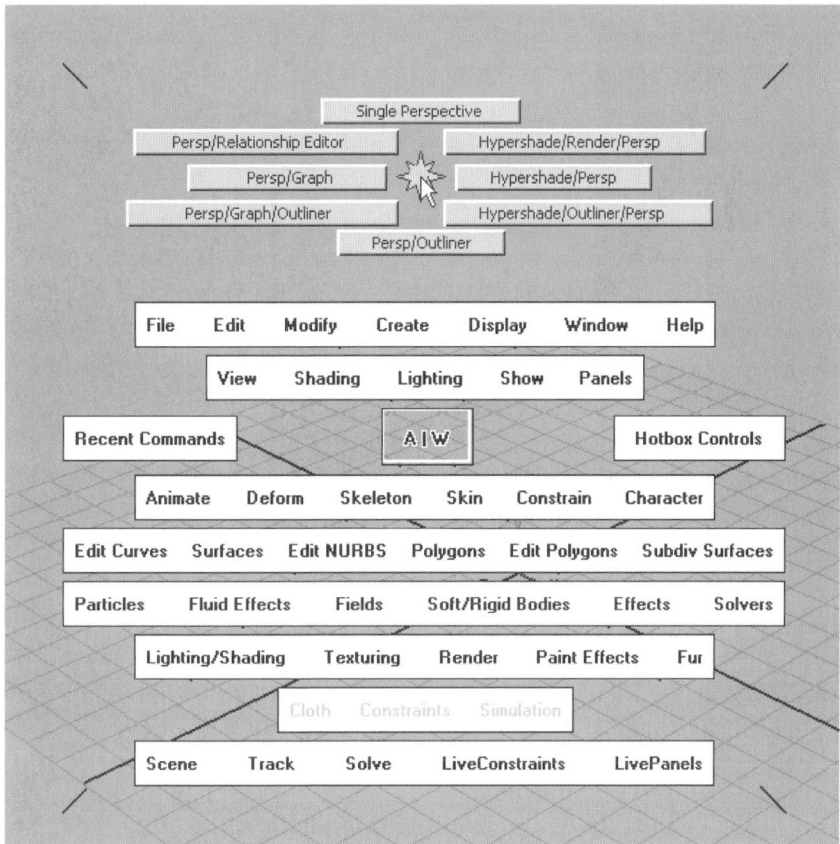

FIGURE B.17   Marking menus around the points of the compass of the hotbox.

For instance, Figure B.17 shows the hotbox activated. By clicking the LMB on the north quadrant of this space, a Marking menu that allows you to choose the panel layout appears. Although we will not go through all the extant Marking menus here, take a minute to look and explore them; they are located around the hotbox.

The important thing that we will talk about here is how to edit the Marking menus that exist. Using Window > Settings/Preferences > Marking Menus, you will be presented with a window that lists the extant Marking menus, where they are, and how they are manipulated when pulled up (Figure B.18).

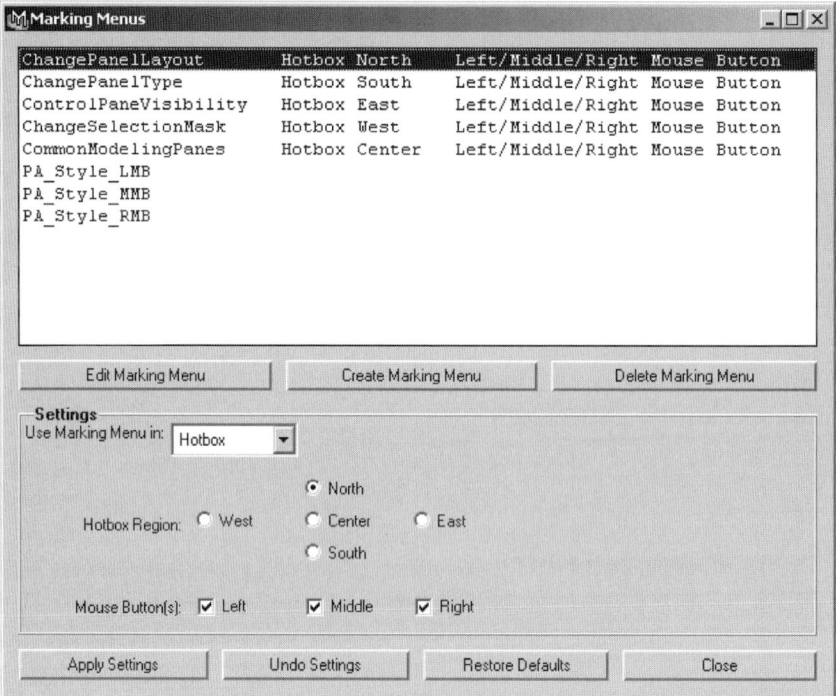

FIGURE B.18 The Marking Menus editing window gives you the opportunity to alter existing Marking menus or even create your own.

To edit an existing Marking menu, simply double-click the name of the menu or select it and hit the Edit Marking Menu button. A new window will open (Figure B.19) that will show the Marking menu. You can test the Marking menu by clicking any of the menu items shown, and Maya will act as though the Marking menu is in use. Or, if you RMB-click on one of the menu items, you will get a pop-up menu allowing you to edit, delete, or add a pop-up submenu to the menu item (Figure B.20).

Notice that the window shown in Figure B.19 also allows you to see what the Marking menu will look like with the box in the bottom-left corner. You may also change the name of a Marking menu.

Click Save to save your changes or Close to discard them.

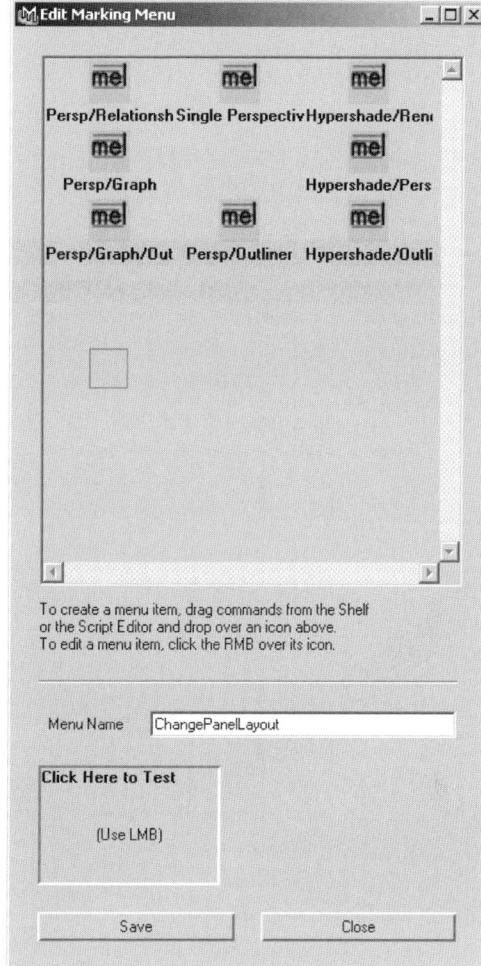

FIGURE B.19   Editing an existing Marking menu.

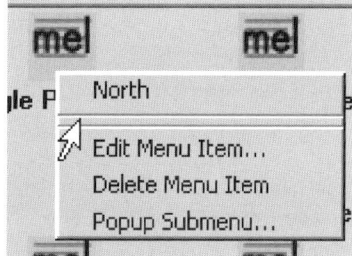

FIGURE B.20   Changing a menu item within a Marking menu.

CREATING MARKING MENUS FROM SCRATCH

In general, it's probably better to leave the existing Marking menus as is. However, the window shown in Figure B.20 can do more than just edit existing menus.

Notice that besides Deleting and Editing Marking Menus, there is also a button for Create Marking Menu. When you click this button a window similar to the editing one shown in Figures B.19 and B.20 opens as a blank canvas (Figure B.21). This allows you to create a Marking menu of your favorite tools from scratch.

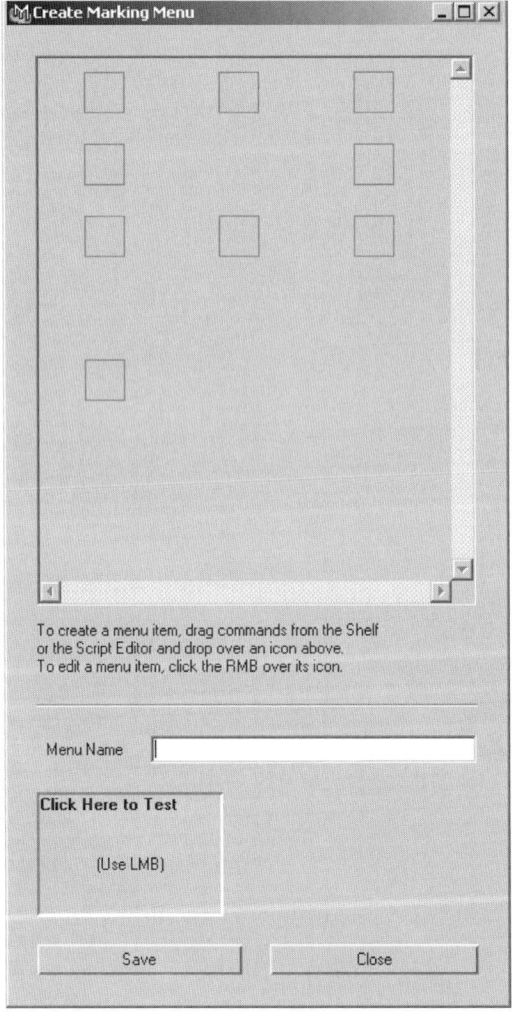

FIGURE B.21 The empty Marking menu window allows you to begin creating your own collection of vital tools.

Each empty menu item box can be filled by MMB-dragging a tool from a Shelf. This, of course, means that if you wish to add any tool to the Marking menu, you must first add it to the Shelf (select the tool while holding down the **Shift-Ctrl-Alt** buttons). You can always delete the tool or item from the Shelf afterward.

Figure B.22 shows a new menu called FrequentPrimitives that has a collection of frequently used shapes. Notice that this new Marking menu's name has no spaces (a typical Maya convention). Also notice that the figure shows a test of how the Marking menu would appear.

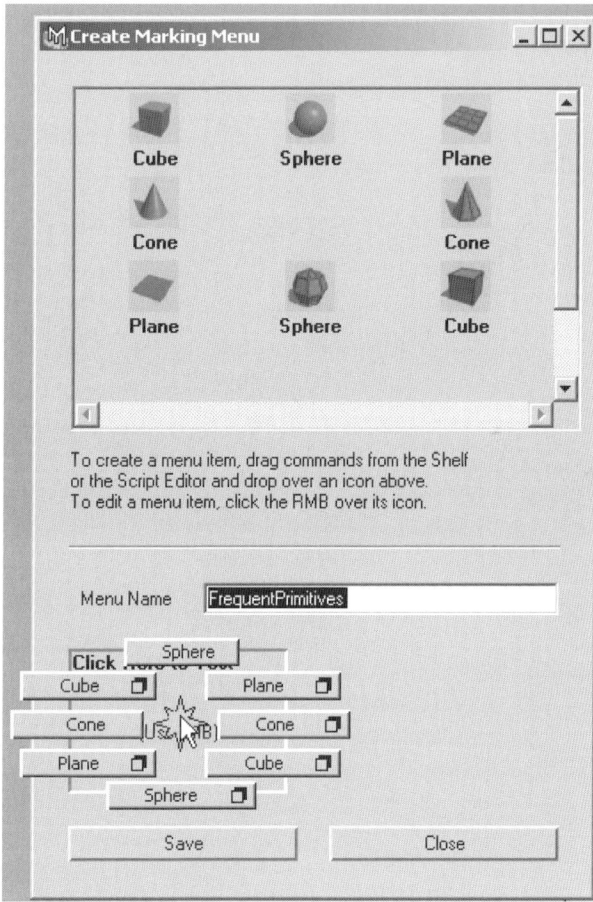

FIGURE B.22   A custom created Marking menu. Each primitive shown here was first added to the Shelf and then MMB-dragged into position within the Marking menu.

After clicking Save and Close, you can decide in the main window how to pull up this Marking menu. In the Settings section, you can choose to have the Marking menu be part of the hotbox or, more effectively, choose to assign it to a new hotkey (Figure B.23).

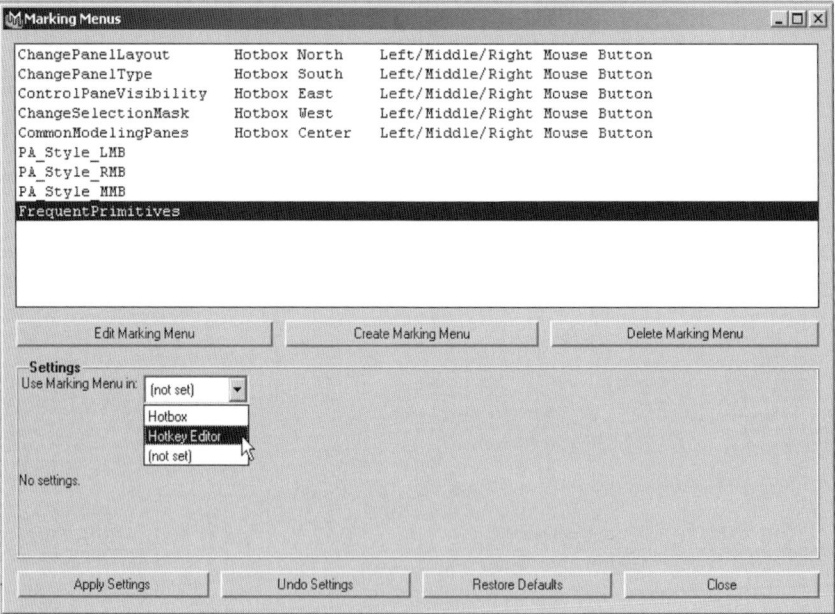

FIGURE B.23   Choosing how to access a Marking menu.

If you choose to assign a Marking menu to a hotkey, you need to be sure and pull up the Hotkey Editor (Window > Setting/Preferences > Hotkeys). Here, you can find User Marking Menus in the Categories column. Select the Marking Menu in the Commands column and then assign your desired hotkey within the Assign New Hotkey area (Figure B.24). Upon saving and closing, your Marking menu is ready to use. In Figure B.25, when pressing **Ctrl-F** (as assigned in the Hotkeys Editor) and LMB-clicking the interface, the Marking menu appears.

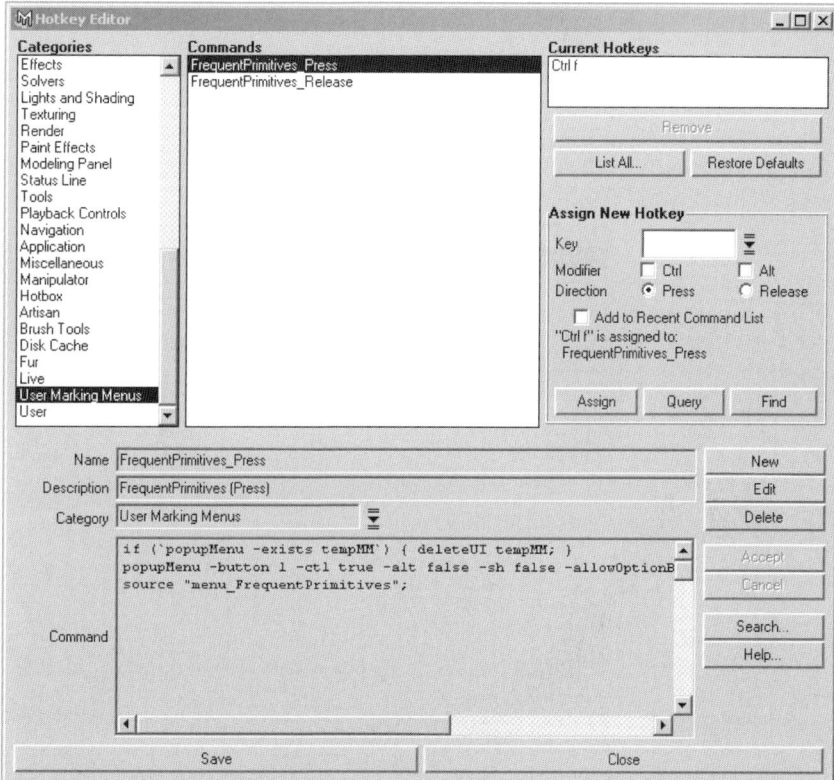

FIGURE B.24   Assigning a hotkey to a newly created Marking menu within the Hotkey Editor.

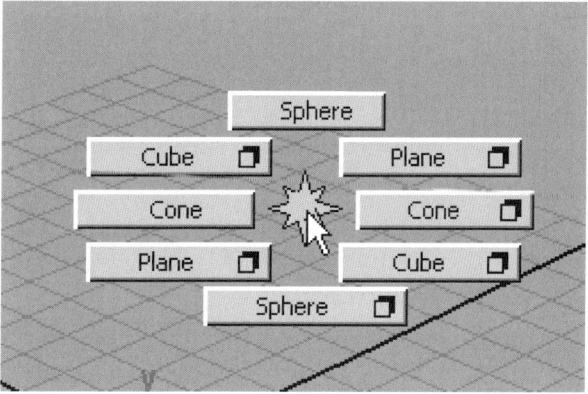

FIGURE B.25   Successful results of creating new Marking menu and assignment of custom hotkey.

CONTROLLING SHELVES

By default, Maya's interface displays the Shelf. The Shelf is a tool where frequently used tools can be stored for quick access. We have looked at how to hide and show this Shelf, and we have alluded to how to add elements to the Shelf while discussing the creation of Marking menus.

Window > Settings > Preferences > Shelves brings up a window that allows for the creation and organization of custom Shelves (Figure B.26). However, because Shelves are a visual tool, this editor is a rather clumsy way of editing a Shelf. Instead, in this section, we will look at how to do the same things within the interface.

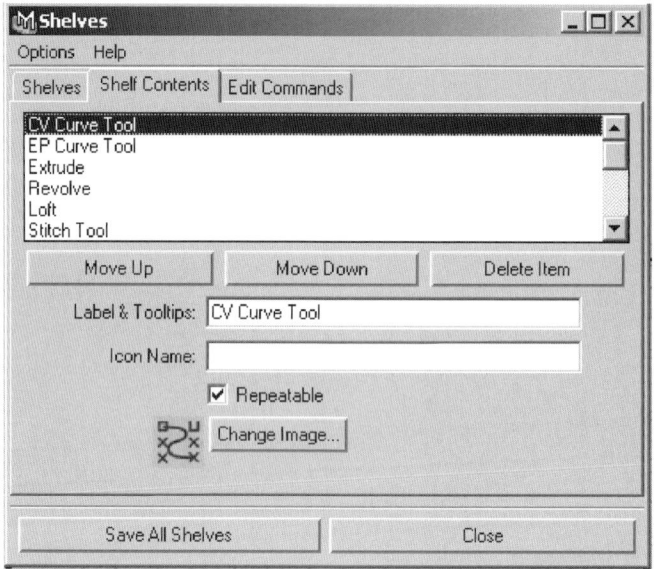

FIGURE B.26   Editing Shelves.

Editing Shelf Content

Figure B.27 shows the default Shelf visible when Maya is first opened. It contains a smattering of commonly used tools from all sorts of modules. To add a tool to the Shelf, hold down **Shift-Ctrl-Alt** and select the tool you wish to add. You can select a tool from any pull-down menu (remember to keep the **Shift-Ctrl-Alt** keys held down). The tool will appear on the Shelf.

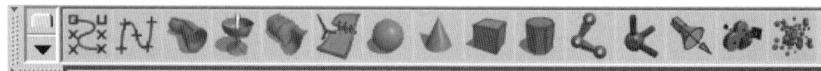

FIGURE B.27   The default Shelf.

Using the MMB, you can click and drag any tool to a new location on the Shelf. This allows you to organize a collection of tools into clusters. Notice that to the far right of the Shelf is a small Trashcan icon. You can remove a tool from the Shelf by MMB-dragging the tool to this Trashcan icon.

Creating New Shelves

At the far left of the Shelf are two small tools (Figure B.28). The bottom allows you to create or edit Shelves (Figure B.29).

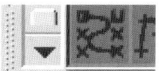

FIGURE B.28   Buttons nesting tools to control the Shelves.

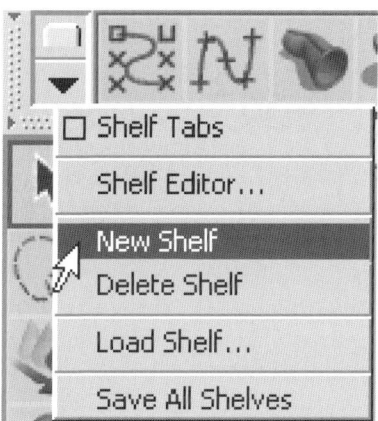

FIGURE B.29   Pop-up menu allowing for creation of new Shelves or editing of extant ones.

Of interest to us is the New Shelf option. Selecting this will prompt you for a name of the new Shelf. You may wish to nest a collection of your favorite modeling or lighting tools. No matter what your Shelf will hold, enter the name with alphanumeric characters and no spaces.

You will then be shown an empty Shelf ready to be filled by using the **Shift-Ctrl-Alt** method.

Once you have begun creating custom Shelves, you can move through them with the top button at the far left of the Shelves. Clicking this pops up the extant shelves allowing you to choose which one to bring forward (Figure B.30).

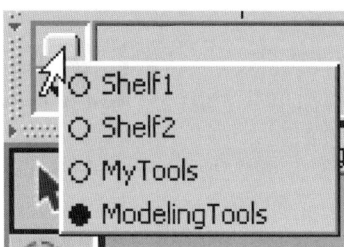

FIGURE B.30   Choosing which Shelf is to be visible.

Remember that all of this could be done with the Shelf Editor but is accomplished more intuitively by using the visual methods listed here.

CONCLUSION

These are not all the ways to alter Maya's interface. However, the methods listed here are by far the most commonly used. In most applications, altering the interface is typically not part of the game plan. However, because of the sheer number of tools within Maya, and the layering and nesting that goes on to get to them, you can increase your productivity tremendously by taking a few moments to organize your panels, windows, and shelves to match your work flow. Notice that in the Shelves Editor (Window > Settings/Preferences > Shelves) and the Panels Editor (Window > Settings/Preferences > Panels), you can save and load previously organized configurations, allowing you to bring your interface organization from project to project—or even machine to machine.

You might not want or need to organize your interface any differently when you are first learning Maya. You will notice that in this book, we are using the default UI organizations. However, as you become more familiar with Maya and your own work flow, customize Maya to your style. Doing so helps make Maya do your bidding and not the other way around.

CREATING EFFECTIVE TEXTURE MAPS

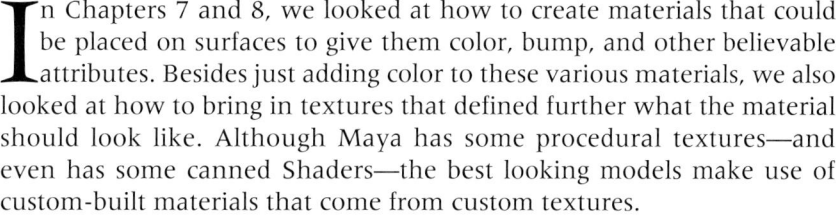

In Chapters 7 and 8, we looked at how to create materials that could be placed on surfaces to give them color, bump, and other believable attributes. Besides just adding color to these various materials, we also looked at how to bring in textures that defined further what the material should look like. Although Maya has some procedural textures—and even has some canned Shaders—the best looking models make use of custom-built materials that come from custom textures.

ON THE CD

In Chapter 8, we spent a bit of time applying a custom texture of a tile floor to our room. That texture was included on the CD-ROM (Tutorials/Chapter08/Textures) and it was set conveniently to lay right on the floor and behave in all the ways it should. However, to get such a texture requires a little bit of work outside of Maya. This appendix is essentially a Photoshop tutorial that discusses how to create textures appropriately.

Creating a believable texture usually starts out with a believable photograph. Figure C.1 is a shot taken with a digital camera of a tile entry way.

This shot has some good things about it and some problems.

Among the good things about this shot, and things that you should keep in mind when taking photos for use as textures, are the following:

- The pattern is fairly straight on. The vertical lines of the grout between the tiles are all parallel to each other. It is important when creating a texture map that you have no perspective visual in the shot at all. You want to let the 3D application do that for you.
- The parallel lines are fairly straight in the frame. This is not a big deal, but you get the most out of a frame if you are careful to have the camera square with any straight elements in the scene.
- The scope is wide. This shot could be focused on one tile, but that would create a fairly unsuccessful texture map. This would be unsuccessful because all the tiles would look exactly the same with no natural variation or interest. If your camera is sufficiently high

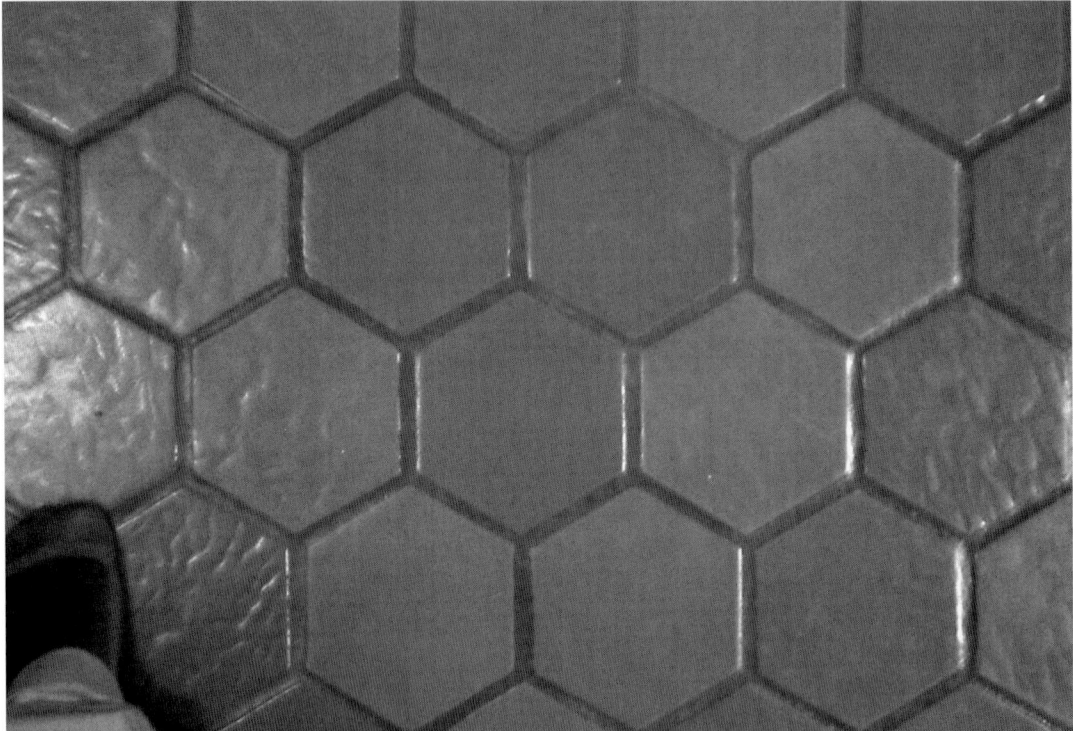

FIGURE C.1 Shot from a digital camera.

resolution, you should get as broad a shot of a texture as you can so you have lots of variation in your pattern.

Some problems with the example photo include the following:

- There are flash highlights. If you look on the left side of the photo, there is a yellow highlight from the light in the room. Similarly, the right side has a bit of a highlight along the edge of the tiles from the light in the next room. Although this helps to define the shapes of the tile to our naked eye visually, it causes great havoc when you need to create bump maps from this image.
- The contrast is relatively low. The image is largely monochromatic. When time comes to create bump maps from it, monochromatic images make it tough to get sufficiently white whites and sufficiently black blacks to get appropriate definition.
- The image is seamed. That is, if you took this photo and then added another where it ended, and another after that (Figure C.2), you would be able to see the seams—definitive lines that show where each copy of the image starts and ends.

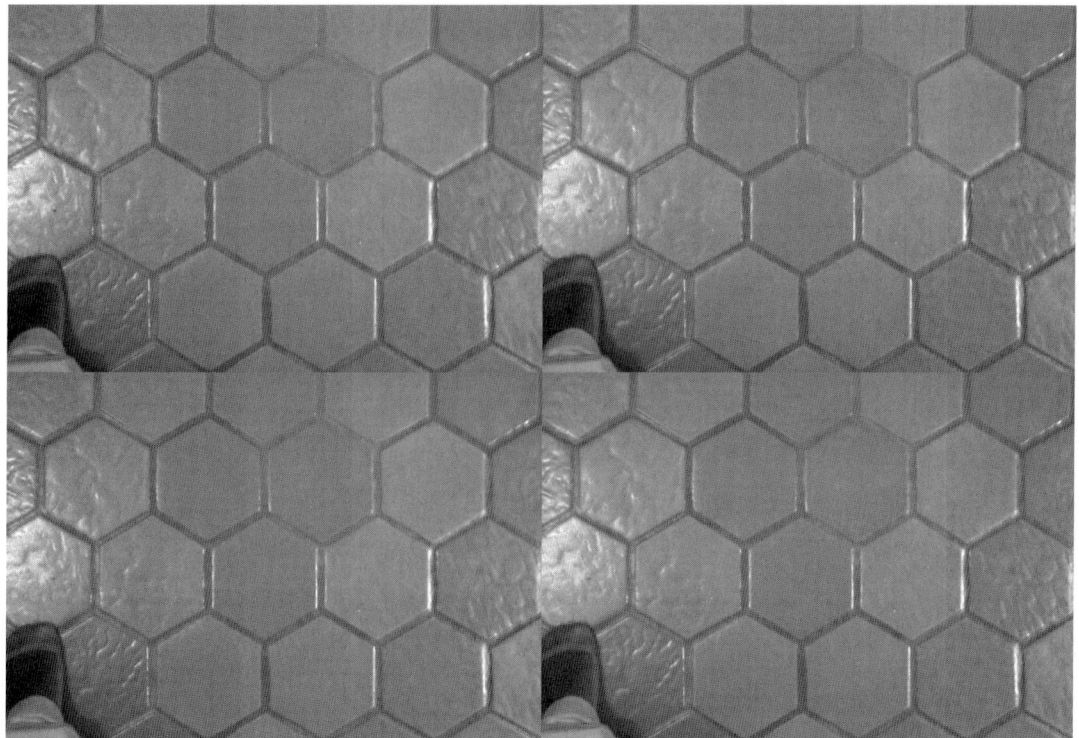

FIGURE C.2   Because this image is not prepared, it is seamed and unfit to be replicated across a surface.

Luckily, none of these drawbacks are terminal. We can fix all of them with a little bit of Photoshop wizardry. Follow the next tutorial to learn how.

TUTORIAL C.1   CREATING SEAMLESS TEXTURES

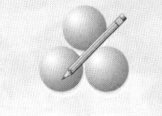

Step 1: Open the file, Raw Photo.tif, from the CD-ROM in Photoshop. It is located at Tutorials/AppendixC.

Step 2: Crop the photo to get rid of feet and bad highlights. The foot in the scene is definitely a problem. Also, the highlights at the extreme left of the image cause some problems. So, to start out, we want to crop those out. Before cropping roughly, take a bit of time to look at how you can find ways to crop so that the edges meet (Figure C.3).

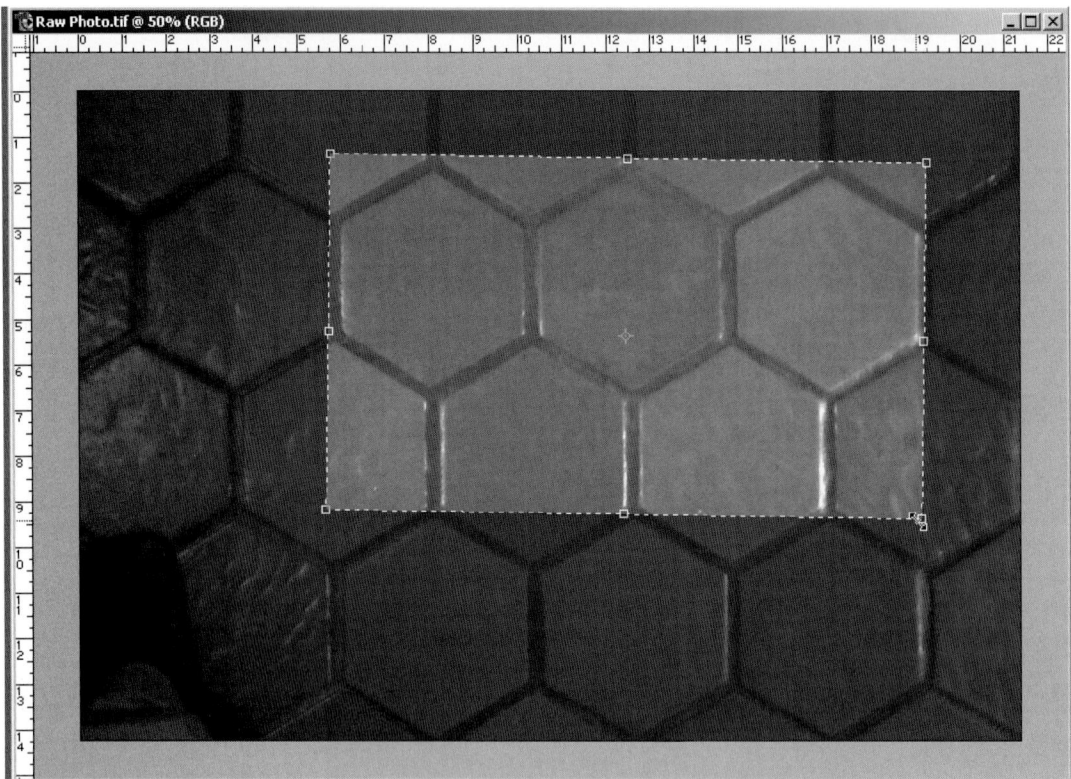

FIGURE C.3   Preparing to crop the image to get rid of poor sections and create roughly seamless imagery.

Notice that on the left side, the cropping bounding box comes to the edge of the grout, while on the right side, it cuts the grout out and comes to the edge of the tile. Similarly, on the top of the image, we have the bottom of the diamonds of tiles, while the bottom corners of the bottom tiles are cropped out. Finally, notice that you might need to rotate the cropping bounding box slightly to make up for any crookedness that might have snuck into the photo from not having the camera straight on. The cropped image is shown in Figure C.4.

Step 3: Offset the image to see the seams. Now, even though we have carefully cropped the image, there are still undoubtedly seams where the right edge of the image does not match up perfectly with the left edge. However, it is difficult to see these problems and work them out when they are on the opposite sides of the image. To move them where we can see them and deal with them, select Filter > Other > Offset.

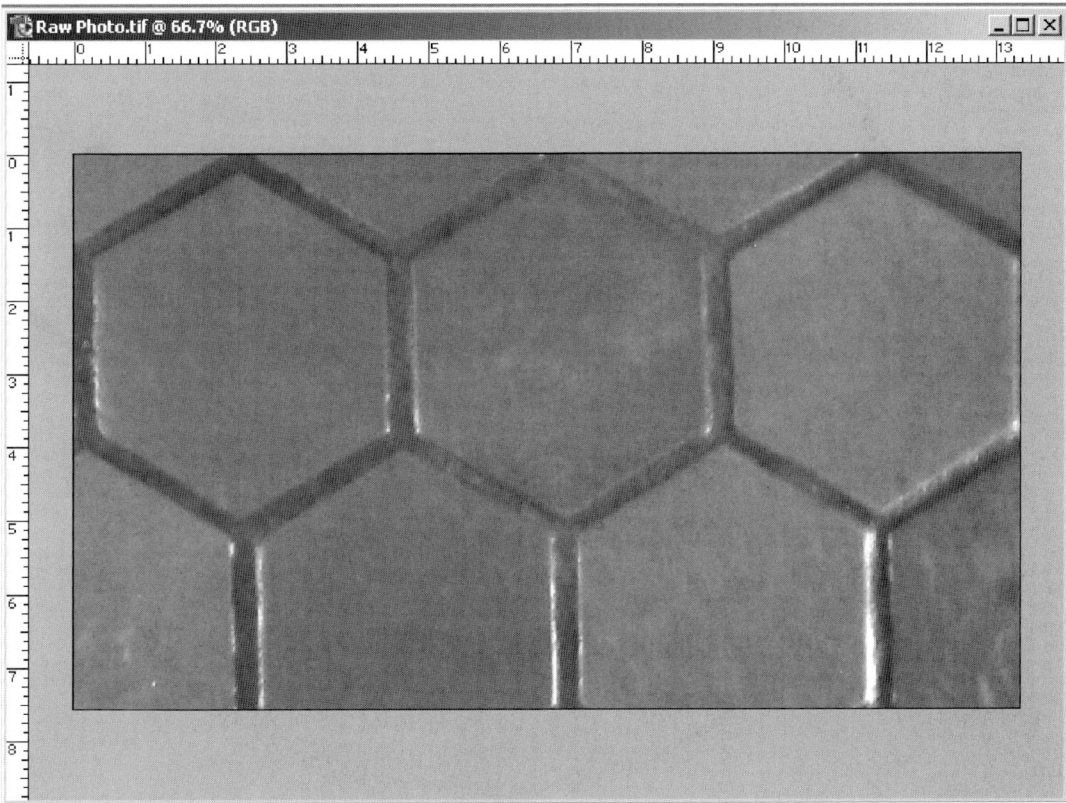

FIGURE C.4   Cropped image.

A new dialog box will appear similar to that in Figure C.5. The values of how far to offset are arbitrary but it is important to have the Wrap Around option checked (Figure C.5).

This takes the image and slides it all sideways off the canvas. However, with the Wrap Around activated, it takes the parts of the image that have been offset off the canvas, wraps them around, and brings them onto the other side. The net effect of this offset in both directions is that the seams of the image are now in the middle of the screen where you can work with them. Meanwhile, the edges of the image now are truly seamless.

You should be able to see the seams fairly clearly, but if not, adjust the levels (or brightness/contrast) until you can see them a bit more clearly.

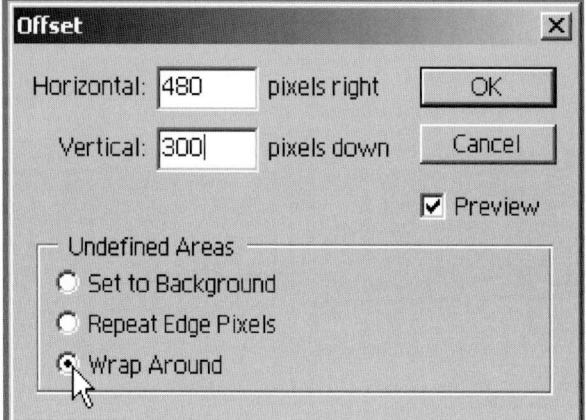

FIGURE C.5 The Offset Filter dialog box.

Step 4: Clone Stamp the seams away. To get rid of the seams, we need to soften the area where they exist. The easiest way to do this is with the Clone Stamp tool (Figure C.6).

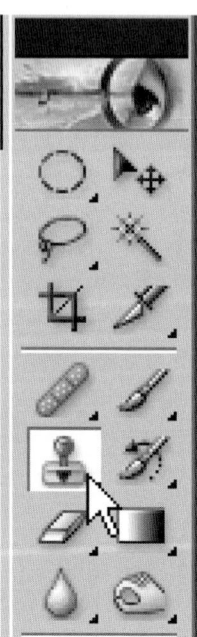

FIGURE C.6 The Clone Stamp tool.

The way this tool works is to define an area you wish to clone from by holding the **Alt** key down (**Option** on a Mac) and LMB-clicking. Then, move the mouse over an area that you wish to clone to and click-drag. This will clone your source pixels to this new location. This works well, because it clones the texture and surfaces of the image (Figure C.7).

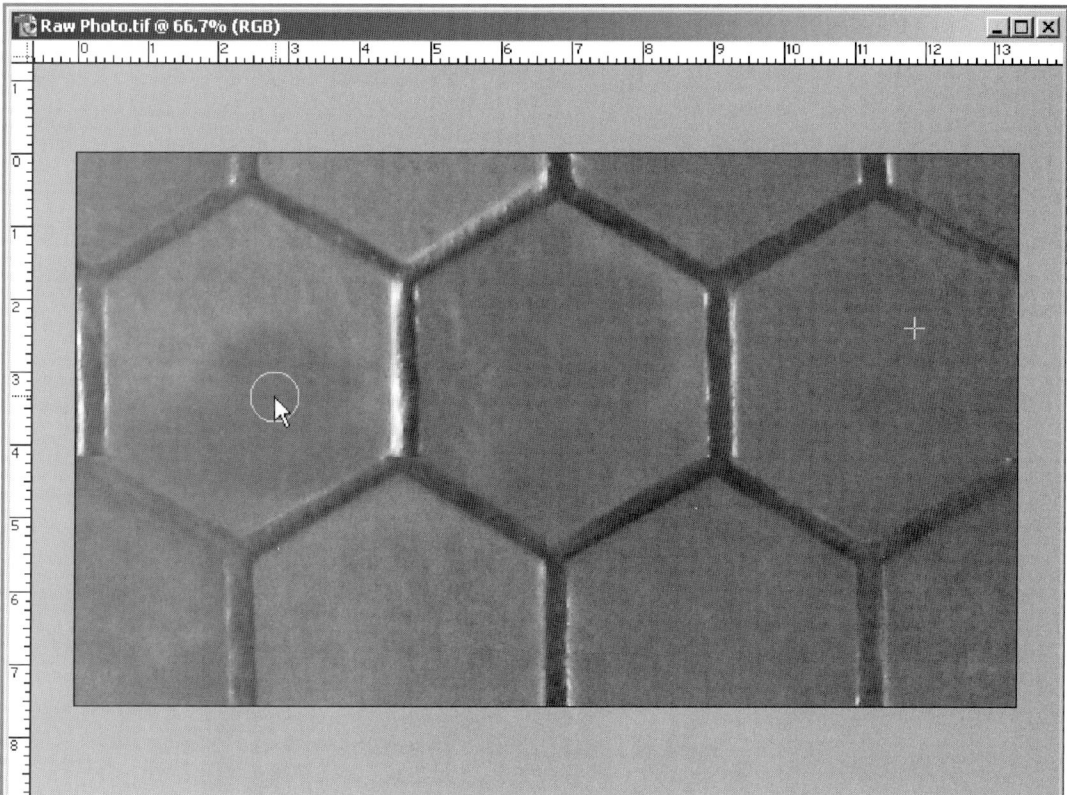

FIGURE C.7   Using the Clone tool to work seams out.

Step 5: Offset again. Sometimes, in the process of working seams out, you can accidentally create new seams if you clone too close to the edges. To make sure that things are clean, select Filter > Other > Offset again and look to see if you can distinguish any seams. If you can, fix them and offset again.

Once all the seams are worked out and repeated offsets reveal a seamless image, you are set. Save the file as TilesColor.tif; make sure you save it as a tiff although jpegs and other formats will work in Maya. This image is what we used in the Color attribute of the material we put on the floor of the room tutorials.

Step 6: Create a bump map from this seamless color map. Although Maya will use colored images as a bump map, the best bump maps are grayscale. Select Image > Mode > Grayscale and hit OK when Photoshop asks you if you wish to discard color information.

Step 7: Work out artificial bumps created through highlights. A nice thing about the grayscale image is the grout is dark already. For some images, such as bricks, the grout is white. Because Maya interprets grayscale images as the whiter the color, the higher the bump while the darker the color, the lower the receding, you often need to invert images where the whites and blacks are backward.

Because this one is alright, there is no need to do this. However, there are some highlights along certain parts of the tiles (circled in Figure C.8). These highlights would be interpreted as actual raised sections when Maya looked at them as a bump map. Because of this, we want to calm down these highlights so they do not create undesired artificial hightlights.

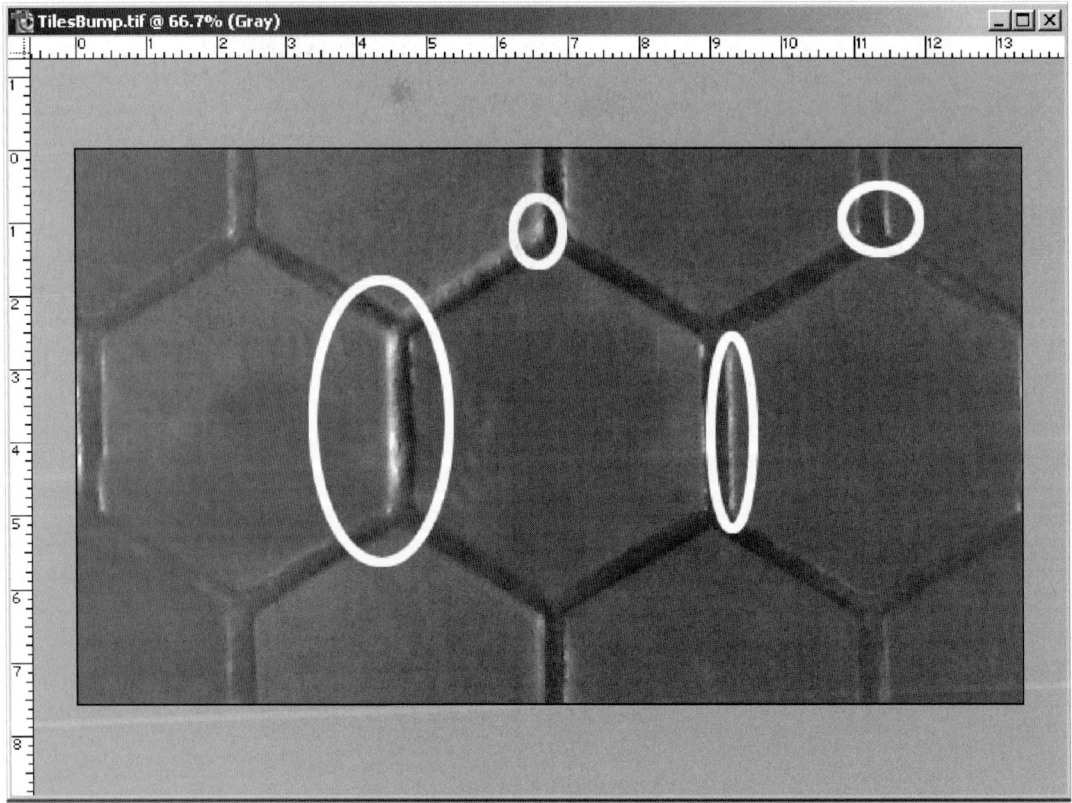

FIGURE C.8 Hightlights created from the light of the photo that will make for inappropriate bumps.

There are several ways to do this, but one of the easiest is to use the Clone tool to clone edges of tiles without highlights (Figure C.9).

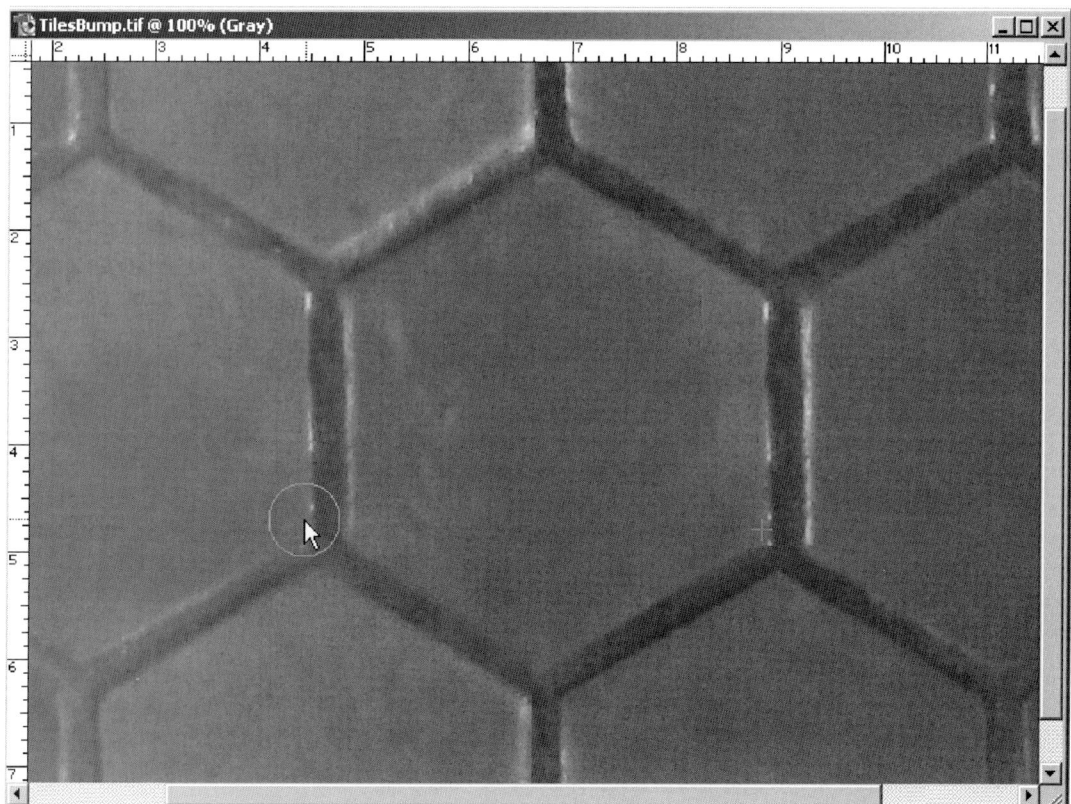

FIGURE C.9   Getting rid of unwanted highlights.

Step 8: Deepen the grout by adjusting levels and using the Burn tool. Select Image > Adjustments > Levels to increase the contrast of the image (Figure C.10). You might find again that after level adjustment, you need to work out some too-high highlights.

Finally, use the Burn tool to darken the grout a bit more. Make sure the Burn brush size is slightly larger than the grout is wide. Also, make sure you have a soft edge on the brush and that you have the opacity set to around 40%. This way, you get gentle edges and you don't blacken anything too quickly (Figure C.11).

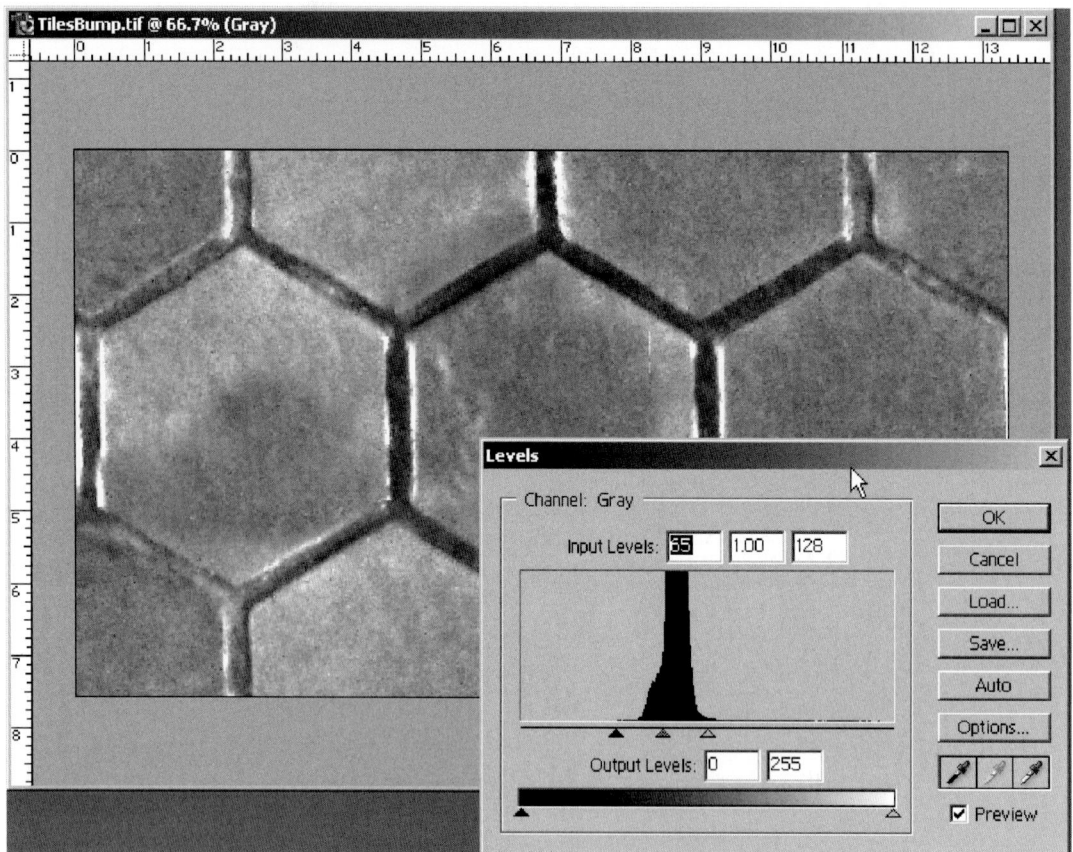

FIGURE C.10 Adjusting levels to create higher contrast.

Step 9: Save this image as TileBump.tif. Of course, this is the image used as the bump map for the Bump attribute for the floor.

Conclusion

Creating good texture maps is an art and takes lots of practice. Remember to prepare the images properly and work out the seams so you will have much more believable images to import as textures. Remember to build each variation texture map off the base color map so that all your various textures imported into attributes line up.

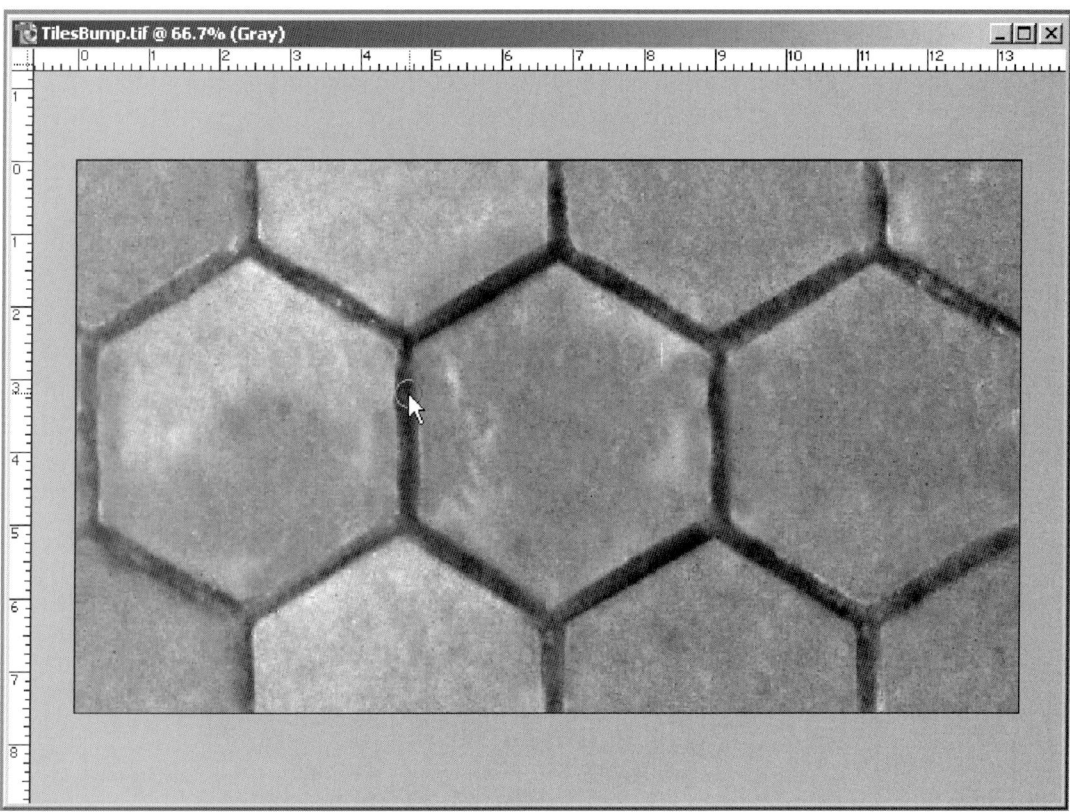

FIGURE C.11   Using the Burn tool to darken the grout.

D

ABOUT THE CD-ROM

Included with this volume is a CD-ROM that includes several important things to help you as you work through the concepts and tutorials. When you first open the CD-ROM, you will see two folders, Images and Tutorials. The Images folder includes all the screenshots contained in the book in full color. For several areas of the book—particularly the ones on texturing and lighting, these full color images are especially important so you may want to have them available as you work.

The second part of the CD-ROM is the Tutorials folder. Contained here are the finished files that show the results of the tutorials with scene files. You may find it helpful to pick apart these files to find details that you feel were left out of the descriptions. Also contained in the Tutorials folder are additional texture maps and other files used in the course of the tutorials.

To use the CD-ROM, just drop it in your CD-ROM drive and open it. All the tutorial files are Maya binaries, and so will only open in Maya. The color images are jpegs and tiffs and so should open with just about any graphics application.

If your machine runs Maya, it will run the disc. Use it often to augment the descriptions and screenshots included in this volume.

SYSTEM REQUIREMENTS

To use the CD-ROM, of course, all you need is a machine with a CD-ROM drive and software to view jpgs/tiffs. OS X is suggested for Mac users for ease of reading the filenames.

However, if you wish to use the Maya binary files included on the CD-ROM, you must have and be aware of the following:

- Maya 6 Complete or Unlimited
- Maya 6 is qualified officially to run on Intel® Pentium III, Pentium 4, AMD Athlon™ Processors, and Apple® G4 or G5 processors.
- Maya 6 will run with Windows XP Professional, Windows 2000 Professional, and Mac OS X.
- Run Maya with as big a video card as you can get. Officially, Maya does not have definitive video card requirements, but if you have less than a 32MB card, you will be too slow to work efficiently.

Remember, Maya has an official list of what hardware setups it will run on. Although these officially "qualified" setups are great to have since you know Maya will run on them, you can run Maya efficiently on other less expensive systems.

INDEX